De natura deorum; Academica; with an English translation by H. Rackham

H 1868-1944 Rackham, Marcus Tullius Cicero

THE LOEB CLASSICAL LIBRARY

FOUNDED BY JAMES LOEB, LL.D.

EDITED BY

E. H. WARMINGTON, M.A., F.R.HIST.SOC.

PREVIOUS EDITORS

T. E. PAGE, C.H., LITT.D. † E. CAPPS, PH.D., LL.D.

W. H. D. ROUSE, LITT.D. L. A. POST, L.H.D.

CICERO

XIX

DE NATURA DEORUM
ACADEMICA

268

CICERO

IN TWENTY-EIGHT VOLUMES

XIX

DE NATURA DEORUM
ACADEMICA

WITH AN ENGLISH TRANSLATION BY

H. RACKHAM, M.A.

UNIVERSITY LECTURER, AND FELLOW AND LECTURER OF CHRIST'S COLLEGE, CAMBRIDGE

CAMBRIDGE, MASSACHUSETTS
HARVARD UNIVERSITY PRESS
LONDON
WILLIAM HEINEMANN LTD
MCMLXVII

First printed 1933
Reprinted 1951, 1956, 1961, 1967

Printed in Great Britain

CONTENTS

DE NATURA DEORUM:

INTRODUCTION— PAGE

Subject of *De Natura Deorum* . . . vii
Post-Aristotelian philosophy . . . vii
Epicurean theology viii
Stoic theology viii
Academic scepticism ix
Cicero's work in philosophy . . . x
Date of composition of *De Natura Deorum* xii
De Natura Deorum unfinished . . . xiii
Summary of *De Natura Deorum* . . xiii
Dramatis personae xiv
Supposed date of the dialogue . . xv
Sources of *De Natura Deorum* . . . xv
MSS. of *De Natura Deorum* . . . xviii
Editions xviii

LIST OF CICERO'S WORKS xxi
BOOK I. 2
BOOK II. 122
BOOK III. 286
FRAGMENTS 384
INDEX 388

CONTENTS

ACADEMICA:

INTRODUCTION— PAGE

Dates of composition and revision . . 399
Subject of *Academica* 400
Dramatis personae 402
Imaginary date of the dialogue . . 403
Sources of *Academica* 404
MSS. of *Academica* 405
Editions 405

DEDICATORY LETTER 406

BOOK I 410

BOOK II 464

INDEX 660

DE NATURA DEORUM

INTRODUCTION

SUBJECT.—In *De Natura Deorum* Cicero put before Roman readers the theological views of the three schools of philosophy that were of chief importance in his day and in the two preceding centuries, the Epicurean, the Stoic, and the Academic.

POST-ARISTOTELIAN PHILOSOPHY.—In spite of the strong antagonism between the Epicureans and the Stoics, their doctrines had features in common which indeed characterized all the thought of the period. From Aristotle onward Greek philosophy became systematic ; it fell into three recognized departments, Logic, Physics, and Ethics, answering the three fundamental questions of the human mind : (1) How do I know the world? (2) What is the nature of the world? (3) The world being what it is, how am I to live in it so as to secure happiness ? And in answer to these questions the Stoics and the Epicureans were agreed (1) that the senses are the sole source of knowledge, (2) that matter is the sole reality, and (3) that happiness depends on peace of mind, undisturbed by passions, fears, and desires. But the ethical systems that they based on these first principles were fundamen-

tally opposed; for Epicurus taught that peace of mind is won by liberating the will from nature's law, the Stoics that it comes by submitting to it. Moreover, though both were materialistic, in their detailed systems of nature they differed widely.

Epicurean Theology.—With both schools alike, Theology fell under the second department of philosophy, Physics. But with Epicurus it was only an appendix to his main theory of nature. This he based upon the atomism of Democritus, holding that the real universe consists in innumerable atoms of matter moving by the force of gravity through an infinity of empty space. Our world and all its contents, and also innumerable other worlds, are temporary clusters of atoms fortuitously collected together in the void; they are constantly forming and constantly dissolving, without plan or purpose. There are gods, because all men believe in them and some men have seen them, and all sensations are true, and so are all beliefs if uncontradicted by sensations. The gods (like everything else) consist of fortuitous clusters of atoms, and our perceptions of them (as of everything else) are caused by atomic films floating off from the surface of their forms and impinging on the atoms of our minds. But it is impious to fancy that the gods are burdened with the labour of upholding or guiding the universe; the worlds go on of themselves, by purely mechanical causation; the gods live a life of undisturbed bliss in the *intermundia*, the empty regions of space between the worlds.

Stoic Theology.—The Stoics, on the contrary, held that the universe is controlled by God, and in the last resort is God. The sole ultimate reality is the divine Mind, which expresses itself in the world-process.

But only matter exists, for only matter can act and be acted upon; mind therefore is matter in its subtlest form, Fire or Breath or Aether. The primal fiery Spirit creates out of itself the world that we know, persists in it as its heat or soul or 'tension,' is the cause of all movement and all life, and ultimately by a universal conflagration will reabsorb the world into itself. But there will be no pause: at once the process will begin again, unity will again pluralize itself, and all will repeat the same course as before. Existence goes on for ever in endlessly recurring cycles, following a fixed law or formula (λόγος); this law is Fate or Providence, ordained by God: the Stoics even said that the 'Logos' *is* God. And the universe is perfectly good: badness is only apparent, evil only means the necessary imperfection of the parts viewed separately from the whole.

The Stoic system then was determinist: but in it nevertheless they found room for freedom of the will. Man's acts like all other occurrences are the necessary effects of causes; yet man's will is free, for it rests with him either willingly to obey necessity, the divine ordinance, or to submit to it with reluctance. His happiness lies in using his divine intellect to understand the laws of the world, and in submitting his will thereto.

Academic Scepticism and the Later Reaction.—The Academic position in Theology was not dogmatic at all, but purely critical. Within a century of Plato's death his school had been completely transformed by Arcesilas, its head in the middle of the third century B.C.; he imported into it the denial of the possibility of knowledge that had been set up as a philosophical system by the Sceptic Pyrrho two

generations before. Arcesilas was regarded as having refounded the school, which was now called the Second or New Academy. Arcesilas's work was carried further a century later by Carneades, who employed his acute logic in demolishing the natural theology of the Stoics. The next head but one, Philo, Cicero's first Academic master, set on foot a reaction to a more dogmatic position ; he asserted that the Academy had not really changed its principles since Plato, and that his predecessors, though attacking the 'criterion' of the Stoics, had not meant to deny all possibility of knowledge : there was a 'clearness' about some sense-impressions that carried conviction of their truth. Philo's successor Antiochus went further and abandoned scepticism altogether ; he maintained that the Academy *had* lost the true doctrine of Plato, and he professed to recover it, calling his school the 'Old Academy.'

Cicero's Work in Philosophy.—Cicero studied philosophy in his youth under the heads of all the three leading schools, for Philo of the Academy, Diodotus the Stoic, and Phaedrus the Epicurean all came to Rome to escape the disturbances of the Mithridatic War. He gave two more years to study in his maturity ; for at the age of twenty-seven he withdrew for a time from public life, spent six months at Athens studying philosophy under the Epicureans Phaedrus and Zeno, and the Academic Antiochus, and then passed on to Rhodes for rhetoric. There he met Posidonius, who was now the leading Stoic, as Diodotus had stayed in Rome as a guest at Cicero's house and resided there till his death. When Cicero went home and resumed his public career, he still continued his studies in his intervals of leisure, as appears

from many passages in his Letters. And when under the Triumvirate his career flagged, he turned more and more to letters. After his return from exile in 57 B.C. he wrote *De Oratore*, *De Republica*, and *De Legibus* (his earliest essay in rhetoric, *De Inventione*, had been written before he was twenty-five). Rhetoric and political science again engaged him on his return to Rome after reconciliation with Caesar in 46 B.C.; and early in 45, after the death of his daughter and the final downfall of Pompey's party at Pharsalus, he retired to a country-house and gave himself entirely to study and to writing. He seems to have conceived the idea of doing a last service to his country by making the treasures of Greek thought accessible to Roman readers. His intention is described in the preface to *De Finibus* (i. 1-13), in which he commends the book to his friend Brutus; no doubt it was presented to Brutus when he visited Cicero in August (*Ad Att.* xiii. 44). Cicero went on with his work through the following year, after the assassination of Caesar in March, till in the autumn he flung himself again into the arena by attacking Antony with the *Philippics*; and this led on to his proscription and his death in December 43.

Thus, excepting the treatises named above, the whole of Cicero's important work in the region of thought was accomplished in 46–44 B.C., within the space of two years.

Cicero's service to philosophy must not be underrated. In writing to Atticus (xii. 52) he himself took a modest view: 'You will say "What is your method in compositions of this kind?" They are mere transcripts, and cost comparatively little labour; I supply only the words, of which I have a copious flow.' But

elsewhere he rates his work rather higher: 'As my habit is, I shall draw from the fountains of the Greeks at my own judgement and discretion' (*Off.* i. 6), and 'I do not merely perform the office of a translator, but apply my own judgement and my own arrangement' (*Fin.* i. 6). His method was unambitious: he took some recent handbook of one or other of the leading schools of philosophy and reproduced it in Latin; but he set passages of continuous exposition in a frame of dialogue, and he added illustrations from Roman history and poetry. His object was to popularize among his fellow-countrymen the work of the great masters of thought; and he had made the masters' thought his own, having read widely and having heard the chief teachers of the day. But to learning and enthusiasm he did not add depth of insight or scientific precision. Nevertheless he performed a notable service to philosophy. With the Greek schools it had now fallen into crabbed technicality: Cicero raised it again to literature, so commending it to all men of culture; and he created a Latin philosophic terminology which has passed into the languages of modern Europe.

N.D.: Date of Composition.—In the preface to *De Divinatione*, book ii., Cicero gives an account of his philosophical authorship. We read there (§ 3) that he finished his three books *De Natura Deorum* after he had published *Tusculan Disputations*; and that then, to complete his treatment of the subject, he began *De Divinatione*, intending to add a treatise *De Fato*. The preface quoted was written soon after Caesar's death, but the work itself before it (*id.* § 7), as was *De Natura Deorum* (see i. 4). Cicero's letter to Atticus dated the Ides of June in 45 B.C. (*Att.* xiii. 8) shows

him engaged upon the whole subject; he requests Atticus to send him 'Brutus's epitome of the works of Caelius,' which he quotes *N.D.* ii. 8 and several times in *De Divinatione*, and 'Philoxenus's copy of Panaetius's Περὶ Προνοίας,' which he follows at *Div.* ii. 97 and quotes *N.D.* ii. 118. In a letter to Atticus a little later (xiii. 8. 1) occur the words 'Before dawn, as I was writing against the Epicureans'—a reference to Cotta's speech in *N.D.* i.; and the next day he writes (*Att.* xiii. 39. 2) 'I am very busy writing; send me . . . Φαίδρου Περὶ Θεῶν'—which he unquestionably required for *N.D.* i. He was therefore engaged on this treatise in the summer of 45 B.C., while at the same time occupied on the *Tusculans*, which he published first.

N.D. NOT COMPLETELY FINISHED.—There is no evidence that he ever actually published *N.D.*; although he speaks of it as 'finished' (*Div.* ii. 3) it clearly lacks his final touches. The dialogue as it stands is one continuous conversation, ending at nightfall (iii. 94), but traces remain suggesting that it was first cast into three conversations held on three successive days, each book containing one; see ii. 73, "As you said yesterday" (with note *ad loc.*); iii. 2, "I hope you have come well prepared"; iii. 18, "All that you said the day before yesterday to prove the existence of the gods."

CONTENTS OF *N.D.*—*De Natura Deorum* opens with a preface dedicating the work to Cicero's friend Brutus. Cicero explains how philosophy occupies his retirement from public life and consoles him in the bereavement of his daughter's death; and how the undogmatic style of the Academic school of thought, of which he was an adherent, was especially suited to the subject of theology. The scene of the dialogue

is then laid and the characters introduced. The theology of Epicurus is taken first. It is expounded by Velleius (§§ 18-56), who precedes his exposition by a preliminary attack on the theology and cosmogony of Plato and the Stoics, and a refutation (§§ 25-41) of the theology of the other schools from Thales downward. He is answered (§§ 57 to end) by the Academic Cotta, who demolishes the Epicurean theology, and pronounces Epicureanism to be really fatal to religion (§ 115).

In Book ii. the Stoic theology is set out by Balbus, who proves (1) the divine existence (§§ 4-44), and expounds (2) the divine nature (§§ 45-72), (3) the providential government of the world (§§ 73-153), and (4) the care of providence for man (§§ 154 to end). Cotta again replies, in Book iii., giving the Academic criticism of the Stoic theology under the same four heads: (1) §§ 7-19, (2) §§ 20-64, (3) § 65 (the rest of this division is lost), (4) §§ 66 to end.

Dramatis Personae.—Thus although as it stands the dialogue is one continuous conversation with the same persons present throughout, it falls into two separate parts, in which two different speakers take the lead; but the rejoinder in both cases is made by Cotta. Velleius the Epicurean speaker and Balbus the Stoic are only known to us from this book, except that *De Oratore* (iii. 78) gives Velleius as a friend of the orator L. Licinius Crassus, and mentions 'duo Balbi' among the Stoics of the day. Both spokesmen, and also Cotta the Academic, are spoken of here as leaders in their schools (i. 16). Cotta had already been commended to Cicero by Atticus (*Att.* xiii. 19. 3), and had been mentioned by Cicero before in *De Oratore* (iii. 145) as having joined the Academy; Cicero

in his youth had listened eagerly to his oratory (*Brutus*, 305, 317); he had been banished in 90 B.C. under the Varian law (*De Or.* iii. 11), had returned to Rome 82 B.C. (*Brut.* 311), and became consul 75 B.C. and then proconsul of Gaul, but died before his triumph. Cicero is almost a κωφὸν πρόσωπον; in the Introduction (i. 16 f.) he makes a complimentary reply to Cotta's greeting, and one other short remark when Velleius says that as another pupil of Philo he will be a valuable ally for Cotta. Cotta in his reply to the Epicurean exposition asks leave (ii. 104) to quote Cicero's translation of the astronomical poem of Aratus, but Cicero gives his consent by silence. At the close of the work (iii. 95) Cicero ends by noting the impression that the debate had made on his own mind.

Supposed Date of the Dialogue.—The imaginary scene of the dialogue may be dated in 77 or 76 B.C. In a list of political murders given by Cotta (iii. 60) the latest is that of Q. Scaevola, which was in 82 B.C. The Stoic professor Posidonius is spoken of as 'the friend of us all' (i. 123), which seems to put the scene after 78 B.C. when Cicero heard him lecture at Rhodes (although he had visited Rome on an embassy from Rhodes in 86 B.C.); but there is no reference to Cotta's consulship, 75 B.C. The date suggested fits in with the reference to P. Vatinius as 'adulescens' (ii. 6); he became quaestor in 63 B.C. when Cicero was consul.

Sources of *N.D.*—It is of interest to try to ascertain the sources from which Cicero gets his materials for the treatise. In the Epicurean's review of the earlier Greek philosophers (i. 25-41) there are references to their works, and later there are allusions to Epicurus's writings (§ 43 Περὶ Κριτηρίου ἢ Κανών, 'a heavenly

volume,' § 49, and §§ 45 and 85 the Κύριαι Δόξαι). But there is nothing to prove that Cicero had read these first-hand authorities, and it is more probable that he followed his usual method of adapting his exposition of each division of his treatise from a single recent writer. For the exposition of Epicureanism which forms the first half of Book i. this was probably a work of his master, Zeno. This conjecture has been supported by a curious accident. Among the papyri discovered at Herculaneum in 1752 is a mutilated Epicurean treatise (fully published in a volume of *Herculanensia* in 1862); there is reason to assign this to Zeno's pupil, Philodemus; and the fragments are enough to show considerable agreement with *N.D.* i. The Epicurean argument in *N.D.* i. has three parts: a general attack on the Platonic and Stoic cosmology, a review of the older philosophers, and an exposition of Epicurean theology. In the papyrus the first part is lost, but it contains the two latter and they correspond very closely with *N.D.*, in spite of some differences; the two books even agree in quotations from Xenophanes, Antisthenes, Aristotle, Chrysippus, and Diogenes of Babylon (*N.D.* i. §§ 31, 32, 33, 41). Mayor thinks that both books take their topics and arguments from Zeno, the teacher of both authors, and as the historical review in both stops at the middle of the second century B.C., Zeno's work may well have been based in turn on one by his predecessor Apollodorus.

Coming to the Academic Cotta's criticism of Epicureanism in the second half of Book i., the Stoic Posidonius is referred to (i. 123) as 'the friend of us all,' and his work *On Nature* is quoted as authority for part of the argument, and may be the source of

the whole; there are Stoic touches throughout (§ 80 the jest at the Academy, § 95 the divinity of the universe, § 100 the teleological argument, § 103 beasts born in fire, § 110 virtue as an active principle, § 115 the definitions of piety and holiness, § 121 the union of man and God). But the Stoic origin of the passage is disputed by some authorities, and it has indeed an Academic colouring: it may possibly come, like Book iii., from Clitomachus, the editor of Carneades, though Carneades is nowhere quoted here as he is in Book iii.

For the Stoic system in Book ii. Cicero probably follows Posidonius. He was unlike most of his school (1) in having literary tastes, and using an easy style with historical illustrations, (2) in being interested in science, and (3) in admiring Plato and Aristotle and adapting Stoicism to suit their doctrines. These features are seen in Cicero's exposition: (1) poetic quotations occur in §§ 4, 65, 89, 104-114, 159, and historical illustrations in §§ 6-11, 61, 69, 165; (2) § 88 refers to the orrery of Posidonius and to astronomical details, tides, the ether, volcanoes, climate, human diet, the kinship of plant, animal, and human life (an Aristotelian touch, conflicting with the older Stoicism), the eternity of the rational soul (which with the early Stoics perished in the universal Conflagration), the origin of civilization (a rationalization of the myth of the Golden Age); (3) Plato is 'the god of philosophers' § 32, and Aristotle is praised §§ 95, 125, and many details are borrowed from him.

The source of the Academic criticism of Stoic theology which occupies Book iii. is certainly Hasdrubal of Carthage, better known under his Greek name of Clitomachus. He was born *c.* 180 B.C. and went to

Athens about the age of twenty-five, becoming the pupil of Carneades and succeeding him as head of the Academy. He left voluminous records of the doctrines of his master, who left none. Carneades was the great source of all criticism of the Stoics, especially of their theology: he 'was fond of tilting at the Stoics,' *N.D.* ii. 162. The proof of the mortality of all animal life, *N.D.* iii. 29-34, and the sorites, §§ 43-52, are explicitly taken from Carneades.

MSS.—There are many MSS. of Cicero containing *De Natura Deorum*, but few are old and none earlier than the ninth century. All go back to one archetype, as is proved by errors, gaps, and transpositions common to all; but none seems to have been copied directly from it, and there appear to have been two lines of tradition from it, exemplified by two of the oldest MSS., which must be deemed the most important; both belonged to Voss and are at Leyden—A dating at the end of the ninth or beginning of the tenth century, and B a little later. They have many errors and some considerable gaps in common, but differ in many readings and transpositions. The other superior MSS. all group with A, viz. V (the Palatine, at Vienna, almost of the same date), N (Bibliothèque Nationale, Paris, twelfth century, descended from V), O (Bodleian, end of twelfth century); and so do all the inferior copies.

The present edition merely notes at the foot of the page a few of the variants of A and B and of the other MSS. (grouped together as *deteriores*) in places where the true reading seems doubtful.

EDITIONS.—For a full view of our evidence for the text the student may be referred to the editions of Plasberg (Leipzig, *ed. major*, 1911, revision announced

1930, *ed. minor,* 1917). The foundation of modern texts is the edition of Orelli and Baiter (1861), based on five MSS., three mentioned above, A, B (called by Orelli P) and V, another at Leyden (Heinsianus, twelfth century), and one at Erlangen, E. The invaluable edition of Joseph Mayor (Cambridge, 1880–1885) also employs evidence collected from twelve other MSS. by various scholars, and the texts of the four editions published at the revival of learning, at Venice (A.D. 1508), Paris (1511), Leipzig (1520), and Basel (1534): the sources of these texts are not entirely known to modern scholars. In addition to his elaborate critical notes Mayor supplies the student with an exhaustive accumulation of explanatory and illustrative commentary.

H. R.

1930.

See also the edition of A. S. Pease, Cambridge. Mass., 1955, 1958.

LIST OF CICERO'S WORKS

SHOWING THEIR DIVISION INTO VOLUMES IN THIS EDITION

VOLUME

A. Rhetorical Treatises. 5 Volumes

I. [Cicero], Rhetorica ad Herennium

II. De Inventione
De Optimo Genere Oratorum
Topica

III. De Oratore, Books I-II

IV. De Oratore, Book III
De Fato
Paradoxa Stoicorum
De Partitione Oratoria

V. Brutus
Orator

LIST OF CICERO'S WORKS

VOLUME

B. Orations. 10 Volumes

VI. Pro Quinctio
Pro Roscio Amerino
Pro Roscio Comoedo
De Lege Agraria Contra Rullum I-III

VII. The Verrine Orations I :
In Q. Caecilium
In C. Verrem Actio I
In C. Verrem Actio II, Books I-II

VIII. The Verrine Orations II :
In C. Verrem Actio II, Books III-V

IX. De Imperio Cn. Pompei (Pro Lege Manilia)
Pro Caecina
Pro Cluentio
Pro Rabirio Perduellionis Reo

X. In Catilinam I-IV
Pro Murena
Pro Sulla
Pro Flacco

XI. Pro Archia
Post Reditum in Senatu
Post Reditum ad Quirites

LIST OF CICERO'S WORKS

VOLUME

De Domo Sua
De Haruspicum Responsis
Pro Cn. Plancio

XII. Pro Sestio
In Vatinium

XIII. Pro Caelio
De Provinciis Consularibus
Pro Balbo

XIV. Pro Milone
In Pisonem
Pro Scauro
Pro Fonteio
Pro Rabirio Postumo
Pro Marcello
Pro Ligario
Pro Rege Deiotaro

XV. Philippics I-XIV

C. Philosophical Treatises 6 Volumes

XVI. De Re Publica
De Legibus

XVII. De Finibus Bonorum et Malorum

LIST OF CICERO'S WORKS

VOLUME

XVIII. Tusculan Disputations

XIX. De Natura Deorum
Academica I and II

XX. Cato Maior de Senectute
Laelius de Amicitia
De Divinatione

XXI. De Officiis

D. Letters. 7 Volumes

XXII. Letters to Atticus, Books I-VI

XXIII. Letters to Atticus, Books VII-XI

XXIV. Letters to Atticus, Books XII-XVI

XXV. Letters to His Friends, Books I-VI

XXVI. Letters to His Friends, Books VII-XII

XXVII. Letters to His Friends, Books XIII-XVI

XXVIII. Letters to His Brother Quintus
Letters to Brutus
Commentariolum Petitionis
Epistula ad Octavianum

DE NATURA DEORUM

M. TULLII CICERONIS DE NATURA DEORUM

AD M. BRUTUM

LIBER PRIMUS

1 I. Cum multae res in philosophia nequaquam satis adhuc explicatae sint, tum perdifficilis, Brute, quod tu minime ignoras, et perobscura quaestio est de natura deorum, quae et ad cognitionem animi pulcherrima est et ad moderandam religionem necessaria. De qua tam variae sunt doctissimorum hominum tamque discrepantes sententiae, ut magno argumento esse debeat causam et principium philosophiae esse inscientiam, prudenterque Academicos a rebus incertis adsensionem cohibuisse : quid est enim temeritate turpius ? aut quid tam temerarium tamque indignum sapientis gravitate atque constantia quam aut falsum sentire aut quod non satis explorate perceptum sit et cognitum sine ulla
2 dubitatione defendere ? Velut in hac quaestione plerique (quod maxime veri simile est et quo omnes

[a] Or perhaps 'which is both of extreme scientific interest.'

MARCUS TULLIUS CICERO
DE NATURA DEORUM

BOOK I

I. There are a number of branches of philosophy that have not as yet been by any means adequately explored; but the inquiry into the nature of the gods, which is both highly interesting in relation to the theory of the soul,[a] and fundamentally important for the regulation of religion, is one of special difficulty and obscurity, as you, Brutus, are well aware. The multiplicity and variety of the opinions held upon this subject by eminent scholars are bound to constitute a strong argument for the view that philosophy has its origin and starting-point in ignorance, and that the Academic School were well-advised in "withholding assent" from beliefs that are uncertain: for what is more unbecoming than ill-considered haste? and what is so ill-considered or so unworthy of the dignity and seriousness proper to a philosopher as to hold an opinion that is not true, or to maintain with unhesitating certainty a proposition not based on adequate examination, comprehension and knowledge? As regards the present subject, for example, most thinkers have affirmed that the gods exist, and this is the most

Preface. Diversity of opinions as to the gods.

Atheism.

duce natura venimus) deos esse dixerunt, dubitare se Protagoras, nullos esse omnino Diagoras Melius et Theodorus Cyrenaicus putaverunt. Qui vero deos esse dixerunt, tanta sunt in varietate et dissensione ut eorum molestum sit enumerare sententias. Nam et de figuris deorum et de locis atque sedibus et de actione vitae multa dicuntur, deque his summa philosophorum dissensione certatur; quod vero maxime rem causamque continet, utrum nihil agant, nihil moliantur, omni curatione et administratione rerum vacent, an contra ab iis et a principio omnia facta et constituta sint et ad infinitum tempus regantur atque moveantur, in primis magna dissensio est, eaque nisi diiudicatur in summo errore necesse est homines atque in maximarum rerum ignoratione
3 versari. II. Sunt enim philosophi et fuerunt qui omnino nullam habere censerent rerum humanarum procurationem deos. Quorum si vera sententia est, quae potest esse pietas, quae sanctitas, quae religio? Haec enim omnia pure atque caste tribuenda deorum numini ita sunt, si animadvertuntur ab iis et si est aliquid a deis inmortalibus hominum generi tributum. Sin autem dei neque possunt nos iuvare nec volunt, nec omnino curant nec quid agamus animadvertunt, nec est quod ab iis ad hominum vitam permanare

probable view and the one to which we are all led by nature's guidance; but Protagoras declared himself uncertain, and Diagoras of Melos and Theodorus of Cyrene held that there are no gods at all. Moreover, the upholders of the divine existence differ and disagree so widely, that it would be a troublesome task to recount their opinions. Many views are put forward about the outward form of the gods, their dwelling-places and abodes, and mode of life, and these topics are debated with the widest variety of opinion among philosophers; but as to the question upon which the whole issue of the dispute principally turns, whether the gods are entirely idle and inactive, taking no part at all in the direction and government of the world, or whether on the contrary all things both were created and ordered by them in the beginning and are controlled and kept in motion by them throughout eternity, here there is the greatest disagreement of all. And until this issue is decided, mankind must continue to labour under the profoundest uncertainty, and to be in ignorance about
3 matters of the highest moment. II. For there are and have been philosophers who hold that the gods exercise no control over human affairs whatever. But if their opinion is the true one, how can piety, reverence or religion exist? For all these are tributes which it is our duty to render in purity and holiness to the divine powers solely on the assumption that they take notice of them, and that some service has been rendered by the immortal gods to the race of men. But if on the contrary the gods have neither the power nor the will to aid us, if they pay no heed to us at all and take no notice of our actions, if they can exert no possible influence upon the life of

Denial of divine providenc

possit, quid est quod ullos deis inmortalibus cultus
honores preces adhibeamus? In specie autem fictae
simulationis sicut reliquae virtutes item pietas inesse
non potest, cum qua simul sanctitatem et religionem
tolli necesse est; quibus sublatis perturbatio vitae
4 sequitur et magna confusio,[1] atque haud scio an
pietate adversus deos sublata fides etiam et societas
generis humani et una excellentissima virtus iustitia
tollatur.

Sunt autem alii philosophi, et ii quidem magni
atque nobiles, qui deorum mente atque ratione
omnem mundum administrari et regi censeant,
neque vero id solum, sed etiam ab isdem hominum
vitae consuli et provideri; nam et fruges et reliqua
quae terra pariat, et tempestates ac temporum varietates caelique mutationes quibus omnia quae terra
gignat maturata pubescant, a dis inmortalibus tribui
generi humano putant, multaque (quae dicentur in
his libris) colligunt quae talia sunt ut ea ipsa dei
inmortales ad usum hominum fabricati paene videantur. Contra quos Carneades ita multa disseruit ut
excitaret homines non socordes ad veri investigandi
5 cupiditatem. Res enim nulla est de qua tantopere
non solum indocti sed etiam docti dissentiant;
quorum opiniones cum tam variae sint tamque inter
se dissidentes, alterum fieri profecto potest ut

[1] quibus . . . confusio *infra post* tollatur *tr. Wyttenbach.*

men, what ground have we for rendering any sort of worship, honour or prayer to the immortal gods? Piety however, like the rest of the virtues, cannot exist in mere outward show and pretence; and, with piety, reverence and religion must likewise disappear. And when these are gone, life soon becomes a welter of disorder and confusion; and in all probability the disappearance of piety towards the gods will entail the disappearance of loyalty and social union among men as well, and of justice itself, the queen of all the virtues.

Belief in providence.

There are however other philosophers, and those of eminence and note, who believe that the whole world is ruled and governed by divine intelligence and reason; and not this only, but also that the gods' providence watches over the life of men; for they think that the corn and other fruits of the earth, and also the weather and the seasons and the changes of the atmosphere by which all the products of the soil are ripened and matured, are the gift of the immortal gods to the human race; and they adduce a number of things, which will be recounted in the books that compose the present treatise, that are of such a nature as almost to appear to have been expressly constructed by the immortal gods for the use of man. This view was controverted at great length by Carneades, in such a manner as to arouse in persons of active mind a keen desire to discover the truth. There is in fact no subject upon which so much difference of opinion exists, not only among the unlearned but also among educated men; and the views entertained are so various and so discrepant, that, while it is no doubt a possible alternative that

earum nulla, alterum certe non potest ut plus una vera sit.

III. Qua quidem in causa et benivolos obiurgatores placare et invidos vituperatores confutare possumus, ut alteros reprehendisse paeniteat, alteri didicisse se gaudeant ; nam qui admonent amice docendi sunt, qui inimice insectantur repellendi.[1]

6 Multum autem fluxisse video de libris nostris, quos compluris brevi tempore edidimus, variumque sermonem partim admirantium unde hoc philosophandi nobis subito studium extitisset, partim quid quaque de re certi haberemus scire cupientium. Multis etiam sensi mirabile videri eam nobis potissimum probatam esse philosophiam quae lucem eriperet et quasi noctem quandam rebus offunderet, desertaeque disciplinae et iam pridem relictae patrocinium necopinatum a nobis esse susceptum.

Nos autem nec subito coepimus philosophari nec mediocrem a primo tempore aetatis in eo studio operam curamque consumpsimus et cum minime videbamur, tum maxime philosophabamur, quod et orationes declarant refertae philosophorum sententiis et doctissimorum hominum familiaritates quibus semper domus nostra floruit, et principes illi Diodotus Philo Antiochus Posidonius a quibus instituti sumus.
7 Et si omnia philosophiae praecepta referuntur ad vitam, arbitramur nos et publicis et privatis in rebus

[1] qua . . . repellendi *infra post* susceptum *tr. Mayor.*

none of them is true, it is certainly impossible that more than one should be so.

III. Upon this issue we are able both to appease kindly critics and to silence malicious fault-finders, causing the latter to repent of their censure and the former to welcome an accession to their knowledge. Friendly remonstrance must be met by explanation, hostile attack by refutation. **Author's reply to critics.**

I observe however that a great deal of talk has been current about the large number of books that I have produced within a short space of time, and that such comment has not been all of one kind; some people have been curious as to the cause of this sudden outburst of philosophical interest on my part, while others have been eager to learn what positive opinions I hold on the various questions. Many also, as I have noticed, are surprised at my choosing to espouse a philosophy that in their view robs the world of daylight and floods it with a darkness as of night; and they wonder at my coming forward so unexpectedly as the champion of a derelict system and one that has long been given up.

[As a matter of fact however I am no new convert to the study of philosophy. From my earliest youth I have devoted no small amount of time and energy to it, and I pursued it most keenly at the very periods when I least appeared to be doing so, witness the philosophical maxims of which my speeches are full, and my intimacy with the learned men who have always graced my household, as well as those eminent professors, Diodotus, Philo, Antiochus and Posidonius, who were my instructors. Moreover, if it be true that all the doctrines of philosophy have a practical bearing, I may claim that in my public and private **Philosophy his lifelong study.**

ea praestitisse quae ratio et doctrina praescripserit.
IV. Sin autem quis requirit quae causa nos inpulerit
ut haec tam sero litteris mandaremus, nihil est quod
expedire tam facile possimus. Nam cum otio lan-
gueremus et is esset rei publicae status ut eam
unius consilio atque cura gubernari necesse esset,
primum ipsius rei publicae causa philosophiam nostris
hominibus explicandam putavi, magni existimans
interesse ad decus et ad laudem civitatis res tam
gravis tamque praeclaras Latinis etiam litteris con-
8 tineri; eoque me minus instituti mei paenitet quod
facile sentio quam multorum non modo discendi sed
etiam scribendi studia commoverim. Complures
enim Graecis institutionibus eruditi ea quae didi-
cerant cum civibus suis communicare non poterant,
quod illa quae a Graecis accepissent Latine dici posse
diffiderent: quo in genere tantum profecisse videmur
ut a Graecis ne verborum quidem copia vincere-
9 mur. Hortata etiam est ut me ad haec conferrem
animi aegritudo fortunae magna et gravi commota
iniuria; cuius si maiorem aliquam levationem reperire
potuissem, non ad hanc potissimum confugissem,
ea vero ipsa nulla ratione melius frui potui quam si
me non modo ad legendos libros sed etiam ad totam

---

[a] The death of his daughter in 45 B.C.

conduct alike I have practised the precepts taught by reason and by theory. IV. If again anyone asks what motive has induced me so late in the day to commit these precepts to writing, there is nothing that I can explain more easily. I was languishing in idle retirement, and the state of public affairs was such that an autocratic form of government had become inevitable. In these circumstances, in the first place I thought that to expound philosophy to my fellow-countrymen was actually my duty in the interests of the commonwealth, since in my judgement it would greatly contribute to the honour and glory of the state to have thoughts so important and so lofty enshrined in Latin literature also; and I am the less inclined to repent of my undertaking because I can clearly perceive what a number of my readers have been stimulated not only to study but to become authors themselves. A great many accomplished students of Greek learning were unable to share their acquisitions with their fellow-citizens, on the ground that they doubted the possibility of conveying in Latin the teachings they had received from the Greeks. In the matter of style however I believe that we have made such progress that even in richness of vocabulary the Greeks do not surpass us. Another thing that urged me to this occupation was the dejection of spirit occasioned by the heavy and crushing blow [a] that had been dealt me by fortune. Had I been able to find any more effective relief from my sorrow, I should not have had recourse to this particular form of consolation; but the best way open to me of enjoying even this consolation to the full extent was to devote myself not only to reading books but also to composing a treatise on the whole

Philosophical writing an occupation for his retirement, a patriotic duty, and a consolation in his bereavement.

philosophiam pertractandam dedissem. Omnes autem eius partes atque omnia membra tum facillume noscuntur cum totae quaestiones scribendo explicantur; est enim admirabilis quaedam continuatio seriesque rerum, ut alia ex alia nexa et omnes inter se aptae conligataeque videantur.

10 V. Qui autem requirunt quid quaque de re ipsi sentiamus, curiosius id faciunt quam necesse est; non enim tam auctoritatis in disputando quam rationis momenta quaerenda sunt. Quin etiam obest plerumque iis qui discere volunt auctoritas eorum qui se docere profitentur; desinunt enim suum iudicium adhibere, id habent ratum quod ab eo quem probant iudicatum vident. Nec vero probare soleo id quod de Pythagoreis accepimus, quos ferunt, si quid adfirmarent in disputando, cum ex eis quaereretur quare ita esset, respondere solitos 'Ipse dixit'[a]; 'ipse' autem erat Pythagoras: tantum opinio praeiudicata poterat, ut etiam sine ratione valeret auctoritas.

11 Qui autem admirantur nos hanc potissimum disciplinam secutos, iis quattuor Academicis libris satis responsum videtur. Nec vero desertarum relictarumque rerum patrocinium suscepimus; non enim hominum interitu sententiae quoque occidunt, sed lucem auctoris fortasse desiderant; ut haec in

---

[a] Αὐτὸς ἔφη: as one might say 'The Master said so.'

of philosophy. Now the readiest mode of imparting a knowledge of the subject in all its departments and branches is to write an exposition of the various methods in their entirety; since it is a striking characteristic of philosophy that its topics all hang together and form a consecutive system; one is seen to be linked to another, and all to be mutually connected and attached.]

Lack of dogmatism justified.

V. Those however who seek to learn my personal opinion on the various questions show an unreasonable degree of curiosity. In discussion it is not so much weight of authority as force of argument that should be demanded. Indeed the authority of those who profess to teach is often a positive hindrance to those who desire to learn; they cease to employ their own judgement, and take what they perceive to be the verdict of their chosen master as settling the question. In fact I am not disposed to approve the practice traditionally ascribed to the Pythagoreans, who, when questioned as to the grounds of any assertion that they advanced in debate, are said to have been accustomed to reply 'He himself said so,'[a] 'he himself' being Pythagoras. So potent was an opinion already decided, making authority prevail unsupported by reason.

Academic doctrine of probability

To those again who are surprised at my choice of a system to which to give my allegiance, I think that a sufficient answer has been given in the four books of my *Academica*. Nor is it the case that I have come forward as the champion of a lost cause and of a position now abandoned. When men die, their doctrines do not perish with them, though perhaps they suffer from the loss of their authoritative exponent. Take for example the philosophical method referred

philosophia ratio contra omnia disserendi nullamque rem aperte iudicandi profecta a Socrate, repetita ab Arcesila, confirmata a Carneade usque ad nostram viguit aetatem; quam nunc prope modum orbam esse in ipsa Graecia intellego. Quod non Academiae vitio sed tarditate hominum arbitror contigisse; nam si singulas disciplinas percipere magnum est, quanto maius omnis? quod facere iis necesse est quibus propositum est veri reperiendi causa et contra omnis
12 philosophos et pro omnibus dicere. Cuius rei tantae tamque difficilis facultatem consecutum esse me non profiteor, secutum esse prae me fero. Nec tamen fieri potest ut qui hac ratione philosophentur ii nihil habeant quod sequantur. Dictum est omnino de hac re alio loco diligentius, sed quia nimis indociles quidam tardique sunt admonendi videntur saepius. Non enim sumus ii quibus nihil verum esse videatur, sed ii qui omnibus veris falsa quaedam adiuncta esse dicamus tanta similitudine ut in iis nulla insit certa iudicandi et adsentiendi nota. Ex quo exstitit illud, multa esse probabilia, quae quamquam non perciperentur, tamen, quia visum quendam haberent insignem et inlustrem iis sapientis vita regeretur.

13 VI. Sed iam, ut omni me invidia liberem, ponam in medio sententias philosophorum de natura deorum.

---

[a] The Stoics on the contrary held that true sensations are distinguished from false ones by an infallible mark (σημεῖον, *nota*, *signum*) and command our instinctive assent to their truth.

to, that of a purely negative dialectic which refrains from pronouncing any positive judgement. This, after being originated by Socrates, revived by Arcesilas, and reinforced by Carneades, has flourished right down to our own period; though I understand that in Greece itself it is now almost bereft of adherents. But this I ascribe not to the fault of the Academy but to the dullness of mankind. If it is a considerable matter to understand any one of the systems of philosophy singly, how much harder is it to master them all! Yet this is the task that confronts those whose principle is to discover the truth by the method of arguing both for and against all the schools. In an undertaking so extensive and so arduous, I do not profess to have attained success, though I do claim to have attempted it. At the same time it would be impossible for the adherents of this method to dispense altogether with any standard of guidance. This matter it is true I have discussed elsewhere more thoroughly; but some people are so dull and slow of apprehension that they appear to require repeated explanations. Our position is not that we hold that nothing is true, but that we assert that all true sensations are associated with false ones so closely resembling them that they contain no infallible mark to guide our judgement and assent.[a] From this followed the corollary, that many sensations are *probable*, that is, though not amounting to a full perception they are yet possessed of a certain distinctness and clearness, and so can serve to direct the conduct of the wise man.

Undogmatic exposition specially appropriate

VI. However, to free myself entirely from ill-disposed criticism, I will now lay before my readers the doctrines of the various schools on the nature

Quo quidem loco convocandi omnes videntur qui quae sit earum vera iudicent; tum demum mihi procax[1] Academia videbitur, si aut consenserint omnes aut erit inventus aliquis qui quid verum sit invenerit. Itaque mihi libet exclamare ut in[2] *Synephebis*:

> pró deum, populárium omnium, <ómnium>[3] adulescéntium
> clámo postulo óbsecro oro plóro atque inploró fidem

non levissuma de re, ut queritur ille ' in civitate ' fieri ' facinora capitalia '—

> ab amico amante argentum accipere meretrix non vult,

14 sed ut adsint cognoscant animadvertant, quid de religione pietate sanctitate caerimoniis fide iure iurando, quid de templis delubris sacrificiisque sollemnibus, quid de ipsis auspiciis quibus nos praesumus existimandum sit (haec enim omnia ad hanc de dis inmortalibus quaestionem referenda sunt): profecto eos ipsos qui se aliquid certi habere arbitrantur addubitare coget doctissimorum hominum de maxuma re tanta dissensio.

15 Quod cum saepe alias, tum maxime animadverti cum apud C. Cottam familiarem meum accurate sane et diligenter de dis inmortalibus disputatum est. Nam cum feriis Latinis ad eum ipsius rogatu arcessi-

[1] pervicax *Reid.*
[2] ut Statius in *dett.*: ut est in, ut ille in *edd., sed nescio an personae nomen exciderit.*
[3] *add. Manutius.*

---

[a] A play of Caecilius Statius translated from Menander.
[b] Cicero was elected a member of the College of Augurs in 53 B.C.

of the gods. This is a topic on which it seems proper to summon all the world to sit in judgement and pronounce which of these doctrines is the true one. If it turn out that all the schools agree, or if any one philosopher be found who has discovered the truth, then but not before I will convict the Academy of captiousness. This being so, I feel disposed to cry, in the words of the *Young Comrades* [a]:

to the subject of this treatise Theology.

> O ye gods and O ye mortals, townsmen, gownsmen, hear my call;
> I invoke, implore, adjure ye, bear ye witness one and all—

not about some frivolous trifle such as that of which a character in the play complains—

> . . . here's a monstrous crime and outrage in the land;
> Here's a lady who declines a guinea from a lover's hand!

but to attend in court, try the case, and deliver their verdict as to what opinions we are to hold about religion, piety and holiness, about ritual, about honour and loyalty to oaths, about temples, shrines and solemn sacrifices, and about the very auspices over which I myself preside [b]; for all of these matters ultimately depend upon this question of the nature of the immortal gods. Surely such wide diversity of opinion among men of the greatest learning on a matter of the highest moment must affect even those who think that they possess certain knowledge with a feeling of doubt.

Introduction to the dialogue.

This has often struck me, but it did so with especial force on one occasion, when the topic of the immortal gods was made the subject of a very searching and thorough discussion at the house of my friend Gaius Cotta. It was the Latin Festival, and I had come at Cotta's express invitation to pay him a visit. I

tuque venissem, offendi eum sedentem in exedra et cum C. Velleio senatore disputantem, ad quem tum Epicurei primas ex nostris hominibus deferebant. Aderat etiam Q. Lucilius Balbus, qui tantos progressus habebat in Stoicis ut cum excellentibus in eo genere Graecis compararetur.

Tum ut me Cotta vidit, " Peropportune " inquit " venis ; oritur enim mihi magna de re altercatio cum Velleio, cui pro tuo studio non est alienum te interesse."

16 VII. " Atqui mihi quoque videor " inquam " venisse ut dicis opportune. Tres enim trium disciplinarum principes convenistis. M. enim[1] Piso si adesset, nullius philosophiae, earum quidem quae in honore sunt, vacaret locus."

Tum Cotta " Si," inquit, " liber Antiochi nostri, qui ab eo nuper ad hunc Balbum missus est, vera loquitur, nihil est quod Pisonem familiarem tuum desideres ; Antiocho enim Stoici cum Peripateticis re concinere videntur, verbis discrepare ; quo de libro, Balbe, velim scire quid sentias."

" Egone ? " inquit ille, " miror Antiochum hominem in primis acutum non vidisse interesse plurimum inter Stoicos, qui honesta a commodis non nomine sed genere toto diiungerent, et Peripateticos, qui honesta commiscerent cum commodis, ut ea inter se magnitudine et quasi gradibus, non genere differrent. Haec enim est non verborum parva sed rerum per-

[1] etiam *Heindorf*, autem *Müller*.

found him sitting in an alcove, engaged in debate with Gaius Velleius, a Member of the Senate, accounted by the Epicureans as their chief Roman adherent at the time. With them was Quintus Lucilius Balbus, who was so accomplished a student of Stoicism as to rank with the leading Greek exponents of that system.

When Cotta saw me, he greeted me with the words: "You come exactly at the right moment, for I am just engaging in a dispute with Velleius on an important topic, in which you with your tastes will be interested to take part."

6 VII. "Well, I too," I replied, "think I have come at the right moment, as you say. For here are you, three leaders of three schools of philosophy, met in congress. In fact we only want Marcus Piso to have every considerable school represented."

"Oh," rejoined Cotta, "if what is said in the book which our master Antiochus lately dedicated to our good Balbus here is true, you have no need to regret the absence of your friend Piso. Antiochus holds the view that the doctrines of the Stoics, though differing in form of expression, agree in substance with those of the Peripatetics. I should like to know your opinion of the book, Balbus."

"My opinion?" said Balbus, "Why, I am surprised that a man of first-rate intellect like Antiochus should have failed to see what a gulf divides the Stoics, who distinguish expediency and right not in name only but in essential nature, from the Peripatetics, who class the right and the expedient together, and only recognize differences of quantity or degree, not of kind, between them. This is not a slight verbal discrepancy, but a fundamental difference of

17 magna dissensio. Verum hoc alias; nunc quod coepimus, si videtur."

"Mihi vero," inquit Cotta, "videtur. Sed ut hic qui intervenit" me intuens "ne ignoret quae res agatur, de natura agebamus deorum, quae cum mihi videretur perobscura, ut semper videri solet, Epicuri ex Velleio sciscitabar sententiam. Quam ob rem," inquit "Vellei, nisi molestum est, repete quae coeperas."

"Repetam vero, quamquam non mihi sed tibi hic venit adiutor; ambo enim" inquit adridens, "ab eodem Philone nihil scire didicistis."

Tum ego: "Quid didicerimus Cotta viderit, tu autem nolo me existimes adiutorem huic venisse sed auditorem, et quidem aequum, libero iudicio, nulla eius modi adstrictum necessitate ut mihi velim nolim sit certa quaedam tuenda sententia."

18 VIII. Tum Velleius fidenter sane, ut solent isti, nihil tam verens quam ne dubitare aliqua de re videretur, tamquam modo ex deorum concilio et ex Epicuri intermundiis descendisset, "Audite" inquit, "non futtilis commenticiasque sententias, non opificem aedificatoremque mundi, Platonis de Timaeo deum, nec anum fatidicam Stoicorum πρόνοιαν, quam Latine licet providentiam dicere, neque vero

[a] Epicurus taught that gods dwelt in empty spaces between the material worlds.

doctrine. However we can discuss this some other time. For the moment we will, if you please, continue the topic which we had begun."

"Agreed," cried Cotta; "but to let the newcomer know what is the subject of discussion"—here he glanced at me—"I will explain that we were debating the nature of the gods: a question which seemed to me, as it always does, an extremely obscure one, and upon which I was therefore inquiring of Velleius as to the opinion of Epicurus. So if you do not mind, Velleius," he continued, "please resume the exposition that you had begun."

"I will do so," replied Velleius, "although it is not I but you who have been reinforced by an ally—since both of you," he said, with a smile in our direction, "are disciples of Philo, and have learned from him to know nothing."

"What we have learned," I rejoined, "shall be Cotta's affair; but pray don't think I have come to act as his ally, but as a listener, and an impartial and unprejudiced listener too, under no sort of bond or obligation willy nilly to uphold some fixed opinion."

Theology of Epicurus expounded by Velleius (§§ 18-56).

VIII. Hereupon Velleius began, in the confident manner (I need not say) that is customary with Epicureans, afraid of nothing so much as lest he should appear to have doubts about anything. One would have supposed he had just come down from the assembly of the gods in the intermundane spaces of Epicurus[a]! "I am not going to expound to you doctrines that are mere baseless figments of the imagination, such as the artisan deity and world-builder of Plato's *Timaeus*, or that old hag of a fortune-teller, the *Pronoia* (which we may render 'Providence') of the Stoics; nor yet a world endowed with a mind and

mundum ipsum animo et sensibus praeditum, rotundum ardentem volubilem deum, portenta et miracula
non disserentium philosophorum sed somniantium.
19 Quibus enim oculis animi[1] intueri potuit vester Plato
fabricam illam tanti operis, qua construi a deo atque
aedificari mundum facit? quae molitio, quae ferramenta, qui vectes, quae machinae, qui ministri tanti
muneris fuerunt? quem ad modum autem oboedire
et parere voluntati architecti aër ignis aqua terra
potuerunt? unde vero ortae illae quinque formae ex
quibus reliqua formantur, apte cadentes ad animum
afficiendum pariendosque sensus? Longum est ad
omnia, quae talia sunt ut optata magis quam inventa
20 videantur; sed illa palmaria,[2] quod qui non modo
natum mundum introduxerit sed etiam manu paene
factum, is eum dixerit fore sempiternum. Hunc
censes primis ut dicitur labris gustasse physiologiam,
id est naturae rationem, qui quicquam quod ortum
sit putet aeternum esse posse? Quae est enim
coagmentatio non dissolubilis? aut quid est cui
principium aliquod sit, nihil sit extremum? Pronoea
vero si vestra est, Lucili, eadem,[3] requiro quae
paulo ante, ministros machinas omnem totius operis
dissignationem atque apparatum; sin alia est, cur
mortalem fecerit mundum, non quem ad modum
21 Platonicus deus sempiternum. IX. Ab utroque au-

[1] animi *om. ed. Veneta.*
[2] palmaria *Davies*: palmaris.
[3] eadem, <eadem> *Heindorf.*

---

[a] Pyramid, cube, octohedron, dodecahedron, eicosihedron; the shapes respectively of the particles of fire, earth, air, aether, water.

senses of its own, a spherical, rotatory god of burning fire; these are the marvels and monstrosities of philosophers who do not reason but dream. What power of mental vision enabled your master Plato to descry the vast and elaborate architectural process which, as he makes out, the deity adopted in building the structure of the universe? What method of engineering was employed? What tools and levers and derricks? What agents carried out so vast an undertaking? And how were air, fire, water and earth enabled to obey and execute the will of the architect? How did the five regular solids,[a] which are the basis of all other forms of matter, come into existence so nicely adapted to make impressions on our minds and produce sensations? It would be a lengthy task to advert upon every detail of a system that is such as to seem the result of idle theorizing rather than of real research; but the prize example is that the thinker who represented the world not merely as having had an origin but even as almost made by hand, also declared that it will exist for ever. Can you suppose that a man can have even dipped into natural philosophy if he imagines that anything that has come into being can be eternal? What composite whole is not capable of dissolution? What thing is there that has a beginning but not an end? While as for your Stoic Providence, Lucilius, if it is the same thing as Plato's creator, I repeat my previous questions, what were its agents and instruments, and how was the entire undertaking planned out and carried through? If on the contrary it is something different, I ask why it made the world mortal, and not everlasting as did Plato's divine creator? IX. Moreover I would put to both of you

Platonic and Stoic theologies and cosmology ridiculed.

tem sciscitor cur mundi aedificatores repente exstiterint, innumerabilia saecla dormierint; non enim, si mundus nullus erat, saecla non erant (saecla nunc dico non ea quae dierum noctiumque numero annuis cursibus conficiuntur, nam fateor ea sine mundi conversione effici non potuisse; sed fuit quaedam ab infinito tempore aeternitas, quam nulla circumscriptio temporum metiebatur, spatio tamen qualis ea fuerit intellegi potest,[1] quod ne in cogitationem quidem cadit ut fuerit tempus aliquod nullum cum
22 tempus esset)—isto igitur tam inmenso spatio quaero, Balbe, cur Pronoea vestra cessaverit. Laboremne fugiebat? At iste nec attingit deum nec erat ullus, cum omnes naturae numini divino, caelum ignes terrae maria, parerent. Quid autem erat quod concupisceret deus mundum signis et luminibus tamquam aedilis ornare? Si ut [deus][2] ipse melius habitaret, antea videlicet tempore infinito in tenebris tamquam in gurgustio habitaverat; post autem varietatene eum delectari putamus qua caelum et terras exornatas videmus? Quae ista potest esse oblectatio deo? quae si esset, non ea tam diu carere
23 potuisset. An haec, ut fere dicitis, hominum causa a deo constituta sunt? Sapientiumne? Propter paucos igitur tanta est facta rerum molitio. An stultorum? At primum causa non fuit cur de inprobis bene mereretur; deinde quid est adsecutus?

[1] intellegi non potest *dett.*
[2] *secl. Ernesti.*

---

[a] There is a play on words in *signis et luminibus*, which denote both the constellations and luminaries of the sky and the statues and illuminations with which the aediles adorned the city for festivals.

the question, why did these deities suddenly awake into activity as world-builders after countless ages of slumber? for though the world did not exist, it does not follow that ages did not exist—meaning by ages, not periods made up of a number of days and nights in annual courses, for ages in this sense I admit could not have been produced without the circular motion of the firmament; but from the infinite past there has existed an eternity not measured by limited divisions of time, but of a nature intelligible in terms of extension; since it is inconceivable that there was ever a
22 time when time did not exist. Well then, Balbus, what I ask is, why did your Providence remain idle all through that extent of time of which you speak? Was it in order to avoid fatigue? But god cannot know fatigue; and also there was no fatigue in question, since all the elements, sky, fire, earth and sea, were obedient to the divine will. Also, why should god take a fancy to decorate the firmament with figures and illuminations,[a] like an aedile? If it was to embellish his own abode, then it seems that he had previously been dwelling for an infinite time in a dark and gloomy hovel! And are we to suppose that thenceforward the varied beauties which we see adorning earth and sky have afforded him pleasure? How can a god take pleasure in things of this sort? And if he did, he could not have dis-
23 pensed with it so long. Or were these beauties designed for the sake of men, as your school usually maintains? For the sake of wise men? If so, all this vast effort of construction took place on account of a handful of people. For the sake of fools then? But in the first place there was no reason for god to do a service to the wicked; and secondly, what good

cum omnes stulti sint sine dubio miserrimi, maxime quod stulti sunt (miserius enim stultitia quid possumus dicere ?), deinde quod ita multa sunt incommoda in vita ut ea sapientes commodorum conpensatione leniant, stulti nec vitare venientia possint nec ferre praesentia ? X. Qui vero mundum ipsum animantem sapientemque esse dixerunt, nullo modo viderunt animi natura intellegentis in quam figuram cadere posset. De quo dicam equidem paulo post,
24 nunc autem hactenus : admirabor eorum tarditatem qui animantem inmortalem et eundem beatum rotundum esse velint quod ea forma neget ullam esse pulchriorem Plato ; at mihi vel cylindri vel quadrati vel coni vel pyramidis videtur esse formosior. Quae vero vita tribuitur isti rotundo deo ? Nempe ut ea celeritate contorqueatur cui par nulla ne cogitari quidem possit ; in qua non video ubinam mens constans et vita beata possit insistere. Quodque in nostro corpore si minima ex parte † significetur[1] molestum sit, cur hoc idem non habeatur molestum in deo ? Terra enim profecto, quoniam mundi pars est, pars est etiam dei ; atqui terrae maxumas regiones inhabitabilis atque incultas videmus, quod pars earum adpulsu solis exarserit, pars obriguerit nive pruinaque longinquo solis abscessu ; quae, si mundus est deus, quoniam mundi partes sunt, dei

[1] sic afficiatur *Schömann* : <frigore aut solis igni> uexetur *Goethe*.

did he do? inasmuch as all fools are beyond question extremely miserable, precisely because they are fools (for what can be mentioned more miserable than folly?), and in the second place because there are so many troubles in life that, though wise men can assuage them by balancing against them life's advantages, fools can neither avoid their approach nor endure their presence. X. Those on the other hand who said that the world is itself endowed with life and with wisdom, failed entirely to discern what shape the nature of an intelligent living being could conceivably possess. I will touch
24 on this a little later; for the present I will confine myself to expressing my surprise at their stupidity in holding that a being who is immortal and also blessed is of a spherical shape, merely on the ground that Plato pronounces a sphere to be the most beautiful of all figures. For my own part, on the score of appearance I prefer either a cylinder or a cube or a cone or a pyramid. Then, what mode of existence is assigned to their spherical deity? Why, he is in a state of rotation, spinning round with a velocity that surpasses all powers of conception. But what room there can be in such an existence for steadfastness of mind and for happiness, I cannot see. Also, why should a condition that is painful in the human body, if even the smallest part of it is affected, be supposed to be painless in the deity? Now clearly the earth, being a part of the world, is also a part of god. Yet we see that vast portions of the earth's surface are uninhabitable deserts, being either scorched by the sun's proximity, or frost-bound and covered with snow owing to its extreme remoteness. But if the world is god, these, being parts of the

membra partim ardentia partim refrigerata dicenda sunt.

25 "Atque haec quidem vestra, Lucili; qualia vero * * est,[1] ab ultimo repetam superiorum. Thales enim Milesius, qui primus de talibus rebus quaesivit, aquam dixit esse initium rerum, deum eam mentem quae ex aqua cuncta fingeret—si[2] di possunt esse sine sensu; et mentem[3] cur aquae adiunxit, si ipsa mens constare potest vacans corpore? Anaximandri autem opinio est nativos esse deos longis intervallis orientis occidentisque, eosque innumerabilis esse mundos. Sed nos deum nisi sempiternum intellegere
26 qui possumus? Post Anaximenes aera deum statuit, eumque gigni esseque inmensum et infinitum et semper in motu: quasi aut aer sine ulla forma deus esse possit, cum praesertim deum non modo aliqua sed pulcherrima specie deceat esse, aut non omne quod ortum sit mortalitas consequatur. XI. Inde Anaxagoras, qui accepit ab Anaximene disciplinam, primus omnium rerum discriptionem et modum mentis infinitae vi ac ratione dissignari et confici voluit; in quo non vidit neque motum sensui iunctum et continentem in infinito[4] ullum esse posse, neque sensum omnino quo non ipsa natura pulsa sentiret. Deinde si mentem istam quasi animal aliquod voluit esse, erit aliquid interius ex quo illud animal nomine-

[1] qualia uero alia sint *B corr.* · *sed veri simile est aliqua verba excidisse.*
[2] si *det.*, sic *A*, *B*.
[3] mentem *B*, mente *cett.*; *post* mente *lacunam edd.*
[4] incontinentem infinito *A*, *B*.

world, must be regarded as limbs of god, undergoing the extremes of heat and cold respectively.

Theology of other schools from Thales downward refuted.

5 "So much, Lucilius, for the doctrines of your school. To show what <the older systems> are like, I will trace their history from the remotest of your predecessors. Thales of Miletus, who was the first person to investigate these matters, said that water was the first principle of things, but that god was the mind that moulded all things out of water—supposing that gods can exist without sensation; and why did he make mind an adjunct of water, if mind can exist by itself, devoid of body? The view of Anaximander is that the gods are not everlasting but are born and perish at long intervals of time, and that they are worlds, countless in number. But how can we conceive of god save as living for ever?
3 Next, Anaximenes held that air is god, and that it has a beginning in time, and is immeasurable and infinite in extent, and is always in motion; just as if formless air could be god, especially seeing that it is proper to god to possess not merely some shape but the most beautiful shape; or as if anything that has had a beginning must not necessarily be mortal. XI. Then there is Anaxagoras, the successor of Anaximenes; he was the first thinker to hold that the orderly disposition of the universe is designed and perfected by the rational power of an infinite mind. But in saying this he failed to see that there can be no such thing as sentient and continuous activity in that which is infinite, and that sensation in general can only occur when the subject itself becomes sentient by the impact of a sensation. Further, if he intended his infinite mind to be a definite living creature, it must have some inner principle of life to justify the name.

tur; quid autem interius mente? cingetur[1] igitur
27 corpore externo; quod quoniam non placet, aperta simplexque mens, nulla re adiuncta qua[2] sentire possit, fugere intellegentiae nostrae vim et notionem videtur. Crotoniates autem Alcmaeo, qui soli et lunae reliquisque sideribus animoque praeterea divinitatem dedit, non sensit sese mortalibus rebus inmortalitatem dare. Nam Pythagoras, qui censuit animum esse per naturam rerum omnem intentum et commeantem ex quo nostri animi carperentur, non vidit distractione humanorum animorum discerpi et lacerari deum, et cum miseri animi essent, quod plerisque contingeret, tum dei partem esse miseram,
28 quod fieri non potest. Cur autem quicquam ignoraret animus hominis, si esset deus? quo modo porro deus iste, si nihil esset nisi animus, aut infixus aut infusus esset in mundo? Tum Xenophanes, qui mente adiuncta omne propterea[3] quod esset infinitum deum voluit esse, de ipsa mente item reprehenditur ut ceteri, de infinitate autem vehementius, in qua nihil neque sentiens neque coniunctum potest esse. Nam Parmenides quidem commenticium quiddam[4] coronae simile efficit (στεφάνην appellat), continentem ardorum[5] lucis orbem qui cingit[6] caelum, quem appellat deum; in quo neque figuram divinam neque sensum quisquam suspicari potest, multaque eiusdem monstra, quippe qui bellum, qui discordiam, qui cupiditatem ceteraque generis eiusdem ad deum revocet, quae vel morbo

[1] cingetur *Ast*: cingatur.
[2] qua *St. Augustine*: quae.
[3] propterea *Reid*: praeterea.
[4] Iam P. quiddam commenticium *? ed.*
[5] ardorum *pr. B*: ardorem.
[6] cingat *Ernesti*.

But mind is itself the innermost principle. Mind therefore will have an outer integument of body. But this Anaxagoras will not allow; yet mind naked and simple, without any material adjunct to serve as an organ of sensation, seems to elude the capacity of our understanding. Alcmaeon of Croton, who attributed divinity to the sun, moon and other heavenly bodies, and also to the soul, did not perceive that he was bestowing immortality on things that are mortal. As for Pythagoras, who believed that the entire substance of the universe is penetrated and pervaded by a soul of which our souls are fragments, he failed to notice that this severance of the souls of men from the world-soul means the dismemberment and rending asunder of god; and that when their souls are unhappy, as happens to most men, then a portion of god is unhappy; which is impossible. Again, if the soul of man is divine, why is it not omniscient? Moreover, if the Pythagorean god is pure soul, how is he implanted in, or diffused throughout, the world? Next, Xenophanes endowed the universe with mind, and held that, as being infinite, it was god. His view of mind is as open to objection as that of the rest; but on the subject of infinity he incurs still severer criticism, for the infinite can have no sensation and no contact with anything outside. As for Parmenides, he invents a purely fanciful something resembling a crown—*stephanè* is his name for it—, an unbroken ring of glowing lights, encircling the sky, which he entitles god; but no one can imagine this to possess divine form, or sensation. He also has many other portentous notions; he deifies war, strife, lust and the like, things which can be destroyed by disease or sleep or forget-

vel somno vel oblivione vel vetustate delentur; eademque de sideribus, quae reprehensa in alio iam
29 in hoc omittantur. XII. Empedocles autem multa alia peccans in deorum opinione turpissume labitur. Quattuor enim naturas ex quibus omnia constare censet divinas esse vult; quas et nasci et extingui perspicuum est et sensu omni carere. Nec vero Protagoras, qui sese negat omnino de deis habere quod liqueat, sint non sint qualesve sint, quicquam videtur de natura deorum suspicari. Quid? Democritus, qui tum imagines earumque circumitus in deorum numerum[1] refert, tum illam naturam quae imagines fundat ac mittat, tum scientiam[2] intellegentiamque nostram, nonne in maximo errore versatur? cum idem omnino, quia nihil semper suo statu maneat, negat[3] esse quicquam sempiternum, nonne deum omnino ita tollit ut nullam opinionem eius reliquam faciat? Quid? aër, quo Diogenes Apolloniates utitur deo, quem sensum habere potest
30 aut quam formam dei? Iam de Platonis inconstantia longum est dicere, qui in Timaeo patrem huius mundi nominari neget posse, in Legum autem libris, quid sit omnino deus anquiri oportere non censeat. Quod[4] vero sine corpore ullo deum vult esse (ut Graeci dicunt ἀσώματον), id quale esse possit intellegi non potest: careat enim sensu necesse est, careat etiam prudentia, careat voluptate; quae omnia una

[1] numerum *Lambinus*: numero.
[2] scientiam *dett.*: sententiam sensum; *ci. Plasberg.*
[3] negat *pr. B*: neget.
[4] Quod . . . comprehendimus *infra post* Idem . . . repugnantia *transponenda Mayor.*

---

[a] See *infra*, § 120 n.
[b] *Timaeus* 28 c.
[c] *Laws* vii. 821.

fulness or lapse of time; and he also deifies the stars, but this has been criticized in another philosopher and need not be dealt with now in the case of
9 Parmenides. XII. Empedocles again among many other blunders comes to grief most disgracefully in his theology. He assigns divinity to the four substances which in his system are the constituent elements of the universe, although manifestly these substances both come into and pass out of existence, and are entirely devoid of sensation. Protagoras also, who declares he has no clear views whatever about the gods, whether they exist or do not exist, or what they are like, seems to have no notion at all of the divine nature. Then in what a maze of error is Democritus [a] involved, who at one moment ranks as gods his roving 'images,' at another the substance that emits and radiates these images, and at another again the scientific intelligence of man! At the same time his denial of immutability, and therefore of eternity, to everything whatsoever surely involves a repudiation of deity so absolute as to leave no conception of a divine being remaining! Diogenes of Apollonia makes air a god; but how can air
30 have sensation, or divinity in any shape? The inconsistencies of Plato are a long story. In the *Timaeus* [b] he says that it is impossible to name the father of this universe; and in the *Laws* [c] he deprecates all inquiry into the nature of the deity. Again,[d] he holds that god is entirely incorporeal (in Greek, *asomatos*); but divine incorporeity is inconceivable, for an incorporeal deity would necessarily be incapable of sensation, and also of practical wisdom, and of pleasure, all of which

[a] This sentence should probably follow the next one.

cum deorum notione comprehendimus. Idem et in Timaeo dicit et in Legibus et mundum deum esse et caelum et astra et terram et animos et eos quos maiorum institutis accepimus; quae et per se sunt falsa perspicue et inter se vehementer repugnantia.
31 Atque etiam Xenophon paucioribus verbis eadem fere peccat; facit enim in iis quae a Socrate dicta rettulit Socratem disputantem formam dei quaeri non oportere, eundemque et solem et animum deum dicere, et modo unum tum autem plures deos; quae sunt isdem in erratis fere quibus ea quae de
32 Platone diximus. XIII. Atque etiam Antisthenes in eo libro qui Physicus inscribitur popularis deos multos naturalem unum esse dicens tollit vim et naturam deorum. Nec multo secus Speusippus Platonem avunculum subsequens et vim quandam dicens qua omnia regantur, eamque animalem, evel-
33 lere ex animis conatur cognitionem deorum. Aristotelesque in tertio de philosophia libro multa turbat a magistro suo[1] Platone <non>[2] dissentiens; modo enim menti tribuit omnem divinitatem, modo mundum ipsum deum dicit esse, modo alium quendam praeficit mundo eique eas partis tribuit ut replicatione quadam mundi motum regat atque tueatur,

[1] suo *dett.*: uno *A*, *B*. [2] *Manutius*.

---

[a] The *Memorabilia*.

[b] One of the popular treatises of Aristotle not now extant, quoted i. 107, ii. 37, 42, 44, 51, 95.

[c] The insertion of the negative is a probable emendation, since the identification of the Peripatetic doctrines with

are attributes essential to our conception of deity. Yet both in the *Timaeus* and the *Laws* he says that the world, the sky, the stars, the earth and our souls are gods, in addition to those in whom we have been taught to believe by ancestral tradition; but it is obvious that these propositions are both inherently false and mutually destructive. Xenophon also commits almost the same errors, though in fewer words; for in his memoir [a] of the sayings of Socrates he represents Socrates as arguing that it is wrong to inquire about the form of god, but also as saying that both the sun and the soul are god, and as speaking at one moment of a single god and at another of several: utterances that involve almost the same mistakes as do those which we quoted from Plato. XIII. Antisthenes also, in his book entitled *The Natural Philosopher*, says that while there are many gods of popular belief, there is one god in nature, so depriving divinity of all meaning or substance. Very similarly Speusippus, following his uncle Plato, and speaking of a certain force that governs all things and is endowed with life, does his best to root out the notion of deity from our minds altogether. And Aristotle in the Third Book of his *Philosophy* [b] has a great many confused notions, <not> [c] disagreeing with the doctrines of his master Plato; at one moment he assigns divinity exclusively to the intellect, at another he says that the world is itself a god, then again he puts some other being over the world, and assigns to this being the rôle of regulating and sustaining the world-motion by means of a sort

those of Plato was made by Antiochus, and is often propounded by Cicero (Mayor); although it is true that it is not appropriate to the Epicurean speaker here (Plasberg).

tum caeli ardorem deum dicit esse, non intellegens caelum mundi esse partem quem alio loco ipse designarit deum. Quo modo autem caeli divinus ille sensus in celeritate tanta conservari potest? ubi deinde illi tot di, si numeramus etiam caelum deum? cum autem sine corpore idem vult esse deum, omni illum sensu privat, <privat>[1] etiam prudentia. Quo porro modo [mundus][2] moveri carens corpore, aut quo modo semper se movens esse quietus et beatus
34 potest? Nec vero eius condiscipulus Xenocrates in hoc genere prudentior, cuius in libris qui sunt de natura deorum nulla species divina describitur; deos enim octo esse dicit, quinque eos qui in stellis vagis moventur,[3] unum qui ex omnibus sideribus quae infixa caelo sunt ex dispersis quasi membris simplex sit putandus deus, septimum solem adiungit octavamque lunam; qui quo sensu beati esse possint, intellegi non potest. Ex eadem Platonis schola Ponticus Heraclides puerilibus fabulis refersit libros et [tamen] modo[4] mundum, tum mentem divinam esse putat, errantibus etiam stellis divinitatem tribuit, sensuque deum privat et eius formam mutabilem esse vult, eodemque in libro rursus terram et caelum refert in
35 deos. Nec vero Theophrasti inconstantia ferenda est; modo enim menti divinum tribuit principatum, modo caelo, tum autem signis sideribusque caelesti-

[1] *ci. Plasberg.* [2] *Heindorf.*
[3] moventur *Reid*: nominantur.
[4] [tamen] modo *edd.*: tum modo, tum *dett.*: modo mundum, tum autem *Dieckhoff.*

---

[a] Aristotle explained the apparently irregular motions of the planets by ascribing to them distinct spheres rotating in opposite directions; the counter-rotation was ἀνέλιξις, of

of inverse rotation[a]; then he says that the celestial heat[b] is god—not realizing that the heavens are a part of that world which elsewhere he himself has entitled god. But how could the divine consciousness which he assigns to the heavens persist in a state of such rapid motion? Where moreover are all the gods of accepted belief, if we count the heavens also as a god? Again, in maintaining that god is incorporeal, he robs him entirely of sensation, and also of wisdom. Moreover, how is motion possible for an incorporeal being, and how, if he is always in motion, can he enjoy tranquillity and bliss? Nor was his fellow-pupil Xenocrates any wiser on this subject. His volumes *On the Nature of the Gods* give no intelligible account of the divine form; for he states that there are eight gods: five inhabiting the planets, and in a state of motion; one consisting of all the fixed stars, which are to be regarded as separate members constituting a single deity; seventh he adds the sun, and eighth the moon. But what sensation of bliss these beings can enjoy it is impossible to conceive. Another member of the school of Plato, Heraclides of Pontus, filled volume after volume with childish fictions; at one moment he deems the world divine, at another the intellect; he also assigns divinity to the planets, and holds that the deity is devoid of sensation and mutable of form; and again in the same volume he reckons earth and sky as gods. Theophrastus also is intolerably inconsistent; at one moment he assigns divine pre-eminence to mind, at another to the heavens, and then again to the constellations and stars

which *replicatio* here is perhaps a translation, although how it could be assigned to the universe is obscure.

[b] The aether.

bus. Nec audiendus eius auditor Strato, is qui physicus appellatur, qui omnem vim divinam in natura sitam esse censet, quae causas gignendi augendi minuendi habeat sed careat omni et sensu et figura.

36 XIV. "Zeno autem, ut iam ad vestros, Balbe, veniam, naturalem legem divinam esse censet, eamque vim obtinere recta imperantem prohibentemque contraria. Quam legem quo modo efficiat animantem intellegere non possumus ; deum autem animantem certe volumus esse. Atque hic idem alio loco aethera deum dicit—si intellegi potest nihil sentiens deus, qui numquam nobis occurrit neque in precibus neque in optatis neque in votis ; aliis autem libris rationem quandam per omnem[1] naturam rerum pertinentem vi divina esse adfectam putat. Idem astris hoc idem tribuit, tum annis mensibus annorumque mutationibus. Cum vero Hesiodi Theogoniam, id est originem deorum, interpretatur, tollit omnino usitatas perceptasque cognitiones deorum ; neque enim Iovem neque Iunonem neque Vestam neque quemquam qui ita appellatur[2] in deorum habet numero, sed rebus inanimis atque mutis per quandam
37 significationem haec docet tributa nomina. Cuius discipuli Aristonis non minus magno in errore sententia est, qui neque formam dei intellegi posse censeat neque in deis sensum esse dicat, dubitetque omnino deus animans necne sit. Cleanthes autem, qui Zenonem audivit una cum eo quem proxime nominavi, tum ipsum mundum deum dicit esse, tum

[1] omnem *dett.* : omnium.
[2] appellatur *dett.* : appelletur.

---

[a] *Cf.* M. Aurelius v. 32 ὁ διὰ τὴν οὐσίαν διήκων λόγος.

in the heavens. Nor is his pupil, Strato, surnamed the Natural Philosopher, worthy of attention; in his view the sole repository of divine power is nature, which contains in itself the causes of birth, growth and decay, but is entirely devoid of sensation and of form.

XIV. "Lastly, Balbus, I come to your Stoic school. Zeno's view is that the law of nature is divine, and that its function is to command what is right and to forbid the opposite. How he makes out this law to be alive passes our comprehension; yet we undoubtedly expect god to be a living being. In another passage however Zeno declares that the aether is god—if there is any meaning in a god without sensation, a form of deity that never presents itself to us when we offer up our prayers and supplications and make our vows. And in other books again he holds the view that a 'reason' which pervades all nature [a] is possessed of divine power. He likewise attributes the same powers to the stars, or at another time to the years, the months and the seasons. Again, in his interpretation of Hesiod's *Theogony* (or Origin of the Gods) he does away with the customary and received ideas of the gods altogether, for he does not reckon either Jupiter, Juno or Vesta as gods, or any being that bears a personal name, but teaches that these names have been assigned allegorically to dumb and lifeless things. Zeno's pupil Aristo holds equally mistaken views. He thinks that the form of the deity cannot be comprehended, and he denies the gods sensation, and in fact is uncertain whether god is a living being at all. Cleanthes, who attended Zeno's lectures at the same time as the last-named, at one moment says that the world itself is god, at another gives this

totius naturae menti atque animo tribuit hoc nomen, tum ultimum et altissimum atque undique circumfusum et extremum omnia cingentem atque conplexum ardorem, qui aether nominetur, certissimum deum iudicat; idemque quasi delirans, in iis libris quos scripsit contra voluptatem, tum fingit formam quandam et speciem deorum, tum divinitatem omnem tribuit astris, tum nihil ratione censet esse divinius. Ita fit ut deus ille quem mente noscimus atque in animi notione tamquam in vestigio volumus
38 reponere nusquam prorsus appareat. XV. At Persaeus eiusdem Zenonis auditor eos esse[1] habitos deos a quibus aliqua magna utilitas ad vitae cultum esset inventa, ipsasque res utiles et salutares deorum esse vocabulis nuncupatas, ut ne hoc quidem diceret, illa inventa esse deorum, sed ipsa divina; quo quid absurdius quam aut res sordidas atque deformis deorum honore adficere aut homines iam morte deletos reponere in deos, quorum omnis cultus esset futurus in luctu?
39 Iam vero Chrysippus, qui Stoicorum somniorum vaferrumus habetur interpres, magnam turbam congregat ignotorum deorum, atque ita ignotorum ut eos ne coniectura quidem informare possimus, cum mens nostra quidvis videatur cogitatione posse depingere, ait enim vim divinam in ratione esse positam et in universae naturae animo atque mente, ipsumque mundum deum dicit esse et eius animi fusionem universam, tum eius ipsius principatum qui in mente et ratione versetur, communemque rerum

[1] eos dicit esse *det.*

name to the mind and soul of the universe, and at another decides that the most unquestionable deity is that remote all-surrounding fiery atmosphere called the aether, which encircles and embraces the universe on its outer side at an exceedingly lofty altitude; while in the books that he wrote to combat hedonism he babbles like one demented, now imagining gods of some definite shape and form, now assigning full divinity to the stars, now pronouncing that nothing is more divine than reason. The result is that the god whom we apprehend by our intelligence, and desire to make to correspond with a mental concept as a seal tallies with its impression, has
3 utterly and entirely vanished. XV. Persaeus, another pupil of Zeno, says that men have deified those persons who have made some discovery of special utility for civilization, and that useful and health-giving things have themselves been called by divine names; he did not even say that they were discoveries of the gods, but speaks of them as actually divine. But what could be more ridiculous than to award divine honours to things mean and ugly, or to give the rank of gods to men now dead and gone, whose worship
9 could only take the form of lamentation? Chrysippus, who is deemed to be the most skilful interpreter of the Stoic dreams, musters an enormous mob of unknown gods—so utterly unknown that even imagination cannot guess at their form and nature, although our mind appears capable of visualizing anything; for he says that divine power resides in reason, and in the soul and mind of the universe; he calls the world itself a god, and also the all-pervading world-soul, and again the guiding principle of that soul, which operates in the intellect and reason, and

naturam [universam] atque[1] omnia continentem, tum fatalem vim[2] et necessitatem rerum futurarum, ignem praeterea [et][3] eum quem ante dixi aethera, tum ea quae natura fluerent atque manarent, ut[4] et aquam et terram et aëra, solem lunam sidera unitatemque[5] rerum qua omnia continerentur, atque etiam homines eos qui inmortalitatem essent con-
40 secuti. Idemque disputat aethera esse eum quem homines Iovem appellarent, quique aër per maria manaret eum esse Neptunum, terramque eam esse quae Ceres diceretur, similique ratione persequitur vocabula reliquorum deorum. Idemque[6] etiam legis perpetuae et aeternae vim, quae quasi dux vitae et magistra officiorum sit, Iovem dicit esse, eandemque fatalem necessitatem appellat <et>[7] sempiternam rerum futurarum veritatem; quorum nihil tale est ut
41 in eo vis divina inesse videatur. Et haec quidem in primo libro de natura deorum; in secundo autem volt Orphei Musaei Hesiodi Homerique fabellas accommodare ad ea quae ipse primo libro de deis inmortalibus dixerat,[8] ut etiam veterrimi poetae, qui haec ne suspicati quidem sint,[9] Stoici fuisse videantur. Quem Diogenes Babylonius consequens in eo libro qui inscribitur de Minerva partum Iovis ortumque virginis ad physiologiam traducens diiungit a fabula.

42 XVI. "Exposui fere non philosophorum iudicia sed delirantium somnia. Nec enim multo absurdiora sunt ea quae poetarum vocibus fusa ipsa suavitate nocuerunt, qui et ira inflammatos et libidine furentis

[1] [universam] atque *Pearson*: universitatemque *Heindorf.*
[2] vim *det.*: orbem; umbram *von Arnim, following best MSS.*
[3] *secl. Bouhier.*
[4] ut <aethera> *ci. Plasberg.*
[5] unitatemque *Pearson*: universitatemque.
[6] eundemque *Roby.*
[7] *add. Bouhier.*
[8] dixerit *A*, *B*: dixit *Nobbe.*
[9] sunt *dett.*

the common and all-embracing nature of things; and also the power of Fate, and the Necessity that governs future events; beside this, the fire that I previously termed aether; and also all fluid and soluble substances, such as water, earth, air, the sun, moon and stars, and the all-embracing unity of things; and even those human beings who have attained immortality. He also argues that the god whom men call Jupiter is the aether, and that Neptune is the air which permeates the sea, and the goddess called Ceres the earth; and he deals in the same way with the whole series of the names of the other gods. He also identifies Jupiter with the mighty Law, everlasting and eternal, which is our guide of life and instructress in duty, and which he entitles Necessity or Fate, and the Everlasting Truth of future events; none of which conceptions is of such a nature as to be deemed to possess divinity. This is what is contained in his *Nature of the Gods*, Book I. In Book II. he aims at reconciling the myths of Orpheus, Musaeus, Hesiod and Homer with his own theology as enunciated in Book I., and so makes out that even the earliest poets of antiquity, who had no notion of these doctrines, were really Stoics. In this he is followed by Diogenes of Babylon, who in his book entitled *Minerva* rationalizes the myth of the birth of the virgin goddess from Jove by explaining it as an allegory of the processes of nature.

Theology of poets and of oriental religion scouted.

XVI. "I have given a rough account of what are more like the dreams of madmen than the considered opinions of philosophers. For they are little less absurd than the outpourings of the poets, harmful as these have been owing to the mere charm of their style. The poets have represented the gods as in-

induxerunt deos feceruntque ut eorum bella proelia pugnas vulnera videremus, odia praeterea discidia discordias, ortus interitus, querellas lamentationes, effusas in omni intemperantia[1] libidines, adulteria, vincula, cum humano genere concubitus mortalisque
43 ex inmortali procreatos. Cum poetarum autem errore coniungere licet portenta magorum Aegyptiorumque in eodem genere dementiam, tum etiam vulgi opiniones, quae in maxima inconstantia veritatis ignoratione versantur.

"Ea qui consideret quam inconsulte ac temere dicantur, venerari Epicurum et in eorum ipsorum numero de quibus haec quaestio est habere debeat.[a] Solus enim vidit primum esse deos, quod in omnium animis eorum notionem inpressisset ipsa natura. Quae est enim gens aut quod genus hominum, quod non habeat sine doctrina anticipationem quandam deorum? quam appellat πρόληψιν Epicurus, id est anteceptam animo rei quandam informationem, sine qua nec intellegi quicquam nec quaeri nec disputari possit.[2] Cuius rationis vim atque utilitatem ex illo caelesti Epicuri de regula et iudicio volumine accepi-
44 mus.[b] XVII. Quod igitur fundamentum huius quaestionis est, id praeclare iactum videtis. Cum enim non instituto aliquo aut more aut lege sit opinio constituta maneatque ad unum omnium firma consensio, intellegi necesse est esse deos, quoniam insitas eorum vel potius innatas cognitiones habemus; de quo autem omnium natura consentit, id verum esse

[1] omnem intemperantiam *? ed.*
[2] possit *dett.*: potest *A*, *B*.

[a] *Cf.* Lucr. v. 8 "deus ille fuit, deus, inclute Memmi."
[b] Diog. L. x. 27 Περὶ κριτηρίου ἢ Κανών.

flamed by anger and maddened by lust, and have displayed to our gaze their wars and battles, their fights and wounds, their hatreds, enmities and quarrels, their births and deaths, their complaints and lamentations, the utter and unbridled licence of their passions, their adulteries and imprisonments, their unions with human beings and the birth of mortal progeny from an immortal parent. With the errors of the poets may be classed the monstrous doctrines of the magi and the insane mythology of Egypt, and also the popular beliefs, which are a mere mass of inconsistencies sprung from ignorance.

Exposition of Epicurean theology. Universal belief a sufficient proof of the gods' existence, and of their immortality and bliss.

"Anyone pondering on the baseless and irrational character of these doctrines ought to regard Epicurus with reverence, and to rank him as one of the very gods about whom we are inquiring.[a] For he alone perceived, first, that the gods exist, because nature herself has imprinted a conception of them on the minds of all mankind. For what nation or what tribe of men is there but possesses untaught some 'preconception' of the gods? Such notions Epicurus designates by the word *prolepsis*, that is, a sort of preconceived mental picture of a thing, without which nothing can be understood or investigated or discussed. The force and value of this argument we learn in that work of genius, Epicurus's *Rule or Standard of Judgement.*[b] XVII You see therefore that the foundation (for such it is) of our inquiry has been well and truly laid. For the belief in the gods has not been established by authority, custom or law, but rests on the unanimous and abiding consensus of mankind; their existence is therefore a necessary inference, since we possess an instinctive or rather an innate concept of them; but a belief which all men by nature share

necesse est ; esse igitur deos confitendum est. Quod quoniam fere constat inter omnis non philosophos solum sed etiam indoctos, fateamur constare illud etiam, hanc nos habere sive anticipationem ut ante dixi sive praenotionem deorum (sunt enim rebus novis nova ponenda nomina, ut Epicurus ipse πρόληψιν appellavit, quam antea nemo eo verbo nominarat)—
45 hanc igitur habemus, ut deos beatos et inmortales putemus. Quae enim nobis natura informationem ipsorum deorum dedit, eadem insculpsit in mentibus ut eos aeternos et beatos haberemus. Quod si ita est, vere exposita illa sententia est ab Epicuro, quod beatum aeternumque sit id nec habere ipsum negotii quicquam nec exhibere alteri, itaque neque ira neque gratia teneri quod quae talia essent imbecilla essent omnia.

"Si nihil aliud quaereremus nisi ut deos pie coleremus et ut superstitione liberaremur, satis erat dictum ; nam et praestans deorum natura hominum pietate coleretur, cum et aeterna esset et beatissima (habet enim venerationem iustam quicquid excellit), et metus omnis a vi atque ira deorum pulsus esset (intellegitur enim a beata inmortalique natura et iram et gratiam segregari, quibus remotis nullos a superis impendere metus). Sed ad hanc confirman-

[a] Diog. L. x. 139 *τὸ μακάριον καὶ ἄφθαρτον οὔτε αὐτὸ πράγματα ἔχει οὔτε ἄλλῳ παρέχει, ὥστε οὔτε ὀργαῖς οὔτε χάρισι συνέχεται· ἐν ἀσθενεῖ γὰρ πᾶν τὸ τοιοῦτον.*

must necessarily be true; therefore it must be admitted that the gods exist. And since this truth is almost universally accepted not only among philosophers but also among the unlearned, we must admit it as also being an accepted truth that we possess a 'preconception,' as I called it above, or 'prior notion,' of the gods. (For we are bound to employ novel terms to denote novel ideas, just as Epicurus himself employed the word *prolepsis* in a sense in which no one had ever used it before.) We have then a preconception of such a nature that we believe the gods to be blessed and immortal. For nature, which bestowed upon us an idea of the gods themselves, also engraved on our minds the belief that they are eternal and blessed. If this is so, the famous maxim [a] of Epicurus truthfully enunciates that 'that which is blessed and eternal can neither know trouble itself nor cause trouble to another, and accordingly cannot feel either anger or favour, since all such things belong only to the weak.'

Such gods are free from passion, and to be worshipped, but not feared.

"If we sought to attain nothing else beside piety in worshipping the gods and freedom from superstition, what has been said had sufficed; since the exalted nature of the gods, being both eternal and supremely blessed, would receive man's pious worship (for what is highest commands the reverence that is its due); and furthermore all fear of the divine power or divine anger would have been banished (since it is understood that anger and favour alike are excluded from the nature of a being at once blessed and immortal, and that these being eliminated we are menaced by no fears in regard to the powers above). But the mind strives to strengthen this belief by

dam opinionem anquirit animus et formam et vitae actionem mentisque agitationem[1] in deo.

46 XVIII. " Ac de forma quidem partim natura nos admonet, partim ratio docet. Nam a natura habemus omnes omnium gentium speciem nullam aliam nisi humanam deorum; quae enim forma alia occurrit umquam aut vigilanti cuiquam aut dormienti? Sed ne omnia revocentur ad primas notiones, ratio hoc
47 idem ipsa declarat. Nam cum praestantissumam naturam, vel quia beata est vel quia sempiterna, convenire videatur eandem esse pulcherrimam, quae conpositio membrorum, quae conformatio liniamentorum, quae figura, quae species humana potest esse pulchrior? Vos quidem, Lucili, soletis (nam Cotta meus modo hoc modo illud), cum artificium effingitis fabricamque divinam, quam sint omnia in hominis figura non modo ad usum verum etiam ad venustatem
48 apta describere. Quodsi omnium animantium formam vincit hominis figura, deus autem animans est, ea figura profecto est quae pulcherrima est omnium, quoniamque deos beatissimos esse constat, beatus autem esse sine virtute nemo potest nec virtus sine ratione constare nec ratio usquam inesse nisi in hominis figura, hominis esse specie deos confitendum
49 est. Nec tamen ea species corpus est, sed quasi corpus, nec habet sanguinem, sed quasi sanguinem.

XIX. " Haec quamquam et inventa sunt acutius et dicta subtilius ab Epicuro, quam ut quivis ea possit agnoscere, tamen fretus intellegentia vestra dissero

[1] vitae . . . agitationem *Beier*: vitam et actionem mentis atque agitationem *MSS.*: vitam et actionem mentisque agitationem *Elvenich*.

trying to discover the form of god, the mode of his activity, and the operation of his intelligence.

46 XVIII. "For the divine form we have the hints of nature supplemented by the teachings of reason. From nature all men of all races derive the notion of gods as having human shape and none other; for in what other shape do they ever appear to anyone, awake or asleep? But not to make primary concepts the sole test of all things, reason itself delivers the

The gods nature; they are in human form, but impercept-ible to sense.

47 same pronouncement. For it seems appropriate that the being who is the most exalted, whether by reason of his happiness or of his eternity, should also be the most beautiful; but what disposition of the limbs, what cast of features, what shape or outline can be more beautiful than the human form? You Stoics at least, Lucilius, (for my friend Cotta says one thing at one time and another at another) are wont to portray the skill of the divine creator by enlarging on the beauty as well as the utility of design displayed

48 in all parts of the human figure. But if the human figure surpasses the form of all other living beings, and god is a living being, god must possess the shape which is the most beautiful of all; and since it is agreed that the gods are supremely happy, and no one can be happy without virtue, and virtue cannot exist without reason, and reason is only found in the human shape, it follows that the gods possess the

49 form of man. Yet their form is not corporeal, but only resembles bodily substance; it does not contain blood, but the semblance of blood.

XIX. "These discoveries of Epicurus are so acute in themselves and so subtly expressed that not everyone would be capable of appreciating them. Still I may rely on your intelligence, and make my exposi-

brevius quam causa desiderat. Epicurus autem, qui res occultas et penitus abditas non modo videat animo sed etiam sic tractet ut manu, docet eam esse vim et naturam deorum ut primum non sensu sed mente cernantur,[1] nec soliditate quadam nec ad numerum, ut ea quae ille propter firmitatem στερέμνια appellat, sed imaginibus similitudine et transitione perceptis, cum infinita simillumarum imaginum series[2] ex innumerabilibus individuis existat et ad deos[3] adfluat, cum maximis voluptatibus in eas imagines mentem intentam infixamque nostram intellegentiam
50 capere quae sit et beata natura et aeterna. Summa vero vis infinitatis et magna ac diligenti contemplatione dignissima est, in qua intellegi necesse est eam esse naturam ut omnia omnibus paribus paria respondeant. Hanc ἰσονομίαν appellat Epicurus, id est aequabilem tributionem. Ex hac igitur illud efficitur, si mortalium tanta multitudo sit, esse inmortalium non minorem, et si quae interimant innumerabilia sint, etiam ea quae conservent infinita esse debere.

"Et quaerere a nobis, Balbe, soletis, quae vita
51 deorum sit quaeque ab iis degatur aetas. Ea videlicet qua nihil beatius, nihil omnibus bonis affluentius cogitari potest. Nihil enim agit, nullis occupationibus est inplicatus, nulla opera molitur, sua sapientia et

[1] cernantur *B*: cernatur.
[2] series *Brieger*: species.
[3] ad eos *B*: a deo, ad nos, a diis ad nos *edd.*

---

[a] Probably to be altered into 'streams to us from the gods.'

tion briefer than the subject demands. Epicurus then, as he not merely discerns abstruse and recondite things with his mind's eye, but handles them as tangible realities, teaches that the substance and nature of the gods is such that, in the first place, it is perceived not by the senses but by the mind, and not materially or individually, like the solid objects which Epicurus in virtue of their substantiality entitles *steremnia*; but by our perceiving images owing to their similarity and succession, because an endless train of precisely similar images arises from the innumerable atoms and streams towards the gods,[a] our mind with the keenest feelings of pleasure fixes its gaze on these images, and so attains an understanding of the nature of a being both blessed and eternal. Moreover there is the supremely potent principle of infinity, which claims the closest and most careful study; we must understand that it has the following property, that in the sum of things everything has its exact match and counterpart. This property is termed by Epicurus *isonomia*, or the principle of uniform distribution. From this principle it follows that if the whole number of mortals be so many, there must exist no less a number of immortals, and if the causes of destruction are beyond count, the causes of conservation also are bound to be infinite.

Divine immortality proved by principle of 'equilibrium.'

"You Stoics are also fond of asking us, Balbus, what is the mode of life of the gods and how they pass their days. The answer is, their life is the happiest conceivable, and the one most bountifully furnished with all good things. God is entirely inactive and free from all ties of occupation; he toils not neither does he labour, but he takes delight in his own wisdom and

The divine bliss not disturbed by creating and directing the world, which goes by nature, through the movement

virtute gaudet, habet exploratum fore se semper cum
52 in maximis tum in aeternis voluptatibus. XX. Hunc deum rite beatum dixerimus, vestrum vero laboriosissimum. Sive enim ipse mundus deus est, quid potest esse minus quietum quam nullo puncto temporis intermisso versari circum axem caeli admirabili celeritate? nisi quietum autem nihil beatum est; sive in [ipso][1] mundo deus inest aliquis qui regat, qui gubernet, qui cursus astrorum mutationes temporum rerum vicissitudines ordinesque conservet,[2] terras et maria contemplans hominum commoda vitasque tueatur, ne ille est inplicatus molestis
53 negotiis et operosis! Nos autem beatam vitam in animi securitate et in omnium vacatione munerum ponimus. Docuit enim nos idem qui cetera, natura effectum esse mundum, nihil opus fuisse fabrica, tamque eam rem esse facilem quam vos effici negatis sine divina posse sollertia, ut innumerabilis natura mundos effectura sit efficiat effecerit. Quod quia quem ad modum natura efficere sine aliqua mente possit non videtis, ut tragici poetae cum explicare argumenti exitum non potestis confugitis ad deum;
54 cuius operam profecto non desideraretis si inmensam et interminatam in omnis partis magnitudinem regionum videretis, in quam se iniciens animus et intendens ita late longeque peregrinatur ut nullam tamen oram ultimi[3] videat in qua possit insistere. In

[1] *Schömann.*
[2] conservet < et > *Davies.*
[3] ultimam *Davies.*

[a] The *deus ex machina* introduced near the end of some Greek tragedies, to cut the knot of the plot, was proverbial.

virtue, and knows with absolute certainty that he of the atoms
will always enjoy pleasures at once consummate and in the void and not by
52 everlasting. XX. This is the god whom we should fate.
call happy in the proper sense of the term; your Stoic god seems to us to be grievously overworked. If the world itself is god, what can be less restful than to revolve at incredible speed round the axis of the heavens without a single moment of respite? but repose is an essential condition of happiness. If on the other hand some god resides within the world as its governor and pilot, maintaining the courses of the stars, the changes of the seasons and all the ordered process of creation, and keeping a watch on land and sea to guard the interests and lives of men, why, what a bondage of irksome and laborious business is his!
53 We for our part deem happiness to consist in tranquillity of mind and entire exemption from all duties. For he who taught us all the rest has also taught us that the world was made by nature, without needing an artificer to construct it, and that the act of creation, which according to you cannot be performed without divine skill, is so easy, that nature will create, is creating and has created worlds without number. You on the contrary cannot see how nature can achieve all this without the aid of some intelligence, and so, like the tragic poets, being unable to bring the plot of your drama to a *dénouement*, you
54 have recourse to a god[a]; whose intervention you assuredly would not require if you would but contemplate the measureless and boundless extent of space that stretches in every direction, into which when the mind projects and propels itself, it journeys onward far and wide without ever sighting any margin or ultimate point where it can stop. Well

hac igitur inmensitate latitudinum longitudinum altitudinum infinita vis innumerabilium volitat atomorum, quae interiecto inani cohaerescunt tamen inter se et aliae alias adprehendentes continuantur; ex quo efficiuntur eae rerum formae et figurac quas vos effici posse sine follibus et incudibus non putatis, itaque inposuistis in cervicibus nostris sempiternum dominum, quem dies et noctes timeremus: quis enim non timeat omnia providentem et cogitantem et animadvertentem et omnia ad se pertinere
55 putantem curiosum et plenum negotii deum? Hinc vobis extitit primum illa fatalis necessitas quam *εἱμαρμένην* dicitis, ut quicquid accidat id ex aeterna veritate causarumque continuatione fluxisse dicatis. Quanti autem haec philosophia aestimanda est cui tamquam aniculis, et iis quidem indoctis, fato fieri videantur omnis? Sequitur *μαντική* vestra, quae Latine divinatio dicitur, qua tanta inbueremur superstitione, si vos audire vellemus, ut haruspices, augures,
56 harioli, vates, coniectores nobis essent colendi. His terroribus ab Epicuro soluti et in libertatem vindicati nec metuimus eos quos intellegimus nec sibi fingere ullam molestiam nec alteri quaerere, et pie sancteque colimus naturam excellentem atque praestantem.

"Sed elatus studio vereor ne longior fuerim. Erat autem difficile rem tantam tamque praeclaram inchoatam relinquere; quamquam non tam dicendi ratio mihi habenda fuit quam audiendi."

57 XXI. Tum Cotta comiter ut solebat: "Atqui,"

then, in this immensity of length and breadth and height there flits an infinite quantity of atoms innumerable, which though separated by void yet cohere together, and taking hold each of another form unions wherefrom are created those shapes and forms of things which you think cannot be created without the aid of bellows and anvils, and so have saddled us with an eternal master, whom day and night we are to fear: for who would not fear a prying busybody of a god, who foresees and thinks of and notices all things, and deems that everything is his concern? An outcome of this theology was first of all your doctrine of Necessity or Fate, *heimarmenē*, as you termed it, the theory that every event is the result of an eternal truth and an unbroken sequence of causation. But what value can be assigned to a philosophy which thinks that everything happens by fate? it is a belief for old women, and ignorant old women at that. And next follows your doctrine of *mantikē*, or Divination, which would so steep us in superstition, if we consented to listen to you, that we should be the devotees of soothsayers, augurs, oracle-mongers, seers and interpreters of dreams. But Epicurus has set us free from superstitious terrors and delivered us out of captivity, so that we have no fear of beings who, we know, create no trouble for themselves and seek to cause none to others, while we worship with pious reverence the transcendent majesty of nature.

"But I fear that enthusiasm for my subject has made me prolix. It was difficult however to leave so vast and splendid a theme unfinished, although really it was not my business to be a speaker so much as a listener."

XXI. Then Cotta took up the discussion. "Well,

inquit, "Vellei, nisi tu aliquid dixisses, nihil sane ex me quidem audire potuisses. Mihi enim non tam facile in mentem venire solet quare verum sit aliquid quam quare falsum; idque cum saepe tum cum te audirem paulo ante contigit. Roges me qualem naturam deorum esse ducam, nihil fortasse respondeam; quaeras putemne talem esse qualis modo a te sit exposita, nihil dicam mihi videri minus. Sed ante quam adgrediar ad ea quae a te disputata sunt,
58 de te ipso dicam quid sentiam. Saepe enim de [L. Crasso][1] familiari illo tuo videor audisse cum te togatis omnibus sine dubio anteferret,[2] paucos tecum Epicureos e Graecia compararet; sed quod ab eo te mirifice diligi intellegebam, arbitrabar illum propter benivolentiam uberius id dicere. Ego autem, etsi vereor laudare praesentem, iudico tamen de re obscura atque difficili a te dictum esse dilucide, neque sententiis solum copiose sed verbis etiam ornatius
59 quam solent vestri. Zenonem, quem Philo noster coryphaeum appellare Epicureorum solebat, cum Athenis essem audiebam frequenter, et quidem ipso auctore Philone—credo ut facilius iudicarem quam illa bene refellerentur cum a principe Epicureorum accepissem quem ad modum dicerentur. Non igitur ille ut plerique, sed isto modo ut tu, distincte graviter

[1] [L. Crasso] *om. A*: *nomen Epicurei cuiusdam excidisse suspicatur Mayor.* [2] anteferret et *dett.*

---

[a] This name is inserted by some MSS., but Crassus in *De oratore*, iii. 77 f., is made to disclaim any special knowledge of philosophy. Probably the name of some philosopher resident in Velleius's house has been lost.

Velleius," he rejoined, with his usual suavity, " unless you had stated a case, you certainly would have had no chance of hearing anything from me. I always find it much easier to think of arguments to prove a thing false than to prove it true. This often happens to me, and did so just now while I was listening to you. Ask me what I think that the divine nature is like, and very probably I shall make no reply ; but inquire whether I believe that it resembles the description of it which you have just given, and I shall say that nothing seems to me less likely. But before proceeding to examine your arguments, I will give my opinion of yourself. I fancy I have often heard that friend of yours [Lucius Crassus] [a] declare that of all the Roman adherents of Epicureanism he placed you unquestionably first, and that few of those from Greece could be ranked beside you ; but knowing his extraordinary esteem for you, I imagined that he was speaking with the partiality of a friend. I myself however, though reluctant to praise you to your face, must nevertheless pronounce that your exposition of an obscure and difficult theme has been most illuminating, and not only exhaustive in its treatment of the subject, but also graced with a charm of style not common in your school. When at Athens, I frequently attended the discourses of Zeno, whom our friend Philo used to call the leader of the Epicurean choir ; in fact it was Philo who suggested that I should go to him—no doubt in order that I might be better able to judge how completely the Epicurean doctrine may be refuted when I had heard an exposition of it from the head of the school. Now Zeno, unlike most Epicureans, had a style as clear, cogent and elegant

Epicurean theology demolished by Cotta (§ 57–end).

He compliments Velleius.

ornate. Sed quod in illo mihi usu saepe venit, idem
modo cum te audirem accidebat, ut moleste ferrem
tantum ingenium (bona venia me audies) in tam
leves, ne dicam in tam ineptas sententias incidisse.
60 Nec ego nunc ipse aliquid adferam melius. Ut enim
modo dixi, omnibus fere in rebus sed maxime in
physicis quid non sit citius quam quid sit dixerim.
XXII. Roges me quid aut quale sit deus, auctore
utar Simonide, de quo cum quaesivisset hoc idem
tyrannus Hiero, deliberandi sibi unum diem postu-
lavit; cum idem ex eo postridie quaereret, biduum
petivit; cum saepius duplicaret numerum dierum
admiransque Hiero requireret cur ita faceret, 'Quia
quanto diutius considero,' inquit, 'tanto mihi res
videtur obscurior.' Sed Simoniden arbitror (non
enim poeta solum suavis verum etiam ceteroqui doctus
sapiensque traditur) quia multa venirent in mentem
acuta atque subtilia, dubitantem quid eorum esset
61 verissimum desperasse omnem veritatem. Epicurus
vero tuus (nam cum illo malo disserere quam tecum)
quid dixit[1] quod non modo philosophia dignum esset
sed mediocri prudentia?

"Quaeritur primum in ea quaestione quae est de natura deorum, sintne di necne sint. 'Difficile est negare.' Credo si in contione quaeratur, sed in huius

[1] dixit (*vel* sit *cum dett.*, *pro* esset) *Lambinus*: dicit.

as your own. But what often occurred to me in his case happened just now while I was listening to you: I felt annoyed that talents so considerable should have chanced to select (if you will forgive my saying it) so trivial, not to say so stupid, a set of doctrines. Not that I propose at the moment to contribute something better of my own. As I said just now, in almost all subjects, but especially in natural philosophy, I am more ready to say what is not true than what is. XXII. Inquire of me as to the being and nature of god, and I shall follow the example of Simonides, who having the same question put to him by the great Hiero, requested a day's grace for consideration; next day, when Hiero repeated the question, he asked for two days, and so went on several times multiplying the number of days by two; and when Hiero in surprise asked why he did so, he replied, 'Because the longer I deliberate the more obscure the matter seems to me.' But Simonides is recorded to have been not only a charming poet but also a man of learning and wisdom in other fields, and I suppose that so many acute and subtle ideas came into his mind that he could not decide which of them was truest, and therefore despaired of truth altogether. But as for your master Epicurus (for I prefer to join issue with him rather than with yourself), which of his utterances is, I do not say worthy of philosophy, but compatible with ordinary common sense?

Cotta's reply will be critical not constructive.

"In an inquiry as to the nature of the gods, the first question that we ask is, do the gods exist or do they not? 'It is difficult to deny their existence.' No doubt it would be if the question were to be asked in a public assembly, but in private conversa-

modi sermone et consessu facillimum. Itaque ego ipse pontifex, qui caerimonias religionesque publicas sanctissime tuendas arbitror, is hoc quod primum est, esse deos, persuaderi mihi non opinione solum sed etiam ad veritatem plane velim. Multa enim occurrunt quae conturbent, ut interdum nulli esse videan-
32 tur. Sed vide quam tecum agam liberaliter: quae communia sunt vobis cum ceteris philosophis non attingam, ut hoc ipsum; placet enim omnibus fere mihique ipsi in primis deos esse, itaque non pugno. Rationem tamen eam quae a te adfertur non satis firmam puto. XXIII. Quod enim omnium gentium generumque hominibus ita videretur, id satis magnum argumentum esse dixisti cur esse deos confiteremur. Quod cum leve per se tum etiam falsum est. Primum enim unde tibi notae sunt opiniones nationum? Equidem arbitror multas esse gentes sic inmanitate effe-
63 ratas ut apud eas nulla suspicio deorum sit. Quid, Diagoras, ἄθεος qui dictus est, posteaque Theodorus nonne aperte deorum naturam sustulerunt? Nam Abderites quidem Protagoras, cuius a te modo mentio facta est, sophistes temporibus illis vel maximus, cum in principio libri sic posuisset, 'De divis, neque ut sint neque ut non sint, habeo dicere,' Atheniensium iussu urbe atque agro est exterminatus librique eius in contione combusti; ex quo equidem existimo

---

[a] Cicero appears to mistranslate the Greek περὶ μὲν θεῶν οὐκ ἔχω εἰδέναι οὔθ' ὡς εἰσὶν οὔθ' ὡς οὐκ εἰσίν Diog. L. ix. 51 ('either *that* they exist or *that* they do not').

tion and in a company like the present it is perfectly easy. This being so, I, who am a high priest, and who hold it to be a duty most solemnly to maintain the rights and doctrines of the established religion, should be glad to be convinced of this fundamental tenet of the divine existence, not as an article of faith merely but as an ascertained fact. For many disturbing reflections occur to my mind, which sometimes make me think that there are no gods at all. But mark how generously I deal with you. I will not attack those tenets which are shared by your school with all other philosophers—for example the one in question, since almost all men, and I myself no less than any other, believe that the gods exist, and this accordingly I do not challenge. At the same time I doubt the adequacy of the argument which you adduce to prove it. XXIII. You said that a sufficient reason for our admitting that the gods exist was the fact that all the nations and races of mankind believe it. But this argument is both inconclusive and untrue. In the first place, how do you know what foreign races believe? For my part I think that there are many nations so uncivilized and barbarous as to have no notion of any gods at all. Again, did not Diagoras, called the Atheist, and later Theodorus openly deny the divine existence? Since as for Protagoras of Abdera, the greatest sophist of that age, to whom you just now alluded, for beginning a book with the words 'About the gods I am unable to affirm either how [a] they exist or how they do not exist,' he was sentenced by a decree of the Athenian assembly to be banished from the city and from the country, and to have his books burnt in the market-place: an example that I can

(1) Argument from universal consent weak, and unfounded in fact.

tardiores ad hanc sententiam profitendam multos esse factos, quippe cum poenam ne dubitatio quidem effugere potuisset. Quid de sacrilegis, quid de impiis periurisque dicemus?

Tubulus si Lucius umquam,
si Lupus aut Carbo aut[1] Neptuni filius,

ut ait Lucilius, putasset esse deos, tam periurus aut
64 tam inpurus fuisset? Non est igitur tam explorata ista ratio ad id quod vultis confirmandum quam videtur. Sed quia commune hoc est argumentum aliorum etiam philosophorum, omittam hoc tempore; ad vestra propria venire malo.

65 "Concedo esse deos; doce me igitur unde sint, ubi sint, quales sint corpore animo vita; haec enim scire desidero. Abuteris ad omnia atomorum regno et licentia; hinc quodcumque in solum venit, ut dicitur, effingis atque efficis. Quae primum nullae sunt. Nihil est enim . . .[2] quod vacet corpore; corporibus autem omnis obsidetur locus; ita nullum inane, nihil esse
66 individuum potest. XXIV. Haec ego nunc physicorum oracula fundo, vera an falsa nescio, sed veri tamen similiora quam vestra. Ista enim flagitia Democriti sive etiam ante Leucippi, esse corpuscula

[1] aut *secl. Jos. Scaliger.* [2] *lacunam Lambinus.*

---

[a] Proverbial for a rough, savage character.
[b] Or perhaps 'that meets the foot.'
[c] A considerable number of words seem to have been lost here.

well believe has discouraged many people since from professing atheism, since the mere expression of doubt did not succeed in escaping punishment. What are we to say about the men guilty of sacrilege or impiety or perjury?

> Suppose that ever Lucius Tubulus,
> Lupus or Carbo, or some son of Neptune,[a]

as Lucilius has it, had believed in the gods, would he have been such a perjurer and scoundrel? We find then that your argument is not so well-established a proof of the view which you uphold as you imagine it to be. Still, as it is a line of reasoning that is followed by other philosophers as well, I will pass it over for the present, and turn rather to doctrines peculiar to your school.

(2) Argument from atomism refuted: atomic doctrine opposed to science,

"I grant the existence of the gods: do you then teach me their origin, their dwelling-place, their bodily and spiritual nature, their mode of life; for these are the things which I want to know. In regard to all of them you make great play with the lawless domination of the atoms; from these you construct and create everything that comes upon the ground,[b] as they say. Now in the first place, there are no such things as atoms. For there is nothing . . . [c] incorporeal, but all space is filled with material bodies; hence there can be no such thing as void, and no such thing as an indivisible body. XXIV. In all of this I speak for the time being only as the mouthpiece of our oracles of natural philosophy; whether their utterances are true or false I do not know, but at all events they are more probable than those of your school. As for the outrageous doctrines of Democritus, or perhaps of his predecessor Leucippus, that

quaedam[1] levia, alia aspera, rotunda alia, partim autem angulata, curvata[2] quaedam et quasi adunca, ex his effectum esse caelum atque terram nulla cogente natura sed concursu quodam fortuito—hanc tu opinionem, C. Vellei, usque ad hanc aetatem perduxisti, priusque te quis de omni vitae statu quam de ista auctoritate deiecerit; ante enim iudicasti Epicureum te esse oportere quam ista cognovisti: ita necesse fuit aut haec flagitia concipere animo aut
67 susceptae philosophiae nomen amittere. Quid enim mereas ut Epicureus esse desinas? 'Nihil equidem' inquis 'ut rationem vitae beatae veritatemque deseram.' Ista igitur est veritas? Nam de vita beata nihil repugno, quam tu ne in deo quidem esse censes nisi plane otio langueat. Sed ubi est veritas? In mundis credo innumerabilibus omnibus minimis temporum punctis aliis nascentibus aliis cadentibus; an in individuis corpusculis tam praeclara opera nulla moderante natura, nulla ratione fingentibus? Sed oblitus liberalitatis meae qua tecum paulo ante uti coeperam, plura complector. Concedam igitur ex individuis constare omnia: quid ad rem? deorum
68 enim natura quaeritur. Sint sane ex atomis; non igitur aeterni. Quod enim ex atomis, id natum aliquando est; si nati,[3] nulli dei ante quam nati;

[1] quaedam, <alia> *Reid.*
[2] curvata *B*: firamata *A*, hamata *edd.*
[3] nati *dett.*, natum *A*, *B*.

there are certain minute particles, some smooth, others rough, some round, some angular, some curved or hook-shaped, and that heaven and earth were created from these, not by compulsion of any natural law but by a sort of accidental colliding—this is the belief to which you, Gaius Velleius, have clung all your life long, and it would be easier to make you alter all your principles of conduct than abandon the teachings of your master; for you made up your mind that Epicureanism claimed your allegiance before you learned these doctrines: so that you were faced with the alternative of either accepting these outrageous notions or surrendering the title of the school of your adoption. For what would you take to cease to be an Epicurean? 'For no consideration,' you reply, 'would I forsake the principles of happiness and the truth.' Then is Epicureanism the truth? For as to happiness I don't join issue, since in your view even divine happiness involves being bored to death with idleness. But where is the truth to be found? I suppose in an infinite number of worlds, some coming to birth and others hurled into ruin at every minutest moment of time? or in the indivisible particles that produce all the marvels of creation without any controlling nature or reason? But I am forgetting the indulgence which I began to show you just now, and am taking too wide a range. I will grant therefore that everything is made out of indivisible bodies; but this takes us no farther, for we are trying to discover the nature of the gods. Suppose we allow that the gods are made of atoms: then it follows that they are not eternal. For what is made of atoms came into existence at some time; but if the gods came into existence, before they came into

inconsistent with divine immortality.

et si ortus est deorum, interitus sit necesse est, ut tu paulo ante de Platonis mundo disputabas. Ubi igitur illud vestrum beatum et aeternum, quibus duobus verbis significatis deum? quod cum efficere vultis, in dumeta conrepitis: ita enim dicebas, non corpus esse in deo sed quasi corpus, nec sanguinem sed tamquam sanguinem.

69 XXV. "Hoc persaepe facitis, ut cum aliquid non veri simile dicatis et effugere reprehensionem velitis adferatis aliquid quod omnino ne fieri quidem possit, ut satius fuerit illud ipsum de quo ambigebatur concedere quam tam inpudenter resistere. Velut Epicurus cum videret, si atomi ferrentur in locum inferiorem suopte pondere, nihil fore in nostra potestate, quod esset earum motus certus et necessarius, invenit quo modo necessitatem effugeret, quod videlicet Democritum fugerat: ait atomum, cum pondere et gravitate directo deorsus feratur, declinare paululum.
70 Hoc dicere turpius est quam illud quod vult non posse defendere. Idem facit contra dialecticos; a quibus cum traditum sit in omnibus diiunctionibus in quibus 'aut etiam aut non' poneretur alterum utrum esse verum, pertimuit ne si concessum esset huius modi aliquid 'aut vivet cras aut non vivet Epicurus,' alterutrum fieret necessarium: totum hoc 'aut etiam

[a] Above, § 49.

existence there were no gods; and if the gods had a beginning, they must also perish, as you were arguing a little time ago about the world as conceived by Plato. Where then do we find that happiness and that eternity which in your system are the two catch-words that denote divinity? When you wish to make this out, you take cover in a thicket of jargon; you gave us the formula just now [a]—God has not body but a semblance of body, not blood but a kind of blood.

XXV. "This is a very common practice with your school. You advance a paradox, and then, when you want to escape censure, you adduce in support of it some absolute impossibility; so that you would have done better to abandon the point in dispute rather than to offer so shameless a defence. For instance, Epicurus saw that if the atoms travelled downwards by their own weight, we should have no freedom of the will, since the motion of the atoms would be determined by necessity. He therefore invented a device to escape from determinism (the point had apparently escaped the notice of Democritus): he said that the atom while travelling vertically downward by the force of gravity makes a very slight swerve to one side. This defence discredits him more than if he had had to abandon his original position. He does the same in his battle with the logicians. Their accepted doctrine is that in every disjunctive proposition of the form 'so-and-so either is or is not,' one of the two alternatives must be true. Epicurus took alarm; if such a proposition as 'Epicurus either will or will not be alive to-morrow' were granted, one or other alternative would be necessary. Accordingly he denied the necessity of a disjunctive proposition

Doctrine of the swerve absurd;

and so is Epicurus's logic.

aut non' negavit esse necessarium; quo quid dici potuit obtusius? Urguebat Arcesilas Zenonem, cum ipse falsa omnia diceret quae sensibus viderentur, Zenon autem nonnulla visa esse falsa, non omnia; timuit Epicurus ne si unum visum esset falsum nullum esset verum: omnis sensus veri nuntios dixit esse. Nihil horum nimis callide[1]; graviorem enim plagam accipiebat ut leviorem repelleret.

71 "Idem facit in natura deorum; dum individuorum corporum concretionem fugit ne interitus et dissipatio consequatur, negat esse corpus deorum sed tamquam corpus, nec sanguinem sed tamquam sanguinem. XXVI. Mirabile videtur quod non rideat haruspex cum haruspicem viderit; hoc mirabilius, quod[2] vos inter vos risum tenere potestis.[3] 'Non est corpus sed quasi corpus': hoc intellegerem quale esset si in ceris[4] fingeretur aut fictilibus figuris; in deo quid sit quasi corpus aut quid sit quasi sanguis intellegere non possum. Ne tu quidem, Vellei, sed non vis fateri.

72 "Ista enim a vobis quasi dictata redduntur quae Epicurus oscitans halucinatus est, cum quidem gloriaretur, ut videmus in scriptis, se magistrum habuisse nullum. Quod etiam[5] non praedicanti tamen facile equidem crederem, sicut mali aedificii domino glorianti se architectum non habuisse; nihil enim olet ex Academia, nihil ex Lycio, nihil ne e puerilibus quidem disciplinis. Xenocraten audire

[1] nimis callide *Allen*: ñ callide, nisi callide *dett.*, nisi ualde *A*, *B*.

[2] quod *det.*: quam (quam <ut> . . . possitis *Plasberg*).

[3] potestis *ed.*: possitis.

[4] cereis *dett.*

[5] etiam *dett.*: et *A*, *B*, ei *Klotz*.

altogether. Now what could be stupider than that? Arcesilas used to attack Zeno because, whereas he himself said that all sense-presentations are false, Zeno said that some were false, but not all. Epicurus feared that if a single sensation were admitted to be false, none would be true: he therefore said that all the senses give a true report. In none of these cases did he behave very cleverly, for to parry a lighter blow he laid himself open to one that was more severe.

(3) Anthropomorphism criticized (§§ 71-102). Quasi-corporeal gods unintelligible.

"He does the same as regards the nature of the gods. In his desire to avoid the assumption of a dense cluster of atoms, which would involve the possibility of destruction and dissipation, he says that the gods have not a body but a semblance of body, and not blood but a semblance of blood. XXVI. It is thought surprising that an augur can see an augur without smiling; but it is more surprising that you Epicureans keep a grave face when by yourselves. 'It is not body but a semblance of body.' I could understand what this supposition meant if it related to waxen images or figures of earthenware, but what 'a semblance of body' or 'a semblance of blood' may mean in the case of god, I cannot understand; nor can you either, Velleius, only you won't admit it.

"The fact is that you people merely repeat by rote the idle vapourings that Epicurus uttered when half asleep; for, as we read in his writings, he boasted that he had never had a teacher. This I for my part could well believe, even if he did not proclaim it, just as I believe the owner of an ill-built house when he boasts that he did not employ an architect! He shows not the faintest trace of the Academy or the Lyceum, or even of the ordinary schoolboy studies. He might have heard Xenocrates—by heaven, what

potuit (quem virum, di immortales); et sunt qui putent audisse, ipse non vult—credo plus nemini. Pamphilum quendam Platonis auditorem ait a se Sami auditum (ibi enim adulescens habitabat cum patre et fratribus, quod in eam[1] pater eius Neocles agripeta venerat, sed cum agellus eum non satis
73 aleret, ut opinor ludi magister fuit); sed hunc Platonicum mirifice contemnit Epicurus: ita metuit ne quid umquam didicisse videatur. In Nausiphane Democriteo tenetur; quem cum a se non neget auditum, vexat tamen omnibus contumeliis; atqui si haec Democritea non audisset, quid audierat? quid enim est[2] in physicis Epicuri non a Democrito? Nam etsi quaedam commutavit, ut quod paulo ante de inclinatione atomorum dixi, tamen pleraque dicit eadem, atomos inane imagines, infinitatem locorum innumerabilitatemque mundorum, eorum ortus interitus, omnia fere quibus naturae ratio continetur.

74 "Nunc istuc 'quasi corpus' et 'quasi sanguinem' quid intellegis? Ego enim te scire ista melius quam me non fateor solum sed etiam facile patior; cum quidem[3] semel dicta sunt, quid est quod Velleius intellegere possit, Cotta non possit? Itaque corpus quid sit, sanguis quid sit intellego, quasi corpus et quasi sanguis quid sit nullo prorsus modo intellego. Neque tu me celas ut Pythagoras solebat alienos,

[1] eam <insulam> *Plasberg*.
[2] enim est *ed.*: est *A*, *B*, enim *dett.*
[3] autem *? ed.*

a master !—and some people think that he did, but he himself denies it, and he ought to know ! He states that he heard a certain Pamphilus, a pupil of Plato, at Samos (where he resided in his youth with his father and brother—his father Neocles had gone there to take up land, but failing to make a living out of his farm, I believe kept a school). However Epicurus pours endless scorn on this Platonist, so afraid is he of appearing ever to have learnt anything from a teacher. He stands convicted in the case of Nausiphanes, a follower of Democritus, whom he does not deny he heard lecture, but whom nevertheless he assails with every sort of abuse. Yet if he had not heard from him these doctrines of Democritus, what had he heard ? for what is there in Epicurus's natural philosophy that does not come from Democritus ? Since even if he introduced some alterations, for instance the swerve of the atoms, of which I spoke just now, yet most of his system is the same, the atoms, the void, the images, the infinity of space, and the countless number of worlds, their births and their destructions, in fact almost everything that is comprised in natural science.

" As to your formula ' a semblance of body ' and ' a semblance of blood,' what meaning do you attach to it ? That you have a better knowledge of the matter than I have I freely admit, and what is more, am quite content that this should be so ; but once it is expressed in words, why should one of us be able to understand it and not the other ? Well then, I do understand what body is and what blood is, but what ' a semblance of body ' and ' a semblance of blood ' are I don't understand in the very least. You are not trying to hide the truth from me, as Pythagoras

nec consulto dicis occulte tamquam Heraclitus, sed,
quod inter nos liceat, ne tu quidem intellegis.
75 XXVII. Illud video pugnare te, species ut quaedam
sit deorum quae nihil concreti habeat nihil solidi
nihil expressi nihil eminentis, sitque pura levis
perlucida. Dicemus igitur idem quod in Venere Coa:
corpus illud non est sed simile corporis, nec ille fusus
et candore mixtus rubor sanguis est sed quaedam
sanguinis similitudo; sic in Epicureo deo non res
sed similitudines rerum esse. Fac id quod ne intellegi
quidem potest mihi esse persuasum; cedo mihi
istorum adumbratorum deorum liniamenta atque
76 formas. Non deest hoc loco copia rationum quibus
docere velitis humanas esse formas deorum; primum
quod ita sit informatum anticipatumque mentibus nostris ut homini, cum de deo cogitet, forma
occurrat humana; deinde quod, quoniam rebus
omnibus excellat natura divina, forma quoque esse
pulcherrima debeat, nec esse humana ullam pulchriorem; tertiam rationem adfertis, quod nulla in
77 alia figura domicilium mentis esse possit. Primum
igitur quidque considera quale sit; arripere enim
mihi videmini quasi vestro iure rem nullo modo
probabilem. ⟨Primum[1]⟩ omnium quis tam caecus
in contemplandis rebus umquam fuit ut non videret
species istas hominum conlatas in deos aut consilio

[1] *Plasberg.*

used to hide it from strangers, nor yet are you speaking obscurely on purpose like Heraclitus, but (to speak candidly between ourselves) you don't understand it yourself any more than I do. XXVII. I am aware that what you maintain is that the gods possess a certain outward appearance, which has no firmness or solidity, no definite shape or outline, and which is free from gross admixture, volatile, transparent. Therefore we shall use the same language as we should of the Venus of Cos: her's is not real flesh but the likeness of flesh, and the mantling blush that dyes her fair cheek is not real blood but something that counterfeits blood; similarly in the god of Epicurus we shall say that there is no real substance but something that counterfeits substance. But assume that I accept as true a dogma that I cannot even understand: exhibit to me, pray, the forms and features of your shadow-deities. On this topic you are at no loss for arguments designed to prove that the gods have the form of men: first because our minds possess a preconceived notion of such a character that, when a man thinks of god, it is the human form that presents itself to him; secondly, because inasmuch as the divine nature surpasses all other things, the divine form also must needs be the most beautiful, and no form is more beautiful than that of man. The third reason you advance is that no other shape is capable of being the abode of intelligence.

Anthropomorphic doctrines due to policy, superstition or vanity.

Well then, take these arguments one by one and consider what they amount to; for in my view they are based on an arbitrary and quite inadmissible assumption on your part. First of all, was there ever any student so blind as not to see that human shape has been thus assigned to the gods either by the deliberate con-

quodam sapientium, quo facilius animos imperitorum ad deorum cultum a vitae pravitate converterent, aut superstitione, ut essent simulacra quae venerantes deos ipsos se adire crederent? Auxerunt autem haec eadem poëtae, pictores, opifices; erat enim non facile agentis aliquid et molientis deos in aliarum formarum imitatione servare. Accessit etiam ista opinio fortasse quod homini homine pulchrius nihil videbatur.[1] Sed tu hoc, physice, non vides, quam blanda conciliatrix et quasi sui sit lena natura? An putas ullam esse terra marique beluam quae non sui generis belua maxime delectetur? Quod ni ita esset, cur non gestiret taurus equae contrectatione, equus vaccae? An tu aquilam aut leonem aut delphinum ullam anteferre censes figuram suae? Quid igitur mirum si hoc eodem modo homini natura praescripsit ut nihil pulchrius quam hominem putaret? . . .[2] eam esse causam cur deos hominum similis putaremus?

78 "Quid censes si ratio[3] esset in beluis? nonne[4] suo quasque generi plurimum tributuras fuisse? XXVIII. At mehercule ego (dicam enim ut sentio) quamvis amem ipse me, tamen non audeo dicere pulchriorem esse me quam ille fuerit taurus qui vexit Europam; non enim hoc loco de ingeniis aut de orationibus[5] nostris sed de specie figuraque quaeritur. Quodsi fingere nobis et iungere formas velimus,

[1] videbatur (*vel* videtur) *Schomann*: videatur.
[2] *lacunam suspic. Mayor.*
[3] oratio *Dumesnil.* [4] nonne *ed.*: non. [5] rationibus ? *ed.*

---

[a] Some words appear to have been lost here.
[b] Perhaps the text should be corrected to 'speech.'
[c] Perhaps the text should be corrected to 'rational.'

trivance of philosophers, the better to enable them to turn the hearts of the ignorant from vicious practices to the observance of religion, or by superstition, to supply images for men to worship in the belief that in so doing they had direct access to the divine presence? These notions moreover have been fostered by poets, painters and artificers, who found it difficult to represent living and active deities in the likeness of any other shape than that of man. Perhaps also man's belief in his own superior beauty, to which you referred, may have contributed to the result. But surely you as a natural philosopher are aware what an insinuating go-between and pander of her own charms nature is! Do you suppose that there is a single creature on land or in the sea which does not prefer an animal of its own species to any other? If this were not so, why should not a bull desire to couple with a mare, or a horse with a cow? Do you imagine that an eagle or lion or dolphin thinks any shape more beautiful than its own? Is it then surprising if nature has likewise taught man to think his own species the most beautiful . . .[a] that this was a reason why we should think the gods resemble man?

Anthropomorphism derogatory to divine perfection.

"Suppose animals possessed reason,[b] do you not think that they would each assign pre-eminence to their own species? XXVIII. For my part I protest (if I am to say what I think) that although I am not lacking in self-esteem yet I don't presume to call myself more beautiful than the famous bull on which Europa rode; for the question is not here of our intellectual and oratorical[c] powers but of our outward form and aspect. Indeed if we choose to make imaginary combinations of shapes, would you

qualis ille maritimus Triton pingitur, natantibus invehens beluis adiunctis humano corpori, nolis esse? Difficili in loco versor; est enim vis tanta naturae ut homo nemo velit nisi hominis similis
79 esse—et quidem formica formicae; sed tamen cuius hominis? quotus enim quisque formosus est? Athenis cum essem, e gregibus epheborum vix singuli reperiebantur—video quid adriseris, sed ita tamen se res habet. Deinde nobis, qui concedentibus philosophis antiquis adulescentulis delectamur, etiam vitia saepe iucunda sunt. 'Naevus in articulo pueri delectat' Alcaeum; at est corporis macula naevus; illi tamen hoc lumen videbatur. Q. Catulus, huius collegae et familiaris nostri pater, dilexit municipem tuum Roscium, in quem etiam illud est eius:

> constiteram exorientem Auroram forte salutans,
> cum subito a laeva Roscius exoritur.
> pace mihi liceat, caelestes, dicere vestra:
> mortalis visust pulchrior esse deo.

Huic deo pulchrior; at erat, sicuti hodie est, perversissimis oculis: quid refert, si hoc ipsum salsum illi et venustum videbatur?

80 "Redeo ad deos. XXIX. Ecquos si non tam[1] strabones at paetulos esse arbitramur, ecquos naevum habere, ecquos silos flaccos frontones capitones, quae

[1] iam *Heinsius*.

---

[a] The Latin is part of a verse from an unknown source.

not like to resemble the merman Triton who is depicted riding upon swimming monsters attached to his man's body? I am on ticklish ground here, for natural instinct is so strong that every man wishes to be like a man and nothing else. Yes, and every ant like an ant! Still, the question is, like what man? How small a percentage of handsome people there are! When I was at Athens, there was scarcely one to be found in each platoon of the training-corps—I see why you smile, but the fact is so all the same. Another point: we, who with the sanction of the philosophers of old are fond of the society of young men, often find even their defects agreeable. Alcaeus 'admires a mole upon his favourite's wrist'[a]; of course a mole is a blemish, but Alcaeus thought it a beauty. Quintus Catulus, the father of our colleague and friend to-day, was warmly attached to your fellow-townsman Roscius, and actually wrote the following verses in his honour:

> By chance abroad at dawn, I stood to pray
> To the uprising deity of day;
> When lo! upon my left—propitious sight—
> Suddenly Roscius dawned in radiance bright.
> Forgive me, heavenly pow'rs, if I declare,
> Meseem'd the mortal than the god more fair.

To Catulus, Roscius was fairer than a god. As a matter of fact he had, as he has to-day, a pronounced squint; but no matter—in the eyes of Catulus this in itself gave him piquancy and charm.

0 "I return to the gods. XXIX. Can we imagine any gods, I do not say as cross-eyed as Roscius, but with a slight cast? Can we picture any of them with a mole, a snub nose, protruding ears, prominent brows and too large a head—defects not unknown among

sunt in nobis? an omnia emendata in illis? Detur id vobis; num etiam una est omnium facies? nam si plures, aliam esse alia pulchriorem necesse est: igitur aliquis non pulcherrimus deus. Si[1] una omnium facies est, florere in caelo Academiam necesse est: si enim nihil inter deum et deum differt, nulla est apud deos cognitio, nulla perceptio.

81 "Quid si etiam, Vellei, falsum illud omnino est, nullam aliam nobis de deo cogitantibus speciem nisi hominis occurrere? tamenne ista tam absurda defendes? Nobis fortasse sic occurrit ut dicis; a parvis enim[2] Iovem Iunonem Minervam Neptunum Vulcanum Apollinem reliquos deos ea facie novimus qua pictores fictoresque voluerunt, neque solum facie sed etiam ornatu aetate vestitu. At non Aegyptii nec Syri nec fere cuncta barbaria; firmiores enim videas apud eos opiniones esse de bestiis quibusdam quam apud nos de sanctissimis templis
82 et simulacris deorum. Etenim fana multa spoliata et simulacra deorum de locis sanctissimis ablata vidimus[3] a nostris, at vero ne fando quidem auditum est crocodilum aut ibin aut faelem violatum ab Aegyptio. Quid igitur censes? Apim illum sanctum Aegyptiorum bovem nonne deum videri Aegyptiis? Tam hercle quam tibi illam vestram Sospitam. Quam tu numquam ne in somnis quidem

[1] sin ? *ed.* [2] a parvis enim *Klotz*: apparuisse. [3] vidimus *Bouhier*: videmus.

us men—, or are they entirely free from personal blemishes? Suppose we grant you that, are we also to say that they are all exactly alike? If not, there will be degrees of beauty among them, and therefore a god can fall short of supreme beauty. If on the other hand they are all alike, then the Academic school must have a large following in heaven, since if there is no difference between one god and another, among the gods knowledge and perception must be impossible.

Anthropomorphic creed not shared by all races

1 "Furthermore, Velleius, what if your assumption, that when we think of god the only form that presents itself to us is that of a man, be entirely untrue? will you nevertheless continue to maintain your absurdities? Very likely we Romans do imagine god as you say, because from our childhood Jupiter, Juno, Minerva, Neptune, Vulcan and Apollo have been known to us with the aspect with which painters and sculptors have chosen to represent them, and not with that aspect only, but having that equipment, age and dress But they are not so known to the Egyptians or Syrians, or any almost of the uncivilized races. Among these you will find a belief in certain animals more firmly established than is reverence for the holiest sanctuaries and images of the gods with
32 us. For we have often seen temples robbed and images of gods carried off from the holiest shrines by our fellow-countrymen, but no one ever even heard of an Egyptian laying profane hands on a crocodile or ibis or cat. What therefore do you infer? that the Egyptians do not believe their sacred bull Apis to be a god? Precisely as much as you believe the Saviour Juno of your native place to be a goddess. You never see her even in your dreams unless

vides nisi cum pelle caprina cum hasta cum scutulo cum calceolis repandis : at non est talis Argia nec Romana Iuno. Ergo alia species Iunonis Argivis, alia Lanuvinis, alia nobis.[1] Et quidem alia nobis
83 Capitolini, alia Afris Hammonis Iovis. XXX. Non pudet igitur physicum, id est speculatorem venatoremque naturae, ab animis consuetudine inbutis petere testimonium veritatis? Isto enim modo dicere licebit Iovem semper barbatum, Apollinem semper inberbem, caesios oculos Minervae, caeruleos esse Neptuni. Et quidem laudamus Athenis Volcanum eum quem fecit Alcamenes, in quo stante atque vestito leviter apparet claudicatio non deformis. Claudum igitur habebimus deum quoniam de Volcano sic accepimus. Age et his vocabulis esse deos faci-
84 mus[2] quibus a nobis nominantur? At primum, quot hominum linguae, tot nomina deorum. Non enim, ut tu Velleius, quocumque veneris, sic idem in Italia Volcanus, idem in Africa, idem in Hispania. Deinde nominum non magnus numerus ne in pontificiis quidem nostris, deorum autem innumerabilis. An sine nominibus sunt? Istud quidem ita vobis dicere necesse est; quid enim attinet, cum una facies sit, plura esse nomina? Quam bellum erat, Vellei, confiteri potius nescire quod nescires,[3] quam ista effutientem nauseare atque ipsum tibi[4] displicere!

[1] alia nobis *det.*, *om. cett.* [2] faciamus *dett.*
[3] nescires *dett.*: nesciris *A*, nescis *corr. B.*
[4] tibi *Manutius*: sibi.

equipped with goat-skin, spear, buckler and slippers turned up at the toe. Yet that is not the aspect of the Argive Juno, nor of the Roman. It follows that Juno has one form for the Argives, another for the people of Lanuvium, and another for us. And indeed our Jupiter of the Capitol is not the same as
3 the Africans' Juppiter Ammon. XXX. Should not the physical philosopher therefore, that is, the explorer and tracker-out of nature, be ashamed to go to minds besotted with habit for evidence of truth? On your principle it will be legitimate to assert that Jupiter always wears a beard and Apollo never, and that Minerva has grey eyes and Neptune blue. Yes, and at Athens there is a much-praised statue of Vulcan made by Alcamenes, a standing figure, draped, which displays a slight lameness, though not enough to be unsightly. We shall therefore deem god to be lame, since tradition represents Vulcan so. Tell me now, do we also make out the gods to have the same names as those by which they are known
4 to us? But in the first place the gods have as many names as mankind has languages. You are Velleius wherever you travel, but Vulcan has a different name in Italy, in Africa and in Spain. Again, the total number of names even in our pontifical books is not great, but there are gods innumerable. Are they without names? You Epicureans at all events are forced to say so, since what is the point of more names when they are all exactly alike? How delightful it would be, Velleius, if when you did not know a thing you would admit your ignorance, instead of uttering this drivel, which must make even your own gorge rise with disgust! Do you really

An tu mei similem putas esse aut tui deum? Profecto non putas.

"Quid ergo, solem dicam aut lunam aut caelum deum? Ergo etiam beatum: quibus fruentem voluptatibus? et sapientem: qui potest esse in eius modi trunco sapientia? Haec vestra sunt.
85 Si igitur nec humano visu, quod docui, nec tali aliquo, quod tibi ita persuasum est, quid dubitas negare deos esse? Non audes. Sapienter id quidem, etsi hoc loco non populum metuis sed ipsos deos: novi ego Epicureos omnia sigilla venerantes,[1] quamquam video non nullis videri Epicurum, ne in offensionem Atheniensium caderet, verbis reliquisse deos, re sustulisse. Itaque in illis selectis eius brevibusque sententiis, quas appellatis κυρίας δόξας, haec ut opinor prima sententia est: 'Quod beatum et inmortale est, id nec habet nec exhibet cuiquam negotium.' XXXI. In hac ita exposita sententia sunt qui existiment, quod ille inscitia plane loquendi fecerit,[2] fecisse consulto; de homine minime vafro male
86 existimant. Dubium est enim utrum dicat aliquid beatum esse et inmortale an, si quid sit, id esse tale.[3] Non animadvertunt hic eum ambigue locutum esse sed multis aliis locis et illum et Metrodorum tam aperte quam paulo ante te. Ille vero deos esse

[1] venerantes *Manutius*: numerantes.
[2] fecerit *A*, *B*: fecerat *corr. A*, *dett.*: fecit? (*ci. sed reiecit Plasberg*). [3] tale *Heindorf*: mortale.

---

[a] Epicurus recorded his principal tenets in a series of brief articles of belief which he called κύριαι δόξαι, *Authoritative Opinions*. Diog. L. x. 139. This one runs τὸ μακάριον καὶ ἄφθαρτον οὔτε αὐτὸ πράγματα ἔχει οὔτε ἄλλῳ παρέχει.

believe that god resembles me, or yourself? Of course you do not.

"What then? Am I to say that the sun is a god, or the moon, or the sky? If so, we must also say that it is happy; but what forms of enjoyment constitute its happiness? and wise; but how can wisdom reside in a senseless bulk like that? These are argu-
5 ments employed by your own school. Well then, if the gods do not possess the appearance of men, as I have proved, nor some such form as that of the heavenly bodies, as you are convinced, why do you hesitate to deny their existence? You do not dare to. Well, that is no doubt wise—although in this matter it is not the public that you fear, but the gods themselves: I personally am acquainted with Epicureans who worship every paltry image, albeit I am aware that according to some people's view Epicurus really abolished the gods, but nominally retained them in order not to offend the people of Athens. Thus the first of his selected aphorisms or maxims, which you call the *Kyriai Doxai*,[a] runs, I believe, thus: *That which is blessed and immortal neither experiences trouble nor causes it to anyone.* XXXI. Now there are people who think that the wording of this maxim was intentional, though really it was due to the author's inability to express himself clearly; their suspicion does an injustice to the most
6 guileless of mankind. It is in fact doubtful whether he means that there *is* a blessed and immortal being, or that, *if* there is, that being is such as he describes. They fail to notice that although his language is ambiguous here, yet in many other places both he and Metrodorus speak as plainly as you yourself did just now. Epicurus however does actually think

Anthropomorphism seriously held by Epicurus himself.

putat, nec quemquam vidi qui magis ea quae timenda esse negaret timeret, mortem dico et deos; quibus mediocres homines non ita valde moventur, his ille clamat omnium mortalium mentes esse perterritas; tot milia latrocinantur morte proposita, alii omnia quae possunt fana conpilant: credo aut illos mortis timor terret aut hos religionis!

87 "Sed quoniam non audes (iam enim cum ipso Epicuro loquar) negare esse deos, quid est quod te inpediat aut solem aut mundum aut mentem aliquam sempiternam in deorum numero[1] ponere? 'Numquam vidi' inquit 'animam rationis consiliique participem in ulla alia nisi humana figura.' Quid? solis numquidnam aut lunae aut quinque errantium siderum simile vidisti? Sol duabus unius orbis ultimis partibus definiens motum cursus annuos conficit; huius hanc lustrationem eiusdem incensa radiis menstruo spatio luna complet; quinque autem stellae eundem orbem tenentes, aliae propius a terris, aliae remotius, ab isdem principiiis dis-
88 paribus temporibus eadem spatia conficiunt. Num quid tale, Epicure, vidisti? Ne sit igitur sol ne luna ne stellae, quoniam nihil esse potest nisi quod attigimus aut vidimus. Quid? deum ipsum numne vidisti? Cur igitur credis esse? Omnia tollamus ergo quae aut historia nobis aut ratio nova adfert.

[1] numero *Walker*: natura.

[a] *i.e.*, have you seen things perform all these motions under your eyes? we see only parts of the courses of the heavenly bodies.

that the gods exist, nor have I ever met anybody more afraid than he was of those things which he says are not terrible at all, I mean death and the gods. Terrors that do not very seriously alarm ordinary people, according to Epicurus haunt the minds of all mortal men: so many thousands commit brigandage, for which the penalty is death, and other men rob temples whenever they have the chance; I suppose the former are haunted by the fear of death and the latter by the terrors of religion!

Rationality not confined to human form.

"But as you have not the courage (for I will now address myself to Epicurus in person) to deny that the gods exist, what should hinder you from reckoning as divine the sun, or the world, or some form of ever-living intelligence? 'I have never seen a mind endowed with reason and with purpose,' he replies, 'that was embodied in any but a human form.' Well, but have you ever seen anything like the sun or the moon or the five planets? The sun, limiting his motion by the two extreme points of one orbit, completes his courses yearly. The moon, lit by the sun's rays, achieves this solar path in the space of a month. The five planets, holding the same orbit, but some nearer to and others farther from the earth, from the same starting-points complete the same distances in different periods of time. Now, Epicurus, have you ever seen anything like this[a]? Well then, let us deny the existence of the sun, moon and planets, inasmuch as nothing can exist save that which we have touched or seen. And what of god himself? You have never seen him, have you? Why then do you believe in his existence? On this principle we must sweep aside everything unusual of which history or science informs us. The next

Ita fit ut mediterranei mare esse non credant. Quae sunt tantae animi angustiae? Ut, si Seriphi natus esses nec umquam egressus ex insula in qua lepusculos vulpeculasque saepe vidisses, non crederes leones et pantheras esse cum tibi quales essent diceretur, si vero de elephanto quis diceret, etiam rideri te putares.[1]

89 "Et tu quidem, Vellei, non vestro more sed dialecticorum, quae funditus gens vestra non novit, argumenti[2] sententiam conclusisti. Beatos esse deos sumpsisti: concedimus. Beatum autem esse sine virtute neminem posse. XXXII. Id quoque damus, et libenter quidem. Virtutem autem sine ratione constare non posse: conveniat id quoque necesse est. Adiungis nec rationem esse nisi in hominis figura: quem tibi hoc daturum putas? si enim ita esset, quid opus erat te gradatim istuc pervenire? sumpsisses tuo iure. Qui[3] autem est istuc gradatim? nam a beatis ad virtutem, a virtute ad rationem video te venisse gradibus: a ratione ad humanam figuram quo modo accedis? Praecipitare istuc quidem est, non descendere.

90 "Nec vero intellego cur maluerit Epicurus deos hominum similes dicere quam homines deorum. Quaeres quid intersit; si enim hoc illi simile sit, esse illud huic. Video, sed hoc dico, non ab hominibus formae figuram venisse ad deos; di enim semper fuerunt, nati numquam sunt, siquidem aeterni sunt

[1] an quicquam . . . numquam vidimus *e* § 97 *huc bene transtulit Hude.*

[2] argumenti *A*, *B*: argumento *dett.*

[3] qui *Schomann*: quid *dett.*, quod *A*, *B* (= quale *Plasberg*).

thing would be for inland races to refuse to believe in the existence of the sea. How can such narrowness of mind be possible? It follows that, if you had been born in Seriphus and had never left the island, where you had been used to seeing nothing larger than hares and foxes, when lions and panthers were described to you, you would refuse to believe in their existence; and if somebody told you about an elephant, you would actually think that he was making fun of you!

"For your part, Velleius, you forsook the practice of your school for that of the logicians—a science of which your clan is entirely ignorant—and expressed the doctrine in the form of a syllogism. You assumed that the gods are happy: we grant it. But no one, you said, can be happy without virtue. XXXII. This also we give you, and willingly. But virtue cannot exist without reason. To this also we must agree. You add, neither can reason exist save embodied in human form. Who do you suppose will grant you this? for if it were true, what need had you to arrive at it by successive steps? you might have taken it for granted. But what about your successive steps? I see how you proceeded step by step from happiness to virtue, from virtue to reason; but how from reason do you arrive at human form? That is not a step, it is a headlong plunge.

"Nor indeed do I understand why Epicurus preferred to say that gods are like men rather than that men are like gods. 'What is the difference?' you will ask me, 'for if A is like B, B is like A.' I am aware of it; but what I mean is, that the gods did not derive the pattern of their form from men; since the gods have always existed, and were never born— **Theomorphism of mankind equally unaccountable.**

futuri ; at homines nati ; ante igitur humana forma quam homines, eaque[1] erant forma di inmortales. Non ergo illorum humana forma sed nostra divina dicenda est.

"Verum hoc quidem ut voletis ; illud quaero, quae fuerit tanta fortuna (nihil enim ratione in rerum natura factum esse vultis)—sed tamen quis iste
91 tantus casus, unde tam felix concursus atomorum, ut repente homines deorum forma nascerentur. Seminane deorum decidisse de caelo putamus in terras et sic homines patrum similes extitisse ? Vellem diceretis ; deorum cognationem agnoscerem non invitus. Nihil tale dicitis, sed casu esse factum ut essemus similes deorum.

"Et nunc argumenta quaerenda sunt quibus hoc refellatur ? Utinam tam facile vera invenire possem quam falsa convincere. XXXIII. Etenim enumerasti memoriter et copiose, ut mihi quidem admirari luberet in homine esse Romano tantam scientiam, usque a Thale Milesio de deorum natura
92 philosophorum sententias. Omnesne tibi illi delirare visi sunt qui sine manibus et pedibus constare deum posse decreverint ? Ne hoc quidem vos movet considerantis, quae sit utilitas quaeque opportunitas in homine membrorum, ut iudicetis membris humanis deos non egere ? Quid enim pedibus opus est sine ingressu, quid manibus si nihil conprehendendum est, quid reliqua discriptione omnium corporis partium, in qua nihil inane, nihil sine causa, nihil

[1] eaque *dett.* : ea qua *A*, *B*.

that is, if they are to be eternal; whereas men were born; therefore the human form existed before mankind, and it was the form of the immortal gods. We ought not to say that the gods have human form, but that our form is divine.

"However, as to that, you may take your choice. What I want to know is, how did such a piece of good luck happen (for according to your school nothing in the universe was caused by design)—but be that as it may, what accident was so potent, how did such a fortunate concourse of atoms come about, that suddenly men were born in the form of gods? Are we to think that divine seed fell from heaven to earth, and that thus men came into being resembling their sires? I wish that this were your story, for I should be glad to acknowledge my divine relations! But you do not say anything of the sort—you say that our likeness to the gods was caused by chance.

"And now is there any need to search for arguments to refute this? I only wish I could discover the truth as easily as I can expose falsehood. XXXIII. For you gave a full and accurate review, which caused me for one to wonder at so much learning in a Roman, of the theological doctrines of the philosophers from Thales of Miletus downward. Did you think they were all out of their minds because they pronounced that god can exist without hands or feet? Does not even a consideration of the adaptation of man's limbs to their functions convince you that the gods do not require human limbs? What need is there for feet without walking, or for hands if nothing has to be grasped, or for the rest of the list of the various parts of the body, in which nothing is useless, nothing without a reason, nothing super-

What use are human limbs to Epicurus's inactive gods?

supervacaneum est, itaque nulla ars imitari sollertiam naturae potest? Habebit igitur linguam deus et non loquetur, dentes palatum fauces nullum ad usum; quaeque procreationis causa natura corpori adfinxit ea frustra habebit deus; nec externa magis quam interiora, cor pulmones iecur cetera, quae detracta utilitate quid habent venustatis?—quandoquidem haec esse in deo propter pulchritudinem voltis.

93 "Istisne fidentes somniis non modo Epicurus et Metrodorus et Hermarchus contra Pythagoram Platonem Empedoclemque dixerunt sed meretricula etiam Leontium contra Theophrastum scribere ausa est? scito illa quidem sermone et Attico, sed tamen: tantum Epicuri hortus habuit licentiae. Et soletis queri; Zeno quidem etiam litigabat; quid dicam Albucium? Nam Phaedro nihil elegantius nihil humanius, sed stomachabatur senex si quid asperius dixeram, cum Epicurus Aristotelem vexarit contumeliosissime, Phaedoni Socratico turpissime male dixerit, Metrodori sodalis sui fratrem Timocraten quia nescio quid in philosophia dissentiret totis voluminibus conciderit, in Democritum ipsum quem secutus est fuerit ingratus, Nausiphanen magistrum suum a quo non[1] nihil didicerat tam male acceperit. XXXIV. Zeno quidem non eos solum qui tum erant, Apollodorum

[1] non *dett.*: *om.* *A*, *B*.

fluous, so that no art can imitate the cunning of nature's handiwork? It seems then that god will have a tongue, and will not speak; teeth, a palate, a throat, for no use; the organs that nature has attached to the body for the object of procreation—these god will possess, but to no purpose; and not only the external but also the internal organs, the heart, lungs, liver and the rest, which if they are not useful are assuredly not beautiful—since your school holds that god possesses bodily parts because of their beauty.

Epicureans ridicule other schools, but their own anthropomorphism is equally ridiculous.

3 "Was it dreams like these that not only encouraged Epicurus and Metrodorus and Hermarchus to contradict Pythagoras, Plato and Empedocles, but actually emboldened a loose woman like Leontium to write a book refuting Theophrastus? Her style no doubt is the neatest of Attic, but all the same!—such was the licence that prevailed in the Garden of Epicurus. And yet you are touchy yourselves, indeed Zeno actually used to invoke the law. I need not mention Albucius. As for Phaedrus, though he was the most refined and courteous of old gentlemen, he used to lose his temper if I spoke too harshly; although Epicurus attacked Aristotle in the most insulting manner, abused Socrates' pupil Phaedo quite outrageously, devoted whole volumes to an onslaught on Timocrates, the brother of his own associate Metrodorus, for differing from him on some point or other of philosophy, showed no gratitude toward Democritus himself, whose system he adopted, and treated so badly his own master Nausiphanes, from whom he had learnt a considerable amount. XXXIV. As for Zeno, he aimed the shafts of his abuse not only at his contemporaries, Apollodorus,

Silum ceteros, figebat maledictis, sed Socraten ipsum parentem philosophiae Latino verbo utens scurram Atticum fuisse dicebat, Chrysippum num-
94 quam nisi Chrysippam vocabat. Tu ipse paulo ante cum tamquam senatum philosophorum recitares, summos viros desipere delirare dementis esse dicebas. Quorum si nemo verum vidit de natura deorum, verendum est ne nulla sit omnino.

"Nam ista quae vos dicitis sunt tota commenticia, vix digna lucubratione anicularum. Non enim sentitis quam multa vobis suscipienda sint si inpetraritis ut concedamus eandem hominum esse et deorum figuram. Omnis cultus et curatio corporis erit eadem adhibenda deo quae adhibetur homini, ingressus cursus accubitio inclinatio sessio conprehensio, ad extremum
95 etiam sermo et oratio; nam quod et maris deos et feminas esse dicitis, quid sequatur videtis. Equidem mirari satis non possum unde ad istas opiniones vester ille princeps venerit. Sed clamare non desinitis retinendum hoc esse, deus ut beatus inmortalisque sit. Quid autem obstat quo minus sit beatus si non sit bipes? aut ista sive beatitas sive beatitudo dicenda est (utrumque omnino durum, sed usu mollienda nobis verba sunt)—verum ea quaecumque est cur aut in solem illum aut in hunc mundum aut in aliquam mentem aeternam figura membrisque
96 corporis vacuam cadere non potest? Nihil aliud dicis nisi: 'Numquam vidi solem aut mundum beatum.'

Silus and the rest, but Socrates himself, the father of philosophy, he declared to have been the Attic equivalent of our Roman buffoons ; and he always alluded to Chrysippus in the feminine gender. You yourself just now, when reeling off the list of philosophers like the censor calling the roll of the Senate, said that all those eminent men were fools, idiots and madmen. But if none of these discerned the truth about the divine nature, it is to be feared that the divine nature is entirely non-existent.

" For as for your school's account of the matter, it is the merest fairy-story, hardly worthy of old wives at work by lamplight. You don't perceive what a number of things you are let in for, if we consent to admit that men and gods have the same form. You will have to assign to god exactly the same physical exercises and care of the person as are proper to men : he will walk, run, recline, bend, sit, hold things in the hand, and lastly even converse and make speeches. As for your saying that the gods are male and female, well, you must see what the consequence of that will be. For my part, I am at a loss to imagine how your great founder arrived at such notions. All the same you never cease vociferating that we must on no account relinquish the divine happiness and immortality. But what prevents god from being happy without having two legs ? and why cannot your ' beatitude ' or ' beatity,' whichever form we are to use—and either is certainly a hard mouthful, but words have to be softened by use—but whatever it is, why can it not apply to the sun yonder, or to this world of ours, or to some eternal intelligence devoid of bodily shape and members ? Your only answer is, ' I have never seen a happy sun or world.' Well,

Quid, mundum praeter hunc umquamne vidisti? Negabis. Cur igitur non sescenta milia esse mundorum sed innumerabilia ausus es dicere? 'Ratio docuit.' Ergo hoc te ratio non docebit, cum praestantissima natura quaeratur eaque beata et aeterna, quae sola divina natura est, ut inmortalitate vincamur[1] ab ea natura sic animi praestantia vinci, atque ut animi item corporis? Cur igitur cum ceteris rebus inferiores simus forma pares sumus? ad similitudinem enim deorum propius accedebat humana virtus
97 quam figura. XXXV. [[2]An quicquam tam puerile dici potest (ut eundem locum diutius urgeam) quam si ea genera beluarum quae in rubro mari Indiave gignuntur[3] nulla esse dicamus? Atqui ne curiosissimi quidem homines exquirendo audire tam multa possunt quam sunt multa quae terra mari paludibus fluminibus exsistunt; quae negemus esse quia numquam vidimus!]

"Ipsa vero quam nihil ad rem pertinet quae vos delectat maxime similitudo! Quid, canis nonne similis lupo?—atque, ut Ennius,

> simia quam similis turpissuma bestia nobis!—

at mores in utroque dispares. Elephanto beluarum
98 nulla prudentior: at figura[4] quae vastior? De bestiis loquor: quid, inter ipsos homines nonne et simillimis formis dispares mores et moribus simillimis[5] figura dissimilis? Etenim si semel, Vellei, suscipimus

[1] vincamur *A, B*: vincimur *dett.*

[2] an quicquam . . . nunquam vidimus *in* § 88 *bene transtulit Hude.*

[3] gignuntur *Schömann*: gignantur.

[4] at figura *det.* (figurā *B*): ad figuram *A.*

[5] simillimis *det.*: *om. A, B*: paribus *Klotz.*

but have you ever seen any other world but this one? No, you will reply. Then why did you venture to assert the existence of, not thousands and thousands, but a countless number of worlds? 'That is what reason teaches.' Then will not reason teach you that when we seek to find a being who shall be supremely excellent, and happy and eternal as well—and nothing else constitutes divinity—, even as that being will surpass us in immortality, so also will it surpass us in mental excellence, and even as in mental excellence, so also in bodily. Why then, if we are inferior to god in all else, are we his equals in form? for man came nearer to the divine image in virtue than in outward aspect. XXXV. [Can you mention anything so childish (to press the same point still further) as to deny the existence of the various species of huge animals that grow in the Red Sea or in India? Yet not even the most diligent investigators could possibly collect information about all the vast multitude of creatures that exist on land and in the sea, the marshes and the rivers: the existence of which we are to deny, because we have never seen them!]

"Then take your favourite argument from resemblance: how utterly pointless it really is! Why, does not a dog resemble a wolf?—and, to quote Ennius,

How like us is that ugly brute, the ape!—

but the two differ in habits. The elephant is the wisest of beasts, but the most ungainly in shape. I speak of animals, but is it not the case even with men that when very much alike in appearance they differ widely in character, and when very much alike in character they are unlike in appearance? In fact,

Why should reason exist only in human form?

genus hoc argumenti, attende quo serpat. Tu enim sumebas nisi in hominis figura rationem inesse non posse; sumet alius nisi in terrestri, nisi in eo qui natus sit, nisi in eo qui adoleverit, nisi in eo qui didicerit, nisi in eo qui ex animo constet et corpore caduco et infirmo, postremo nisi in homine atque mortali. Quodsi in omnibus his rebus obsistis, quid est quod te forma una conturbet? His enim omnibus quae proposui adiunctis in homine rationem esse et mentem videbas; quibus detractis deum tamen nosse te dicis, modo liniamenta maneant. Hoc est non considerare sed quasi sortiri quid loquare.
99 Nisi forte ne hoc quidem attendis, non modo in homine sed etiam in arbore quicquid supervacaneum sit aut usum non habeat obstare. Quam molestum est uno digito plus habere! Quid ita? Quia nec ad speciem nec ad[1] usum alium quinque desiderant. Tuus autem deus non digito uno redundat sed capite collo cervicibus lateribus alvo tergo poplitibus manibus pedibus feminibus cruribus. Si ut inmortalis sit, quid haec ad vitam membra pertinent? quid ipsa facies? Magis illa, cerebrum cor pulmones iecur: haec enim sunt domicilia vitae; oris quidem habitus ad vitae firmitatem nihil pertinet.

100 XXXVI. "Et eos vituperabas qui ex operibus magnificis atque praeclaris, cum ipsum mundum, cum eius membra caelum terras maria, cumque horum insignia

[1] ad . . . ad *om. A, B.*

Velleius, if once we embark on this line of argument, see how far it takes us. You claimed it as axiomatic that reason can only exist in human form ; but some-one else will claim that it can only exist in a terrestrial creature, in one that has been born, has grown up, has been educated, consists of a soul and a body liable to decay and disease—in fine, that it can only exist in a mortal man. If you stand out against each of these assumptions, why be troubled about shape only ? Rational intelligence exists in man, as you saw, only in conjunction with all the attributes that I have set out ; yet you say that you can recognize god even with all these attributes stripped off, provided that the outward form remains. This is not to weigh the question, it is to toss up for what you are to say. Unless indeed you happen never to have observed this either, that not only in a man but even in a tree whatever is superfluous or without a use is harmful. What a nuisance it is to have a single finger too many ! Why is this ? Because, given five fingers, there is no need of another either for appearance or for use. But your god has got not merely one finger more than he wants, but a head, neck, spine, sides, belly, back, flanks, hands, feet, thighs, legs. If this is to secure him immortality, what have these members to do with life ? What has even the face ? It depends more on the brain, heart, lungs and liver, for they are the abode of life : a man's countenance and features have nothing to do with his vitality.

Why have the gods limbs if they are inactive?

XXXVI. " Then you censured those who argued from the splendour and the beauty of creation, and who, observing the world itself, and the parts of the world, the sky and earth and sea, and the sun, moon

solem lunam stellasque vidissent, cumque temporum maturitates mutationes vicissitudinesque cognovissent, suspicati essent aliquam excellentem esse praestantemque naturam quae haec effecisset moveret regeret gubernaret. Qui etiam si aberrant a[1] coniectura, video tamen quid sequantur; tu quod opus tandem magnum et egregium habes quod effectum divina mente videatur, ex quo esse deos suspicere? 'Habemus'[2] inquis 'in animo insitam informationem quandam dei.' Et barbati quidem Iovis, galeatae
101 Minervae: num igitur esse talis putas? Quanto melius haec vulgus imperitorum, qui non membra solum hominis deo tribuant sed usum etiam membrorum. Dant enim arcum sagittas hastam clipeum fuscinam fulmen, et si actiones quae sint deorum non vident, nihil agentem tamen deum non queunt cogitare. Ipsi qui inridentur Aegyptii nullam beluam nisi ob aliquam utilitatem quam ex ea caperent consecraverunt; velut ibes maximam vim serpentium conficiunt, cum sint aves excelsae, cruribus rigidis, corneo proceroque rostro; avertunt pestem ab Aegypto, cum volucris anguis ex vastitate Libyae vento Africo invectas interficiunt atque consumunt, ex quo fit ut illae nec morsu vivae noceant nec odore mortuae. Possum de ichneumonum utilitate de crocodilorum de faelium dicere, sed nolo esse longus. Ita concludam, tamen beluas a barbaris propter beneficium consecratas, vestrorum deorum non modo beneficium nullum exstare sed ne factum quidem

[1] a *om. Walker.* [2] habemus *dett.*: habebam *A, B.*

and stars that adorn them, and discovering the laws of the seasons and their periodic successions, conjectured that there must exist some supreme and transcendent being who had created these things, and who imparted motion to them and guided and governed them. Though this guess may be wide of the mark, I can see what they are after; but as for you, what mighty masterpiece pray do you adduce as apparently the creation of divine intelligence, leading you to conjecture that gods exist? 'We have an idea of god implanted in our minds,' you say. Yes, and an idea of Jupiter with a beard, and Minerva in a helmet; but do you therefore believe that those deities are really like that? The unlearned multitude are surely wiser here—they assign to god not only a man's limbs, but the use of those limbs. For they give him bow, arrows, spear, shield, trident, thunderbolt; and if they cannot see what actions the gods perform, yet they cannot conceive of god as entirely inactive. Even the Egyptians, whom we laugh at, deified animals solely on the score of some utility which they derived from them; for instance, the ibis, being a tall bird with stiff legs and a long horny beak, destroys a great quantity of snakes: it protects Egypt from plague, by killing and eating the flying serpents that are brought from the Libyan desert by the south-west wind, and so preventing them from harming the natives by their bite while alive and their stench when dead. I might describe the utility of the ichneumon, the crocodile and the cat, but I do not wish to be tedious. I will make my point thus: these animals are at all events deified by the barbarians for the benefits which they confer, but your gods not only do no service that you can point to, but

102 omnino. 'Nihil habet' inquit[1] 'negotii.' Profecto Epicurus quasi pueri delicati nihil cessatione melius existimat. XXXVII. At ipsi tamen pueri etiam cum cessant exercitatione aliqua ludicra delectantur: deum sic feriatum volumus cessatione torpere ut si se commoverit vereamur ne beatus esse non possit? Haec oratio non modo deos spoliat motu et actione divina[2] sed etiam homines inertis efficit, si quidem agens aliquid ne deus quidem esse beatus potest.

103 "Verum sit sane ut vultis deus effigies hominis et imago: quod eius est domicilium, quae sedes, qui locus, quae deinde actio vitae? quibus rebus id quod vultis beatus est? Utatur enim suis bonis oportet et fruatur qui beatus futurus est. Nam locus quidem iis etiam naturis quae sine animis sunt suus est cuique proprius, ut terra infimum teneat, hanc inundet aqua, superior aeri, aetheriis[3] ignibus altissima ora reddatur. Bestiarum autem terrenae sunt aliae, partim aquatiles, aliae quasi ancipites in utraque sede viventes; sunt quaedam etiam quae igne nasci putentur appareant-
104 que in ardentibus fornacibus saepe volitantes. Quaero igitur vester deus primum ubi habitet, deinde quae causa eum loco moveat, si modo movetur aliquando, porro,[4] cum hoc proprium sit animantium ut aliquid adpetant quod sit naturae accommodatum, deus quid

[1] inquis? (*cf.* § 109) *ed.* [2] divina *secl. Reinhardt.*
[3] superior aeri, aetheriis *Müller*: superi aetheri *B*, superi aether *A*. [4] porro *Heindorf*: postremo.

[a] This is stated by Aristotle, *Gen. An.* iii. 9, *Hist. An.* v. 19, and Pliny, *N.H.* xi. 42.

2 they don't do anything at all. 'God,' he says, 'is free from trouble.' Obviously Epicurus thinks, as spoilt children do, that idleness is the best thing there is. XXXVII. Yet these very children even when idle amuse themselves with some active game: are we to suppose that god enjoys so complete a holiday, and is so sunk in sloth, that we must fear lest the least movement may jeopardize his happiness? This language not merely robs the gods of the movements and activities suitable to the divine nature, but also tends to make men slothful, if even god cannot be happy when actively employed.

(4) Even granting the 'images,' this does not prove the reality of the gods, or their existence as happy and eternal beings.

3 "However, granting your view that god is the image and the likeness of man, what is his dwelling-place and local habitation? in what activities does he spend his life? what constitutes that happiness which you attribute to him? For a person who is to be happy must actively enjoy his blessings. As for locality, even the inanimate elements each have their own particular region: earth occupies the lowest place, water covers the earth, to air is assigned the upper realm, and the ethereal fires occupy the highest confines of all. Animals again are divided into those that live on land and those that live in the water, while a third class are amphibious and dwell in both regions, and there are also some that are believed to be born from fire, and are occasionally seen fluttering
4 about in glowing furnaces.[a] About your deity therefore I want to know, first, where he dwells; secondly, what motive he has for moving in space, that is, if he ever does so move; thirdly, it being a special characteristic of animate beings to desire some end that is appropriate to their nature, what is the thing that god desires; fourthly, upon what subject does he

appetat, ad quam denique rem motu mentis ac ratione
utatur, postremo quo modo beatus sit quo modo
aeternus. Quicquid enim horum attigeris,[1] ulcus est:
ita male instituta ratio exitum reperire non potest.
105 Sic enim dicebas, speciem dei percipi cogitatione non
sensu, nec esse in ea ullam soliditatem, neque
eandem ad numerum permanere, eamque esse eius
visionem ut similitudine et transitione cernatur neque
deficiat umquam ex infinitis corporibus similium[2]
accessio, ex eoque fieri ut in haec intenta mens
nostra beatam illam naturam et sempiternam putet.
XXXVIII. Hoc per ipsos deos, de quibus loquimur,
quale tandem est? Nam si tantum modo ad cogitationem valent nec habent ullam soliditatem nec
eminentiam, quid interest utrum de Hippocentauro
an de deo cogitemus? omnem enim talem conforma-
tionem animi ceteri philosophi motum inanem vocant,
vos autem adventum in animos et introitum ima-
106 ginum dicitis. Ut igitur[3] Ti. Gracchum cum videor
contionantem[4] in Capitolio videre de[5] M. Octavio
deferentem sitellam tum eum motum animi dico esse
inanem, tu autem et Gracchi et Octavii imagines re-
manere quae in Capitolium cum pervenerim[6] tum ad
animum meum referantur[7]: hoc idem fieri in deo, cuius
crebra facie pellantur animi, ex quo esse beati atque
107 aeterni intellegantur. Fac imagines esse quibus pul-

[1] attigeris *dett.*: attigerit *A*, *B*, attigeritis *Reid*.
[2] similium <imaginum> *Goethe*.
[3] igitur *secl. Madvig*. [4] contionans*?* *ed*. [5] <et> de *Bouhier*.
[6] pervenerim *dett.*: pervenerint *A*, *B*. [7] deferantur *Ernesti*.

---

[a] *i.e.*, permanent identity: it does not continue one and the same.

[b] Perhaps the Latin should be altered to give 'images: just as, when while making a speech in the Capitol I seem to see Tiberius Gracchus producing . . .'

employ his mental activity and reason; and lastly, how is he happy, and how eternal? For whichever of these questions you raise, you touch a tender spot. An argument based on such insecure premisses can
5 come to no valid conclusion. Your assertion was that the form of god is perceived by thought and not by the senses, that it has no solidity nor numerical persistence,[a] and that our perception of it is such that it is seen owing to similarity and succession, a never-ceasing stream of similar forms arriving continually from the infinite number of atoms, and that thus it results that our mind, when its attention is fixed on these forms, conceives the divine nature to be happy and eternal. XXXVIII. Now in the name of the very gods about whom we are talking, what can possibly be the meaning of this? If the gods only appeal to the faculty of thought, and have no solidity or definite outline, what difference does it make whether we think of a god or of a hippocentaur? Such mental pictures are called by all other philosophers mere empty imaginations, but you say they are the arrival and entrance into our minds of certain
6 images.[b] Well then, when I seem to see Tiberius Gracchus in the middle of his speech in the Capitol producing the ballot-box for the vote on Marcus Octavius, I explain this as an empty imagination of the mind, but your explanation is that the images of Gracchus and Octavius have actually remained on the spot, so that when I come to the Capitol these images are borne to my mind; the same thing happens, you say, in the case of god, whose appearance repeatedly impinges on men's minds, and so gives rise to the belief in happy and eternal deities.
7 Suppose that there are such images constantly im-

sentur animi: species dumtaxat obicitur quaedam—num etiam cur ea beata sit cur aeterna?

"Quae autem istae imagines vestrae aut unde? A Democrito omnino haec licentia; sed et ille reprehensus a multis est, nec vos exitum reperitis, totaque res vacillat et claudicat. Nam quid est quod minus probari possit, quam omnino[1] in me incidere imagines Homeri Archilochi Romuli Numae Pythagorae Platonis—nedum ea[2] forma qua illi[3] fuerunt? Quo modo illae[4] ergo et quorum imagines[5]? Orpheum poetam docet Aristoteles numquam fuisse, et hoc Orphicum carmen Pythagorei ferunt cuiusdam fuisse Cercopis; at Orpheus, id est imago eius ut vos vultis, in animum meum saepe
108 incurrit. Quid quod eiusdem hominis in meum aliae, aliae in tuum? quid quod earum rerum quae numquam omnino fuerunt neque esse potuerunt, ut Scyllae, ut Chimaerae? quid quod hominum locorum urbium earum quas numquam vidimus? quid quod simul ac mihi collibitum est praesto est imago? quid quod etiam ad dormientem veniunt invocatae? Tota res, Vellei, nugatoria est. Vos autem non modo oculis imagines sed etiam animis inculcatis:
109 tanta est inpunitas garriendi. XXXIX. At quam licenter! Fluentium frequenter transitio fit visionum, ut e multis una videatur. Puderet me dicere non

[1] quam omnino *Reid*: quam hominum *dett.*, omnium *A*, *B*: quam omnium hominum *? ed.*
[2] nedum ea *ed.*: nec ea *Ald.*, nec ex *MSS.*: nedum *Reid.*
[3] ipsi *? ed.* [4] illac *Reid*: illi. [5] imagines *secl. Earle.*

[a] See note on i. 33.

pinging on our minds: but that is only the presentation of a certain form—surely not also of a reason for supposing that this form is happy and eternal?

"But what is the nature of these images of yours, and whence do they arise? This extravagance, it is true, is borrowed from Democritus; but he has been widely criticized, nor can you find a satisfactory explanation, and the whole affair is a lame and impotent business. For what can be more improbable than that images of Homer, Archilochus, Romulus, Numa, Pythagoras and Plato should impinge on me at all—much less that they should do so in the actual shape that those men really bore? How then do those images arise? and of whom are they the images? Aristotle[a] tells us that the poet Orpheus never existed, and the Pythagoreans say that the Orphic poem which we possess was the work of a certain Cercops; yet Orpheus, that is, according to you, the image of him, often comes into my mind. What of the fact that different images of the same person enter my mind and yours? or that images come to us of things that never existed at all and never can have existed—for instance, Scylla, and the Chimaera? or of people, places and cities which we have never seen? What of the fact that I can call up an image instantaneously, the very moment that I choose to do so? or that they come to me unbidden, even when I am asleep? Velleius, the whole affair is humbug. Yet you stamp these images not only on our eyes but also on our minds—so irresponsibly do you babble. XXXIX. And how extravagantly! There is a constant passage or stream of visual presentations which collectively produce a single visual impression. I should be ashamed to say that

'Equilibrium' (§ 50) might equally prove the immortality of men.

intellegere, si vos ipsi intellegeretis qui ista defenditis. Quo modo enim probas continenter imagines ferri, aut si continenter quo modo aeternae? 'Innumerabilitas' inquis[1] 'suppeditat atomorum.' Num eadem ergo ista faciet ut sint omnia sempiterna? Confugis ad aequilibritatem (sic enim ἰσονομίαν si placet appellemus) et ais quoniam sit natura mortalis inmortalem etiam esse oportere. Isto modo quoniam homines mortales sunt sunt[2] aliqui inmortales, et quoniam nascuntur in terra nascuntur[3] in aqua. 'Et quia sunt quae interimant, sunt[4] quae conservent.' Sint sane, sed ea[5] conservent quae sunt:
110 deos istos esse non sentio. Omnis tamen ista rerum[6] effigies ex individuis quo modo corporibus oritur? quae etiamsi essent, quae nulla sunt, pellere se ipsa et agitari[7] inter se concursu fortasse possent, formare figurare colorare animare non possent. Nullo igitur modo inmortalem deum efficitis.

XL. "Videamus nunc de beato. Sine virtute certe nullo modo; virtus autem actuosa, et deus vester nihil agens; expers virtutis igitur; ita ne beatus quidem.
111 Quae ergo vita? 'Suppeditatio' inquis 'bonorum nullo malorum interventu.' Quorum tandem bonorum? Voluptatum credo nempe ad corpus pertinentium: nullam enim novistis nisi profectam

[1] inquis *dett.*: inquit *A*, *B*. [2] sunt *ed.*: sint.
[3] nascuntur *pr. B*, *dett.*: nascantur *A*.
[4] sunt *dett.*: sint *A*, *B*. [5] ea: ea quae *dett.*
[6] rerum: deorum *Goethe*. [7] agitare *det.*

[a] Perhaps Cicero wrote 'pictures of the gods.'

I do not understand the doctrine, if you who maintain it understood it yourselves! How can you prove that the stream of images is continuous, or if it is, how are the images eternal? You say that there is an innumerable supply of atoms. Are you going to argue then that everything is eternal, for the same reason? You take refuge in the principle of 'equilibrium' (for so with your consent we will translate *isonomia*), and you say that because there is mortal substance there must also be immortal substance. On that showing, because there are mortal men, there are also some that are immortal, and because there are men born on land, there are men born in the water. 'And because there are forces of destruction, there are also forces of preservation.' Suppose there were, they would only preserve things that already exist; but I am not aware that your gods do exist. But be that as it may, how do all your pictures of objects[a] arise out of the atoms? even if the atoms existed, which they do not, they might conceivably be capable of pushing and jostling one another about by their collisions, but they could not create form, shape, colour, life. You fail entirely therefore to prove divine immortality.

How can happiness go with inactivity (and therefore absence of virtue), or without pleasures of sense, or with constant danger of dissolution?

XL. "Now let us consider divine happiness. Happiness is admittedly impossible without virtue. But virtue is in its nature active, and your god is entirely inactive. Therefore he is devoid of virtue. Therefore he is not happy either. In what then does his life consist? 'In a constant succession of things good,' you reply, 'without any admixture of evils.' Things good—what things? Pleasures, I suppose—that is, of course, pleasures of the body, for your school recognizes no pleasures of the mind that do

a corpore et redeuntem ad corpus animi voluptatem. Non arbitror te, Vellei, similem esse Epicureorum reliquorum[1] quos pudeat quarundam Epicuri vocum, quibus ille testatur se ne intellegere quidem ullum bonum quod sit seiunctum a delicatis et obscenis voluptatibus, quas quidem non erubescens perse-
112 quitur omnis nominatim. Quem cibum igitur aut quas potiones aut quas vocum aut florum[2] varietates aut quos tactus quos odores adhibebis ad deos, ut eos perfundas voluptatibus? Et poetae quidem nectar ambrosiam <que>[3] <in>[4] epulas conparant et aut Iuventatem aut Ganymedem pocula ministrantem, tu autem, Epicure, quid facies? neque enim unde habeat ista deus tuus video nec quo modo utatur. Locupletior igitur hominum natura ad beate vivendum est quam deorum, quod pluribus generibus fruitur voluptatum.
113 At has leviores ducis voluptates, quibus quasi titillatio (Epicuri enim hoc verbum est) adhibetur sensibus. Quousque ludis? Nam etiam Philo noster ferre non poterat aspernari Epicureos mollis et delicatas voluptates; summa enim memoria pronuntiabat plurimas Epicuri sententias iis ipsis verbis quibus erant scriptae; Metrodori vero, qui est Epicuri collega sapientiae, multa[5] inpudentiora recitabat: accusat enim Timocratem fratrem suum Metrodorus quod dubitet omnia quae ad beatam vitam pertineant ventre metiri, neque id semel dicit sed saepius. Adnuere te video, nota enim tibi sunt; proferrem libros si negares. Neque

[1] aliquorum *Bouhier*. [2] colorum *Walker*.
[3] *add. Vict.* [4] *add. Reid.*
[5] multo *? Plasberg*.

[a] His phrase was γαργαλισμοὶ σώματος (Athenaeus xii. 546).

not arise from and come back to the body. I don't suppose that you, Velleius, are like the rest of the Epicureans, who are ashamed of certain utterances of Epicurus, in which he protests that he cannot conceive any good that is unconnected with the pleasures of the voluptuary and the sensualist, pleasures which in fact he proceeds without a blush to enumerate by
2 name. Well then, what viands and beverages, what harmonies of music and flowers of various hue, what delights of touch and smell will you assign to the gods, so as to keep them steeped in pleasure? The poets array banquets of nectar and ambrosia, with Hebe or Ganymede in attendance as cup-bearer; but what will you do, Epicurean? I don't see either where your god is to procure these delights or how he is to enjoy them. It appears then that mankind is more bountifully equipped for happiness than is the deity, since man can experience a wider range of pleasures.
3 You tell me that you consider these pleasures inferior, which merely 'tickle' the senses (the expression is that of Epicurus[a]). When will you cease jesting? Why, even our friend Philo was impatient with the Epicureans for affecting to despise the pleasures of sensual indulgence; for he had an excellent memory and could quote verbatim a number of maxims from the actual writings of Epicurus. As for Metrodorus, Epicurus's co-partner in philosophy, he supplied him with many still more outspoken quotations; in fact Metrodorus takes his brother Timocrates to task for hesitating to measure every element of happiness by the standard of the belly, nor is this an isolated utterance, but he repeats it several times. I see you nod your assent, as you are acquainted with the passages; and did you deny it, I would produce

nunc reprehendo quod ad voluptatem omnia referantur (alia est ea quaestio), sed doceo deos vestros esse voluptatis expertes, ita vestro iudicio ne beatos quidem.

114 XLI. 'At dolore vacant.' Satin est id ad illam abundantem bonis vitam beatissimam? 'Cogitat' inquiunt 'adsidue beatum esse se; habet enim nihil aliud quod agitet in mente.' Conprehende igitur animo et propone ante oculos deum nihil aliud in omni aeternitate nisi 'Mihi pulchre est' et 'Ego beatus sum' cogitantem. Nec tamen video quo modo non vereatur iste deus beatus ne intereat, cum sine ulla intermissione pulsetur agiteturque atomorum incursione sempiterna, cumque ex ipso imagines semper afluant. Ita nec beatus est vester deus nec aeternus.

115 "'At etiam de sanctitate, de pietate adversus deos libros scripsit Epicurus.' At quo modo in his loquitur? Ut T. Coruncanium aut P. Scaevolam pontifices maximos te audire dicas, non eum qui sustulerit omnem funditus religionem nec manibus ut Xerxes sed rationibus deorum inmortalium templa et aras everterit. Quid est enim, cur deos ab hominibus colendos dicas, cum dei non modo homines non
116 colant[1] sed omnino nihil curent nihil agant? 'At est eorum eximia quaedam praestansque natura, ut ea debeat ipsa per se ad se colendam allicere sapientem.' An quicquam eximium potest esse in

[1] hominibus non consulant *Manutius*.

---

[a] Diogenes Laertius x. 29 mentions a treatise of Epicurus Περὶ ὁσιότητος.

[b] The Latin runs 'do not worship men,' and perhaps should be altered to give, 'do not study men's interests.'

the volumes. Not that I am at the moment criticizing your making pleasure the sole standard of value—that belongs to another inquiry. What I am trying to prove is that your gods are incapable of pleasure, and therefore by your verdict can have no happiness either. XLI. 'But they are free from pain.' Does that satisfy the ideal of perfect bliss, overflowing with good things? 'God is engaged (they say) in ceaseless contemplation of his own happiness, for he has no other object for his thoughts.' I beg of you to realize in your imagination a vivid picture of a deity solely occupied for all eternity in reflecting 'What a good time I am having! How happy I am!' And yet I can't see how this happy god of yours is not to fear destruction, since he is subjected without a moment's respite to the buffeting and jostling of a horde of atoms that eternally assail him, while from his own person a ceaseless stream of images is given off. Your god is therefore neither happy nor eternal.

(5) Epicurean principles really fatal to religion.

"'Yes, but Epicurus actually wrote books about holiness[a] and piety.' But what is the language of these books? Such that you think you are listening to a Coruncanius or a Scaevola, high priests, not to the man who destroyed the very foundations of religion, and overthrew—not by main force like Xerxes, but by argument—the temples and the altars of the immortal gods. Why, what reason have you for maintaining that men owe worship to the gods, if the gods not only pay no respect to men,[b] but care for nothing and do nothing at all? 'But deity possesses an excellence and pre-eminence which must of its own nature attract the worship of the wise.' Now how can there be any excellence in a being so

ea natura quae sua voluptate laetans nihil nec actura sit umquam neque agat neque egerit? quae porro pietas ei debetur a quo nihil acceperis? aut quid omnino cuius nullum meritum sit ei deberi potest? Est enim pietas iustitia adversum deos; cum quibus quid potest nobis esse iuris, cum homini nulla cum deo sit communitas? Sanctitas autem est scientia colendorum deorum; qui quam ob rem colendi sint non intellego nullo nec accepto ab iis nec sperato
117 bono. XLII. Quid est autem quod deos veneremur propter admirationem eius naturae in qua egregium nihil videmus[1]?

"Nam superstitione, quod gloriari soletis, facile est liberari cum sustuleris omnem vim deorum; nisi forte Diagoram aut Theodorum qui omnino deos esse negabant censes superstitiosos esse potuisse; ego ne Protagoram quidem, cui neutrum licuerit, nec esse deos nec non esse. Horum enim sententiae omnium non modo superstitionem tollunt in qua inest timor inanis deorum, sed etiam religionem quae deorum
118 cultu pio continetur. Quid, ii qui dixerunt totam de dis inmortalibus opinionem fictam esse ab hominibus sapientibus rei publicae causa, ut quos ratio non posset eos ad officium religio duceret, nonne omnem religionem funditus sustulerunt? Quid, Prodicus Cius, qui ea quae prodessent hominum vitae deorum

[1] videamus *Alan.*

engrossed in the delights of his own pleasure that he always has been, is, and will continue to be entirely idle and inactive? Furthermore how can you owe piety to a person who has bestowed nothing upon you? or how can you owe anything at all to one who has done you no service? Piety is justice towards the gods; but how can any claims of justice exist between us and them, if god and man have nothing in common? Holiness is the science of divine worship; but I fail to see why the gods should be worshipped if we neither have received nor hope to receive benefit from them. XLII. On the other hand what reason is there for adoring the gods on the ground of our admiration for the divine nature, if we cannot see that that nature possesses any special excellence?

"As for freedom from superstition, which is the favourite boast of your school, that is easy to attain when you have deprived the gods of all power; unless perchance you think that it was possible for Diagoras or Theodorus to be superstitious, who denied the existence of the gods altogether. For my part, I don't see how it was possible even for Protagoras, who was not certain either that the gods exist or that they do not. For the doctrines of all these thinkers abolish not only superstition, which implies a groundless fear of the gods, but also religion, which consists in piously worshipping them. Take again those who have asserted that the entire notion of the immortal gods is a fiction invented by wise men in the interest of the state, to the end that those whom reason was powerless to control might be led in the path of duty by religion; surely this view was absolutely and entirely destructive of religion. Or Prodicus of Cos, who said that the gods were personifications of things

in numero habita esse dixit, quam tandem religionem
119 reliquit? Quid, qui aut fortis aut claros aut potentis viros tradunt post mortem ad deos pervenisse, eosque esse ipsos quos nos colere precari venerarique soleamus, nonne expertes sunt religionum omnium? quae ratio maxime tractata ab Euhemero est, quem noster et interpretatus et secutus est praeter ceteros Ennius; ab Euhemero autem et mortes et sepulturae demonstrantur deorum; utrum igitur hic confirmasse videtur religionem an penitus totam sustulisse? Omitto Eleusinem sanctam illam et augustam,

> ubi initiantur gentes orarum ultimae,

praetereo Samothraciam eaque quae Lemni

> nocturno aditu occulta coluntur
> silvestribus saepibus densa,

quibus explicatis ad rationemque revocatis rerum magis natura cognoscitur quam deorum.

120 XLIII. "Mihi quidem etiam Democritus vir magnus in primis, cuius fontibus Epicurus hortulos suos inrigavit, nutare videtur in natura deorum. Tum enim censet imagines divinitate praeditas inesse in universitate rerum, tum principia mentis quae sint[1] in eodem universo deos esse dicit, tum animantes imagines quae vel prodesse nobis soleant[2] vel

[1] sint *Heindorf*: sunt. [2] soleant *dett.*: solent *A*, *B*.

---

[a] The source of this verse is unknown.
[b] Probably from the *Philoctetes* of Attius.

beneficial to the life of man—pray what religion was left by his theory? Or those who teach that brave or famous or powerful men have been deified after death, and that it is these who are the real objects of the worship, prayers and adoration which we are accustomed to offer—are not they entirely devoid of all sense of religion? This theory was chiefly developed by Euhemerus, who was translated and imitated especially by our poet Ennius. Yet Euhemerus describes the death and burial of certain gods; are we then to think of him as upholding religion, or rather as utterly and entirely destroying it? I say nothing of the holy and awe-inspiring sanctuary of Eleusis,

> Where tribes from earth's remotest confines seek
> Initiation,[a]

and I pass over Samothrace and those

> occult mysteries
> Which throngs of worshippers at dead of night
> In forest coverts deep do celebrate[b]

at Lemnos, since such mysteries when interpreted and rationalized prove to have more to do with natural science than with theology.

XLIII. "For my own part I believe that even that very eminent man Democritus, the fountain-head from which Epicurus derived the streams that watered his little garden, has no fixed opinion about the nature of the gods. At one moment he holds the view that the universe includes images endowed with divinity; at another he says that there exist in this same universe the elements from which the mind is compounded, and that these are gods; at another, that they are animate images, which are wont to exercise a beneficent or harmful influence over us; and again

Democritus also really had no theology.

nocere, tum ingentis quasdam imagines tantasque
ut universum mundum conplectantur extrinsecus.
Quae quidem omnia sunt patria Democriti quam
121 Democrito digniora; quis enim istas imagines con-
prehendere animo potest, quis admirari, quis aut
cultu aut religione dignas iudicare?

"Epicurus vero ex animis hominum extraxit radici-
tus religionem cum dis inmortalibus et opem et
gratiam sustulit. Cum enim optimam et praestan-
tissimam naturam dei dicat esse, negat idem esse
in deo gratiam: tollit id quod maxime proprium
est optimae praestantissimaeque naturae. Quid
enim melius aut quid praestantius bonitate et bene-
ficentia? Qua cum carere deum vultis, neminem
deo nec deum nec hominem carum,[1] neminem ab eo
amari, neminem diligi vultis. Ita fit ut non modo
homines a deis sed ipsi dei inter se [ab aliis alii][2]
neglegantur. XLIV. Quanto Stoici melius, qui a
vobis reprehenduntur: censent autem sapientes
sapientibus etiam ignotis esse amicos; nihil est
enim virtute amabilius, quam qui adeptus erit, ubicum-
122 que erit gentium a nobis diligetur. Vos autem quid
mali datis cum <in>[3] inbecillitate gratificationem et
benivolentiam ponitis! Ut enim omittam vim et
naturam deorum, ne homines quidem censetis nisi in-
becilli essent futuros beneficos et benignos fuisse?
Nulla est caritas naturalis inter bonos? Carum

[1] carum <esse> ? *ed.* [2] *Cobet.* [3] *Lambinus.*

---

[a] In the actual teaching of Democritus these scattered doctrines formed a consistent whole: the basis of the world is particles of divine fire, floating in space; groups of them form deities, vast beings of long life but not everlasting; some of the particles floating off from these enter the mind,

that they are certain vast images of such a size as to envelop and enfold the entire world.[a] All these fancies are more worthy of Democritus's native city[b] than of himself; for who could form a mental picture of such images? who could adore them and deem them worthy of worship or reverence?

Epicureanism denies divine and decries human benevolence.

"Epicurus however, in abolishing divine beneficence and divine benevolence. uprooted and exterminated all religion from the human heart. For while asserting the supreme goodness and excellence of the divine nature, he yet denies to god the attribute of benevolence—that is to say, he does away with that which is the most essential element of supreme goodness and excellence. For what can be better or more excellent than kindness and beneficence? Make out god to be devoid of either, and you make him devoid of all love, affection or esteem for any other being, human or divine. It follows not merely that the gods do not care for mankind, but that they have no care for one another. XLIV. How much more truth there is in the Stoics, whom you censure! They hold that all wise men are friends, even when strangers to each other, since nothing is more lovable than virtue, and he that attains to it will have our esteem in whatever country he dwells. But as for you, what mischief you cause when you reckon kindness and benevolence as weaknesses! Apart altogether from the nature and attributes of deity, do you think that even human beneficence and benignity are solely due to human infirmity? Is there no natural affection between the good? There is some-

itself composed of similar particles, and give us knowledge of the gods.

[b] Abdera in Thrace had a reputation for stupidity.

ipsum verbum est amoris, ex quo amicitiae nomen est ductum ; quam si ad fructum nostrum referemus[1] non ad illius commoda quem diligimus,[2] non erit ista amicitia sed mercatura quaedam utilitatum suarum. Prata et arva et pecudum greges diliguntur isto modo, quod fructus ex iis capiuntur, hominum caritas et amicitia gratuita est ; quanto igitur magis deorum, qui nulla re egentes et inter se diligunt et hominibus consulunt. Quod[3] ni[4] ita est,[5] quid veneramur quid precamur deos, cur sacris pontifices cur auspiciis augures praesunt, quid optamus a deis inmortalibus, quid vovemus? 'At etiam liber est
23 Epicuri de sanctitate.' Ludimur ab homine non tam faceto quam ad scribendi licentiam libero. Quae enim potest esse sanctitas si dei humana non curant, quae autem animans natura nihil curans?

"Verius est igitur nimirum illud quod familiaris omnium nostrum Posidonius disseruit in libro quinto de natura deorum, nullos esse deos Epicuro videri, quaeque is de deis inmortalibus dixerit invidiae detestandae gratia dixisse ; neque enim tam desipiens fuisset ut homunculi similem deum fingeret, liniamentis dumtaxat extremis non habitu solido, membris hominis praeditum omnibus usu membrorum ne minimo quidem, exilem quendam atque perlucidum, nihil cuiquam tribuentem nihil gratificantem,

[1] referemus *A* : referimus *pr. B.*
[2] diligimus *dett.* : diligemus.
[3] quod *Mayor* : quid.
[4] ni *dett.* : ne *A, B.* [5] est *? Mayor* : sit.

thing attractive in the very sound of the word 'love,' from which the Latin term for friendship is derived. If we base our friendship on its profit to ourselves, and not on its advantage to those whom we love, it will not be friendship at all, but a mere bartering of selfish interests. That is our standard of value for meadows and fields and herds of cattle: we esteem them for the profits that we derive from them; but affection and friendship between men is disinterested; how much more so therefore is that of the gods, who, although in need of nothing, yet both love each other and care for the interests of men. If this be not so, why do we worship and pray to them? why have pontiffs and augurs to preside over our sacrifices and auspices? why make petitions and vow offerings to heaven? 'Why, but Epicurus (you tell me) actually wrote a treatise on holiness.' Epicurus is making fun of us, though he is not so much a humorist as a loose and careless writer. For how can holiness exist if the gods pay no heed to man's affairs? Yet what is the meaning of an animate being that pays no heed to anything?

Epicurus feigned piety to avoid popular odium.

"It is doubtless therefore truer to say, as the good friend of us all, Posidonius, argued in the fifth book of his *On the Nature of the Gods*, that Epicurus does not really believe in the gods at all, and that he said what he did about the immortal gods only for the sake of deprecating popular odium. Indeed he could not have been so senseless as really to imagine god to be like a feeble human being, but resembling him only in outline and surface, not in solid substance, and possessing all man's limbs but entirely incapable of using them, an emaciated and transparent being, showing no kindness or beneficence to anybody,

omnino nihil curantem nihil agentem. Quae natura primum nulla esse potest, idque videns Epicurus re
124 tollit oratione relinquit deos; deinde si maxime talis est deus ut nulla gratia nulla hominum caritate teneatur, valeat—quid enim dicam 'propitius sit'? esse enim propitius potest nemini, quoniam ut dicitis omnis in inbecillitate est et gratia et caritas."

---

[a] The formula of ceremonious farewell to a deity, in contrast with *vale*, used in taking leave of a human being.

caring for nothing and doing nothing at all. In the first place, a being of this nature is an absolute impossibility, and Epicurus was aware of this, and so actually abolishes the gods, although professedly
4 retaining them. Secondly, even if god exists, yet is of such a nature that he feels no benevolence or affection towards men, good-bye to him, say I—not 'God be gracious to me,'[a] why should I say that? for he cannot be gracious to anybody, since, as you tell us, all benevolence and affection is a mark of weakness."

LIBER SECUNDUS

1 I. Quae cum Cotta dixisset, tum Velleius "Ne ego" inquit "incautus qui cum Academico et eodem rhetore congredi conatus sim. Nam neque indisertum Academicum pertimuissem nec sine ista philosophia rhetorem quamvis eloquentem; neque enim flumine conturbor inanium verborum, nec subtilitate sententiarum si orationis est siccitas. Tu autem Cotta utraque re valuisti; corona tibi et iudices defuerunt. Sed ad ista alias: nunc Lucilium, si ipsi commodum est, audiamus."

2 Tum Balbus: "Eundem equidem malim audire Cottam, dum qua eloquentia falsos deos sustulit eadem veros inducat. Est enim et philosophi et pontificis et Cottae de dis inmortalibus habere non errantem et vagam ut Academici sed ut nostri stabilem certamque sententiam. Nam contra Epicurum satis superque dictum est. Sed aveo audire tu ipse Cotta quid sentias."

"An" inquit "oblitus es quid initio dixerim, facilius me, talibus praesertim de rebus, quid non

---

• The Academic logic was famous.

BOOK II

I. Cotta having thus spoken, Velleius replied. "I am indeed a rash person," he said, "to attempt to join issue with a pupil of the Academy [a] who is also a trained orator. An Academic unversed in rhetoric I should not have been much afraid of, nor yet an orator however eloquent who was not reinforced by that system of philosophy; for I am not disconcerted by a mere stream of empty verbiage, nor yet by subtlety of thought if expressed in a jejune style. You however, Cotta, were strong in both points; you only lacked a public audience and a jury to listen to you. But my answer to your arguments may wait until another time; let us now hear Lucilius, if he himself is agreeable."

Exposition of Stoic theology undertaken by Lucilius Balbus.

"For my part," rejoined Balbus, "I had rather listen to Cotta again, using the same eloquence that he employed in abolishing false gods to present a picture of the true ones. A philosopher, a pontiff and a Cotta should possess not a shifting and unsettled conception of the immortal gods, like the Academics, but a firm and definite one like our school. As for refuting Epicurus, that has been accomplished and more than accomplished already. But I am eager to hear what you think yourself, Cotta."

"Have you forgotten," said Cotta, "what I said at the outset, that I find it more easy, especially on

3 sentirem quam quid sentirem posse dicere? Quodsi haberem aliquid quod liqueret, tamen te vicissim audire vellem, cum ipse tam multa dixissem."

Tum Balbus: "Geram tibi morem; et agam quam brevissume potero, etenim convictis Epicuri erroribus longa de mea disputatione detracta oratio est. Omnino dividunt nostri totam istam de dis inmortalibus quaestionem in partis quattuor: primum docent esse deos, deinde quales sint, tum mundum ab iis administrari, postremo consulere eos rebus humanis. Nos autem hoc sermone quae priora duo sunt sumamus; tertium et quartum, quia maiora sunt, puto esse in aliud tempus differenda."

"Minime vero" inquit Cotta; "nam et otiosi sumus et iis de rebus agimus quae sunt etiam negotiis anteponendae."

4 II. Tum Lucilius "Ne egere quidem videtur" inquit "oratione prima pars. Quid enim potest esse tam apertum tamque perspicuum, cum caelum suspeximus caelestiaque contemplati sumus, quam esse aliquod numen praestantissimae mentis quo haec regantur? Quod ni ita esset, qui potuisset adsensu omnium dicere Ennius:

> Aspice hoc sublime candens, quem invocant omnes Iovem,

illum vero et Iovem et dominatorem rerum et omnia nutu regentem et, ut idem Ennius,

> patrem divumque hominumque,

such subjects as these, to say what I don't think than what I do? Even if I had any clear view, I should still prefer to hear you speak in your turn, now that I have said so much myself."

"Well," replied Balbus, "I will yield to your wish; and I shall be as brief as I can, for indeed when the errors of Epicurus have been refuted, my argument is robbed of all occasion for prolixity. To take a general view, the topic of the immortal gods which you raise is divided by our school into four parts: first they prove that the gods exist; next they explain their nature; then they show that the world is governed by them; and lastly that they care for the fortunes of mankind. In our present discourse however let us take the first two of these heads; the third and fourth, being questions of greater magnitude, had better I think be put off to another time."

Division of the subject into four parts.

"No, no," cried Cotta, "we are at leisure now, and moreover the subjects which we are discussing might fitly claim precedence even of matters of business."

II. "The first point," resumed Lucilius, "seems not even to require arguing. For when we gaze upward to the sky and contemplate the heavenly bodies, what can be so obvious and so manifest as that there must exist some power possessing transcendent intelligence by whom these things are ruled? Were it not so, how comes it that the words of Ennius carry conviction to all readers—

I. Proof of the Divine existence (§§ 4–44). (1) The gods' existence proved from observation of the heavens;

> Behold this dazzling vault of heaven, which all mankind
> as Jove invoke,

ay, and not only as Jove but as sovereign of the world, ruling all things with his nod, and as Ennius likewise says—

> father of gods and men,

et praesentem ac praepotentem deum? Quod qui dubitet, haud sane intellego cur non idem sol sit an
5 nullus sit dubitare possit; qui enim est hoc illo evidentius? Quod nisi cognitum conprehensumque animis haberemus, non tam stabilis opinio permaneret nec confirmaretur diuturnitate temporis nec una cum saeclis aetatibusque hominum inveterari potuisset. Etenim videmus ceteras opiniones fictas atque vanas diuturnitate extabuisse. Quis enim Hippocentaurum fuisse aut Chimaeram putat, quaeve anus tam excors inveniri potest quae illa quae quondam credebantur apud inferos portenta extimescat? Opinionis[1] enim commenta delet dies, naturae iudicia confirmat.

"Itaque et in nostro populo et in ceteris deorum cultus religionumque sanctitates exsistunt in dies
6 maiores atque meliores, idque evenit non temere nec casu, sed quod et praesentes saepe di vim suam declarant, ut et apud Regillum bello Latinorum, cum A. Postumius dictator cum Octavio Mamilio Tusculano proelio dimicaret, in nostra acie Castor et Pollux ex equis pugnare visi sunt, et recentiore memoria iidem Tyndaridae Persem victum nuntiaverunt. P. enim Vatinius, avus huius adulescentis, cum e[2] praefectura Reatina Romam venienti noctu duo iuvenes cum equis albis dixissent regem Persem illo die captum,

[1] opinionis *det.*: -ne *A*, *B*, -num B *corr.*
[2] <ei> e *Heindorf.*

a deity omnipresent and omnipotent? If a man
doubts this, I really cannot see why he should not
also be capable of doubting the existence of the sun;
5 how is the latter fact more evident than the former? (2) from the consensus of mankind;
Nothing but the presence in our minds of a firmly
grasped concept of the deity could account for the
stability and permanence of our belief in him, a
belief which is only strengthened by the passage of
the ages and grows more deeply rooted with each
successive generation of mankind. In every other
case we see that fictitious and unfounded opinions
have dwindled away with lapse of time. Who believes that the Hippocentaur or the Chimaera ever
existed? Where can you find an old wife senseless
enough to be afraid of the monsters of the lower
world that were once believed in? The years obliterate the inventions of the imagination, but confirm the
judgements of nature.

"Hence both in our own nation and among all others
reverence for the gods and respect for religion grow
6 continually stronger and more profound. Nor is this (3) from recorded epiphanies;
unaccountable or accidental; it is the result, firstly,
of the fact that the gods often manifest their power
in bodily presence. For instance in the Latin War,
at the critical battle of Lake Regillus between the
dictator Aulus Postumius and Octavius Mamilius of
Tusculum, Castor and Pollux were seen fighting on
horseback in our ranks. And in more modern history
likewise these sons of Tyndareus brought the news
of the defeat of Perses. What happened was that
Publius Vatinius, the grandfather of our young contemporary, was returning to Rome by night from
Reate, of which he was governor, when he was informed by two young warriors on white horses that

<cum>[1] senatui[2] nuntiavisset,[3] primo quasi temere de re publica locutus in carcerem coniectus est, post a Paulo litteris allatis cum idem dies constitisset, et agro a senatu et vacatione donatus est. Atque etiam cum ad fluvium Sagram Crotoniatas Locri maximo proelio devicissent, eo ipso die auditam esse eam pugnam ludis Olympiae memoriae proditum est. Saepe Faunorum voces exauditae, saepe visae formae deorum quemvis non aut hebetem aut impium deos praesentes esse confiteri coëgerunt.

7 III. "Praedictiones vero et praesensiones rerum futurarum quid aliud declarant nisi hominibus[4] ea quae futura[5] sint ostendi monstrari portendi praedici? ex quo illa ostenta monstra portenta prodigia dicuntur. Quodsi ea[6] ficta credimus licentia fabularum, Mopsum Tiresiam Amphiaraum Calchantem Helenum (quos tamen augures ne ipsae quidem fabulae adscivissent si res omnino repudiaret), ne domesticis quidem exemplis docti numen deorum conprobabimus? Nihil nos P. Claudi bello Punico primo temeritas movebit? qui etiam per iocum deos inridens, cum cavea liberati pulli non pascerentur mergi eos in aquam iussit, ut biberent quoniam esse nollent; qui risus classe devicta multas ipsi lacrimas,

[1] *add. Vahlen.* [2] senatuique *dett.*
[3] nuntiavit et *det.* [4] hominibus <divinitus> *Brieger.*
[5] futura *om. A, B* (quae . . . sint *om. edd.*).
[6] externa *Heindorf.*

King Perses had that very day been taken prisoner. When Vatinius carried the news to the Senate, at first he was flung into gaol on the charge of spreading an unfounded report on a matter of national concern; but afterwards a dispatch arrived from Paulus, and the date was found to tally, so the Senate bestowed upon Vatinius both a grant of land and exemption from military service. It is also recorded in history that when the Locrians won their great victory over the people of Crotona at the important battle of the River Sagra, news of the engagement was reported at the Olympic Games on the very same day. Often has the sound of the voices of the Fauns, often has the apparition of a divine form compelled anyone that is not either feeble-minded or impious to admit the real presence of the gods.

III. "Again, prophecies and premonitions of future events cannot but be taken as proofs that the future may appear or be foretold as a warning or portended or predicted to mankind—hence the very words 'apparition,' 'warning,' 'portent,' 'prodigy.' Even if we think that the stories of Mopsus, Tiresias, Amphiaraus, Calchas and Helenus are mere baseless fictions of romance (though their powers of divination would not even have been incorporated in the legends had they been entirely repugnant to fact), shall not even the instances from our own native history teach us to acknowledge the divine power? shall we be unmoved by the story of the recklessness of Publius Claudius in the first Punic War? Claudius merely in jest mocked at the gods: when the chickens on being released from their cage refused to feed, he ordered them to be thrown into the water, so that as they would not eat they might drink; but the joke

(4) from the fact of divination.

magnam populo Romano cladem attulit. Quid? collega eius Iunius eodem bello nonne tempestate classem amisit cum auspiciis non paruisset? Itaque Claudius a populo condemnatus est, Iunius necem
8 sibi ipse conscivit. C. Flaminium Caelius religione neglecta cecidisse apud Trasumenum scribit cum magno rei publicae vulnere. Quorum exitio intellegi potest eorum imperiis rem publicam amplificatam qui religionibus paruissent. Et si conferre volumus nostra cum externis, ceteris rebus aut pares aut etiam inferiores reperiemur, religione id est cultu
9 deorum multo superiores. An Atti Navii lituus ille, quo ad investigandum suem regiones vineae terminavit, contemnendus est? Crederem, nisi eius augurio rex Hostilius maxima bella gessisset. Sed neglegentia nobilitatis augurii disciplina omissa veritas auspiciorum spreta est, species tantum retenta; itaque maximae rei publicae partes, in his bella quibus rei publicae salus continetur, nullis auspiciis administrantur, nulla peremnia servantur, nulla ex acuminibus, nulla cum[1] viri vocantur (ex quo in procinctu

[1] nulla cum *Schömann*: nulli.

[a] Cicero's memory has played him false over *suem* and *uvam*. In *Div.* i. 3, ii. 80, he says Attus (in the reign of Tarquinius Priscus) had vowed to the Lares the largest bunch of grapes in his vineyard if he found a strayed pig. He found it, and then discovered by augury in which quarter of the vineyard to look for the largest bunch.

cost the jester himself many tears and the Roman people a great disaster, for the fleet was severely defeated. Moreover did not his colleague Junius during the same war lose his fleet in a storm after failing to comply with the auspices? In consequence of these disasters Claudius was tried and condemned for high treason and Junius committed suicide. Caelius writes that Gaius Flaminius after ignoring the claims of religion fell at the battle of Trasimene, when a serious blow was inflicted on the state. The fate of these men may serve to indicate that our empire was won by those commanders who obeyed the dictates of religion. Moreover if we care to compare our national characteristics with those of foreign peoples, we shall find that, while in all other respects we are only the equals or even the inferiors of others, yet in the sense of religion, that is, in reverence for the gods, we are far superior. Or are we to make light of the famous augural staff of Attus Navius, wherewith he marked out the vineyard into sections for the purpose of discovering the pig[a]? I would agree that we might do so, had not King Hostilius fought great and glorious wars under the guidance of Attus's augury. But owing to the carelessness of our nobility the augural lore has been forgotten, and the reality of the auspices has fallen into contempt, only the outward show being retained; and in consequence highly important departments of public administration, and in particular the conduct of wars upon which the safety of the state depends, are carried on without any auspices at all; no taking of omens when crossing rivers, none when lights flash from the points of the javelins, none when men are called to arms (owing to which wills made on

testamenta perierunt, tum enim bella gerere nostri
10 duces incipiunt cum auspicia posuerunt). At vero apud maiores tanta religionis vis fuit ut quidam imperatores etiam se ipsos dis inmortalibus capite velato verbis certis pro re publica devoverent. Multa ex Sibyllinis vaticinationibus multa ex haruspicum responsis commemorare possum quibus ea confirmentur quae dubia nemini debent esse. IV. Atqui et nostrorum augurum et Etruscorum haruspicum disciplinam P. Scipione[1] C. Figulo consulibus res ipsa probavit; quos cum Ti. Gracchus consul iterum crearet, primus rogator ut eos rettulit ibidem est repente mortuus. Gracchus cum comitia nihilo minus peregisset remque illam in religionem populo venisse sentiret, ad senatum rettulit. Senatus 'quos ad soleret' referendum censuit. Haruspices introducti responderunt non fuisse iustum comitiorum
11 rogatorem. Tum Gracchus, ut e patre audiebam, incensus ira: 'Itane vero? ego non iustus, qui et consul rogavi et augur et auspicato? an vos Tusci ac barbari auspiciorum populi Romani ius tenetis et interpretes esse comitiorum potestis?' Itaque tum illos exire iussit; post autem e provincia litteras ad collegium misit se cum legeret libros recordatum esse

[1] <in> P. Scipione <et> *Bouhier.*

---

[a] The Etruscans differed from the Graeco-Italic races in customs, religion, and language.

active service have gone out of existence, since our generals only enter on their military command when they have laid down their augural powers).
0 But among our ancestors religion was so powerful that some commanders actually offered themselves as victims to the immortal gods on behalf of the state, veiling their heads and formally vowing themselves to death. I could quote numerous passages from the Sibylline prophecies and from the oracles of soothsayers in confirmation of facts that no one really ought to question. IV. Why, in the consulship of Publius Scipio and Gaius Figulus both our Roman augural lore and that of the Etruscan soothsayers were confirmed by the evidence of actual fact. Tiberius Gracchus, then consul for the second time, was holding the election of his successors. The first returning officer in the very act of reporting the persons named as elected suddenly fell dead. Gracchus nevertheless proceeded with the election. Perceiving that the scruples of the public had been aroused by the occurrence, he referred the matter to the Senate. The Senate voted that it be referred 'to the customary officials.' Soothsayers were sent for, and pronounced that the returning officer for the
1 elections had not been in order. Thereupon Gracchus, so my father used to tell me, burst into a rage. 'How now?' he cried, 'was I not in order? I put the names to the vote as consul, as augur, and with auspices taken. Who are you, Tuscan barbarians,[a] to know the Roman constitution, and to be able to lay down the law as to our elections?' And accordingly he then sent them about their business. Afterwards however he sent a dispatch from his province to the College of Augurs to say that while reading the sacred

vitio sibi tabernaculum captum fuisse hortos[1] Scipionis, quod cum pomerium postea intrasset habendi senatus causa in redeundo cum idem pomerium transiret auspicari esset oblitus; itaque vitio creatos consules esse. Augures rem ad senatum; senatus ut abdicarent consules; abdicaverunt. Quae quaerimus exempla maiora? Vir sapientissimus atque haud sciam an omnium praestantissimus peccatum suum quod celari posset confiteri maluit quam haerere in re publica religionem, consules summum imperium statim deponere quam id tenere punctum temporis
12 contra religionem. Magna augurum auctoritas; quid, haruspicum ars nonne divina? Haec et innumerabilia ex eodem genere qui videat nonne cogatur confiteri deos esse? Quorum enim interpretes sunt eos ipsos esse certe necesse est; deorum autem interpretes sunt; deos igitur esse fateamur. At fortasse non omnia eveniunt quae praedicta sunt. Ne aegri quidem quia non omnes convalescunt idcirco ars nulla medicina est. Signa ostenduntur a dis rerum futurarum; in his si qui erraverunt, non deorum natura sed hominum coniectura peccavit.

"Itaque inter omnis omnium gentium summa constat; omnibus enim innatum est et in animo
13 quasi insculptum esse deos. V. Quales sint varium

[1] <ad> hortos *Schömann*, in hortis *Lambinus*.

---

[a] The validity of the military auspices expired when the magistrates returned within the city.

books it had come to his mind that there had been an irregularity when he took Scipio's park as the site for his augural tent, for he had subsequently entered the city bounds to hold a meeting of the Senate and when crossing the bounds again on his return had forgotten to take the auspices [a]; and that therefore the consuls had not been duly elected. The College of Augurs referred the matter to the Senate; the Senate decided that the consuls must resign; they did so. What more striking instances can we demand? A man of the greatest wisdom and I may say unrivalled distinction of character preferred to make public confession of an offence that he might have concealed rather than that the stain of impiety should cling to the commonwealth; the consuls preferred to retire on the spot from the highest office of the state rather than hold it for one moment of time in violation of
2 religion. The augur's office is one of high dignity; surely the soothsayer's art also is divinely inspired. Is not one who considers these and countless similar facts compelled to admit that the gods exist? If there be persons who interpret the will of certain beings, it follows that those beings must themselves exist; but there are persons who interpret the will of the gods; therefore we must admit that the gods exist. But perhaps it may be argued that not all prophecies come true. Nor do all sick persons get well, but that does not prove that there is no art of medicine. Signs of future events are manifested by the gods; men may have mistaken these signs, but the fault lay with man's powers of inference, not with the divine nature.

"Hence the main issue is agreed among all men of all nations, inasmuch as all have engraved in their minds an innate belief that the gods exist.

est, esse nemo negat. Cleanthes quidem noster quattuor de causis dixit in animis hominum informatas deorum esse notiones. Primam posuit eam de qua modo dixi, quae orta esset ex praesensione rerum futurarum; alteram, quam ceperimus[1] ex magnitudine commodorum quae percipiuntur caeli temperatione fecunditate terrarum aliarumque com-
14 moditatum conplurium copia; tertiam, quae terreret animos fulminibus tempestatibus nimbis nivibus grandinibus vastitate pestilentia terrae motibus et saepe fremitibus lapideisque imbribus et guttis imbrium quasi cruentis, tum labibus aut repentinis terrarum hiatibus, tum praeter naturam hominum pecudumque portentis, tum facibus visis caelestibus, tum stellis iis quas Graeci cometas nostri cincinnatas vocant, quae nuper bello Octaviano magnarum fuerunt calamitatum praenuntiae, tum sole geminato, quod ut e patre audivi Tuditano et Aquilio consulibus evenerat, quo quidem anno P. Africanus sol alter extinctus est, quibus exterriti homines vim quandam
15 esse caelestem et divinam suspicati sunt; quartam causam esse eamque vel maximam aequabilitatem motus conversionumque[2] caeli, solis lunae siderumque omnium distinctionem varietatem pulchritudinem ordinem, quarum rerum aspectus ipse satis indicaret non esse ea fortuita. Ut, si quis in domum aliquam

[1] caperemus *Bake.*

[2] conversionumque *Ernesti*: conversionem MSS.: <constantiamque> conversionum *Regenhart.*

---

[a] Gn. Octavius, cos. 87 B.C., was a partisan of Sulla, who was then at war with Mithridates; the other consul Cinna supported Marius. Fighting took place between them and Octavius fell.

[b] The proscriptions of Marius and Sulla.

V. As to their nature there are various opinions, but their existence nobody denies. Indeed our master Cleanthes gave four reasons to account for the formation in men's minds of their ideas of the gods. He put first the argument of which I spoke just now, the one arising from our foreknowledge of future events; second, the one drawn from the magnitude of the benefits which we derive from our temperate climate, from the earth's fertility, and from a vast abundance of other blessings; third, the awe inspired by lightning, storms, rain, snow, hail, floods, pestilences, earthquakes and occasionally subterranean rumblings, showers of stones and raindrops the colour of blood, also landslips and chasms suddenly opening in the ground, also unnatural monstrosities human and animal, and also the appearance of meteoric lights and what are called by the Greeks 'comets,' and in our language 'long-haired stars,' such as recently during the Octavian War [a] appeared as harbingers of dire disasters,[b] and the doubling of the sun, which my father told me had happened in the consulship of Tuditanus and Aquilius, the year [c] in which the light was quenched of Publius Africanus, that second sun of Rome: all of which alarming portents have suggested to mankind the idea of the existence of some celestial and divine power. And the fourth and most potent cause of the belief he said was the uniform motion and revolution of the heavens, and the varied groupings and ordered beauty of the sun, moon and stars, the very sight of which was in itself enough to prove that these things are not the mere effect of chance. When a man goes into a house,

(5) Consensus of mankind explained by Cleanthes

[c] 129 B.C. He was found dead in his bed, but the murderer was not discovered; *cf.* iii. 80.

aut in gymnasium aut in forum venerit, cum videat omnium rerum rationem modum disciplinam non possit ea sine causa fieri iudicare sed esse aliquem intellegat qui praesit et cui pareatur, multo magis in tantis motionibus tantisque vicissitudinibus, tam multarum rerum atque tantarum ordinibus, in quibus nihil umquam inmensa et infinita vetustas mentita sit, statuat necesse est ab aliqua mente tantos naturae motus gubernari.

16 VI. "Chrysippus quidem, quamquam est acerrimo ingenio, tamen ea dicit ut ab ipsa natura didicisse non ut ipse repperisse videatur. 'Si enim' inquit 'est aliquid in rerum natura quod hominis mens quod ratio quod vis quod potestas humana efficere non possit, est certe id quod illud efficit homine melius; atqui res caelestes omnesque eae quarum est ordo sempiternus ab homine confici non possunt; est igitur id quo[1] illa conficiuntur homine melius; id autem quid potius dixeris quam deum? Etenim si di non sunt, quid esse potest in rerum natura homine melius? in eo enim solo est ratio, qua nihil potest esse praestantius; esse autem hominem qui nihil in omni mundo melius esse quam se putet desipientis adrogantiae est; ergo est aliquid melius; est igitur profecto deus.'

17 An vero si domum magnam pulchramque videris non possis adduci ut etiamsi dominum non videas

[1] a quo *dett.*

a wrestling-school or a public assembly and observes in all that goes on arrangement, regularity and system, he cannot possibly suppose that these things come about without a cause: he realizes that there is someone who presides and controls. Far more therefore with the vast movements and phases of the heavenly bodies, and these ordered processes of a multitude of enormous masses of matter, which throughout the countless ages of the infinite past have never in the smallest degree played false, is he compelled to infer that these mighty world-motions are regulated by some Mind.

(6) Proof of Chrysippus: the universe shows the operation of more than human power.

VI. "Extremely acute of intellect as is Chrysippus, nevertheless his utterance here might well appear to have been learnt from the very lips of Nature, and not discovered by himself. 'If (he says) there be something in the world that man's mind and human reason, strength and power are incapable of producing, that which produces it must necessarily be superior to man; now the heavenly bodies and all those things that display a never-ending regularity cannot be created by man; therefore that which creates them is superior to man; yet what better name is there for this than "god"? Indeed, if gods do not exist, what can there be in the universe superior to man? for he alone possesses reason, which is the most excellent thing that can exist; but for any human being in existence to think that there is nothing in the whole world superior to himself would be an insane piece of arrogance; therefore there is something superior to man; therefore God does exist.' Again, if you see a spacious and beautiful house, you could not be induced to believe, even though you could not see its master, that it was built

(7) The aether is suited for superhuman inhabitants.

muribus illam et mustelis aedificatam putes:—tantum ergo ornatum mundi, tantam varietatem pulchritudinemque rerum caelestium, tantam vim et magnitudinem maris atque terrarum si tuum ac non deorum inmortalium domicilium putes, nonne plane desipere videare? An ne hoc quidem intellegimus, omnia supera esse meliora, terram autem esse infimam, quam crassissimus circumfundat aër? ut ob eam ipsam causam quod etiam quibusdam regionibus atque urbibus contingere videmus hebetiora ut sint hominum ingenia propter caeli pleniorem[1] naturam, hoc idem generi humano evenerit quod in terra hoc est in crassissima regione mundi
18 conlocati sint. Et tamen ex ipsa hominum sollertia esse aliquam[2] mentem et eam quidem acriorem et divinam existimare debemus. Unde enim hanc homo 'arripuit' (ut ait apud Xenophontem Socrates)? Quin et umorem et calorem qui est fusus in corpore et terrenam ipsam viscerum soliditatem, animum denique illum spirabilem si quis quaerat unde habeamus, apparet quod[3] aliud a terra sumpsimus aliud ab umore aliud ab igni aliud ab aëre eo quem spiritu[4] ducimus.[5] VII. Illud autem quod vincit haec omnia, rationem dico et, si placet pluribus verbis, mentem consilium cogitationem prudentiam, ubi invenimus, unde sustulimus? An cetera mundus habebit omnia, hoc unum quod plurimi est non habebit? Atqui certe nihil omnium rerum melius est mundo nihil praestabilius nihil pulcrius,

[1] pleniorem <umore> *Usener.*
[2] aliam quam *Schömann* : aliquam <mundi> *Mayor.*
[3] quod : quorum *Plasberg.*
[4] spiritu *edd.* : spiritum *MSS.*
[5] ducimus *dett.* : dicimus *A, B.*

[a] συναρπάσαι Xen. *Mem.* i. 4. 8.

by mice and weasels ; if then you were to imagine that this elaborate universe, with all the variety and beauty of the heavenly bodies and the vast quantity and extent of sea and land, were your abode and not that of the gods, would you not be thought absolutely insane ? Again, do we not also understand that everything in a higher position is of greater value, and that the earth is the lowest thing, and is enveloped by a layer of the densest kind of air ? Hence for the same reason what we observe to be the case with certain districts and cities, I mean that their inhabitants are duller-witted than the average owing to the more compressed quality of the atmosphere, has also befallen the human race as a whole owing to its being located on the earth, that is, in the densest region of the world.

(8) Man's reason, like his other elements, is derived from the universe.

Yet even man's intelligence must lead us to infer the existence of a mind <in the universe>, and that a mind of surpassing ability, and in fact divine. Otherwise, whence did man 'pick up'[a] (as Socrates says in Xenophon) the intelligence that he possesses ? If anyone asks the question, whence do we get the moisture and the heat diffused throughout the body, and the actual earthy substance of the flesh, and lastly the breath of life within us, it is manifest that we have derived the one from earth, the other from water, and the other from the air which we inhale in breathing.

(9) Reason is essential to the perfection of the universe.

VII. But where did we find, whence did we abstract, that other part of us which surpasses all of these, I mean our reason, or, if you like to employ several terms to denote it, our intelligence, deliberation, thought, wisdom ? Is the world to contain each of the other elements but not this one, the most precious of them all ? Yet beyond question nothing exists among all things that is superior to the world,

nec solum nihil est sed ne cogitari quidem quicquam melius potest. Et si ratione et sapientia nihil est melius, necesse est haec inesse in eo quod optimum
19 esse concedimus. Quid vero, tanta rerum consentiens conspirans continuata cognatio quem non coget ea quae dicuntur a me conprobare? Possetne uno[1] tempore florere, dein vicissim horrere terra, aut tot rebus ipsis se inmutantibus solis accessus discessusque solstitiis brumisque cognosci, aut aestus maritimi fretorumque angustiae ortu aut obitu lunae commoveri, aut una totius caeli conversione cursus astrorum dispares conservari? Haec ita fieri omnibus inter se concinentibus mundi partibus profecto non possent nisi ea uno divino et continuato spiritu continerentur.

20 "Atque haec cum uberius disputantur et fusius, ut mihi est in animo facere, facilius effugiunt Academicorum calumniam; cum autem, ut Zeno solebat, brevius angustiusque concluduntur, tum apertiora sunt ad reprendendum. Nam ut profluens amnis aut vix aut nullo modo, conclusa autem aqua facile conrumpitur, sic orationis flumine reprensoris convicia diluuntur, angustia autem conclusae rationis non facile se ipsa tutatur. Haec enim quae dilatantur a
21 nobis Zeno sic premebat: VIII. 'Quod ratione utitur id melius est quam id quod ratione non utitur;

[1] uno: verno *Bouhier*, suo *Reizenstein*.

nothing that is more excellent or more beautiful; and not merely does nothing superior to it exist, but nothing superior can even be conceived. And if there be nothing superior to reason and wisdom, these faculties must necessarily be possessed by that being which we admit to be superior to all others. Again, consider the sympathetic agreement, interconnexion and affinity of things: whom will this not compel to approve the truth of what I say? Would it be possible for the earth at one definite time to be gay with flowers and then in turn all bare and stark, or for the spontaneous transformation of so many things about us to signal the approach and the retirement of the sun at the summer and the winter solstices, or for the tides to flow and ebb in the seas and straits with the rising and setting of the moon, or for the different courses of the stars to be maintained by the one revolution of the entire sky? These processes and this musical harmony of all the parts of the world assuredly could not go on were they not maintained in unison by a single divine and all-pervading spirit.

(10) The sympathy pervading the parts of the world proves the operation of divine spirit.

"When one expounds these doctrines in a fuller and more flowing style, as I propose to do, it is easier for them to evade the captious objections of the Academy; but when they are reduced to brief syllogistic form, as was the practice of Zeno, they lie more open to criticism. A running river can almost or quite entirely escape pollution, whereas an enclosed pool is easily sullied; similarly a flowing stream of eloquence sweeps aside the censures of the critic, but a closely reasoned argument defends itself with difficulty. The thoughts that we expound at length Zeno used to compress into this form: VIII. 'That which has the faculty of reason is superior to that

(11) Zeno proved the world's rationality (and therefore its divinity).

nihil autem mundo melius; ratione igitur mundus utitur.' Similiter effici potest sapientem esse mundum, similiter beatum, similiter aeternum; omnia enim haec meliora sunt quam ea quae sunt his carentia, nec mundo quicquam melius. Ex quo efficietur esse mundum deum. Idemque hoc modo:
22 'Nullius sensu carentis pars aliqua potest esse sentiens; mundi autem partes sentientes sunt; non igitur caret sensu mundus.' Pergit idem et urget angustius: 'Nihil' inquit 'quod animi quodque rationis est expers, id generare ex se potest animantem conpotemque rationis; mundus autem generat animantis compotesque rationis; animans est igitur mundus composque rationis.' Idemque similitudine ut saepe solet rationem conclusit[1] hoc modo: 'Si ex oliva modulate canentes tibiae nascerentur, num dubitares quin inesset in oliva tibicinii quaedam scientia? Quid si platani fidiculas ferrent numerose sonantes? idem scilicet censeres in platanis inesse musicam. Cur igitur mundus non animans sapiensque iudicetur, cum ex se procreet animantis atque sapientis?'

23 IX. "Sed quoniam coepi secus agere atque initio dixeram (negaram enim hanc primam partem egere oratione, quod esset omnibus perspicuum deos esse), tamen id ipsum rationibus physicis (id est naturalibus[2]) confirmare[3] volo. Sic enim res se habet ut omnia quae alantur[4] et quae crescant[5] contineant in

[1] concludit *dett.* [2] id . . . naturalibus *om. Ald.*
[3] confirmare *dett.*: -ri *A*, *B*. [4] aluntur *dett.*
[5] crescunt *dett.*

which has not the faculty of reason; but nothing is superior to the world; therefore the world has the faculty of reason.' A similar argument can be used to prove that the world is wise, and happy, and eternal; for things possessed of each of these attributes are superior to things devoid of them, and nothing is superior to the world. From this it will follow that the world is god. Zeno also argued thus: 'Nothing devoid of sensation can have a part of itself that is sentient; but the world has parts that are sentient; therefore the world is not devoid of sensation.' He also proceeds to press the argument more closely: 'Nothing,' he says, 'that is inanimate and irrational can give birth to an animate and rational being; but the world gives birth to animate and rational beings; therefore the world is animate and rational.' Furthermore he proved his argument by means of one of his favourite comparisons, as follows: 'If flutes playing musical tunes grew on an olive-tree, surely you would not question that the olive-tree possessed some knowledge of the art of flute-playing; or if plane-trees bore well-tuned lutes, doubtless you would likewise infer that the plane-trees possessed the art of music; why then should we not judge the world to be animate and endowed with wisdom, when it produces animate and wise offspring?'

(12) Arguments from Physics: heat is the cause of motion, and light pervades the world;

IX. "However, having begun to treat the subject in a different way from that which I proposed at the beginning (for I said that this part required no discussion, since the existence of god was manifest to everybody), in spite of this I should like to prove even this point by means of arguments drawn from Physics or Natural Philosophy. It is a law of Nature that all things capable of nurture and growth contain within

se vim caloris, sine qua neque ali possent nec crescere; nam omne quod est calidum et igneum cietur et agitur motu suo ; quod autem alitur et crescit motu quodam utitur certo et aequabili ; qui quam diu remanet in nobis tam diu sensus et vita remanet, refrigerato autem et extincto calore occidimus ipsi
24 et extinguimur. Quod quidem Cleanthes his etiam argumentis docet, quanta vis insit caloris in omni corpore : negat enim esse ullum cibum tam gravem quin is nocte et die concoquatur ; cuius etiam in reliquiis inest[1] calor iis quas natura respuerit. Iam vero venae et arteriae micare non desinunt quasi quodam igneo motu, animadversumque saepe est cum cor animantis alicuius evolsum ita mobiliter palpitaret ut imitaretur igneam celeritatem. Omne igitur quod vivit, sive animal sive terra editum, id vivit propter inclusum in eo calorem. Ex quo intellegi debet eam caloris naturam vim habere in se vitalem per omnem mundum pertinentem.

25 "Atque id facilius cernemus toto genere hoc igneo quod tranat omnia subtilius explicato. Omnes igitur partes mundi (tangam autem maximas) calore fultae sustinentur. Quod primum in terrena natura perspici potest. Nam et lapidum conflictu atque tritu elici ignem videmus et recenti fossione 'terram fumare calentem,' atque etiam ex puteis iugibus aquam calidam trahi, et id maxime fieri temporibus hibernis, quod magna vis terrae cavernis contineatur[2]

[1] insit *Heindorf.* [2] continetur *dett.*

[a] Mayor detected here a verse-quotation from an unknown source.

them a supply of heat, without which their nurture and growth would not be possible; for everything of a hot, fiery nature supplies its own source of motion and activity; but that which is nourished and grows possesses a definite and uniform motion; and as long as this motion remains within us, so long sensation and life remain, whereas so soon as our heat is cooled and quenched we ourselves perish and are extinguished. This doctrine Cleanthes enforces by these further arguments, to show how great is the supply of heat in every living body: he states that there is no food so heavy that it is not digested in twenty-four hours; and even the residue of our food which nature rejects contains heat. Again, the veins and arteries never cease throbbing with a flame-like pulse, and frequent cases have been observed when the heart of an animal on being torn out of its body has continued to beat with a rapid motion resembling the flickering of fire. Every living thing therefore, whether animal or vegetable, owes its vitality to the heat contained within it. From this it must be inferred that this element of heat possesses in itself a vital force that pervades the whole world.

matter shows signs of heat as its ruling principle, and therefore the world possesses reason,

"We shall discern the truth of this more readily from a more detailed account of this all-permeating fiery element as a whole. All the parts of the world (I will however only specify the most important) are supported and sustained by heat. This can be perceived first of all in the element of earth. We see fire produced by striking or rubbing stones together; and when newly dug, 'the earth doth steam with warmth'[a]; and also warm water is drawn from running springs, and this occurs most of all in the winter-time, because a great store of heat is confined

caloris eaque hieme sit[1] densior ob eamque causam calorem insitum in terris contineat[2] artius. X.
26 Longa est oratio multaeque rationes quibus doceri possit omnia quae terra concipiat semina quaeque ipsa ex se generata stirpibus infixa contineat ea temperatione caloris et oriri et augescere. Atque aquae etiam admixtum esse calorem primum ipse liquor aquae declarat [effusio],[3] quae neque conglaciaret frigoribus neque nive pruinaque concresceret nisi eadem se admixto calore liquefacta et dilapsa diffunderet; itaque et aquilonibus[4] reliquisque frigoribus adiectis[5] durescit umor et idem vicissim mollitur tepefactus et tabescit calore. Atque etiam maria agitata ventis ita tepescunt ut intellegi facile possit in tantis illis umoribus esse inclusum calorem; nec enim ille externus et adventicius habendus est tepor sed ex intimis maris partibus agitatione excitatus, quod nostris quoque corporibus contingit cum motu atque exercitatione recalescunt. Ipse vero aer, qui natura est maxime frigidus, minime est expers calo-
27 ris; ille vero et multo quidem calore admixtus est, ipse enim oritur ex respiratione aquarum, earum enim quasi vapor quidam aer habendus est, is autem existit motu eius caloris qui aquis continetur, quam similitudinem cernere possumus in iis aquis[6] quae effervescunt subditis ignibus. Iam vero reliqua quarta pars mundi: ea et ipsa tota natura fervida est et

[1] fit *dett.*
[2] continet *Heindorf.*
[3] effusio *om. det.*: effusae *B*, et fusio *Gruter.*
[4] aquiloniis *? ed.*
[5] adstrictus *Heindorf.*
[6] iis aquis *ed. Rom.*: his aquis *MSS.*, aeneis *Allen* (aeneis, aenis *post* quae *addunt dett.*).

in the caverns of the earth, which in winter is denser and therefore confines more closely the heat stored
6 in the soil. X. It would require a long discourse and a great many arguments to enable me to show that all the seeds that earth receives in her womb, and all the plants which she spontaneously generates and holds fixed by their roots in the ground, owe both their origin and growth to this warm temperature of the soil. That water also contains an admixture of heat is shown first of all by its liquid nature; water would neither be frozen into ice by cold nor congealed into snow and hoar-frost unless it could also become fluid when liquefied and thawed by the admixture of heat; this is why moisture both hardens when exposed to a north wind or a frost from some other quarter, and also in turn softens when warmed, and evaporates with heat. Also the sea when violently stirred by the wind becomes warm, so that it can readily be realized that this great body of fluid contains heat; for we must not suppose the warmth in question to be derived from some external source, but stirred up from the lowest depths of the sea by violent motion, just as happens to our bodies when they are restored to warmth by movement and exercise. Indeed the air itself, though by nature the coldest of the elements, is by no means entirely devoid of heat;
7 indeed it contains even a considerable admixture of heat, for it is itself generated by exhalation from water, since air must be deemed to be a sort of vaporized water, and this vaporization is caused by the motion of the heat contained in the water. We may see an example of the same process when water is made to boil by placing fire beneath it.—There remains the fourth element: this is itself by nature

ceteris naturis omnibus salutarem inpertit et vitalem
28 calorem. Ex quo concluditur, cum omnes mundi partes sustineantur calore, mundum etiam ipsum simili parique natura in tanta diuturnitate servari, eoque magis quod intellegi debet calidum illud atque igneum ita in omni fusum esse natura ut in eo insit procreandi vis et causa gignendi, a quo et animantia omnia et ea quorum stirpes terra continentur et nasci sit necesse et augescere.

29 XI. "Natura est igitur[1] quae contineat mundum omnem eumque tueatur, et ea quidem non sine sensu atque ratione; omnem enim naturam necesse est quae non solitaria sit neque simplex sed cum alio iuncta atque conexa habere aliquem in se principatum, ut in homine mentem, in belua quiddam simile mentis unde oriantur rerum adpetitus; in arborum autem et earum rerum quae gignuntur e terra radicibus inesse principatus putatur. Principatum autem id dico quod Graeci ἡγεμονικόν vocant, quo nihil in quoque genere nec potest nec debet esse praestantius; ita necesse est illud etiam in quo sit totius naturae principatus esse omnium optimum omniumque rerum potestate dominatuque dignissimum.
30 Videmus autem in partibus mundi (nihil est enim in omni mundo quod non pars universi sit) inesse sensum atque rationem. In ea parte igitur in qua

[1] <ignea> igitur ? *Mayor.*

[a] Mayor would alter the Latin to give 'It is therefore the element of fire that . . .'

glowing hot throughout and also imparts the warmth of health and life to all other substances. Hence from the fact that all the parts of the world are sustained by heat the inference follows that the world itself also owes its continued preservation for so long a time to the same or a similar substance, and all the more so because it must be understood that this hot and fiery principle is interfused with the whole of nature in such a way as to constitute the male and female generative principles, and so to be the necessary cause of both the birth and the growth of all living creatures, whether animals or those whose roots are planted in the earth.

XI. "There is therefore an element that holds [a] the whole world together and preserves it, and this an element possessed of sensation and reason; since every natural object that is not a homogeneous and simple substance but a complex and composite one must contain within it some ruling principle, for example in man the intelligence, in the lower animals something resembling intelligence that is the source of appetition. With trees and plants the ruling principle is believed to be located in the roots. I use the term 'ruling principle' as the equivalent of the Greek *hēgemonikon*, meaning that part of anything which must and ought to have supremacy in a thing of that sort. Thus it follows that the element which contains the ruling principle of the whole of nature must also be the most excellent of all things and the most deserving of authority and sovereignty over all things. Now we observe that the parts of the world (and nothing exists in all the world which is not a part of the whole world) possess sensation and reason. Therefore it follows that that part which contains the

mundi inest principatus haec inesse necesse est, et acriora quidem atque maiora. Quocirca sapientem esse mundum necesse est, naturamque eam quae res omnes conplexa teneat perfectione rationis excellere, eoque deum esse mundum omnemque vim mundi natura divina contineri.

"Atque etiam mundi ille fervor purior perlucidior
mobiliorque multo ob easque causas aptior ad sensus
commovendos quam hic noster calor quo haec quae
31 nota nobis sunt retinentur et vigent. Absurdum
igitur est dicere, cum homines bestiaeque hoc calore
teneantur et propterea moveantur ac sentiant,
mundum esse sine sensu qui integro et libero et
puro eodemque acerrimo et mobilissimo ardore
teneatur, praesertim cum is ardor qui est mundi non
agitatus ab alio neque externo pulsu sed per se ipse
ac sua sponte moveatur; nam quid potest esse
mundo[1] valentius, quod pellat atque moveat calorem
32 eum quo ille teneatur? XII. Audiamus enim
Platonem quasi quendam deum philosophorum; cui
duo placet esse[2] motus, unum suum alterum exter-
num, esse autem divinius quod ipsum ex se sua sponte
moveatur quam quod pulsu agitetur alieno. Hunc
autem motum in solis animis esse ponit, ab hisque
principium motus esse ductum putat. Quapropter
quoniam ex mundi ardore motus omnis oritur,
is autem ardor non alieno inpulsu sed sua sponte

[1] <in> mundo *Goethe.* [2] esse <genera> *Plasberg.*

[a] *Timaeus* 89.

ruling principle of the world must necessarily possess sensation and reason, and these in a more intense and higher form. Hence it follows that the world possesses wisdom, and that the element which holds all things in its embrace is pre-eminently and perfectly rational, and therefore that the world is god, and all the forces of the world are held together by the divine nature.

"Moreover that glowing heat of the world is far purer and more brilliant and far more mobile, and therefore more stimulating to the senses, than this warmth of ours by which the things that we know are preserved and vitalized. As therefore man and the animals are possessed by this warmth and owe to this their motion and sensation, it is absurd to say that the world is devoid of sensation, considering that it is possessed by an intense heat that is stainless, free and pure, and also penetrating and mobile in the extreme; especially as this intense world-heat does not derive its motion from the operation of some other force from outside, but is self-moved and spontaneous in its activity: for how can there be anything more powerful than the world, to impart motion and activity to the warmth by which the world is held together? XII. For let us hear Plato,[a] that divine philosopher, for so almost he is to be deemed. He holds that motion is of two sorts, one spontaneous, the other derived from without; and that that which moves of itself spontaneously is more divine than that which has motion imparted to it by some force not its own. The former kind of motion he deems to reside only in the soul, which he considers to be the only source and origin of motion. Hence, since all motion springs from the world-heat, and since that heat moves spon-

since the world-heat is purer than ours, and is self-moved, and therefore possesses soul;

movetur, animus sit necesse est; ex quo efficitur animantem esse mundum.

"Atque ex hoc quoque intellegi poterit in eo inesse intellegentiam, quod certe est mundus melior quam ulla natura; ut enim nulla pars est corporis nostri quae non minoris sit quam nosmet ipsi sumus, sic mundum universum pluris esse necesse est quam partem aliquam universi; quod si ita est, sapiens sit mundus necesse est, nam ni ita esset, hominem qui esset[1] mundi pars, quoniam rationis esset[1] particeps, pluris esse quam mundum omnem oporteret.

33 "Atque etiam si a primis inchoatisque naturis ad ultimas perfectasque volumus procedere, ad deorum naturam perveniamus necesse est. Prima[2] enim animadvertimus a natura sustineri ea quae gignantur e terra, quibus natura nihil tribuit amplius quam ut
34 ea alendo atque augendo tueretur. Bestiis autem sensum et motum dedit et cum quodam adpetitu accessum ad res salutares a pestiferis recessum; hoc homini amplius quod addidit rationem, qua regerentur animi adpetitus, qui tum remitterentur tum continerentur. XIII. Quartus autem gradus est et altissimus eorum qui natura boni sapientesque gignuntur, quibus a principio innascitur ratio recta constansque, quae supra hominem putanda est deoque tribuenda, id est mundo, in quo necesse est perfectam illam atque absolutam inesse rationem.

[1] est *dett.* [2] primo, primum *dett.*

taneously and not by any impulse from something else, it follows that that heat is soul; which proves that the world is an animate being.

for the whole world must be superior to its parts.

"Another proof that the world possesses intelligence is supplied by the fact that the world is unquestionably better than any of its elements; for even as there is no part of our body that is not of less value than we are ourselves, so the whole universe must needs be of higher worth than any portion of the universe; and if this be so, it follows that the world must be endowed with wisdom, for, if it were not, man, although a part of the world, being possessed of reason would necessarily be of higher worth than the world as a whole.

(13) Arguments from the scale of existence Vegetables, animals and man suggest deity above them.

"Again, if we wish to proceed from the first rudimentary orders of being to the last and most perfect, we shall necessarily arrive in the end at deity. We notice the sustaining power of nature first in the members of the vegetable kingdom, towards which her bounty was limited to providing for their preservation by means of the faculties of nurture and growth. Upon the animals she bestowed sensation and motion, and an appetite or impulse to approach things wholesome and retire from things harmful. For man she amplified her gift by the addition of reason, whereby the appetites might be controlled, and alternately indulged and held in check. XIII. But the fourth and highest grade is that of beings born by nature good and wise, and endowed from the outset with the innate attributes of right reason and consistency; this must be held to be above the level of man: it is the attribute of god, that is, of the world, which must needs possess that perfect and absolute reason of which I spoke. Again, it is un-

35 Neque enim dici potest in ulla rerum institutione non
esse aliquid extremum atque perfectum. Ut enim
in vite ut in pecude nisi quae vis obstitit videmus
naturam suo quodam itinere ad ultimum pervenire,
atque ut pictura et fabrica ceteraeque artes habent
quendam absoluti operis effectum, sic in omni natura
ac multo etiam magis necesse est absolvi aliquid
ac perfici. Etenim ceteris naturis multa externa
quo minus perficiantur possunt obsistere, universam
autem naturam nulla res potest impedire, propterea
quod omnis naturas ipsa cohibet et continet. Quocirca necesse est esse quartum illum et altissimum
36 gradum quo nulla vis possit accedere. Is autem
est gradus in quo rerum omnium natura ponitur;
quae quoniam talis est ut et praesit omnibus et eam
nulla res possit inpedire, necesse est intellegentem
esse mundum et quidem etiam sapientem.

"Quid autem est inscitius quam[1] eam naturam quae omnis res sit conplexa non optumam dici, aut cum sit optuma non primum animantem esse, deinde rationis et consilii compotem, postremo sapientem? Qui enim potest aliter esse optuma? Neque enim si stirpium similis sit aut etiam bestiarum, optuma putanda sit potius quam deterruma; nec vero si rationis particeps sit nec sit tamen a principio sapiens, non sit deterior mundi potius quam humana condicio; homo enim sapiens fieri potest, mundus autem si in aeterno praeteriti temporis spatio fuit insipiens, numquam profecto sapientiam con-

[1] quam <aut> *Manutius*.

deniable that every organic whole must have an ultimate ideal of perfection. As in vines or in cattle we see that, unless obstructed by some force, nature progresses on a certain path of her own to her goal of full development, and as in painting, architecture and the other arts and crafts there is an ideal of perfect workmanship, even so and far more in the world of nature as a whole there must be a process towards completeness and perfection. The various limited modes of being may encounter many external obstacles to hinder their perfect realization, but there can be nothing that can frustrate nature as a whole, since she embraces and contains within herself all modes of being. Hence it follows that there must exist this fourth and highest grade, unassailable by any external force. Now this is the grade on which universal nature stands; and since she is of such a character as to be superior to all things and incapable of frustration by any, it follows of necessity that the world is an intelligent being, and indeed also a wise being.

All things strive for perfection, but universal nature alone can attain it.

The world, as containing all things and therefore being supremely good, must possess wisdom and divinity.

"Again, what can be more illogical than to deny that the being which embraces all things must be the best of all things, or, admitting this, to deny that it must be, first, possessed of life, secondly, rational and intelligent, and lastly, endowed with wisdom? How else can it be the best of all things? If it resembles plants or even animals, so far from being highest, it must be reckoned lowest in the scale of being. If again it be capable of reason yet has not been wise from the beginning, the world must be in a worse condition than mankind; for a man can become wise, but if in all the eternity of past time the world has been foolish, obviously it will never attain wisdom;

sequetur; ita erit homine deterior. Quod quoniam absurdum est, et sapiens a principio mundus et deus habendus est.

37 "Neque enim est quicquam aliud praeter mundum cui nihil absit quodque undique aptum atque perfectum expletumque sit omnibus suis numeris et partibus. XIV. Scite enim Chrysippus, ut clipei causa involucrum vaginam autem gladii, sic praeter mundum cetera omnia aliorum causa esse generata, ut eas fruges atque fructus quos terra gignit animantium causa, animantes autem hominum, ut equum vehendi causa arandi bovem venandi et custodiendi canem; ipse autem homo ortus est ad mundum contemplandum et imitandum, nullo modo
38 perfectus, sed est quaedam particula perfecti. Sed mundus quoniam omnia conplexus est neque est quicquam quod non insit in eo, perfectus undique est; qui igitur potest ei deesse id quod est optimum? nihil autem est mente et ratione melius; ergo haec mundo deesse non possunt. Bene igitur idem Chrysippus, qui similitudines adiungens omnia in perfectis et maturis docet esse meliora, ut in equo quam in eculeo, in cane quam in catulo, in viro quam in puero; item quod in omni mundo optimum sit id in perfecto
39 aliquo atque absoluto esse debere; est autem nihil mundo perfectius, nihil virtute melius; igitur mundi est propria virtus. Nec vero hominis natura perfecta est, et efficitur tamen in homine virtus; quanto igitur

---

[a] Mayor would transfer this sentence to the end of § 37.
[b] This probably comes from Aristotle's lost dialogue *De Philosophia*, see i. 33 n.

and so it will be inferior to man. Which is absurd. Therefore the world must be deemed to have been wise from the beginning, and divine.

The world alone is perfect, and therefore virtuous, rational and divine.

"In fact[a] there is nothing else beside the world that has nothing wanting, but is fully equipped and complete and perfect in all its details and parts. XIV. For as Chrysippus cleverly put it,[b] just as a shield-case is made for the sake of a shield and a sheath for the sake of a sword, so everything else except the world was created for the sake of some other thing; thus the corn and fruits produced by the earth were created for the sake of animals, and animals for the sake of man: for example the horse for riding, the ox for ploughing, the dog for hunting and keeping guard; man himself however came into existence for the purpose of contemplating and imitating the world; he is by no means perfect, but he is 'a small fragment of that which is perfect.' The world on the contrary, since it embraces all things and since nothing exists which is not within it, is entirely perfect; how then can it fail to possess that which is the best? but there is nothing better than intelligence and reason; the world therefore cannot fail to possess them. Chrysippus therefore also well shows by the aid of illustrations that in the perfect and mature specimen of its kind everything is better than in the imperfect, for instance in a horse than in a foal, in a dog than in a puppy, in a man than in a boy; and that similarly a perfect and complete being is bound to possess that which is the best thing in all the world; but no being is more perfect than the world, and nothing is better than virtue; therefore virtue is an essential attribute of the world. Again, man's nature is not perfect, yet virtue may be realized in man;

in mundo facilius; est ergo in eo virtus. Sapiens est igitur, et propterea deus.

XV. "Atque hac mundi divinitate perspecta tribuenda est sideribus eadem divinitas, quae ex mobilissima purissimaque aetheris parte gignuntur neque ulla praeterea sunt admixta natura totaque sunt calida atque perlucida, ut ea quoque rectissime et animantia esse et sentire atque intellegere dicantur.
40 Atque ea quidem tota esse ignea duorum sensuum testimonio confirmari Cleanthes putat, tactus et oculorum. Nam solis et candor[1] inlustrior est quam ullius ignis, quippe qui inmenso mundo tam longe lateque conluceat, et is eius tactus est non ut tepefaciat solum sed etiam saepe comburat, quorum neutrum faceret nisi esset igneus. 'Ergo' inquit 'cum sol igneus sit, Oceanique alatur umoribus quia nullus ignis sine pastu aliquo posset permanere, necesse est aut ei similis sit igni quem adhibemus ad usum atque victum aut et qui corporibus animantium
41 continetur. Atqui hic noster ignis quem usus vitae requirit confector est et consumptor omnium, idemque quocumque invasit cuncta disturbat ac dissipat; contra ille corporeus vitalis et salutaris omnia conservat alit auget sustinet sensuque adficit.' Negat ergo esse dubium horum ignium sol utri similis sit, cum is quoque efficiat ut omnia floreant

[1] et candor *Klotz* : calor et candor *A*, *B*, candor *dett.*

how much more readily then in the world! therefore the world possesses virtue. Therefore it is wise, and consequently divine.

(14) Divinity of the stars: (a) because they are composed of aether, the source of life;

XV. "Having thus perceived the divinity of the world, we must also assign the same divinity to the stars, which are formed from the most mobile and the purest part of the aether, and are not compounded of any other element besides; they are of a fiery heat and translucent throughout. Hence they too have the fullest right to be pronounced to be living beings endowed with sensation and intelligence. That the stars consist entirely of fire Cleanthes holds to be established by the evidence of two of the senses, those of touch and sight. For the radiance of the sun is more brilliant than that of any fire, inasmuch as it casts its light so far and wide over the boundless universe; and the contact of its rays is so powerful that it not merely warms but often actually burns, neither of which things could it do if it were not made of fire. 'Therefore,' Cleanthes proceeds, 'since the sun is made of fire, and is nourished by the vapours exhaled from the ocean because no fire could continue to exist without sustenance of some sort, it follows that it resembles either that fire which we employ in ordinary life or that which is contained in the bodies of living creatures. Now our ordinary fire that serves the needs of daily life is a destructive agency, consuming everything, and also wherever it spreads it routs and scatters everything. On the other hand the fire of the body is the glow of life and health; it is the universal preservative, giving nourishment, fostering growth, sustaining, bestowing sensation.' He therefore maintains that there can be no doubt which of the two kinds of fire the sun resembles, for the sun

et in suo quaeque genere pubescant. Quare cum
solis ignis similis eorum ignium sit qui sunt in
corporibus animantium, solem quoque animantem
esse oportet, et quidem reliqua astra quae oriantur in ardore caelesti qui aether vel caelum nomi-
42 natur. Cum igitur aliorum animantium ortus in
terra sit, aliorum in aqua, in aëre aliorum, absurdum
esse Aristoteli videtur in ea parte quae sit ad gi-
gnenda animantia aptissima animal gigni nullum putare. Sidera autem aetherium locum obtinent, qui
quoniam tenuissimus est et semper agitatur et viget,
necesse est quod animal in eo gignatur id et sensu
acerrimo et mobilitate celerrima esse ; quare cum in
aethere astra gignantur, consentaneum est in iis
sensum inesse et intellegentiam. Ex quo efficitur in
deorum numero astra esse ducenda. XVI. Etenim
licet videre acutiora ingenia et ad intellegendum
aptiora eorum qui terras incolant eas in quibus aër sit
purus ac tenuis, quam illorum qui utantur crasso caelo
43 atque concreto ; quin etiam cibo quo utare interesse
aliquid ad mentis aciem putant ; probabile est igitur
praestantem intellegentiam in sideribus esse, quae et
aetheriam partem mundi incolant et marinis terrenis-
que umoribus longo intervallo extenuatis alantur.
Sensum autem astrorum atque intellegentiam maxume declarat ordo eorum atque constantia ; nihil est
enim quod ratione et numero moveri possit sine consilio, in quo nihil est temerarium nihil varium nihil

[a] Doubtless in the lost *De Philosophia*, see i. 32 n.

also causes all things to flourish and to bring forth increase each after its kind. Hence since the sun resembles those fires which are contained in the bodies of living creatures, the sun also must be alive; and so too the other heavenly bodies, since they have their origin in the fiery heat of heaven that is entitled the aether or sky. Since therefore some living creatures are born on the earth, others in the water and others in the air, it is absurd, so Aristotle [a] holds, to suppose that no living animal is born in that element which is most adapted for the generation of living things. But the stars occupy the region of aether, and as this has a very rarefied substance and is always in lively motion, it follows that the animal born in this region has the keenest senses and the swiftest power of movement; hence since the stars come into existence in the aether, it is reasonable to suppose that they possess sensation and intelligence. And from this it follows that the stars are to be reckoned as gods. XVI. For it may be observed that the inhabitants of those countries in which the air is pure and rarefied have keener wits and greater powers of understanding than persons who live in a dense and heavy climate; moreover the substance employed as food is also believed to have some influence on mental acuteness; it is therefore likely that the stars possess surpassing intelligence, since they inhabit the ethereal region of the world and also are nourished by the moist vapours of sea and earth, rarefied in their passage through the wide intervening space. Again, the consciousness and intelligence of the stars is most clearly evinced by their order and regularity; for regular and rhythmical motion is impossible without design, which contains no trace of casual or acci-

(b) because the inhabitants of aether probably possess the keenest intellect;

(c) the intelligence of the stars is shown by their ordered motion, which is due to their own freewill.

fortuitum; ordo autem siderum et in omni aeternitate constantia neque naturam significat (est enim plena rationis) neque fortunam quae amica varietati constantiam respuit; sequitur ergo ut ipsa sua
44 sponte suo sensu ac divinitate moveantur. Nec vero Aristoteles non laudandus est in eo quod omnia quae moventur aut natura moveri censuit aut vi aut voluntate; moveri autem solem et lunam et sidera omnia; quae autem natura moverentur haec aut pondere deorsum aut levitate in sublime ferri, quorum neutrum astris contingeret. propterea quod eorum motus in orbem circumque ferretur; nec vero dici potest vi quadam maiore fieri ut contra naturam astra moveantur; quae enim potest maior esse? restat igitur ut motus astrorum sit voluntarius.

"Quae qui videat non indocte solum verum etiam impie faciat si deos esse neget. Nec sane multum interest utrum id neget an eos omni procuratione atque actione privet; mihi enim qui nihil agit esse omnino non videtur. Esse igitur deos ita perspicuum est ut id qui neget vix eum sanae mentis existimem.

45 XVII. "Restat ut qualis eorum natura sit consideremus; in quo nihil est difficilius quam a consuetudine oculorum aciem mentis abducere. Ea difficultas induxit et vulgo inperitos et similes philosophos

---

[a] Probably as in § 42.

dental variation; now the order and eternal regularity of the constellations indicates neither a process of nature, for it is highly rational, nor chance, for chance loves variation and abhors regularity; it follows therefore that the stars move of their own free-will and because of their intelligence and divinity. Aristotle is also to be commended for his view[a] that the motion of all living bodies is due to one of three causes, nature, force, or will; now the sun and moon and all the stars are in motion, and bodies moved by nature travel either downwards owing to their weight or upwards owing to their lightness; but neither (he argued) is the case with the heavenly bodies, because their motion is revolution in a circle; nor yet can it be said that some stronger force compels the heavenly bodies to travel in a manner contrary to their nature, for what stronger force can there be? it remains therefore that the motion of the heavenly bodies is voluntary.

"Anyone who sees this truth would show not only ignorance but wickedness if he denied the existence of the gods. Nor indeed does it make much difference whether he denies their existence or deprives them entirely of providential care and of activity; since to my mind an entirely inactive being cannot be said to exist at all. Therefore the existence of the gods is so manifest that I can scarcely deem one who denies it to be of sound mind.

II. The Divine Nature (§§ 45–72).

XVII. "It remains for us to consider the qualities of the divine nature; and on this subject nothing is more difficult than to divert the eye of the mind from following the practice of bodily sight. This difficulty has caused both uneducated people generally and

inperitorum ut nisi figuris hominum constitutis nihil possent de dis inmortalibus cogitare; cuius opinionis levitas confutata a Cotta non desiderat orationem meam. Sed cum talem esse deum certa notione animi praesentiamus, primum ut sit animans, deinde ut in omni natura nihil eo sit praestantius, ad hanc praesensionem notionemque nostram nihil video quod potius accommodem quam ut primum hunc ipsum mundum quo nihil excellentius fieri potest animantem
46 esse et deum iudicem. His quam volet Epicurus iocetur, homo non aptissimus ad iocandum minimeque resipiens[1] patriam, et dicat se non posse intellegere qualis sit volubilis et rotundus deus, tamen ex hoc quod etiam ipse probat numquam me movebit: placet enim illi esse deos, quia necesse sit praestantem esse aliquam naturam qua nihil sit melius. Mundo autem certe nihil est melius. Nec dubium quin quod animans sit habeatque sensum et rationem et mentem id sit melius quam id quod
47 his careat. Ita efficitur animantem, sensus mentis rationis mundum esse compotem; qua ratione deum esse mundum concluditur.

"Sed haec paulo post facilius cognoscentur ex iis rebus ipsis quas mundus efficit. XVIII. Interea, Vellei, noli quaeso prae te ferre vos plane expertes esse doctrinae. Conum tibi ais et cylindrum et

[1] resipiens *dett.*: respiciens *A*, *B*.

(1) The divine form is spherical, as is seen in the world which is divine.

those philosophers who resemble the uneducated to be unable to conceive of the immortal gods without setting before themselves the forms of men: a shallow mode of thought which Cotta has exposed and which therefore calls for no discussion from me. But assuming that we have a definite and preconceived idea of a deity as, first, a living being, and secondly, a being unsurpassed in excellence by anything else in the whole of nature, I can see nothing that satisfies this preconception or idea of ours more fully than, first, the judgement that this world, which must necessarily be the most excellent of all things, is itself a living being and a god. Let Epicurus jest at this notion as he will—and he is a person who jokes with difficulty, and has but the slightest smack of his native Attic wit,—let him protest his inability to conceive of god as a round and rotating body. Nevertheless he will never dislodge me from one belief which even he himself accepts: he holds that gods exist, on the ground that there must necessarily be some mode of being of outstanding and supreme excellence; now clearly nothing can be more excellent than the world. Nor can it be doubted that a living being endowed with sensation, reason and intelligence must excel a being devoid of those attributes; hence it follows that the world is a living being and possesses sensation, intelligence and reason; and this argument leads to the conclusion that the world is god.

"But these points will appear more readily a little later merely from a consideration of the creatures that the world produces. XVIII. In the meantime, pray, Velleius, do not parade your school's utter ignorance of science. You say that you think a cone, a cylinder

pyramidem pulchriorem quam sphaeram videri. Novum etiam oculorum iudicium habetis! Sed sint ista pulchriora dumtaxat aspectu,—quod mihi tamen ipsum non videtur, quid enim pulchrius ea figura quae sola omnis alias figuras complexa continet, quaeque nihil asperitatis habere nihil offensionis potest, nihil incisum angulis nihil anfractibus nihil eminens nihil lacunosum? cumque duae formae praestantes sint, ex solidis globus (sic enim σφαῖραν interpretari placet), ex planis autem circulus aut orbis, qui κύκλος Graece dicitur, his duabus formis contingit solis ut omnes earum partes sint inter se simillumae a medioque tantundem[1] absit <omne>[2]
48 extremum, quo nihil fieri potest aptius—sed si haec non videtis, quia numquam eruditum illum pulverem attigistis, ne hoc quidem physici intellegere potuistis, hanc aequabilitatem motus constantiamque ordinum in alia figura non potuisse servari? Itaque nihil potest esse indoctius quam quod a vobis adfirmari solet: nec enim hunc ipsum mundum pro certo rotundum esse dicitis, nam posse fieri ut sit alia figura, innumerabilesque mundos alios aliarum
49 esse formarum. Quae si bis bina quot essent didicisset Epicurus certe non diceret; sed dum palato quid sit optimum iudicat, 'caeli palatum,' ut ait Ennius, non suspexit.

XIX. "Nam cum duo sint genera siderum, quorum

[1] tantundem *Madvig*: tantum. [2] *add. Brieger.*

---

[a] Ancient geometricians drew their diagrams in dust sprinkled on a board, or on the ground.

and a pyramid more beautiful than a sphere. Why, even in matters of taste you Epicureans have a criterion of your own! However, assuming that the figures which you mention are more beautiful to the eye—though for my part I don't think them so, for what can be more beautiful than the figure that encircles and encloses in itself all other figures, and that can possess no roughness or point of collision on its surface, no indentation or concavity, no protuberance or depression? There are two forms that excel all others, among solid bodies the globe (for so we may translate the Greek *sphaera*), and among plane figures the round or circle, the Greek *kyklos*; well then, these two forms alone possess the property of absolute uniformity in all their parts and of having every point on the circumference equidistant from the centre; and nothing can be more compact than
48 that. Still, if you Epicureans cannot see this, as you have never meddled with that learned dust,[a] could you not have grasped even so much of natural philosophy as to understand that the uniform motion and regular disposition of the heavenly bodies could not have been maintained with any other shape? Hence nothing could be more unscientific than your favourite assertion, that it is not certain that our world itself is round, since it may possibly have some other form, and there are countless numbers of worlds, all of
49 different shapes. Had but Epicurus learnt that twice two are four he certainly would not talk like that; but while making his palate the test of the chief good, he forgets to lift up his eyes to what Ennius calls 'the palate of the sky.'

XIX. "For there are two kinds of heavenly

alterum spatiis inmutabilibus ab ortu ad occasum commeans nullum umquam cursus sui vestigium inflectat, alterum autem continuas conversiones duas isdem spatiis cursibusque conficiat, ex utraque re et mundi volubilitas, quae nisi in globosa forma esse non posset, et stellarum rotundi ambitus cognoscuntur.

"Primusque sol, qui astrorum tenet principatum, ita movetur ut cum terras larga luce compleverit easdem modo his modo illis ex partibus opacet; ipsa enim umbra terrae soli officiens noctem efficit. Nocturnorum autem spatiorum eadem est aequabilitas quae diurnorum. Eiusdemque solis tum accessus modici tum recessus et frigoris et caloris modum temperant. Circumitus enim solis orbium quinque et sexaginta et trecentorum quarta fere diei parte addita conversionem conficiunt annuam; inflectens autem sol cursum tum ad septem triones tum ad meridiem aestates et hiemes efficit et ea duo tempora quorum alterum hiemi senescenti adiunctum est alterum aestati. Ita ex quattuor temporum mutationibus omnium quae terra marique gignuntur initia causaeque ducuntur.

50 "Iam solis annuos cursus spatiis menstruis luna consequitur, cuius tenuissimum lumen facit proximus accessus ad solem, digressus autem longissimus quisque plenissimum. Neque solum eius species ac forma mutatur tum crescendo tum defectibus in initia recurrendo, sed etiam regio, quae tum est

[a] The fixed stars are carried round the polar axis by the general celestial movement, while the planets have two simultaneous motions, (1) that of the fixed stars, (2) a movement of their own, by which they revolve (as was supposed) round the earth.

bodies,[a] some that travel from east to west in unchanging paths, without ever making the slightest deviation in their course, while the others perform two unbroken revolutions in the same paths and courses. Now both of these facts indicate at once the rotatory motion of the firmament, which is only possible with a spherical shape, and the circular revolutions of the heavenly bodies.

(2) The divine activity is rotatory motion, as shown in the heavenly bodies:

" Take first of all the sun, which is the chief of the celestial bodies. Its motion is such that it first fills the countries of the earth with a flood of light, and then leaves them in darkness now on one side and now on the other ; for night is caused merely by the shadow of the earth, which intercepts the light of the sun. Its daily and nightly paths have the same regularity. Also the sun by at one time slightly approaching and at another time slightly receding causes a moderate variation of temperature. For the passage of about 365¼ diurnal revolutions of the sun completes the circuit of a year ; and by bending its course now towards the north and now towards the south the sun causes summers and winters and the two seasons of which one follows the waning of winter and the other that of summer. Thus from the changes of the four seasons are derived the origins and causes of all those creatures which come into existence on land and in the sea.

the sun,

" Again the moon in her monthly paths overtakes the yearly course of the sun ; and her light wanes to its minimum when she approaches nearest to the sun, and waxes to its maximum each time that she recedes farthest from him. And not only is her shape and outline altered by her alternate waxing and waning or returning to her starting-point, but also her posi-

the moon,

aquilonia tum[1] australis. In[2] lunae quoque cursu est et brumae quaedam et solstitii similitudo, multaque ab ea manant et fluunt quibus et animantes alantur augescantque et pubescant maturitatemque adsequantur quae oriuntur e terra.

51 XX. "Maxume vero sunt admirabiles motus earum quinque stellarum quae falso vocantur errantes—nihil enim errat quod in omni aeternitate conservat progressus et regressus reliquosque motus constantis et ratos. Quod eo est admirabilius in his stellis quas dicimus, quia tum occultantur tum rursus aperiuntur, tum adeunt tum recedunt, tum antecedunt tum autem subsequuntur, tum celerius moventur tum tardius tum omnino ne moventur quidem sed ad quoddam tempus insistunt. Quarum ex disparibus motionibus magnum annum mathematici nominaverunt, qui tum efficitur cum solis et lunae et quinque errantium ad eandem inter se comparationem confectis omnium spatiis est facta conversio.

52 Quae quam longa sit magna quaestio est, esse vero certam et definitam necesse est. Nam ea quae Saturni stella dicitur Φαίνωνque a Graecis nominatur, quae a terra abest plurimum, triginta fere annis cursum suum conficit, in quo cursu multa mirabiliter efficiens tum antecedendo tum retardando, tum vespertinis temporibus delitiscendo tum matutinis rursum se aperiendo, nihil inmutat sempiternis

[1] tum *det.*: aut *A*, *B*.

[2] <inde> *vel* <nam> *vel* <ita> in *edd.*

---

[a] Perhaps from Aristotle's lost *De Philosophia*, see i. 33 n. The Cosmic Year is attributed to the Pythagoreans and to Heraclitus: Plato, *Timaeus* 39, gives it as 10,000 years.

[b] Herschel's figures, given by Mayor, are (omitting hours):

tion in the sky, which at one time is in the north and another in the south. The moon's course also has a sort of winter and summer solstice; and she emits many streams of influence, which supply animal creatures with nourishment and stimulate their growth and which cause plants to flourish and attain maturity.

XX. "Most marvellous are the motions of the five stars, falsely called planets or wandering stars—for a thing cannot be said to wander if it preserves for all eternity fixed and regular motions, forward, backward and in other directions. And this regularity is all the more marvellous in the case of the stars we speak of, because at one time they are hidden and at another they are uncovered again; now they approach, now retire; now precede, now follow; now move faster, now slower, now do not move at all but remain for a time stationary. On the diverse motions of the planets the mathematicians have based what they call the Great Year,[a] which is completed when the sun, moon and five planets having all finished their courses have returned to the same positions relative to one another. The length of this period is hotly debated, but it must necessarily be a fixed and definite time.[b] For the planet called Saturn's, the Greek name of which is *Phaenon* (the shiner), which is the farthest away from the earth, completes its orbit in about thirty years, in the course of which period it passes through a number of remarkable phases, at one time accelerating and at another time retarding its velocity, now disappearing in the evening, then reappearing in the morning, yet without varying in the the planets

Saturn 29 years 174 days, Jupiter 11 years 315 days, Mars 1 year 321 days, Venus 224 days, Mercury 87 days.

saeclorum aetatibus quin eadem isdem temporibus efficiat. Infra autem hanc propius a terra Iovis stella fertur quae Φαέθων dicitur, eaque eundem duodecim signorum orbem annis duodecim conficit easdemque quas Saturni stella efficit in cursu varie-
53 tates. Huic autem proximum inferiorem orbem tenet Πυρόεις, quae stella Martis appellatur, eaque quattuor et viginti mensibus sex ut opinor diebus minus eundem lustrat orbem quem duae superiores. Infra hanc autem stella Mercurii est (ea Στίλβων appellatur a Graecis), quae anno fere vertente signiferum lustrat orbem neque a sole longius umquam unius signi intervallo discedit tum antevertens tum subsequens. Infima est quinque errantium terraeque proxima stella Veneris, quae Φωσφόρος Graece Lucifer Latine dicitur cum antegreditur solem, cum subsequitur autem Ἕσπερος; ea cursum anno conficit et latitudinem lustrans signiferi orbis et longitudinem, quod idem faciunt stellae superiores, neque umquam ab sole duorum signorum intervallo longius discedit tum antecedens tum subsequens.

54 XXI. "Hanc igitur in stellis constantiam, hanc tantam tam variis cursibus in omni aeternitate convenientiam temporum non possum intellegere sine mente ratione consilio. Quae cum in sideribus inesse videamus, non possumus ea ipsa non in deorum numero reponere.

"Nec vero eae stellae quae inerrantes vocantur non significant eandem mentem atque prudentiam,

least degree throughout all the ages of eternity, but always doing the same things at the same times. Below this and nearer to the earth moves the star of Jupiter, called *Phaëthon* (the blazing star), which completes the same circuit of the twelve signs of the zodiac in twelve years, and makes the same variations during its course as the star of Saturn. The orbit next below is that of *Pyroeis* (the fiery), which is called the star of Mars, and this covers the same orbit as the two planets above it in twenty-four months all but (I think) six days. Below this in turn is the star of Mercury, called by the Greeks *Stilbōn* (the gleaming), which completes the circuit of the zodiac in about the period of a year, and is never distant from the sun more than the space of a single sign, though it sometimes precedes the sun and sometimes follows it. Lowest of the five planets and nearest to the earth is the star of Venus, called in Greek *Phosphoros* (the light-bringer) and in Latin Lucifer when it precedes the sun, but when it follows it *Hesperos*; this planet completes its orbit in a year, traversing the zodiac with a zigzag movement as do the planets above it, and never distant more than the space of two signs from the sun, though sometimes in front of it and sometimes behind it.

XXI. "This regularity therefore in the stars, this exact punctuality throughout all eternity notwithstanding the great variety of their courses, is to me incomprehensible without rational intelligence and purpose. And if we observe these attributes in the planets, we cannot fail to enrol even them among the number of the gods.

"Moreover the so-called fixed stars also indicate the same intelligence and wisdom. Their revolutions

and the fixed stars.

quarum est cotidiana conveniens constansque conversio nec habent aetherios cursus neque caelo inhaerentes, ut plerique dicunt physicae rationis ignari; non est enim aetheris ea natura ut vi sua stellas conplexa contorqueat, nam tenuis ac perlucens et aequabili calore suffusus aether non satis aptus
55 ad stellas continendas videtur; habent igitur suam sphaeram stellae inerrantes ab aetheria coniunctione secretam et liberam. Earum autem perennes cursus atque perpetui cum admirabili incredibilique constantia declarant in his vim et mentem esse divinam, ut haec ipsa qui non sentiat deorum vim habere is nihil omnino sensurus esse videatur.

56 "Nulla igitur in caelo nec fortuna nec temeritas nec erratio nec vanitas inest contraque omnis ordo veritas ratio constantia; quaeque his vacant ementita et falsa plenaque erroris, ea circum terras infra lunam (quae omnium ultima est) in terrisque versantur. Caelestium[1] ergo admirabilem ordinem incredibilemque constantiam, ex qua conservatio et salus omnium omnis oritur, qui vacare mente putat is ipse mentis expers habendus est.

57 "Haud ergo, ut opinor, erravero si a principe investigandae veritatis huius disputationis principium duxero. XXII. Zeno igitur naturam ita definit ut eam dicat ignem esse artificiosum, ad gignendum

[1] caelestium *dett.*: caelestem *A, B.*

recur daily with exact regularity. It is not the case
that they are carried along by the aether or that their
courses are fixed in the firmament, as most people
ignorant of natural philosophy aver ; for the aether
is not of such a nature as to hold the stars and cause
them to revolve by its own force, since being rare and
translucent and of uniform diffused heat, the aether
does not appear to be well adapted to contain the
5 stars. Therefore the fixed stars have a sphere of
their own, separate from and not attached to the
aether. Now the continual and unceasing revolutions
of these stars, marvellously and incredibly regular as
they are, clearly show that these are endowed with
divine power and intelligence ; so that anyone who
cannot perceive that they themselves possess divinity
would seem to be incapable of understanding anything at all.

3 "In the heavens therefore there is nothing of chance or hazard, no error, no frustration, but absolute order, accuracy, calculation and regularity. Whatever lacks these qualities, whatever is false and spurious and full of error, belongs to the region between the earth and the moon (the last of all the heavenly bodies), and to the surface of the earth. Anyone therefore who thinks that the marvellous order and incredible regularity of the heavenly bodies, which is the sole source of preservation and safety for all things, is not rational, himself cannot be deemed a rational being.

7 "I therefore believe that I shall not be wrong if in discussing this subject I take my first principle from the prince of seekers after truth, Zeno himself.
XXII. Now Zeno gives this definition of nature : 'nature (he says) is a craftsmanlike fire, proceeding

(3) The divinity of nature shown in its creative, artistic and providential activity.

progredientem via. Censet enim artis maxume proprium esse creare et gignere, quodque in operibus nostrarum artium manus efficiat id multo artificiosius naturam efficere, id est ut dixi ignem artificiosum, magistrum artium reliquarum. Atque hac quidem ratione omnis natura artificiosa est, quod habet quasi
58 viam quandam et sectam quam sequatur; ipsius vero mundi, qui omnia conplexu suo coërcet et continet, natura non artificiosa solum sed plane artifex ab eodem Zenone dicitur, consultrix et provida utilitatum opportunitatumque omnium. Atque ut ceterae naturae suis seminibus quaeque gignuntur augescunt continentur, sic natura mundi omnes motus habet voluntarios conatusque et adpetitiones quas *ὁρμάς* Graeci vocant, et his consentaneas actiones sic adhibet ut nosmet ipsi qui animis movemur et sensibus. Talis igitur mens mundi cum sit ob eamque causam vel prudentia vel providentia appellari recte possit (Graece enim *πρόνοια* dicitur), haec potissimum providet et in his maxime est occupata, primum ut mundus quam aptissimus sit ad permanendum, deinde ut nulla re egeat, maxume autem ut in eo eximia pulchritudo sit atque omnis ornatus.

59 XXIII. "Dictum est de universo mundo, dictum etiam est de sideribus, ut iam prope modum appareat multitudo nec cessantium deorum nec ea quae agant molientium cum labore operoso ac molesto. Non

---

[a] Diogenes Laertius vii. 156 *πῦρ τεχνικὸν ὁδῷ βάδιζον εἰς γένεσιν.*

[b] Aristotle, *Phys.* ii. 2 *ἡ τέχνη μιμεῖται τὴν φύσιν.*

[c] Diogenes L. vii. 86 *τεχνίτης ὁ λόγος τῆς ὁρμῆς.*

methodically to the work of generation.'[a] For he holds that the special function of an art or craft is to create and generate, and that what in the processes of our arts is done by the hand is done with far more skilful craftsmanship by nature,[b] that is, as I said, by that 'craftsmanlike' fire which is the teacher of the other arts. And on this theory, while each department of nature is 'craftsmanlike,' in the sense of having a method or path marked out for it to follow,
8 the nature of the world itself, which encloses and contains all things in its embrace, is styled by Zeno not merely 'craftsmanlike' but actually 'a craftsman,'[c] whose foresight plans out the work to serve its use and purpose in every detail. And as the other natural substances are generated, reared and sustained each by its own seeds, so the world-nature experiences all those motions of the will, those impulses of conation and desire, that the Greeks call *hormae,* and follows these up with the appropriate actions in the same way as do we ourselves, who experience emotions and sensations. Such being the nature of the world-mind, it can therefore correctly be designated as prudence or providence (for in Greek it is termed *pronoia*); and this providence is chiefly directed and concentrated upon three objects, namely to secure for the world, first, the structure best fitted for survival; next, absolute completeness; but chiefly, consummate beauty and embellishment of every kind.

9 XXIII. "We have discussed the world as a whole, and we have also discussed the heavenly bodies; so that there now stands fairly well revealed to our view a vast company of gods who are neither idle nor yet perform their activities with irksome and laborious

enim venis et nervis et ossibus continentur nec iis escis aut potionibus vescuntur ut aut nimis acres aut nimis concretos umores colligant, nec iis corporibus sunt ut casus aut ictus extimescant aut morbos metuant ex defetigatione membrorum, quae verens Epicurus monogrammos deos et nihil agentes com-
60 mentus est. Illi autem pulcherrima forma praediti purissimaque in regione caeli collocati ita feruntur moderanturque cursus ut ad omnia conservanda et tuenda consensisse videantur.

"Multae autem aliae naturae deorum ex magnis beneficiis eorum non sine causa et a Graeciae sapientissimis et a maioribus nostris constitutae nominataeque sunt. Quicquid enim magnam utilitatem generi adferret humano, id non sine divina bonitate erga homines fieri arbitrabantur. Itaque tum illud quod erat a deo natum[1] nomine ipsius dei nuncupabant, ut cum fruges Cererem appellamus vinum autem Liberum, ex quo illud Terentii:

> sine Cerere et Libero friget Venus,

61 tum autem res ipsa in qua vis inest maior aliqua sic appellatur ut ea ipsa[2] nominetur deus, ut Fides, ut Mens, quas in Capitolio dedicatas videmus proxime a M. Aemilio Scauro, ante autem ab A. Atilio Calatino erat Fides consecrata. Vides Virtutis templum, vides Honoris a M. Marcello renovatum quod

[1] datum *vel* donatum *Davies*.
[2] ipsa *B*: ipsa vis *A*, ipsa res *dett.*

---

[a] A probable correction reads 'given by,' *cf.* i. 38 and 118.

[b] The language seems to indicate that the building was visible from the *exedra* of Cotta's mansion, where the discussion took place (i. 14). A temple near the Porta Capena was dedicated to Honos by Fabius Cunctator, and later enlarged by Marcellus and dedicated to Honos and Virtus

toil. For they have no framework of veins and sinews and bones; nor do they consume such kinds of food and drink as to make them contract too sharp or too sluggish a condition of the humours; nor are their bodies such as to make them fear falls or blows or apprehend disease from exhaustion of their members —dangers which led Epicurus to invent his unsubstantial, do-nothing gods On the contrary, they are endowed with supreme beauty of form, they are situated in the purest region of the sky, and they so control their motions and courses as to seem to be conspiring together to preserve and to protect the universe.

"Many other divinities however have with good reason been recognized and named both by the wisest men of Greece and by our ancestors from the great benefits that they bestow. For it was thought that whatever confers great utility on the human race must be due to the operation of divine benevolence towards men. Thus sometimes a thing sprung from [a] a god was called by the name of the god himself; as when we speak of corn as Ceres, of wine as Liber, so that Terence writes:

(4) The gods of popular worship are the divine gifts to man deified, or virtues and passions personified,

> when Ceres and when Liber fail,
> Venus is cold.

In other cases some exceptionally potent force is itself designated by a title of divinity, for example Faith and Mind; we see the shrines on the Capitol lately dedicated to them both by Marcus Aemilius Scaurus, and Faith had previously been deified by Aulus Atilius Calatinus. You see [b] the temple of Virtue, restored as the temple of Honour by Marcus

jointly. Another temple dedicated to these two deities by Marius stood on the Capitol.

multis ante annis erat bello Ligustico a Q. Maximo dedicatum. Quid Opis, quid Salutis, quid Concordiae Libertatis Victoriae? quarum omnium rerum quia vis erat tanta ut sine deo regi[1] non posset, ipsa res deorum nomen obtinuit. Quo ex genere Cupidinis et Voluptatis et Lubentinae Veneris vocabula consecrata sunt, vitiosarum rerum neque naturalium (quamquam Velleius aliter existimat), sed tamen ea ipsa vitia natura[2] vehementius saepe pulsant.
62 Utilitatum igitur magnitudine constituti sunt ei di qui utilitates quasque gignebant, atque his quidem nominibus quae paulo ante dicta sunt quae vis sit in quoque declaratur deo.

XXIV. "Suscepit autem vita hominum consuetudoque communis ut beneficiis excellentis viros in caelum fama ac voluntate tollerent. Hinc Hercules hinc Castor et Pollux hinc Aesculapius hinc Liber etiam (hunc dico Liberum Semela natum, non eum quem nostri maiores auguste sancteque [Liberum][3] cum Cerere et Libera consecraverunt, quod quale sit ex mysteriis intellegi potest; sed quod ex nobis natos liberos appellamus, idcirco Cerere nati nominati sunt Liber et Libera, quod in Libera[4] servant, in Libero[5] non item)—hinc etiam Romulus,[6] quem quidem eundem esse Quirinum putant, quorum cum remanerent animi atque aeternitate fruerentur, rite di sunt habiti, cum et optimi essent et aeterni.

63 "Alia quoque ex ratione et quidem physica magna fluxit multitudo deorum qui induti specie humana

[1] intellegi *Goethe*.
[2] natura *A*, *B*: naturam *B corr.*
[3] Liberum *om. dett.* [4] Libero *dett.* [5] Libera *dett.*
[6] Romulus *Marsus*: Romulum.

Marcellus, but founded many years before by Quintus Maximus in the time of the Ligurian war. Again, there are the temples of Wealth, Safety, Concord, Liberty and Victory, all of which things, being so powerful as necessarily to imply divine governance, were themselves designated as gods. In the same class the names of Desire, Pleasure and Venus Lubentina have been deified—things vicious and unnatural (although Velleius thinks otherwise), yet the urge of these vices often overpowers natural instinct. Those gods therefore who were the authors of various benefits owed their deification to the value of the benefits which they bestowed, and indeed the names that I just now enumerated express the various powers of the gods that bear them.

or departed human benefactors,

XXIV. "Human experience moreover and general custom have made it a practice to confer the deification of renown and gratitude upon distinguished benefactors. This is the origin of Hercules, of Castor and Pollux, of Aesculapius, and also of Liber (I mean Liber the son of Semele, not the Liber whom our ancestors solemnly and devoutly consecrated with Ceres and Libera, the import of which joint consecration may be gathered from the mysteries; but Liber and Libera were so named as Ceres' offspring, that being the meaning of our Latin word *liberi*—a use which has survived in the case of Libera but not of Liber)—and this is also the origin of Romulus, who is believed to be the same as Quirinus. And these benefactors were duly deemed divine, as being both supremely good and immortal, because their souls survived and enjoyed eternal life.

3 "Another theory also, and that a scientific one, has been the source of a number of deities, who clad

fabulas poetis suppeditaverunt, hominum autem vitam superstitione omni referserunt. Atque hic locus a Zenone tractatus post a Cleanthe et Chrysippo pluribus verbis explicatus est. Nam cum[1] vetus haec opinio Graeciam opplevisset,[2] exsectum Caelum a filio Saturno, vinctum autem Saturnum ipsum a
64 filio Iove, physica ratio non inelegans inclusa est in impias fabulas. Caelestem enim altissimam aetheriamque naturam, id est igneam, quae per sese omnia gigneret, vacare voluerunt ea parte corporis quae coniunctione alterius egeret ad procreandum. XXV. Saturnum autem eum esse voluerunt qui cursum et conversionem spatiorum ac temporum contineret; qui deus Graece id ipsum nomen habet: Κρόνος enim dicitur, qui est idem χρόνος, id est spatium temporis. Saturnus autem est appellatus quod saturaretur annis; ex se enim natos comesse fingitur solitus, quia consumit aetas temporum spatia annisque praeteritis insaturabiliter expletur; vinctus autem a Iove ne inmoderatos cursus haberet atque ut eum siderum vinclis alligaret. Sed ipse Iuppiter—id est iuvans pater, quem conversis casibus appellamus a iuvando Iovem, a poetis 'pater divomque hominumque' dicitur, a maioribus autem nostris optumus maxumus, et quidem ante optumus, id est beneficentissimus, quam maxumus quia maius est certeque gratius prodesse omnibus quam opes magnas habere

[1] cum *A corr.*: *om. cett.*

[2] opplevisset *A*, *B*: opplevit *det.*, opplevit esse *Heindorf.*

[a] *i.e.*, Uranus.

in human form have furnished the poets with legends and have filled man's life with superstitions of all sorts. This subject was handled by Zeno and was later explained more fully by Cleanthes and Chrysippus. For example, an ancient belief prevailed throughout Greece that Caelus [a] was mutilated by his son Saturn, and Saturn himself thrown into bondage by his son Jove: now these immoral fables enshrined a decidedly clever scientific theory. Their meaning was that the highest element of celestial ether or fire, which by itself generates all things, is devoid of that bodily part which requires union with another for the work of procreation. XXV. By Saturn again they denoted that being who maintains the course and revolution of seasons and periods of time, the deity actually so designated in Greek, for Saturn's Greek name is *Kronos*, which is the same as *chronos*, a space of time. The Latin designation 'Saturn' on the other hand is due to the fact that he is 'saturated' or 'satiated with years' (*anni*); the fable is that he was in the habit of devouring his sons—meaning that Time devours the ages and gorges himself insatiably with the years that are past. Saturn was bound by Jove in order that Time's courses might not be unlimited, and that Jove might fetter him by the bonds of the stars. But Jupiter himself—the name means 'the helping father,' whom with a change of inflexion we style Jove, from *iuvare* 'to help'; the poets call him 'father of gods and men,' and our ancestors entitled him 'best and greatest,' putting the title 'best,' that is most beneficent, before that of 'greatest,' because universal beneficence is greater, or at least more lovable, than the possession of great wealth—

or personified forces of nature (this explains most of the gods of the mythology).

65 — hunc igitur Ennius ut supra dixi nuncupat ita dicens:

aspice hoc sublime candens quem invocant omnes Iovem,

planius quam alio loco idem:

cui[1] quod in me est exsecrabor hoc quod lucet quicquid est;

hunc etiam augures nostri, cum dicunt 'Iove fulgente, tonante': dicunt enim 'caelo fulgente et[2] tonante.' Euripides autem ut multa praeclare sic hoc breviter:

vides sublime fusum inmoderatum aethera,
qui terram tenero circumiectu amplectitur:
hunc summum habeto divum, hunc perhibeto Iovem.

66 XXVI. "Aër autem, ut Stoici disputant, interiectus inter mare et caelum Iunonis nomine consecratur, quae est soror et coniunx Iovis, quod ei[3] similitudo est aetheris et cum eo summa coniunctio; effeminarunt autem eum Iunonique tribuerunt quod nihil est eo mollius. (Sed Iunonem a iuvando credo nominatam.) Aqua restabat et terra, ut essent ex fabulis tria regna divisa. Datum est igitur Neptuno alterum,[4] Iovis ut volunt[5] fratri, maritimum omne regnum, nomenque productum ut Portunus a portu sic Neptunus a nando paulum primis litteris immutatis. Terrena autem vis omnis atque natura Diti patri dedicata est (qui Dives, ut apud Graecos Πλούτων), quia et recidunt omnia in terras et oriuntur

[1] qui *dett.* [2] et *om. dett.*
[3] ei *Probus*: et *MSS.*, ei et *Heindorf.*
[4] alteri *A corr.* [5] volumus *pr. A*, *pr. B.*

[a] § 4.
[b] Euripides fr. 386:

ὁρᾷς τὸν ὑψοῦ τόνδ' ἄπειρον αἰθέρα
καὶ γῆν πέριξ ἔχονθ' ὑγραῖς ἐν ἀγκάλαις·
τοῦτον νόμιζε Ζῆνα, τόνδ' ἡγοῦ θεόν.

[c] Hera.

5 it is he then who is addressed by Ennius in the following terms, as I said before [a]:

> Behold this dazzling vault of heaven, which all mankind
> as Jove invoke—

more explicitly than in another passage of the same poet:

> Now by whatever pow'r it be that sheds
> This light of day, I'll lay my curse upon him!

It is he also whom our augurs mean by their formula 'should Jove lighten and thunder,' meaning 'should the sky lighten and thunder.' Euripides among many fine passages has this brief invocation:

> Thou seest the boundless aether's spreading vault,
> Whose soft embrace encompasseth the earth:
> This deem thou god of gods, the supreme Jove.[b]

6 XXVI. "The air, lying between the sea and sky, is according to the Stoic theory deified under the name belonging to Juno,[c] sister and wife of Jove, because it resembles and is closely connected with the aether; they made it female and assigned it to Juno because of its extreme softness. (The name of Juno however I believe to be derived from *iuvare* 'to help'). There remained water and earth, to complete the fabled partition of the three kingdoms. Accordingly the second kingdom, the entire realm of the sea, was assigned to Neptune, Jove's brother as they hold; his name is derived from *nare* 'to swim,' with a slight alteration of the earlier letters and with the suffix seen in *Portunus* (the harbour god), derived from *portus* 'a harbour.' The entire bulk and substance of the earth was dedicated to father Dis (that is, Dives, 'the rich,' and so in Greek *Plouton*), because all things fall back into the earth and also arise from the earth.

e terris. Cui nuptam dicunt[1] Proserpinam (quod Graecorum nomen est, ea enim est quae Περσεφόνη Graece nominatur) — quam frugum semen esse volunt absconditamque quaeri a matre fingunt.
67 Mater autem est a gerendis frugibus Ceres (tamquam Geres, casuque prima littera itidem immutata ut a Graecis; nam ab illis quoque Δημήτηρ quasi γῆ μήτηρ nominata est). Iam qui magna verteret Mavors, Minerva autem quae vel minueret vel minaretur. XXVII. Cumque in omnibus rebus vim haberent maxumam prima et extrema, principem in sacrificando Ianum esse voluerunt, quod ab eundo nomen est ductum, ex quo transitiones perviae iani foresque in liminibus profanarum aedium ianuae nominantur. Iam[2] Vestae nomen a Graecis; ea est enim quae ab illis Ἑστία dicitur; vis autem eius ad aras et focos pertinet, itaque in ea dea, quod est rerum custos intumarum, omnis et precatio
68 et sacrificatio extrema est. Nec longe absunt ab hac vi di[3] Penates sive a penu ducto nomine (est enim omne quo vescuntur homines penus) sive ab eo quod penitus insident, ex quo etiam penetrales a poetis vocantur. Iam Apollinis nomen est Graecum, quem solem esse volunt, Dianam autem et lunam eandem esse putant. cum[4] sol dictus sit vel quia solus ex omnibus sideribus est tantus vel quia cum est exortus obscuratis omnibus solus apparet,

[1] nuptam dicunt *om. A, B.* [2] iam *Wölfflein:* nam. [3] vi di: divi *B corr.* [4] cumque *Mayor.*

[a] Euripides, *Phaethon*, fr. 775:

ὦ καλλιφεγγὲς Ἥλι', ὥς μ' ἀπώλεσας
καὶ τόνδ'· Ἀπόλλω δ' ἐν βροτοῖς σ' ὀρθῶς καλεῖ
ὅστις τὰ σιγῶντ' ὀνόματ' οἶδε δαιμόνων.

But Plato, *Cratylus*, 405 Ἀπόλλων = ἅμα ποδῶν . . . τὴν ὁμοῦ πόλησιν καὶ περὶ τὸν οὐρανὸν . . . καὶ περὶ τὴν ἐν τῇ ᾠδῇ ἁρμονίαν.

He is said to have married Proserpina (really a Greek name, for she is the same as the goddess called *Persephone* in Greek)—they think that she represents the seed of corn, and fable that she was hidden away,
67 and sought for by her mother. The mother is Ceres, a corruption of 'Geres,' from *gero*, because she *bears* the crops; the same accidental change of the first letter is also seen in her Greek name *Dēmētēr*, a corruption of *gē mētēr* (' mother earth '). Mavors again is from *magna vertere*, ' the overturner of the great,' while Minerva is either ' she who minishes ' or ' she who is minatory.' XXVII. Also, as the beginning and the end are the most important parts of all affairs, they held that Janus is the leader in a sacrifice, the name being derived from *ire* (' to go '), hence the names *jani* for archways and *januae* for the front doors of secular buildings. Again, the name Vesta comes from the Greeks, for she is the goddess whom they call *Hestia*. Her power extends over altars and hearths, and therefore all prayers and all sacrifices end with this goddess, because she is the guardian of
8 the innermost things. Closely related to this function are the Penates or household gods, a name derived either from *penus*, which means a store of human food of any kind, or from the fact that they reside *penitus*, in the recesses of the house, owing to which they are also called *penetrales* by the poets. The name Apollo again is Greek; they say that he is the sun,[a] and Diana they identify with the moon; the word *sol* being from *solus*, either because the sun ' alone ' of all the heavenly bodies is of that magnitude, or because when the sun rises all the stars are dimmed and it ' alone ' is visible; while the name *luna* is derived

Luna a lucendo nominata sit[1]; eadem est enim Lucina, itaque, ut apud Graecos Dianam eamque Luciferam, sic apud nostros Iunonem Lucinam in pariendo invocant. Quae eadem Diana Omnivaga dicitur non a venando sed quod in septem
69 numeratur tamquam vagantibus. Diana[2] dicta quia noctu quasi diem efficeret. Adhibetur autem ad partus quod ii maturescunt aut septem non numquam aut ut plerumque novem lunae cursibus, qui quia mensa spatia conficiunt menses nominantur; concinneque ut multa Timaeus, qui cum in historia dixisset qua nocte natus Alexander esset eadem Dianae Ephesiae templum deflagravisse, adiunxit minime id esse mirandum, quod Diana cum in partu Olympiadis adesse voluisset afuisset domo. Quae autem dea ad res omnes veniret Venerem nostri nominaverunt, atque[3] ex ea potius venustas quam Venus ex venustate.

70 XXVIII. "Videtisne igitur ut a physicis rebus bene atque utiliter inventis tracta ratio sit ad commenticios et fictos deos? quae res genuit falsas opiniones erroresque turbulentos et superstitiones paene aniles. Et formae enim nobis deorum et aetates et vestitus ornatusque noti sunt, genera praeterea coniugia cognationes, omniaque traducta ad similitudinem inbecillitatis humanae. Nam et perturbatis animis inducuntur: accepimus[4] enim deorum cupiditates aegritudines iracundias; nec

[1] sit: est *Mayor.*
[2] <sed> Diana *Mayor.* [3] estque *Mayor.*
[4] accepimus *dett.*: accipimus *A*, *B*.

from *lucere* 'to shine'; for it is the same word as *Lucina*, and therefore in our country Juno Lucina is invoked in childbirth, as is Diana in her manifestation as Lucifera (the light-bringer) among the Greeks. She is also called Diana *Omnivaga* (wide-wandering), not from her hunting, but because she is counted one of the seven planets or 'wanderers' (*vagari*). She was called Diana because she made a sort of *day* in the night-time. She is invoked to assist at the birth of children, because the period of gestation is either occasionally seven, or more usually nine, lunar revolutions, and these are called *menses* (months), because they cover measured (*mensa*) spaces. Timaeus in his history with his usual aptness adds to his account of the burning of the temple of Diana of Ephesus on the night on which Alexander was born the remark that this need cause no surprise, since Diana was away from home, wishing to be present when Olympias was brought to bed. Venus was so named by our countrymen as the goddess who 'comes' (*venire*) to all things; her name is not derived from the word *venustas* (beauty) but rather *venustas* from it.

XXVIII. "Do you see therefore how from a true and valuable philosophy of nature has been evolved this imaginary and fanciful pantheon? The perversion has been a fruitful source of false beliefs, crazy errors and superstitions hardly above the level of old wives' tales. We know what the gods look like and how old they are, their dress and their equipment, and also their genealogies, marriages and relationships, and all about them is distorted into the likeness of human frailty. They are actually represented as liable to passions and emotions—we hear of their being in love, sorrowful, angry; according to the myths they even

vero ut fabulae ferunt bellis proeliisque caruerunt, nec solum ut apud Homerum cum duo exercitus contrarios alii dei ex alia parte defenderent, sed etiam ut cum Titanis ut cum Gigantibus sua propria bella gesserunt. Haec et dicuntur et creduntur stultissime et plena sunt futtilitatis summaeque
71 levitatis. Sed tamen his fabulis spretis ac repudiatis deus pertinens per naturam cuiusque rei, per terras Ceres per maria Neptunus alii per alia, poterunt intellegi qui qualesque sint, quoque eos nomine consuetudo nuncupaverit, hoc eos[1] et venerari et colere debemus. Cultus autem deorum est optimus idemque castissimus atque sanctissimus plenissimusque pietatis ut eos semper pura integra incorrupta et mente et voce veneremur. Non enim philosophi solum verum etiam maiores nostri superstitionem a
72 religione separaverunt. Nam qui totos dies precabantur et immolabant ut sibi sui liberi superstites essent superstitiosi sunt appellati, quod nomen patuit postea latius; qui autem omnia quae ad cultum deorum pertinerent diligenter retractarent et tamquam relegerent, ‹hi›[2] sunt dicti religiosi ex relegendo, ut elegantes ex eligendo ex diligendo diligentes ex intellegendo intellegentes; his enim in verbis omnibus inest vis legendi eadem quae in religioso. Ita factum est in superstitioso et religioso alterum vitii nomen alterum laudis. Ac mihi videor satis et esse deos et quales essent ostendisse.

[1] hoc eos *Keil*: hos deos. [2] *add. Nonius.*

---

[a] Scholars are divided as to whether this etymology is correct or whether *religio* is connected with *ligare*, as Cicero himself suggests elsewhere by his phrases *religione obstringere, impedire, solvi*.

engage in wars and battles, and that not only when as in Homer two armies are contending and the gods take sides and intervene on their behalf, but they actually fought wars of their own, for instance with the Titans and with the Giants. These stories and these beliefs are utterly foolish; they are stuffed with nonsense and absurdity of all sorts. But though repudiating these myths with contempt, we shall nevertheless be able to understand the personality and the nature of the divinities pervading the substance of the several elements, Ceres permeating earth, Neptune the sea, and so on; and it is our duty to revere and worship these gods under the names which custom has bestowed upon them. But the best and also the purest, holiest and most pious way of worshipping the gods is ever to venerate them with purity, sincerity and innocence both of thought and of speech. For religion has been distinguished from superstition not only by philosophers but by our ancestors. Persons who spent whole days in prayer and sacrifice to ensure that their children should outlive them were termed 'superstitious' (from *superstes*, a survivor), and the word later acquired a wider application. Those on the other hand who carefully reviewed and so to speak retraced all the lore of ritual were called 'religious' from *relegere* (to retrace or re-read), like 'elegant' from *eligere* (to select), 'diligent' from *diligere* (to care for), 'intelligent' from *intellegere* (to understand); for all these words contain the same sense of 'picking out' (*legere*) that is present in 'religious.'[a] Hence 'superstitious' and 'religious' came to be terms of censure and approval respectively. I think that I have said enough to prove the existence of the gods and their nature.

True religion.

73 XXIX. "Proximum est ut doceam deorum providentia mundum administrari. Magnus sane locus est[1] et a vestris, Cotta, vexatus, ac nimirum vobiscum omne certamen est. Nam vobis, Vellei, minus notum est quem ad modum quidque dicatur; vestra enim solum legitis, vestra amatis, ceteros causa incognita condemnatis. Velut a te ipso hesterno die dictum est anum fatidicam πρόνοιαν a Stoicis induci, id est providentiam; quod eo errore dixisti quia existumas ab iis providentiam fingi quasi quandam deam singularem quae mundum omnem gubernet et
74 regat. Sed id praecise dicitur: ut, si quis dicat Atheniensium rem publicam consilio regi, desit illud 'Areopagi,[2]' sic cum dicimus providentia mundum administrari deesse arbitrato 'deorum,' plene autem et perfecte sic dici existimato, providentia deorum mundum administrari. Ita salem istum, quo caret vestra natio, in inridendis nobis nolitote consumere, et mehercle si me audiatis ne experiamini quidem; non decet, non datum est, non potestis. Nec vero hoc in te unum[3] convenit, moribus domesticis ac nostrorum hominum urbanitate limatum,[4] sed cum in reliquos vestros tum in eum maxime qui ista peperit, hominem sine arte sine litteris, insultantem in omnes, sine acumine ullo sine
75 auctoritate sine lepore. XXX. Dico igitur pro-

[1] est *om. dett.*
[2] Ariopagi *A corr.*: Arpagi *cett.*, Ariipagi *Plasberg.*
[3] unum *Manutius* (*post* convenit *Kindervater*): uno.
[4] limatum *Manutius*: limato.

[a] See i. 18, 20, 22. The language here and at iii. 18 implies that the work was planned to fall into three separate conversations held on three successive days: an indication that it lacks the author's final revision.

II. Providential government of the world (§§ 73-153) Introductory: Epicurean sneers are grounded in ignorance.

3 XXIX. "Next I have to show that the world is
governed by divine providence. This is of course a
vast topic; the doctrine is hotly contested by your
school, Cotta, and it is they no doubt that are my
chief adversaries here. As for you and your friends,
Velleius, you scarcely understand the vocabulary of
the subject; for you only read your own writings, and
are so enamoured of them that you pass judgement
against all the other schools without giving them a
hearing. For instance, you yourself told us yesterday[a]
that the Stoics present *Pronoia* or providence in the
guise of an old hag of a fortune-teller; this was due
to your mistaken notion that they imagine providence
as a kind of special deity who rules and governs the
universe. But as a matter of fact 'providence' is an
4 elliptical expression; when one says 'the Athenian
state is ruled by the council,' the words 'of the
Areopagus' are omitted: so when we speak of the
world as governed by providence, you must understand the words 'of the gods' and must conceive that
the full and complete statement would be 'the world
is governed by the providence of the gods.' So do not
you and your friends waste your wit on making fun
of us,—your tribe is none too well off for that commodity. Indeed if your school would take my advice
you would give up all attempts at humour; it sits ill
upon you, for it is not your forte and you can't bring
it off. This does not, it is true, apply to you in particular,—you have the polished manners of your family
and the urbanity of a Roman; but it does apply to
all the rest of you, and especially to the parent of the
system, an uncultivated, illiterate person, who tilts
at everybody and is entirely devoid of penetration,
5 authority or charm. XXX. I therefore declare that

videntia deorum mundum et omnes mundi partes et initio constitutas esse et omni tempore administrari; eamque disputationem tris in partes nostri fere dividunt, quarum prima pars est quae ducitur ab ea ratione quae docet esse deos; quo concesso confitendum est eorum consilio mundum administrari. Secunda est autem quae docet omnes res subiectas esse naturae sentienti ab eaque omnia pulcherrume geri; quo constituto sequitur ab animantibus principiis ea esse generata.[1] Tertius est locus qui ducitur ex admiratione rerum caelestium atque terrestrium.

76 "Primum igitur aut negandum est esse deos, quod et Democritus simulacra et Epicurus imagines inducens quodam pacto negat, aut qui deos esse concedant iis fatendum est eos aliquid agere idque praeclarum; nihil est autem praeclarius mundi administratione; deorum igitur consilio administratur. Quod si aliter est, aliquid profecto sit necesse est melius et maiore vi praeditum quam deus, quale id cumque est, sive inanima natura sive necessitas vi magna incitata haec

77 pulcherrima opera efficiens quae videmus; non est igitur natura deorum praepotens neque excellens, siquidem ea subiecta est ei vel necessitati vel naturae qua caelum maria terrae regantur. Nihil est autem praestantius deo; ab eo igitur mundum necesse est regi; nulli igitur est naturae oboediens aut subiectus deus, omnem ergo regit ipse naturam. Etenim si

[1] ea esse generata *dett.*: eam e. generatam *A*, *B*, omnia e. generata *Heindorf*, eum e. generatum *Walker*.

the world and all its parts were set in order at the beginning and have been governed for all time by divine providence: a thesis which our school usually divides into three sections. The first is based on the argument proving that the gods exist; if this be granted, it must be admitted that the world is governed by their wisdom. The second proves that all things are under the sway of sentient nature, and that by it the universe is carried on in the most beautiful manner; and this proved, it follows that the universe was generated from living first causes. The third topic is the argument from the wonder that we feel at the marvel of creation, celestial and terrestrial.

Division of the subject.

"In the first place therefore one must either deny the existence of the gods, which in a manner is done by Democritus when he represents them as 'apparitions' and by Epicurus with his 'images'; or anybody who admits that the gods exist must allow them activity, and activity of the most distinguished sort; now nothing can be more distinguished than the government of the world; therefore the world is governed by the wisdom of the gods. If this is not so, there must clearly be something better and more powerful than god, be it what it may, whether inanimate nature or necessity speeding on with mighty force to create the supremely beautiful objects that we see; in that case the nature of the gods is not superior to all else in power, inasmuch as it is subject to a necessity or nature that rules the sky, sea and land. But as a matter of fact nothing exists that is superior to god; it follows therefore that the world is ruled by him; therefore god is not obedient or subject to any form of nature, and therefore he himself rules all nature. In fact if we concede divine intelli-

(1) Providential government inferred from the divine wisdom and power.

concedimus intellegentes esse deos, concedimus etiam providentes et rerum quidem maxumarum. Ergo utrum ignorant quae res maxumae sint quoque eae modo tractandae et tuendae, an vim non habent qua tantas res sustineant et gerant? At et ignoratio rerum aliena naturae deorum est et sustinendi muneris propter inbecillitatem difficultas minime cadit in maiestatem deorum. Ex quo efficitur id quod volumus, deorum providentia mundum admini-
78 strari. XXXI. Atqui necesse est cum sint di (si modo sunt, ut profecto sunt) animantis esse, nec solum animantis sed etiam rationis compotes inter seque quasi civili conciliatione et societate coniunctos, unum mundum ut communem rem publicam atque
79 urbem aliquam regentis. Sequitur ut eadem sit in iis quae humano in genere ratio, eadem veritas utrobique sit eademque lex, quae est recti praeceptio pravique depulsio. Ex quo intellegitur prudentiam quoque et mentem a deis ad homines pervenisse; ob eamque causam maiorum institutis Mens Fides Virtus Concordia consecratae et publice dedicatae sunt, quae qui convenit penes deos esse negare cum earum[1] augusta et sancta simulacra veneremur? Quodsi inest in hominum genere mens fides virtus concordia, unde haec in terram nisi ab superis defluere potuerunt? Cumque sint in nobis consilium ratio prudentia, necesse est deos haec ipsa habere maiora, nec habere solum sed etiam iis uti in maxumis et

[1] earum *ed.*: eorum.

gence, we concede also divine providence, and providence exercised in things of the highest moment. Are then the gods ignorant what things are of the highest moment and how these are to be directed and upheld, or do they lack the strength to undertake and to perform duties so vast? But ignorance is foreign to the divine nature, and weakness, with a consequent incapacity to perform one's office, in no way suits with the divine majesty. This proves our thesis that the world is governed by divine providence.

78 XXXI. And yet from the fact of the gods' existence (assuming that they exist, as they certainly do) it necessarily follows that they are animate beings, and not only animate but possessed of reason and united together in a sort of social community or fellowship, ruling the one world as a united commonwealth or
79 state. It follows that they possess the same faculty of reason as the human race, and that both have the same apprehension of truth and the same law enjoining what is right and rejecting what is wrong. Hence we see that wisdom and intelligence also have been derived by men from the gods; and this explains why it was the practice of our ancestors to deify Mind, Faith, Virtue and Concord, and to set up temples to them at the public charge, and how can we consistently deny that they exist with the gods, when we worship their majestic and holy images? And if mankind possesses intelligence, faith, virtue and concord, whence can these things have flowed down upon the earth if not from the powers above? Also since we possess wisdom, reason and prudence, the gods must needs possess them too in greater perfection, and not possess them merely but also exercise them upon matters of the

80 optumis rebus ; nihil autem nec maius nec melius mundo ; necesse est ergo eum deorum consilio et providentia administrari. Postremo cum satis docuerimus hos esse deos quorum insignem vim et inlustrem faciem videremus, solem dico et lunam et vagas stellas et inerrantes et caelum et mundum ipsum et earum rerum vim quae inessent in omni mundo cum magno usu et commoditate generis humani, efficitur omnia regi divina mente atque prudentia. Ac de prima quidem parte satis dictum est.

81 XXXII. " Sequitur ut doceam omnia subiecta esse naturae eaque ab ea pulcherrime geri.[1] Sed quid sit ipsa natura explicandum est ante breviter, quo facilius id quod docere volumus intellegi possit. Namque alii naturam esse censent vim quandam sine ratione cientem motus in corporibus necessarios, alii autem vim participem rationis atque ordinis tamquam via progredientem declarantemque quid cuiusque rei causa efficiat quid sequatur, cuius sollertiam nulla ars nulla manus nemo opifex consequi possit imitando ; seminis enim vim esse tantam ut id, quamquam sit perexiguum, tamen si inciderit in concipientem conprendentemque naturam nanctumque sit materiam qua ali augerique possit, ita fingat et efficiat in suo quidque genere, partim ut tantum modo per stirpes alantur suas, partim ut moveri etiam et sentire et appetere possint et ex sese
82 similia sui gignere. Sunt autem qui omnia naturae

[1] geri *A*, *B* : regi *dett.*

greatest magnitude and value; but nothing is of greater magnitude and value than the universe; it follows therefore that the universe is governed by the wisdom and providence of the gods. Finally, since we have conclusively proved the divinity of those beings whose glorious might and shining aspect we behold, I mean the sun and moon and the planets and fixed stars, and the sky and the world itself, and all that mighty multitude of objects contained in all the world which are of great service and benefit to the human race, the conclusion is that all things are ruled by divine intelligence and wisdom. So much for the first division of my subject.

(2) Providential government inferred from the nature of the world. The meaning of 'nature.'

XXXII. "Next I have to show that all things are under the sway of nature and are carried on by her in the most excellent manner. But first I must briefly explain the meaning of the term 'nature' itself, to make our doctrine more easily intelligible. Some persons define nature as a non-rational force that causes necessary motions in material bodies; others as a rational and ordered force, proceeding by method and plainly displaying the means that she takes to produce each result and the end at which she aims, and possessed of a skill that no handiwork of artist or craftsman can rival or reproduce. For a seed, they point out, has such potency that, tiny though it is in size, nevertheless if it falls into some substance that conceives and enfolds it, and obtains suitable material to foster its nurture and growth, it fashions and produces the various creatures after their kinds, some designed merely to absorb nourishment through their roots, and others capable of motion, sensation, appetition and reproduction of their species. Some thinkers again denote by the term 'nature' the whole

nomine appellent, ut Epicurus, qui ita dividit: omnium quae sint naturam esse corpora et inane quaeque his accidant. Sed nos cum dicimus natura constare administrarique mundum, non ita dicimus ut glaebam aut fragmentum lapidis aut aliquid eius modi sola[1] cohaerendi natura, sed ut arborem ut animal, in quibus nulla temeritas sed ordo apparet et artis quaedam similitudo.

83 XXXIII. "Quodsi ea quae a terra stirpibus continentur arte naturae vivunt et vigent, profecto ipsa terra eadem vi continetur [arte naturae],[2] quippe quae gravidata seminibus omnia pariat et fundat ex sese, stirpes amplexa alat et augeat ipsaque alatur vicissim a superis externisque naturis. Eiusdemque exspirationibus et aër alitur et aether et omnia supera. Ita si terra natura tenetur et viget eadem ratio in reliquo mundo est; stirpes enim terrae inhaerent, animantes autem adspiratione aëris sustinentur, ipseque aër nobiscum videt nobiscum audit nobiscum sonat, nihil enim eorum sine eo fieri potest; quin etiam movetur nobiscum, quacumque enim imus quacumque[3] move-
84 mur videtur quasi locum dare et cedere. Quaeque in medium locum mundi qui est infimus[4] et quae a medio in superum quaeque conversione rotunda circum medium feruntur, ea continentem mundi efficiunt unamque naturam. Et cum quattuor genera sint corporum, vicissitudine eorum mundi

[1] sola *Walker*: nulla MSS., una *vel* nuda *Davies*, nulla <nisi> *Heindorf*. [2] *om. Davies*.
[3] quacunque *B corr.*: qua.
[4] <in rotundo> infimus *Plasberg*.

[a] The MSS. give "which possesses no natural principle of cohesion."

of existence—for example Epicurus, who divides the nature of all existing things into atoms, void, and the attributes of these. When we on the other hand speak of nature as the sustaining and governing principle of the world, we do not mean that the world is like a clod of earth or lump of stone or something else of that sort, which possesses only [a] the natural principle of cohesion, but like a tree or an animal, displaying no haphazard structure, but order and a certain semblance of design.

XXXIII. "But if the plants fixed and rooted in the earth owe their life and vigour to nature's art, surely the earth herself must be sustained by the same power, inasmuch as when impregnated with seeds she brings forth from her womb all things in profusion, nourishes their roots in her bosom and causes them to grow, and herself in turn is nourished by the upper and outer elements. Her exhalations moreover give nourishment to the air, the ether and all the heavenly bodies. Thus if earth is upheld and invigorated by nature, the same principle must hold good of the rest of the world, for plants are rooted in the earth, animals are sustained by breathing air, and the air itself is our partner in seeing, hearing and uttering sounds, since none of these actions can be performed without its aid; nay, it even moves as we move, for wherever we go or move our limbs, it seems as it were to give place and retire before us. And those things which travel towards the centre of the earth which is its lowest point, those which move from the centre upwards, and those which rotate in circles round the centre, constitute the one continuous nature of the world. Again the continuum of the world's nature is constituted by the cyclic transmutations of the four

The world a vast organism governed by an intelligent nature.

continuata natura est. Nam ex terra aqua ex aqua
oritur aër ex aëre aether, deinde retrorsum vicissim
ex aethere aër, inde aqua, ex aqua terra infima.
Sic naturis his ex quibus omnia constant sursus
deorsus ultro citro commeantibus mundi partium
85 coniunctio continetur. Quae aut sempiterna sit
necesse est hoc eodem ornatu quem videmus, aut
certe perdiuturna, permanens ad longinquum et
inmensum paene tempus. Quorum utrumvis ut sit,
sequitur natura mundum administrari. Quae enim
classium navigatio aut quae instructio exercitus aut,
rursus ut ea quae natura efficit conferamus, quae
procreatio vitis aut arboris, quae porro animantis
figura conformatioque membrorum tantam naturae
sollertiam significat quantam ipse mundus? Aut
igitur nihil est quod sentiente natura regatur, aut
86 mundum regi confitendum est. Etenim qui reliquas
naturas omnes earumque semina contineat qui potest
ipse non natura administrari? ut si qui dentes et
pubertatem natura dicat existere, ipsum autem
hominem cui ea existant non constare natura, non
intellegat ea quae ecferant aliquid ex sese perfec-
tiores habere naturas quam ea quae ex iis ecferantur.
XXXIV. Omnium autem rerum quae natura administrantur seminator et sator et parens ut ita
dicam atque educator et altor est mundus omniaque
sicut membra et partes suas nutricatur et continet.

kinds of matter. For earth turns into water, water into air, air into aether, and then the process is reversed, and aether becomes air, air water, and water earth, the lowest of the four. Thus the parts of the world are held in union by the constant passage up and down, to and fro, of these four elements of which
85 all things are composed. And this world-structure must either be everlasting in this same form in which we see it or at all events extremely durable, and destined to endure for an almost immeasurably protracted period of time. Whichever alternative be true, the inference follows that the world is governed by nature. For consider the navigation of a fleet, the marshalling of an army, or (to return to instances from the processes of nature) the budding of a vine or of a tree, or even the shape and structure of the limbs of an animal—when do these ever evidence such a degree of skill in nature as does the world itself? Either therefore there is nothing that is ruled by a sentient nature, or we must admit that the
86 world is so ruled. Indeed, how is it possible that the universe, which contains within itself all the other natures and their seeds, should not itself be governed by nature? Thus if anyone declared that a man's teeth and the hair on his body are a natural growth but that the man himself to whom they belong is not a natural organism, he would fail to see that things which produce something from within them must have more perfect natures than the things which are produced from them. XXXIV. But the sower and planter and begetter, so to speak, of all the things that nature governs, their trainer and nourisher, is the world; the world gives nutriment and sustenance to all its limbs as it were, or parts. But if the parts

Quodsi mundi partes natura administrantur, necesse est mundum ipsum natura administrari. Cuius quidem administratio nihil habet in se quod reprehendi possit ; ex iis enim naturis quae erant quod effici
87 optimum potuit effectum est. Doceat ergo aliquis potuisse melius ; sed nemo umquam docebit, et si quis corrigere aliquid volet aut deterius faciet aut id quod fieri non potuerit desiderabit.

"Quodsi omnes mundi partes ita constitutae sunt ut neque ad usum meliores potuerint esse neque ad speciem pulcriores, videamus utrum ea fortuitane sint an eo statu quo cohaerere nullo modo potuerint nisi sensu moderante divinaque providentia. Si igitur meliora sunt ea quae natura quam illa quae arte perfecta sunt, nec ars efficit quicquam sine ratione, ne natura quidem rationis expers est habenda. Qui igitur convenit, signum aut tabulam pictam cum aspexeris, scire adhibitam esse artem, cumque procul cursum navigii videris, non dubitare quin id ratione atque arte moveatur, aut cum solarium vel descriptum vel ex aqua contemplere, intellegere declarari horas arte non casu, mundum autem, qui et has ipsas artes et earum artifices et cuncta conplectatur, consilii et rationis esse expertem
88 putare ? Quodsi in Scythiam aut in Britanniam sphaeram aliquis tulerit hanc quam nuper familiaris noster effecit Posidonius, cuius singulae conversiones idem efficiunt in sole et in luna et in quinque stellis

of the world are governed by nature, the world itself must needs be governed by nature. Now the government of the world contains nothing that could possibly be censured; given the existing elements, the best that could be produced from them has been produced. Let someone therefore prove that it could have been better. But no one will ever prove this, and anyone who essays to improve some detail will either make it worse or will be demanding an improvement impossible in the nature of things.

The world's perfection must be the work of intelligence (that of a divine ruler).

"But if the structure of the world in all its parts is such that it could not have been better whether in point of utility or beauty, let us consider whether this is the result of chance, or whether on the contrary the parts of the world are in such a condition that they could not possibly have cohered together if they were not controlled by intelligence and by divine providence. If then the products of nature are better than those of art, and if art produces nothing without reason, nature too cannot be deemed to be without reason. When you see a statue or a painting, you recognize the exercise of art; when you observe from a distance the course of a ship, you do not hesitate to assume that its motion is guided by reason and by art; when you look at a sun-dial or a water-clock, you infer that it tells the time by art and not by chance; how then can it be consistent to suppose that the world, which includes both the works of art in question, the craftsmen who made them, and everything else besides, can be devoid of purpose and of reason? Suppose a traveller to carry into Scythia or Britain the orrery recently constructed by our friend Posidonius, which at each revolution reproduces the same motions of the sun, the moon and the

errantibus quod efficitur in caelo singulis diebus et noctibus, quis in illa barbaria dubitet quin ea sphaera sit perfecta ratione? XXXV. Hi autem dubitant de mundo ex quo et oriuntur et fiunt omnia, casune ipse sit effectus aut necessitate aliqua an ratione ac mente divina, et Archimedem arbitrantur plus valuisse in imitandis sphaerae conversionibus quam naturam in efficiendis, praesertim cum multis partibus sint illa perfecta quam haec simulata sollertius.
89 Utque[1] ille apud Accium pastor qui navem numquam ante vidisset, ut procul divinum et novum vehiculum Argonautarum e monte conspexit, primo admirans et perterritus hoc modo loquitur:

tanta moles labitur
fremibunda ex alto ingenti sonitu et spiritu[2]:
prae se undas volvit, vertices vi suscitat,
ruit prolapsa, pelagus respergit reflat;
ita dum interruptum credas nimbum volvier,
dum quod sublime ventis expulsum rapi
saxum aut procellis, vel globosos turbines
existere ictos undis concursantibus,
nisi quas terrestris pontus strages conciet,
aut forte Triton fuscina evertens specus
subter radices penitus undanti in freto
molem ex profundo saxeam ad caelum eruit.

Dubitat primo quae sit ea natura quam cernit ignotam; idemque iuvenibus visis auditoque nautico cantu:

[sicut][3] inciti atque alacres rostris perfremunt
delphini—

item alia multa—

[1] utque *Plasberg*: atque *A*, *B*, atqui *dett.*
[2] spiritu *Priscian*: strepitu.
[3] sicut *non habuit pr. B* (*Dieckhoff*).

[a] Born 170 B.C. The lines came from his *Medea*.

five planets that take place in the heavens every twenty-four hours, would any single native doubt that this orrery was the work of a rational being? XXXV. These thinkers however raise doubts about the world itself from which all things arise and have their being, and debate whether it is the product of chance or necessity of some sort, or of divine reason and intelligence; they think more highly of the achievement of Archimedes in making a model of the revolutions of the firmament than of that of nature in creating them, although the perfection of the original shows a craftsmanship many times as great as does the counterfeit. Just as the shepherd in Accius [a] who had never seen a ship before, on descrying in the distance from his mountain-top the strange vessel of the Argonauts, built by the gods, in his first amazement and alarm cries out:

so huge a bulk
Glides from the deep with the roar of a whistling wind:
Waves roll before, and eddies surge and swirl;
Hurtling headlong, it snorts and sprays the foam.
Now might one deem a bursting storm-cloud rolled,
Now that a rock flew skyward, flung aloft
By wind and storm, or whirling waterspout
Rose from the clash of wave with warring wave;
Save 'twere land-havoc wrought by ocean-flood,
Or Triton's trident, heaving up the roots
Of cavernous vaults beneath the billowy sea,
Hurled from the depth heaven-high a massy crag.

At first he wonders what the unknown creature that he beholds may be. Then when he sees the warriors and hears the singing of the sailors, he goes on:

the sportive dolphins swift
Forge snorting through the foam—

and so on and so on—

Silvani melo
consimilem ad aures cantum et auditum refert.

90 Ergo ut hic primo aspectu inanimum quiddam sensuque vacuum se putat cernere, post autem signis certioribus quale sit id de quo dubitaverat incipit suspicari, sic philosophi debuerunt, si forte eos primus aspectus mundi conturbaverat, postea, cum vidissent motus eius finitos et aequabiles omniaque ratis ordinibus moderata inmutabilique constantia, intellegere inesse aliquem non solum habitatorem in hac caelesti ac divina domo sed etiam rectorem et moderatorem et tamquam architectum tanti operis tantique muneris.

XXXVI. "Nunc autem mihi videntur ne suspicari quidem quanta sit admirabilitas caelestium rerum
91 atque terrestrium. Principio enim terra sita in media parte mundi circumfusa undique est hac animali spirabilique natura cui nomen est aer—Graecum illud quidem sed perceptum iam tamen usu a nostris ; tritum est enim pro Latino. Hunc rursus amplectitur inmensus aether, qui constat ex altissimis ignibus—mutuemur hoc quoque verbum, dicaturque tam aether Latine quam dicitur aer, etsi interpretatur Pacuvius :

hoc quod memoro nostri caelum, Graii perhibent aethera—

quasi vero non Graius hoc dicat ! 'At Latine loqui-

Brings to my ears and hearing such a tune
As old Silvanus piped.

90 Well then, even as the shepherd at the first sight thinks he sees some lifeless and inanimate object, but afterwards is led by clearer indications to begin to suspect the true nature of the thing about which he had previously been uncertain, so it would have been the proper course for the philosophers, if it so happened that the first sight of the world perplexed them, afterwards when they had seen its definite and regular motions, and all its phenomena controlled by fixed system and unchanging uniformity, to infer the presence not merely of an inhabitant of this celestial and divine abode, but also of a ruler and governor, the architect as it were of this mighty and monumental structure.

XXXVI. "But as it is they appear to me to have no suspicion even of the marvels of the celestial and
91 terrestrial creation. For in the first place the earth, which is situated in the centre of the world, is surrounded on all sides by this living and respirable substance named the air. 'Air' is a Greek word, but yet it has by this time been accepted in use by our race, and in fact passes current as Latin. The air in turn is embraced by the immeasurable aether, which consists of the most elevated portions of fire. The term 'aether' also we may borrow, and employ it like 'air' as a Latin word, though Pacuvius provides his readers with a translation:

What I speak of, we call heaven, but the Greeks it 'aether' call—

just as though the man who says this were not a Greek! 'Well, he is talking Latin,' you may say.

tur.' Si quidem nos non quasi Graece loquentem audiamus; docet idem alio loco:

Graiugena: de isto[1] aperit ipsa oratio.

92 Sed ad maiora redeamus. Ex aethere igitur innumerabiles flammae siderum exsistunt, quorum est princeps sol omnia clarissima luce conlustrans, multis partibus maior atque amplior quam terra universa, deinde reliqua sidera magnitudinibus inmensis. Atque hi tanti ignes tamque multi non modo nihil nocent terris rebusque terrestribus, sed ita prosunt ut si moti[2] loco sint conflagrare terras necesse sit a tantis ardoribus moderatione et temperatione sublata.

93 XXXVII. "Hic ego non mirer esse quemquam qui sibi persuadeat corpora quaedam solida atque individua vi[3] et gravitate ferri mundumque effici ornatissimum et pulcherrimum ex eorum corporum concursione fortuita? Hoc qui existimat fieri potuisse, non intellego cur non idem putet, si innumerabiles unius et viginti formae litterarum vel aureae vel qualeslibet aliquo coiciantur, posse ex iis in terram excussis annales Ennii ut deinceps legi possint effici; quod nescio an ne in uno quidem
94 versu possit tantum valere fortuna. Isti autem quem ad modum adseverant ex corpusculis non calore non qualitate aliqua (quam ποιότητα Graeci

[1] istoc *Bothe.* [2] moti *dett.*: mota *A*, *B.* [3] <sua> vi *Lambinus.*

Just so, if we won't suppose we are hearing him talk Greek ; in another passage Pacuvius tells us :

A Grecian born : my speech discloses that.

2 But let us return to more important matters. From aether then arise the innumerable fires of the heavenly bodies, chief of which is the sun, who illumines all things with most brilliant light, and is many times greater and vaster than the whole earth ; and after him the other stars of unmeasured magnitudes. And these vast and numerous fires not merely do no harm to the earth and to terrestrial things, but are actually beneficial, though with the qualification that were their positions altered, the earth would inevitably be burnt up by such enormous volumes of heat when uncontrolled and untempered.

The world's order cannot result from a fortuitous concourse of atoms.

3 XXXVII. "At this point must I not marvel that there should be anyone who can persuade himself that there are certain solid and indivisible particles of matter borne along by the force of gravity, and that the fortuitous collision of those particles produces this elaborate and beautiful world ? I cannot understand why he who considers it possible for this to have occurred should not also think that, if a countless number of copies of the one-and-twenty letters of the alphabet, made of gold or what you will, were thrown together into some receptacle and then shaken out on to the ground, it would be possible that they should produce the *Annals* of Ennius, all ready for the reader. I doubt whether chance could possibly succeed in
4 producing even a single verse ! Yet according to the assertion of your friends, that out of particles of matter not endowed with heat, nor with any 'quality' (the Greek term *poiotes*), nor with sense, but colliding

vocant) non sensu praeditis sed concurrentibus temere atque casu mundum esse perfectum, vel innumerabiles potius in omni puncto temporis alios nasci alios interire,—quodsi mundum efficere potest concursus atomorum, cur porticum cur templum cur domum cur urbem non potest, quae sunt minus operosa et multo[1] quidem [faciliora][2]? Certe ita temere de mundo effutiunt ut mihi quidem numquam hunc admirabilem caeli ornatum (qui locus est proximus) suspexisse videantur. Praeclare ergo Aristoteles
95 'Si essent' inquit 'qui sub terra semper habitavissent bonis et inlustribus domiciliis quae essent ornata signis atque picturis instructaque rebus iis omnibus quibus abundant ii qui beati putantur, nec tamen exissent umquam supra terram, accepissent autem fama et auditione esse quoddam numen et vim deorum, deinde aliquo tempore patefactis terrae faucibus ex illis abditis sedibus evadere in haec loca quae nos incolimus atque exire potuissent: cum repente terram et maria caelumque vidissent, nubium magnitudinem ventorumque vim cognovissent aspexissentque solem eiusque cum magnitudinem pulchritudinemque tum etiam efficientiam cognovissent, quod is diem efficeret toto caelo luce diffusa, cum autem terras nox opacasset, tum caelum totum cernerent astris distinctum et ornatum lunaeque luminum varietatem tum crescentis tum senescentis eorumque omnium ortus et occasus atque in omni aeternitate ratos inmutabilosque cursus — quae cum viderent, profecto et esse

[1] multa *B*. [2] *secl. Madvig.*

[a] In the lost dialogue *De Philosophia*, see i. 33 n.

together at haphazard and by chance, the world has emerged complete, or rather a countless number of worlds are some of them being born and some perishing at every moment of time—yet if the clash of atoms can create a world, why can it not produce a colonnade, a temple, a house, a city, which are less and indeed much less difficult things to make? The fact is, they indulge in such random babbling about the world that for my part I cannot think that they have ever looked up at this marvellously beautiful sky—which is my next topic. So Aristotle says[a] brilliantly: 'If there were beings who had always lived beneath the earth, in comfortable, well-lit dwellings, decorated with statues and pictures and furnished with all the luxuries enjoyed by persons thought to be supremely happy, and who though they had never come forth above the ground had learnt by report and by hearsay of the existence of certain deities or divine powers; and then if at some time the jaws of the earth were opened and they were able to escape from their hidden abode and to come forth into the regions which we inhabit; when they suddenly had sight of the earth and the seas and the sky, and came to know of the vast clouds and mighty winds, and beheld the sun, and realized not only its size and beauty but also its potency in causing the day by shedding light over all the sky, and, after night had darkened the earth, they then saw the whole sky spangled and adorned with stars, and the changing phases of the moon's light, now waxing and now waning, and the risings and settings of all these heavenly bodies and their courses fixed and changeless throughout all eternity,—when they saw these things, surely they would think that the gods exist

Only familiarity blinds us to the divine marvels of nature.

deos et haec tanta opera deorum esse arbitrarentur.'

96 XXXVIII. Atque haec quidem ille; nos autem tenebras cogitemus tantas quantae quondam eruptione Aetnaeorum ignium finitimas regiones obscuravisse dicuntur, ut per biduum nemo hominem homo agnosceret, cum autem tertio die sol inluxisset tum ut revixisse sibi viderentur: quodsi hoc idem ex aeternis tenebris contingeret ut subito lucem aspiceremus, quaenam species caeli videretur? Sed adsiduitate cotidiana et consuetudine oculorum adsuescunt animi, neque admirantur neque requirunt rationes earum rerum quas semper vident, proinde quasi novitas nos magis quam magnitudo rerum debeat
97 ad exquirendas causas excitare. Quis enim hunc hominem dixerit qui, cum tam certos caeli motus tam ratos astrorum ordines tamque inter se omnia conexa et apta viderit, neget in his ullam inesse rationem, eaque casu fieri dicat quae quanto consilio gerantur nullo consilio adsequi possumus? An, cum machinatione quadam moveri aliquid videmus, ut sphaeram ut horas ut alia permulta, non dubitamus quin illa opera sint rationis, cum autem impetum caeli cum admirabili celeritate moveri vertique videamus[1] constantissime conficientem vicissitudines anniversarias cum summa salute et conservatione rerum omnium, dubitamus quin ea

[1] videmus *dett.*

and that these mighty marvels are their handiwork.'

96 XXXVIII. Thus far Aristotle; let us for our part imagine a darkness as dense as that which is said to have once covered the neighbouring districts on the occasion of an eruption of the volcano Etna, so that for two days no man could recognize his fellow, and when on the third day the sun shone upon them, they felt as if they had come to life again: well, suppose that after darkness had prevailed from the beginning of time, it similarly happened to ourselves suddenly to behold the light of day, what should we think of the splendour of the heavens? But daily recurrence and habit familiarize our minds with the sight, and we feel no surprise or curiosity as to the reasons for things that we see always; just as if it were the novelty and not rather the importance of phenomena that ought to arouse us to inquire into their causes.

97 Who would not deny the name of human being to a man who, on seeing the regular motions of the heaven and the fixed order of the stars and the accurate interconnexion and interrelation of all things, can deny that these things possess any rational design, and can maintain that phenomena, the wisdom of whose ordering transcends the capacity of our wisdom to understand it, take place by chance? When we see something moved by machinery, like an orrery or clock or many other such things, we do not doubt that these contrivances are the work of reason; when therefore we behold the whole compass of the heaven moving with revolutions of marvellous velocity and executing with perfect regularity the annual changes of the seasons with absolute safety and security for all things, how can we doubt that all this is effected

non solum ratione fiant sed etiam excellenti divinaque ratione?

98 "Licet enim iam remota subtilitate disputandi oculis quodam modo contemplari pulchritudinem rerum earum quas divina providentia dicimus constitutas. XXXIX. Ac principio terra universa cernatur, locata in media sede mundi, solida et globosa et undique ipsa in sese nutibus suis conglobata, vestita floribus herbis arboribus frugibus, quorum omnium incredibilis multitudo insatiabili varietate distinguitur. Adde huc fontium gelidas perennitates, liquores perlucidos amnium, riparum vestitus viridissimos, speluncarum concavas altitudines, saxorum asperitates, inpendentium montium altitudines inmensitatesque camporum; adde etiam reconditas auri
99 argentique venas infinitamque vim marmoris. Quae vero et quam varia genera bestiarum vel cicurum vel ferarum! qui volucrium lapsus atque cantus! qui pecudum pastus! quae vita silvestrium! Quid iam de hominum genere dicam? qui quasi cultores terrae constituti non patiuntur eam nec inmanitate beluarum efferari nec stirpium asperitate vastari, quorumque operibus agri, insulae litoraque collucent distincta tectis et urbibus. Quae si ut animis sic oculis videre possemus, nemo cunctam intuens
100 terram de divina ratione dubitaret. At vero quanta maris est pulchritudo! quae species universi! quae multitudo et varietas insularum! quae amoenitates orarum ac litorum! quot genera quamque disparia partim submersarum, partim fluitantium et

not merely by reason, but by a reason that is transcendent and divine?

"For we may now put aside elaborate argument and gaze as it were with our eyes upon the beauty of the creations of divine providence, as we declare them to be. XXXIX. And first let us behold the whole earth, situated in the centre of the world, a solid spherical mass gathered into a globe by the natural gravitation of all its parts, clothed with flowers and grass and trees and corn, forms of vegetation all of them incredibly numerous and inexhaustibly varied and diverse. Add to these cool fountains ever flowing, transparent streams and rivers, their banks clad in brighest verdure, deep vaulted caverns, craggy rocks, sheer mountain heights and plains of immeasurable extent: add also the hidden veins of gold and silver, and marble in unlimited quantity. Think of all the various species of animals, both tame and wild! think of the flights and songs of birds! of the pastures filled with cattle, and the teeming life of the woodlands! Then why need I speak of the race of men? who are as it were the appointed tillers of the soil, and who suffer it not to become a savage haunt of monstrous beasts of prey nor a barren waste of thickets and brambles, and whose industry diversifies and adorns the lands and islands and coasts with houses and cities. Could we but behold these things with our eyes as we can picture them in our minds, no one taking in the whole earth at one view could doubt the divine reason. Then how great is the beauty of the sea! how glorious the aspect of its vast expanse! how many and how diverse its islands! how lovely the scenery of its coasts and shores! how numerous and how different the species of marine animals, some dwelling in

(3) Detailed review of the wonders of nature (§§ 98–153).

The earth and the other elements

innantium beluarum, partim ad saxa nativis testis inhaerentium! Ipsum autem mare sic terram appetens litoribus alludit ut una ex duabus naturis conflata
101 videatur. Exin mari finitumus aer die et nocte distinguitur, isque tum fusus et extenuatus sublime fertur, tum autem concretus in nubes cogitur umoremque colligens terram auget imbribus, tum effluens huc et illuc ventos efficit. Idem annuas frigorum et calorum facit varietates, idemque et volatus alitum sustinet et spiritu[1] ductus alit et sustentat animantes. XL. Restat ultimus et a domiciliis nostris altissimus omnia cingens et coercens caeli complexus, qui idem aether vocatur, extrema ora et determinatio mundi, in quo cum admirabilitate maxima igneae formae
102 cursus ordinatos definiunt. E quibus sol, cuius magnitudine multis partibus terra superatur, circum eam ipsam volvitur, isque oriens et occidens diem noctemque conficit, et modo accedens tum autem recedens binas in singulis annis reversiones ab extremo contrarias facit, quarum in intervallo tum quasi tristitia quadam contrahit terram, tum vicissim laetificat ut
103 cum caelo hilarata videatur. Luna autem, quae est, ut ostendunt mathematici, maior quam dimidia pars terrae, isdem spatiis vagatur quibus sol, sed tum congrediens cum sole tum digrediens et eam lucem quam a sole accepit mittit in terras et varias ipsa

[1] spiritu *det.*: spiritus.

the depths, some floating and swimming on the surface, some clinging in their own shells to the rocks! And the sea itself, yearning for the earth, sports against her shores in such a fashion that the two
101 elements appear to be fused into one. Next the air bordering on the sea undergoes the alternations of day and night, and now rises upward melted and rarefied, now is condensed and compressed into clouds and gathering moisture enriches the earth with rain, now flows forth in currents to and fro and produces winds. Likewise it causes the yearly variations of cold and heat, and it also both supports the flight of birds and inhaled by breathing nourishes and sustains the animal race. XL. There remains the element that is most distant and highest removed from our abodes, the all-engirdling, all-confining circuit of the sky, also named the aether, the farthest coast and frontier of the world, wherein those fiery shapes most
102 marvellously trace out their ordered courses. Of these the sun, which many times surpasses the earth in magnitude, revolves about her, and by his rising and setting causes day and night, and now approaching, then again retiring, twice each year makes returns in opposite directions from his farthest point, and in the period of those returns at one time causes the face of the earth as it were to contract with a gloomy frown, and at another restores her to gladness till she seems to smile in sympathy with the sky.
103 Again the moon, which is, as the mathematicians prove, more than half the size of the earth, roams in the same courses as the sun, but at one time converging with the sun and at another diverging from it, both bestows upon the earth the light that it has borrowed from the sun and itself undergoes divers

The sun, moon and planets.

lucis mutationes habet, atque etiam tum subiecta atque opposita soli radios eius et lumen obscurat, tum ipsa incidens in umbram terrae, cum est e regione solis, interpositu interiectuque terrae repente deficit. Isdemque spatiis eae stellae quas vagas dicimus circum terram feruntur eodemque modo oriuntur et occidunt, quarum motus tum incitantur, tum retardantur,
104 saepe etiam insistunt. Quo spectaculo nihil potest admirabilius esse, nihil pulchrius. Sequitur stellarum inerrantium maxima multitudo, quarum ita discripta distinctio est ut ex notarum figurarum similitudine nomina invenerint."[1] XLI. Atque hoc loco me intuens: " Utar," inquit, " carminibus Arateis, quae a te admodum adulescentulo conversa ita me delectant quia Latina sunt ut multa ex iis memoria teneam. Ergo, ut oculis adsidue videmus, sine ulla mutatione aut varietate

cetera labuntur celeri caelestia motu
cum caeloque simul noctesque diesque feruntur,

105 quorum contemplatione nullius expleri potest animus naturae constantiam videre cupientis;

extremusque adeo duplici de cardine vertex
dicitur esse polus.

Hunc circum Arctoe duae feruntur numquam occidentes;

ex his altera apud Graios Cynosura vocatur,
altera dicitur esse Helice,

[1] *huc c. xliii. init.* atque ita . . . appareat *Mayor transponit.*

[a] Aratus of Soli in Cilicia, *fl.* late 3rd cent. B.C. at the Macedonian court, versified the astronomy of Plato's pupil Eudoxus, and weather-forecasts, in two poems, *Phaenomena* and *Diosemeia*. Of Cicero's translation of the former two-thirds, of the latter (*Prognostica*) a few lines survive.

changes of its light, and also at one time is in conjunction and hides the sun, darkening the light of its rays, at another itself comes into the shadow of the earth, being opposite to the sun, and owing to the interposition and interference of the earth is suddenly extinguished. And the so-called wandering stars (planets) travel in the same courses round the earth, and rise and set in the same way, with motions now accelerated, now retarded, and sometimes even ceasing altogether. Nothing can be more marvellous or more beautiful than this spectacle. Next comes the vast multitude of the fixed stars, grouped in constellations so clearly defined that they have received names derived from their resemblance to familiar objects." XLI. Here he looked at me and said, "I will make use of the poems of Aratus,[a] as translated by yourself when quite a young man, which because of their Latin dress give me such pleasure that I retain many of them in memory. Well then, as we continually see with our own eyes, without any change or variation

The constellations.

> Swiftly the other heavenly bodies glide,
> All day and night travelling with the sky,

and no one who loves to contemplate the uniformity of nature can ever be tired of gazing at them.

> The furthest tip of either axle-end
> Is called the pole.

Round the pole circle the two Bears, which never set;

> One of these twain the Greeks call Cynosure,[b]
> The other Helicē[c] is named;

[b] 'Dog's tail,' perhaps the curve of the three stars.
[c] 'The spiral,' perhaps of its motion round the pole.

cuius quidem clarissimas stellas totis noctibus cernimus,

quas nostri Septem soliti vocitare Triones;

106 paribusque[1] stellis similiter distinctis eundem caeli verticem lustrat parva Cynosura:

hac fidunt duce nocturna Phoenices in alto;
sed prior illa magis stellis distincta refulget
et late prima confestim a nocte videtur,
haec vero parva est, sed nautis usus in hac est,
nam cursu interiore brevi convertitur orbe.

XLII. Et quo sit earum stellarum admirabilior aspectus,

has inter, veluti rapido cum gurgite flumen,
torvus Draco serpit subter superaque revolvens
sese conficiensque sinus e corpore flexos.

107 Eius cum totius est praeclara species, <tum>[2] in primis aspicienda est figura capitis atque ardor oculorum:

huic non una modo caput ornans stella relucet,
verum tempora sunt duplici fulgore notata
e trucibusque oculis duo fervida lumina flagrant
atque uno mentum radianti sidere lucet;
obstipum caput at tereti cervice reflexum
obtutum in cauda maioris figere dicas.

108 Et reliquum quidem corpus Draconis totis noctibus cernimus:

hoc caput hic paulum sese subito aequore condit,[3]
ortus ubi atque obitus partem[4] admiscetur in unam.[5]

Id autem caput

attingens defessa velut maerentis imago
vertitur,

[1] propiusque *? Plasberg.* [2] *add. Manutius.*
[3] subito aequore condit *Grotius*: subitoque recondit.
[4] partem *det.*: partim *A*, *B*, parti *Cochanovius.*
[5] unam *H. Stephanus*: una.

[a] Said to mean 'threshing-oxen.'

and the latter's extremely bright stars, visible to us all night long,

> Our countrymen the Seven Triones [a] call ;

6 and the little Cynosure consists of an equal number of stars similarly grouped, and revolves round the same pole :

> Phoenician sailors place in this their trust
> To guide their course by night ; albeit the other
> Shines out before and with more radiant stars
> At earliest night-fall far and wide is seen,
> Yet small though this one is, the mariner
> On this relies, since it revolves upon
> An inner circle and a shorter path.

XLII. Also the further to enhance the beauty of those constellations,

> Between them, like a river flowing swift,
> The fierce-eyed Serpent winds ; in sinuous coils
> Over and under twines his snaky frame.

7 His whole appearance is very remarkable, but the most striking part of him is the shape of his head and the brilliance of his eyes :

> No single shining star his head adorns,
> His brows are by a double radiance marked,
> And from his cruel eyes two lights flash out,
> The while his chin gleams with one flashing star ;
> His graceful neck is bent, his head reclined,
> As if at gaze upon the Great Bear's tail.

8 And while the rest of the Serpent's body is visible all night long,

> This head a moment sinks beneath the sea,
> Where meet its setting and its rise in one.

Next to its head however

> The weary figure of a man in sorrow
> Revolves,

quam quidem Graeci

Engonasin vocitant, genibus quia nixa feratur.
hic illa eximio posita est fulgore Corona.

Atque haec quidem a tergo, propter caput autem Anguitenens,

109 quem claro perhibent Ophiuchum nomine Graii.
hic pressu duplici palmarum continet Anguem,
atque eius ipse manet religatus corpore torto,
namque virum medium serpens sub pectora cingit.
ille tamen nitens graviter vestigia ponit
atque oculos urguet pedibus pectusque Nepaï.

Septentriones autem sequitur

Arctophylax, vulgo qui dicitur esse Bootes,
quod quasi temoni adiunctam prae se quatit Arctum.

110 Dein quae sequuntur[1]: huic enim[2] Booti

subter praecordia fixa videtur
stella micans radiis, Arcturus nomine claro,

cuius <pedibus>[3] subiecta fertur

spicum inlustre tenens splendenti corpore Virgo.

XLIII. Atque ita dimetata signa sunt ut in tantis discriptionibus divina sollertia appareat[4]:

et natos Geminos invises sub caput Arcti,
subiectus mediae est Cancer, pedibusque tenetur
magnus Leo tremulam quatiens e corpore flammam.

Auriga

sub laeva Geminorum obductus parte feretur;
adversum caput huic Helicae truculenta tuetur,
at Capra laevum umerum clara obtinet.

[Tum quae sequuntur :][5]

verum haec est magno atque inlustri praedita signo,
contra Haedi exiguum iaciunt mortalibus ignem.

[1] dein . . . sequuntur *Mayor tr. post* Virgo *infra.*
[2] enim *om. Mayor.* [3] *add. Davies.*
[4] atque . . . appareat *Mayor in c. xl. fin. tr.* [5] *Heindorf.*

[a] Perhaps the harvest began under this sign.

which the Greeks

> Engónasin call, as travelling "on his knees."
> Here is the Crown, of radiance supreme.

This is in the rear of the Serpent, while at its head is the Serpent-holder,

109
> By Greeks called Ophiúchus, famous name!
> Firm between both his hands he "holds the Snake,"
> Himself in bondage by its body held,
> For serpent round the waist engirdles man.
> Yet treads he firm and presses all his weight,
> Trampling upon the Scorpion's eyes and breast.

After the Septentriones comes

> The Bear-ward, commonly Boötes called,
> Because he drives the Bear yoked to a pole.

110 And then the following lines: for with this Boötes

> beneath his bosom fixed appears
> A glittering star, Arcturus, famous name,

and below his feet moves

> The Virgin bright, holding her ear of corn •
> Resplendent.

XLIII. And the constellations are so accurately spaced out that their vast and ordered array clearly displays the skill of a divine creator:

> By the Bear's head you will descry the Twins,
> Beneath its belly the Crab, and in its claws
> The Lion's bulk emits a twinkling ray.

The Charioteer

> Hidden beneath the Twins' left flank will glide;
> Him Helicē confronts with aspect fierce;
> At his left shoulder the bright She-goat stands.

[And then the following:]

> A constellation vast and brilliant she,
> Whereas the Kids emit a scanty light
> Upon mankind.

Cuius sub pedibus

corniger est valido conixus[1] corpore Taurus.

111 Eius caput stellis conspersum est frequentibus:

has Graeci stellas Hyadas vocitare suērunt,

a pluendo (ὕειν enim est pluere), nostri imperite Suculas, quasi a subus essent, non ab imbribus nominatae. Minorem autem Septentrionem Cepheus passis palmis a tergo[2] subsequitur:

namque ipsum ad tergum Cynosurae vertitur Arcti.

Hunc antecedit

obscura specie stellarum Cassiepia.
hanc autem inlustri versatur corpore propter
Andromeda aufugiens aspectum maesta parentis.
huic Equus ille iubam quatiens fulgore micanti
summum contingit caput alvo, stellaque iungens
una tenet duplices communi lumine formas
aeternum ex astris cupiens conectere nodum.
exin contortis Aries cum cornibus haeret;

quem propter

Pisces, quorum alter paulum praelabitur ante
et magis horriferis Aquilonis tangitur auris.

112 XLIV. Ad pedes Andromedae Perseus describitur,

quem summa <a>[3] regione aquilonis flamina pulsant;

cuius

propter laevum genus[4] omni ex parte locatas
parvas[5] Vergilias tenui cum luce videbis.
inde Fides posita et leviter convexa videtur,
inde est ales Avis lato sub tegmine caeli.

Capiti autem Equi proxima est Aquarii dextra totusque deinceps Aquarius.

[1] connixus *dett.*: conexus *A*, *B*.
[2] terga *A*, *B*, <post> terga *Plasberg*.
[3] *Baiter*: ab *B corr.*
[4] genus *B corr.*: genum.
[5] omni . . . parvas *B corr.*: *om. cett.*

[a] See above, § 105.

Beneath her feet

Crouches the hornéd Bull, a mighty frame.

His head is bespangled with a multitude of stars:

The Greeks were wont to call them Hyades,

from their bringing rain, the Greek for which is *hyein*, while our nation stupidly names them the Sucking-pigs, as though the name Hyades were derived from the word for 'pig' and not from 'rain.' Behind the Lesser Septentrio follows Cepheus, with open hands outstretched;

For close behind the Bear, the Cynosure,[a]
He wheels.

Before him comes

Cassiepía with her darkling stars,
And next to her roams a bright shape, the sad
Andromeda, shunning her mother's sight.
The belly of the Horse touches her head,
Proudly he tosses high his glittering mane;
One common star holds their twin shapes conjoint
And constellations linked indissolubly.
Close by them stands the Ram with wreathéd horns;

and next to him

The Fishes gliding, one some space in front
And nearer to the North Wind's shuddering breath.

XLIV. At the feet of Andromeda Perseus is outlined,

Assailed by all the zenith's northern blasts:

and by him

at his left knee placed on every side
The tiny Pleiads dim you will descry.
And, slightly sloping, next the Lyre is seen,
Next the winged Bird 'neath heaven's wide canopy.

Close to the Horse's head is the right hand of Aquarius, and then his whole figure.

tum gelidum valido de pectore frigus anhelans
corpore semifero magno Capricornus in orbe;
quem cum perpetuo vestivit lumine Titan,
brumali flectens contorquet tempore currum.

113 Hic autem aspicitur

ut sese ostendens emergit Scorpios alte
posteriore trahens plexum[1] vi corporis Arcum,
quem propter nitens pinnis convolvitur Ales,
at propter se Aquila ardenti cum corpore portat.

Deinde Delphinus,

exinde Orion obliquo corpore nitens.

114 Quem subsequens

fervidus ille Canis stellarum luce refulget.

Post Lepus subsequitur,

curriculum numquam defesso corpore sedans;
at Canis ad caudam serpens prolabitur Argo.
hanc Aries tegit et squamoso corpore Pisces
Fluminis inlustri tangentem corpore[2] ripas.

Quem longe serpentem et manantem aspicies,

proceraque Vincla videbis,
quae retinent Pisces caudarum a parte locata . . .
inde Nepae cernes propter fulgentis acumen
Aram, quam flatu permulcet spiritus Austri.

Propterque Centaurus

cedit Equi partis properans subiungere Chelis.
hic dextram porgens, quadrupes qua vasta tenetur,
tendit et inlustrem truculentus cedit ad Aram;
hic sese infernis e partibus erigit Hydra,

cuius longe corpus est fusum,

in medioque sinu fulgens Cratera relucet,
extremam nitens plumato corpore Corvus
rostro tundit; et hic Geminis est ille sub ipsis
Ante-Canem,[3] Προκύων Graio qui nomine fertur.

[1] flexum *A corr.*, *B corr.* [2] pectore *Heinsius.*
[3] Antecanis *Lambinus.*

Next in the mighty zone comes Capricorn,
Half-brute, half-man ; his mighty bosom breathes
An icy chill ; and when the Titan sun
Arrayeth him with never-ceasing light,
He turns his car to climb the wintry sky.

13 Here we behold

How there appears the Scorpion rising high,
His mighty tail trailing the bended Bow ;
Near which on soaring pinions wheels the Bird
And near to this the burning Eagle flies.

Then the Dolphin,

And then Orion slopes his stooping frame.

14 Following him

The glowing Dog-star radiantly shines.

After this follows the Hare,

Who never resteth weary from her race ;
At the Dog's tail meandering Argo glides.
Her the Ram covers, and the scaly Fishes,
And her bright breast touches the River's[a] banks.

Its long winding current you will observe,

And in the zenith you will see the Chains
That bind the Fishes, hanging at their tails. . . .
Then you'll descry, near the bright Scorpion's sting,
The Altar, fanned by Auster's gentle breath.

And by it the Centaur

Proceeds, in haste to join the Horse's parts
Unto the Claws ; extending his right hand,
That grasps the mighty beast, he marches on
And grimly strides towards the Altar bright.
Here Hydra rises from the nether realms,

her body widely outstretched ;

And in her midmost coil the Wine-bowl gleams,
While pressing at her tail the feathered Crow
Pecks with his beak ; and here, hard by the Twins,
The Hound's Forerunner, in Greek named *Prokyon*.

[a] Called Eridanus, and identified with the Po or the Nile.

115 Haec omnis discriptio siderum atque hic tantus caeli ornatus ex corporibus huc et illuc casu et temere cursantibus potuisse effici cuiquam sano videri potest? an[1] vero alia quae natura mentis et rationis expers haec efficere potuit? quae non modo ut fierent ratione eguerunt sed intellegi qualia sint sine summa ratione non possunt.

XLV. "Nec vero haec solum admirabilia, sed nihil maius quam quod ita stabilis est mundus atque ita cohaeret, ad permanendum ut nihil ne excogitari quidem possit aptius. Omnes enim partes eius undique medium locum capessentes nituntur aequaliter. Maxime autem corpora inter se iuncta permanent cum quasi quodam vinculo circumdato colligantur; quod facit ea natura quae per omnem mundum omnia mente et ratione conficiens funditur
116 et ad medium rapit et convertit extrema. Quocirca si mundus globosus est ob eamque causam omnes eius partes undique aequabiles ipsae per se atque inter se continentur, contingere idem terrae necesse est, ut omnibus eius partibus in medium vergentibus (id autem medium infimum in sphaera est) nihil interrumpat quo labefactari possit tanta contentio gravitatis et ponderum. Eademque ratione mare, cum supra terram sit, medium tamen terrae locum expetens conglobatur undique aequabiliter neque
117 redundat umquam neque effunditur. Huic autem continens aër fertur ille quidem levitate sublimis,[2] sed tamen in omnes partes se ipse fundit; itaque

[1] an *G*, aut *cett.*
[2] sublimis *B*, sublimi *cett.*, sublime *Orelli*.

Can any sane person believe that all this array of stars and this vast celestial adornment could have been created out of atoms rushing to and fro fortuitously and at random? or could any other being devoid of intelligence and reason have created them? Not merely did their creation postulate intelligence, but it is impossible to understand their nature without intelligence of a high order.

The world and its parts held together by centripetal force.

XLV. "But not only are these things marvellous, but nothing is more remarkable than the stability and coherence of the world, which is such that it is impossible even to imagine anything better adapted to endure. For all its parts in every direction gravitate with a uniform pressure towards the centre. Moreover bodies conjoined maintain their union most permanently when they have some bond encompassing them to bind them together; and this function is fulfilled by that rational and intelligent substance which pervades the whole world as the efficient cause of all things and which draws and collects the outermost particles towards the centre. Hence if the world is round and therefore all its parts are held together by and with each other in universal equilibrium, the same must be the case with the earth, so that all its parts must converge towards the centre (which in a sphere is the lowest point) without anything to break the continuity and so threaten its vast complex of gravitational forces and masses with dissolution. And on the same principle the sea, although above the earth, nevertheless seeks the earth's centre and so is massed into a sphere uniform on all sides, and never floods its bounds and overflows. Its neighbour the air travels upward it is true in virtue of its lightness, but at the same time spreads horizontally in all

et mari continuatus et iunctus est et natura fertur ad caelum, cuius tenuitate et calore temperatus vitalem et salutarem spiritum praebet animantibus. Quem complexa summa pars caeli, quae aetheria dicitur, et suum retinet ardorem tenuem et nulla admixtione concretum et cum aëris extremitate coniungitur. XLVI. In aethere autem astra volvuntur, quae se et nisu suo conglobata continent et forma ipsa figuraque sua momenta sustentant; sunt enim rotunda, quibus formis, ut ante dixisse videor,
118 minime noceri potest. Sunt autem stellae natura flammeae, quocirca terrae maris aquarum[1] vaporibus aluntur iis qui a sole ex agris tepefactis et ex aquis excitantur; quibus altae renovataeque stellae atque omnis aether refundunt eadem et rursum trahunt indidem, nihil ut fere intereat aut admodum paululum quod astrorum ignis et aetheris flamma consumit. Ex quo eventurum nostri putant id de quo Panaetium addubitare dicebant, ut ad extremum omnis mundus ignesceret, cum umore consumpto neque terra ali posset nec remearet aër, cuius ortus aqua omni exhausta esse non posset; ita relinqui nihil praeter ignem, a quo rursum animante ac deo renovatio

[1] aquarumque reliquarum *Probus*, *Plasberg*.

[a] See § 47.

directions; and thus while contiguous and conjoined with the sea it has a natural tendency to rise to the sky, and by receiving an admixture of the sky's tenuity and heat furnishes to living creatures the breath of life and health. The air is enfolded by the highest part of the sky, termed the ethereal part; this both retains its own tenuous warmth uncongealed by any admixture and unites with the outer surface of the air. XLVI. In the aether the stars revolve in their courses; these maintain their spherical form by their own internal gravitation, and also sustain their motions by virtue of their very shape and conformation; for they are round, and this is the shape, as I believe I remarked before,[a] that is least capable of
18 receiving injury. But the stars are of a fiery substance, and for this reason they are nourished by the vapours of the earth, the sea and the waters, which are raised up by the sun out of the fields which it warms and out of the waters; and when nourished and renewed by these vapours the stars and the whole aether shed them back again, and then once more draw them up from the same source, with the loss of none of their matter, or only of an extremely small part which is consumed by the fire of the stars and the flame of the aether. As a consequence of this, so our school believe, though it used to be said that Panaetius questioned the doctrine, there will ultimately occur a conflagration of the whole world, because when the moisture has been used up neither can the earth be nourished nor will the air continue to flow, being unable to rise upward after it has drunk up all the water; thus nothing will remain but fire, by which, as a living being and a god, once again a new world may be created and the ordered universe

The cyclical regeneration of the earth.

119 mundi fieret atque idem ornatus oreretur. Nolo in stellarum ratione multus vobis videri, maximeque earum quae errare dicuntur; quarum tantus est concentus ex dissimillimis motibus ut, cum summa Saturni refrigeret, media Martis incendat, his interiecta Iovis inlustret et temperet infraque Martem duae soli oboediant, ipse sol mundum omnem sua luce compleat ab eoque luna inluminata graviditates et partus adferat maturitatesque gignendi. Quae copulatio rerum et quasi consentiens ad mundi incolumitatem coagmentatio naturae quem non movet, hunc horum nihil umquam reputavisse certo scio.

120 XLVII. "Age ut a caelestibus rebus ad terrestres veniamus, quid est in his in quo non naturae ratio intellegentis appareat? Principio eorum quae gignuntur e terra stirpes et stabilitatem dant iis quae sustinent et e terra sucum trahunt quo alantur ea quae radicibus continentur; obducunturque libro aut cortice trunci quo sint a frigoribus et caloribus tutiores. Iam vero vites sic claviculis adminicula tamquam manibus adprehendunt atque ita se erigunt ut animantes. Quin etiam a caulibus,[1] si propter sati sint, ut a pestiferis et nocentibus refugere dicuntur nec eos ulla ex parte contingere.

121 Animantium vero quanta varietas est, quanta ad eam rem vis ut in suo quaeque genere permaneat! Quarum aliae coriis tectae sunt aliae villis vestitae aliae spinis hirsutae; pluma alias alias

[1] caulibus *det.*: caulibus brassicis *A*, *B*, c. brassicae *Plasberg*.

19 be restored as before. I would not have you think that I dwell too long upon astronomy, and particularly upon the system of the stars called planets; these with the most diverse movements work in such mutual harmony that the uppermost, that of Saturn, has a cooling influence, the middle planet, that of Mars, imparts heat, the one between them, that of Jove, gives light and a moderate warmth, while the two beneath Mars obey the sun, and the sun itself fills all the world with light, and also illuminates the moon, which is the source of conception and birth and of growth and maturity. If any man is not impressed by this co-ordination of things and this harmonious combination of nature to secure the preservation of the world, I know for certain that he has never given any consideration to these matters.

Co-operation of the planets.

20 XLVII. "To come now from things celestial to things terrestrial, which is there among these latter which does not clearly display the rational design of an intelligent being? In the first place, with the vegetation that springs from the earth, the stocks both give stability to the parts which they sustain and draw from the ground the sap to nourish the parts upheld by the roots; and the trunks are covered with bark or rind, the better to protect them against cold and heat. Again the vines cling to their props with their tendrils as with hands, and thus raise themselves erect like animals. Nay more, it is said that if planted near cabbages they shun them like pestilential and noxious things, and will not touch them at any
21 point. Again what a variety there is of animals, and what capacity they possess of persisting true to their various kinds! Some of them are protected by hides, others are clothed with fleeces, others bristle

The wonders of vegetable life.

The wonders of animal life: its adaptation for the preservation of the individual.

squama videmus obductas, alias esse cornibus armatas, alias habere effugia pinnarum. Pastum autem animantibus large et copiose natura eum qui cuique aptus erat comparavit. Enumerare possum ad eum pastum capessendum conficiendumque quae sit in figuris animantium et quam sollers subtilisque discriptio partium quamque admirabilis fabrica membrorum. Omnia enim, quae quidem intus inclusa sunt, ita nata atque ita locata sunt ut nihil eorum supervacaneum sit, nihil ad vitam retinendam
122 non necessarium. Dedit autem eadem natura beluis et sensum et appetitum, ut altero conatum haberent ad naturales pastus capessendos, altero secernerent pestifera a salutaribus. Iam vero alia animalia gradiendo alia serpendo ad pastum accedunt, alia volando alia nando, cibumque partim oris hiatu et dentibus ipsis capessunt, partim unguium tenacitate arripiunt, partim aduncitate rostrorum, alia sugunt alia carpunt alia vorant alia mandunt. Atque etiam aliorum ea est humilitas ut cibum terrestrem rostris
123 facile contingant; quae autem altiora sunt, ut anseres ut cygni ut grues ut cameli, adiuvantur proceritate collorum; manus etiam data elephanto est, quia propter magnitudinem corporis difficiles aditus habebat ad pastum. XLVIII. At quibus bestiis erat is cibus ut alius[1] generis bestiis[2] vescerentur, aut vires natura dedit aut celeritatem. Data est

[1] alius *det.*: aliis.
[2] bestiis *dett.*: escis *A*, *B* (animalis generis escis ? *Plasberg*).

with spines; some we see covered with feathers, some with scales, some armed with horns, some equipped with wings to escape their foes. Nature, however, has provided with bounteous plenty for each species of animal that food which is suited to it. I might show in detail what provision has been made in the forms of the animals for appropriating and assimilating this food, how skilful and exact is the disposition of the various parts, how marvellous the structure of the limbs. For all the organs, at least those contained within the body, are so formed and so placed that none of them is superfluous or not neces-
2 sary for the preservation of life. But nature has also bestowed upon the beasts both sensation and desire, the one to arouse in them the impulse to appropriate their natural foods, the other to enable them to distinguish things harmful from things wholesome. Again, some animals approach their food by walking, some by crawling, some by flying, some by swimming; and some seize their nutriment with their gaping mouth and with the teeth themselves, others snatch it in the grasp of their claws, others with their curved beaks, some suck, others graze, some swallow it whole, others chew it. Also some are of such lowly stature that they easily reach their food upon the
3 ground with their jaws; whereas the taller species, such as geese, swans, cranes and camels, are aided by the length of their necks; the elephant is even provided with a hand, because his body is so large that it was difficult for him to reach his food. XLVIII. Those beasts on the other hand whose mode of sustenance was to feed on animals of another species received from nature the gift either of strength or swiftness. Upon certain creatures

quibusdam etiam machinatio quaedam atque sollertia, ut in araneolis aliae quasi rete texunt, ut si quid inhaeserit conficiant, aliae autem ut[1] . . . ex inopinato observant et si quid incidit arripiunt idque consumunt. Pina vero (sic enim Graece dicitur) duabus grandibus patula conchis cum parva squilla quasi societatem coit comparandi cibi, itaque cum pisciculi parvi in concham hiantem innataverunt, tum admonita <a>[2] squilla[3] pina morsu[4] comprimit conchas; sic dissimillimis bestiolis communiter cibus quaeritur.
124 In quo admirandum est congressune aliquo inter se an iam inde ab ortu natura ipsa congregatae sint. Est etiam admiratio non nulla in bestiis aquatilibus iis quae gignuntur in terra: veluti crocodili fluviatilesque testudines quaedamque serpentes ortae extra aquam simul ac primum niti possunt aquam persequuntur. Quin etiam anitum ova gallinis saepe supponimus, e quibus pulli orti primo aluntur ab iis ut a matribus a quibus exclusi fotique sunt, deinde eas relinquunt et effugiunt sequentes, cum primum aquam quasi naturalem domum videre potuerunt: tantam ingenuit animantibus conservandi sui natura custodiam. XLIX. Legi etiam scriptum esse avem quandam quae platalea nominaretur; eam sibi cibum quaerere advolantem ad eas avis quae se in mari mergerent, quae cum emersissent piscemque cepissent, usque eo premere earum capita mordicus dum illae captum amitterent, in quod

[1] ut *om. det.*: *lacunam indicavit Mayor.*
[2] <a> *add. det.* [3] squillae *ed. vet.*
[4] morsus *MSS.*: squillae morsu pina *Heindorf.*

[a] A variant gives "the shrimp draws the attention of the mussel by giving it a nip, and the mussel shuts up its shells."
[b] Aristotle, *Hist. An.* ix. 10.

there was bestowed even a sort of craft or cunning: for instance, one species of the spider tribe weaves a kind of net, in order to dispatch anything that is caught in it; another in order to . . . stealthily keeps watch, and, snatching anything that falls into it, devours it. The mussel, or *pina* as it is called in Greek, is a large bivalve which enters into a sort of partnership with the tiny shrimp to procure food, and so, when little fishes swim into the gaping shell, the shrimp draws the attention of the mussel and the mussel shuts up its shells with a snap [a]; thus two very dissimilar creatures obtain their food in
124 common. In this case we are curious to know whether their association is due to a sort of mutual compact, or whether it was brought about by nature herself and goes back to the moment of their birth. Our wonder is also considerably excited by those aquatic animals which are born on land—crocodiles, for instance, and water-tortoises and certain snakes, which are born on dry land but as soon as they can first crawl make for the water. Again we often place ducks' eggs beneath hens, and the chicks that spring from the eggs are at first fed and mothered by the hens that hatched and reared them, but later on they leave their foster-mothers, and run away when they pursue them, as soon as they have had an opportunity of seeing the water, their natural home. So powerful an instinct of self-preservation has nature implanted in living creatures. XLIX. I have even read in a book [b] that there is a bird called the spoonbill, which procures its food by flying after those birds which dive in the sea, and upon their coming to the surface with a fish that they have caught, pressing their heads down with its beak until they drop their prey, which

ipsa invaderet. Eademque haec avis scribitur conchis se solere complere easque cum stomachi calore
concoxerit evomere, atque ita eligere ex iis quae sunt[1]
125 esculenta. Ranae autem marinae dicuntur obruere
sese harena solere et moveri prope aquam, ad quas
quasi ad escam pisces cum accesserint confici a ranis
atque consumi. Miluo est quoddam bellum quasi
naturale cum corvo; ergo alter alterius ubicumque
nanctus est ova frangit. Illud vero (ab Aristotele
animadversum a quo pleraque) quis potest non
mirari, grues cum loca calidiora petentes maria
transmittant trianguli efficere formam? eius autem
summo angulo aër ab iis adversus pellitur, deinde
sensim ab utroque latere tamquam remis ita pinnis
cursus avium levatur; basis autem trianguli, quem[2]
efficiunt grues, ea tamquam a puppi ventis adiuvatur;
eaeque in tergo praevolantium colla et capita
reponunt; quod quia ipse dux facere non potest,
quia non habet ubi nitatur, revolat ut ipse quoque
quiescat, in eius locum succedit ex iis quae adquie-
runt, eaque vicissitudo in omni cursu conservatur.
126 Multa eius modi proferre possum, sed genus ipsum
videtis. Iam vero illa etiam notiora, quanto se opere
custodiant bestiae, ut in pastu circumspectent, ut in
cubilibus delitiscant. L. Atque illa mirabilia,
quod—ea quae nuper, id est paucis ante saeclis,[3]

[1] sint *Ernesti.*
[2] quem *dett.*: quam. [3] id . . . saeclis *secl. Cobet.*

[a] Cicero seems to have omitted or misunderstood something in Aristotle; the passage quoted is not in his extant works. Pliny, *N.H.* x. 63, tells the same thing of wild geese and swans, saying *a tergo sensim dilatante se cuneo porrigitur agmen*, 'the column widens out at the rear with the gradual broadening of the wedge.'

it pounces on for itself. It is also recorded of this bird that it is in the habit of gorging itself with shell-fish, which it digests by means of the heat of its stomach and then brings up again, and so picks out from them
25 the parts that are good to eat. Sea-frogs again are said to be in the habit of covering themselves with sand and creeping along at the water's edge, and then when fishes approach them thinking they are something to eat, these are killed and devoured by the frogs. The kite and the crow live in a state of natural war as it were with one another, and therefore each destroys the other's eggs wherever it finds them. Another fact (observed by Aristotle, from whom most of these cases are cited) cannot but awaken our surprise, namely that cranes when crossing the seas on the way to warmer climates fly in a triangular formation. With the apex of the triangle they force aside the air in front of them, and then gradually on either side [a] by means of their wings acting as oars the birds' onward flight is sustained, while the base of the triangle formed by the cranes gets the assistance of the wind when it is so to speak astern. The birds rest their necks and heads on the backs of those flying in front of them ; and the leader, being himself unable to do this as he has no one to lean on, flies to the rear that he himself also may have a rest, while one of those already rested takes his place,
26 and so they keep turns throughout the journey. I could adduce a number of similar instances, but you see the general idea. Another even better known class of stories illustrates the precautions taken by animals for their security, the watch they keep while feeding, their skill in hiding in their lairs. L. Other remarkable facts are that dogs cure themselves by

medicorum ingeniis reperta sunt—vomitione canes,
purgando[1] autem alvo se ibes[2] Aegyptiae curant.
Auditum est pantheras, quae in barbaria venenata
carne caperentur, remedium quoddam habere quo
cum essent usae non morerentur, capras autem in
Creta feras, cum essent confixae venenatis sagittis,
herbam quaerere quae dictamnus vocaretur, quam
cum gustavissent sagittas excidere dicunt e corpore.
127 Cervaeque paulo ante partum perpurgant se quadam
herbula quae seselis dicitur. Iam illa cernimus, ut
contra vim et metum suis se armis quaeque defendant cornibus tauri, apri dentibus, morsu leones ;
aliae fuga se aliae occultatione tutantur, atramenti
effusione sepiae torpore torpedines, multae etiam in-
sectantis odoris intolerabili foeditate depellunt.

LI. " Ut vero perpetuus mundi esset ornatus, magna
adhibita cura est a providentia deorum ut semper
essent et bestiarum genera et arborum omniumque rerum quae a terra stirpibus continerentur. Quae
quidem omnia eam vim seminis habent in se ut ex
uno plura generentur, idque semen inclusum est in
intuma parte earum bacarum quae ex quaque stirpe
funduntur ; isdemque seminibus et homines adfatim
vescuntur et terrae eiusdem generis stirpium renova-
128 tione conplentur. Quid loquar quanta ratio in bestiis ad perpetuam conservationem earum generis
appareat ? Nam primum aliae mares aliae feminae
sunt, quod perpetuitatis causa machinata natura est,

[1] purgando *Plasberg* : purgante, purgantes *MSS.*
[2] alvo sibis *etc. MSS.* : purgantes autem alvos ibes Aegyptiae curantur *Madvig.*

vomiting and ibises in Egypt by purging—modes of treatment only recently, that is, a few generations ago, discovered by the talent of the medical profession. It has been reported that panthers, which in foreign countries are caught by means of poisoned meat, have a remedy which they employ to save themselves from dying; and that wild goats in Crete, when pierced with poisoned arrows, seek a herb called dittany, and on their swallowing this the arrows, it is said, drop out of their bodies. Does, shortly before giving birth to their young, thoroughly purge themselves with a herb called hartwort. Again we observe how various species defend themselves against violence and danger with their own weapons, bulls with their horns, boars with their tusks, lions with their bite; some species protect themselves by flight, some by hiding, the cuttle-fish by emitting an inky fluid, the sting-ray by causing cramp, and also a number of creatures drive away their pursuers by their insufferably disgusting odour.

The adaptation of vegetable and animal nature for the perpetuation of species.

LI. "In order to secure the everlasting duration of the world-order, divine providence has made most careful provision to ensure the perpetuation of the families of animals and of trees and all the vegetable species. The latter all contain within them seed possessing the property of multiplying the species; this seed is enclosed in the innermost part of the fruits that grow from each plant; and the same seeds supply mankind with an abundance of food, besides replenishing the earth with a fresh stock of plants of the same kind. Why should I speak of the amount of rational design displayed in animals to secure the perpetual preservation of their kind? To begin with some are male and some female, a device of nature

deinde partes corporis et ad procreandum et ad concipiendum aptissimae, et in mare et in femina commiscendorum corporum mirae libidines. Cum autem in locis semen insedit, rapit omnem fere cibum ad sese eoque saeptum[1] fingit animal; quod cum ex utero elapsum excidit, in iis animantibus quae lacte aluntur omnis fere cibus matrum lactescere incipit, eaque quae paulo ante nata sunt sine magistro duce natura mammas appetunt earumque ubertate saturantur. Atque ut intellegamus nihil horum esse fortuitum et haec omnia esse opera providae sollertisque naturae, quae multiplices fetus procreant, ut sues ut canes, iis mammarum data est multitudo, quas easdem paucas habent eae bestiae quae pauca gignunt.

129 Quid dicam quantus amor bestiarum sit in educandis custodiendisque iis quae procreaverunt, usque ad eum finem dum possint se ipsa defendere? etsi pisces, ut aiunt, ova cum genuerunt relinquunt, facile enim illa aqua et sustinentur et fetum fundunt. LII. Testudines autem et crocodilos dicunt, cum in terra partum ediderint, obruere ova, deinde discedere; ita et nascuntur et educantur ipsa per sese. Iam gallinae avesque reliquae et quietum requirunt ad pariendum locum et cubilia sibi nidosque construunt eosque quam possunt mollissume substernunt, ut quam facillume ova serventur; e quibus pullos cum excuderunt, ita tuentur ut et pinnis foveant ne frigore laedantur et

[1] ex eoque conceptum (*vel* coeptum) ? *Mayor.*

[a] Perhaps the text should be emended to give, 'and fashions a living creature conceived therefrom.'

to perpetuate the species. Then parts of their bodies are most skilfully contrived to serve the purposes of procreation and of conception, and both male and female possess marvellous desires for copulation. And when the seed has settled in its place, it draws almost all the nutriment to itself and hedged within it fashions a living creature[a]; when this has been dropped from the womb and has emerged, in the mammalian species almost all the nourishment received by the mother turns to milk, and the young just born, untaught and by nature's guidance, seek for the teats and satisfy their cravings with their bounty. And to show to us that none of these things merely happens by chance and that all are the work of nature's providence and skill, species that produce large litters of offspring, such as swine and dogs, have bestowed upon them a large number of teats, while those animals which bear only a few young have only a few teats. Why should I describe the affection shown by animals in rearing and protecting the offspring to which they have given birth, up to the point when they are able to defend themselves? although fishes, it is said, abandon their eggs when they have laid them, since these easily float and hatch out in the water. LII. Turtles and crocodiles are said to lay their eggs on land and bury them and then go away, leaving their young to hatch and rear themselves. Hens and other birds find a quiet place in which to lay, and build themselves nests to sit on, covering these with the softest possible bedding in order to preserve the eggs most easily; and when they have hatched out their chicks they protect them by cherishing them with their wings so that they may not be injured by cold, and by shading them

si est calor a sole se opponant. Cum autem pulli
pinnulis uti possunt, tum volatus eorum matres
130 prosequuntur, reliqua cura liberantur. Accedit ad
non nullorum animantium et earum rerum quas terra
gignit conservationem et salutem hominum etiam
sollertia et diligentia. Nam multae et pecudes et
stirpes sunt quae sine procuratione hominum salvae
esse non possunt.

"Magnae etiam opportunitates ad cultum hominum atque abundantiam aliae aliis in locis reperiuntur. Aegyptum Nilus inrigat et, cum tota aestate obrutam oppletamque tenuit, tum recedit mollitosque et oblimatos agros ad serendum relinquit. Mesopotamiam fertilem efficit Euphrates, in quam quotannis[1] quasi novos agros invehit. Indus vero, qui est omnium fluminum maximus, non aqua solum agros laetificat et mitigat sed eos etiam conserit; magnam enim vim seminum secum frumenti similium
131 dicitur deportare. Multaque alia in aliis locis commemorabilia proferre possum, multos fertiles agros
alios aliorum fructuum. LIII. Sed illa quanta
benignitas naturae, quod tam multa ad vescendum,
tam varia et tam iucunda gignit, neque ea uno
tempore anni, ut semper et novitate delectemur
et copia! Quam tempestivos autem dedit, quam
salutares non modo hominum sed etiam pecudum
generi, iis denique omnibus quae oriuntur e terra,
ventos Etesias! quorum flatu nimii temperantur
calores, ab isdem etiam maritimi cursus celeres et
certi deriguntur. Multa praetereunda sunt [et

[1] quotannis *Rom.*: quod annos, quot annos *MSS.*

[a] Trade-winds blowing periodically (ἔτος, 'year') from N.-W. and other quarters.

against the heat of the sun. When the young birds are able to use their sprouting wings, their mothers escort them in their flights, but are released from any
0 further tendance upon them. Moreover the skill and industry of man also contribute to the preservation and security of certain animals and plants. For there are many species of both which could not survive without man's care.

The adaptation of external nature for the preservation and convenience of man.

"Also a plentiful variety of conveniences is found in different regions for the productive cultivation of the soil by man. Egypt is watered by the Nile, which keeps the land completely flooded all the summer and afterwards retires leaving the soil soft and covered with mud, in readiness for sowing. Mesopotamia is fertilized by the Euphrates, which as it were imports into it new fields every year. The Indus, the largest river in the world, not only manures and softens the soil but actually sows it with seed, for it is said to bring down with it a great quantity of seeds
1 resembling corn. And I could produce a number of other remarkable examples in a variety of places, and instance a variety of lands each prolific in a different kind of produce. LIII. But how great is the benevolence of nature, in giving birth to such an abundance and variety of delicious articles of food, and that not at one season only of the year, so that we have continually the delights of both novelty and plenty! How seasonable moreover and how wholesome not for the human race alone but also for the animal and the various vegetable species is her gift of the Etesian winds [a]! their breath moderates the excessive heat of summer, and they also guide our ships across the sea upon a swift and steady course. Many instances must be passed over [and yet many are

132 tamen multa dicuntur].[1] Enumerari enim non possunt fluminum opportunitates, aestus maritimi multum†[2] accedentes et recedentes, montes vestiti atque silvestres, salinae ab ora maritima remotissimae, medicamentorum salutarium plenissimae terrae, artes[3] denique innumerabiles ad victum et ad vitam necessariae. Iam diei noctisque vicissitudo conservat animantes tribuens aliud agendi tempus aliud quiescendi. Sic undique omni ratione concluditur mente consilioque divino omnia in hoc mundo ad salutem omnium conservationemque admirabiliter administrari.

133 "Hic[4] quaeret quispiam, cuiusnam causa tantarum rerum molitio facta sit? Arborumne et herbarum, quae quamquam sine sensu sunt tamen a natura sustinentur? At id quidem absurdum est. An bestiarum? Nihilo probabilius deos mutorum[5] et nihil intellegentium causa tantum laborasse. Quorum igitur causa quis dixerit effectum esse mundum? Eorum scilicet animantium quae ratione utuntur; hi sunt di et homines, quibus profecto nihil est melius, ratio est enim quae praestet omnibus. Ita fit credibile deorum et hominum causa factum esse mundum quaeque in eo [mundo][6] sint omnia.

LIV. "Faciliusque intellegetur a dis inmortalibus hominibus esse provisum si erit tota hominis fabricatio perspecta omnisque humanae naturae figura atque

[1] *secl. Muller.*
[2] multum† : ⟨si⟩mul cum ⟨luna⟩ *Plasberg* (cum luna simul *Alan*).
[3] utilitates *Koch.*
[4] hic *dett.*, sin *A, B.*
[5] mutorum *Davies*: mutarum.
[6] [mundo] *edd.*, *om. E, L, O.*

[a] Probably an interpolated note.

given].[a] For it is impossible to recount the conveniences afforded by rivers, the ebb and flow [b] . . . of the tides of the sea, the mountains clothed with forests, the salt-beds lying far inland from the sea-coast, the copious stores of health-giving medicines that the earth contains, and all the countless arts necessary for livelihood and for life. Again the alternation of day and night contributes to the preservation of living creatures by affording one time for activity and another for repose. Thus every line of reasoning goes to prove that all things in this world of ours are marvellously governed by divine intelligence and wisdom for the safety and preservation of all.

"Here somebody will ask, for whose sake was all this vast system contrived? For the sake of the trees and plants, for these, though without sensation, have their sustenance from nature? But this at any rate is absurd. Then for the sake of the animals? It is no more likely that the gods took all this trouble for the sake of dumb, irrational creatures. For whose sake then shall one pronounce the world to have been created? Doubtless for the sake of those living beings which have the use of reason; these are the gods and mankind, who assuredly surpass all other things in excellence, since the most excellent of all things is reason. Thus we are led to believe that the world and all the things that it contains were made for the sake of gods and men.

The hand of Providence seen in the structure and nature of man:

LIV. "And that man has been cared for by divine providence will be more readily understood if we survey the whole structure of man and all the conformation and perfection of human nature. There are

[b] The text may have been corrupted, and may have run 'ebb and flow with the moon.'

134 perfectio. Nam cum tribus rebus animantium vita teneatur, cibo potione spiritu, ad haec omnia percipienda os est aptissimum, quod adiunctis naribus spiritu augetur. Dentibus autem in ore constructis manditur[1] atque ab iis[2] extenuatur et mollitur cibus. Eorum adversi acuti morsu dividunt escas, intimi autem conficiunt qui genuini vocantur, quae confectio
135 etiam a lingua adiuvari videtur. Linguam autem ad radices eius haerens excipit stomachus, quo primum inlabuntur ea quae accepta sunt ore. Is utraque ex parte tosillas attingens palato extremo atque intimo terminatur. Atque is agitatione et motibus linguae cum depulsum et quasi detrusum cibum accepit, depellit: ipsius autem partes eae quae sunt infra quam id quod devoratur dilatantur, quae autem supra
136 contrahuntur. Sed cum aspera arteria—sic enim a medicis appellatur—ostium habeat adiunctum linguae radicibus paulo supra quam ad linguam stomachus adnectitur, eaque ad pulmones usque pertineat excipiatque animam eam quae ducta est spiritu, eandemque a pulmonibus respiret et reddat, tegitur quodam quasi operculo, quod ob eam causam datum est ne si quid in eam cibi forte incidisset spiritus impediretur. Sed cum alvi natura subiecta stomacho cibi et potionis sit receptaculum, pulmones autem et cor extrinsecus spiritum ducant, in alvo multa sunt mirabiliter effecta, quae constat fere e

[1] mandatur *ci. Alan.* [2] ab iis *secl. Baiter.*

[a] A plausible emendation of the text gives 'Within the mouth is the structure of the teeth, to which the food is handed over (*mandatur*) and by which it is divided up and softened.'

[b] The Greek *tracheia arteria*, 'rough artery' (air-ducts and blood-vessels not being distinguished).

three things requisite for the maintenance of animal life, food, drink and breath; and for the reception of all of these the mouth is most consummately adapted, receiving as it does an abundant supply of breath through the nostrils which communicate with it. The structure of the teeth within the mouth serves to chew the food, and it is divided up and softened by them.[a] The front teeth are sharp, and bite our viands into pieces; the back teeth, called molars, masticate them, the process of mastication apparently being assisted also by the tongue. Next to the tongue comes the gullet, which is attached to its roots, and into which in the first place pass the substances that have been received in the mouth. The gullet is adjacent to the tonsils on either side of it, and reaches as far as the back or innermost part of the palate. The action and movements of the tongue drive and thrust the food down into the gullet, which receives it and drives it further down, the parts of the gullet below the food that is being swallowed dilating and the parts above it contracting. The windpipe, or trachea[b] as it is termed by physicians, has an orifice attached to the roots of the tongue a little above the point where the tongue is joined to the gullet; it reaches to the lungs, and receives the air inhaled by breathing, and also exhales it and passes it out from the lungs; it is covered by a sort of lid, provided for the purpose of preventing a morsel of food from accidentally falling into it and impeding the breath. Below the gullet lies the stomach, which is constructed as the receptacle of food and drink, whereas breath is inhaled by the lungs and heart. The stomach performs a number of remarkable operations; its structure consists principally of muscular fibres, and it is

provision for the support of his life by food and air;

nervis, est autem multiplex et tortuosa, arcetque et continet sive illud aridum est sive umidum quod recepit, ut id mutari et concoqui possit, eaque tum astringitur tum relaxatur, atque omne quod accepit cogit et confundit, ut facile et calore, quem multum habet, et terendo cibo et praeterea spiritu omnia cocta atque confecta in reliquum corpus dividantur. LV. In pulmonibus autem inest raritas quaedam et adsimilis spongiis mollitudo ad hauriendum spiritum aptissima, qui tum se contrahunt adspirantes, tum in respiratu dilatantur, ut frequenter ducatur cibus
137 animalis quo maxime aluntur animantes. Ex intestinis autem alvo[1] secretus a reliquo cibo sucus is quo alimur permanat ad iecur per quasdam a medio intestino usque ad portas iecoris (sic enim appellantur) ductas et derectas vias, quae pertinent ad iecur eique adhaerent; atque inde aliae <alio>[2] pertinentes sunt, per quas cadit cibus a iecore dilapsus. Ab eo cibo cum est secreta bilis eique umores qui e renibus profunduntur, reliqua se in sanguinem vertunt ad easdemque portas iecoris confluunt, ad quas omnes eius viae pertinent; per quas lapsus cibus in hoc ipso loco in eam venam quae cava appellatur confunditur perque eam ad cor confectus iam coctusque[3] perlabitur; a corde autem in totum corpus distribuitur per venas admodum multas in omnes partes corporis pertinentes.
138 Quem ad modum autem reliquiae cibi depellantur tum astringentibus se intestinis tum relaxantibus,

[1] alvo *om. dett.* [2] *Heindorf*: <ad renes> *Ascensius.*
[3] *Ascensius*: coactusque MSS., concoctusque *Madvig.*

[a] The *phleps koilé*, the great trunk vein.

manifold and twisted ; it compresses and contains
the dry or moist nutriment that it receives, enabling
it to be assimilated and digested ; at one moment it
is astricted and at another relaxed, thus pressing and
mixing together all that is passed into it, so that by
means of the abundant heat which it possesses, and by
its crushing the food, and also by the operation of the
breath, everything is digested and worked up so as to
be easily distributed throughout the rest of the body.
LV. The lungs on the contrary are soft and of a loose
and spongy consistency, well adapted to absorb the
breath ; which they inhale and exhale by alternately
contracting and expanding, to provide frequent
draughts of that aerial nutriment which is the chief
37 support of animal life. The alimentary juice secreted
from the rest of the food by the stomach flows from
the bowels to the liver through certain ducts or
channels reaching to the liver, to which they are
attached, and connecting up what are called the
doorways of the liver with the middle intestine.
From the liver different channels pass in different
directions, and through these falls the food passed
down from the liver. From this food is secreted bile,
and the liquids excreted by the kidneys ; the residue
turns into blood and flows to the aforesaid doorways
of the liver, to which all its channels lead. Flowing
through these doorways the food at this very point
pours into the so-called *vena cava* or hollow vein,[a] and
through this, being now completely worked up and
digested, flows to the heart, and from the heart is
distributed all over the body through a rather large
number of veins that reach to every part of the frame.
38 It would not be difficult to indicate the way in which
the residue of the food is excreted by the alternate

haud sane difficile dictu est, sed tamen praetereundum est ne quid habeat iniucunditatis oratio. Illa potius explicetur incredibilis fabrica naturae: nam quae spiritu in pulmones anima ducitur, ea calescit primum ipso ab spiritu, deinde contagione pulmonum, ex eaque pars redditur respirando, pars concipitur cordis parte quadam quem ventriculum cordis appellant, cui similis alter adiunctus est in quem sanguis a iecore per venam illam cavam influit; eoque modo ex his partibus et sanguis per venas in omne corpus diffunditur et spiritus per arterias; utraeque autem crebrae multaeque toto corpore intextae vim quandam incredibilem artificiosi operis divinique testantur.

139 Quid dicam de ossibus? quae subiecta corpori mirabiles commissuras habent et ad stabilitatem aptas et ad artus finiendos adcommodatas et ad motum et ad omnem corporis actionem. Huc adde nervos, a quibus artus continentur, eorumque inplicationem corpore toto pertinentem, qui sicut venae et arteriae a corde tracti et profecti[1] in corpus omne ducuntur.

140 LVI. "Ad hanc providentiam naturae tam diligentem tamque sollertem adiungi multa possunt e quibus intellegatur quantae res hominibus a dis[2] quamque eximiae tributae sint. Quae[3] primum eos humo excitatos celsos et erectos constituit,[4] ut deorum cognitionem caelum intuentes capere possent. Sunt

[1] *sic edd.*; tractae et profectae *MSS.*
[2] a dis *secl. Schomann.* [3] quae *Asconius*: qui *MSS.*
[4] constituerunt *dett.*

[a] The Greeks used the same word *neuroi* for both, and did not clearly distinguish them.

astriction and relaxation of the bowels; however this topic must be passed over lest my discourse should be somewhat offensive. Rather let me unfold the following instance of the incredible skilfulness of nature's handiwork. The air drawn into the lungs by breathing is warmed in the first instance by the breath itself and then by contact with the lungs; part of it is returned by the act of respiration, and part is received by a certain part of the heart called the cardiac ventricle, adjacent to which is a second similar vessel into which the blood flows from the liver through the *vena cava* mentioned above; and in this manner from these organs both the blood is diffused through the veins and the breath through the arteries all over the body. Both of these sets of vessels are very numerous and are closely interwoven with the tissues of the entire body; they testify to an extraordinary degree of skilful and divine craftsmanship. Why need I speak about the bones, which are the framework of the body? their marvellous cartilages are nicely adapted to secure stability, and fitted to end off the joints and to allow of movement and bodily activity of every sort. Add thereto the nerves or sinews[a] which hold the joints together and whose ramifications pervade the entire body; like the veins and arteries these lead from the heart as their starting-point and pass to all parts of the body.

the structure of man's body;

LVI. "Many further illustrations could be given of this wise and careful providence of nature, to illustrate the lavishness and splendour of the gifts bestowed by the gods on men. First, she has raised them from the ground to stand tall and upright, so that they might be able to behold the sky and so gain a knowledge of the gods. For men are sprung from

man's erect position;

enim ex terra homines non ut incolae atque habitatores sed quasi spectatores superarum rerum atque caelestium, quarum spectaculum ad nullum aliud genus animantium pertinet. Sensus autem interpretes ac nuntii rerum in capite tamquam in arce mirifice ad usus necessarios et facti et conlocati sunt. Nam oculi tamquam speculatores altissimum locum obtinent, ex quo plurima conspicientes fungantur suo
141 munere; et aures, cum sonum percipere debeant qui natura in[1] sublime fertur, recte in altis corporum partibus collocatae sunt; itemque nares et quod omnis odor ad supera fertur recte sursum sunt et quod cibi et potionis iudicium magnum earum est non sine causa vicinitatem oris secutae sunt. Iam gustatus, qui sentire eorum quibus vescimur genera debet,[2] habitat in ea parte oris qua esculentis et potulentis iter natura patefecit. Tactus autem toto corpore aequabiliter fusus est, ut omnes ictus omnesque minimos[3] et frigoris et caloris adpulsus sentire possimus. Atque ut in aedificiis architecti avertunt ab oculis naribusque dominorum ea quae profluentia necessario taetri essent aliquid habitura, sic natura res similis procul amandavit a sensibus.

142 LVII. "Quis vero opifex praeter naturam, qua nihil potest esse callidius, tantam sollertiam persequi potuisset in sensibus? quae primum oculos membranis tenuissimis vestivit et saepsit, quas pri-

[1] in *om. dett.* [2] debet *dett.*: deberet *A*, *B*.
[3] minimos *dett.*: nimios *A*, *B*.

the earth not as its inhabitants and denizens, but to be as it were the spectators of things supernal and heavenly, in the contemplation whereof no other species of animals participates. Next, the senses, posted in the citadel of the head as the reporters and messengers of the outer world, both in structure and position are marvellously adapted to their necessary services. The eyes as the watchmen have the highest station, to give them the widest outlook for the performance of their function. The ears also, having the duty of perceiving sound, the nature of which is to rise, are rightly placed in the upper part of the body. The nostrils likewise are rightly placed high inasmuch as all smells travel upwards, but also, because they have much to do with discriminating food and drink, they have with good reason been brought into the neighbourhood of the mouth. Taste, which has the function of distinguishing the flavours of our various viands, is situated in that part of the face where nature has made an aperture for the passage of food and drink. The sense of touch is evenly diffused over all the body, to enable us to perceive all sorts of contacts and even the minutest impacts of both cold and heat. And just as architects relegate the drains of houses to the rear, away from the eyes and nose of the masters, since otherwise they would inevitably be somewhat offensive, so nature has banished the corresponding organs of the body far away from the neighbourhood of the senses. **man's organs of sense;**

LVII. "Again what artificer but nature, who is unsurpassed in her cunning, could have attained such skilfulness in the construction of the senses? First, she has clothed and walled the eyes with membranes of the finest texture, which she has made on the one

mum perlucidas fecit ut per eas cerni posset, firmas autem ut continerent[1]; sed lubricos oculos fecit et mobiles, ut et declinarent si quid noceret et aspectum quo vellent facile converterent; aciesque ipsa qua cernimus, quae pupula vocatur, ita parva est ut ea quae nocere possint facile vitet, palpebraeque, quae sunt tegmenta oculorum, mollissimae tactu ne laederent aciem, aptissime factae[2] et ad claudendas pupulas ne quid incideret et ad aperiendas, idque providit ut identidem fieri posset cum maxima celeri-
143 tate. Munitaeque sunt palpebrae tamquam vallo pilorum, quibus et apertis oculis si quid incideret repelleretur et somno coniventibus, cum oculis ad cernendum non egeremus,†[3] ut qui tamquam involuti quiescerent. Latent praeterea utiliter et excelsis undique partibus saepiuntur; primum enim superiora superciliis obducta sudorem a capite et fronte defluentem repellunt; genae deinde ab inferiore parte tutantur subiectae leniterque eminentes; nasusque ita locatus est ut quasi murus oculis interiectus esse
144 videatur. Auditus autem semper patet, eius enim sensu etiam dormientes egemus, a quo cum sonus est acceptus etiam e somno excitamur. Flexuosum iter habet, ne quid intrare possit si simplex et derectum pateret; provisum etiam ut si qua minima bestiola

[1] continerent *Lambinus*: continerentur.
[2] et aptissimae factae sunt *Heindorf*.
[3] *locum corruptum edd. varie sanant.*

[a] *Pupa*, κόρη, so called from its reflecting a small image of a person who looks into it.

hand transparent so that we may be able to see through them, and on the other hand firm of substance, to serve as the outer cover of the eye. The eyes she has made mobile and smoothly turning, so as both to avoid any threatened injury and to direct their gaze easily in any direction they desire. The actual organ of vision, called the pupil or 'little doll,'[a] is so small as easily to avoid objects that might injure it; and the lids, which are the covers of the eyes, are very soft to the touch so as not to hurt the pupil, and very neatly constructed so as to be able both to shut the eyes in order that nothing may impinge upon them and to open them; and nature has provided that this process can be repeated again and again with extreme rapidity. The eyelids are furnished with a palisade of hairs, whereby to ward off any impinging object while the eyes are open, and so that while they are closed in sleep, when we do not need the eyes for seeing, they may be as it were tucked up for repose. Moreover the eyes are in an advantageously retired position, and shielded on all sides by surrounding prominences; for first the parts above them are covered by the eyebrows which prevent sweat from flowing down from the scalp and forehead; then the cheeks, which are placed beneath them and which slightly project, protect them from below; and the nose is so placed as to seem to be a wall separating the eyes from one another. The organ of hearing on the other hand is always open, since we require this sense even when asleep, and when it receives a sound, we are aroused even from sleep. The auditory passage is winding, to prevent anything from being able to enter, as it might if the passage were clear and straight; it has further been

conaretur inrumpere[1] in sordibus aurium tamquam in visco inhaeresceret. Extra autem eminent quae appellantur aures, et tegendi causa factae tutandique sensus et ne adiectae voces laberentur atque errarent prius quam sensus ab iis pulsus esset. Sed duros et quasi corneolos habent introitus multisque cum flexibus, quod his naturis relatus amplificatur sonus; quocirca et in fidibus testudine resonatur aut cornu, et ex tortuosis locis et inclusis <soni>[2] referuntur
145 ampliores. Similiter nares, quae semper propter necessarias utilitates patent, contractiores habent introitus, ne quid in eas quod noceat possit pervadere; umoremque semper habent ad pulverem multaque alia depellenda non inutilem. Gustatus praeclare saeptus est, ore enim continetur et ad usum apte et ad incolumitatis custodiam.

LVIII. "Omnesque[3] sensus hominum multo antecellunt[4] sensibus bestiarum. Primum enim oculi in iis artibus quarum iudicium est oculorum, in pictis fictis[5] caelatisque formis, in corporum etiam motione atque gestu multa[6] cernunt subtilius, colorum enim[7] et figurarum [tum][8] venustatem atque ordinem et ut ita dicam decentiam oculi iudicant; atque etiam alia maiora, nam et virtutes et vitia cognoscunt, iratum propitium, laetantem dolentem, fortem ignavum, au-
146 dacem timidumque[9] [cognoscunt].[10] Auriumque item est admirabile quoddam artificiosumque iudicium, quo

[1] irrepere *quidam apud Lambinum.*
[2] <soni> *Lambinus, post* referuntur *dett.*
[3] omnisque *A corr.*
[4] antecellunt *B corr.*: antecellit.
[5] *An ut dittographia secludendum? cf.* § 150 *ed.*
[6] multo *? ed.*
[7] enim *Heindorf*: etiam.
[8] *secl. Manutius*: <orna>tum *vel* <habi>tum *Plasberg.*
[9] que *om. Ald.*
[10] *secl. Baiter.*

provided that even the tiniest insect that may attempt to intrude may be caught in the sticky wax of the ears. On the outside project the organs which we call ears, which are constructed both to cover and protect the sense-organ and to prevent the sounds that reach them from sliding past and being lost before they strike the sense. The apertures of the ears are hard and gristly, and much convoluted, because things with these qualities reflect and amplify sound; this is why tortoise-shell or horn gives resonance to a lyre, and also why winding passages and enclosures have an echo which is louder than the
5 original sound. Similarly the nostrils, which to serve the purposes required of them have to be always open, have narrower apertures, to prevent the entrance of anything that may harm them; and they are always moist, which is useful to guard them against dust and many other things. The sense of taste is admirably shielded, being enclosed in the mouth in a manner well suited for the performance of its function and for its protection against harm.

LVIII. "And all the senses of man far excel those of the lower animals. In the first place our eyes have a finer perception of many things in the arts which appeal to the sense of sight, painting, modelling and sculpture, and also in bodily movements and gestures; since the eyes judge beauty and arrangement and so to speak propriety of colour and shape; and also other more important matters, for they also recognize virtues and vices, the angry and the friendly, the joyful and the sad, the brave man and the coward,
6 the bold and the craven. The ears are likewise marvellously skilful organs of discrimination; they

iudicatur et in vocis et in tibiarum nervorumque cantibus varietas sonorum intervalla distinctio, et vocis genera permulta, canorum fuscum, leve asperum, grave acutum, flexibile durum, quae hominum solum auribus iudicantur. Nariumque item et gustandi et <quadam ex>[1] parte tangendi magna iudicia sunt. Ad quos sensus capiendos et perfruendos plures etiam quam vellem artes repertae sunt. Perspicuum est enim quo conpositiones unguentorum, quo ciborum conditiones, quo corporum lenocinia processerint.

147 LIX. " Iam vero animum ipsum mentemque hominis rationem consilium prudentiam qui non divina cura perfecta esse perspicit, is his ipsis rebus mihi videtur carere. De quo dum disputarem tuam mihi dari vellem, Cotta, eloquentiam. Quo enim tu illa modo diceres quanta primum intellegentia, deinde consequentium rerum cum primis coniunctio et conprehensio esset in nobis ; ex quo videlicet iudicamus[2] quid ex quibusque rebus efficiatur idque ratione concludimus, singulasque res definimus circumscripteque complectimur ; ex quo scientia intellegitur quam vim habeat qualis<que>[3] sit, qua ne in deo quidem est res ulla praestantior. Quanta vero illa sunt, quae vos Academici infirmatis et tollitis, quod et sensibus et animo ea quae extra sunt percipimus

148 atque conprendimus ; ex quibus conlatis inter se et

[1] *ci. Plasberg.*

[2] (videlicet iudicamus *Plasberg*: iudicamus videlicet *Vahlen*): videlicet *A*, videmus *B*.

[3] *Moser.*

[a] It is quite possible that the three words *varietas*, *intervalla*, *distinctio* are merely a periphrasis for the single term

judge differences of tone, of pitch and of key [a] in the music of the voice and of wind and stringed instruments, and many different qualities of voice, sonorous and dull, smooth and rough, bass and treble, flexible and hard, distinctions discriminated by the human ear alone. Likewise the nostrils, the taste and in some measure the touch have highly sensitive faculties of discrimination. And the arts invented to appeal to and indulge these senses are even more numerous than I could wish. The developments of perfumery and cookery and of the meretricious adornment of the person are obvious examples.

LIX. "Coming now to the actual mind and intellect of man, his reason, wisdom and foresight, one who cannot see that these owe their perfection to divine providence must in my view himself be devoid of these very faculties. While discussing this topic I could wish, Cotta, that I had the gift of your eloquence. How could not you describe first our powers of understanding, and then our faculty of conjoining premisses and consequences in a single act of apprehension, the faculty I mean that enables us to judge what conclusion follows from any given propositions and to put the inference in syllogistic form, and also to delimit particular terms in a succinct definition; whence we arrive at an understanding of the potency and the nature of knowledge, which is the most excellent part even of the divine nature. Again, how remarkable are the faculties which you Academics invalidate and abolish, our sensory and intellectual perception and comprehension of external objects; it is by collating and comparing our percepts that we also

man's divine gift of reason;

[a] διαστήματα, 'differences of pitch,' in contrast with differences of quality which follow.

conparatis artes quoque efficimus partim ad usum vitae partim ad oblectationem necessarias. Iam vero domina rerum, ut vos soletis dicere, eloquendi vis quam est praeclara quamque divina: quae primum efficit ut et ea quae ignoramus discere et ea quae scimus alios docere possimus: deinde hac cohortamur hac persuademus, hac consolamur afflictos hac deducimus perterritos a timore, hac gestientes conprimimus hac cupiditates iracundiasque restinguimus, haec nos iuris legum urbium societate devinxit,
149 haec a vita inmani et fera segregavit. Ad usum autem orationis incredibile est, si[1] diligenter attenderis, quanta opera machinata natura sit. Primum enim a pulmonibus arteria usque ad os intimum pertinet, per quam vox principium a mente ducens percipitur et funditur. Deinde in ore sita lingua est finita[2] dentibus; ea vocem inmoderate profusam fingit et terminat atque sonos vocis distinctos et pressos efficit cum et[3] dentes et[4] alias partes pellit oris. Itaque plectri similem linguam nostri solent dicere, chordarum dentes, nares cornibus iis qui ad nervos resonant in cantibus.

150 LX. "Quam vero aptas quamque multarum artium ministras manus natura homini dedit. Digitorum enim contractio facilis facilisque porrectio propter molles commissuras et artus nullo in motu laborat. Itaque ad pingendum, ‹ad›[5] fingendum, ad scalpendum, ad nervorum eliciendos sonos ac tibiarum apta manus est admotione digitorum. Atque haec

[1] si *Madvig*: nisi. [2] munita *Baenemann*.
[3] et ad *A corr.* [4] et ad *A*.
[5] *add. Ald.*: [fingendum] *? cf.* § 145 *ed.*

[a] The vibration of the hollow horns no doubt intensified the sound of the strings.

create the arts that serve either practical necessities or the purpose of amusement. Then take the gift of speech, the queen of arts as you are fond of calling it—what a glorious, what a divine faculty it is! In the first place it enables us both to learn things we do not know and to teach things we do know to others; secondly it is our instrument for exhortation and persuasion, for consoling the afflicted and assuaging the fears of the terrified, for curbing passion and quenching appetite and anger; it is this that has united us in the bonds of justice, law and civil order, this that has separated us from savagery and barbarism. Now careful consideration will show that the mechanism of speech displays a skill on nature's part that surpasses belief. In the first place there is an artery passing from the lungs to the back of the mouth, which is the channel by which the voice, originating from the mind, is caught and uttered. Next, the tongue is placed in the mouth and confined by the teeth; it modulates and defines the inarticulate flow of the voice and renders its sounds distinct and clear by striking the teeth and other parts of the mouth. Accordingly my school is fond of comparing the tongue to the quill of a lyre, the teeth to the strings, and the nostrils to the horns which echo [a] the notes of the strings when the instrument is played.

man's gift of speech and its organs;

LX. "Then what clever servants for a great variety of arts are the hands which nature has bestowed on man! The flexibility of the joints enables the fingers to close and open with equal ease, and to perform every motion without difficulty. Thus by the manipulation of the fingers the hand is enabled to paint, to model, to carve, and to draw forth the notes of the lyre and of the flute. And beside these

the mechanism of man's hand, and his capacity for the arts and crafts;

oblectationis, illa necessitatis, cultus dico agrorum extructionesque tectorum, tegumenta corporum vel texta vel suta omnemque fabricam aeris et ferri ; ex quo intellegitur ad inventa animo, percepta sensibus adhibitis opificum manibus omnia nos consecutos, ut tecti ut vestiti ut salvi esse possemus, urbes
151 muros domicilia delubra haberemus. Iam vero operibus hominum, id est manibus, cibi etiam varietas invenitur et copia. Nam et agri multa efferunt manu quaesita quae vel statim consumantur vel mandentur condita vetustati, et praeterea vescimur bestiis et terrenis et aquatilibus et volantibus partim capiendo partim alendo. Efficimus etiam domitu nostro quadripedum vectiones, quorum celeritas atque vis nobis ipsis adfert vim et celeritatem ; nos onera quibusdam bestiis nos iuga inponimus, nos elephantorum acutissumis sensibus nos sagacitate canum ad utilitatem nostram abutimur, nos e terrae cavernis ferrum eligimus rem ad colendos agros necessariam, nos aeris argenti auri venas penitus abditas invenimus et ad usum aptas et ad ornatum decoras. Arborum autem consectione omnique materia et culta et silvestri partim ad calficiendum corpus igni adhibito et ad mitigandum cibum utimur, partim ad aedificandum ut tectis saepti frigora ca-
152 loresque pellamus ; magnos vero usus adfert ad navigia facienda, quorum cursibus subpeditantur omnes undique ad vitam copiae ; quasque res violentissimas

arts of recreation there are those of utility, I mean agriculture and building, the weaving and stitching of garments, and the various modes of working bronze and iron; hence we realize that it was by applying the hand of the artificer to the discoveries of thought and observations of the senses that all our conveniences were attained, and we were enabled to have shelter, clothing and protection, and possessed cities, fortifi-
51 cations, houses and temples. Moreover men's industry, that is to say the work of their hands, procures us also our food in variety and abundance. It is the hand that gathers the divers products of the fields, whether to be consumed immediately or to be stored in repositories for the days to come; and our diet also includes flesh, fish and fowl, obtained partly by the chase and partly by breeding. We also tame the four-footed animals to carry us on their backs, their swiftness and strength bestowing strength and swiftness upon ourselves. We cause certain beasts to bear our burdens or to carry a yoke, we divert to our service the marvellously acute senses of elephants and the keen scent of hounds; we collect from the caves of the earth the iron which we need for tilling the land, we discover the deeply hidden veins of copper, silver and gold which serve us both for use and for adornment; we cut up a multitude of trees both wild and cultivated for timber which we employ partly by setting fire to it to warm our bodies and cook our food, partly for building so as to shelter ourselves
52 with houses and banish heat and cold. Timber moreover is of great value for constructing ships, whose voyages supply an abundance of sustenance of all sorts from all parts of the earth; and we alone have the power of controlling the most violent of nature's

natura genuit earum moderationem nos soli habemus, maris atque ventorum, propter nauticarum rerum scientiam, plurimisque maritimis rebus fruimur atque utimur. Terrenorum item commodorum omnis est in homine dominatus: nos campis nos montibus fruimur, nostri sunt amnes nostri lacus, nos fruges serimus nos arbores, nos aquarum inductionibus terris fecunditatem damus, nos flumina arcemus derigimus avertimus, nostris denique manibus in rerum natura quasi alteram naturam efficere conamur.

153 LXI. "Quid vero? hominum ratio non in caelum usque penetravit? Soli enim ex animantibus nos astrorum ortus obitus cursusque cognovimus, ab hominum genere finitus est dies mensis annus, defectiones solis et lunae cognitae praedictaeque in omne posterum tempus, quae quantae quando futurae sint. Quae contuens animus accedit ad cognitionem deorum, e qua oritur pietas, cui coniuncta iustitia est reliquaeque virtutes, e quibus vita beata existit par et similis deorum, nulla alia re nisi inmortalitate, quae nihil ad bene vivendum pertinet, cedens caelestibus. Quibus rebus expositis satis docuisse videor hominis natura quanto omnis anteiret animantes; ex quo debet intellegi nec figuram situmque membrorum nec ingenii mentisque vim talem effici potuisse fortuna.

154 "Restat ut doceam atque aliquando perorem, omnia quae sint in hoc mundo quibus utantur homines hominum causa facta esse et parata.

offspring, the sea and the winds, thanks to the science of navigation, and we use and enjoy many products of the sea. Likewise the entire command of the commodities produced on land is vested in mankind. We enjoy the fruits of the plains and of the mountains, the rivers and the lakes are ours, we sow corn, we plant trees, we fertilize the soil by irrigation, we confine the rivers and straighten or divert their courses. In fine, by means of our hands we essay to create as it were a second world within the world of nature.

LXI. "Then moreover has not man's reason penetrated even to the sky? We alone of living creatures know the risings and settings and the courses of the stars, the human race has set limits to the day, the month and the year, and has learnt the eclipses of the sun and moon and foretold for all future time their occurrence, their extent and their dates. And contemplating the heavenly bodies the mind arrives at a knowledge of the gods, from which arises piety, with its comrades justice and the rest of the virtues, the sources of a life of happiness that vies with and resembles the divine existence and leaves us inferior to the celestial beings in nothing else save immortality, which is immaterial for happiness. I think that my exposition of these matters has been sufficient to prove how widely man's nature surpasses all other living creatures; and this should make it clear that neither such a conformation and arrangement of the members nor such power of mind and intellect can possibly have been created by chance.

man's capacity to observe the heavens and to worship the gods.

"It remains for me to show, in coming finally to a conclusion, that all the things in this world which men employ have been created and provided for the sake of men.

IV. Providential care for man (§154 to end).

LXII. " Principio ipse mundus deorum hominumque causa factus est, quaeque in eo sunt ea parata ad
fructum hominum et inventa sunt. Est enim mundus
quasi communis deorum atque hominum domus, aut
urbs utrorumque ; soli enim ratione utentes iure ac
lege vivunt. Ut igitur Athenas et Lacedaemonem
Atheniensium Lacedaemoniorumque causa putandum est conditas esse, omniaque quae sint in his
urbibus eorum populorum recte esse dicuntur, sic
quaecumque sunt in omni mundo deorum atque
155 hominum putanda sunt. Iam vero circumitus solis
et lunae reliquorumque siderum, quamquam etiam
ad mundi cohaerentiam pertinent, tamen et spectaculum hominibus praebent ; nulla est enim insatiabilior
species, nulla pulchrior et ad rationem sollertiamque
praestantior ; eorum enim cursus dimetati maturitates temporum et varietates mutationesque cognovimus ; quae si hominibus solis nota sunt, hominum
156 facta esse causa iudicandum est. Terra vero feta
frugibus et vario leguminum genere, quae cum
maxuma largitate fundit, ea ferarumne an hominum
causa gignere videtur ? Quid de vitibus olivetisque
dicam, quarum uberrumi laetissumique fructus
nihil omnino ad bestias pertinent ? Neque enim
serendi neque colendi nec tempestive demetendi
percipiendique fructus neque condendi ac reponendi

LXII. "In the first place the world itself was created for the sake of gods and men, and the things that it contains were provided and contrived for the enjoyment of men. For the world is as it were the common dwelling-place of gods and men, or the city that belongs to both; for they alone have the use of reason and live by justice and by law. As therefore Athens and Sparta must be deemed to have been founded for the sake of the Athenians and the Spartans, and all the things contained in those cities are rightly said to belong to those peoples, so whatever things are contained in all the world must be deemed to belong to the gods and to men. Again the revolutions of the sun and moon and other heavenly bodies, although also contributing to the maintenance of the structure of the world, nevertheless also afford a spectacle for man to behold; for there is no sight of which it is more impossible to grow weary, none more beautiful nor displaying a more surpassing wisdom and skill; for by measuring the courses of the stars we know when the seasons will come round, and when their variations and changes will occur; and if these things are known to men alone, they must be judged to have been created for the sake of men. Then the earth, teeming with grain and vegetables of various kinds, which she pours forth in lavish abundance—does she appear to give birth to this produce for the sake of the wild beasts or for the sake of men? What shall I say of the vines and olives, whose bounteous and delightful fruits do not concern the lower animals at all? In fact the beasts of the field are entirely ignorant of the arts of sowing and cultivating, and of reaping and gathering the fruits of the earth in due season and storing them

The world and the heavenly bodies exist for the sake of gods and men.

The vegetable kingdom is provided for the use of man.

ulla pecudum scientia est, earumque omnium rerum
157 hominum est et usus et cura. LXIII. Ut fides igitur et tibias eorum causa factas dicendum est qui illis uti possent, sic ea quae dixi iis solis confitendum est esse parata qui utuntur, nec si quae bestiae furantur aliquid ex iis aut rapiunt, illarum quoque causa ea nata esse dicemus. Neque enim homines murum aut formicarum causa frumentum condunt sed coniugum et liberorum et familiarum suarum; itaque bestiae furtim ut dixi fruuntur, domini
158 palam et libere. Hominum igitur causa eas rerum copias comparatas fatendum est, nisi forte tanta ubertas et varietas pomorum eorumque iucundus non gustatus solum sed odoratus etiam et aspectus dubitationem adfert quin hominibus solis ea natura donaverit. Tantumque abest ut haec bestiarum etiam causa parata sint, ut ipsas bestias hominum gratia generatas esse videamus. Quid enim oves aliud adferunt nisi ut earum villis confectis atque contextis homines vestiantur? quae quidem neque ali neque sustentari neque ullum fructum edere ex se sine cultu hominum et curatione potuissent. Canum vero tam fida custodia tamque amans dominorum adulatio tantumque odium in externos, et tam incredibilis ad investigandum sagacitas narium tanta alacritas in venando quid significat[1] aliud nisi se ad hominum commoditates esse generatos?
159 Quid de bubus loquar? quorum ipsa terga declarant

[1] significant? *ed.*

in garners; all these products are both enjoyed and tended by men. LXIII. Just as therefore we are bound to say that lyres and flutes were made for the sake of those who can use them, so it must be agreed that the things of which I have spoken have been provided for those only who make use of them, and even if some portion of them is filched or plundered by some of the lower animals, we shall not admit that they were created for the sake of these animals also. Men do not store up corn for the sake of mice and ants but for their wives and children and households; so the animals share these fruits of the earth only by stealth as I have said, whereas their masters enjoy them openly and freely. It must therefore be admitted that all this abundance was provided for the sake of men, unless perchance the bounteous plenty and variety of our orchard fruit and the delightfulness not only of its flavour but also of its scent and appearance lead us to doubt whether nature intended this gift for man alone! So far is it from being true that the fruits of the earth were provided for the sake of animals as well as men, that the animals themselves, as we may see, were created for the benefit of men. What other use have sheep save that their fleeces are dressed and woven into clothing for men? and in fact they could not have been reared nor sustained nor have produced anything of value without man's care and tendance. Then think of the dog, with its trusty watchfulness, its fawning affection for its master and hatred of strangers, its incredible keenness of scent in following a trail and its eagerness in hunting—what do these qualities imply except that they were created to serve the conveniences of men? Why should I speak of oxen? the very shape of their backs makes

and the animals also are created for his use,

non esse se ad onus accipiendum figurata, cervices autem natae ad iugum, tum vires umerorum et latitudines ad aratra [ex]trahenda.[1] Quibus cum terrae subigerentur fissione glebarum, ab illo aureo genere, ut poetae loquuntur, vis nulla umquam adferebatur;

> ferrea tum vero proles exorta repente est,
> ausaque funestum prima est fabricarier ensem
> et gustare manu vinctum domitumque iuvencum.

Tanta putabatur utilitas percipi e bubus ut eorum visceribus vesci scelus haberetur.

LXIV. "Longum est mulorum persequi utilitates et asinorum, quae certe ad hominum usum paratae
160 sunt. Sus vero quid habet praeter escam? cui quidem ne putesceret animam ipsam pro sale datam dicit esse Chrysippus; qua pecude, quod erat ad vescendum hominibus apta, nihil genuit natura fecundius. Quid multitudinem suavitatemque piscium dicam? quid avium, ex quibus tanta percipitur voluptas ut interdum Pronoea nostra Epicurea fuisse videatur? atque eae ne caperentur quidem nisi hominum ratione atque sollertia;—quamquam avis quasdam, et alites et oscines, ut nostri augures appellant, rerum augurandarum causa esse natas
161 putamus. Iam vero immanes et feras beluas nanciscimur venando, ut et vescamur iis et exerceamur

[1] trahenda *Ernesti.*

[a] Cicero's translation of Aratus's *Phaenomena*, 129 ff.

[b] Clement of Alexandria, *Strom.* vii. 34 Κλεάνθης φησὶν

it clear that they were not destined to carry burdens, whereas their necks were born for the yoke and their broad powerful shoulders for drawing the plough. And as it was by their means that the earth was brought under tillage by breaking up its clods, no violence was ever used towards them, so the poets say, by the men of that Golden Age;

> But then the iron race sprang into being,
> And first did dare to forge the deadly sword,
> And taste the ox its hand had tamed to bondage.[a]

So valuable was deemed the service that man received from oxen that to eat their flesh was held a crime.

LXIV. "It would be a long story to tell of the services rendered by mules and asses, which were un-
160 doubtedly created for the use of men. As for the pig, it can only furnish food; indeed Chrysippus[b] actually says that its soul was given it to serve as salt and keep it from putrefaction; and because this animal was fitted for the food of man, nature made it the most prolific of all her offspring. Why should I speak of the teeming swarms of delicious fish? or of birds, which afford us so much pleasure that our Stoic Providence appears to have been at times a disciple of Epicurus? and they could not even be caught save by man's intelligence and cunning;—although some birds, birds of flight and birds of utterance as our augurs call them, we believe to have been created for the
161 purpose of giving omens. The great beasts of the forest again we take by hunting, both for food and in order to exercise ourselves in the mimic warfare of the

ἀνθ' ἁλῶν αὐτοὺς (τοὺς ὗς) ἔχειν τὴν ψυχήν, ἵνα μὴ σαπῇ τὰ κρέα; but Cicero is probably right in giving it to Chrysippus.

in venando ad similitudinem bellicae disciplinae, et utamur domitis et condocefactis, ut elephantis, multaque ex earum corporibus remedia morbis et vulneribus eligamus, sicut ex quibusdam stirpibus et herbis quarum utilitates longinqui temporis usu et periclitatione percepimus. Totam licet animis tamquam oculis lustrare terram mariaque omnia: cernes iam spatia frugifera atque inmensa camporum vestitusque densissimos montium, pecudum pastus,
162 tum incredibili cursus maritimos celeritate. Nec vero supra terram sed etiam in intumis eius tenebris plurimarum rerum latet utilitas quae ad usum hominum orta ab hominibus solis invenitur.

LXV. "Illud vero, quod uterque vestrum arripiet fortasse ad reprendendum, Cotta quia Carneades lubenter in Stoicos invehebatur, Velleius quia nihil tam inridet Epicurus quam praedictionem rerum futurarum, mihi videtur vel maxume confirmare deorum providentia consuli rebus humanis. Est enim profecto divinatio, quae multis locis rebus temporibus apparet cum [in][1] privatis tum maxume
163 publicis. Multa cernunt haruspices, multa augures provident, multa oraclis declarantur multa vaticinationibus multa somniis multa portentis; quibus cognitis multae saepe res ex[2] hominum sententia atque utilitate partae, multa etiam pericula depulsa sunt. Haec igitur sive vis sive ars sive natura ad scientiam rerum futurarum homini profecto est nec alii cuiquam a dis inmortalibus data.

[1] *secl. Muller.* [2] ex *dett.*: *om. A, B.*

chase, and also, as in the case of elephants, to train and discipline them for our employment, and to procure from their bodies a variety of medicines for diseases and wounds, as also we do from certain roots and herbs whose values we have learnt by long-continued use and trial. Let the mind's eye survey the whole earth and all the seas, and you will behold now fruitful plains of measureless extent and mountains thickly clad with forests and pastures filled with flocks, now vessels sailing with marvellous swiftness across the sea. Nor only on the surface of the earth, but also in its darkest recesses there lurks an abundance of commodities which were created for men's use and which men alone discover.

and so is the inorganic world.

LXV. "The next subject is one which each of you perhaps will seize upon for censure, Cotta because Carneades used to enjoy tilting at the Stoics, Velleius because nothing provokes the ridicule of Epicurus so much as the art of prophecy; but in my view it affords the very strongest proof that man's welfare is studied by divine providence. I refer of course to Divination, which we see practised in many regions and upon various matters and occasions both private and more especially public. Many observations are made by those who inspect the victims at sacrifices, many events are foreseen by augurs or revealed in oracles and prophecies, dreams and portents, a knowledge of which has often led to the acquisition of many things gratifying men's wishes and requirements, and also to the avoidance of many dangers. This power or art or instinct therefore has clearly been bestowed by the immortal gods on man, and on no other creature, for the ascertainment of future events.

Divination is possessed solely by man.

"Quae si singula vos forte non movent, universa certe tamen inter se conexa atque coniuncta movere debebunt.[1]

164 "Nec vero universo generi hominum solum sed etiam singulis a dis inmortalibus consuli et provideri solet. Licet enim contrahere universitatem generis humani, eamque gradatim ad pauciores, postremo deducere ad singulos. LXVI. Nam si omnibus hominibus qui ubique sunt quacumque in ora ac parte terrarum ab huiusce terrae quam nos incolimus continuatione distantium deos consulere censemus ob eas causas quas ante diximus, his quoque hominibus consulunt qui has nobiscum terras ab
165 oriente ad occidentem colunt. Sin autem his consulunt[2] qui quasi magnam quandam insulam incolunt quam nos orbem terrae vocamus, etiam illis consulunt qui partes eius insulae tenent, Europam Asiam Africam. Ergo et earum partes diligunt, ut Romam Athenas Spartam Rhodum, et earum urbium separatim ab universis singulos diligunt, ut Pyrrhi bello Curium Fabricium Coruncanium, primo Punico Calatinum Duellium Metellum Lutatium, secundo Maxumum Marcellum Africanum, post hos Paulum Gracchum Catonem, patrumve memoria Scipionem Laelium; multosque praeterea et nostra civitas et Graecia tulit singulares viros, quorum neminem nisi iuvante deo talem fuisse creden-
166 dum est. Quae ratio poetas maxumeque Homerum inpulit ut principibus heroum, Ulixi Diomedi Aga-

[1] debebant *nonnulli.*

[2] his consulunt *Ald.*: consulunt iis *dett.*

"And if perchance these arguments separately fail to convince you, nevertheless in combination their collective weight will be bound to do so.

"Nor is the care and providence of the immortal gods bestowed only upon the human race in its entirety, but it is also wont to be extended to individuals. We may narrow down the entirety of the human race and bring it gradually down to smaller and smaller groups, and finally to single individuals. LXVI. For if we believe, for the reasons that we have spoken of before, that the gods care for all human beings everywhere in every coast and region of the lands remote from this continent in which we dwell, then they care also for the men who inhabit with us these lands between the sunrise and the sunset. But if they care for these who inhabit that sort of vast island which we call the round earth, they also care for those who occupy the divisions of that island, Europe, Asia and Africa. Therefore they also cherish the divisions of those divisions, for instance Rome, Athens, Sparta and Rhodes; and they cherish the individual citizens of those cities regarded separately from the whole body collectively, for example, Curius, Fabricius and Coruncanius in the war with Pyrrhus, Calatinus, Duellius, Metellus and Lutatius in the First Punic War, and Maximus, Marcellus and Africanus in the Second, and at a later date Paulus, Gracchus and Cato, or in our fathers' time Scipio and Laelius; and many remarkable men besides both our own country and Greece have given birth to, none of whom could conceivably have been what he was save by god's aid. It was this reason which drove the poets, and especially Homer, to attach to their chief heroes, Ulysses, Diomede,

Divine care extends to individual men.

memnoni Achilli, certos deos discriminum et periculorum comites adiungeret. Praeterea ipsorum deorum saepe praesentiae, quales supra commemoravi, declarant ab iis et civitatibus et singulis hominibus consuli. Quod quidem intellegitur etiam significationibus rerum futurarum quae tum dormientibus tum vigilantibus portenduntur; multa praeterea ostentis multa extis admonemur, multisque rebus aliis quas diuturnus usus ita notavit ut artem
167 divinationis efficeret. Nemo igitur vir magnus sine aliquo adflatu divino umquam fuit. Nec vero <id>[1] ita refellendum est ut, si segetibus aut vinetis cuiuspiam tempestas nocuerit, aut si quid e vitae commodis casus abstulerit, eum cui quid horum acciderit aut invisum deo aut neglectum a deo iudicemus. Magna di curant, parva neglegunt. Magnis autem viris prosperae semper omnes res, siquidem satis a nostris et a principe philosophiae Socrate dictum est de ubertatibus virtutis et copiis.
168 LXVII. "Haec mihi fere in mentem veniebant quae dicenda putarem de natura deorum. Tu autem, Cotta, si me audias, eandem causam agas teque et principem civem et pontificem esse cogites et, quoniam in utramque partem vobis licet disputare, hanc

[1] *add. Heindorf.*

[a] In *De Divinatione* Cicero's brother Quintus sets out in Book I. these two kinds of divination, natural, by means of dreams and ecstasies, and artificial, through the observation of entrails of victims, birds' flight, lightning and other portents; in Book II. Cicero replies, denying divination altogether.

Agamemnon or Achilles, certain gods as the companions of their perils and adventures; moreover the gods have often appeared to men in person, as in the cases which I have mentioned above, so testifying that they care both for communities and for individuals.[a] And the same is proved by the portents of future occurrences that are vouchsafed to men sometimes when they are asleep and sometimes when they are awake. Moreover we receive a number of warnings by means of signs and of the entrails of victims, and by many other things that long-continued usage has noted in such a manner as to create the art of divination. Therefore no great man ever existed who did not enjoy some portion of divine inspiration. Nor yet is this argument to be disproved by pointing to cases where a man's cornfields or vineyards have been damaged by a storm, or an accident has robbed him of some commodity of value, and inferring that the victim of one of these misfortunes is the object of god's hatred or neglect. The gods attend to great matters; they neglect small ones. Now great men always prosper in all their affairs, assuming that the teachers of our school and Socrates, the prince of philosophy, have satisfactorily discoursed upon the bounteous abundance of wealth that virtue bestows.

LXVII. "These are more or less the things that occurred to me which I thought proper to be said upon the subject of the nature of the gods. And for your part, Cotta, would you but listen to me, you would plead the same cause, and reflect that you are a leading citizen and a pontiff, and you would take advantage of the liberty enjoyed by your school of arguing both *pro* and *contra* to choose to espouse my **Conclusion.**

potius sumas, eamque facultatem disserendi quam tibi a rhetoricis exercitationibus acceptam amplificavit Academia potius huc conferas. Mala enim et impia consuetudo est contra deos disputandi, sive ex animo id fit sive simulate."

side, and preferably to devote to this purpose those powers of eloquence which your rhetorical exercises have bestowed upon you and which the Academy has fostered. For the habit of arguing in support of atheism, whether it be done from conviction or in pretence, is a wicked and an impious practice."

LIBER TERTIUS

1 I. Quae cum Balbus dixisset, tum adridens Cotta "Sero" inquit "mihi Balbe praecipis quid defendam; ego enim te disputante quid contra dicerem mecum ipse meditabar, neque tam refellendi tui causa quam ea quae minus intellegebam requirendi. Cum autem suo cuique iudicio sit utendum, difficile factu est me id sentire quod tu velis."

2 Hic Velleius "Nescis" inquit "quanta cum exspectatione Cotta sim te auditurus. Iucundus enim Balbo nostro sermo tuus contra Epicurum fuit; praebebo igitur ego me tibi vicissim attentum contra Stoicos auditorem. Spero enim te ut soles bene paratum venire."

3 Tum Cotta "Sic mehercule" inquit "Vellei; neque enim mihi par ratio cum Lucilio est ac tecum fuit."

"Qui tandem?" inquit ille.

"Quia mihi videtur Epicurus vester de dis inmortalibus non magnopere pugnare: tantum modo negare deos esse non audet ne quid invidiae subeat aut criminis. Cum vero deos nihil agere nihil curare

BOOK III

I. Cotta smiled when Balbus said this. "It is too late, Balbus," he rejoined, "for you to tell me what view I am to support, for while you were discoursing I was pondering what arguments I could bring against you, though not so much for the purpose of refuting you as of asking for an explanation of the points which I could not quite understand. However, each man must use his own judgement, and it is a difficult task for me to take the view which you would like me to take."

Academic criticism of Stoic theology. Introduction: Cotta admits the force of Balbus's exposition, but is content with the ancestral religion of Rome.

Hereupon Velleius broke in: "You cannot think, Cotta," said he, "how eager I am to hear you. Our good friend Balbus enjoyed your discourse against Epicurus; so I in my turn will give you an attentive hearing against the Stoics. For I hope that you come well equipped, as you usually do."

"Yes, to be sure, Velleius," replied Cotta; "for I have a very different business before me with Lucilius from what I had with you."

"How so, pray?" said Velleius.

"Because I think that your master Epicurus does not put up a very strong fight on the question of the immortal gods; he only does not venture to deny their existence so that he may not encounter any ill-feeling or reproach. But when he asserts that the gods do nothing and care for nothing, and that though

confirmat, membrisque humanis esse praeditos sed eorum membrorum usum nullum habere, ludere videtur, satisque putare si dixerit esse quandam
4 beatam naturam et aeternam. A Balbo autem animadvertisti credo quam multa dicta sint, quamque etiamsi minus vera tamen apta inter se et cohaerentia. Itaque cogito ut dixi non tam refellere eius orationem quam ea quae minus intellexi requirere. Quare Balbe tibi permitto, responderene mihi malis de singulis rebus quaerenti ex te ea quae parum accepi, an universam audire orationem meam."

Tum Balbus "Ego vero si quid explanari tibi voles respondere malo, sin me interrogare non tam intellegendi causa quam refellendi, utrum voles faciam: vel ad singula quae requires statim respondebo vel cum peroraris ad omnia."

5 Tum Cotta "Optıme" inquit; "quam ob rem sic agamus ut nos ipsa ducet oratio. II. Sed ante quam de re, pauca de me. Nom enim mediocriter moveor auctoritate tua, Balbe, orationeque ea quae me in perorando cohortabatur ut meminissem me et Cottam esse et pontificem; quod eo credo valebat, ut opiniones quas a maioribus accepimus de dis inmortalibus, sacra caerimonias religionesque defenderem. Ego vero eas defendam semper semperque

they possess limbs like those of men they make no use of those limbs, he seems not to be speaking seriously, and to think it enough if he affirms the existence of blessed and everlasting beings of some sort. But as for Balbus, I am sure you must have noticed how much he had to say, and how though lacking in truth it was yet consistent and systematic. Hence what I have in mind, as I said, is not so much to refute his discourse as to ask for an explanation of the things that I could not quite understand. Accordingly, I offer you the choice, Balbus, whether you would prefer that I should question you and you reply upon each of the points singly as to which I did not quite agree, or that you should hear out my entire discourse."

"Oh," answered Balbus, "I had rather reply about any point which you desire to have explained to you; or if you want to question me with a view not so much to understanding as to refuting me, I will do whichever you wish, and will either reply to each of your inquiries at once, or answer them all when you have completed your speech."

5 "Very well," rejoined Cotta, "let us then proceed as the argument itself may lead us. II. But before we come to the subject, let me say a few words about myself. I am considerably influenced by your authority, Balbus, and by the plea that you put forward at the conclusion of your discourse, when you exhorted me to remember that I am both a Cotta and a pontiff. This no doubt meant that I ought to uphold the beliefs about the immortal gods which have come down to us from our ancestors, and the rites and ceremonies and duties of religion. For my part I always shall uphold them and always have

defendi, nec me ex ea opinione quam a maioribus accepi de cultu deorum inmortalium ullius umquam oratio aut docti aut indocti movebit. Sed cum de religione agitur, Ti. Coruncanium P. Scipionem P. Scaevolam pontifices maximos, non Zenonem aut Cleanthen aut Chrysippum sequor, habeoque C. Laelium augurem eundemque sapientem, quem potius audiam dicentem de religione in illa oratione nobili quam quemquam principem Stoicorum. Cumque omnis populi Romani religio in sacra et in auspicia divisa sit, tertium adiunctum sit si quid praedictionis causa ex portentis et monstris Sibyllae interpretes haruspicesve monuerunt, harum ego religionum nullam umquam contemnendam putavi, mihique ita persuasi, Romulum auspiciis Numam sacris constitutis fundamenta iecisse nostrae civitatis, quae numquam profecto sine summa placatione deo-
6 rum inmortalium tanta esse potuisset. Habes Balbe quid Cotta quid pontifex sentiat; fac nunc ego intellegam tu quid sentias. A te enim philosopho rationem accipere debeo religionis, maioribus autem nostris etiam nulla ratione reddita credere."

III. Tum Balbus "Quam igitur a me rationem" inquit "Cotta, desideras?"

Et ille "Quadripertita" inquit "fuit divisio tua, primum ut velles docere deos esse, deinde quales essent, tum ab iis mundum regi, postremo consulere

---

[a] Laelius when praetor, 143 B.C., successfully opposed a proposal to transfer the election of the augurs to the people, instead of their being co-opted. *Cf.* § 43.

done so, and no eloquence of anybody, learned or unlearned, shall ever dislodge me from the belief as to the worship of the immortal gods which I have inherited from our forefathers. But on any question of religion I am guided by the high pontiffs, Titus Coruncanius, Publius Scipio and Publius Scaevola, not by Zeno or Cleanthes or Chrysippus; and I have Gaius Laelius, who was both an augur and a philosopher, to whose discourse upon religion, in his famous oration,[a] I would rather listen than to any leader of the Stoics. The religion of the Roman people comprises ritual, auspices, and the third additional division consisting of all such prophetic warnings as the interpreters of the Sybil or the soothsayers have derived from portents and prodigies. Well, I have always thought that none of these departments of religion was to be despised, and I have held the conviction that Romulus by his auspices and Numa by his establishment of our ritual laid the foundations of our state, which assuredly could never have been as great as it is had not the fullest measure of divine favour been obtained for it. There, Balbus, is the opinion of a Cotta and a pontiff; now oblige me by letting me know yours. You are a philosopher, and I ought to receive from you a proof of your religion, whereas I must believe the word of our ancestors even without proof."

III. "What proof then do you require of me, Cotta?" replied Balbus.

"You divided your discourse under four heads," said Cotta; "first you designed to prove the existence of the gods; secondly, to describe their nature; thirdly, to show that the world is governed by them; and lastly, that they care for the welfare of men.

The four divisions of the subject.

eos rebus humanis: haec, si recte memini, partitio fuit."

"Rectissume" inquit Balbus, "sed expecto quid requiras."

7 Tum Cotta "Primum quidque videamus" inquit, "et si id est primum quod inter omnis nisi admodum impios convenit, mihi quidem ex animo excuti non potest esse deos, id tamen ipsum, quod mihi persuasum est auctoritate maiorum, cur ita sit, nihil tu me doces."

"Quid est" inquit Balbus, "si tibi persuasum est, cur a me velis discere?"

Tum Cotta "Quia sic adgredior" inquit "ad hanc disputationem quasi nihil umquam audierim de dis inmortalibus nihil cogitaverim; rudem me et integrum discipulum accipe et ea quae requiro doce."

8 "Dic igitur" inquit "quid requiras."

"Egone? primum illud, cur, quom[1] [perspicuum in][2] istam partem[3] ne egere quidem oratione dixisses, quod esset perspicuum et inter omnis constaret ‹deos esse›,[4] de eo ipso tam multa dixeris."

"Quia te quoque" inquit "animadverti, Cotta, saepe cum in foro diceres quam plurimis posses argumentis onerare iudicem, si modo eam facultatem tibi daret causa. Atque hoc idem et philosophi faciunt et ego ut potui feci. Tu autem qui id[5] quaeris similiter facis ac si me roges cur te duobus contuear

[1] quom *Forchhammer*: quod. [2] *secl. Plasberg.*
[3] in ista partitione *Heindorf.* [4] *add. Plasberg.*
[5] qui id *dett.*: quod.

These, if I remember rightly, were the headings that you laid down."

"You are quite right," said Balbus; "but now tell me what it is that you want to know."

"Let us take each point in turn," replied Cotta, "and if the first one is the doctrine which is universally accepted save by absolute infidels, although I for my part cannot be persuaded to surrender my belief that the gods exist, nevertheless you teach me no reason why this belief, of which I am convinced on the authority of our forefathers, should be true."

I. The divine existence (§§ 7-19).

"If you are convinced of it," said Balbus, "what reason is there for your wanting me to teach you?"

"Because," said Cotta, "I am entering on this discussion as if I had never been taught anything or reflected at all about the immortal gods. Accept me as a pupil who is a novice and entirely untutored, and teach me what I want to know."

"Tell me then," said he, "what do you want to know?"

If the belief in the gods is necessary and universal, argument is needless, and may awaken doubt.

"What do I want to know? First of all, why it was that after saying that this part of your subject did not even need discussion, because the fact of the divine existence was manifest and universally admitted, you nevertheless discoursed at such great length on that very point."

"It was because I have often noticed that you too, Cotta, when speaking in court, overwhelmed the judge with all the arguments you could think of, provided the case gave you an opportunity to do so. Well, the Greek philosophers do likewise, and so did I also, to the best of my ability. But for you to ask me this question is just the same as if you were to ask me why I look at you with two eyes instead of closing

oculis et non altero coniveam, cum idem uno adsequi possim."

9 IV. Tum Cotta "Quam simile istud sit" inquit "tu videris. Nam ego neque in causis, si quid est evidens de quo inter omnis conveniat, argumentari soleo (perspicuitas enim argumentatione elevatur), nec si id facerem in causis forensibus idem facerem in hac subtilitate sermonis. Cur coniveres[1] autem altero oculo causa non esset, cum idem obtutus esset amborum, et cum rerum natura, quam tu sapientem esse vis, duo lumina ab animo ad oculos perforata nos habere voluisset. Sed quia non confidebas tam esse id perspicuum quam tu velles, propterea multis argumentis deos esse docere voluisti. Mihi enim unum sat erat, ita nobis maiores nostros tradidisse. Sed tu

10 auctoritates contemnis, ratione pugnas; patere igitur rationem meam cum tua ratione contendere.

"Adfers haec omnia argumenta cur di sint, remque mea sententia minime dubiam argumentando dubiam facis. Mandavi enim memoriae non numerum solum sed etiam ordinem argumentorum tuorum. Primum fuit, cum caelum suspexissemus statim nos intellegere esse aliquod numen quo haec regantur. Ex hoc illud etiam:

[1] *Madvig*: contueres.

one of them, seeing that I could achieve the same result with one eye as with two."

IV. "How far your comparison really holds good," rejoined Cotta, "is a question that I will leave to you. As a matter of fact in law-suits it is not my practice to argue a point that is self-evident and admitted by all parties, for argument would only diminish its clearness; and besides, if I did do this in pleading cases in the courts, I should not do the same thing in an abstract discussion like the present. But there would be no real reason for your shutting one eye, since both eyes have the same field of vision, and since the nature of things, which you declare to be possessed of wisdom, has willed that we should possess two windows pierced from the mind to the eyes. You did not really feel confident that the doctrine of the divine existence was as self-evident as you could wish, and for that reason you attempted to prove it with a number of arguments. For my part a single argument would have sufficed, namely that it has been handed down to us by our forefathers. But you despise authority, and fight your battles with the weapon of reason. Give permission therefore for my reason to join issue with yours.

"You adduce all these arguments to prove that the gods exist, and by arguing you render doubtful a matter which in my opinion admits of no doubt at all. For I have committed to memory not only the number but also the order of your arguments. The first was that when we look up at the sky, we at once perceive that some power exists whereby the heavenly bodies are governed. And from this you went on to quote[a]:

Not true that the sight of the heavens leads to a belief in a God of Nature; and common belief is unreliable.

[a] Book II. 4.

aspice hoc sublime candens, quem invocant omnes Iovem;

11 quasi vero quisquam nostrum istum potius quam Capitolinum Iovem appellet, aut hoc perspicuum sit constetque inter omnis, eos esse deos quos tibi Velleius multique praeterea ne animantis quidem esse concedant. Grave etiam argumentum tibi videbatur quod opinio de dis inmortalibus et omnium esset et cotidie cresceret: placet igitur tantas res opinione stultorum iudicari, vobis praesertim qui illos insanos esse dicatis? V. 'At enim praesentis videmus deos, ut apud Regillum Postumius, in Salaria Vatinius'; nescio quid etiam de Locrorum apud Sagram proelio. Quos igitur tu Tyndaridas appellabas, id est homines homine natos, et quos Homerus, qui recens ab illorum aetate fuit, sepultos esse dicit Lacedaemone, eos tu cantheriis albis nullis calonibus ob viam Vatinio venisse existimas et victoriam populi Romani Vatinio potius homini rustico quam M. Catoni qui tum erat princeps nuntiavisse? Ergo et illud in silice quod hodie apparet apud Regillum tamquam vestigium un-
12 gulae, Castoris equi credis esse? Nonne mavis illud credere quod probari potest, animos praeclarorum hominum, quales isti Tyndaridae fuerunt, divinos esse et aeternos, quam eos qui semel cremati essent

[a] *i.e.*, the heavenly bodies. [b] Book II 6.

Behold this dazzling vault of heaven, which all mankind
as Jove invoke;

11 just as if anyone among us really gave the name of Jove to your heaven rather than to Jove of the Capitol, or as if it were self-evident and universally agreed that those beings [a] are divine whom Velleius and many others beside will not even grant you to be alive at all! Also you thought it a weighty argument that the belief in the immortal gods is universally held and is spreading every day. Then is anybody content that questions of such moment should be decided by the beliefs of the foolish? and particularly yourselves, who say that all the foolish are mad?

The stories of gods appearing are mere rumour.

V. "But you say [b] that the gods appear to us in bodily presence—for instance, they did to Postumius at Lake Regillus and to Vatinius on the Via Salaria; and also some story or other about the battle of the Locrians on the Sagra. Then do you really think that the beings whom you call the sons of Tyndareus, that is mortal men of mortal parentage, and whom Homer, who lived not long after their period, states to have been buried at Sparta, came riding on white hacks with no retainers, and met Vatinius, and selected a rough countryman like him to whom to bring the news of a great national victory, instead of Marcus Cato, who was the chief senator at the time? Well then, do you also believe that the mark in the rock resembling a hoof-print, to be seen at the present day on the shore of Lake Regillus, was made by
12 Castor's horse? Would you not prefer to believe the perfectly credible doctrine that the souls of famous men, like the sons of Tyndareus you speak of, are divine and live for ever, rather than that men who had been once for all burnt on a funeral pyre were

equitare et in acie pugnare potuisse? aut si hoc fieri potuisse dicis, doceas oportet quo modo, nec fabellas aniles proferas."

13 Tum Lucilius "An tibi" inquit "fabellae videntur? Nonne ab A. Postumio aedem Castori et Polluci in foro dedicatam, nonne senatus consultum de Vatinio vides? Nam de Sagra Graecorum etiam est volgare proverbium, qui quae adfirmant certiora esse dicunt quam illa quae apud Sagram. His igitur auctoribus nonne debes moveri?"

Tum Cotta "Rumoribus" inquit "mecum pugnas, Balbe, ego autem a te rationes requiro . . .[1]

14 VI. ". . . sequuntur quae futura sunt; effugere enim nemo id potest quod futurum est. Saepe autem ne utile quidem est scire quid futurum sit; miserum est enim nihil proficientem angi nec habere ne spei quidem extremum et tamen commune solacium, praesertim cum vos iidem fato fieri dicatis omnia, quod autem semper ex omni aeternitate verum fuerit id esse fatum: quid igitur iuvat aut quid adfert ad cavendum scire aliquid futurum, cum id certe futurum sit? Unde porro ista divinatio? Quis invenit fissum iecoris, quis cornicis cantum notavit, quis sortis? Quibus ego credo, nec possum Atti Navii quem commemorabas lituum contemnere; sed qui ista intel-

[1] *lacunam signavit Victorius.*

---

[a] A part of Cotta's argument has here been lost, including a transition to the subject of prophecies and presentiments. *Cf. infr.* 16 and Book II. 7. [b] Book II. 9.

able to ride on horseback and fight in a battle? Or if you maintain that this was possible, then you have got to explain how it was possible, and not merely bring forward old wives' tales."

"Do you really think them old wives' tales?" rejoined Lucilius. "Are you not aware of the temple in the forum dedicated to Castor and Pollux by Aulus Postumius, or of the resolution of the senate concerning Vatinius? As for the Sagra, the Greeks actually have a proverbial saying about it: when they make an assertion they say that it is 'more certain than the affair on the Sagra.' Surely their authority must carry weight with you?"

"Ah, Balbus," replied Cotta, "you combat me with hearsay for your weapon, but what I ask of you is proof. . . .[a]

Divination even if true would be useless, and it cannot prove the gods' existence.

VI. ". . . the events that are going to happen follow; for no one can escape what is going to happen. But often it is not even an advantage to know what is going to happen; for it is miserable to suffer unavailing torments, and to lack even the last, yet universal, consolation of hope, especially when your school also asserts that all events are fated, fate meaning that which has always from all eternity been true: what good is it therefore to know that something is going to happen, or how does it help us to avoid it, when it certainly will happen? Moreover whence was your art of divination derived? Who found out the cleft in the liver? Who took note of the raven's croaking, or the way in which the lots fall? Not that I don't believe in these things, or care to scoff at Attus Navius's crosier of which you were speaking[b]; but how did these modes of divination come to be understood? this is what the philosophers

lecta sint a philosophis debeo discere, praesertim cum
15 plurimis de rebus divini[1] isti mentiantur. 'At medici quoque' (ita enim dicebas) 'saepe falluntur.' Quid simile medicina, cuius ego rationem video, et divinatio, quae unde oriatur non intellego? Tu autem etiam Deciorum devotionibus placatos deos esse censes. Quae fuit eorum tanta iniquitas ut placari populo Romano non possent nisi viri tales occidissent? Consilium illud imperatorium fuit, quod Graeci *στρατήγημα* appellant, sed eorum imperatorum qui patriae consulerent vitae non parcerent; rebantur enim fore ut exercitus imperatorem equo incitato se in hostem inmittentem persequeretur, id quod evenit. Nam Fauni vocem equidem numquam audivi: tibi si audivisse te dicis credam, etsi Faunus omnino quid sit nescio. VII. Non igitur adhuc, quantum quidem in te est, Balbe, intellego deos esse; quos equidem credo esse, sed nihil docent Stoici.

16 "Nam Cleanthes ut dicebas quattuor modis formatas in animis hominum putat deorum esse notiones. Unus ex his is[2] modus est de quo satis dixi, qui est susceptus ex praesensione rerum futurarum; alter ex perturbationibus tempestatum et reliquis motibus; tertius ex commoditate rerum quas percipimus et copia; quartus ex astrorum ordine caelique constantia. De praesensione diximus. De perturbationibus

[1] *det.*: divinis *A*, *B*.
[2] *Dieckhoff*: unus is *A*, unus ex his *B*.

[a] Book II. 12. [b] Book II. 6.

must teach me, especially as your diviners tell such a pack of lies. 'Well, but physicians also are often wrong'—this was your argument.[a] But what resemblance is there between medicine, whose rational basis I can see, and divination, the source of which I cannot understand? Again, you think that the gods were actually propitiated by the sacrifice of the Decii. But how can the gods have been so unjust that their wrath against the Roman people could only be appeased by the death of heroes like the Decii? No, the sacrifice of the Decii was a device of generalship, or *stratēgēma* as it is termed in Greek, though a device for generals who were ready to give their lives in their country's service; their notion was that if a commander rode full gallop against the foe his troops would follow him, and so it proved. As for the utterances of a Faun,[b] I never heard one, but if you say you have, I will take your word for it, although what on earth a Faun may be I do not know. VII. As yet therefore, Balbus, so far as it depends on you I do not understand the divine existence; I believe in it, but the Stoics do not in the least explain it.

Invalidity of Cleanthes' argument from the awe-inspiring phenomena of nature.

"As for Cleanthes, his view is, as you were telling us, that ideas of the gods are formed in men's minds in four ways. One of these ways I have sufficiently discussed, the one derived from our foreknowledge of future events; the second is based on meteorological disturbances and the other changes of the weather; the third on the utility and abundance of the commodities which are at our disposal; and the fourth on the orderly movements of the stars and the regularity of the heavens. About foreknowledge we have spoken. As for meteorological disturbances by land

caelestibus et maritimis et terrenis non possumus dicere, cum ea fiant, non esse multos qui illa metuant
17 et a dis inmortalibus fieri existument; sed non id quaeritur, sintne aliqui qui deos esse putent: di utrum sint necne sint quaeritur. Nam reliquae causae quas Cleanthes adfert, quarum una est de commodorum quae capimus copia, altera de temporum ordine caelique constantia, tum tractabuntur a nobis cum disputabimus de providentia deorum, de qua plurima
18 a te, Balbe, dicta sunt; eodemque illa etiam differemus, quod Chrysippum dicere aiebas, quoniam esset aliquid in rerum natura quod ab homine effici non posset, esse aliquid homine melius, quaeque in domo pulchra cum pulchritudine mundi comparabas, et cum totius mundi convenientiam consensumque adferebas; Zenonisque brevis et acutulas conclusiones in eam partem sermonis quam modo dixi differemus, eodemque tempore illa omnia quae a te physice dicta sunt de vi ignea deque eo calore ex quo omnia generari dicebas, loco suo quaerentur; omniaque quae a te nudius tertius dicta sunt, cum docere velles deos esse, quare et mundus universus et sol et luna et stellae sensum ac mentem haberent,
19 in idem tempus reservabo. A te autem idem illud etiam atque etiam quaeram, quibus rationibus tibi persuadeas deos esse."

VIII. Tum Balbus: "Equidem attulisse rationes

and sea, we cannot deny that there are many people who are afraid of these occurrences and think them
7 to be caused by the immortal gods; but the question is not, are there any people who think that the gods exist,—the question is, do the gods exist or do they not? As for the remaining reasons adduced by Cleanthes, the one derived from the abundance of the commodities bestowed upon us, and the other from the ordered sequence of the seasons and the regularity of the heavens, we will treat of these when we come to discuss divine providence, about which you,
8 Balbus, said a great deal; and we defer to the same time the argument which you attributed to Chrysippus, that since there exists something in the universe which could not be created by man, some being must exist of a higher order than man; as also your comparison of the beautiful furniture in a house with the beauty of the world, and your reference to the harmony and common purpose of the whole world; and Zeno's terse and pointed little syllogisms we will postpone to that part of my discourse which I have just mentioned; and at the same time all your arguments of a scientific nature about the fiery force and heat which you alleged to be the universal source of generation shall be examined in their place; and all that you said the day before yesterday, when attempting to prove the divine existence, to show that both the world as a whole and the sun and moon and stars possess sensation and intelligence, I will keep
9 for the same occasion. But the question I shall have to ask you over and over again, as before, is this: what are your reasons for believing that the gods exist?"

Other arguments adduced by Balbus deferred.

VIII. "Why," replied Balbus, "I really think I

mihi videor, sed eas tu ita refellis ut, cum me interrogaturus esse videare et ego me ad respondendum compararim, repente avertas orationem nec des respondendi locum. Itaque maximae res tacitae praeterierunt, de divinatione de fato, quibus de quaestionibus tu quidem strictim nostri autem multa solent dicere, sed ab hac ea quaestione quae nunc in manibus est separantur ; quare si videtur noli agere confuse, ut hoc explicemus hac disputatione quod quaeritur."

20 "Optime" inquit Cotta. "Itaque quoniam quattuor in partes totam quaestionem divisisti de primaque diximus, consideremus secundam ; quae mihi talis videtur fuisse, ut, cum ostendere velles quales di essent, ostenderes nullos esse. A consuetudine enim oculorum animum abducere difficillimum dicebas; sed, cum deo nihil praestantius esset, non dubitabas quin mundus esset deus, quo nihil in rerum natura melius esset. Modo possemus eum animantem cogitare, vel potius ut cetera oculis sic animo hoc
21 cernere! Sed cum mundo negas quicquam esse melius, quid dicis melius ? Si pulchrius, adsentior ; si aptius ad utilitates nostras, id quoque adsentior ; sin autem id dicis, nihil esse mundo sapientius, nullo modo prorsus adsentior, non quod difficile sit mentem ab

have produced my reasons, but so far from your refuting them, every time when you seem to be on the point of subjecting me to an examination and I get ready to reply, you suddenly switch off the discussion, and do not give me an opportunity of answering. And so matters of the first importance have passed without remark—such as divination, and fate, subjects which you dismiss very briefly, whereas our school is accustomed to say a great deal about them, though they are quite distinct from the topic with which we are now dealing. Please therefore adopt an orderly mode of procedure, and in this debate let us clear up this question that is now before us."

"By all means," said Cotta; "and accordingly, as you divided the whole subject into four parts, and we have spoken about the first part, let us consider the second. It seems to me to have amounted to this: you intended to show what the gods are like, but you actually showed them to be non-existent. For you said that it is very difficult to divert the mind from its association with the eyes; yet you did not hesitate to argue that, since nothing is more excellent than god, the world must be god, because there is nothing in the universe superior to the world. Yes, if we could but imagine the world to be alive, or rather, if we could but discern this truth with our minds exactly as we see external objects with our eyes! But when you say that nothing is superior to the world, what do you mean by superior? If you mean more beautiful, I agree; if more suited to our convenience, I agree to that too; but if what you mean is that nothing is wiser than the world, I entirely and absolutely disagree; not because it is difficult to divorce the mind from the eyes, but

II. The divine nature (§§ 20-64). The world is beautiful but why therefore wise?

oculis sevocare, sed quo magis sevoco eo minus id quod tu vis possum mente comprehendere. IX. 'Nihil est mundo melius in rerum natura.' Ne in terris quidem urbe nostra: num igitur idcirco in urbe esse rationem cogitationem mentem putas, aut, quoniam non sit, num idcirco existimas formicam anteponendam esse huic pulcherrumae urbi, quod in urbe sensus sit nullus, in formica non modo sensus sed etiam mens ratio memoria? Videre oportet, Balbe, quid tibi
22 concedatur, non te ipsum quod velis sumere. Istum enim locum totum illa vetus Zenonis brevis et ut tibi videbatur acuta conclusio dilatavit. Zeno enim ita concludit: 'Quod ratione utitur id melius est quam id quod ratione non utitur; nihil autem mundo me-
23 lius; ratione igitur mundus utitur.' Hoc si placet, iam efficies ut mundus optime librum legere videatur; Zenonis enim vestigiis hoc modo rationem poteris concludere: 'Quod litteratum est id est melius quam quod non est litteratum; nihil autem mundo melius; litteratus igitur est mundus.' Isto modo etiam disertus et quidem mathematicus, musicus, omni denique doctrina eruditus, postremo philosophus.[1] Saepe dixisti nihil fieri nisi ex eo, nec illam vim esse naturae ut sui dissimilia posset effingere: concedam non modo animantem et sapientem esse mundum sed fidicinem etiam et tubicinem, quoniam earum quoque artium homines ex eo procreantur? Nihil igitur

[1] *post* philosophus *addit* erit mundus *det.*

[a] The text is certainly corrupt, being self-contradictory and contradicting ii. 20.

because the more I do so, the less my mind succeeds in grasping your meaning. IX. 'There is nothing in the universe superior to the world.' No more is there anything on earth superior to our city; but you do not therefore think that our city possesses a reasoning, thinking mind? or, because it does not, you do not therefore consider, do you, that an ant is to be rated more highly than this supremely beautiful city, on the ground that a city does not possess sensation whereas an ant has not only sensation, but also a mind that reasons and remembers? You ought to see what you can get your opponent to admit, Balbus, not take for granted anything you like. The whole of this topic of yours was expanded[a] tersely, and as you thought effectively, by the famous old syllogism of Zeno. Zeno puts the argument thus: 'That which is rational is superior to that which is not rational; but nothing is superior to the world; therefore the world is rational.' If you accept this conclusion, you will go on to prove that the world is perfectly able to read a book; for following in Zeno's footsteps you will be able to construct a syllogism as follows: 'That which is literate is superior to that which is illiterate; but nothing is superior to the world; therefore the world is literate.' By this mode of reasoning the world will also be an orator, and even a mathematician, a musician, and in fact an expert in every branch of learning, in fine a philosopher. You kept repeating that the world is the sole source of all created things, and that nature's capacity does not include the power to create things unlike herself: am I to admit that the world is not only a living being, and wise, but also a harper and a flute-player, because it gives birth also to men skilled in these arts?

Zeno proves too much.

adfert pater iste Stoicorum quare mundum ratione
uti putemus, ne cur animantem quidem esse. Non
est igitur mundus deus; et tamen nihil est eo melius,
nihil est enim eo pulchrius, nihil salutarius nobis,
nihil ornatius aspectu motuque constantius.

"Quodsi mundus universus non est deus, ne stellae
quidem, quas tu innumerabilis in deorum numero
reponebas. Quarum te cursus aequabiles aeternique
delectabant, nec mehercule iniuria, sunt enim ad-
24 mirabili incredibilique constantia. Sed non omnia,
Balbe, quae cursus certos et constantis habent ea
deo potius tribuenda sunt quam naturae. X. Quid
Chalcidico Euripo in motu identidem reciprocando
putas fieri posse constantius, quid freto Siciliensi,
quid Oceani fervore illis in locis

Europam Libyamque rapax ubi dividit unda?

Quid? aestus maritimi vel Hispanienses vel Britan-
nici eorumque certis temporibus vel accessus vel
recessus sine deo fieri non possunt? Vide, quaeso,
si omnes motus omniaque quae certis temporibus
ordinem suum conservant divina dicimus, ne tertianas
quoque febres et quartanas divinas esse dicendum sit,
quarum reversione et motu quid potest esse constantius? Sed omnium talium rerum ratio reddenda
25 est; quod vos cum facere non potestis, tamquam in
aram confugitis ad deum.

"Et Chrysippus tibi acute dicere videbatur, homo

Well then, your father of the Stoic school really adduces no reason why we should think that the world is rational, or even alive. Therefore the world is not god ; and nevertheless there is nothing superior to the world, for there is nothing more beautiful than it, nothing more conducive to our health, nothing more ornate to the view, or more regular in motion.

"And if the world as a whole is not god, neither are the stars, which in all their countless numbers you wanted to reckon as gods, enlarging with delight upon their uniform and everlasting movements, and I protest with good reason, for they display a marvellous and extraordinary regularity. But not all things, Balbus, that have fixed and regular courses are to be accredited to a god rather than to nature.

The regularity of the stars the work of nature.

X. What occurrence do you think could possibly be more regular than the repeated alternation of flow in the Euripus at Chalcis ? or in the Straits of Messina ? or than the eddying ocean-currents in the region where

> Europe and Libya by the hurrying wave
> Are sundered ?

Cannot the tides on the coasts of Spain or Britain ebb and flow at fixed intervals of time without a god's intervention ? Why, if all motions and all occurrences that preserve a constant periodic regularity are declared to be divine, pray shall we not be obliged to say that tertian and quartan agues are divine too, for nothing can be more regular than the process of their recurrence ? But all such phenomena call for a rational explanation ; and in your inability to give such an explanation you fly for refuge to a god.

"Also you admired the cleverness of an argument of Chrysippus, who was undoubtedly an adroit and

Chrysippus's arguments

sine dubio versutus et callidus (versutos eos appello quorum celeriter mens versatur, callidos autem quorum tamquam manus opere sic animus usu concalluit); is igitur 'Si aliquid est' inquit 'quod homo efficere non possit, qui id efficit melior est homine; homo autem haec quae in mundo sunt efficere non potest; qui potuit igitur is praestat homini; homini autem praestare quis possit nisi deus? est igitur deus.' Haec omnia in eodem quo illa Zenonis errore
26 versantur; quid enim sit melius, quid praestabilius, quid inter naturam et rationem intersit, non distinguitur. Idemque, si dei non sint, negat esse in omni natura quicquam homine melius; id autem putare quemquam hominem, nihil homine esse melius, summae adrogantiae censet esse. Sit sane adrogantis pluris se putare quam mundum; at illud non modo non adrogantis sed potius prudentis, intellegere se habere sensum et rationem, haec eadem Orionem et Caniculam non habere. Et 'Si domus pulchra sit, intellegamus eam dominis' inquit 'aedificatam esse, non muribus; sic igitur mundum deorum domum existimare debemus.' Ita prorsus existimarem, si illum aedificatum esse, non quem ad modum docebo a natura conformatum putarem.

27 XI. "At enim quaerit apud Xenophontem Socrates unde animum arripuerimus si nullus fuerit in mundo. Et ego quaero unde orationem unde numeros unde

---

[a] *Callidus*, 'clever,' is actually derived from *callum*, 'hardened skin,' as Cicero suggests, and so means 'practised,' 'expert.'

[b] The passage here anticipated is lost. [c] See ii. 18.

hardy [a] thinker (I apply the adjective 'adroit' to persons of nimble wit, and 'hardy' to those whose minds have grown hard with use as the hand is hardened by work); well, Chrysippus argues thus: 'If anything exists that man is not capable of creating, he that creates that thing is superior to man; but man is not capable of creating the objects that we see in the world; therefore he that was capable of so doing surpasses man; but who could surpass man save god? therefore god exists.' The whole of this is involved in the same mistake as the argument of Zeno; no definition is given of the meaning of 'superior' and 'more excellent,' or of the distinction between nature and reason. Chrysippus furthermore declares that, if there be no gods, the natural universe contains nothing superior to man; but for any man to think that there is nothing superior to man he deems to be the height of arrogance. Let us grant that it is a mark of arrogance to value oneself more highly than the world; but not merely is it not a mark of arrogance, rather is it a mark of wisdom, to realize that one is a conscious and rational being, and that Orion and Canicula are not. Again, he says 'If we saw a handsome mansion, we should infer that it was built for its masters and not for mice; so therefore we must deem the world to be the mansion of the gods.' Assuredly I should so deem it if I thought it had been built like a house, and not constructed by nature, as I shall show that it was.[b]

as to man's superiority equally invalid.

XI. "But then you tell me that Socrates in Xenophon asks the question, if the world contains no rational soul, where did we pick up ours? [c] And I too ask the question, where did we get the faculty of speech, the knowledge of numbers, the art of music? unless

Socrates refuted: man's reason is due to nature, and so is nature's own harmony.

cantus; nisi vero loqui solem cum luna putamus cum propius accesserit, aut ad harmoniam canere mundum ut Pythagoras existimat. Naturae ista sunt, Balbe, naturae non artificiose ambulantis ut ait Zeno, quod quidem quale sit, iam videbimus, sed omnia cientis
28 et agitantis motibus et mutationibus suis. Itaque illa mihi placebat oratio de convenientia consensuque naturae, quam quasi cognatione continuata conspirare dicebas: illud non probabam, quod negabas id accidere potuisse nisi ea uno divino spiritu contineretur. Illa vero cohaeret et permanet naturae viribus, non deorum, estque in ea iste quasi consensus, quam *συμπάθειαν* Graeci vocant, sed ea quo sua sponte maior est eo minus divina ratione fieri existimanda est.

29 XII. "Illa autem, quae Carneades adferebat, quem ad modum dissolvitis? Si nullum corpus inmortale sit, nullum esse corpus[1] sempiternum; corpus autem inmortale nullum esse, ne individuum quidem nec quod dirimi distrahive non possit. Cumque omne animal patibilem naturam habeat, nullum est eorum quod effugiat accipiendi aliquid extrinsecus, id est quasi ferendi et patiendi, necessitatem, et si omne animal tale est inmortale nullum est. Ergo itidem, si omne animal secari ac dividi potest, nullum est eorum individuum, nullum aeternum; atqui omne animal ad accipiendam vim externam et ferundam paratum est;

[1] corpus: animal (*auctore Madvig*) *Baiter*.

[a] For the 'music of the spheres' *cf.* ii. 19, and Plato, *Rep.* x. 617 B. [b] See ii. 57. [c] i. 54.

indeed we suppose that the sun holds conversation with the moon when their courses approximate, or that the world makes a harmonious music,[a] as Pythagoras believes. These faculties, Balbus, are the gifts of nature—not nature 'walking in craftsmanlike manner' as Zeno[b] says (and what this means we will consider in a moment), but nature by its own motions and mutations imparting motion and activity
28 to all things. And so I fully agreed with the part of your discourse[c] that dealt with nature's punctual regularity, and what you termed its concordant interconnexion and correlation; but I could not accept your assertion that this could not have come about were it not held together by a single divine breath. On the contrary, the system's coherence and persistence is due to nature's forces and not to divine power; she does possess that 'concord' (the Greek term is *sympatheia*) of which you spoke, but the greater this is as a spontaneous growth, the less possible is it to suppose that it was created by divine reason.

Carneades proved that every living thing is mortal, because (i.) corporeal, (ii.) impressionable,

29 XII. "Then, how does your school refute the following arguments of Carneades? If no body is not liable to death, no body can be everlasting; but no body is not liable to death, nor even indiscerptible nor incapable of decomposition and dissolution. And every living thing is by its nature capable of feeling; therefore there is no living thing that can escape the unavoidable liability to undergo impressions from without, that is to suffer and to feel; and if every living thing is liable to suffering, no living thing is not liable to death. Therefore likewise, if every living thing can be cut up into parts, no living thing is indivisible, and none is everlasting. But every living thing is so constructed as to be liable to undergo and to suffer

mortale igitur omne animal et dissolubile et dividuum
30 sit necesse est. Ut enim,[1] si omnis cera commutabilis esset, nihil esset cereum quod commutari non posset, item nihil argenteum nihil aëneum si commutabilis esset natura argenti et aeris — similiter igitur, si omnia [quae sunt][2] e quibus cuncta constant mutabilia sunt, nullum corpus esse potest non mutabile; mutabilia autem sunt illa ex quibus omnia constant, ut vobis videtur; omne igitur corpus mutabile est. At si esset corpus aliquod inmortale, non esset omne mutabile. Ita efficitur ut omne corpus mortale sit. Etenim omne corpus aut aqua aut aër aut ignis aut terra est, aut id quod est concretum ex his aut ex aliqua parte eorum; horum autem nihil est quin
31 intereat; nam et terrenum omne dividitur, et umor ita mollis est ut facile premi conlidique possit, ignis vero et aër omni pulsu facillime pellitur naturaque cedens est maxume et dissupabilis; praetereaque omnia haec tum intereunt cum in naturam aliam convertuntur, quod fit cum terra in aquam se vertit et cum ex aqua oritur aër, ex aëre aether, cumque eadem vicissim retro commeant; quodsi ea intereunt e quibus constat omne animal, nullum est animal
32 sempiternum. XIII. Et ut haec omittamus, tamen animal nullum inveniri potest quod neque natum umquam sit et semper sit futurum; omne enim animal sensus habet; sentit igitur et calida et frigida et

[1] necesset enim *pr. B*: necesse est. etenim *ci. Plasberg.*
[2] *secl. Schömann*: si omnia e quibus quae sunt cuncta constant *Heindorf*: si ea e quibus constant omnia quae sunt *Mayor*: *lacunam signat Plasberg.*

violence from without; it therefore follows that every living thing is liable to death and dissolution, and is divisible. For just as, if all wax were capable of change, nothing made of wax would be incapable of change, and likewise nothing made of silver or bronze if silver and bronze were substances capable of change, therefore similarly, if all the elements of which all things are composed are liable to change, there can be no body not liable to change; but the elements of which, according to your school, all things are composed are liable to change; therefore every body is liable to change. But if any body were not liable to death, then not every body would be liable to change. Hence it follows that every body is liable to death. In fact every body consists of either water or air or fire or earth, or of a combination of these elements or some of them; but none of these elements is exempt from destruction; for everything of an earthy nature is divisible, and also liquid substance is soft and therefore easily crushed and broken up, while fire and air are very readily impelled by impacts of all kinds, and are of a consistency that is extremely yielding and easily dissipated; and besides, all these elements perish when they undergo transmutation, which occurs when earth turns into water, and when from water arises air, and from air aether, and when alternately the same processes are reversed; but if those elements of which every living thing consists can perish, no living thing is everlasting. XIII. And, to drop this line of argument, nevertheless no living thing can be found which either was never born or will live for ever. For every living thing has sensation; therefore it perceives both heat and cold, both sweetness and sourness—it cannot through any of the

(iii.) composed of elements themselves mutable and destructible,

(iv.) susceptible of pleasure and pain

dulcia et amara nec potest ullo sensu iucunda accipere, non accipere contraria; si igitur voluptatis sensum capit, doloris etiam capit; quod autem dolorem accipit, id accipiat etiam interitum necesse est; omne
33 igitur animal confitendum est esse mortale. Praeterea, si quid est quod nec voluptatem sentiat nec dolorem, id animal esse non potest, sin autem quid animal est, id illa necesse est sentiat; et quod ea sentit non potest esse aeternum; et omne animal sentit; nullum igitur animal aeternum est. Praeterea nullum potest esse animal in quo non et adpetitio sit et declinatio naturalis; appetuntur autem quae secundum naturam sunt, declinantur contraria; et omne animal adpetit quaedam et fugit a quibusdam, quod autem refugit, id contra naturam est, et quod est contra naturam, id habet vim interimendi; omne ergo animal intereat necesse est.
34 Innumerabilia sunt ex quibus effici cogique possit nihil esse quod sensum habeat quin id intereat; etenim ea ipsa quae sentiuntur, ut frigus ut calor ut voluptas ut dolor ut cetera, cum amplificata sunt interimunt; nec ullum animal est sine sensu; nullum igitur animal aeternum est. XIV. Etenim aut simplex est natura animantis, ut vel terrena sit vel ignea vel animalis vel umida, quod quale sit ne intellegi quidem potest; aut concreta ex pluribus

senses receive pleasant sensations and not receive their opposites; if therefore it is capable of feeling pleasure, it is also capable of feeling pain; but a being which can experience pleasure must necessarily also be liable to destruction; therefore it must be admitted that every living thing is liable to death.

33 Besides, if there be anything that cannot feel either pleasure or pain, this cannot be a living thing, and if on the other hand anything is alive, this must necessarily feel pleasure and pain; and that which feels pleasure and pain cannot be everlasting; and every living thing feels them; therefore no living thing is everlasting. Besides, there can be no living thing which does not possess natural instincts of appetition and avoidance; but the objects of appetition are the things which are in accordance with nature, and the objects of avoidance are the contrary; and every living thing seeks certain things and flees from certain things, but that which it flees from is contrary to nature, and that which is contrary to nature has the power of destruction; therefore every living thing must of necessity perish.

(v.) possessed of likes and dislikes, and what it dislikes is destructive.

34 There are proofs too numerous to count by which it can be irrefragably established that there is nothing possessed of sensation that does not perish; in fact the actual objects of sensation, such as cold and heat, pleasure and pain, and the rest, when felt in an intense degree cause destruction; nor is any living thing devoid of sensation; therefore no living thing is everlasting. XIV. For every living thing must either be of a simple substance, and composed of either earth or fire or breath or moisture—and such an animal is inconceivable—, or else of a substance compounded of several elements, each having its own

(vi.) capable of intense sensation,

(vii.) composite and therefore dissoluble.

naturis, quarum suum quaeque locum habeat quo naturae vi feratur, alia infimum alia summum alia medium: haec ad quoddam tempus cohaerere possunt, semper autem nullo modo possunt, necesse est enim in suum quaeque locum natura rapiatur; nullum igitur animal est sempiternum.

35 "Sed omnia vestri, Balbe, solent ad igneam vim referre, Heraclitum ut opinor sequentes, quem ipsum non omnes interpretantur uno modo; qui quoniam quid diceret intellegi noluit, omittamus; vos autem ita dicitis, omnem vim esse igneam, itaque et animantis cum calor defecerit tum interire et in omni natura rerum id vivere id vigere quod caleat. Ego autem non intellego quo modo calore extincto corpora intereant, non intereant umore aut spiritu amisso,
36 praesertim cum intereant etiam nimio calore; quam ob rem id quidem commune est de calido; verum tamen videamus exitum. Ita voltis opinor, nihil esse animal intrinsecus in natura atque mundo praeter ignem: qui magis quam praeter animam, unde animantium quoque constet animus, ex quo animal dicitur? Quo modo autem hoc quasi concedatur sumitis, nihil esse animum nisi ignem? probabilius enim videtur tale quiddam esse animum ut sit ex igni atque anima temperatum. Quodsi ignis ex sese ipse animal est nulla se alia admiscente natura, quoniam is, cum inest in corporibus nostris, efficit ut sentiamus, non potest ipse esse sine sensu. Rursus eadem dici

---

[a] A fragment of Heraclitus runs 'The same world of all things none of the gods nor any man did make, but it always was and is and will be ever-living fire, being kindled by measures and extinguished by measures.'

[b] He was called 'the dark'; *clarus ob obscuram linguam* Lucretius i. 639.

place towards which it travels by natural impulsion, one to the bottom, another to the top and another to the middle; such elements can cohere for a certain time, but cannot possibly do so for ever, for each must of necessity be borne away by nature to its own place; therefore no living thing is everlasting.

35 "But your school, Balbus, is wont to trace all things back to an elemental force of a fiery nature, herein as I believe following Heraclitus,[a] although all do not interpret the master in one way; however, as he did not wish his meaning to be understood,[b] let us leave him out; but your doctrine is that all force is of the nature of fire, and that because of this animal creatures perish when their heat fails and also in every realm of nature a thing is alive and vigorous if it is warm. But I for my part do not understand how organisms should perish if their heat is quenched without perishing if deprived of moisture or air, especi-

Fire is not specially essential to life;

36 ally as they also perish from excessive heat; therefore what you say about heat applies also to the other elements. However, let us see what follows. Your view, I believe, is that there is no animate being contained within the whole universe of nature except fire. Why fire any more than air (*anima*), of which also the soul (*animus*) of animate beings consists, from which the term 'animate' is derived? On what ground moreover do you take it for granted that there is no soul except fire? It seems more reasonable to hold that soul is of a composite nature, and consists of fire and air combined. However, if fire is animate in and by itself, without the admixture of any other element, it is the presence of fire in our own bodies that causes us to possess sensation, and therefore fire itself cannot be devoid of sensation. Here we can

but if it is the source of feeling, it must be destructible,

possunt: quidquid est enim quod sensum habeat, id necesse est sentiat et voluptatem et dolorem, ad quem autem dolor veniat ad eundem etiam interitum venire; ita fit ut ne ignem quidem efficere possitis aeternum.

37 Quid enim? non eisdem vobis placet omnem ignem pastus indigere, nec permanere ullo modo posse nisi alatur? ali autem solem, lunam, reliqua astra aquis, alia dulcibus, alia marinis? Eamque causam Cleanthes adfert

> cur se sol referat nec longius progrediatur
> solstitiali orbi,

itemque brumali, ne longius discedat a cibo. Hoc totum quale sit mox; nunc autem concludatur illud: quod interire possit id aeternum non esse natura; ignem autem interiturum esse nisi alatur; non esse igitur natura ignem sempiternum.

38 XV. "Qualem autem deum intellegere nos possumus nulla virtute praeditum? Quid enim? prudentiamne deo tribuemus, quae constat ex scientia rerum bonarum et malarum et nec bonarum nec malarum? cui mali nihil est nec esse potest, quid huic opus est dilectu bonorum et malorum? Quid autem ratione, quid intellegentia? quibus utimur ad eam rem ut apertis obscura adsequamur; at obscurum deo nihil potest esse. Nam iustitia, quae suum cuique distribuit, quid pertinet ad deos? hominum enim societas et communitas, ut vos dicitis, iustitiam procreavit. Temperantia autem

---

[a] See § 32.

[b] Mayor detected this verse quotation from an unknown source. *Cf.* ii. 25.

repeat the argument employed before [a]: whatever has sensation must necessarily feel both pleasure and pain, but he who is liable to pain must also be liable to destruction; from this it follows that you are

37 unable to prove fire also to be everlasting. Moreover, do you not also hold that all fire requires fuel, and cannot possibly endure unless it is fed? and that the sun, moon and other heavenly bodies draw sustenance in some cases from bodies of fresh water and in other cases from the sea? This is the reason given by Cleanthes to explain why

especially as it requires fuel.

> The sun turns back, nor farther doth proceed
> Upon his summer curve,[b]

and upon his winter one likewise; it is that he may not travel too far away from his food. We will defer consideration of the whole of this subject; for the present let us end with the following syllogism: That which can perish cannot be an eternal substance; but fire will perish if it is not fed; therefore fire is not an eternal substance.

38 XV. "But what can we make of a god not endowed with any virtue? Well, are we to assign to god prudence, which consists in the knowledge of things good, things evil, and things neither good nor evil? to a being who experiences and can experience nothing evil, what need is there of the power to choose between things good and evil? Or of reason, or of intelligence? these faculties we employ for the purpose of proceeding from the known to the obscure; but nothing can be obscure to god. Then justice, which assigns to each his own—what has this to do with the gods? justice, as you tell us, is the offspring of human society and of the commonwealth of man. And

The recognized virtues incompatible with a divine nature, but deity without virtue inconceivable

constat ex praetermittendis voluptatibus corporis, cui si locus in caelo est, est etiam voluptatibus. Nam fortis deus intellegi qui potest? in dolore? an in labore? an in periculo? quorum deum nihil attingit.
39 Nec ratione igitur utentem nec virtute ulla praeditum deum intellegere qui possumus?

"Nec vero volgi atque imperitorum inscitiam despicere possum, cum ea considero quae dicuntur a Stoicis. Sunt enim illa imperitorum: piscem Syri venerantur, omne fere genus bestiarum Aegyptii consecraverunt; iam vero in Graecia multos habent ex hominibus deos, Alabandum Alabandis, Tenedii Tennen, Leucotheam quae fuit Ino et eius Palaemonem filium cuncta Graecia, Herculem Aesculapium Tyndaridas; Romulum nostri aliosque compluris, quos quasi novos et adscripticios cives in
40 caelum receptos putant. XVI. Haec igitur indocti; quid vos philosophi? qui meliora? Omitto illa, sunt enim praeclara: sit sane deus ipse mundus—hoc credo illud esse

sublime candens, quem invocant omnes Iovem.

Quare igitur pluris adiungimus deos? Quanta autem est eorum multitudo! Mihi quidem sane multi videntur; singulas enim stellas numeras deos eosque aut beluarum nomine appellas, ut Capram ut Nepam

---

[a] The conclusion implied is that no god exists.

[b] Atargatis or Derceto (Dagon), a fish with a woman's face, worshipped at Ascalon.

temperance consists in forgoing bodily pleasures; so if there is room for temperance in heaven, there is also room for pleasure. As for courage, how can god be conceived as brave? in enduring pain? or toil? or danger? to none of these is god liable. God then is neither rational nor possessed of any of the virtues: but such a god is inconceivable[a]!

Popular mythology not more irrational than Stoic deification of stars, of corn and wine, and of dead men (often there are several of the same name).

"In fact, when I reflect upon the utterances of the Stoics, I cannot despise the stupidity of the vulgar and the ignorant. With the ignorant you get superstitions like the Syrians' worship of a fish,[b] and the Egyptians' deification of almost every species of animal; nay, even in Greece they worship a number of deified human beings, Alabandus at Alabanda, Tennes at Tenedos, Leucothea, formerly Ino, and her son Palaemon throughout the whole of Greece, as also Hercules, Aesculapius, the sons of Tyndareus; and with our own people Romulus and many others, who are believed to have been admitted to celestial citizenship in recent times, by a sort of extension of the franchise! XVI. Well, those are the superstitions of the unlearned; but what of you philosophers? how are your dogmas any better? I pass over the rest of them, for they are remarkable indeed! but take it as true that the world is itself god—for this, I suppose, is the meaning of the line

> Yon dazzling vault of heaven, which all mankind
> As Jove invoke.

Why then are we to add a number of other gods as well? And what a crowd of them there is! At least there seems to me to be a great lot of them; for you reckon each of the stars a god, and either call them by the names of animals such as She-goat, Scorpion,

ut Taurum ut Leonem, aut rerum inanimarum, ut
41 Argo ut Aram ut Coronam. Sed ut haec concedantur, reliqua qui tandem non modo concedi sed omnino intellegi possunt? Cum fruges Cererem, vinum Liberum dicimus, genere nos quidem sermonis utimur usitato, sed ecquem tam amentem esse putas qui illud quo vescatur deum credat esse? Nam quos ab hominibus pervenisse dicis ad deos, tu reddes rationem quem ad modum id fieri potuerit aut cur fieri desierit, et ego discam libenter; quo modo nunc quidem est, non video quo pacto ille cui 'in monte Oetaeo illatae lampades' fuerint, ut ait Accius, 'in domum aeternam patris' ex illo ardore pervenerit; quem tamen Homerus apud inferos conveniri facit ab Ulixe, sicut ceteros qui excesserant vita.

42 "Quamquam quem potissimum Herculem colamus scire sane velim; pluris enim tradunt nobis ii qui interiores scrutantur et reconditas litteras, antiquissimum Iove natum sed item Iove antiquissimo—nam Ioves quoque pluris in priscis Graecorum litteris invenimus: ex eo igitur et Lysithoë est is Hercules quem concertavisse cum Apolline de tripode accepimus. Alter traditur Nilo natus Aegyptius, quem aiunt Phrygias litteras conscripsisse. Tertius est ex Idaeis Digitis, cui inferias adferunt.[1] Quartus

[1] adferunt *dett.*: adferunt qui *A*, *B*, adferunt Coi *Gronovius.*

[a] *Od.* xi. 600 ff. Our text of Homer adds in ll. 602-604 that what Odysseus met was a wraith (εἴδωλον), but that Heracles himself was feasting with the gods and wedded to Hebe. These lines, however, were obelized by Aristarchus as non-Homeric and inconsistent with the *Iliad*, which

Bull, Lion, or of inanimate things such as the Argo,
41 the Altar, the Crown. But allowing these, how pray can one possibly, I do not say allow, but make head or tail of the remainder? When we speak of corn as Ceres and wine as Liber, we employ a familiar figure of speech, but do you suppose that anybody can be so insane as to believe that the food he eats is a god? As for the cases you allege of men who have risen to the status of divinity, you shall explain, and I shall be glad to learn, how this apotheosis was possible, or why it has ceased to take place now. As at present informed, I do not see how the hero to whose body

On Oeta's mount the torches were applied,

as Accius has it, can have passed from that burning pyre to

The everlasting mansions of his Sire—,

in spite of the fact that Homer [a] represents Ulysses as meeting him, among the rest of those who had departed this life, in the world below!

42 "Nevertheless I should like to know what particular Hercules it is that we worship; for we are told of several by the students of esoteric and recondite writings, the most ancient being the son of Jupiter, that is of the most ancient Jupiter likewise, for we find several Jupiters also in the early writings of the Greeks. That Jupiter then and Lysithoë were the parents of the Hercules who is recorded to have had a tussle with Apollo about a tripod! We hear of another in Egypt, a son of the Nile, who is said to have compiled the sacred books of Phrygia. A third comes from the Digiti of Mount Ida, who offer sacri-

speaks of Heracles as killed by the wrath of Hera, and of Hebe as a virgin.

Iovis est ⟨et⟩[1] Asteriae Latonae sororis, qui Tyri maxime colitur, cuius Karthaginem filiam ferunt. Quintus in India qui Belus dicitur. Sextus hic ex Alcmena quem Iuppiter genuit, sed tertius Iuppiter quoniam ut iam docebo pluris Ioves etiam accepimus.

43 XVII. "Quando enim me in hunc locum deduxit oratio, docebo meliora me didicisse de colendis dis inmortalibus iure pontificio et more maiorum capedunculis iis quas Numa nobis reliquit, de quibus in illa aureola oratiuncula dicit Laelius, quam rationibus Stoicorum. Si enim vos sequar, dic quid ei respondeam qui me sic roget: 'Si di sunt,[2] suntne etiam Nymphae deae? si Nymphae, Panisci etiam et Satyri; hi autem non sunt; ne Nymphae [deae][3] quidem igitur. At earum templa sunt publice vota et dedicata; ne ceteri quidem ergo di, quorum templa sunt dedicata? Age porro: Iovem et Neptunum deos[4] numeras; ergo etiam Orcus frater eorum deus; et illi qui fluere apud inferos dicuntur, Acheron Cocytus Pyriphlegethon, tum Charon tum Cerberus
44 di putandi. At id quidem repudiandum; ne Orcus quidem igitur; quid dicitis ergo de fratribus?' Haec Carneades aiebat, non ut deos tolleret (quid enim philosopho minus conveniens?) sed ut Stoicos

[1] *add. Heindorf.* [2] *post* sunt *lacunam signat Mayor.* [3] deae *om. dett.* [4] deos *dett.*: deum *A*, *B*.

---

[a] The argument goes on at § 53, and perhaps §§ 43–52 should be transposed after § 60 (although the first sentence of § 43 seems to belong neither here nor there).

[b] See § 6 n.

fices at his tomb. A fourth is the son of Jupiter and Asteria, the sister of Latona; he is chiefly worshipped at Tyre, and is said to have been the father of the nymph Carthago. There is a fifth in India, named Belus. The sixth is our friend the son of Alcmena, whose male progenitor was Jupiter, that is Jupiter number three, since, as I will now explain, tradition tells us of several Jupiters also.[a]

Carneades by a sorites proved it impossible to draw a line between the divine and the human or the natural.

XVII. "For as my discourse has led me to this topic, I will show that I have learnt more about the proper way of worshipping the gods, according to pontifical law and the customs of our ancestors, from the poor little pots bequeathed to us by Numa, which Laelius discusses in that dear little golden speech[b] of his, than from the theories of the Stoics. For if I adopt your doctrines, tell me what answer I am to make to one who questions me thus: 'If gods exist, are the nymphs also goddesses? if the nymphs are, the Pans and Satyrs also are gods; but they are not gods; therefore the nymphs also are not. Yet they possess temples vowed and dedicated to them by the nation; are the other gods also therefore who have had temples dedicated to them not gods either? Come tell me further: you reckon Jupiter and Neptune gods, therefore their brother Orcus is also a god; and the fabled streams of the lower world, Acheron, Cocytus and Pyriphlegethon, and also Charon and also Cerberus are to be deemed gods. No, you say, we must draw the line at that; well then, Orcus is not a god either; what are you to say about his brothers then?' These arguments were advanced by Carneades, not with the object of establishing atheism (for what could less befit a philosopher?) but

nihil de dis explicare convinceret; itaque insequebatur: 'Quid enim?' aiebat 'si hi fratres sunt in numero deorum, num de patre eorum Saturno negari potest, quem volgo maxime colunt ad occidentem? Qui si est deus, patrem quoque eius Caelum esse deum confitendum est. Quod si ita est, Caeli quoque parentes di habendi sunt, Aether et Dies, eorumque fratres et sorores, qui a genealogis antiquis sic nominantur, Amor Dolus Metus[1] Labor Invidentia Fatum Senectus Mors Tenebrae Miseria Querella Gratia Fraus Pertinacia Parcae Hesperides Somnia, quos omnis Erebo et Nocte natos ferunt.' Aut igitur haec monstra probanda sunt aut prima illa
45 tollenda. XVIII. Quid? Apollinem Volcanum
Mercurium ceteros deos esse dices, de Hercule Aesculapio Libero Castore Polluce dubitabis? At hi quidem coluntur aeque atque illi, apud quosdam etiam multo magis. Ergo hi dei sunt habendi mortalibus nati matribus? Quid? Aristaeus, qui olivae dicitur inventor, Apollinis filius, Theseus Neptuni, reliqui quorum patres di, non erunt in deorum numero? Quid quorum matres? Opinor etiam magis; ut enim iure civili qui est matre libera liber est, item iure naturae qui dea matre est deus sit necesse est. Itaque Achillem Astypalaeenses insulani sanctissume colunt; qui si deus est, et Orpheus et Rhesus di sunt,

[1] Metus *dett.*: Morbus *dett.*, modus *A*, *B*.

in order to prove the Stoic theology worthless; accordingly he used to pursue his inquiry thus: 'Well
now,' he would say, 'if these brothers are included
among the gods, can we deny the divinity of their
father Saturn, who is held in the highest reverence
by the common people in the west? And if he is
a god, we must also admit that his father Caelus is a
god. And if so, the parents of Caelus, the Aether
and the Day, must be held to be gods, and their
brothers and sisters, whom the ancient genealogists
name Love, Guile, Fear, Toil, Envy, Fate, Old Age,
Death, Darkness, Misery, Lamentation, Favour,
Fraud, Obstinacy, the Parcae, the Daughters of
Hesperus, the Dreams: all of these are fabled to be
the children of Erebus and Night.' Either therefore
you must accept these monstrosities or you must dis-
15 card the first claimants also. XVIII. Again, if you
call Apollo, Vulcan, Mercury and the rest gods, will
you have doubts about Hercules, Aesculapius, Liber,
Castor and Pollux? But these are worshipped just
as much as those, and indeed in some places very
much more than they. Are we then to deem these
gods, the sons of mortal mothers? Well then, will
not Aristaeus, the reputed discoverer of the olive,
who was the son of Apollo, Theseus the son of Neptune, and all the other sons of gods, also be reckoned
as gods? What about the sons of goddesses? I
think they have an even better claim; for just as by
the civil law one whose mother is a freewoman is a
freeman, so by the law of nature one whose mother is
a goddess must be a god. And in the island of Astypalaea Achilles is most devoutly worshipped by the
inhabitants on these grounds; but if Achilles is a
god, so are Orpheus and Rhesus, whose mother was a

Musa matre nati, nisi forte maritumae nuptiae terrenis anteponuntur. Si hi di non sunt, quia nusquam
46 coluntur, quo modo illi sunt? Vide igitur ne virtutibus hominum isti honores habeantur, non immortalitatibus; quod tu quoque, Balbe, visus es dicere. Quo modo autem potes, si Latonam deam putas, Hecatam non putare, quae matre Asteria est, sorore Latonae? An haec quoque dea est? vidimus enim eius aras delubraque in Graecia. Sin haec dea est, cur non Eumenides? Quae si deae sunt, quarum et Athenis fanum est et apud nos, ut ego interpretor, lucus Furinae, Furiae deae sunt, speculatrices credo et vindices
47 facinorum et sceleris. Quodsi tales dei sunt ut rebus humanis intersint, Natio quoque dea putanda est, cui cum fana circumimus in agro Ardeati rem divinam facere solemus; quae quia partus matronarum tueatur[1] a nascentibus Natio nominata est. Ea si dea est, di omnes illi qui commemorabantur a te, Honos Fides Mens Concordia, ergo etiam Spes Moneta omniaque quae cogitatione nobismet ipsi[2] possumus fingere. Quod si veri simile non est, ne illud quidem est haec unde fluxerunt. XIX. Quid autem dicis, si di sunt illi quos colimus et accepimus, cur non eodem in genere Serapim Isimque numeremus? quod si facimus, cur barbarorum deos repudiemus? Boves

[1] tuetur *B corr.* [2] ipsi *Davies*: ipsis.

[a] There was a special worship of Venus at Ardea, an old Latin city once important but long before Cicero's time insignificant.

Muse, unless perhaps a marriage at the bottom of the sea counts higher than a marriage on dry land! If these are not gods, because they are nowhere wor-
46 shipped, how can the others be gods? Is not the explanation this, that divine honours are paid to men's virtues, not to their immortality? as you too, Balbus, appeared to indicate. Then, if you think Latona a goddess, how can you not think that Hecate is one, who is the daughter of Latona's sister Asteria? Is Hecate a goddess too? we have seen altars and shrines belonging to her in Greece. But if Hecate is a goddess, why are not the Eumenides? and if they are goddesses,—and they have a temple at Athens, and the Grove of Furina at Rome, if I interpret that name aright, also belongs to them,—then the Furies are goddesses, presumably in their capacity of de-
47 tectors and avengers of crime and wickedness. And if it is the nature of the gods to intervene in man's affairs, the Birth-Spirit also must be deemed divine, to whom it is our custom to offer sacrifice when we make the round of the shrines in the Territory of Ardea[a]: she is named Natio from the word for being born (*nasci*), because she is believed to watch over married women in travail. If she is divine, so are all those abstractions that you mentioned, Honour, Faith, Intellect, Concord, and therefore also Faith, the Spirit of Money and all the possible creations of our own imagination. If this supposition is unlikely, so also is the former one, from which all these instances flow. XIX. Then, if the traditional gods whom we worship are really divine, what reason can you give why we should not include Isis and Osiris in the same category? And if we do so, why should we repudiate the gods of the barbarians? We shall

igitur et equos, ibis accipitres aspidas crocodilos pisces canes lupos faelis multas praeterea beluas in deorum numerum reponemus. Quae si reicimus,[1]
48 illa quoque unde haec nata sunt reiciemus. Quid deinde? Ino dea ducetur et Λευκοθέα a Graecis a nobis Matuta dicetur cum sit Cadmi filia, Circe autem et Pasiphaë et Aeeta[2] e Perseide Oceani filia nati patre Sole in deorum numero non habebuntur? quamquam Circen quoque coloni nostri Circeienses religiose colunt. Ergo hanc deam duces[3]: quid Medeae respondebis, quae duobus[4] avis Sole et Oceano, Aeeta patre matre Idyia procreata est? quid huius Absyrto fratri (qui est apud Pacuvium Aegialeus, sed illud nomen veterum litteris usitatius)? qui si di non sunt, vereor quid agat
49 Ino; haec enim omnia ex eodem fonte fluxerunt. An Amphiaraus erit deus et Trophonius? Nostri quidem publicani, cum essent agri in Boeotia deorum inmortalium excepti lege censoria, negabant inmortalis esse ullos qui aliquando homines fuissent. Sed si sunt hi di, est certe Erechtheus, cuius Athenis et delubrum vidimus et sacerdotem. Quem si deum facimus, quid aut de Codro dubitare possumus aut de ceteris qui pugnantes pro patriae libertate ceciderunt? quod si probabile non est, ne illa quidem superiora unde
50 haec manant probanda sunt. Atque in plerisque

[1] reicimus *Mayor*: reiciamus *MSS.*, reiciemus *? ed.*
[2] Aeetae *Baiter*: eae e *A*, eae *B*.
[3] duces *Baiter*: ducis, dicis, dices *MSS.*
[4] duobus <dis> *Alan.*

[a] As well as Matuta.

therefore have to admit to the list of gods oxen and horses, ibises, hawks, asps, crocodiles, fishes, dogs, wolves, cats and many beasts besides. Or if we reject these, we shall also reject those others from whom
48 their claim springs. What next? If Ino is to be deemed divine, under the title of Leucothea in Greece and Matuta at Rome, because she is the daughter of Cadmus, are Circe and Pasiphaë and Aeetes, the children of Perseis the daughter of Oceanus by the Sun, to be not counted in the list of gods? in spite of the fact that Circe too[a] is devoutly worshipped at the Roman colony of Circei. If you therefore deem her divine, what answer will you give to Medea, who, as her father was Aeetes and her mother Idyia, had as her two grandfathers the Sun and Oceanus? or to her brother Absyrtus (who appears in Pacuvius as Aegialeus, though the former name is commoner in ancient literature)? if these are not divine, I have my fears as to what will become of Ino, for the claims of all of them derive from the same source.
49 Or if we allow Ino, are we going to make Amphiaraus and Trophonius divine? The Roman tax-farmers, finding that lands in Boeotia belonging to the immortal gods were exempted by the censor's regulations, used to maintain that nobody was immortal who had once upon a time been a human being. But if these are divine, so undoubtedly is Erechtheus, whose shrine and whose priest also we saw when at Athens. And if we make him out to be divine, what doubts can we feel about Codrus or any other persons who fell fighting for their country's freedom? if we stick at this, we must reject the earlier cases too,
50 from which these follow. Also it is easy to see that in most states the memory of brave men has been

civitatibus intellegi potest augendae virtutis gratia, quo[1] libentius rei publicae causa periculum adiret optimus quisque, virorum fortium memoriam honore deorum immortalium consecratam. Ob eam enim ipsam causam Erechtheus Athenis filiaeque eius in numero deorum sunt; itemque Leonaticum est delubrum Athenis, quod Λεωκόριον nominatur. Alabandenses quidem sanctius Alabandum colunt, a quo est urbs illa condita, quam quemquam nobilium deorum; apud quos non inurbane Stratonicus ut multa, cum quidam ei molestus Alabandum deum esse confirmaret, Herculem negaret, 'Ergo' inquit
51 'mihi Alabandus tibi Hercules sit iratus.' XX. Illa autem, Balbe, quae tu a caelo astrisque ducebas, quam longe serpant non vides? Solem deum esse lunamque, quorum alterum Apollinem Graeci alteram Dianam putant. Quodsi Luna dea est, ergo etiam Lucifer ceteraeque errantes numerum deorum obtinebunt; igitur etiam inerrantes. Cur autem Arqui species non in deorum numero reponatur? est enim pulcher, et ob eam causam quia speciem habeat[2] admirabilem Thaumante dicitur ‹Iris›[3] esse nata. Cuius si divina natura est, quid facies nubibus? Arcus enim ipse e nubibus efficitur quodam modo coloratis; quarum una etiam Centauros peperisse dicitur. Quodsi nubes rettuleris in deos, referendae certe erunt tempestates, quae populi Romani ritibus consecratae sunt. Ergo imbres nimbi procellae turbines dei putandi. Nostri qui-

[1] ‹aut› quo *Lactantius*.
[2] habet *dett.* [3] *add. Antonius Augustinus.*

[a] Editors suspect this unknown name: Cicero can hardly have coined it to translate the Greek.

sanctified with divine honours for the purpose of promoting valour, to make the best men more willing to encounter danger for their country's sake. This is the reason why Erechtheus and his daughters have been deified at Athens, and likewise there is the Leonatic[a] shrine at Athens, which is named *Leōcorion.* The people of Alabanda indeed worship Alabandus, the founder of that city, more devoutly than any of the famous deities. And it was there that Stratonicus uttered one of his many witty sayings; some person obnoxious to him swore that Alabandus was divine and Hercules was not: 'Well and good,' said Stratonicus, 'let the wrath of Alabandus fall on
51 me and that of Hercules on you.' XX. As for your deriving religion from the sky and stars, do you not see what a long way this takes you? You say that the sun and moon are deities, and the Greeks identify the former with Apollo and the latter with Diana. But if the Moon is a goddess, then Lucifer also and the rest of the planets will have to be counted gods; and if so, then the fixed stars as well. But why should not the glorious Rainbow be included among the gods? it is beautiful enough, and its marvellous loveliness has given rise to the legend that Iris is the daughter of Thaumas.[b] And if the rainbow is a divinity, what will you do about the clouds? The rainbow itself is caused by some coloration of the clouds; and also a cloud is fabled to have given birth to the Centaurs. But if you enroll the clouds among the gods, you will undoubtedly have to enroll the seasons, which have been deified in the national ritual of Rome. If so, then rain and tempest, storm and whirlwind must be deemed divine. At any rate

[b] From θαῦμα, wonder.

dem duces mare ingredientes inmolare hostiam
52 fluctibus consuerunt. Iam si est Ceres a gerendo (ita enim dicebas), terra ipsa dea est (et ita habetur; quae est enim alia Tellus?) Sin terra, mare etiam, quem Neptunum esse dicebas; ergo et flumina et fontes. Itaque et Fontis delubrum Maso ex Corsica dedicavit, et in augurum precatione Tiberinum Spinonem Almonem Nodinum alia propinquorum fluminum nomina videmus. Ergo hoc aut in inmensum serpet, aut nihil horum recipiemus; nec illa infinita ratio superstitionis probabitur; nihil ergo horum probandum est.

53 XXI. "Dicamus igitur, Balbe, oportet contra illos etiam qui hos deos ex hominum genere in caelum translatos non re sed opinione esse dicunt, quos auguste omnes sancteque veneramur. . . . Principio Ioves tres numerant ii qui theologi nominantur, ex quibus primum et secundum natos in Arcadia, alterum patre Aethere, ex quo etiam Proserpinam natam ferunt et Liberum, alterum patre Caelo, qui genuisse Minervam dicitur, quam principem et inventricem belli ferunt, tertium Cretensem Saturni filium, cuius in illa insula sepulcrum ostenditur. Διόσκουροι etiam apud Graios multis modis nominantur: primi tres, qui appellantur Anaces[1] Athenis, ex rege Iove antiquissimo et Proserpina nati, Trito-

[1] Anaces *Marsus*: Anaktes.

---

[a] *Cf.* ii. 67. [b] *Cf.* ii. 66.

[c] §§ 53-60 Mayor transposes to the end of § 42, thus supplying a reference for the words 'these gods' in the second line. But the topic of the first sentence is nowhere pursued, and perhaps it should be kept where it stands, with a mark indicating the loss of a passage that it introduced, and the rest of §§ 53-60 transferred to § 42.

it has been the custom of our generals when embarking on a sea-voyage to sacrifice a victim to the waves. Again, if the name of Ceres is derived from her bearing fruit, as you said,[a] the earth itself is a goddess (and so she is believed to be, for she is the same as the deity Tellus). But if the earth is divine, so also is the sea, which you identified with Neptune[b]; and therefore the rivers and springs too. This is borne out by the facts that Maso dedicated a Temple of Fons out of his Corsican spoils, and that the Augurs' litany includes as we may see the names of Tiberinus, Spino, Almo, Nodinus, and other rivers in the neighbourhood of Rome. Either therefore this process will go on indefinitely, or we shall admit none of these; and this unlimited claim of superstition will not be accepted; therefore none of these is to be accepted.

Refutation of the theory that deified human beings exist only in thought.

XXI. "Accordingly,[c] Balbus, we also ought to refute the theory that these gods, who are deified human beings, and who are the objects of our most devout and universal veneration, exist not in reality but in imagination. . . In the first place, the so-called theologians enumerate three Jupiters, of whom the first and second were born, they say, in Arcadia, the father of one being Aether, who is also fabled to be the progenitor of Proserpine and Liber, and of the other Caelus, and this one is said to have begotten Minerva, the fabled patroness and originator of warfare; the third is the Cretan Jove, son of Saturn; his tomb is shown in that island. The Dioscuri also have a number of titles in Greece. The first set, called Anaces at Athens, the sons of the very ancient King Jupiter and Proserpine, are Tritopatreus, Eubuleus and

List of divine names each shared by several individuals.

patreus Eubuleus Dionysus, secundi Iove tertio nati et Leda Castor et Pollux, tertii dicuntur a non nullis Alco et Melampus et Tmolus, Atrei filii, qui Pelope
54 natus fuit. Iam Musae primae quattuor Iove altero natae, Thelxinoë Aoede Arche Melete, secundae Iove tertio et Mnemosyne procreatae novem, tertiae Piero natae et Antiopa, quas Pieridas et Pierias solent poëtae appellare, isdem nominibus et eodem numero quo proximae superiores. Cumque tu Solem quia solus esset appellatum esse dicas, Soles ipsi quam multi a theologis proferuntur. Unus eorum Iove natus nepos Aetheris, alter Hyperione, tertius Volcano Nili filio, cuius urbem Aegyptii volunt esse eam quae Heliopolis appellatur, quartus is quem heroicis temporibus Acantho Rhodi peperisse dicitur, <pater>[1] Ialysi Camiri Lindi Rhodi, quintus qui Colchis fertur Aeetam et Circam procreavisse.
55 XXII. Volcani item complures: primus Caelo natus, ex quo et Minerva Apollinem eum[2] cuius in tutela Athenas antiqui historici esse voluerunt, secundus Nilo natus, Phthas[3] ut Aegyptii appellant, quem custodem esse Aegypti volunt, tertius ex tertio Iove et Iunone, qui Lemni fabricae traditur praefuisse, quartus Memalio natus, qui tenuit insulas propter
56 Siciliam quae Volcaniae nominabantur. Mercurius unus Caelo patre Die matre natus, cuius obscenius

[1] *add. Davies.* [2] Apollinum is *Davies.*
[3] Phthas *Gyraldus*: Opas.

---

[a] See ii. 68.
[b] *i.e.*, volcanic: the Lipari are meant.

Dionysus. The second set, the sons of the third Jove and Leda, are Castor and Pollux. The third are named by some people Alco, Melampus and Tmolus,
54 and are the sons of Atreus the son of Pelops. Again, the first set of Muses are four, the daughters of the second Jupiter, Thelxinoë, Aoede, Arche and Melete; the second set are the offspring of the third Jupiter and Mnemosyne, nine in number; the third set are the daughters of Pierus and Antiope, and are usually called by the poets the Pierides or Pierian Maidens; they are the same in number and have the same names as the next preceding set. The sun's name Sol you derive[a] from his being sole of his kind, but the theologians produce a number even of Suns! One is the son of Jove and grandson of Aether; another the son of Hyperion; the third of Vulcan the son of Nile,—this is the one who the Egyptians say is lord of the city named Heliopolis; the fourth is the one to whom Acanthe is said to have given birth at Rhodes in the heroic age, the father of Ialysus, Camirus, Lindus and Rhodus; the fifth is the one said to have be-
55 gotten Aeetes and Circe at Colchi. XXII. There are also several Vulcans; the first, the son of the Sky, was reputed the father by Minerva of the Apollo said by the ancient historians to be the tutelary deity of Athens; the second, the son of Nile, is named by the Egyptians Phthas, and is deemed the guardian of Egypt; the third is the son of the third Jupiter and of Juno, and is fabled to have been the master of a smithy at Lemnos; the fourth is the son of Memalius, and lord of the islands near Sicily which used to be
56 named the Isles of Vulcan.[b] One Mercury has the Sky for father and the Day for mother; he is represented in a state of sexual excitation traditionally

excitata natura traditur quod aspectu Proserpinae commotus sit, alter Valentis et Phoronidis[1] filius is qui sub terris habetur idem Trophonius, tertius Iove tertio natus et Maia, ex quo et Penelopa Pananatum ferunt, quartus Nilo patre, quem Aegyptii nefas habent nominare, quintus quem colunt Pheneatae, qui Argum dicitur interemisse ob eamque causam Aegyptum profugisse atque Aegyptiis leges et litteras tradidisse: hunc Aegyptii Theuth[2] appellant, eodemque nomine anni primus mensis apud eos
57 vocatur. Aesculapiorum primus Apollinis, quem Arcades colunt, qui specillum invenisse primusque volnus dicitur obligavisse, secundus secundi Mercurii frater: is fulmine percussus dicitur humatus esse Cynosuris; tertius Arsippi et Arsinoae, qui primus purgationem alvi dentisque evolsionem ut ferunt invenit, cuius in Arcadia non longe a Lusio flumine sepulcrum et lucus ostenditur. XXIII. Apollinum antiquissimus is quem paulo antea[3] e Vulcano natum esse dixi custodem Athenarum, alter Corybantis filius natus in Creta, cuius de illa insula cum Iove ipso certamen fuisse traditur, tertius Iove tertio natus et Latona, quem ex Hyperboreis Delphos ferunt advenisse, quartus in Arcadia, quem Arcades Νόμιον[4] appellant quod ab eo se leges ferunt accepisse.
58 Dianae item plures: prima Iovis et Proserpinae,

[1] Coronidis *Davies.*
[2] Theuth *Baiter*: Theyn.
[3] ante *ci. Plasberg.*
[4] Νόμιον *Huet*: nomionem.

said to be due to passion inspired by the sight of
Proserpine. Another is the son of Valens and
Phoronis; this is the subterranean Mercury identified with Trophonius. The third, the son of the
third Jove and of Maia, the legends make the father
of Pan by Penelope. The fourth has Nile for father;
the Egyptians deem it sinful to pronounce his name.
The fifth, worshipped by the people of Pheneus, is
said to have killed Argus and consequently to have
fled in exile to Egypt, where he gave the Egyptians
their laws and letters. His Egyptian name is Theuth,
which is also the name in the Egyptian calendar for
57 the first month of the year. Of the various Aesculapii
the first is the son of Apollo, and is worshipped by the
Arcadians; he is reputed to have invented the probe
and to have been the first surgeon to employ splints.
The second is the brother of the second Mercury; he
is said to have been struck by lightning and buried at
Cynosura. The third is the son of Arsippus and
Arsinoë, and is said to have first invented the use of
purges and the extraction of teeth; his tomb and
grove are shown in Arcadia, not far from the river
Lusius. XXIII. The most ancient of the Apollos is
the one whom I stated just before to be the son of
Vulcan and the guardian of Athens. The second is
the son of Corybas, and was born in Crete; tradition
says that he fought with Jupiter himself for the
possession of that island. The third is the son of the
third Jupiter and of Latona, and is reputed to have
come to Delphi from the Hyperboreans. The fourth
belongs to Arcadia, and is called by the Arcadians
58 *Nomios*, as being their traditional lawgiver. Likewise there are several Dianas. The first, daughter of
Jupiter and Proserpine, is said to have given birth to

quae pinnatum Cupidinem genuisse dicitur; secunda notior, quam Iove tertio et Latona natam accepimus; tertiae pater Upis traditur Glauce mater: eam saepe Graeci Upim paterno nomine appellant. Dionysos multos habemus: primum Iove et Proserpina natum, secundum Nilo, qui Nysam dicitur interemisse, tertium Cabiro patre, eumque regem Asiae praefuisse dicunt, cui Sabazia sunt instituta, quartum Iove et Luna, cui sacra Orphica putantur confici, quintum Niso natum et Thyone, a quo Trieterides
59 constitutae putantur. Venus prima Caelo et Die nata, cuius Elide delubrum vidimus, altera spuma procreata, ex qua et Mercurio Cupidinem secundum natum accepimus, tertia Iove nata et Diona, quae nupsit Volcano, sed ex ea et Marte natus Anteros dicitur, quarta Syria Cyproque concepta,[1] quae Astarte vocatur, quam Adonidi nupsisse proditum est. Minerva prima, quam Apollinis matrem supra diximus, secunda orta Nilo, quam Aegyptii Saïtae colunt, tertia illa quam a Iove generatam supra diximus, quarta Iove nata et Coryphe Oceani filia, quam Arcades Κορίαν nominant et quadrigarum inventricem ferunt, quinta Pallantis, quae patrem dicitur interemisse virginitatem suam violare conantem, cui pin-
60 narum talaria adfigunt. Cupido primus Mercurio et

[1] a Syria Cyproque accepta ? *Mayor.*

---

[a] Perhaps the Latin should be altered to give 'we obtained from Syria and Cyprus.'

the winged Cupid. The second is more celebrated; tradition makes her the daughter of the third Jupiter and of Latona. The father of the third is recorded to have been Upis, and her mother Glauce; the Greeks often call her by her father's name of Upis. We have a number of Dionysi. The first is the son of Jupiter and Proserpine; the second of Nile—he is the fabled slayer of Nysa. The father of the third is Cabirus; it is stated that he was king over Asia, and the Sabazia were instituted in his honour. The fourth is the son of Jupiter and Luna; the Orphic rites are believed to be celebrated in his honour. The fifth is the son of Nisus and Thyone, and is believed to have
9 established the Trieterid festival. The first Venus is the daughter of the Sky and the Day; I have seen her temple at Elis. The second was engendered from the sea-foam, and as we are told became the mother by Mercury of the second Cupid. The third is the daughter of Jupiter and Dione, who wedded Vulcan, but who is said to have been the mother of Anteros by Mars. The fourth was conceived of Syria and Cyprus,[a] and is called Astarte; it is recorded that she married Adonis. The first Minerva is the one whom we mentioned above as the mother of Apollo. The second sprang from the Nile, and is worshipped by the Egyptians of Sais. The third is she whom we mentioned above as begotten by Jupiter. The fourth is the daughter of Jupiter and Coryphe the daughter of Oceanus, and is called *Koria* by the Arcadians, who say that she was the inventor of the four-horsed chariot. The fifth is Pallas, who is said to have slain her father when he attempted to violate her maidenhood; she is represented with wings attached to her
0 ankles. The first Cupid is said to be the son of Mer-

Diana prima natus dicitur, secundus Mercurio et Venere secunda, tertius qui idem est Anteros Marte et Venere tertia. Atque haec quidem aliaque eius modi ex vetere Graeciae fama collecta sunt, quibus intellegis resistendum esse ne perturbentur religiones; vestri autem non modo haec non refellunt verum etiam confirmant interpretando quorsum quidque pertineat. Sed eo iam unde huc digressi sumus revertamur.

61 XXIV. " . . . Num censes igitur subtiliore ratione opus esse ad haec refellenda? Nam mentem fidem spem virtutem honorem victoriam salutem concordiam ceteraque eius modi rerum vim habere videmus, non deorum. Aut enim in nobismet insunt ipsis, ut mens ut spes ut fides ut virtus ut concordia, aut optandae nobis sunt, ut honos ut salus ut victoria; quarum rerum utilitatem video, video etiam consecrata simulacra, quare autem in iis vis deorum insit tum intellegam cum[1] cognovero. Quo in genere vel maxime est Fortuna numeranda, quam nemo ab inconstantia et temeritate seiunget, quae digna certe non sunt deo.

62 "Iam vero quid vos illa delectat explicatio fabularum et enodatio nominum? Exsectum a filio Caelum, vinctum itidem a filio Saturnum, haec et alia generis eiusdem ita defenditis ut ii qui ista finxerunt non

[1] cum <ex te> *Bouhier*.

[a] See note on § 53. The introduction of the next topic seems to have been lost.

cury and the first Diana, the second of Mercury and the second Venus, and the third, who is the same as Anteros, of Mars and the third Venus.

"These and other similar fables have been culled from the ancient traditions of Greece; you are aware that we ought to combat them, so that religion may not be undermined. Your school however not merely do not refute them, but actually confirm them by interpreting their respective meanings. But let us now return to the point from which we digressed to this topic.

XXIV. [a]" . . . Do you then think that any more subtle argument is needed to refute these notions? Intelligence, faith, hope, virtue, honour, victory, safety, concord and the other things of this nature are obviously abstractions, not personal deities. For they are either properties inherent in ourselves, for instance intelligence, hope, faith, virtue, concord, or objects of our desire, for instance honour, safety, victory. I see that they have value, and I am also aware that statues are dedicated to them; but why they should be held to possess divinity is a thing that I cannot understand without further enlightenment. Fortune has a very strong claim to be counted in this list, and nobody will dissociate fortune from inconstancy and haphazard action, which are certainly unworthy of a deity.

For the Stoics' deified abstractions are absurd, and so are their allegorizations and strained etymologies.

"Again, why are you so fond of those allegorizing and etymological methods of explaining the mythology? The mutilation of Caelus by his son, and likewise the imprisonment of Saturn by his, these and similar figments you rationalize so effectively as to

modo non insani sed etiam fuisse sapientes videantur. In enodandis autem nominibus quod miserandum sit laboratis: 'Saturnus quia se saturat annis, Mavors quia magna vertit, Minerva quia minuit aut quia minatur, Venus quia venit ad omnia, Ceres a gerendo.' Quam periculosa consuetudo; in multis enim nominibus haerebitis: quid Veiovi facies, quid Volcano? quamquam quoniam Neptunum a nando appellatum putas, nullum erit nomen quod non possis una littera explicare unde ductum sit; in quo quidem magis tu
63 mihi natare visus es quam ipse Neptunus. Magnam molestiam suscepit et minime necessariam primus Zeno post Cleanthes deinde Chrysippus, commenticiarum fabularum reddere rationem, vocabulorum[1] cur quidque ita appellatum sit causas explicare. Quod cum facitis, illud profecto confitemini, longe aliter se rem habere atque hominum opinio sit; eos enim qui di appellantur rerum naturas esse non figuras deorum. XXV. Qui tantus error fuit ut perniciosis etiam rebus non modo nomen deorum tribueretur sed etiam sacra constituerentur; Febris enim fanum in Palatio et <Orbonae ad>[2] aedem Larum et aram Malae Fortunae Esquiliis consecra-
64 tam videmus. Omnis igitur talis a philosophia pellatur error ut cum de dis inmortalibus disputemus dicamus indigna[3] dis immortalibus; de quibus habeo ipse quod[4] sentiam, non habeo autem quod[4] tibi adsentiar. Neptunum esse dicis animum cum intelle-

[1] vocabulorumque *dett.*
[2] *add. ed. Bononiensis* 1494.
[3] indigna *det.*: digna *B*, *cett. valde corrupti.*
[4] quod . . . quod *Ernesti*: quid . . . quid.

[a] For this and the following etymologies see ii. 64-67.
[b] Or perhaps 'find out the derivation by the light of one letter.'

make out their authors to have been not only not idiots, but actually philosophers. But as for your strained etymologies, one can only pity your misplaced ingenuity! Saturnus is so called because he is 'sated with years,' [a] Mavors because he 'subverts the great,' Minerva because she 'minishes,' or because she is 'minatory,' Venus because she 'visits' all things, Ceres from *gero* 'to bear.' What a dangerous practice! with a great many names you will be in difficulties. What will you make of Vejovis, or Vulcan? though since you think the name Neptune comes from *nare* 'to swim,' there will be no name of which you could not make the derivation clear by altering one letter [b]: in this matter you seem to me to be
63 more at sea than Neptune himself! A great deal of quite unnecessary trouble was taken first by Zeno, then by Cleanthes and lastly by Chrysippus, to rationalize these purely fanciful myths and explain the reasons for the names by which the various deities are called. But in so doing you clearly admit that the facts are widely different from men's belief, since the so-called gods are really properties of things, not divine persons at all. XXV. So far did this sort of error go, that even harmful things were not only given the names of gods but actually had forms of worship instituted in their honour: witness the temple to Fever on the Palatine, that of Orbona the goddess of bereavement close to the shrine of the Lares, and the altar conse-
64 crated to Misfortune on the Esquiline. Let us therefore banish from philosophy entirely the error of making assertions in discussing the immortal gods that are derogatory to their dignity: a subject on which I know what views to hold myself, but do not know how to agree to your views. You say that Nep-

gentia per mare pertinentem, idem de Cerere; istam autem intellegentiam aut maris aut terrae non modo comprehendere animo sed ne suspicione quidem possum attingere. Itaque aliunde mihi quaerendum est ut et esse deos et quales sint di discere possim; qualis tu eos esse vis <vide ne esse
65 non possint. Nunc>[1] videamus ea quae sequuntur, primum deorum<ne> providentia mundus regatur, deinde consulantne di rebus humanis. Haec enim mihi ex tua partitione restant duo; de quibus si vobis videtur accuratius disserendum puto."

"Mihi vero" inquit Velleius "valde videtur; nam et maiora exspecto et iis quae dicta sunt vehementer adsentior."

Tum Balbus "Interpellare te" inquit "Cotta, nolo, sed sumemus tempus aliud; efficiam profecto ut fateare. Sed . . .

. . . . .

nequaquam istuc istac ibit; magna inest certatio.
nam ut ego illi supplicarem tanta blandiloquentia,
ni ob rem[2]—

66 XXVI. Parumne ratiocinari videtur et sibi ipsa nefariam pestem machinari? Illud vero quam callida ratione:

qui volt[3] quod volt, ita dat se res ut operam dabit—

[1] *supplet Plasberg.*
[2] ni ob rem *Vahlen*: niobem. [3] volt esse *dett.*

---

[a] A considerable passage has been lost, part of it being according to Plasberg the fragments preserved by Lactantius; see p. 384.

[b] These verses are from the *Medea* of Ennius, and correspond to Euripides, *Medea* 365 ff.

tune is the rational soul that pervades the sea; and similarly for Ceres; but your notion of the sea or the land possessing a rational intelligence is not merely something that I cannot fully understand, but I have not the slightest inkling what it means. Accordingly I must seek elsewhere for instruction both as to the existence and as to the nature of the gods; as for your account of them <perhaps it may be impossible. Now> let us consider the next topics—first whether the world is ruled by divine providence, and then whether the gods have regard for the affairs of mankind. For these are the two that I have left of the heads into which you divided the subject; and if you gentlemen approve, I feel that they require a somewhat detailed discussion."

III. Providential government of the universe (§ 65).

"For my part," said Velleius, "I approve entirely, for I anticipate something more important still to come, and I also strongly agree with what has been said already."

"I do not want to interrupt you with questions," added Balbus, "we will take another time for that: I warrant I will bring you to agree. But . . .[a]

. . . . .

IV. Providential care for man (§ 65 to end). The gift of reason an injury rather than a benefit. Examples from tragedy.

> Nay, 'twill not be; a struggle is in store,
> What, should I fawn on him and speak him fair,
> Save for my purpose—[b]

XXVI. Is there any lack of reasoning here, think you, and is she not plotting dire disaster for herself? Again, how cleverly reasoned is the saying:

> For him that wills that which he wills, the event
> Shall be as he shall make it![c]

[c] 'Where there's a will there's a way.' The quotation is assigned to Ennius.

qui est versus omnium seminator malorum.

ille traversa mente mi hodie tradidit repagula
quibus ego iram omnem recludam atque illi perniciem dabo,
mihi maerores illi luctum, exitium illi exilium mihi.

Hanc videlicet rationem, quam vos divino beneficio homini solum tributam dicitis, bestiae non habent ;
67 videsne igitur quanto munere deorum simus adfecti ? Atque eadem Medea patrem patriamque fugiens,

postquam pater
adpropinquat iamque paene ut conprehendatur parat,
puerum interea obtruncat membraque articulatim dividit
perque agros passim dispergit corpus : id ea gratia
ut, dum nati dissipatos artus captaret parens,
ipsa interea effugeret, illum ut maeror tardaret sequi,
sibi salutem ut familiari pareret parricidio.

68 Huic ut scelus sic ne ratio quidem defuit. Quid ? ille funestas epulas fratri conparans nonne versat huc et illuc cogitatione rationem ?

maior mihi moles, maius miscendumst malum,
qui illius acerbum cor contundam et conprimam.

XXVII. Nec tamen ille ipse est praetereundus

qui non sat habuit coniugem inlexe in stuprum,

de quo recte et verissume loquitur Atreus :

---

[a] Again from the *Medea* of Ennius ; *cf.* Eur. *Med.* 371 f., 394 ff.

[b] Possibly from the *Medea* of Accius, *cf.* ii. 89. This part of the story is not in Euripides.

[c] This and the three following quotations are from the *Atreus* of Accius. Atreus deliberates how to take vengeance on his brother Thyestes for seducing his wife Aerope.

Yet this verse contains the seeds of every kind of mischief.

> He with misguided mind
> This day hath put the keys into my hand
> Wherewith I will unlock my utmost wrath
> And work his ruin ; grief shall be my portion
> And sorrow his : mine exile, his extinction.[a]

This gift of reason forsooth, which according to your school divine beneficence has bestowed on man alone,
67 the beasts do not possess ; do you see then how great a boon the gods have vouchsafed to us ? And Medea likewise, when flying from her father and her fatherland,

> when her sire drew near,
> And now was all but in the act to seize her,
> Her boy she did behead, and joint by joint
> Severed his limbs, and all about the fields
> His body strewed : the same with this intent,
> That, while her father strove to gather up
> Her son's dismember'd members, in the meantime
> She might herself escape, so that his grief
> Should hinder his pursuit, and she win safety
> By most unnatural murder of her kin.[b]

68 Medea was criminal, but also she was perfectly rational. Again, does not the hero plotting the direful banquet for his brother turn the design this way and that in his thoughts ?

> More must I moil and bigger bale must brew,
> Whereby to quell and crush his cruel heart.[c]

XXVII. Nor must we pass over Thyestes himself, who

> Was not content to tempt my wife to sin—

an offence of which Atreus speaks correctly and with perfect truth—

. . . quod re in summa summum esse arbitror
periclum, matres coinquinari regias,
contaminari stirpem ac misceri[1] genus.

At id ipsum quam callide, qui regnum adulterio quaereret:

adde[2] (inquit) huc, quod mihi portento caelestum pater
prodigium misit, regni stabilimen mei,
agnum inter pecudes aurea clarum coma
quondam Thyestem clepere ausum esse e regia,
qua in re adiutricem coniugem cepit sibi.

69 Videturne summa inprobitate usus non sine summa esse ratione? Nec vero scaena solum referta est his sceleribus, sed multo[3] vita communis paene maioribus. Sentit domus unius cuiusque, sentit forum, sentit curia campus socii provinciae, ut quem ad modum ratione recte fiat sic ratione peccetur, alterumque et a paucis et raro, alterum et saepe et a plurimis, ut satius fuerit nullam omnino nobis a dis inmortalibus datam esse rationem quam tanta cum pernicie datam. Ut vinum aegrotis, quia prodest raro nocet saepissime, melius est non adhibere omnino quam spe dubiae salutis in apertam perniciem incurrere, sic haud scio an melius fuerit humano generi motum istum celerem cogitationis, acumen, sollertiam, quam rationem vocamus, quoniam pestifera est multis, admodum paucis salutaris, non dari

[1] ac misceri *Ribbeck*: admisceri.
[2] adde *Scriverius*: addo.
[3] multo <magis> ? *Mayor*.

the which I deem the height of peril
In matters of high state, if royal mothers
Shall be debauched, the royal blood corrupted,
The lineage mixed.

But how craftily this very crime is plotted by his brother, employing adultery as a means to gain the throne :

Thereto withal (says Atreus) the heavenly sire did send me
A warning portent, to confirm my reign—
A lamb, conspicuous among the flock
With fleece of gold, Thyestes once did dare
To steal from out my palace, and in this deed
My consort did suborn as his accomplice.

69 Do you see that Thyestes, while acting with extreme wickedness, displayed complete rationality as well? And not only does the stage teem with crimes of this sort, but ordinary life even more so, and with almost worse crimes. Our private homes ; the law-courts, the senate, the hustings ; our allies, our provinces—all have cause to know that just as right actions may be guided by reason, so also may wrong ones, and that whereas few men do the former, and on rare occasions, so very many do the latter, and frequently ; so that it would have been better if the immortal gods had not bestowed upon us any reasoning faculty at all than that they should have bestowed it with such mischievous results. Wine is seldom beneficial and very often harmful to the sick, and therefore it is better not to give it to them at all than to run a certain risk of injury in the doubtful hope of a cure ; similarly it would perhaps have been better if that nimbleness and penetration and cleverness of thought which we term 'reason,' being as it is disastrous to many and wholesome to but few, had never been given to the human race at all, than that it should have been

70 omnino quam tam munifice et tam large dari. Quam ob rem si mens voluntasque divina idcirco consuluit hominibus quod iis est largita rationem, iis solis consuluit quos bona ratione donavit, quos videmus si modo ulli sunt esse perpaucos. Non placet autem paucis a dis inmortalibus esse consultum; sequitur ergo ut nemini consultum sit.

XXVIII. "Huic loco sic soletis occurrere: non idcirco non optume nobis a dis esse provisum quod multi eorum beneficio perverse uterentur; etiam patrimoniis multos male uti, nec ob eam causam eos beneficium a patribus nullum habere. Quisquamne istuc negat? aut quae est in collatione ista similitudo? Nec enim Herculi nocere Deianira voluit cum ei tunicam sanguine Centauri tinctam dedit, nec prodesse Pheraeo Iasoni is qui gladio vomicam eius aperuit quam sanare medici non potuerant. Multi enim et cum obesse vellent profuerunt et cum prodesse obfuerunt; ita non fit ex eo quod datur ut voluntas eius qui dederit appareat, nec si is qui accepit bene utitur, idcirco is qui dedit amice dedit.
71 Quae enim libido quae avaritia quod facinus aut suscipitur nisi consilio capto aut sine animi motu et cogitatione, id est ratione, perficitur? Nam omnis opinio ratio est, et quidem bona ratio si vera, mala autem si falsa est opinio. Sed a deo tantum rationem habemus, si modo habemus, bonam autem

[a] Pliny, *N.H.* vii. 51, implies that this was a wound inflicted by an enemy in battle: Seneca, *Benef.* ii. 18. 8, seems to speak of the attempt of an assassin.

given in such bounteous abundance. If therefore the divine intelligence and will displayed care for men's welfare because it bestowed upon them reason, it cared for the welfare of those only to whom it gave virtuous reason, whom we see to be very few, if not entirely non-existent. We cannot, however, suppose that the immortal gods have cared for only a few; it follows therefore that they have cared for none.

Only the virtuous use of reason is beneficial, and that depends on ourselves.

XXVIII. "This line of argument is usually met by your school thus: it does not follow, you say, that the gods have not made the best provision for us because many men employ their bounty wrongly; many men make bad use of their inheritances, but this does not prove that they have received no benefit from their fathers. Does anybody deny this? and where is the analogy in your comparison? When Deianira gave Hercules the shirt soaked in the Centaur's blood, she did not intend to injure him. When the soldier with a stroke of his sword opened Jason of Pherae's tumour which the physicians had failed to cure, he did not intend to do him good.[a] Plenty of people have done good when they intended to do harm and harm when they intended to do good. The nature of the gift does not disclose the will of the giver, and the fact that the recipient makes good use of it does not prove that the giver gave it with friendly intentions. Is there a single act of lust, of avarice or of crime, which is not entered on deliberately or which is not carried out with active exercise of thought, that is, by aid of the reason? inasmuch as every belief is an activity of reason—and of reason that is a good thing if the belief is true, but a bad thing if it is false. But god bestows upon us (if indeed he does) merely reason—it is we who make

rationem aut non bonam a nobis. Non enim ut patrimonium relinquitur sic ratio est homini beneficio deorum data ; quid enim potius hominibus dedissent si iis nocere voluissent ? iniustitiae autem intemperantiae timiditatis quae semina essent, si his vitiis ratio non subesset ?

XXIX. "Medea modo et Atreus commemorabantur a nobis, heroicae personae, inita subductaque
72 ratione nefaria scelera meditantes. Quid ? levitates comicae parumne semper in ratione versantur ? parumne subtiliter disputat ille in Eunucho :

> quid igitur faciam ? . . .
> exclusit, revocat ; redeam ? non si me obsecret.

Ille vero in Synephebis Academicorum more contra communem opinionem non dubitat pugnare ratione, qui 'in amore summo' 'summaque inopia' suave esse dicit

> parentem habere avarum, inlepidum, in liberos
> difficilem, qui te nec amet nec studeat tui—

73 atque huic incredibili sententiae ratiunculas suggerit :

> aut tu illum fructu fallas aut per litteras
> avertas aliquod nomen aut per servolum
> percutias pavidum ; postremo a parco patre
> quod sumas, quanto dissipes libentius !

Idemque facilem et liberalem patrem incommodum esse amanti filio disputat :

---

[a] Terence, *Eun.* Act i. *init.*
[b] See on i. 13.

it good or the reverse. The divine bestowal of reason upon man is not in itself an act of beneficence, like the bequest of an estate; for what other gift could the gods have given to men in preference if their intention had been to do them harm? and from what seeds could injustice, intemperance and cowardice spring, if these vices had not a basis in reason?

XXIX. "We alluded just now to Medea and Atreus, characters of heroic legend, planning their atrocious crimes with a cool calculation of profit and loss. But what of the frivolous scenes of comedy? do not these show the reasoning faculty constantly employed? Does not that young man in the *Eunuch* [a] argue subtly enough: Examples of the abuse of reason from comedy,

> What shall I do then? . . .
> She shut me out, and now she calls me back;
> Well, shall I go? No, not if she implores me.

While the one in the *Young Comrades* [b] does not hesitate to employ the weapon of reason, in true Academic style, to combat received opinion, when he says

> 'Tis sweet, when deep in love and deep in debt,
> To have a niggardly and ungracious sire,
> Who loves you not and cares not for your weal—

an extraordinary dictum for which he subjoins some reasons of a sort:

> Then either you may cheat him of a rent,
> Or forge a document and intercept
> A debt that's due to him, or send your page-boy
> To trick him with some scare; and last of all,
> How much more fun it is to squander money
> Which you have screwed out of a stingy father!

And he proceeds to argue that a kind and generous father is a positive inconvenience to a son in love:

quem neque quo pacto fallam nec quid inde auferam
nec quem dolum ad eum aut machinam commoliar
scio quicquam : ita omnes meos dolos fallacias
praestrigias praestrinxit commoditas patris.

Quid ergo isti doli, quid machinae, quid fallaciae praestrigiaeque num sine ratione esse potuerunt ? O praeclarum munus deorum, ut Phormio possit dicere :

cedo senem ; iam instructa sunt mi in corde consilia omnia !

74 XXX. " Sed exeamus e theatro, veniamus in forum. Sessum it praetor. Quid ut iudicetur ? Qui tabularium incenderit. Quod facinus occultius ? at[1] se Q. Sosius splendidus eques Romanus ex agro Piceno fecisse confessus est. Qui transscripserit tabulas publicas. Id quoque L. Alenus fecit, cum chirographum sex primorum imitatus est : quid hoc homine sollertius ? Cognosce alias quaestiones, auri Tolossani, coniurationis Iugurthinae ; repete superiora, Tubuli de pecunia capta ob rem iudicandam, posteriora, de incestu rogatione Peducaea, tum haec cotidiana, sicae veneni[2] peculatus, testamentorum etiam, lege nova quaestiones. Inde illa actio 'ope consilioque tuo furtum aio factum esse,' inde tot iudicia de fide mala, tutelae, mandati, pro socio, fiduciae, reliqua quae ex empto aut vendito aut conducto aut locato contra fidem fiunt, inde iudicium

[1] at *B* : ad *A*, id *Davies*, at id *Schutz.*
[2] veneni *dett.* : venena *A*, *B*.

[a] Toulouse joined the Cimbri in their revolt, and was sacked by Q. Servilius Caepio, 106 B.C.; the temples contained large stores of gold. Caepio was most severely punished for sacrilege on his return to Rome.

How I'm to cheat him, what to levy off him,
What plot to plan or trick to play upon him,
I can't imagine: all my tricks and dodges
My father's generosity has out-tricked.

Well then, how can those plots and devices, those dodges and tricks have come into existence without reasoning? What a noble gift of the gods, that enables Phormio to say:

Produce the old boy—my plans are all prepared!

XXX. "But let us quit the theatre and visit the law-courts. The praetor is about to take his seat. What is the trial to be about? To find out who set fire to the record office. How could you have a craftier crime? yet Quintus Socius, a distinguished Roman knight, confessed he had done it. To find out who tampered with the public accounts. Well, this again was done by Lucius Alenus, when he forged the handwriting of the six senior treasury clerks; what could be craftier than this fellow? Note other trials—the affair of the gold from Toulouse,[a] Jugurtha's conspiracy; go back to an earlier period, and take the trial of Tubulus for giving a bribed verdict, or to a later one, and take the trial for incest on Peducaeus's motion, and then the trials under the new law, the cases of assassination, poisoning, embezzlement and forgery of wills, that are daily occurrences at the present time. Reason is the source of the charge 'I declare that with your aid and counsel a theft was committed'; hence spring all the trials for breach of trust as to a guardianship, commission, in virtue of partnership, trusteeship, and all the other cases arising from breach of faith in purchase or sale or hire or lease; hence procedure on the public behalf in a private suit

and from the law-courts.

publicum rei privatae lege Plaetoria, inde everriculum malitiarum omnium iudicium de dolo malo, quod C. Aquillius familiaris noster protulit, quem dolum idem Aquillius tum teneri putat cum aliud sit simu-
75 latum aliud actum. Hanc igitur tantam a dis inmortalibus arbitramur malorum sementim esse factam? Si enim rationem hominibus di dederunt, malitiam dederunt; est enim malitia versuta et fallax ratio nocendi; iidem etiam di fraudem dederunt, facinus ceteraque, quorum nihil nec suscipi sine ratione nec effici potest. Utinam igitur, ut illa anus optat

ne in nemore Pelio securibus
caesae accidissent abiegnae ad terram trabes,

sic istam calliditatem hominibus di ne dedissent! qua perpauci bene utuntur, qui tamen ipsi saepe a male utentibus opprimuntur, innumerabiles autem improbe utuntur, ut donum hoc divinum rationis et consilii ad fraudem hominibus, non ad bonitatem impertitum esse videatur.

76 XXXI. "Sed urgetis identidem hominum esse istam culpam, non deorum — ut si medicus gravitatem morbi, gubernator vim tempestatis accuset; etsi hi quidem homunculi, sed tamen ridiculi: 'Quis enim te adhibuisset' dixerit quispiam 'si ista non essent?' Contra deum licet disputare liberius: 'In hominum vitiis ais esse culpam: eam dedisses hominibus ratio-

[a] This law made the cheating of young men by money-lenders a criminal offence, conviction carrying ineligibility for public office.

[b] Probably this gave action for forms of fraud not coming under any previous formula.

[c] The opening lines of Ennius's *Medea*, translated from Euripides: εἴθ' ὤφελε . . . μηδ' ἐν νάπαισι Πηλίου πεσεῖν ποτε τμηθεῖσα πεύκη.

under the law of Plaetorius [a]; hence that net to catch wrong-doing of all sorts, the 'action for malicious fraud' [b] promulgated by our friend Gaius Aquillius, a charge of fraud that Aquillius likewise holds to be proved when a man has pretended to do one thing and has done another. Do we then really think that this enormous crop of evil was sown by the immortal gods? For if the gods gave man reason, they gave him malice, for malice is the crafty and covert planning of harm; and likewise also the gods gave him trickery and crime and all the other wickednesses, none of which can be either planned or executed without reasoning. 'If only,' as the old nurse prays in the tragedy,

> Pelion's glades had never seen
> The axe fell to the earth the pine-tree trunks,[c]

so if only the gods had never given to man that cunning which you speak of! Which very few use well, and even these themselves are all the same often crushed by those who use it badly; whereas countless numbers use it wickedly, and make it seem that this divine gift of reason and of wisdom was imparted to man for the purpose of deception and not of honest dealing.

XXXI. "But you keep insisting that mankind and not the gods are to blame for this. That is as if a physician should plead the severity of the disease, or a helmsman the violence of the storm. Though these are mere men—but even for them it would be an absurd plea: 'if it were not so,' anybody would rejoin, 'who would have employed you?' But a god one might rebut more roundly: 'You say that the fault lies in men's vices; you ought to have given men a rational faculty of such a nature as would have

Providence must have foreseen that man would abuse reason, and should not have bestowed it.

nem, quae vitia culpamque excluderet.' Ubi igitur locus fuit errori deorum? Nam patrimonia spe bene tradendi relinquimus, qua possumus falli; deus falli qui potuit? An ut Sol in currum cum Phaëthontem filium sustulit, aut Neptunus cum Theseus Hippolytum perdidit, cum ter optandi a Neptuno patre
77 habuisset potestatem? Poetarum ista sunt, nos autem philosophi esse volumus, rerum auctores, non fabularum. Atque hi tamen ipsi di poetici si scissent perniciosa fore illa filiis, peccasse in beneficio putarentur. Ut[1] si verum est quod Aristo Chius dicere solebat, nocere audientibus philosophos iis qui bene dicta male interpretarentur (posse enim asotos ex Aristippi, acerbos e Zenonis schola exire), prorsus, si qui audierunt vitiosi essent discessuri quod perverse philosophorum disputationem interpretarentur, tacere praestaret philosophos[2] quam iis qui se audis-
78 sent nocere: sic, si homines rationem bono consilio a dis immortalibus datam in fraudem malitiamque convertunt, non dari illam quam dari humano generi melius fuit. Ut, si medicus sciat eum aegrotum qui iussus sit vinum sumere meracius sumpturum statimque periturum, magna sit in culpa, sic vestra ista providentia reprehendenda, quae rationem dederit

[1] ut *Davies*: et.
[2] philosophos *dett.*: philosophis *A*, *B*.

[a] Poseidon gave his son Theseus, King of Athens, three wishes. Theseus wished the death of his son Hippolytus, falsely accused by his step-mother Phaedra of love for her. Poseidon sent a sea-bull that scared Hippolytus's chariot-horses, and he was killed.

precluded vice and crime.' What room therefore was there for error on the part of the gods? We men bequeath legacies in the hope of bestowing them beneficially, a hope in which we may be deceived; but how could god be deceived? As the Sun was, when he gave his son Phaëthon a ride in his chariot? or Neptune, when his bestowal on his son of permission for three wishes resulted in Theseus' causing the
77 death of Hippolytus[a]? These are fables of the poets, whereas we aim at being philosophers, who set down facts, not fictions. And all the same, even these gods of poetry would be held guilty of mistaken kindness if they knew that their gifts would bring their sons disaster. Just as, if a favourite saying of Aristo of Chios was true, that philosophers are harmful to their hearers when the hearers put a bad interpretation on doctrines good in themselves (for he allowed it was possible to leave the school of Aristippus a profligate, or that of Zeno cantankerous), then clearly, if their pupils were likely to go away depraved because they misinterpreted the philosophers' discourses, it would be better for the philosophers to keep silence than to do harm to those who heard
78 them: similarly, if men abuse the faculty of reason, bestowed on them with a good intention by the immortal gods, by employing it to cheat and wrong their fellows, it would have been better for it not to be bestowed upon the human race than to be bestowed. Just as, supposing a doctor to know that a patient for whom he prescribes wine will be certain to drink it with too little water and will die on the spot, that doctor would be greatly to blame, so your Stoic providence is to be censured for bestowing reason upon those whom it knew to be going to use

iis quos scierit ea perverse et inprobe usuros. Nisi forte dicitis eam nescisse. Utinam quidem! sed non audebitis, non enim ignoro quanti eius nomen putetis.

79 XXXII. "Sed hic quidem locus concludi iam potest. Nam si stultitia consensu omnium philosophorum maius est malum quam si omnia mala et fortunae et corporis ex altera parte ponantur, sapientiam autem nemo adsequitur, in summis malis omnes sumus quibus vos optume consultum a dis inmortalibus dicitis. Nam ut nihil interest utrum nemo valeat an nemo possit valere, sic non intellego quid intersit utrum nemo sit sapiens an nemo esse possit.

"Ac nos quidem nimis multa de re apertissuma; Telamo autem uno versu locum totum conficit cur di homines neglegant:

> nam si curent, bene bonis sit, male malis; quod nunc abest.

Debebant illi quidem omnis bonos efficere, siquidem
80 hominum generi consulebant; sin id minus, bonis quidem certe consulere debebant. Cur igitur duo Scipiones, fortissimos et optimos viros, in Hispania Poenus oppressit? cur Maximus extulit filium consularem? cur Marcellum Hannibal interemit? cur Paulum Cannae sustulerunt? cur Poenorum crudelitati Reguli corpus est praebitum? cur Africanum domestici parietes non texerunt? Sed haec vetera

---

[a] From Ennius's *Telamon*: the hero is bewailing the death of Ajax.

[b] See ii. 14 note *c*.

it wrongly and evilly. Unless perhaps you say that providence did *not* know. I only wish you would! but you will not dare to, for I am well aware how highly you esteem its name.

XXXII. "But this topic we may now bring to an end. For if by the general consent of all philosophers folly is a greater evil than all the ills of fortune and of the body when placed in the scale against it, and if wisdom on the other hand is attained by nobody, we, for whose welfare you say that the gods have cared most fully, are really in the depth of misfortune. For just as it makes no difference whether no one *is* in good health or no one *can be* in good health, so I do not understand what difference it makes whether no one *is* wise or no one *can be* wise.

Man's lack of wisdom proves the indifference of God; as do the misfortunes of the good and the triumphs of the wicked

"However, we are dwelling too long on a point that is perfectly clear. Telamo dispatches the whole topic of proving that the gods pay no heed to man in a single verse:

> For if they cared for men, good men would prosper
> And bad men come to grief; but this is not so.[a]

Indeed the gods ought to have made all men good, if they really cared for the human race; or failing that, they certainly ought at all events to have cared for the good. Why then were the two Scipios, the bravest and noblest of men, utterly defeated by the Carthaginians in Spain? why did Maximus bury his son, a man of consular rank? why did Hannibal slay Marcellus? why did Cannae prove the ruin of Paulus? why was the person of Regulus surrendered to the cruelty of the Carthaginians? why was not Africanus shielded by the walls of his home[b]? But these and numerous other instances are of long

et alia permulta; propiora videamus. Cur avunculus meus, vir innocentissumus idemque doctissumus P. Rutilius, in exilio est? cur sodalis meus interfectus domi suae Drusus? cur temperantiae prudentiaeque specimen ante simulacrum Vestae pontifex maximus est Q. Scaevola trucidatus? cur ante etiam tot civitatis principes a Cinna interempti? cur omnium perfidiosissimus C. Marius Q. Catulum praestantissuma dignitate virum mori potuit
81 iubere? Dies deficiat si velim enumerare[1] quibus bonis male evenerit, nec minus si commemorem quibus improbis optime. Cur enim Marius tam feliciter septimum consul domi suae senex est mortuus? cur omnium crudelissimus tam diu Cinna regnavit? At dedit poenas. XXXIII. Prohiberi melius fuit impedirique ne tot summos viros interficeret quam ipsum aliquando poenas dare. Summo cruciatu supplicioque Q. Varius, homo importunissumus, periit; si quia Drusum ferro Metellum veneno sustulerat, illos conservari melius fuit quam poenas sceleris Varium pendere. Duodequadraginta annos Dionysius tyrannus fuit opulentissumae et beatissumae
82 civitatis; quam multos ante hunc in ipso Graeciae flore Pisistratus! 'At Phalaris, at Apollodorus poenas sustulit.' Multis quidem ante cruciatis et necatis. Et praedones multi saepe poenas dant, nec tamen possumus dicere non pluris captivos

[1] enumerare *Ernesti*: numerare.

ago; let us look at more recent cases. Why is my uncle Publius Rutilius, a man of stainless honour and also of consummate learning, now in exile? why was my comrade Drusus murdered in his own home? why was that pattern of high principle and of wisdom, the chief pontiff Quintus Scaevola, assassinated in front of the statue of Vesta? why before that were so many leading citizens also made away with by Cinna? why had that monster of treachery Gaius Marius the power to order the death of that noblest
81 of mankind, Quintus Catulus? The day would be too short if I desired to recount the good men visited by misfortune; and equally so were I to mention the wicked who have prospered exceedingly. For why did Marius die so happily in his own home, an old man and consul for the seventh time? why did that monster of cruelty Cinna lord it for so long? You will say that he was punished. XXXIII. It would have been better for him to be hindered and prevented from murdering so many eminent men, than finally to be punished in his turn. That barbarous creature Quintus Varius was executed with the most painful torture: if this was for stabbing Drusus and poisoning Metellus, it would have been better for their lives to be preserved than for Varius to be punished for his crime. Dionysius was despot of a most wealthy and prosperous city for thirty-eight
82 years; and before him, for how many years was Pisistratus tyrant of Athens, the very flower of Greece! 'Ah but Phalaris (you say) met with punishment, and so did Apollodorus.' Yes, but not till after they had tortured and killed many victims. Many brigands too are frequently punished, but still we cannot say that the captives cruelly murdered do not outnumber

acerbe quam praedones necatos. Anaxarchum Democriteum a Cyprio tyranno excarnificatum accepimus, Zenonem Eleatem[1] in tormentis necatum; quid dicam de Socrate, cuius morti inlacrimare[2] soleo Platonem legens? Videsne igitur deorum iudicio, si vident res humanas, discrimen esse sublatum?
83 XXXIV. Diogenes quidem Cynicus dicere solebat Harpalum, qui temporibus illis praedo felix habebatur, contra deos testimonium dicere quod in illa fortuna tam diu viveret. Dionysius, de quo ante dixi, cum fanum Proserpinae Locris expilavisset navigabat Syracusas, isque cum secundissumo vento cursum teneret, ridens 'Videtisne' inquit, 'amici, quam bona a dis inmortalibus navigatio sacrilegis detur?' Idque[3] homo acutus cum bene planeque percepisset, in eadem sententia perseverabat; qui cum ad Peloponnesum classem appulisset et in fanum venisset Iovis Olympii, aureum ei detraxit amiculum grandi pondere, quo Iovem ornarat e manubiis Karthaginiensium tyrannus Gelo, atque in eo etiam cavillatus est aestate grave esse aureum amiculum, hieme frigidum, eique laneum pallium iniecit, cum id esse[4] ad omne anni tempus[5] diceret. Idemque Aesculapii Epidauri barbam auream demi iussit, neque enim convenire barbatum esse filium cum in
84 omnibus fanis pater inberbis esset. Etiam mensas argenteas de omnibus delubris iussit auferri, in quibus cum more veteris Graeciae inscriptum esset

[1] Eleatem *Marsus*: Elete *A*, Elee *B*, Eleae *dett.*
[2] inlacrimare *det.*: -ri *A*, *B*. [3] idque *Lambinus*: atque.
[4] esse aptum *dett.* [5] tempus aptum *dett.*

[a] *sc.* the *Phaedo.* [b] Apollo.

the brigands executed. It is related that Anaxarchus the disciple of Democritus was cruelly butchered by the tyrant of Cyprus, and Zeno of Elea tortured to death. Why need I mention Socrates, whose death when I read Plato[a] never fails to move me to tears? Do you see then that the verdict of the gods, if they do regard men's fortunes, has destroyed all distinc-
83 tion between them? XXXIV. Indeed Diogenes the Cynic used to say that Harpalus, a brigand of the day who passed as fortunate, was a standing witness against the gods, because he lived and prospered as he did for so long. Dionysius, whom I mentioned before, having plundered the temple of Proserpine at Locri, was sailing back to Syracuse, and as he ran before a very favourable wind, remarked with a smile, 'See you, my friends, what a good crossing the immortal gods bestow on men guilty of sacrilege?' He was a clever fellow, and grasped the truth so well and clearly that he remained in the same belief continuously; for touching with his fleet on the coast of the Peloponnese and arriving at the temple of Olympian Zeus, he stripped him of his gold mantle, an adornment consisting of a great weight of metal, bestowed upon the god by the tyrant Gelo out of the spoils of the Carthaginians, and actually made a jest about it, saying that a golden mantle was oppressive in summer and cold in winter, and he threw on the god a woollen cloak, saying it was for every season of the year. He also gave orders for the removal of the golden beard of Aesculapius at Epidaurus, saying it was not fitting for the son to wear a beard when his
84 father[b] appeared in all his temples beardless. He even ordered the silver tables to be carried off from all the shrines, saying that as they bore the inscription 'the

'bonorum deorum,' uti se eorum bonitate velle
dicebat. Idem Victoriolas aureas et pateras coronas-
que quae simulacrorum porrectis manibus sustine-
bantur sine dubitatione tollebat, eaque se accipere
non auferre dicebat, esse enim stultitiam a quibus
bona precaremur ab iis porrigentibus et dantibus
nolle sumere. Eundemque ferunt haec quae dixi sublata de fanis in forum protulisse et per praeconem
vendidisse, exactaque pecunia edixisse ut quod quisque a sacris[1] haberet id ante diem certam in suum
quidque fanum referret; ita ad impietatem in deos
in homines adiunxit iniuriam. XXXV. Hunc igitur
nec Olympius Iuppiter fulmine percussit nec Aesculapius misero diuturnoque morbo tabescentem interemit, atque in suo lectulo mortuus in † tyrannidis[2]
rogum inlatus est, eamque potestatem quam
ipse per scelus erat nanctus quasi iustam et legiti-
85 mam hereditatis loco filio tradidit. Invita in hoc
loco versatur oratio, videtur enim auctoritatem ad-
ferre peccandi: recte videretur, nisi et virtutis et
vitiorum sine ulla divina ratione grave ipsius con-
scientiae pondus esset. Qua sublata iacent omnia;
ut enim nec domus nec res publica ratione quadam
et disciplina dissignata videatur si in ea nec recte
factis praemia extent ulla nec supplicia peccatis,
sic mundi divina [in homines][3] moderatio profecto

[1] a sacris: sacri *B*.
[2] tyranni dis *B*: typanidis *A*.
[3] *Bouhier*.

[a] *i.e.*, kindness, bounty, *bonté*.
[b] The text is probably corrupt.

property of the good gods,' he desired to profit by their goodness.[a] Also he used to have no scruples in removing the little gold images of Victory and the gold cups and crowns carried in the outstretched hands of statues, and he used to say that he did not take them but accepted them, for it was folly to pray to certain beings for benefits and then when they proffered them as a gift to refuse to receive them. It is also related that he produced in the market-place the spoils of the temples which I have mentioned and sold them by auction, and after he had got the money issued a proclamation that anybody who possessed any article taken from a holy place must restore that article before a fixed date to the shrine to which it belonged; thus to impiety towards the gods he added injustice towards men. XXXV. Well, Dionysius was not struck dead with a thunderbolt by Olympian Jupiter, nor did Aesculapius cause him to waste away and perish of some painful and lingering disease. He died in his bed and was laid upon a royal[b] pyre, and the power which he had himself secured by crime he handed on as an inheritance to his son as a just and
85 lawful sovereignty. It is with reluctance that I enlarge upon this topic, since you may think that my discourse lends authority to sin; and you would be justified in so thinking, were not an innocent or guilty conscience so powerful a force in itself, without the assumption of any divine design. Destroy this, and everything collapses; for just as a household or a state appears to lack all rational system and order if in it there are no rewards for right conduct and no punishments for transgression, so there is no such thing at all as the divine governance of the world if

nulla est si in ea discrimen nullum est bonorum et malorum.

86 "'At enim minora di neglegunt, neque agellos singulorum nec viticulas persequuntur, nec si uredo aut grando quippiam nocuit, id Iovi animadvertendum fuit; ne in regnis quidem reges omnia minima curant': sic enim dicitis. Quasi ego paulo ante[a] de fundo Formiano P. Rutilii sim questus, non de amissa salute. XXXVI. Atque hoc quidem omnes mortales sic habent, externas commoditates, vineta segetes oliveta, ubertatem frugum et fructuum, omnem denique commoditatem prosperitatemque vitae a dis se habere; virtutem autem nemo umquam

87 acceptam deo rettulit. Nimirum recte; propter virtutem enim iure laudamur et in virtute recte gloriamur, quod non contingeret, si id donum a deo non a nobis haberemus. At vero aut honoribus aucti aut re familiari aut si aliud quippiam nacti sumus fortuiti boni aut depulimus mali, tum dis gratias agimus, tum nihil nostrae laudi adsumptum arbitramur. Num quis quod bonus vir esset gratias dis egit umquam? at quod dives, quod honoratus, quod incolumis. Iovemque optumum et maxumum ob eas res appellant, non quod nos iustos temperatos sapientes efficiat, sed quod salvos incolumis opulentos copiosos.

88 Neque Herculi quisquam decumam[b] vovit umquam si sapiens factus esset — quamquam Pythagoras cum in

[a] § 80.

[b] A tenth part of spoils of war and of treasure-trove was devoted to Hercules as god of treasures.

that governance makes no distinction between the good and the wicked.

Man's life and liberty are not small matters. External goods may be, but these God bestows; whereas virtue a man must win for himself.

" 'But,' it may be objected, 'the gods disregard smaller matters, and do not pay attention to the petty farms and paltry vines of individuals, and any trifling damage done by blight or hail cannot have been a matter for the notice of Jupiter; even kings do not attend to all the petty affairs in their kingdoms': this is how you argue. As if forsooth it was Publius Rutilius's estate at Formiae about which I complained a little time ago,[a] and not his loss of all security! XXXVI. But this is the way with all mortals: their external goods, their vineyards, cornfields and olive-yards, with their abundant harvests and fruits, and in short all the comfort and prosperity of their lives, they think of as coming to them from the gods; but virtue no one ever imputed to a god's bounty. And doubtless with good reason; for our virtue is a just ground for others' praise and a right reason for our own pride, and this would not be so if the gift of virtue came to us from a god and not from ourselves. On the other hand when we achieve some honour or some accession to our estate, or obtain any other of the goods or avoid any of the evils of fortune, it is then that we render thanks to the gods, and do not think that our own credit has been enhanced. Did anyone ever render thanks to the gods because he was a good man? No, but because he was rich, honoured, secure. The reason why men give to Jupiter the titles of Best and Greatest is not that they think that he makes us just, temperate or wise, but safe, secure, wealthy and opulent. Nor did anyone ever vow to pay a tithe to Hercules[b] if he became a wise man! It is true there is a story that Pyth-

geometria quiddam novi invenisset Musis bovem immolasse dicitur; sed id quidem non credo, quoniam ille ne Apollini quidem Delio hostiam immolare voluit ne aram sanguine aspergeret. Ad rem autem ut redeam, iudicium hoc omnium mortalium est, fortunam a deo petendam, a se ipso sumendam esse sapientiam. Quamvis licet Menti delubra et Virtuti et Fidei[1] consecremus, tamen haec in nobis ipsis sita videmus; spei salutis opis victoriae facultas a dis expetenda est. Inproborum igitur prosperitates secundaeque res redarguunt, ut Diogenes dicebat,
89 vim omnem deorum ac potestatem. XXXVII. 'At non numquam bonos exitus habent boni.' Eos quidem arripimus attribuimusque sine ulla ratione dis inmortalibus. At Diagoras cum Samothracam venisset, ἄθεος ille qui dicitur, atque ei quidam amicus 'Tu, qui deos putas humana neglegere, nonne animadvertis ex tot tabulis pictis quam multi votis vim tempestatis effugerint in portumque salvi pervenerint?' 'Ita fit' inquit, 'illi enim nusquam picti sunt qui naufragia fecerunt in marique perierunt.' Idemque, cum ei naviganti vectores adversa tempestate timidi et perterriti dicerent non iniuria sibi illud accidere qui illum in eandem navem recepissent, ostendit eis in eodem cursu multas alias laborantis quaesivitque num etiam in iis navibus Diagoram vehi crederent. Sic enim res se habet ut ad

[1] Fidei *secl.* <et Spei> (*del. infra* spei) *Pearce.*

[a] "Hope" should probably be transferred to the preceding list, after "Faith," *cf.* § 61.

agoras used to sacrifice an ox to the Muses when he had made a new discovery in geometry! but I don't believe it, since Pythagoras refused even to sacrifice a victim to Apollo of Delos, for fear of sprinkling the altar with blood. However, to return to my point, it is the considered belief of all mankind that they must pray to god for fortune but obtain wisdom for themselves. Let us dedicate temples as we will to Intellect, Virtue and Faith, yet we perceive that these things are within ourselves; hope,[a] safety, wealth, victory are blessings which we must seek from the gods. Accordingly the prosperity and good fortune of the wicked, as Diogenes used to say, disprove the might and power of the gods entirely. XXXVII. 'But sometimes good men come to good ends.' Yes, and we seize upon these cases and impute them with no reason to the immortal gods. Diagoras, named the Atheist, once came to Samothrace, and a certain friend said to him, 'You who think that the gods disregard men's affairs, do you not remark all the votive pictures that prove how many persons have escaped the violence of the storm, and come safe to port, by dint of vows to the gods?' 'That is so,' replied Diagoras; 'it is because there are nowhere any pictures of those who have been shipwrecked and drowned at sea.' On another voyage he encountered a storm which threw the crew of the vessel into a panic, and in their terror they told him that they had brought it on themselves by having taken him on board their ship. He pointed out to them a number of other vessels making heavy weather on the same course, and inquired whether they supposed that those ships also had a Diagoras on board. The fact really is that your character and past life make no

Virtue is not rewarded by heaven and vice is punished by man if at all.

prosperam adversamve fortunam qualis sis aut quem ad modum vixeris nihil intersit.

90 " 'Non animadvertunt' inquit 'omnia di, ne reges quidem.' Quid est simile? Reges enim si scientes praetermittunt, magna culpa est; XXXVIII. at deo ne excusatio quidem est inscientiae. Quem vos praeclare defenditis, cum dicitis eam vim deorum esse ut etiamsi quis morte poenas sceleris effugerit expetantur eae poenae a liberis a nepotibus a posteris. O miram aequitatem deorum: ferretne civitas ulla latorem istius modi legis, ut condemnaretur filius aut nepos si pater aut avus deliquisset?

> quinam Tantalidarum internecioni modus
> paretur, aut quaenam umquam ob mortem Myrtili
> poenis luendis dabitur satias supplici?

91 Utrum poëtae Stoicos depravarint an Stoici poëtis dederint auctoritatem non facile dixerim; portenta enim ab utrisque et flagitia dicuntur. Neque enim quem Hipponactis iambus laeserat aut qui erat Archilochi versu volneratus, a deo inmissum dolorem, non conceptum a se ipso continebat, nec cum Aegisthi libidinem aut cum Paridis videmus a deo causam requirimus, cum culpae paene vocem audiamus, nec ego multorum aegrorum salutem non ab Hippocrate potius quam ab Aesculapio datam iudico, nec Lacedaemoniorum disciplinam dicam umquam ab Apolline potius Spartae quam a Lycurgo datam. Critolaus inquam evertit Corinthum, Karthaginem Hasdrubal:

---

[a] By Attius, probably from *Thyestes*.

[b] Viz. of the death of Agamemnon, and the fall of Troy.

[c] General of the Achaean League, defeated by the Romans 147 B.C.; next year Corinth was taken and destroyed.

difference whatever as regards your fortune good or bad.

90 " 'The gods do not take notice of everything, any more than do human rulers,' says our friend. Where is the parallel? If human rulers knowingly overlook a fault they are greatly to blame; XXXVIII. but as for god, he cannot even offer the excuse of ignorance. And how remarkably you champion his cause, when you declare that the divine power is such that even if a person has escaped punishment by dying, the punishment is visited on his children and grandchildren and their descendants! What a remarkable instance of the divine justice! Would any state tolerate a lawgiver who should enact that a son or grandson was to be sentenced for the transgression of a father or grandfather?

> Where shall the Tantalids' vendetta end?
> What penalty for Myrtilus's murder
> Shall ever glut the appetite of vengeance?[a]

91 Whether the Stoic philosophers were led astray by the poets, or the poets relied on the authority of the Stoics, I should find it hard to say; for both tell some monstrous and outrageous tales. For the victim lashed by the lampoons of Hipponax or the verses of Archilochus nursed a wound not inflicted by a god but received from himself; and we do not look for any heaven-sent cause[b] when we view the licentiousness of Aegisthus or of Paris, since their guilt almost cries aloud in our ears; and the bestowal of health upon many sick persons I ascribe to Hippocrates rather than to Aesculapius; and I will never allow that Sparta received the Lacedaemonian rule of life from Apollo rather than from Lycurgus. It was Critolaus,[c] I aver, who overthrew Corinth, and

hi duo illos oculos orae maritumae effoderunt, non iratus aliqui quem omnino irasci posse negatis, deus.
92 At subvenire certe potuit et conservare urbis tantas atque talis; XXXIX. vos enim ipsi dicere soletis nihil esse quod deus efficere non possit, et quidem sine labore ullo; ut enim hominum membra nulla contentione mente ipsa ac voluntate moveantur, sic numine deorum omnia fingi moveri mutarique posse. Neque id dicitis superstitiose atque aniliter sed physica constantique ratione; materiam enim rerum, ex qua et in qua omnia sint, totam esse flexibilem et commutabilem, ut nihil sit quod non ex ea quamvis subito fingi convertique possit; eius autem universae fictricem et moderatricem divinam esse providentiam; hanc igitur, quocumque se moveat, efficere posse quicquid velit. Itaque aut nescit quid possit, aut neglegit res humanas, aut quid sit optimum non
93 potest iudicare. 'Non curat singulos homines.' Non mirum: ne civitates quidem. Non eas[1]? Ne nationes quidem et gentes. Quodsi has etiam contemnet, quid mirum est omne ab ea genus humanum esse contemptum? Sed quo modo iidem dicitis non omnia deos persequi, iidem voltis a dis inmortalibus hominibus dispertiri ac dividi somnia? idcirco haec tecum quia vestra est de somniorum veritate sententia. Atque iidem etiam vota suscipi dicitis

[1] non <modo> eas *Muller*.

Hasdrubal Carthage: those two glories of the sea-coast were extinguished by these mortals, not by some angry god—who according to your school is entirely incapable of anger. But at all events a god could have come to the aid of those great and splendid cities and have preserved them—XXXIX. for you yourselves are fond of saying that there is nothing that a god cannot accomplish, and that without any toil; as man's limbs are effortlessly moved merely by his mind and will, so, as you say, the gods' power can mould and move and alter all things. Nor do you say this as some superstitious fable or old wives' tale, but you give a scientific and systematic account of it: you allege that matter, which constitutes and contains all things, is in its entirety flexible and subject to change, so that there is nothing that cannot be moulded and transmuted out of it however suddenly, but the moulder and manipulator of this universal substance is divine providence, and therefore providence, whithersoever it moves, is able to perform whatever it will. Accordingly either providence does not know its own powers, or it does not regard human affairs, or it lacks power of judgement to discern what is the best. 'It does not care for individuals.' This is no wonder; no more does it care for cities. Not for these? Not for tribes or nations either. And if it shall appear that it despises even nations, what wonder is it that it has scorned the entire human race? But how can you both maintain that the gods do not pay attention to everything and also believe that dreams are distributed and doled out to men by the immortal gods? I argue this with you because the belief in the truth of dreams is a tenet of your school. And do you also say that it is proper

God, if incapable of anger, might still care for the good, if not individuals, then nations, or humanity at large: you profess to believe in divination, and your idle gods have time to spare.

oportere? Nempe singuli vovent: audit igitur mens divina etiam de singulis; videtis ergo non esse eam tam occupatam quam putabatis? Fac esse distentam, caelum versantem terram tuentem maria moderantem: cur tam multos deos nihil agere et cessare patitur? cur non rebus humanis aliquos otiosos deos praeficit qui a te, Balbe, innumerabiles explicati sunt?

"Haec fere dicere habui de natura deorum, non ut eam tollerem sed ut intellegeretis quam esset obscura et quam difficilis explicatus haberet."

94 XL. Quae cum dixisset, Cotta finem. Lucilius autem "Vehementius" inquit, "Cotta, tu quidem invectus es in eam Stoicorum rationem quae de providentia deorum ab illis sanctissume et providentissume constituta est. Sed quoniam advesperascit, dabis nobis diem aliquem ut contra ista dicamus. Est enim mihi tecum pro aris et focis certamen et pro deorum templis atque delubris proque urbis muris, quos vos pontifices sanctos esse dicitis diligentiusque urbem religione quam ipsis moenibus cingitis; quae deseri a me, dum quidem spirare potero, nefas iudico."

95 Tum Cotta: "Ego vero et opto redargui me, Balbe, et ea quae disputavi disserere malui quam iudicare, et facile me a te vinci posse certo scio."

for men to take vows upon themselves? Well, but vows are made by individuals; therefore the divine mind gives a hearing even to the concerns of individuals; do you see therefore that it is not so engrossed in business as you thought? Grant that it is distracted between moving the heavens and watching the earth and controlling the seas: why does it suffer so many gods to be idle and keep holiday? why does it not appoint some of the leisured gods whose countless numbers you expounded, Balbus, to superintend human affairs?

"This more or less is what I have to say about the nature of the gods; it is not my design to disprove it, but to bring you to understand how obscure it is and how difficult to explain."

94 XL. So saying, Cotta ended. But Lucilius said: Conclusion.
"You have indeed made a slashing attack upon the most reverently and wisely constructed Stoic doctrine of the divine providence. But as evening is now approaching, you will assign us a day on which to make our answer to your views. For I have to fight against you on behalf of our altars and hearths, of the temples and shrines of the gods, and of the city-walls, which you as pontiffs declare to be sacred and are more careful to hedge the city round with religious ceremonies than even with fortifications; and my conscience forbids me to abandon their cause so long as I yet can breathe."

95 "I on my side," replied Cotta, "only desire to be refuted. My purpose was rather to discuss the doctrines I have expounded than to pronounce judgement upon them, and I am confident that you can easily defeat me."

"Quippe" inquit Velleius "qui etiam somnia putet ad nos mitti ab Iove, quae ipsa tamen tam levia non sunt quam est Stoicorum de natura deorum oratio."

Haec cum essent dicta, ita discessimus ut Velleio Cottae disputatio verior, mihi Balbi ad veritatis similitudinem videretur esse propensior.

"Oh, no doubt," interposed Velleius; "why, he thinks that even our dreams are sent to us by Jupiter —though dreams themselves are not so unsubstantial as a Stoic disquisition on the nature of the gods."

Here the conversation ended, and we parted, Velleius thinking Cotta's discourse to be the truer, while I felt that that of Balbus approximated more nearly to a semblance of the truth.

FRAGMENTA

Ex Libro de Natura Deorum tertio

1. *Lactant. Inst. div. ii. 3. 2 Intellegebat Cicero falsa esse quae homines adorarent. Nam cum multa dixisset quae ad eversionem religionum valerent, ait tamen* non esse illa vulgo disputanda, ne susceptas publice religiones disputatio talis exstinguat.

2. *Ib. ii. 8. 10 Cicero de natura deorum disputans sic ait :* Primum igitur non est probabile eam materiam rerum unde orta sunt omnia esse divina providentia effectam, sed habere et habuisse vim et naturam suam. Ut igitur faber cum quid aedificaturus est non ipse facit materiam sed ea utitur quae sit parata, fictorque item cera, sic isti providentiae divinae materiam praesto esse oportuit non quam ipsa[1] faceret sed quam haberet paratam. Quodsi non est a deo materia facta, ne terra quidem et aqua et aër et ignis a deo factus est.

3. *Maii vett. interpr. Virg. p. 45 ed. Med. apud Ciceronem de natura deorum LT, ubi de* Cleomene Lacedaemonio . . .

4. *Diomedes i. p. 313. 10 Keil. Cicero de deorum natura tertio :* homines omnibus bestiis antecedunt.

[1] ipsa *edd.* : ipse *MSS.*

[a] This and the three following fragments Plasberg inserts in Book III. § 65.

FRAGMENTS

Fragments of Book III

1.[a] *Lactantius, Divine Institutions ii. 32. Cicero was aware that the objects of men's worship were false. For after saying a number of things tending to subvert religion, he adds nevertheless that* these matters ought not to be discussed in public, lest such discussion destroy the established religion of the nation.

2. *Ib. ii. 8. 10. Cicero in discussing the nature of the gods says thus :* First therefore it is not probable that the material substance from which all things are derived was created by divine providence, but that it has and has had a force and nature of its own. As therefore the carpenter when about to build a house does not himself make timber but employs that which has been prepared, and the same with the modeller and his wax, so your divine providence ought to have been supplied with matter not made by itself but given to it ready-made. But if matter was not made by god, earth, water, air and fire also were not made by god.

3. *Maius' Ancient Interpreters of Virgil, p. 45, ed. Milan. In Cicero's de Natura Deorum bk. III., where speaking of* Cleomenes of Sparta . . .

4. *Diomedes i. p. 313. 10 Keil. Cicero de Natura Deorum bk. III* Men surpass all the lower animals.

CICERO

Ex Libris incertis

5. *Serv. ad Verg. Aen. iii.* 284 *Tullius in libro de natura deorum* tria milia annorum *dixit* magnum annum tenere.

6. *Serv. ad Verg. Aen. iii.* 600 *spirabile . . . est sermo Ciceronis, quanquam ille* spiritabile *dixerit in libris de deorum natura.*

7. *Serv. ad Verg. Aen. vi.* 894 *Per portam corneam oculi significantur, qui et cornei sunt et duriores ceteris membris, nam frigus non sentiunt sicut etiam Cicero dixit in libris de natura deorum.*

---

[a] See ii. 51 f., where, however, the length of the Great Year is stated to be uncertain. In *Hortensius*, fr. 26, Cicero gave it as 12954 years.

[b] One MS. of Servius has *spiritale*, which is probably

Fragments of uncertain Origin

5. *Servius on Virgil Aen. iii. 284. Tully in his book on the nature of the gods said that* the Great Year contains three thousand years.[a]

6. *Id. on Aen. iii. 600. 'Spirabile' . . . is in the style of Cicero, although he said* 'spiritabile'[b] *in his books on the nature of the gods.*

7. *Id. on Aen. vi. 894. By 'the gate of horn' the eyes are meant, which are both horny and harder than the other parts of the body, for they do not feel cold, as Cicero also said in his books on the nature of the gods.*[c]

correct. In *N.D.* ii. 18 we find *spiritalem*, with a less well attested variant *spiritabilem*, presumably a mere error. The usual form is *spiritualis*.

[c] There is nothing like this about the eyes in Cicero, though in ii. 144 he says "the ears have hard and so to speak horny entrances."

INDEX TO DE NATURA DEORUM

Absyrtus (brother of Medea, killed by her), iii. 48
Academica, Cicero's, i. 11
Academy, non-dogmatic, i. 1-14; doctrine of *epochē*, i. 11; of probability, i. 12; rhetoric of, ii. 168
Accius (Roman tragic author, 170–?100 B.C.), quoted, ii. 89; iii. 41, 68, 90
accommodare (συνοικειοῦν), i. 41, 104; ii. 45, 139
Acheron (river in Hades), iii. 43
Achilles, worship of, iii. 45
adaptation of animals to environment, ii. 121 ff., for propagation of species, ii. 128 ff., for use of man, ii. 158 ff.; of man's structure, ii. 134 ff.; of nature for use of man, ii. 130 ff., 154 ff.
Adonis, iii. 59
Aegialeus (=Absyrtus), iii. 48
Aegisthus, iii. 91
aequabilis tributio, *aequilibritas* (ἰσονομία), i. 50, 109
Aesculapii, three, iii. 57
Aesculapius, human benefactor deified, ii. 62; iii. 39, 45, 91; Epidaurian, his gold beard, iii. 83
aether, a foreign word, ii. 91, 101; divine, i. 36; =Jove, ii. 65; source of soul and life, ii. 18, 39 ff.; fiery heat, i. 33, 37; ii. 41, 53; holds world together, ii. 101, 115; inhabited, ii. 43
Aether, father of Caelus, iii. 44; father of Jove, iii. 53 f.
Africanus. See Scipio
air, =Juno, ii. 66; properties of, i. 40; ii. 17, 26 f., 42, 83, 101, 117; iii. 30
Alabanda (city in Caria, named from hero Alabandus), iii. 39, 50
Albucius (praetor in Sardinia 105 B.C., condemned *de repetundis*, retired to Athens and Epicurean philosophy), i. 93
Alcaeus (Greek lyric poet of Mitylene, *fl.* 600 B.C.), quoted in Latin, i. 79
Alcamenes (Athenian sculptor, *fl.* 440–400 B.C., pupil of Pheidias), i. 83
Alcmaeo (philosopher of Crotona in Italy, younger contemporary of Pythagoras, end of 6th cent. B.C.), i. 27
Alco, one of the Dioscuri, iii. 53
Alexander the Great, ii. 69
allegory, Stoic use of, i. 36 f., 41; ii. 62 ff.; iii. 62 ff.
Almo (a small tributary of the Tiber), iii. 52
alphabet, the Latin, ii. 93
Amor, iii. 44
Amphiaraus, a legendary augur, ii. 7; iii. 49
Anactes ('Kings'), iii. 53
Anaxagoras (Ionian philosopher 500–428 B.C., teacher of Pericles and Euripides), i. 26
Anaxarchus (a philosopher of Abdera, accompanied Alexander into Asia; incurred the hatred of Nicocreon, king of Salamis in Cyprus, by his free speaking, and pounded to death in a mortar), iii. 83
Anaximander (of Miletus, 610–547 B.C.), i. 25
Anaximenes (of Miletus, *fl.* end of 6th cent. B.C.), i. 26

INDEX TO DE NATURA DEORUM

animal life, wonders of, ii. 121 ff.
Annus magnus, ii. 51
Anteros, iii. 60
anthropomorphism, i. 46 ff., 71 ff., 102
Antiope, iii. 54
Antisthenes (pupil of Socrates, founder of Cynic school), i. 32
Aoede, iii. 54
Apis, i. 82
Apollo (meaning of name), ii. 68; iii. 55, 57, 88, 91
Apollodorus (minor Stoic philosopher), i. 93
Apollodorus (tyrant of Cassandria, formerly Potidaea, *c.* 280 B.C., overthrown by Antigonus Gonatas), iii. 82
Aquillius (C. Gallus, praetor with Cicero 66 B.C.), iii. 74
Aratus, ii. 104 ff. (see note), 159
Arcesilas (*c.* 315–240 B.C., founder of second Academy), i. 11, 70
Arche, iii. 54
Archilochus (of Paros, *fl.* 700 B.C., invented iambic metre; lampooned Lycambes for breaking his promise to give him a daughter in marriage; she and her sisters hanged themselves for shame), iii. 91
Archimedes (mathematician and astronomer of Syracuse, 287–212 B.C.: his orrery brought to Rome by Marcellus), ii. 88
Arctoe, ii. 105
Arctophylae, ii. 109
Arcturus, ii. 110
Arctus, ii. 109 ff.
Ardea (ancient town in Latium), iii. 47
Areopagus, ii. 74
Argo, ii. 89, 114
Argus, iii. 56
Aristaeus, iii. 45
Aristippus (of Cyrene, pupil of Socrates, founder of Cyrenaic school of hedonism), iii. 77
Aristo (of Chios, Stoic, reacted towards Cynicism), i. 37; iii. 77
Aristotle (385–322 B.C.), quoted, ii. 42, 44, 51, 95, 125; Epicurean criticism of, i. 20, 33, 93; dialogue *On Philosophy* (lost), i. 33, 107
Arsinoë, iii. 57
Arsippus, iii. 57
Asia (under K. Dionysus), iii. 58
asomata, i. 30
Astarte (Venus), iii. 59
Asteria (mother of Hercules), iii. 42; (of Hecate), iii. 46
astronomy, heliocentric, i. 24; ii. 53, 119; geocentric, ii. 91, 98; the planets, ii. 51 ff., 103, 119; exhalation, ii. 40, 83, 118; iii. 37
Astypalaea (one of Cyclades islands near Cos), iii. 45
atheism, i. 62 f., 118; iii. 89
Atheos (Diogenes), i. 62
Atreus, iii. 53, 68, 76
Attic wit, i. 93
Attus Navius, ii. 9; iii. 14
augury, ii. 7 ff., 55, 160; iii. 52

Belus, iii. 42
Boeotia, iii. 49
Bootes, ii. 109 f.
botany, ii. 29, 33, 120, 127
Britain, barbarism of, ii. 88; tides in, iii. 24

Cabirus, iii. 58
Cadmus, iii. 48
Caelius Antipater (Roman jurist *fl.* end of 2nd century B.C., wrote history of Punic wars), ii. 8
Caelus (Uranus), ii. 63; iii. 44, 53 ff.
Calatinus, Atilius (consul 258 and 254 B.C., defeated Carthaginians in 1st Punic war), ii. 61, 165
Calchas, ii. 7
Camirus (city in Rhodes), iii. 54
Cancer, ii. 110
Canicula (Sirius), iii. 26
Cannae (death of Paullus at battle of, 216 B.C.), iii. 80
Carbo (C. Papirius, partisan of Gracchi, but defended murderer of Gaius), i. 64
Carneades (of Cyrene, 214–129 B.C., head of Middle Academy; Athenian ambassador to Rome 155 B.C.), i. 4, 11; ii. 162; iii. 29, 44
Carthage, iii. 42, 83, 91

INDEX TO DE NATURA DEORUM

Castor and Pollux, ii. 6; iii. 11 ff., 53
cat deified in Egypt, i. 82, 101; iii. 47
Cato (censor 184 B.C.), i. 71; ii. 165; iii. 11
Catulus the elder (consul 102 B.C., died in Marian proscription 87 B.C.), i. 79; iii. 80
Catulus the younger (consul 78 B.C.), i. 79
Centaurs, iii. 51
centripetal universe, ii. 115 ff.
Cerberus, iii. 43
Cercops, i. 107
Ceres (= earth), i. 40; ii. 67; iii. 52, 62; (= corn), ii. 60; iii. 41, 52
Charon, iii. 43
Chimaera, i. 108; ii. 5
Chronos (= Kronos), ii. 64
Chrysippus (280–206 B.C., third head of Stoic school), i. 39; ii. 16, 37, 63, 160; iii. 18, 25, 63; nicknamed Chrysippa, i. 93
Cicero, biographical details, i. 14, 59, 79, 93; iii. 46, 59, 83; philosophical studies, i. 5-12
Cinna (consul 87 B.C., leader in Marian massacre), iii. 80 f.
Circe, iii. 48, 54
Cleanthes (succeeded Zeno as head of Stoic school *c.* 260 B.C.), i. 37; ii. 13, 24, 40, 63; iii. 16, 63
Cocytus, iii. 43
Codrus, iii. 49
Concord (temple on Capitol built 367 B.C. on passing of Licinian laws), ii. 61; iii. 47, 61
conscience a witness to God, iii. 46, 85
Corinth, fall of, 146 B.C., iii. 91 (see note)
Coronis, iii. 56 (see crit. n.)
Coruncanius i. 115; ii. 165; iii. 5
Cotta (see Introd. p. xiv), i. 15; ii. 168; iii. 5, 95
creation of world inconceivable, i. 19 ff.
Critolaus, iii. 91 n.
crocodile, i. 82, 101; ii. 124, 129; iii. 47
Cronos, ii. 64
Crotona (see Locri), ii. 6
Cupidines, iii. 59 ff.
Cupido, ii. 61; iii. 58
Curius, ii. 165
cycle of existence of world, ii. 118

Decii (P. Decius Mus immolated himself in Latin war 340 B.C.; son of same name fell at Sentinum in Etruscan war 295 B.C.; grandson fell at Asculum in war against Pyrrhus 279 B.C.), iii. 15; *cf.* ii. 10
Deianeira (wife of Hercules), iii. 70
deification of abstractions, ii. 60 ff., 79
Delphi, iii. 57
Democritus (of Abdera in Thrace, *c.* 460–361 B.C., atomist), i. 29, 75, 93, 107, 120; ii. 76; doctrine of design, ii. 120 ff.
Diagoras (of Melos, 'the Atheist,' pupil of Democritus, fled from Athens when prosecuted for impiety 411 B.C.), i. 2, 63, 117; iii. 89
Diana, ii. 68 f.; iii. 58
Digiti (*Dactyli*, 'Fingers,' five wise men of Mt. Ida in Crete or Phrygia, Hercules being the eldest), iii. 42
Diodotus (Stoic philosopher, lived with Cicero from 84 to his death 59 B.C.), i. 6
Diogenes of Apollonia (natural philosopher, 5th cent. B.C.), i. 29
Diogenes of Babylon (fourth head of Stoic school, mid. 2nd cent. B.C.), i. 41
Diogenes the Cynic (d. 323 B.C.), iii. 83, 88
Dionysius (the elder, tyrant of Syracuse, 405–368 B.C.), iii. 82 ff.
Dioscuri, iii. 53
'Dis,' from *dives*, ii. 66
divination (*mantikê*), i. 55; ii. 4 ff., 162 f., 166; iii. 5, 11 ff., 95
Drusus (reformer, murdered 91 B.C.), iii. 80 f.
Duellius, ii. 165

ἡγεμονικόν. See *hegemonikon*.
Egyptian mythology, i. 43
εἱμαρμενή. See *heimarmenê*.

INDEX TO DE NATURA DEORUM

elements, denizens of, i. 103; ii. 42
elephant, ii. 151, 161
Eleusis, i. 119
Empedocles (philosopher and statesman of Agrigentum, *fl.* 490 B.C.), i. 29, 93
Engonasin (ἐν γόνασιν, constellation of a kneeling man), ii. 108
Ennius (Roman epic poet 239–169 B.C.), i. 119; ii. 4, 65, 93; iii. 10, 40, 65 f., 75, 79
Epicurus, his theology expounded, i. 18 ff.; demolished, i. 57 ff.
epiphanies, i. 36, 46, 76; ii. 6, 166; iii. 11 ff.
epochē, i. 11
Erebus, iii. 44
Erechtheus (legendary king of Athens, to secure whose victory in war his daughters offered their lives in sacrifice), iii. 49 f.
Ἕσπερος. See *Hesperos*
Ἑστία. See *Hestia*
eternity, the notion of, i. 22
Etna, eruption of, ii. 96
Etruscan augury, ii. 10 ff.
Eubouleus, iii. 53
Euhemerus (Greek rationalizing mythologist, *fl.* 300 B.C.), i. 119
Eumenides, iii. 46
Euripides, quoted, ii. 65
Europa, i. 78; ii. 165; iii. 24
Eviolus (?), iii. 53

Fabius, Q. Maximus Cunctator (dedicated temple to Honos 233 B.C., hero of 2nd Punic war), ii. 61, 165; iii. 80
Fabricius, ii. 165
Faunus, ii. 6; iii. 15
fire, vital properties of, i. 103; ii. 40, 42; Heraclitus's primary, refuted, iii. 35 ff.
fish, worship of, iii. 39, 47
Flaminius, C. (consul, fell in battle with Hannibal at Trasimene 217 B.C.), ii. 8
flux, basis of life, i. 39; ii. 84; iii. 30
Fons (god of wells, son of Janus), iii. 52
Formiae (Mola di Gaieta: ruins of Cicero's villa still shown), iii. 86
friendship, utilitarian, i. 122
Furies, Furina, iii. 46

Gelo (tyrant of Syracuse 491–478 B.C.), iii. 83
Gēmētēr, ii. 67
Gigas, ii. 70
Glauce, iii. 58
Gracchus, Ti. Sempronius (consul 177 and 163 B.C., father of the tribunes), i. 106; ii. 10, 11, 165
gravitation, ii. 115

Haedi ('Kids,' constellation), ii. 110
hand, mechanism of, ii. 150 ff.
Hannibal, iii. 80
Harpalus (profligate treasurer of Alexander, fled to Athens 324 B.C.), iii. 83
Hasdrubal, iii. 91
hawk, ii. 125
heat vital, ii. 23 ff.
hedonism refuted, i. 111 ff.
hēgemonikon, ii. 29
heimarmenē, i. 55
Helenus (son of Priam, foretold fortunes of Aeneas), ii. 7
Helicē ('screw'), ii. 105, 110
Heliopolis (city on Nile), iii. 54
Heraclides of Pontus (pupil of Plato and Aristotle), i. 34
Heraclitus ('the obscure,' philosopher of Ephesus, late 6th cent. B.C.) i. 74; iii. 35
Hercules, ii. 62; iii. 39, 41 f., 50, 70, 88
Hermarchus (of Mitylene, succeeded Epicurus), i. 93
Hesiod, i. 41; ii. 159; iii. 44
Hesperides, iii. 44
Hesperos, ii. 53
Hestia, ii. 67
Hiero (tyrant of Syracuse 478–467 B.C.), i. 60
Hippocentaur, i. 105; ii. 5
Hippocrates (*fl.* 400 B.C.), iii. 91
Hippolytus, iii. 76
Hipponax (of Ephesus, late 6th cent. B.C., invented *scazon* or limping iambus, satirized sculptors Bupalus and Athenis who had caricatured him), iii. 91

INDEX TO DE NATURA DEORUM

Homer, i. 41 ; ii. 70, 165 ; iii. 11, 41
Honor, ii. 61 ; iii. 47, 61
hormai (impulses of will), ii. 58
Hyades, ii. 111
Hyperion, iii. 54

Ialysus, iii. 54
iambus. See Hipponax
Ianus, ii. 67
Iason (tyrant of Pherae in Thessaly, assassinated 370 B.C.), iii. 70
ibis, i. 82, 101 ; ii. 126 ; iii. 47
ichneumon, i. 101
Idyia, iii. 48
imagines, i. 29, 49, 73, 106 ff., 120 ; ii. 76
India, i. 88, 97
Indus, greatest of rivers, ii. 130
Ino (sea goddess, gave Odysseus veil on which he floated after shipwreck, *Od.* v. 333 ff.), iii. 48
intermundia, i. 18
Iris, iii. 51
Isis, iii. 47
isonomia, i. 50, 109
Iuno, i. 82 ; ii. 66
Iupiter, derivation, ii. 64 ; Stoic, the supreme law, i. 40 ; the sky, ii. 4, 65, 119 ; Capitolinus, i. 82 ; Hammon, i. 82 ; planet, ii. 119 ; Olympian, iii. 83 ; source of dreams, iii. 95 ; three Jupiters, iii. 53
Iuventus (Hebe), i. 112

Kronos = *chronos*, ii. 64
kyklos, ii. 47
Kyriai Doxai, i. 85

Labor, iii. 44
Laelius (C. Sapiens, friend of younger Africanus, and chief speaker in *De Amicitia*), ii. 165 ; iii. 5, 43
Latona, iii. 46, 57 f.
Leda, iii. 53
Lemnos, i. 119 ; iii. 55
Leontium (pupil of Epicurus), i. 94
Leucippus (atomic physicist, forerunner of Democritus, date uncertain), i. 66
Leucothea (epithet of Ino), iii. 39, 48
Liber, ii. 60, 62 ; iii. 41, 53
Libera, ii. 63
Libya, iii. 24
liver, ii. 137 ; iii. 14
Locri, ii. 6 ; iii. 11, 83
Lubentina (or Libitina, a form of Venus, and goddess of death because deaths were registered in her temple at Rome), ii. 61
Lucifer, ii. 53 ; iii. 51
Lucilius (satirist, 148–103 B.C.), i. 64
Lucina, ii. 68
Luna, ii. 68 ; iii. 51, 58
Lutatius (C. Lutatius, defeated Carthaginian fleet off Aegates islands and ended 1st Punic war, 241 B.C.), ii. 165
Lyceum (shrine at Athens, its grove, *peripatos*, the resort of Aristotle), i. 72
Lycurgus (lawgiver of Sparta), iii. 91
Lysithoë, iii. 42

machina, deus ex, i. 53
magi, i. 43
Mala Fortuna, iii. 63
man, image of God, i. 90 ; noblest work of God, ii. 133 ff. ; world made for, ii. 154 ff. ; belittled, ii. 17, 34 ff., 79 ; bodily structure, ii. 134 ff., 139 ff.
mantikē, i. 55
Marcellus, M. (defeated Gauls at Clastidium 222 B.C., besieged Syracuse in 2nd Punic war, fell at Venusia 208 B.C.), ii. 61, 165 ; iii. 80
Marius, C. (democratic leader, 157–86 B.C.), iii. 80 f.
Mars, ii. 53, 67, 119 ; iii. 59, 62
Maso (C. Papirius, defeated Corsicans 231 B.C.), iii. 52
matter, iii. 29 f., 92
'Mavors,' etymology of, ii. 67 ; iii. 62
Medea, iii. 48 ; *Medea* of Ennius, iii. 65 f., 75 ; of Accius, ii. 89 ; iii. 67
Melete, iii. 54
'menses' from *mensa*, ii. 69
Mercury, iii. 56 ff.
Metellus (consul 250 B.C.), ii. 265 ; his murder (otherwise unknown), iii. 81

INDEX TO DE NATURA DEORUM

Metrodorus (Epicurus's most distinguished pupil, d. 277 B.C.), i. 86, 93, 113
mind in matter, i. 25 f. ; ii. 18, 58, 61 ; iii. 47, 61, 88
Minerva, i. 81, 83, 100 ; ii. 67 ; iii. 53, 55, 59, 63
Miseria, iii. 44
Mnemosyne, iii. 54
mole, i. 79 f.
Moneta, iii. 47
monogrammos deos, ii. 59
moon, ii. 19, 50, 103, 119
Mopsus, ii. 7
Musae, iii. 45, 54, 88
Musaeas (mythical poet), i. 41
mysteries, i. 119 ; ii. 62 ; iii. 58
mythology, personification of natural forces, ii. 62 ; popular, ridiculed, ii. 70 ; iii. 11, 16

nature, blind force of Epicurus and New Academy, i. 35, 53 ; ii. 43, 76, 81 f. ; iii. 27 f. ; rational, of Stoics, ii. 36 ff., 57, 76 ; surpasses art, i. 92 ; ii. 35, 57 f., 82 ff. ; deification of forces of, ii. 63
Nausiphanes (teacher of Epicurus), i. 73, 93
Navius. See Attus
necessity = God, i. 39 ; opposed to reason, ii. 76 f., 88
Neptune, i. 40 ; ii. 60, 66, 71 ; iii. 43, 52, 62, 64, 76
Nilus, ii. 130 ; iii. 42, 54, 56, 58 f.
Nisus (nursed infant Bacchus), iii. 58
Nodinus (unknown stream near Rome), iii. 52
Nomios (*nomos*, law), iii. 57
Numa (second king of Rome), iii. 5, 43
Nymphae, iii. 43

Octavian war (Gn. Octavius, consul 87 B.C., fought for Sulla against the Marian consul Cinna), ii. 14
Olympias (mother of Alexander the Great), ii. 69
Ophiuchus ('snake-holder'), ii. 109
Ops (wife of Saturn, goddess of earth and wealth, had temple on Capitol), ii. 61 ; iii. 88
optimism of Stoics, ii. 18, 86 f.
Orbona (goddess of bereavement), iii. 63
Orion, ii. 113 ; iii. 26
ὁρμαί (impulses of will), ii. 58
Orpheus, i. 41, 107 ; iii. 45, 58
orreries, ii. 88

Pacuvius (Roman tragedian, b. *c* 220 B.C.), iii. 48
Palaemon, iii. 39
Pallas, father of Minerva, iii. 59
Pamphilus, teacher of Epicurus, i. 72
Pan, iii. 56
Panaetius (of Rhodes, 180–111 B.C., eclectic Stoic, friend of Scipio, wrote Περὶ τοῦ καθήκοντος, the basis of Cicero's *De Officiis*), ii. 118
Panisci, iii. 43
pantheism ridiculed, i. 25, 52 f.
panther, i. 88 ; ii. 126
Parcae (the fates), iii. 44
Paris, iii. 91
Parmenides (idealist philosopher of Elea, 5th cent. B.C., pupil of Xenophanes, wrote didactic poem *On Nature*, frags. extant), i. 28
Pasiphaë, iii. 48
Paulus (L. Aemilius Macedonicus, defeated Perses, last king of Macedon, at Pydna, 168 B.C.), ii. 6, 165 ; his father defeated at Cannae (by Hannibal, 216 B.C.), iii. 80
Peducaea rogatio, iii. 74
Pelops, iii. 53
Penates, etymology of, ii. 68
Penelopa, iii. 56
Peripatetics, i. 16
Persaeus, Stoic philosopher, i. 38
Perseis, daughter of Oceanus, iii. 48
Persephone, ii. 66
Perses. See Paullus
Pertinacia, iii. 44
pessimism of Epicurus, i. 23 Academic, iii. 79 f.
Phaedo, i. 93 ; iii. 82 (n.)
Phaedrus (head of Epicurean school, d. 70 B.C.), i. 93
Phaenon = Saturn, ii. 52

INDEX TO DE NATURA DEORUM

Phaëthon, ii. 52; iii. 76
Phalaris (tyrant of Agrigentum 560–540 B.C.), iii. 82
Pheneatae (Arcadian tribe), iii. 56
Philo (founder of New Academy, teacher of Cicero), i. 6, 11, 17, 59, 113
Philodemus, i. 45, 49
philosophy, value of, i. 6 f.; ii. 1, 3, 168; four schools of, i. 16
Phōsphoros, ii. 53
Phthas, iii. 55
physicists, the early, their theology refuted, i. 25 ff.
physiology, human, ii. 134 ff.
Pierides, Pierus, iii. 54
Pisistratus (three times tyrant of Athens, d. 527 B.C.), iii. 82
Piso (M. Pupius Calpurnius, consul 61 B.C., expounder of Peripatetic system in *De Finibus* v.), i. 16
planets, ii. 51 f.
Plato on creation, i. 19 ff.; inconsistency of, i. 30; 'divine,' ii. 32; *Timaeus*, i. 19; *Phaedo*, iii. 82
Pluto, ii. 66
poiotes, ii. 96
Portunus, ii. 66
Posidonius (eclectic Stoic at Rhodes, where Cicero attended his lectures), i. 6, 123; ii. 88
Postumius, Aulus (dictator in early republic), iii. 13
probability, i. 12
Prodicus (of Ceos, b. 470 B.C., sophist at Athens), i. 118
progress (*prokopē*), iii. 79
prolēpsis, i. 43
pronoia, i. 18, 20; ii. 58, 73, 160
Proserpine, iii. 79
Protagoras (of Abdera, 490–415 B.C., sophist, banished from Athens for impiety), i. 2, 20, 63
providence, proved, ii. 73-153; in structure of world, ii. 154 ff.; refuted, iii. 65 ff.; care for individual men, ii. 164 ff.; refuted, iii. 79 ff.
Punic war, first (264–242 B.C.), ii. 71; second (218–202 B.C.), ii. 65
Pyrrhus (king of Epirus, at war with Rome in Italy, 280–276 B.C.), ii. 165
Pythagoras (born 529 B.C. at Samos, taught at Crotona in Italy, founded religious brotherhood), i. 10, 74, 107; iii. 88

qualitas, ii. 96
Querella, iii. 44

rationality of universe, ii. 16 ff.
reason, human, ii. 157; not necessarily beneficial, iii. 70 ff.
Regillus (lake in Latium, where Romans defeated Latins, 498 B.C.), ii. 6
Regulus (hero of 1st Punic war), ii. 80
'religio,' etymology of, iii. 72
Rhesus (son of a Muse and of Strymon the king and river of Thrace), iii. 45
Romulus, founder of augury, ii. 9; iii. 5; deification of, ii. 62; iii. 39
Roscius (actor), i. 79
rotation the divine motion, ii. 99 ff.
Rutilius (*legatus* in Asia, exiled on false charge of peculation, *c.* 98 B.C.), iii. 80, 86

Sabazius (identified with Dionysus), iii. 58
Sagra (small river in S. Italy, scene of victory of Locrian settlers over Crotona, *c.* 560 B.C.), ii. 6
Salaria (*via*), iii. 11
Samothrace (island in N. Aegean, seat of Cabeiric mystery ritual), ii. 6
Saturn, etymology of name, ii. 64; iii. 53, 62; worship of, iii. 44; the planet, ii. 52, 119
Scaevola, P. (consul 123 B.C.), i. 115; iii. 5
Scaevola, Q. (son of above, assassinated 82 B.C.), iii. 80
Scaurus (163–90 B.C., leader of Optimates), ii. 61
scepticism, i. 1, 63, 117; justified, i. 10 ff.
Scipio, P. Cornelius Africanus Major, ii. 165; Minor (his murder foretold by prodigies, 129 B.C.), ii. 14; iii. 80
Scipio, P. Cornelius Nasica (consul 162 B.C.), ii. 10; iii. 5

INDEX TO DE NATURA DEORUM

Scipio, P. and Cn. (brothers, fell in Spain 212 B.C.), iii. 80
sense organs, man's, ii. 140 ff.
Septentriones, ii. 105, 109 f.
Serapis, iii. 47
Seriphus (one of Cyclades islands), i. 88
Sibyllae, ii. 10; iii. 5
sight, theory of, ii. 88, 144 f.
Silvanus, ii. 89
Simonides (lyric poet of Ceos, 550–470 B.C.), at court of Hiero, tyrant of Syracuse, i. 60
Socrates, i. 95
'sol,' ii. 66
Sosius (unknown), iii. 74
Sospita (Juno 'the saviour'), temple of, at Lanuvium, i. 82
soul of man, i. 27, 91; ii. 18, 79; iii. 12; of the world, i. 25 ff., 36 ff.; ii. 24 ff., 57; iii. 28 ff.
sound, ii. 83, 144, 146, 149
Sparta, ii. 165; iii. 91
speech, organs of, ii. 148 ff.
Speusippus (nephew of Plato), i. 33
sphaera, ii. 47, 55; (orrery) ii. 88, 97
spherical form divine, ii. 45 ff.
spider, ii. 123
Spino, a river (unknown), iii. 52
stars, divine, ii. 39; motions of, ii. 51 ff., 103
Stephanē of Parmenides, i. 28
steremnia, i. 49
Stoics, i. 4; iii. 77; theology refuted, i. 36 ff.; defended, ii.
Strato (became head of Lyceum, 287 B.C.), i. 35
Stratonicus (Athenian musician in time of Alexander), iii. 50
sun, ii. 29, 40 ff., 79, 102, 118 f.; iii. 37; mock suns, ii. 14
'superstitio,' etymology of, ii. 72
swerve of atoms, i. 69
Syrian fish-worship, iii. 39

Tantalidae, iii. 90
teeth, ii. 127, 134; iii. 57
Tellus, iii. 52
Terence quoted, ii. 60; iii. 72 f.
Thaumas, iii. 51
Thelxinoë, iii. 54
Theodorus (Cyrenaic philosopher, end of 4th cent. B.C.), i. 2, 63, 117
theophanies denied, iii. 11 ff.
Theophrastus (succeeded Aristotle as head of Lyceum, d. 278 B.C.), i. 35
Theseus, iii. 45, 76
Theuth, iii. 56
Thyestes (brother of Atreus), iii. 68
Thyone (name of deified Semele, mother of Dionysus), iii. 58
Tiberinus (deity of river Tiber), iii. 52
tides, ii. 19; iii. 23 f.
Timocrates (pupil of Epicurus), i. 93
Tiresias (mythical blind seer), ii. 7
transubstantiation, iii. 41
Trasimene (Etruscan lake near Perusia), ii. 8
Trieterides (biennial festival at Thebes), iii. 58
Triton, i. 78; ii. 89
Trophonius (built temple of Delphi, after death worshipped as hero and had oracular cave in Boeotia), iii. 49, 56
Tubulus (praetor 142 B.C.), i. 63; iii. 74
Tyndaridae, iii. 11

Ulixes, ii. 166
undogmatic theology defended, i. 10 f.
Upis, iii. 58
Uranus. See Caelus

Valens (Ἴσχυς, son of Elatus), iii. 56
Varius (tribune 91 B.C., tool of Equites against Drusus), his death (otherwise unknown), iii. 81
vegetarianism, ii. 159; iii. 88
Veiovis (ancient Sabine and Latin god), iii. 62
Venus, ii. 60 f., 69 (etymology); iii. 62; four of the name, iii. 57
Vesta, ii. 67, 80
Victoria, ii. 61; iii. 61, 88
Victoriolae, iii. 84
Vulcan, i. 81, 83 f.; iii. 54 f., 59, 62

weazel, ii. 17
Wolf-god in Egypt, iii. 47

INDEX TO DE NATURA DEORUM

Xenocrates (396–314 B.C., third head of Academy), i. 34, 72
Xenophanes (c. 576–480 B.C., born at Colophon, poet, founder of Eleatic school of philosophy), i. 28
Xenophon, i. 31; ii. 18 (*Memorabilia* quoted); iii. 27
Xerxes, i. 115

Zeno the Eleatic (pupil of Parmenides, died in attempting to put down tyranny at Elea), iii 82
Zeno, the Epicurean (b. at Sidon), i. 59
Zeno, the founder of Stoicism (b. at Citium in Cyprus 3rd cent. B.C. *ad fin.*), i. 36, 57, 63, 70; ii. 20, 57, 63; iii. 18, 22, 63, 77
zodiac, ii. 53

ACADEMICA

ACADEMICA

INTRODUCTION

Dates of Composition and Revision.—In Cicero's letters to Atticus written during the summer of 45 B.C., when he was in retirement from public life (see p. xi), there are many references to his work on this treatise. Writing from Astura on May 13, and alluding to the death of his daughter, he says: 'Ego hic duo magna συντάγματα absolvi; nullo enim alio modo a miseria quasi aberrare possum' (*Att.* xii. 45. 1). On May 29, he writes from Tusculum (*Att.* xiii. 32 3): 'Torquatus Romaest; misi ut tibi daretur. Catulum et Lucullum ut opinor antea; his libris nova prohoemia sunt addita quibus eorum uterque laudatur.' Here 'Torquatus' means the first two books of *De Finibus*, and 'Catulus' the first and 'Lucullus' the second book of *Academica* in its first shape; so it is the latter treatise, and not *De Finibus* I. and II., that is probably referred to by the modest expression in the preceding quotation 'two big compilations.' We infer that *Academica* in its first form was so far finished by the latter half of May that a copy was sent to Atticus, new prefaces being added a little later. Cicero refers to the treatise

as 'Illam 'Ακαδημικὴν σύνταξιν' (*Att.* xiii. 6. 1), but the two volumes were actually named *Catulus* and *Lucullus*, after the leading interlocutors in each. Hortensius also figured in *Catulus*, and Cicero in both.

But Cicero was not satisfied with his work as it stood, and began at once to revise it, improving the style and making the treatment more concise; he also divided the two volumes into four. He writes of these alterations with great satisfaction (*Att.* xiii. 13. 1, June 26): 'ex duobus libris contuli in quattuor: grandiores sunt omnino quam erant illi, sed tamen multa detracta.' Also (*Att.* xiii. 12. 3) Atticus seems to have suggested that a literary compliment was due to Varro, who had promised to dedicate an important work to Cicero (this was his *De Lingua Latina*); and Cicero writes that although two years had passed without Varro's having got on a yard with the work ('adsiduo cursu cubitum nullum processerit'), he has decided to transfer to him the dedication of *Academica*, and to postpone paying a compliment to Catulus, Lucullus and Hortensius, 'homines nobiles illi quidem sed nullo modo philologi' (*ibid.*), in fact, well known, not indeed for ἀπαιδευσία (want of education), but for ἀτριψία (lack of special training) in these subjects (*Att.* xiii. 13. 1).

Contents.—In Cicero's encyclopaedia of philosophy *Academica* is the article on Epistemology, the theory of knowledge. In his earlier draft of the work, in Book I., *Catulus*, the scepticism of Carneades (Middle Academy) and his doctrine of 'probability' were

expounded by Catulus ; Hortensius countered with the dogmatism of Antiochus (Old Academy), and Cicero put the case of Philo (Middle Academy), that 'probability' is consistent with Platonism. In Book II., *Lucullus*, Lucullus defended the cause of Antiochus by attacking Scepticism, and then Scepticism was defended by Cicero. In the second edition Cicero and Varro were the sole interlocutors ; Cicero championed the Middle Academy as well as the New, and the Old Academy was assigned to Varro.

It is to this second edition that Cicero refers in his letters in all allusions to the work after the alteration was made ; its title was now *Academica*, though he also describes it as 'Academici libri.' But he seems not to have succeeded in entirely suppressing the first edition ; and by a curious accident the second half of the first edition has come down to us, while of the second edition only the first quarter and a few fragments of the remainder have survived. We therefore have only three quarters of the whole work, and only one quarter of it in the form finally authorized by the writer. Some modern editors have designated the extant part of Edition I. 'Academica Priora' and that of Edition II. 'Academica Posteriora,' but so far as I know the significance intended to be conveyed by the adjectives in those titles has no classical authority.

The position can be most clearly exhibited in tabular form ; the parts of the editions that are not now extant and the names of the speakers in those parts are printed in italics :

INTRODUCTION TO ACADEMICA

Subjects.	Exponents. Ed. I.	Ed. II.
	(' *Catulus* ')	(' Academica, Liber I.')
Carneades's scepticism : ' Probability.'	*Catulus.*	
Antiochus's dogmatism.	*Hortensius.*	Varro.
Philo's ' Probability Platonic.'	*Cicero.*	Cicero.
		(*Liber II.*)
Carneades's scepticism.		*Cicero.*
	(' Lucullus.')	(*Liber III.*)
Antiochus's polemic against scepticism.	Lucullus.	*Varro.*
		(*Liber IV.*)
Defence of scepticism.	Cicero.	*Cicero.*

Dramatis Personae.—Q. Lutatius Catulus, a distinguished leader of the aristocracy, was consul with Lepidus in 78 B.C., when he resisted his colleague's efforts to abrogate the acts of Sulla, and next year defeated him in the battle of the Milvian Bridge. He opposed the conferment of extraordinary powers on Pompey in 67 and 66, and was censor with Crassus in 65. He died in 60. There is no evidence that he was interested in philosophy. In the dialogue he professes merely to put forward the views of his father, the famous colleague of Marius. The elder Catulus was a man of great culture and learning, but Cicero could not introduce him into the dialogue for reasons of chronology : he died in 87, committing suicide to escape the proscription of Marius.

L. Licinius Lucullus (*c.* 110–57 B.C.) was also a

supporter of Sulla, and was famous as the conqueror of Mithridates. He was superseded in his command by Pompey in 66, and gradually withdrew from public life. He had amassed great wealth on his Asiatic campaigns, and was famous for the splendour of his establishments. He had literary tastes and was a generous patron of letters.

Q. Hortensius (114–50 B.C.) made a career and a fortune by his oratorical ability. An adherent of Sulla and the aristocratic party, he was consul in 69; but in the previous year the trial of Verres for peculation in Sicily had transferred the primacy in oratory from Verres' defender, Hortensius, to his prosecutor, Cicero. Hortensius was an opponent of Pompey, and on Pompey's coalition with Crassus and Caesar in 60 he retired from politics.

M. Terentius Varro (116–28 B.C.) was the most learned of scholars and the most encyclopaedic of writers. His works included agriculture, grammar, religious and political antiquities, biography, philosophy, geography and law; some parts of his books on the first two subjects alone survive. He also had a public career; he held naval command against the pirates and against Mithridates, and he supported Pompey in the civil war, but after Pharsalia Caesar forgave him, and employed his talents in collecting books for a great public library.

The Imaginary Date of the dialogues in the first edition falls between 63 B.C., the year of Cicero's consulship (alluded to *Ac.* ii. 62), and 60, when Catulus died. The scene of the first conversation (now lost) was the sea-side villa of Catulus at Cumae, west of Naples; that of the second (our *Academica* II.), a day later, is Hortensius's villa at Bauli, a little

place on the Gulf of Puteoli (Pozzuoli), just east of Cumae. In the second edition the scene is laid at Varro's villa near the Lucrine Lake, the enclosed recess of the Gulf of Puteoli. The imaginary date is near the actual time of composition in 45 B.C. ('nuper,' *Ac.* i. 1).

Sources of *Academica*.—Cicero frequently states that his arguments for dogmatism are those of his old teacher, Antiochus of Ascalon; and it is pretty clear that he merely transcribed them from some book or books of this authority. For dramatic effect, at *Ac.* ii. 11 f. he makes Lucullus profess to be producing arguments from his recollection of discussions in which Antiochus had taken part; but there is no doubt that actually he is writing with a book of Antiochus in front of him, probably *Sosus* (see *Ac.* ii. 12 note), a dialogue in which Antiochus combated his old teacher Philo.

The arguments in defence of scepticism come partly from a work of Philo twice referred to, though not by its name (*Ac.* i. 13, ii. 11): this doubtless supplied Cicero with the historical justification of the New Academy which concludes Book I., and probably also with the historical references with which he begins his speech that ends the work (*Ac.* ii. 66–78). The destructive arguments that these follow are very likely taken from Clitomachus, who succeeded Carneades as head of the New Academy in 129 B.C. The constructive doctrines of Carneades that come next are drawn from two works of Clitomachus mentioned by their names (ii. 98, 103); and the historical passage that concludes is doubtless also from Clitomachus, who wrote a book Περὶ Αἱρέσεων (Diogenes Laertius ii. 92).

INTRODUCTION TO ACADEMICA

Manuscripts.—Scholars range the mss. of *Academica* I. in two families, derived from two archetypes of the twelfth century or older. Of the former family, one ms., 'codex Puteanus,' Parisinus 6331 (which contains *De Finibus* also), is placed by recent critics in the twelfth century, and several mss. related to it belong to the fourteenth or fifteenth century. Of the latter family, all are fourteenth or fifteenth century. In the present edition only a few specially interesting variants are given, the readings of Puteanus being quoted as P, but the other mss. not being distinguished.

Academica II. is contained in the same mss. as *De Natura Deorum*, for which see p. xviii.

Editions.—J. S. Reid's edition of 1884 (London) is a most valuable resource ; it contains an exhaustive introduction and commentary.

The newest text is that of Plasberg (Teubner, Leipzig, 1922). In this the evidence for the text is fully set out ; also the preface gives in full all the passages in Cicero's Letters that refer to *Academica*, and a valuable study of the relation between Cicero's two editions.

Literary students will also be grateful to Mr. Plasberg for two quotations that grace the back of his title-page—one from Pliny (*Nat. Hist.* xxxi. 6) which shows that Cicero actually named his villa at Puteoli (Pozzuoli) 'Academia,' and the other from Copernicus, writing to Pope Paul III. in 1543 and saying that the earliest suggestion which he had seen that the earth is in motion was a statement that he quotes from Cicero (viz. *Ac.* ii. 123).

H. R.

1932.

CICERO, *AD FAMILIARES*, IX. VIII.

CICERO VARRONI

1 ETSI munus[a] flagitare, quamvis quis ostenderit, ne populus quidem solet nisi concitatus, tamen ego exspectatione promissi tui[b] moveor ut admoneam te, non ut flagitem. Misi autem ad te quattuor admonitores[c] non nimis verecundos—nosti enim profecto os huius adulescentioris Academiae[d]—ex ea igitur media excitatos misi, qui metuo ne te forte flagitent, ego autem mandavi ut rogarent. Exspectabam omnino iam diu, meque sustinebam ne ad te prius ipse quid scriberem quam aliquid accepissem, ut possem te remunerari quam simillimo munere. Sed cum tu tardius faceres, id est (ut ego interpretor) diligentius, teneri non potui quin coniunctionem studiorum amorisque nostri quo possem litterarum genere declararem. Feci igitur sermonem inter nos habitum in

---

[a] *Munus* denotes specially a gladiatorial show.

[b] Varro had promised to dedicate to Cicero his treatise *De Lingua Latina*, at which he was now working.

[c] The four volumes of *Academica*, second edition, of which the first volume forms Book I. of the extant text.

[d] This hints at the 'young-mannishness' and self-assertion of the New Academy.

LETTER DEDICATING SECOND EDITION TO VARRO

Cicero to Varro

1 Even the public, unless stirred up to do so, does not as a rule actually demand a gift,[a] although somebody has held out an offer of one; yet in my case eagerness for the present that you promised [b] prompts me to send you, not a demand, but a reminder. But the four emissaries that I am sending to remind you [c] are not excessively modest ones—for no doubt you are acquainted with the 'cheek' of this junior [d] Academy —well, it is from the very heart of that School that my messengers have been summoned; and I am afraid that they may perhaps present a demand to you, although my instructions to them are to make a request. Anyway I have now been a long time waiting and keeping myself from writing anything to you on my side before I had received something from you, so as to have the opportunity of making you as nearly as possible a repayment in kind. But as you have been acting rather slowly, that is (as I construe it) rather carefully, I have been unable to keep myself from making public, in such literary form as was within my powers, the community of studies and of affection that unites us. I have accordingly composed a dialogue, held between us at my place at

Cumano, cum esset una Pomponius ; tibi dedi partes Antiochinas, quas a te probari intellexisse mihi videbar, mihi sumpsi Philonis. Puto fore ut cum legeris mirere nos id locutos esse inter nos quod numquam
2 locuti sumus ; sed nosti morem dialogorum. Posthac autem, mi Varro, quam plurima si videtur et de nobis inter nos ; sero fortasse, sed superiorum temporum fortuna rei publicae causam sustineat, haec ipsi praestare debemus. Atque utinam quietis temporibus atque aliquo si non bono at saltem certo statu civitatis haec inter nos studia exercere possemus ! quamquam tum quidem vel aliae quaepiam rationes honestas nobis et curas et actiones darent ; nunc autem quid est sine his cur vivere velimus ? mihi vero cum his ipsis vix, his autem detractis ne vix quidem. Sed haec coram et saepius. Migrationem et emptionem feliciter evenire volo, tuumque in ea re consilium probo. Cura ut valeas.

---

[a] What Cicero refers to is not recorded.

Cumae, with Pomponius as one of the party ; I have cast you for the part of champion of Antiochus, whose doctrine I think I have understood you to approve of, while I have taken the rôle of Philo myself. When you read it I fancy you will be surprised at our holding a conversation that never actually took place ; but
2 you know the convention as to dialogues. On some later occasion, my dear Varro, we will if you think fit have a very full talk together about our personal affairs as well ; too late, perhaps, but let the destiny of the commonwealth bear the responsibility for the days that are past, it is our duty to answer for the present. And would that we had the power to carry on these joint studies in a period of tranquillity, and with the affairs of state settled in some definite if not satisfactory manner ! although in that case indeed perhaps certain other interests would afford us honourable subjects of thought and honourable fields of action ; whereas now without our present studies what reason have we to wish to be alive? For my own part, even with them scarcely any, but if they be taken from me, not even scarcely ! But we will discuss this when we meet, and repeatedly. I hope the move and the sale [a] are turning out a success : I approve of your policy in that business. Good-bye.

ACADEMICA

LIBER PRIMUS

(EDITIO POSTERIOR)[a]

1 I. In Cumano nuper cum mecum Atticus noster esset, nuntiatum est nobis a M. Varrone venisse eum Roma pridie vesperi et nisi de via fessus esset continuo ad nos venturum fuisse. Quod cum audissemus, nullam moram interponendam putavimus quin videremus hominem nobiscum et studiis eisdem et vetustate amicitiae coniunctum; itaque confestim ad eum ire perreximus, paulumque cum ab[1] eius villa abessemus ipsum ad nos venientem vidimus; atque illum complexi ut mos amicorum est, satis eum longo
2 intervallo ad suam villam reduximus. Hic pauca primo atque ea percontantibus nobis ecquid forte Roma novi; tum[2] Atticus "Omitte ista, quae nec percontari nec audire sine molestia possumus, quaeso," inquit, "et quaere potius ecquid ipse novi; silent enim diutius Musae Varronis quam solebant, nec tamen

[1] ab *inseruit Wesenberg.*
[2] tum *inseruit Reid.*

[a] This Book as we have it belongs to the second edition of Cicero's work, and is therefore entitled *Academica Posteriora* by some editors.

ACADEMICA

BOOK I[a]

ANTIOCHUS'S DOGMATISM *v.* PHILO'S 'PROBABILITY'

1 I. My friend Atticus was staying with me lately at my country-place at Cumae, when a message came to us from Marcus Varro's house that he had arrived from Rome on the evening of the day before, and if not fatigued from the journey intended to come straight on to us. On hearing this, we thought that no obstacle must intervene to delay our seeing a person united to us by identity of studies as well as by old friendship; so we hastily set out to go to him, and were only a short distance from his country-house when we saw him coming towards us in person. We gave our Varro a friend's embrace, and after a fairly long interval we escorted him back to his own

Introduction. Scene of the dialogue.

2 house. Here there was first a little conversation, and that arising out of my asking whether Rome happened to have been doing anything new; and then Atticus said, "Do pray drop those subjects, about which we can neither ask questions nor hear the answers without distress; inquire of him instead whether he himself has done anything new. For Varro's Muses have kept silent for a longer time than they used, but all the same my belief is that your

istum cessare sed celare quae scribat existimo." "Minime vero," inquit ille, "intemperantis enim arbitror esse scribere quod occultari velit; sed habeo opus magnum in manibus, idque[1] iam pridem; ad hunc enim ipsum"—me autem dicebat—"quaedam institui, quae et sunt magna sane et limantur

3 a me politius." Et ego "Ista quidem" inquam "Varro, iam diu exspectans non audeo tamen flagitare; audivi enim e Libone nostro (cuius nosti studium)—nihil enim eum eius modi celare possumus —non te ea intermittere sed accuratius tractare nec de manibus umquam deponere. Illud autem mihi ante hoc tempus numquam in mentem venit a te requirere, sed nunc postea quam sum ingressus res eas quas tecum simul didici mandare monumentis, philosophiamque veterem illam a Socrate ortam Latinis litteris illustrare, quaero quid sit cur cum multa scribas hoc genus praetermittas, praesertim cum et ipse in eo excellas et id studium totaque ea res longe ceteris et studiis et artibus antecedat."

4 II. Tum ille: "Rem a me saepe deliberatam et multum agitatam requiris; itaque non haesitans respondebo sed ea dicam quae mihi sunt in promptu, quod ista ipsa de re multum, ut dixi, et diu cogitavi.

[1] idque *Christ*: que *vel* quae *codd.*

---

[a] Varro's *De Lingua Latina*, see Introduction p. 400.

friend is not taking a holiday but is hiding what he writes." "Oh no, certainly not," said Varro, "for I think that to put in writing what one wants to be kept hidden is sheer recklessness; but I have got a big task in hand, and have had for a long time: I have begun on a work[a] dedicated to our friend here himself"—meaning me—"which is a big thing I can assure you, and which is getting a good deal of
3 touching up and polishing at my hands." At this I said, "As to that work of yours, Varro, I have been waiting for it a long time now, but all the same I don't venture to demand it; for I have heard (since we cannot hide anything of that kind) from our friend Libo, an enthusiastic student as you know, that you are not leaving it off, but are giving it increased attention, and never lay it out of your hands. However, there is a question that it has never occurred to me to put to you before the present moment, but now, after I have embarked on the task of placing upon record the doctrines that I have learnt in common with you, and of expounding in Latin literary form the famous old system of philosophy that took its rise from Socrates, I do put the question why, though you write a great deal, you pass over this class of subject, especially when you yourself are distinguished in it, and also when this interest and this whole subject far outstrip all other interests and other sciences?"

Varro would leave philosophical authorship to Greeks.

4 II. "The question that you ask," rejoined Varro, "is one which I have often pondered and considered deeply. And so I will not beat about the bush in my reply, but will say what at once occurs to me, because I have, as I said, thought much and long upon the very point that you raise. For as I saw that

Nam cum philosophiam viderem diligentissime Graecis litteris explicatam, existimavi si qui de nostris eius studio tenerentur, si essent Graecis doctrinis eruditi, Graeca potius quam nostra lecturos; sin a Graecorum artibus et disciplinis abhorrerent, ne haec quidem curaturos quae sine eruditione Graeca intellegi non possunt; itaque ea nolui scribere quae nec indocti intellegere possent nec docti legere curarent.
5 Vides autem (eadem enim ipse didicisti) non posse nos Amafini aut Rabiri similes esse, qui nulla arte adhibita de rebus ante oculos positis vulgari sermone disputant, nihil definiunt, nihil partiuntur, nihil apta interrogatione concludunt, nullam denique artem esse nec dicendi nec disserendi putant. Nos autem praeceptis dialecticorum et oratorum etiam, quoniam utramque vim virtutem esse nostri putant, sic parentes ut legibus, verbis quoque novis cogimur uti, quae docti, ut dixi, a Graecis petere malent, indocti ne a nobis quidem accipient, ut frustra omnis suscipiatur labor.
6 Iam vero physica, si Epicurum, id est si Democritum probarem, possem scribere ita plane ut Amafinius; quid est enim magnum, cum causas rerum efficien-

---

[a] Epicurean writers with a large sale; their works are now entirely lost. Epicurus himself decried the use of technical language in philosophy. The speaker here touches on the three accepted departments of philosophy in their established order, Logic, Physics, Ethics, which study respectively the questions, how we know the facts of the world, what those facts are, and consequently what conduct will secure our welfare? 'Physics' for the ancients has not the limited sense that the term bears now, but denotes the whole of Natural Science, including Biology, which is indeed specially suggested by the term, as φύεσθαι often means 'to grow,' of a living organism.

[b] *Interrogatio* is a synonym for *ratio*, and renders ἐρώτημα,

philosophy had been most carefully expounded in Greek treatises, I judged that any persons from our nation that felt an interest in the subject, if they were learned in the teachings of the Greeks, would sooner read Greek writings than ours, and if on the other hand they shrank from the sciences and systems of the Greeks, they would not care even for philosophy, which cannot be understood without Greek learning: and therefore I was unwilling to write what the unlearned would not be able to understand and the learned would not take the trouble to read.
5 But you are aware (for you have passed through the same course of study yourself) that we Academics cannot be like Amafinius or Rabirius,[a] who discuss matters that lie open to the view in ordinary language, without employing any technicality and entirely dispensing with definition and division and neat syllogistic proof,[b] and who in fact believe that no science of rhetoric or logic exists. But we for our part while obeying the rules of the logicians and of the orators also as if they were laws, for our school considers each of these faculties a merit, are compelled to employ novel terms as well, for which the learned, as I said, will prefer to go to the Greeks, while the unlearned will not accept them even from us, so that **Logic**
6 all our toil will be undertaken in vain. Then as **Physics.**
for natural philosophy, if I accepted the system of Epicurus, that is of Democritus, I could write about it as lucidly as Amafinius; for when once you have abolished causation, in the sense of efficient causes,

properly denoting an argument developed in a series of questions, but also used for any form of proof, ἀπόδειξις *Concludere* = συλλογίζεσθαι, denoting logical inference, and specially deduction.

tium[1] sustuleris, de corpusculorum (ita enim appellat atomos) concursione fortuita loqui? Nostra tu physica nosti, quae cum contineantur ex effectione et ex materia ea quam fingit et format effectio, adhibenda etiam geometria[a] est; quam quibusnam quisquam enuntiare verbis aut quem ad intellegendum poterit adducere? Haec[2] ipsa de vita et moribus et de expetendis fugiendisque rebus illi simpliciter, pecudis enim et hominis idem bonum esse censent, apud nostros autem[3] non ignoras quae sit et quanta subtili-
7 tas: sive enim Zenonem sequare, magnum est efficere ut quis intellegat quid sit illud verum et simplex bonum quod non possit ab honestate seiungi, quod bonum quale sit omnino negat Epicurus se[4] sine voluptatibus sensum moventibus ne suspicari quidem[5]; si vero Academiam veterem persequamur, quam nos, ut scis, probamus, quam erit illa acute explicanda nobis! quam argute, quam obscure etiam contra Stoicos disserendum! Totum igitur illud philosophiae studium mihi quidem ipse sumo et ad vitae constantiam quantum possum et ad delectationem animi, nec ullum arbitror, ut apud Platonem est, maius aut melius a dis datum munus homini.[b]
8 Sed meos amicos in quibus id[6] est studium in Graeciam mitto, id est, ad Graecos ire iubeo, ut ex[7] fontibus potius hauriant quam rivulos consectentur; quae

[1] efficientes *Lambinus.*
[2] *lacunam ante* haec *codd.*: <ecce> haec *Reid.*
[3] autem *Lambinus*: enim *codd.*
[4] se *inseruit Lambinus.*
[5] ne suspicari quidem *Durand*: nec suspicari *codd.*
[6] id *inseruit Durand.*
[7] ex *Halm*: ea a *codd.*

[a] *i.e.*, (with arithmetic) the whole of mathematics so far as then discovered. [b] *Timaeus* 47 B.

what is there remarkable in talking about the accidental collision of minute bodies—that is his name for atoms? The natural science of my school you know; being a system that combines the efficient force and the matter which is fashioned and shaped by the efficient force, it must also bring in geometry [a]; but what terminology, pray, will anybody have to use in explaining geometry, or whom will he be able to bring to understand it? Even this Ethics.
department of ethics and the subject of moral choice and avoidance that school handles quite simply, for it frankly identifies the good of man with the good of cattle, but what a vast amount of what minute precision the teachers of our school display is not
7 unknown to you. For if one is a follower of Zeno, it is a great task to make anybody understand the meaning of the real and simple good that is inseparable from morality, because Epicurus entirely denies that he can even guess what sort of a thing good is without pleasures that excite the sense; but if we should follow the lead of the Old Academy, the school that I as you know approve, how acutely we shall have to expound that system! How subtly, how profoundly even, we shall have to argue against the Stoics! Accordingly for my own part I adopt the great pursuit of philosophy in its entirety both (so far as I am able) as a guiding principle of life and as an intellectual pleasure, and I agree with the dictum of Plato [b] that no greater and better gift has been
8 bestowed by the gods upon mankind. But my friends who possess an interest in this study I send to Greece, that is, I bid them go to the Greeks, so that they may draw from the fountain-heads rather than seek out mere rivulets; while doctrines which nobody had

autem nemo adhuc docuerat nec erat unde studiosi scire possent, ea quantum potui (nihil enim magnopere meorum miror) feci ut essent nota nostris: a Graecis enim peti non poterant ac post L. Aelii nostri occasum ne a Latinis quidem. Et tamen in illis veteribus nostris quae Menippum imitati, non interpretati, quadam hilaritate conspersimus, multa admixta ex intima philosophia, multa dicta dialectice; quae cum[1] facilius minus docti intellegerent iucunditate quadam ad legendum invitati[2] in laudationibus, in his ipsis antiquitatum prooemiis philosophis scribere voluimus, si modo consecuti sumus."

9 III. Tum ego, "Sunt," inquam, "ista, Varro; nam nos in nostra urbe peregrinantis errantisque tamquam hospites tui libri quasi domum reduxerunt, ut possemus aliquando qui et ubi essemus agnoscere. Tu aetatem patriae, tu discriptiones temporum, tu sacrorum iura, tu sacerdotum,[3] tu domesticam, tu bellicam disciplinam, tu sedem regionum, locorum, tu omnium divinarum humanarumque rerum nomina, genera, officia, causas aperuisti, plurimumque idem poëtis nostris omninoque Latinis et litteris luminis et verbis attulisti, atque ipse varium et elegans omni fere numero poëma fecisti, philosophiamque multis locis

[1] cum *Reid*: quo *codd.*
[2] *hic interponit lacunam Casaubon.*
[3] sacerdotum <munera> *Lambinus.*

[a] Only fragments are extant of Varro's *Menippean Satires.* Menippus was a Cynic philosopher and satirist living at Gadara in the middle of the second century B.C.
[b] *i.e.*, Ethics, see p. 414 note *a*.

been teaching up till now, and for which there was nobody available from whom those interested could learn them, I have done as much as lay in my power (for I have no great admiration for any of my own achievements) to make them known to our fellow-countrymen; for these doctrines could not be obtained from the Greeks, nor from the Latins either since the demise of our countryman Lucius Aelius. And nevertheless in those old writers of our country whom in my imitation[a] (it is not a translation) of Menippus I treated with a certain amount of ridicule, there is a copious admixture of elements derived from the inmost depths of philosophy,[b] and many utterances in good logical form; and though in my funeral orations these were more easily intelligible to less learned readers if they were tempted to peruse them by a certain attractiveness of style, when we come to the prefaces to my *Antiquities*, in these my aim was, if only I attained it, to write for philosophers."

Cicero defends Latin philosophy.

9 III. "What you say, Varro, is true," I rejoined, "for we were wandering and straying about like visitors in our own city, and your books led us, so to speak, right home, and enabled us at last to realize who and where we were. You have revealed the age of our native city, the chronology of its history, the laws of its religion and its priesthood, its civil and its military institutions, the topography of its districts and its sites, the terminology, classification and moral and rational basis of all our religious and secular institutions, and you have likewise shed a flood of light upon our poets and generally on Latin literature and the Latin language, and you have yourself composed graceful poetry of various styles in almost every metre, and have sketched an outline of philosophy

incohasti, ad impellendum satis, ad edocendum parum.
10 Causam autem probabilem tu quidem adfers, aut
enim Graeca legere malent qui erunt eruditi, aut ne
haec quidem qui illa nesciunt; sed da mihi nunc—
satisne probas? Immo vero et haec qui illa non
poterunt et qui Graeca poterunt non contemnent sua.
Quid enim causae est cur poëtas Latinos Graecis
litteris eruditi legant, philosophos non legant? An
quia delectat Ennius, Pacuvius, Attius, multi alii, qui
non verba sed vim Graecorum expresserunt poëtarum?
Quanto magis philosophi delectabunt, si, ut illi
Aeschylum, Sophoclem, Euripidem, sic hi Platonem
imitentur, Aristotelem, Theophrastum? Oratores
quidem laudari video, si qui e nostris Hyperidem sint
11 aut Demosthenem imitati. Ego autem (dicam enim
ut res est), dum me ambitio, dum honores, dum
causae, dum rei publicae non solum cura sed quaedam
etiam procuratio multis officiis implicatum et con-
strictum tenebat, haec inclusa habebam, et ne obsole-
scerent renovabam cum licebat legendo; nunc vero
et fortunae gravissimo percussus vulnere et administratione rei publicae liberatus doloris medicinam a
philosophia peto et oti oblectationem hanc honestissi-

[a] The death of his daughter Tullia.

in many departments that is enough to stimulate the student though not enough to complete his
10 instruction. But though it is true that the case you bring forward has some probability, as accomplished students on the one hand will prefer to read the Greek writings, and on the other hand people who do not know those will not read these either, still, tell me now—do you quite prove your point? The truth rather is that both those who cannot read the Greek books will read these and those who can read the Greek will not overlook the works of their own nation. For what reason is there why accomplished Grecians should read Latin poets and not read Latin philosophers? Is it because they get pleasure from Ennius, Pacuvius, Accius and many others, who have reproduced not the words but the meaning of the Greek poets? How much more pleasure will they get from philosophers, if these imitate Plato, Aristotle and Theophrastus in the same way as those poets imitated Aeschylus, Sophocles and Euripides? At all events I see that any of our orators that have imitated Hyperides or Demosthenes are praised.
11 But for my own part (for I will speak frankly), so long as I was held entangled and fettered by the multifarious duties of ambition, office, litigation, political interests and even some political responsibility, I used to keep these studies within close bounds, and relied merely on reading, when I had the opportunity, to revive them and prevent their fading away; but now that I have been smitten by a grievously heavy blow[a] of fortune and also released from taking part in the government of the country, I seek from philosophy a cure for my grief and I deem this to be the most honourable mode of amusing my leisure.

mam iudico. Aut enim huic aetati hoc maxime aptum est, aut iis rebus si quas dignas laude gessimus hoc in primis consentaneum, aut etiam ad nostros cives erudiendos nihil utilius, aut si haec ita non sunt, nihil
12 aliud video quod agere possimus. Brutus quidem noster, excellens omni genere laudis, sic philosophiam Latinis litteris persequitur nihil ut iisdem de rebus Graeca desideres,[1] et eandem quidem sententiam sequitur quam tu, nam Aristum Athenis audivit aliquamdiu, cuius tu fratrem Antiochum. Quam ob rem da, quaeso, te huic etiam generi litterarum."

13 IV. Tum ille "Istuc quidem considerabo, nec vero sine te. Sed de te ipso quid est," inquit, "quod audio?" "Quanam," inquam, "de re?" "Relictam a te veterem Academiam,[2]" inquit, "tractari autem novam." "Quid ergo?" inquam, "Antiocho id magis licuerit nostro familiari, remigrare in domum veterem e nova, quam nobis in novam e vetere? Certe enim recentissima quaeque sunt correcta et emendata maxime; quamquam Antiochi magister Philo, magnus vir ut tu existimas ipse, negat in libris, quod coram etiam ex ipso audiebamus, duas Academias esse, erroremque eorum qui ita putarunt coarguit." "Est," inquit, "ut dicis, sed ignorare te non arbitror quae contra ea[3] Philonis Antiochus
14 scripserit." "Immo vero et ista et totam veterem

[1] *Aldus*: Graecia desideret *codd.*
[2] Academiam *Bentley*: illam *Madvig*: iam *codd.*
[3] ea *inseruit Reid.*

[a] Succeeded Antiochus as head of the Old Academy.
[b] *i.e.*, from Atticus.

For this occupation is the one most suited to my age; or it is the one more in harmony than any other with such praiseworthy achievements as I can claim; or else it is the most useful means of educating our fellow-citizens also; or, if these things are not the case, I see no other occupation that is within our power. At all events our friend Brutus, who is eminent for every kind of distinction, is so successful an exponent of philosophy in a Latin dress that one could not feel the least need for Greek writings on the same subjects, and indeed he is an adherent of the same doctrine as yourself, as for a considerable time he heard the lectures of Aristus [a] at Athens, whose brother Antiochus you attended. Pray therefore devote yourself to this field of literature also."

IV. "I will deal with your point," he rejoined, "although I shall require your assistance. But what is this news that I hear [b] about yourself?"

Varro following Antiochus defends Old Academy against New; Cicero siding with Philo maintains that they agree.

"What about, exactly?" said I. "That you have abandoned the Old Academy, and are dealing with the New." "What then?" I said. "Is our friend Antiochus to have had more liberty to return from the new school to the old, than we are to have to move out of the old one into the new? Why, there is no question that the newest theories are always most correct and free from error; although Philo, Antiochus's master, a great man as you yourself judge him, makes an assertion in his books which we used also to hear from his own lips,—he says that there are not two Academies, and proves that those who thought so were mistaken." "What you say is true," said he, "but I think that you are not unacquainted with what Antiochus wrote to combat those statements of Philo." "On the contrary, I should like

Academiam, a qua absum iam diu, renovari a te, nisi molestum est, velim ; et simul adsidamus," inquam, "si videtur." "Sane istud quidem," inquit, "sum enim admodum infirmus ; sed videamus idemne Attico placeat fieri a me quod te velle video." "Mihi vero," ille, "quid est enim quod malim quam ex Antiocho iam pridem audita recordari, et simul videre satisne ea commode dici possint Latine ?" Quae cum essent[1] dicta, in conspectu consedimus omnes.[2]

15 Tum Varro ita exorsus est : "Socrates mihi videtur, id quod constat inter omnes, primus a rebus occultis et ab ipsa natura involutis, in quibus omnes ante eum philosophi occupati fuerunt, avocavisse philosophiam et ad vitam communem adduxisse, ut de virtutibus et vitiis omninoque de bonis rebus et malis quaereret, caelestia autem vel procul esse a nostra cognitione censeret vel, si maxime cognita essent,
16 nihil tamen ad bene vivendum. Hic in omnibus fere sermonibus qui ab iis qui illum audierunt perscripti varie copioseque sunt ita disputat ut nihil adfirmet ipse, refellat alios, nihil se scire dicat nisi id ipsum, eoque praestare ceteris quod illi quae nesciant scire se putent, ipse se nihil scire, id unum sciat, ob eamque rem se arbitrari ab Apolline omnium sapientissimum

[1] sint *codd. plerique : delent edd. plerique.*
[2] omnes *delet Reid (metri tollendi causa).*

you, if you do not mind, to recapitulate the arguments to which you refer, and also the whole theory of the Old Academy, with which I have been out of touch for a long while now ; and at the same time," I said, " let us if you please sit down for our talk." " Let us sit down by all means," he said, " for I am in rather weak health. But let us see whether Atticus would like me to undertake the same task that I see you want me to." " To be sure I should," said Atticus, " for what could I like better than to recall to memory the doctrines that I heard long ago from Antiochus, and at the same time to see if they can be satisfactorily expressed in Latin ? " After these remarks we took our seats in full view of one another.

Varro expounds Antiochus's dogmatism (§§ 15-42). (1) historical : it descends from Socrates.

Then Varro began as follows : " It is my view, and it is universally agreed, that Socrates was the first person who summoned philosophy away from mysteries veiled in concealment by nature herself, upon which all philosophers before him had been engaged, and led it to the subject of ordinary life, in order to investigate the virtues and vices, and good and evil generally, and to realize that heavenly matters are either remote from our knowledge or else, however fully known, have nothing to do with the good life. The method of discussion pursued by Socrates in almost all the dialogues so diversely and so fully recorded by his hearers is to affirm nothing himself but to refute others, to assert that he knows nothing except the fact of his own ignorance, and that he surpassed all other people in that they think they know things that they do not know but he himself thinks he knows nothing, and that he believed this to have been the reason why Apollo declared him to be the

esse dictum quod haec esset una omnis[1] sapientia, non arbitrari se scire quod nesciat. Quae cum diceret constanter et in ea sententia permaneret, omnis eius oratio tamen[2] in virtute laudanda et in hominibus ad virtutis studium cohortandis consumebatur, ut e Socraticorum libris maximeque Platonis intellegi
17 potest. Platonis autem auctoritate, qui varius et multiplex et copiosus fuit, una et consentiens duobus vocabulis philosophiae forma instituta est, Academicorum et Peripateticorum, qui rebus congruentes nominibus differebant; nam cum Speusippum sororis filium Plato philosophiae quasi heredem reliquisset, duos autem praestantissimo studio atque doctrina, Xenocratem Calchedonium et Aristotelem Stagiriten, qui erant cum Aristotele Peripatetici dicti sunt quia disputabant inambulantes in Lycio, illi autem quia[3] Platonis instituto in Academia, quod est alterum gymnasium, coetus erant et sermones habere soliti, e loci vocabulo nomen habuerunt. Sed utrique Platonis ubertate completi certam quandam disciplinae formulam composuerunt et eam quidem plenam ac refertam, illam autem Socraticam dubitanter[4] de omnibus rebus et nulla adfirmatione adhibita consuetudinem disserendi reliquerunt. Ita facta est, quod minime Socrates probabat, ars quaedam philosophiae et rerum
18 ordo et descriptio disciplinae. Quae quidem erat

[1] hominis *Lambinus*. [2] *Gruter*: tam *codd.*
[3] quia *? Reid*: qui a, qui *codd.*
[4] *Baiter*: dubitantem, dubitationem *codd.*

[a] Plato, *Apology*, 21 A.
[b] Cicero is translating διάδοχος.
[c] At the entrance to the Bosporus, nearly opposite to Byzantium. [d] On the coast of Macedon.
[e] This famous Athenian gymnasium had a much-frequented *peripatos* or promenade.

wisest of all men,[a] because all wisdom consists solely in not thinking that you know what you do not know. He used to say this regularly, and remained firm in this opinion, yet nevertheless the whole of his discourses were spent in praising virtue and in exhorting mankind to the zealous pursuit of virtue, as can be gathered from the books of members of the Socratic
17 school, and particularly from those of Plato. But originating with Plato, a thinker of manifold variety and fertility, there was established a philosophy that, though it had two appellations, was really a single uniform system, that of the Academic and the Peripatetic schools, which while agreeing in doctrine differed in name; for Plato left his sister's son Speusippus as 'heir'[b] to his system, but two pupils of outstanding zeal and learning, Xenocrates, a native of Calchedon,[c] and Aristotle, a native of Stagira[d]; and accordingly the associates of Aristotle were called the Peripatetics, because they used to debate while walking in the Lyceum,[e] while the others, because they carried on Plato's practice of assembling and conversing in the Academy, which is another gymnasium, got their appellation from the name of the place. But both schools drew plentiful supplies from Plato's abundance, and both framed a definitely formulated rule of doctrine, and this fully and copiously set forth, whereas they abandoned the famous Socratic custom of discussing everything in a doubting manner and without the admission of any positive statement. Thus was produced something that Socrates had been in the habit of reprobating entirely, a definite science of philosophy, with a regular arrangement of subjects and a formulated
18 system of doctrine. At the outset it is true this was

primo duobus, ut dixi, nominibus una, nihil enim inter Peripateticos et illam veterem Academiam differebat: abundantia quadam ingenii praestabat, ut mihi quidem videtur, Aristoteles, sed idem fons erat utrisque et eadem rerum expetendarum fugiendarumque partitio.

V. "Sed quid ago?" inquit "aut sumne sanus qui haec vos doceo? nam etsi non sus Minervam, ut aiunt, tamen inepte quisquis Minervam docet." Tum Atticus, "Tu vero," inquit, "perge, Varro; valde enim amo nostra atque nostros, meque ista delectant cum Latine dicuntur et isto modo." "Quid me," inquam, "putas, qui philosophiam iam professus sim populo nostro exhibiturum?" "Pergamus igitur,"
19 inquit, "quoniam placet. Fuit ergo iam accepta a Platone philosophandi ratio triplex, una de vita et moribus, altera de natura et rebus occultis, tertia de disserendo et quid verum,[1] quid falsum, quid rectum in oratione pravumve, quid consentiens, quid repugnans esset[2] iudicando. Ac primum illam partem bene vivendi a natura petebant[3] eique parendum esse dicebant, neque ulla alia in re nisi in natura quaerendum esse illud summum bonum quo omnia referrentur, constituebantque extremum esse rerum expetendarum et finem bonorum adeptum esse omnia e natura et animo et corpore et vita.

[1] verum et *codd. plurimi*: verum sit *Reid.*
[2] repugnans esset *Müller*: repugnet *codd.*
[3] repetebant *Reid.*

[a] A proverb of Greek origin; the story on which it was based does not seem to be recorded. Theocritus has it in a rather different form, ὗς ποτ' Ἀθηναίαν ἔριν ἤρισεν (5. 23), suggesting perhaps a challenge to a competition in music.
[b] *i.e.*, the original Academy.
[c] *Vita* denotes ἐκτὸς ἀγαθά, 'external goods.'

a single system with two names, as I said, for there was no difference between the Peripatetics and the Old Academy of those days. Aristotle excelled, as I at all events think, in a certain copiousness of intellect, but both schools drew from the same source, and both made the same classification of things as desirable and to be avoided.

V. " But what am I about ? " he said, " am I quite all there, who teach these things to you ? Even if it is not a case of the proverbial pig teaching Minerva,[a] anyway whoever teaches Minerva is doing a silly thing." " Do pray go on, Varro," rejoined Atticus, " for I love our literature and our fellow-countrymen profoundly, and I delight in the doctrines of your school when set forth in Latin and as you are setting them forth." " What do you suppose that I feel about it," said I, " seeing that I have already offered myself as an exponent of philosophy to our nation ? "

(2) Antiochus's Ethics: goods are mental, bodily and external.

" Well then, let us proceed," said he, " as we are
9 agreed. There already existed, then, a threefold scheme of philosophy inherited from Plato: one division dealt with conduct and morals, the second with the secrets of nature, the third with dialectic and with judgement of truth and falsehood, correctness and incorrectness, consistency and inconsistency, in rhetorical discourse. And for the first of these sections, the one dealing with the right conduct of life, they [b] went for a starting-point to nature, and declared that her orders must be followed, and that the chief good which is the ultimate aim of all things is to be sought in nature and in nature only ; and they laid it down that to have attained complete accordance with nature in mind, body and estate [c] is the limit of things desirable and the End of goods.

Corporis autem alia ponebant esse in toto, alia in
partibus, valetudinem vires pulchritudinem in toto,
in partibus autem sensus integros et praestantiam
aliquam partium singularum, ut in pedibus celeritatem, vim in manibus, claritatem in voce, in lingua
20 etiam explanatam vocum impressionem. Animi
autem quae essent ad comprehendendam virtutem
idonea, eaque ab eis in naturam et mores divide-
bantur: naturae celeritatem ad discendum et memoriam dabant, quorum utrumque mentis esset proprium et ingenii, morum autem putabant studia esse
et quasi consuetudinem, quam partim adsiduitate
exercitationis, partim ratione formabant, in quibus
erat ipsa philosophia. In qua quod incohatum est
neque absolutum progressio quaedam ad virtutem
appellatur, quod autem absolutum, id est virtus, quasi
perfectio naturae omniumque rerum quas in animis
21 ponunt una res optima. Ergo haec animorum. Vitae
autem (id enim erat tertium) adiuncta esse dicebant
quae ad virtutis usum valerent. Nam virtus in animi
bonis et in corporis cernitur et in quibusdam quae
non tam naturae quam beatae vitae adiuncta sunt.
Hominem esse censebant quasi partem quandam
civitatis et universi generis humani, eumque esse
coniunctum cum hominibus humana quadam societate.
Ac de summo quidem atque naturali bono sic agunt;

[a] *Quasi* marks *consuetudo* as a translation of *ἔθος* and suggests its relation to *ἦθος*.

[b] This translates Zeno's term *προκοπή*.

[c] *τελείωσις*.

[d] Translates *μέρος*.

[e] *ἡ ἀνθρωπινὴ κοινωνία*.

Among goods of the body they laid it down that some resided in the whole frame and others in the parts: health, strength and beauty were goods of the whole, goods of the parts were sound senses and the particular excellences of the parts severally, for instance speed in the feet, power in the hands, clearness in the voice, and also an even and distinct articulation of
20 sounds as a quality of the tongue. Goodness of the mind consisted in the qualities conducive to the comprehension of virtue; these they divided into gifts of nature and features of the moral character—quickness of apprehension and memory they assigned to nature, each of them being a mental and intellectual property, while to the moral character they deemed to belong the interests or 'habit'[a] which they moulded partly by diligent practice and partly by reason, practice and reason being the domain of philosophy itself. In this philosophy a commencement not carried to completion is called 'progress'[b] towards virtue, but the completed course is virtue, which is the 'consummation'[c] of nature, and is the most supremely excellent of all the faculties of the mind as they define them. This then is their account
21 of the mind. To 'estate'—that was the third division—they said belonged certain properties that influenced the exercise of virtue. For virtue is displayed in connexion with the goods of the mind and those of the body, and with some that are the attributes not so much of nature as of happiness. Man they deemed to be, so to say, a 'part'[d] of the state and of the human race as a whole, and they held that a man was conjoined with his fellow-men by the 'partnership of humanity.'[e] And this being their treatment of the supreme good as bestowed by

cetera autem pertinere ad id putant aut adaugendum aut tuendum,[1] ut divitias, ut opes, ut gloriam, ut gratiam. Ita tripartita ab iis inducitur ratio bonorum.

22 VI. "Atque haec illa sunt tria genera quae putant plerique Peripateticos dicere. Id quidem non falso, est enim haec partitio illorum; illud imprudenter, si alios esse Academicos qui tum[2] appellarentur, alios Peripateticos arbitrantur. Communis haec ratio et utrisque hic bonorum finis videbatur, adipisci quae essent prima natura quaeque ipsa per sese expetenda, aut omnia aut maxima; ea sunt autem maxima quae in ipso animo atque in ipsa virtute versantur. Itaque omnis illa antiqua philosophia sensit in una virtute esse positam beatam vitam, nec tamen beatissimam nisi adiungerentur et corporis et cetera quae supra
23 dicta sunt ad virtutis usum idonea. Ex hac descriptione agendi quoque aliquid in vita et offici ipsius initium reperiebatur, quod erat in conservatione earum rerum quas natura praescriberet. Hinc gignebatur fuga desidiae voluptatumque contemptio, ex quo laborum dolorumque susceptio multorum magnorumque recti honestique causa et earum rerum quae erant congruentes cum descriptione naturae, unde et amicitia exsistebat et iustitia atque aequitas, eaeque et voluptatibus et multis vitae commodis anteponebantur. Haec quidem fuit apud eos morum institutio et eius partis quam primam posui forma atque descriptio.
24 "De natura autem (id enim sequebatur) ita dice-

[1] *Lambinus*: tenendum *codd.*
[2] *Reid*: dum *codd.*

[a] A dual rendering of τὸ καλόν.

nature, all other goods they considered to be factors contributing either to its increase or to its protection, for instance wealth, resources, fame, influence. Thus they introduced a triple classification of goods.

22 VI. "And this corresponds with the three classes of goods which most people think to be intended by the Peripatetics. This is indeed correct, for this classification is theirs, but it is a mistake if people suppose that the Academics quoted above and the Peripatetics were different schools. This theory was common to both, and both held that the end of goods was to acquire either all or the greatest of the things that are by nature primary, and are intrinsically worthy of desire; and the greatest of these are the ones which have their being in the mind itself and in virtue itself. Accordingly the whole of the great philosophy of antiquity held that happiness lies in virtue alone, yet that happiness is not supreme without the addition of the goods of the body and all the other goods suitable for the employment of virtue that

Virtue a conduct

23 were specified above. From this scheme they used also to arrive at a first principle of conduct in life and of duty itself, which principle lay in safeguarding the things that nature prescribed. Hence sprang the duty of avoiding idleness and of disregarding pleasures, leading on to the undergoing of many great toils and pains for the sake of the right and noble,[a] and of the objects in harmony with the plan marked out by nature, from which sprang friendship, and also justice and fairness; and these they rated higher than pleasures and an abundance of the good things of life. This then was their system of ethics, the plan and outline of the department that I placed first.

24 "The subject of nature (for that came next) they

bant ut eam dividerent in res duas, ut altera esset efficiens, altera autem quasi huic se praebens, ex qua[1] efficeretur aliquid. In eo quod efficeret vim esse censebant, in eo autem quod efficeretur materiam quandam; in utroque tamen utrumque, neque enim materiam ipsam cohaerere potuisse si nulla vi contineretur, neque vim sine aliqua materia (nihil est enim quod non alicubi esse cogatur). Sed quod ex utroque, id iam corpus et quasi qualitatem quandam nominabant—dabitis enim profecto ut in rebus inusitatis, quod Graeci ipsi faciunt a quibus haec iam diu tractantur, utamur verbis interdum inauditis."

25 VII. "Nos vero," inquit Atticus; "quin etiam Graecis licebit utare cum voles, si te Latina forte deficient." "Bene sane facis; sed enitar ut Latine loquar, nisi in huiusce modi verbis, ut philosophiam aut rhetoricam aut physicam aut dialecticam appellem, quibus ut aliis multis consuetudo iam utitur pro Latinis. Qualitates igitur appellavi quas ποιότητας Graeci vocant, quod ipsum apud Graecos non est

[1] ex qua *Turnebus*: eaque *codd.*: ex eaque *Mdv.*

[a] The two ἀρχαί, ποιητική and παθητική. *Quasi* marks *huic se praebens* as a translation of the latter.

[b] *Quandam* apologizes for the use of *materia*, 'timber,' as a philosophical term to translate ὕλη.

[c] This clause explains the preceding clause only and is traceable ultimately to *Timaeus* 52 B φάμεν ἀναγκαῖον εἶναί που τὸ ὂν ἅπαν ἔν τινι τόπῳ. Apparently Antiochus with Plato identified matter and space.

[d] *i.e.*, organized matter, *materia* being matter as yet unformed.

[e] Cicero apologizes for coining the word *qualitas* to render ποιότης, 'what-sort-ness,' a term coined by Plato, *Theaetetus*, 189 A; the Latin abstract noun, like the Greek, is used for the concrete, 'a thing of a certain quality,' an object possessing certain properties.

dealt with by the method of dividing nature into two principles,[a] the one the active, and the other the 'passive,' on which the active operated and out of which an entity was created. The active principle they deemed to constitute force, the one acted on, a sort of 'material'[b]; yet they held that each of the two was present in the combination of both, for matter could not have formed a concrete whole by itself with no force to hold it together, nor yet force without some matter (for nothing exists that is not necessarily somewhere[c]). But when they got to the product of both force and matter, they called this 'body,'[d] and, if I may use the term, 'quality'[e]—as we are dealing with unusual subjects you will of course allow us occasionally to employ words never heard before, as do the Greeks themselves, who have now been handling these topics for a long time."

(3) Antiochus's Physics: entities are matter informed by force.

VII. "To be sure we will," said Atticus; "indeed you shall be permitted to employ even Greek words if Latin ones happen to fail you." "That is certainly kind of you, but I will do my best to talk Latin, except in the case of words of the sort now in question, so as to employ the term 'philosophy' or 'rhetoric' or 'physics'[f] or 'dialectic,'[g] which like many others are now habitually used as Latin words. I have therefore given the name of 'qualities' to the things that the Greeks call *poiotētes*; even among the Greeks it is not a word in ordinary use, but

[f] *i.e.*, the whole of natural science, of which physics in the modern sense is a part.

[g] *i.e.*, logic (including both formal logic and epistemology or the theory of knowledge, *cf.* ii. 142); λογική included both διαλεκτική and ῥητορική. *Cf.* § 30 n.

vulgi verbum sed philosophorum; atque id in multis. Dialecticorum vero verba nulla sunt publica, suis utuntur; et id quidem commune omnium fere est artium, aut enim nova sunt rerum novarum facienda nomina aut ex aliis transferenda. Quod si Graeci faciunt qui in his rebus tot iam saecula versantur, quanto id magis nobis concedendum est qui haec nunc primum
26 tractare conamur?" "Tu vero," inquam, "Varro, bene etiam meriturus mihi videris de tuis civibus si eos non modo copia rerum auxeris, ut fecisti,[1] sed etiam verborum." "Audebimus ergo," inquit, "novis verbis uti te auctore si necesse erit. Earum igitur qualitatum sunt aliae principes, aliae ex his ortae. Principes sunt unius modi et simplices; ex his autem variae ortae sunt et quasi multiformes. Itaque aer (hoc quoque utimur iam[2] pro Latino) et ignis et aqua et terra prima sunt; ex his autem ortae animantium formae earumque rerum quae gignuntur e terra. Ergo illa initia et (ut e Graeco vertam) elementa dicuntur; e quibus aer et ignis movendi vim habent et efficiendi, reliquae[3] partes accipiendi et quasi patiendi, aquam dico et terram. Quintum genus, e quo essent astra mentesque, singulare eorumque quattuor quae supra dixi dissimile Aristoteles quoddam esse

[1] ut effecisti *codd. fere omnes*: uti fecisti *Klotz.*
[2] *Halm*: enim *codd.*
[3] reliqua *Halm.*

---

[a] *i.e.*, 'qualified objects,' classes of things, abstract for concrete, *cf.* § 24.
[b] πολυειδής.
[c] A literal translation of φυτά—the vegetable kingdom.
[d] ἀρχαί.
[e] στοιχεῖα.
[f] Halm's emendation gives 'and the remaining elements . . . the receptive and passive rôle.' But *cf. Tusc.* i. 40 'terram et mare . . . reliquae duae partes.'

belongs to the philosophers, and this is the case with many terms. But the dialecticians' vocabulary is none of it the popular language, they use words of their own; and indeed this is a feature shared by almost all the sciences: either new names have to be coined for new things, or names taken from other things have to be used metaphorically. This being the practice of the Greeks, who have now been engaged in these studies for so many generations, how much more ought it to be allowed to us, who are now attempting to handle these subjects for the first
26 time!" "Indeed, Varro," said I, "I think you will actually be doing a service to your fellow-countrymen if you not only enlarge their store of facts, as you have done, but of words also." "Then on your authority we will venture to employ new words, if we have to. Well then, those qualities[a] are of two sorts, primary and derivative. Things of primary quality are homogeneous and simple; those derived from them are varied and 'multiform.'[b] Accordingly air (this word also we now use as Latin) and fire and water and earth are primary; while their derivatives are the species of living creatures and of the things that grow out of the earth.[c] Therefore those things are termed first principles[d] and (to translate from the Greek) elements[e]; and among them air and fire have motive and efficient force, and the remaining divisions, I mean water and earth, receptive and 'passive' capacity.[f] Aristotle deemed that there existed a certain fifth sort of element,[g] in a class by itself and unlike the four that I have mentioned above, which was the source of the stars and of thinking

The elements

[g] This πέμπτη οὐσία, *quinta essentia*, has floated down to us in the word 'quintessence.'

27 rebatur. Sed subiectam putant omnibus sine ulla specie atque carentem omni illa qualitate (faciamus enim tractando usitatius hoc verbum et tritius) materiam quandam, e qua omnia expressa atque efficta sint, quae una omnia accipere possit omnibusque modis mutari atque ex omni parte, atque etiam interire, non in nihilum sed in suas partes, quae infinite secari ac dividi possint, cum sit nihil omnino in rerum natura minimum quod dividi nequeat; quae autem moveantur, omnia intervallis moveri, quae intervalla item
28 infinite dividi possint. Et cum ita moveatur illa vis quam qualitatem esse diximus et cum sic ultro citroque versetur, et materiam ipsam totam penitus commutari putant et illa effici quae appellant qualia, e quibus in omni natura cohaerente et continuata cum omnibus suis partibus unum effectum esse mundum, extra quem nulla pars materiae sit nullumque corpus, partes autem esse mundi omnia quae insint in eo quae natura sentiente teneantur, in qua ratio perfecta insit quae sit eadem sempiterna (nihil enim
29 valentius esse a quo intereat); quam vim animum esse dicunt mundi, eandemque esse mentem sapientiamque perfectam, quem deum appellant, omniumque rerum quae sint ei subiectae quasi prudentiam quandam, procurantem caelestia maxime, deinde in terris ea quae pertineant ad homines; quam inter-

---

[a] *i.e.*, spaces of void or vacuum that are between the solids and enable them to move.

[b] See § 25 n. The Stoics asserted that everything real has two components, the active and the passive, force and matter, and they expressed the former as 'quality'; but they emphasized their materialism by sometimes speaking of the qualifying force as a current of air.

[c] *ποιά.* [d] *Natura* = *οὐσία* = *ὕλη*, *cf.* ii. 118.

[e] *Cf. N.D.* ii. 22, 75, 85.

27 minds. But they hold that underlying all things is Matter and space infinitely divisible.
a substance called 'matter,' entirely formless and
devoid of all 'quality' (for let us make this word
more familiar and manageable by handling), and that
out of it all things have been formed and produced,
so that this matter can in its totality receive all
things and undergo every sort of transformation
throughout every part of it, and in fact even suffer
dissolution, not into nothingness but into its own
parts, which are capable of infinite section and division,
since there exists nothing whatever in the nature of
things that is an absolute least, incapable of division;
but that all things that are in motion move by
means of interspaces,[a] these likewise being infinitely
28 divisible. And since the force that we have called The *Cosmos*.
'quality'[b] moves in this manner and since it thus
vibrates to and fro, they think that the whole of
matter also is itself in a state of complete change
throughout, and is made into the things which they
term 'qualified,'[c] out of which in the concrete
whole of substance,[d] a continuum united with all its
parts, has been produced one world, outside of which
there is no portion of matter and no body, while all
the things that are in the world are parts of it. held
together by a sentient being,[e] in which perfect reason,
is immanent, and which is immutable[f] and eternal
since nothing stronger exists to cause it to perish;
29 and this force they say is the soul of the world, and The all-pervading Reason.
is also perfect intelligence and wisdom, which they
entitle God, and is a sort of 'providence'[g] knowing
the things that fall within its province, governing
especially the heavenly bodies, and then those things
on earth that concern mankind; and this force they

[f] *Eadem* denotes self-identity. [g] πρόνοια.

dum eandem necessitatem appellant, quia nihil aliter possit[1] atque ab ea constitutum sit inter[2] quasi fatalem et immutabilem continuationem ordinis sempiterni; non numquam quidem eandem fortunam, quod efficiat multa improvisa ac necopinata nobis propter obscuritatem ignorationemque causarum.

30 VIII. "Tertia deinde philosophiae pars, quae erat in ratione et in disserendo, sic tractabatur ab utrisque. Quamquam oriretur a sensibus, tamen non esse iudicium veritatis in sensibus: mentem volebant rerum esse iudicem; solam censebant idoneam cui crederetur, quia sola cerneret id quod semper esset simplex et unius modi et tale quale esset. Hanc illi ἰδέαν appellant, iam a Platone ita nominatam, nos

31 recte speciem possumus dicere. Sensus autem omnes hebetes et tardos esse arbitrabantur nec percipere ullo modo res ullas quae subiectae sensibus viderentur, quod aut ita essent parvae ut sub sensum cadere non possent, aut ita mobiles et concitatae ut nihil umquam unum esset[3] constans, ne idem quidem, quia continenter laberentur et fluerent omnia; itaque hanc

32 omnem partem rerum opinabilem appellabant. Scientiam autem nusquam esse censebant nisi in animi notionibus atque rationibus; qua de causa definitiones rerum probabant et has ad omnia de quibus disceptabatur adhibebant. Verborum etiam explicatio probabatur, id est, qua de causa quaeque essent ita nominata, quam ἐτυμολογίαν appellabant; post

[1] <esse> possit? *ed.* [2] inter: evenire *Turnebus.*
[3] esset <et> *edd.*, esset <aut> *Reid.*

[a] κατηναγκασμένην τινὰ καὶ ἀπαράβατον συμπλοκήν.

[b] A dual rendering of λογική, or perhaps of διαλεκτική. See § 27 n. [c] *i.e.*, definition of *res*, things, not of words.

also sometimes call Necessity, because nothing can happen otherwise than has been ordained by it under a 'fated and unchangeable concatenation of everlasting order'[a]; although they sometimes also term it Fortune, because many of its operations are unforeseen and unexpected by us on account of their obscurity and our ignorance of causes.

30 VIII. "Then the third part of philosophy, consisting in reason and in discussion,[b] was treated by them both as follows. The criterion of truth arose indeed from the senses, yet was not in the senses: the judge of things was, they held, the mind—they thought that it alone deserves credence, because it alone perceives that which is eternally simple and uniform and true to its own quality. This thing they call the *Idea*, a name already given it by Plato; we
31 can correctly term it *form*. All the senses on the other hand they deemed to be dull and sluggish, and entirely unperceptive of all the things supposed to fall within the province of the senses, which were either so small as to be imperceptible by sense, or in such a violent state of motion that no single thing was ever stationary, nor even remained the same thing, because all things were in continual ebb and flow; accordingly all this portion of things they
32 called the object of opinion. Knowledge on the other hand they deemed to exist nowhere except in the notions and reasonings of the mind; and consequently they approved the method of defining *things*, and applied this 'real definition'[c] to all the subjects that they discussed. They also gave approval to derivation of words, that is, the statement of the reason why each class of things bears the name that it does—the subject termed by them etymology

(4) Antiochus's Logic.

argumentis quibusdam[1] et quasi rerum notis ducibus[a] utebantur ad probandum et ad concludendum id quod explanari volebant; in quo[2] tradebatur omnis dialecticae disciplina, id est, orationis ratione conclusae; huic quasi ex altera parte oratoria vis dicendi adhibebatur,[b] explicatrix orationis perpetuae ad persuadendum accommodatae.

33 "Haec erat illis prima forma[3] a Platone tradita; cuius quas acceperim immutationes,[4] si vultis, exponam." "Nos vero volumus," inquam, "ut pro Attico etiam respondeam." "Et recte," inquit, "respondes; praeclare enim explicatur Peripateticorum et Academiae veteris auctoritas."

IX. "Aristoteles[5] primus species quas paulo ante dixi labefactavit, quas mirifice Plato erat amplexatus, ut in iis quiddam divinum esse diceret. Theophrastus autem, vir et oratione suavis et ita moratus ut probitatem quandam prae se et ingenuitatem ferat, vehementius etiam fregit quodam modo auctoritatem veteris disciplinae; spoliavit enim virtutem suo decore imbecillamque reddidit quod negavit in ea
34 sola positum esse beate vivere. Nam Strato eius auditor, quamquam fuit acri ingenio, tamen ab ea disciplina omnino semovendus est, qui cum maxime necessariam partem philosophiae, quae posita est in virtute et moribus, reliquisset totumque se ad investigationem naturae contulisset, in ea ipsa plurimum dissedit a suis. Speusippus autem et Xenocrates, qui

[1] quibusdam *delendum?* (*om. codd. nonnulli*).
[2] *Manutius*: qua *codd.*
[3] prima forma *Reid*: prima *codd.*: forma *Mdv.*
[4] *Davies*: disputationes *codd.*
[5] Aristoteles igitur *cod. unus.*

[a] *Quasi* marks *notis* as an explanation of *argumentis* used to translate σύμβολα. [b] ἀντίστροφον.

and then they used derivations as 'tokens' or so to say marks [a] of things, as guides for arriving at proofs or conclusions as to anything of which they desired an explanation; and under this head was imparted their whole doctrine of Dialectic, that is, speech cast in the form of logical argument; to this as a 'counterpart' [b] was added the faculty of Rhetoric, which sets out a continuous speech adapted to the purpose of persuasion.

3 "This was their primary system, inherited from Plato; and if you wish I will expound the modifications of it that have reached me." "Of course we wish it," said I, "if I may reply for Atticus as well." "And you reply correctly," said Atticus, "for he is giving a brilliant exposition of the doctrine of the Peripatetics and the Old Academy."

Departures from the old doctrine

IX. "Aristotle was the first to undermine the Forms of which I spoke a little while before, which had been so marvellously embodied in the system of Plato, who spoke of them as containing an element of divinity. Theophrastus, who has a charming style and also a certain conspicuous uprightness and nobility of character, in a way made an even more violent breach in the authority of the old doctrine; for he robbed virtue of her beauty and weakened her strength by denying that the happy life is placed in
4 her alone. As for his pupil Strato, although he had a penetrating intellect nevertheless he must be kept altogether separate from that school; he abandoned the most essential part of philosophy, which consists in ethics, to devote himself entirely to research in natural science, and even in this he differed very widely from his friends. On the other hand Speusippus and Xenocrates, the first inheritors of the system

primi Platonis rationem auctoritatemque susceperant, et post eos Polemo et Crates unaque Crantor in Academia congregati diligenter ea quae a superiori-
35 bus acceperant tuebantur. Iam Polemonem audiverant adsidue Zeno et Arcesilas ; sed Zeno cum Arcesilam anteiret aetate valdeque subtiliter dissereret et peracute moveretur, corrigere conatus est disciplinam. Eam quoque, si videtur, correctionem explicabo, sicut solebat Antiochus." "Mihi vero," inquam, "videtur, quod vides idem significare Pomponium."

X. "Zeno igitur nullo modo is erat qui ut Theophrastus nervos virtutis inciderit, sed contra qui omnia quae ad beatam vitam pertinerent in una virtute poneret nec quidquam aliud numeraret in bonis, idque appellaret honestum, quod esset simplex
36 quoddam et solum et unum bonum. Cetera autem etsi nec bona nec mala essent, tamen alia secundum naturam dicebat,[1] alia naturae esse[2] contraria ; his ipsis alia interiecta et media numerabat. Quae autem secundum naturam essent, ea sumenda et quadam aestimatione dignanda docebat, contraque contraria, neutra autem in mediis relinquebat. In
37 quibus ponebat nihil omnino esse momenti, sed quae essent sumenda,[3] ex iis alia pluris esse aestimanda, alia minoris : quae pluris ea praeposita appellabat, reiecta autem quae minoris. Atque ut haec non tam rebus quam vocabulis commutaverat, sic inter recte

[1] *Lambinus* : docebat *codd.* [2] [esse] *Ernesti.*
[3] sumenda : media *Davies* : <non> sumenda *? ed.*

[a] τὸ καλόν.
[b] *Sumenda* is carelessly put for *neutra*—unless indeed the text should be corrected by inserting "*not* to be chosen."
[c] *i.e.*, of minus value, in grades of undesirability : this inaccuracy occurs in the Greek authorities.

and authority of Plato, and after them Polemo and Crates, and also Crantor, gathered in the one fold of the Academy, were assiduous defenders of the doctrines that they had received from their predecessors.

35 Finally, Polemo had had diligent pupils in Zeno and Arcesilas, but Zeno, who was Arcesilas's senior in age and an extremely subtle dialectician and very acute thinker, instituted a reform of the system. This remodelled doctrine also I will expound, if you approve, as it used to be expounded by Antiochus." "I do approve," said I, "and Pomponius, as you see, indicates his agreement."

countered by Zeno.

X. "Well, Zeno was by no means the man ever to hamstring virtue, as Theophrastus had done, but on the contrary to make it his practice to place all the constituents of happiness in virtue alone, and to include nothing else in the category of Good, entitling virtue 'the noble,'[a] which denoted a sort of uniform,

Zeno's Ethics: classification of values; virtue the sole good.

36 unique and solitary good. All other things, he said, were neither good nor bad, but nevertheless some of them were in accordance with nature and others contrary to nature; also among these he counted another interposed or 'intermediate' class of things. He taught that things in accordance with nature were to be chosen and estimated as having a certain value, and their opposites the opposite, while things that were neither he left in the 'intermediate' class. These he declared to possess no motive force whatever,

37 but among things to be chosen[b] some were to be deemed of more value and others of less[c]: the more valuable he termed 'preferred,' the less valuable, 'rejected.' And just as with these he had made an alteration of terminology rather than of substance,

factum atque peccatum officium et contra officium media locabat quaedam, recte facta sola in bonis [actionibus][1] ponens, prave, id est peccata, in malis; officia autem[2] servata praetermissaque media putabat,
38 ut dixi. Cumque superiores non omnem virtutem in ratione esse dicerent sed quasdam virtutes natura aut more perfectas, hic omnes in ratione ponebat; cumque illi ea genera virtutum quae supra dixi seiungi posse arbitrarentur, hic nec id ullo modo fieri posse disserebat nec virtutis usum modo, ut superiores, sed ipsum habitum per se esse praeclarum, nec tamen virtutem cuiquam adesse quin ea semper uteretur. Cumque perturbationem animi illi ex homine non tollerent, naturaque et condolescere et concupiscere et extimescere et efferri laetitia dicerent, sed ea contraherent in angustumque deducerent, hic omnibus
39 his quasi morbis voluit carere sapientem; cumque eas perturbationes antiqui naturales esse dicerent et rationis expertes, aliaque in parte animi cupiditatem, alia rationem collocarent, ne his quidem adsentiebatur, nam et perturbationes voluntarias esse putabat opinionisque iudicio suscipi et omnium perturbationum matrem esse arbitrabatur immoderatam quandam intemperantiam. Haec fere de moribus.

XI. " De naturis autem sic sentiebat, primum ut in quattuor initiis rerum illis quintam hanc naturam ex qua superiores sensus et mentem effici rebantur non

[1] *ed.* [2] autem *Lambinus* : autem et *codd.*

---

[a] *Officium* is Cicero's rendering of καθῆκον, 'a suitable act,' formally right in the circumstances, whatever the motive of the agent. [b] *i.e.*, καλόν.

[c] So, in a later theology, faith is manifested in works.

[d] *Morbus* is a translation of πάθος.

[e] *i.e.*, the elements. [f] See § 26.

so between a right action and a sin he placed appropriate action [a] and action violating propriety as things intermediate, classing only actions rightly done as goods and actions wrongly done, that is sins, as evils, whereas the observance or neglect of appropriate
38 acts he deemed intermediate, as I said. And whereas his predecessors said that not all virtue resides in the reason, but that certain virtues are perfected by nature or by habit, he placed all the virtues in reason; and whereas they thought that the kinds of virtues that I have stated above can be classed apart, he argued that this is absolutely impossible, and that not merely the exercise of virtue, as his predecessors held, but the mere state of virtue is in itself a splendid thing,[b] although no body possesses virtue without continuously exercising it.[c] Also whereas they did not remove emotion out of humanity altogether, and said that sorrow and desire and fear and delight were natural, but curbed them and narrowed their range, Zeno held that the wise man was devoid of all these
39 'diseases'[d]; and whereas the older generation said that these emotions were natural and non-rational, and placed desire and reason in different regions of the mind, he did not agree with these doctrines either, for he thought that even the emotions were voluntary and were experienced owing to a judgement of opinion, and he held that the mother of all the emotions was a sort of intemperance and lack of moderation. These more or less were his ethical doctrines.

XI. "His views as to the natural substances [e] were as follows. First, in dealing with the four recognized primary elements he did not add this fifth substance [f] which his predecessors deemed to be the source of

Zeno's Physics.

adhiberet ; statuebat enim ignem esse ipsam naturam quae quidque gigneret, etiam[1] mentem atque sensus. Discrepabat etiam ab iisdem quod nullo modo arbitrabatur quidquam effici posse ab ea quae expers esset corporis, cuius generis Xenocrates et superiores etiam animum esse dixerant, nec vero aut quod efficeret aliquid aut quod efficeretur posse esse non
40 corpus. Plurima autem in illa tertia philosophiae parte mutavit : in qua primum de sensibus ipsis quaedam dixit nova, quos iunctos esse censuit e quadam quasi impulsione oblata extrinsecus (quam ille *φαντασίαν*, nos visum appellemus licet, et teneamus hoc quidem verbum, erit enim utendum in reliquo sermone saepius),—sed ad haec quae visa sunt et quasi accepta sensibus adsensionem adiungit animorum quam esse vult in nobis positam et voluntariam.
41 Visis non omnibus adiungebat fidem sed iis solum quae propriam quandam haberent declarationem earum rerum quae viderentur ; id autem visum cum ipsum per se cerneretur, comprendibile—feretis haec ? " " Nos vero," inquit ; " quonam enim alio modo *καταληπτόν* diceres ? " " Sed cum acceptum iam et approbatum esset, comprehensionem appellabat, similem iis rebus quae manu prenderentur—ex quo etiam nomen hoc duxerat, cum eo verbo antea nemo tali in re usus esset, plurimisque idem novis verbis (nova enim dicebat) usus est. Quod autem erat sensu comprensum, id ipsum sensum appellabat, et si ita erat comprensum ut

[1] *Reid* : et *codd.*

---

[a] *i.e.*, a combination of external impression or presentation and internal assent ; but the sentence is interrupted by a parenthesis. [b] *ἐνάργεια*, see ii. 18 n.

[c] *Comprehensio* is used for *comprehensum*, as *κατάληψις* was for *καταληπτικὴ φαντασία*. See ii. 145.

sensation and of intellect; for he laid it down that the natural substance that was the parent of all things, even of the senses and the mind, was itself fire. He also differed from the same thinkers in holding that an incorporeal substance, such as Xenocrates and the older thinkers also had pronounced the mind to be, was incapable of any activity, whereas anything capable of acting, or being acted upon in any way could not be incorporeal. In the third department of philosophy he made a number of changes. Here first of all he made some new pronouncements about sensation itself, which he held to be a combination [a] of a sort of impact offered from outside (which he called *phantasia* and we may call a presentation, and let us retain this term at all events, for we shall have to employ it several times in the remainder of my discourse),—well, to these presentations received by the senses he joins the act of mental assent which he makes out to reside within us and to be a voluntary act. He held that not all presentations are trustworthy but only those that have a 'manifestation,' [b] peculiar to themselves, of the objects presented; and a trustworthy presentation, being perceived as such by its own intrinsic nature, he termed 'graspable'—will you endure these coinages?" "Indeed we will," said Atticus, "for how else could you express '*catalēpton*'?" "But after it had been received and accepted as true, he termed it a 'grasp,' [c] resembling objects gripped in the hand—and in fact he had derived the actual term from manual prehension, nobody before having used the word in such a sense, and he also used a number of new terms (for his doctrines were new). Well, a thing grasped by sensation he called itself a sensation, and a sensation so firmly grasped as to be

Zeno's Logic: sense-data judged true by reason constitute knowledge

convelli ratione non posset, scientiam, sin aliter, inscientiam nominabat, ex qua exsisteret etiam opinio, quae esset imbecilla et cum falso incognitoque com-
42 munis. Sed inter scientiam et inscientiam comprehensionem illam quam dixi collocabat, eamque neque in rectis neque in pravis numerabat sed solum ei[1] credendum esse dicebat. E quo sensibus etiam fidem tribuebat, quod, ut supra dixi, comprehensio facta sensibus et vera esse illi et fidelis videbatur, non quod omnia quae essent in re comprehenderet, sed quia nihil quod cadere in eam posset relinqueret, quodque natura quasi normam scientiae et principium sui dedisset unde postea notiones rerum in animis imprimerentur, e quibus non principia solum sed latiores quaedam ad rationem inveniendam viae aperirentur.[2] Errorem autem et temeritatem et ignorantiam et opinationem et suspicionem, et uno nomine omnia quae essent aliena firmae et constantis adsensionis, a virtute sapientiaque removebat. Atque in his fere commutatio constitit omnis dissensioque Zenonis a superioribus."

43 XII. Quae cum dixisset, "Breviter sane minimeque obscure exposita est," inquam, "a te, Varro, et veteris Academiae ratio et Stoicorum; verum esse autem arbitror, ut Antiocho nostro familiari placebat, correctionem veteris Academiae potius quam novam aliquam disciplinam putandam." Tum Varro, "Tuae sunt nunc partes," inquit, "qui ab antiquorum ratione desciscis et ea quae ab Arcesila novata sunt probas,

[1] solum ei *Christ*: soli *codd.*
[2] *Davies*: reperiuntur *codd.*

[a] The MSS. give 'that it alone was credible.'
[b] A translation of γνώμων or κανών.

irremovable by reasoning he termed knowledge, but a sensation not so grasped he termed ignorance, and this was the source also of opinion, an unstable impression akin to falsehood and ignorance. But as a stage between knowledge and ignorance he placed that 'grasp' of which I have spoken, and he reckoned it neither as a right nor as a wrong impression, but said that it was only [a] 'credible.' On the strength of this he deemed the senses also trustworthy, because, as I said above, he held that a grasp achieved by the senses was both true and trustworthy, not because it grasped all the properties of the thing, but because it let go nothing that was capable of being its object, and because nature had bestowed as it were a 'measuring-rod' [b] of knowledge and a first principle of itself from which subsequently notions of things could be impressed upon the mind, out of which not first principles only but certain broader roads to the discovery of reasoned truth were opened up. On the other hand error, rashness, ignorance, opinion, suspicion, and in a word all the things alien to firm and steady assent, Zeno set apart from virtue and wisdom. And it is on these points more or less that all Zeno's departure and disagreement from the doctrine of his predecessors turned."

Wisdom and virtue.

XII. When he had said this, I remarked: "You have certainly given a short and very lucid exposition of the theory both of the Old Academy and of the Stoics; though I think it to be true, as our friend Antiochus used to hold, that the Stoic theory should be deemed a correction of the Old Academy rather than actually a new system." "It is now your rôle," rejoined Varro, "as a seceder from the theory of the older period and a supporter of the innovations

Cicero replies for Philo's 'Probability = Platonism.

docere quod et qua de causa discidium factum sit, ut
44 videamus satisne ista sit iusta defectio." Tum ego, "Cum Zenone," inquam, "ut accepimus, Arcesilas sibi omne certamen instituit, non pertinacia aut studio vincendi, ut mihi quidem videtur, sed earum rerum obscuritate quae ad confessionem ignorationis adduxerant Socratem et iam ante Socratem Democritum, Anaxagoram, Empedoclem, omnes paene veteres, qui nihil cognosci, nihil percipi, nihil sciri posse dixerunt, angustos sensus, imbecillos animos, brevia curricula vitae, et, ut Democritus, in profundo veritatem esse demersam, opinionibus et institutis omnia teneri, nihil veritati relinqui, deinceps omnia tenebris circum-
45 fusa esse dixerunt. Itaque Arcesilas negabat esse quidquam quod sciri posset, ne illud quidem ipsum, quod Socrates sibi reliquisset: sic omnia latere censebat in occulto, neque esse quidquam quod cerni aut intellegi posset; quibus de causis nihil oportere neque profiteri neque adfirmare quemquam neque adsensione approbare, cohibereque semper et ab omni lapsu continere temeritatem, quae tum esset insignis cum aut falsa aut incognita res approbaretur, neque hoc quidquam esse turpius quam cognitioni et perceptioni adsensionem approbationemque praecurrere. Huic rationi quod erat consentaneum faciebat, ut contra omnium sententias disserens in eam[1] plerosque deduceret, ut cum in eadem re paria contrariis in

[1] in eam *Madvig*: dies iam *codd.* (de sua *unus*).

[a] ἐν βυθῷ ἡ ἀλήθεια Diog. L. ix. 72.

[b] We do not even know that nothing can be known: *cf.* ii. 73.

of Arcesilas, to explain the nature and the reason of the rupture that took place, so as to enable us to see
44 whether the secession was fully justified." "It was entirely with Zeno, so we have been told," I replied, "that Arcesilas set on foot his battle, not from obstinacy or desire for victory, as it seems to me at all events, but because of the obscurity of the facts that had led Socrates to a confession of ignorance, as also previously his predecessors Democritus, Anaxagoras, Empedocles, and almost all the old philosophers, who utterly denied all possibility of cognition or perception or knowledge, and maintained that the senses are limited, the mind feeble, the span of life short, and that truth (in Democritus's phrase) is sunk in an abyss,[a] opinion and custom are all-prevailing, no place is left for truth, all things successively are
45 wrapped in darkness. Accordingly Arcesilas said that there is nothing that can be known, not even that residuum of knowledge that Socrates had left himself—the truth of this very dictum[b]: so hidden in obscurity did he believe that everything lies, nor is there anything that can be perceived or understood, and for these reasons, he said, no one must make any positive statement or affirmation or give the approval of his assent to any proposition, and a man must always restrain his rashness and hold it back from every slip, as it would be glaring rashness to give assent either to a falsehood or to something not certainly known, and nothing is more disgraceful than for assent and approval to outstrip knowledge and perception. His practice was consistent with this theory—he led most of his hearers to accept it by arguing against the opinions of all men, so that when equally weighty reasons were found on

Developments of Arcesilas justified;

partibus momenta rationum invenirentur, facilius ab
46 utraque parte adsensio sustineretur. Hanc Academiam novam appellant, quae mihi vetus videtur, siquidem Platonem ex illa vetere numeramus, cuius in libris nihil adfirmatur et in utramque partem multa disseruntur, de omnibus quaeritur, nihil certi dicitur; sed tamen illa quam exposuisti vetus, haec nova nominetur; quae usque ad Carneadem perducta, qui quartus ab Arcesila fuit, in eadem Arcesilae ratione permansit. Carneades autem nullius philosophiae partis ignarus et, ut cognovi ex iis qui illum audierant maximeque ex Epicureo Zenone, qui cum ab eo plurimum dissentiret, unum tamen praeter ceteros mirabatur, incredibili quadam fuit facultate. . . ."

[a] See ii. 16.

[b] The contemporary of Cicero, who heard him at Athens.

opposite sides on the same subject, it was easier to
46 withhold assent from either side. They call this school the New Academy,—to me it seems old, at all events if we count Plato a member of the Old Academy, in whose books nothing is stated positively and there is much arguing both *pro* and *contra*, all things are inquired into and no certain statement is made ; but nevertheless let the Academy that you expounded be named the Old and this one the New ; and right down to Carneades, who was fourth [a] in succession from Arcesilas, it continued to remain true to the same theory of Arcesilas. Carneades however was acquainted with every department of philosophy, and as I have learnt from his actual hearers, and especially from the Epicurean Zeno,[b] who though disagreeing very much with Carneades, nevertheless had an exceptional admiration for him, he possessed an incredible facility. . . ."

they were carried on by Carneades

FRAGMENTA EDITIONIS POSTERIORIS

Libri I

1. *Nonius p.* 65. *Digladiari dictum est dissentire et dissidere, dictum a gladiis. Cicero Academicorum lib. I.:* Quid autem stomachatur Mnesarchus? quid Antipater digladiatur cum Carneade tot voluminibus?

2. *Non. p.* 43 (s.v. *concinnare*). *Idem in Academicis lib. I.:* Quicum similitudine verbi concinere maxime sibi videretur . . .

Libri II

3. *Non. p.* 65. *Aequor ab aequo et plano Cicero Academicorum lib. II. vocabulum accepisse confirmat:* Quid tam planum videtur quam mare? e quo etiam aequor illud poëtae vocant.

4. *Non. p.* 69. *Adamare. Cicero Academicorum lib. II.:* Qui enim serius honores adamaverunt vix admittuntur ad eos nec satis commendati multitudini possunt esse.

5. *Non. p.* 104. *Exponere pro exempla boni ostentare. Cicero Academicis lib. II.:* Frangere avaritiam, scelera ponere, vitam suam exponere ad imitandum iuventuti.

6. *Non. p.* 121. *Hebes positum pro obscuro aut obtuso.*

FRAGMENTS, SECOND EDITION

From Book I

1. *Digladiari* has been used in the sense of 'to disagree,' 'dissent': it is derived from 'swords.' Cicero, *Academica*, Bk. I.: 'But why is Mnesarchus resentful? Why does Antipater cross swords with Carneades in so many volumes?'

2. (Under *concinnare.*) The same author in *Academica* Bk. I.: 'With whom by reason of the similarity of the word he seemed to himself to be completely in harmony . . .'

From Book II

3. The view that *aequor* is derived from *aequum*, 'level,' is supported by Cicero, *Academica*, Book II.: 'What seems so level as the sea? This is actually the reason why the word for it in poetry is *aequor*.'

4. *Adamare.* 'For those who have fallen in love with office too late gain admission to it with difficulty, and cannot be enough in favour with the multitude.'

5. *Exponere* meaning 'to show examples of good': 'To crush avarice, to put away crime, to exhibit one's own life for the young to imitate.'

6. *Hebes*, 'dull,' used in the sense of 'dark,' or

Cicero Academ. lib. II.: Quid? lunae quae liniamenta sunt? potesne dicere? cuius et nascentis et senescentis alias hebetiora, alias acutiora videntur cornua.

7. *Non. p.* 162. *Purpurascit. Cicero Acad. lib. II.:* Quid? mare nonne caeruleum? at eius unda cum est pulsa remis purpurascit, et quidem aquae tinctum quodam modo et infectum . . .

8. *Non. p.* 162. *Perpendicula et normae. Cicero Acad. lib. II.:* Atqui si id crederemus, non egeremus perpendiculis, non normis, non regulis.

9. *Non. p.* 394. *Siccum dicitur aridum et sine humore. . . . Siccum dicitur et sobrium, immadidum. Cicero Acad. lib. II.:* Alius (color) adultis, alius adulescentibus, alius aegris, <alius sanis>, alius siccis, alius vinulentis.

10. *Non. p.* 474. *Urinantur. Cicero in Academicis lib. II.:* Si quando enim nos demersimus ut qui urinantur, aut nihil superum aut obscure admodum cernimus.

11. *Non. p.* 545. *Alabaster. Cicero Acad. lib. II.:* Quibus etiam alabaster plenus unguenti puter esse videtur.

Libri III

12. *Non. p.* 65. *Digladiari . . . idem tertio:* Digladiari autem semper et depugnare in facinorosis et audacibus quis non cum miserrimum tum etiam stultissimum dixerit?

13. *Non. p.* 65. *Exultare dictum est exilire. Cicero Acad. lib. III.:* Et ut nos nunc sedemus ad Lucrinum pisciculosque exultantes videmus . . .

14. *Non. p.* 123. *Ingeneraretur ut innasceretur. Cicero Acad. lib. III.:* In tanta animantium varietate

else 'blunt': 'Well, what are the outlines of the moon? Can you say? The horns of the moon both when rising and setting sometimes seem duller, sometimes sharper.'

7. *Purpurascit.* 'What, is not the sea blue? But when its water is struck by oars it purples, and indeed a sort of dye and stain having come to the water's . . .'

8. *Perpendicula* and *normae.* 'Yet if we believed that, we should not require plumblines or rods or rulers.'

9. *Siccum* means 'dried up,' devoid of moisture. . . . *Siccum* also means 'sober,' not a soaker. 'We notice a different complexion in grown-up people and the young, in invalids and the healthy, in the dry and in wine-bibbers.'

10. *Urinantur.* 'For whenever we stoop like men making water, we see nothing above us or only quite dimly.'

11. *Alabaster.* 'People who think even a scent-bottle full of perfume a stinking thing.'

From Book III

12. *Digladiari.* . . . Cicero also writes in Book III.: 'But to be always crossing swords and fighting to the end among criminals and desperadoes—who would not call this a most pitiable and also a most foolish occupation?'

13. *Exultare* means 'to jump out.' 'And just as we are now sitting by the Lucrine Lake and see the little fishes jumping out of the water . . .'

14. *Ingeneraretur* in the sense of 'might be born in.' 'That in man alone among all this variety of

homini ut soli cupiditas ingeneraretur cognitionis et scientiae!

15. *Non. p.* 419. *Vindicare, trahere, liberare.* . . . *Cicero Acad. lib. III.* : Aliqua potestas sit, vindicet se in libertatem.

16. *Lactant. Inst. vi.* 24. *Cicero . . . cuius haec in Academico tertio verba sunt :* Quod si liceret, ut iis qui in itinere deerravissent, sic vitam deviam secutis corrigere errorem paenitendo, facilior esset emendatio temeritatis.

17. *Diomedes p.* 377 *ed. Keil. Varro ad Ciceronem tertio* fixum *et Cicero Academicorum tertio* malcho in opera adfixa.

Librorum incertorum

18. *Lactant. Inst. iii.* 14. *Haec tua verba sunt (Cicero) :* Mihi autem non modo ad sapientiam caeci videmur sed ad ea ipsa quae aliqua ex parte cerni videantur hebetes et obtusi.

19. *Augustin. c. Academicos ii.* 26 Talia, *inquit Academicus*, mihi videntur omnia quae probabilia vel veri similia putavi nominanda ; quae tu si alio nomine vis vocare, nihil repugno, satis enim mihi est te iam bene accepisse quid dicam, id est, quibus rebus haec nomina imponam : non enim vocabulorum opificem sed rerum inquisitorem decet esse sapientem.

20. *August. c. Acad. iii.* 15 *sq. Est in libris Ciceronis quos in huius causae patrocinium scripsit locus quidam, ut mihi videtur, mira urbanitate conditus, ut non nullis*

---

[a] *Malleo*, Reid's conjecture for the unknown word *malcho* of the MSS.

living creatures might be born a desire for learning and knowledge.'

15. *Vindicare* 'to draw,' 'to set free.' 'Let him show some capacity, let him champion himself into freedom.'

16. Cicero . . . who in his third Academic volume has these words: 'Whereas if those who have pursued a devious path in life were allowed, like travellers who had wandered from the road, to remedy their mistake by repenting, the correction of recklessness would be easier.'

17. Varro in his third book dedicated to Cicero uses *fixum*, and Cicero in *Academica*, Book III. 'adfixed on the work with a hammer.' [a]

Fragments of uncertain Context

18. These are your own words, (Cicero): 'To me however we seem not only blind to wisdom but dull and blunted even towards things that are in some measure visible.'

19. 'Such,' says the Academic speaker, 'seem to me to be all the things that I have thought fit to entitle "probable" or possessed of verisimilitude; if you want to call them by another name I make no objection, for it satisfies me that you have already well grasped my meaning, that is, the things to which I assign these names: since it becomes the wise man to be not a manufacturer of words but a researcher into things.'

20. The books of Cicero that he wrote to champion this cause contain a certain passage that seems to me to have a remarkably witty flavour, while some people

autem, etiam firmitate roboratus. Difficile est prorsus ut quemquam non moveat quod ibi dictum est, Academico sapienti ab omnibus ceterarum sectarum qui sibi sapientes videntur secundas partes dari, cum primas sibi quemque vindicare necesse sit; ex quo posse probabiliter confici eum recte primum esse suo iudicio qui omnium ceterorum iudicio sit secundus.

21. *August. c. Acad. iii.* 20. 43 *Ait enim* (*Cicero*) illis morem fuisse occultandi sententiam suam nec eam cuiquam nisi qui secum ad senectutem usque vixissent aperire consuesse.

22. *August. de civ. Dei vi.* 2 *Denique et ipse Tullius huic* (*M. Varroni*) *tale testimonium perhibet ut in libris Academicis dicat eam quae ibi versatur disputationem se habuisse cum M. Varrone,* homine, *inquit,* omnium facile acutissimo et sine ulla dubitatione doctissimo.

think it actually a powerful and strong piece of writing. Indeed it is hard to see how anybody could fail to be impressed by what is said there, that 'the Wise Man of the Academy is given the second rôle by all the adherents of the other schools that seem wise in their own eyes, though of course they each claim the first part for themselves; and that from this the probable inference may be drawn that, since he is second by everybody else's verdict, his own verdict is right in placing him first.'

[There follows a page of imaginary dialogue between Zeno, Epicurus and an Academic, which some editors print as a verbatim quotation from Cicero; but the style makes this unlikely, and it is not introduced as a quotation, as is the passage above.]

21. For he (Cicero) says that they 'had a habit of concealing their opinion, and did not usually disclose it to anybody except those that had lived with them right up to old age.'

22. Finally Tully himself also bears such witness to this man (Marcus Varro) as to say in *Academica* that the discussion there set out took place between himself and Marcus Varro, 'a person who was easily the most penetrating of all men, and without any doubt extremely learned.'

LIBER SECUNDUS. LUCULLUS

(EDITIO PRIOR)

1 I. Magnum ingenium L. Luculli magnumque optimarum artium studium, tum omnis liberalis et digna homine nobili ab eo percepta doctrina, quibus temporibus florere in foro maxime potuit caruit omnino rebus urbanis. Ut enim admodum adulescens cum fratre pari pietate et industria praedito paternas inimicitias magna cum gloria est persecutus, in Asiam quaestor profectus ibi permultos annos admirabili quadam laude provinciae praefuit; deinde absens factus aedilis, continuo praetor (licebat enim celerius legis praemio), post in Africam, inde ad consulatum, quem ita gessit ut diligentiam admirarentur omnes, ingenium agnoscerent. Post ad Mithridaticum bellum missus a senatu non modo opinionem vicit omnium quae de virtute eius erat sed etiam gloriam
2 superiorum; idque eo fuit mirabilius quod ab eo laus

[a] This Book belongs to the first edition of the work (in which it was dedicated to Lucullus and entitled by his name), and it is therefore designated *Academica Priora* by some editors.

[b] The elder Lucullus had been tried and found guilty of misconduct when commanding in the slave-war in Sicily, 103 B.C. His sons (in accordance with the Roman sentiment of filial duty) did their best to ruin his prosecutor Servilius.

[c] Probably Sulla, when re-enacting the old *lex annalis* by his *lex de magistratibus*, inserted a clause exempting his own officers as a special privilege, to reward their services.

BOOK II.[a] LUCULLUS

ANTIOCHUS'S ATTACK ON SCEPTICISM EXPOUNDED AND ANSWERED

1 I. The great talents of Lucius Lucullus and his great devotion to the best sciences, with all his acquisitions in that liberal learning which becomes a person of high station, were entirely cut off from public life at Rome in the period when he might have won the greatest distinction at the bar. For when as quite a youth, in co-operation with a brother possessed of equal filial affection and devotion, he had carried on with great distinction the personal feuds of his father,[b] he went out as quaestor to Asia, and there for a great many years presided over the province with quite remarkable credit; then in his absence he was elected aedile, and next praetor (since by a statutory grant[c] this was permitted before the usual time); later he was appointed to Africa, and then to the consulship, which he so administered as to win universal admiration for his devotion to duty and universal recognition of his ability. Later the senate commissioned him to the war with Mithridates,[d] in which he not only surpassed everybody's previous estimation of his valour but even the glory
2 of his predecessors; and this was the more remark-

Introduction. Lucullus the scholar-statesman.

[d] The third Mithridatic War, beginning 74 B.C., when Lucullus was consul.

imperatoria non admodum exspectabatur qui adulescentiam in forensi opera, quaesturae diuturnum tempus Murena bellum in Ponto gerente in Asia pace consumpserat. Sed incredibilis quaedam ingenii magnitudo non desideravit indocilem usus disciplinam. Itaque cum totum iter et navigationem consumpsisset partim in percontando a peritis, partim in rebus gestis legendis, in Asiam factus imperator venit, cum esset Roma profectus rei militaris rudis. Habuit enim divinam quandam memoriam rerum, verborum maiorem Hortensius, sed quo plus in negotiis gerendis res quam verba prosunt, hoc erat memoria illa praestantior; quam fuisse in Themistocle, quem facile Graeciae principem ponimus, singularem ferunt, qui quidem etiam pollicenti cuidam se artem ei memoriae quae tum primum proferebatur traditurum respondisse dicitur oblivisci se malle discere—credo quod haerebant in memoria quaecumque audierat et viderat. Tali ingenio praeditus Lucullus adiunxerat etiam illam quam Themistocles spreverat disciplinam, itaque, ut litteris consignamus quae monumentis mandare volumus, sic ille in animo res insculptas
3 habebat. Tantus ergo imperator in omni genere belli fuit, proeliis, oppugnationibus, navalibus pugnis, totiusque belli instrumento et adparatu, ut ille rex post Alexandrum maxumus hunc a se maiorem ducem cognitum quam quemquam eorum quos legisset

---

[a] The second Mithridatic War, 83–82 B.C.

[b] *i.e.*, the training provided by experience and not by study.

[c] The lyric poet Simonides of Ceos (556–467 B.C.), the inventor of the system.

[d] Mithridates the Great (120–63 B.C.), king of Pontus.

able because military distinction was not particularly anticipated from one who had spent his youth in practice at the bar, and the long period of his quaestorship peacefully in Asia, while Murena was carrying on the war in Pontus.[a] But intellectual gifts that even surpassed belief had no need of the unschooled training that is given by experience.[b] Accordingly after spending the whole of his journey by land and sea partly in cross-questioning those who were experts and partly in reading military history, he arrived in Asia a made general, although he had started from Rome a tiro in military matters. For he had a memory for facts that was positively inspired, although Hortensius had a better memory for words, but Lucullus's memory was the more valuable, inasmuch as in the conduct of business facts are of more assistance than words; and this form of memory is recorded as having been present in a remarkable degree in Themistocles, whom we rank as easily the greatest man of Greece, and of whom the story is told that when somebody[c] offered to impart to him the *memoria technica* that was then first coming into vogue, he replied that he would sooner learn to forget—no doubt this was because whatever he heard or saw remained fixed in his memory. Gifted with such natural endowments, Lucullus had also added the training which Themistocles had despised, and thus he kept facts engraved on his mind just as we enshrine in writing things
3 that we desire to record. Consequently he was so great a commander in every class of warfare, battles, sieges, sea-fights, and in the entire field of military equipment and commissariat, that the greatest king[d] since the time of Alexander admitted that he had discovered Lucullus to be a greater general than any

fateretur. In eodem tanta prudentia fuit in constituendis temperandisque civitatibus, tanta aequitas, ut hodie stet Asia Luculli institutis servandis et quasi vestigiis persequendis. Sed etsi magna cum utilitate rei publicae, tamen diutius quam vellem tanta vis virtutis atque ingeni peregrinata afuit ab oculis et fori et curiae. Quin etiam cum victor a Mithridatico bello revertisset, inimicorum calumnia triennio tardius quam debuerat triumphavit; nos enim consules introduximus paene in urbem currum clarissimi viri; cuius mihi consilium et auctoritas quid tum in maximis rebus profuissent[1] dicerem nisi de me ipso dicendum esset, quod hoc tempore non est necesse; itaque privabo potius illum debito testimonio quam id cum mea laude communicem.

4 II. Sed quae populari gloria decorari in Lucullo debuerunt, ea fere sunt et Graecis litteris celebrata et Latinis. Nos autem illa externa cum multis, haec interiora cum paucis ex ipso saepe cognovimus; maiore enim studio Lucullus cum omni litterarum generi tum philosophiae deditus fuit quam qui illum ignorabant arbitrabantur, nec vero ineunte aetate solum sed et pro quaestore aliquot annos et in ipso bello, in quo ita magna rei militaris esse occupatio solet ut non multum imperatori sub ipsis pellibus otii relinquatur. Cum autem e philosophis ingenio

[1] profuisset *codd. fere omnes.*

---

[a] At the end of 67 B.C.

[b] Cicero is doubtless thinking chiefly of the suppression of the revolutionary conspiracy led by Catiline.

of those that he had read of. He also possessed so much wisdom and justice in the work of establishing and reforming governments that Asia to-day continues to observe the institutions and follow in the footsteps of Lucullus. But although greatly to the advantage of the state, nevertheless those vast powers of character and of intellect were absent abroad, out of the sight of both the law-courts and the senate, for a longer time than I could have wished. Moreover when he returned [a] victorious from the Mithridatic War, the chicanery of his enemies postponed his triumph three years later than it ought to have taken place; for it was I as consul who virtually led into the city the chariot of this glorious hero, of the value to me of whose advice and influence at that period in the most important affairs [b] I might speak if it did not involve speaking about myself, which at this time is not necessary; and so I will rob him of the tribute due to him rather than combine it with my own praise.

4 II. However, the things in Lucullus's career that deserved the honour of a national celebration have fairly well won their tribute of fame in both Greek and Latin records. But my knowledge of these facts about his public life I share with many persons; the following more private details I have often learnt from himself in company with few others—for Lucullus was more ardently devoted both to letters of all sorts and to philosophy than persons who did not know him supposed, and indeed not only at an early age but also for some years during his proquaestorship, and even on active service, when military duties are usually so engrossing as to leave a commander not much leisure when actually under canvas. But as Philo's pupil Antiochus was deemed

scientiaque putaretur Antiochus Philonis auditor excellere, eum secum et quaestor habuit et post aliquot annos imperator, quique esset ea memoria quam ante dixi, ea saepe audiendo facile cognovit quae vel semel audita meminisse potuisset. Delectabatur autem mirifice lectione librorum de quibus audiebat.[1]

5 Ac vereor interdum ne talium personarum cum amplificare velim minuam etiam gloriam. Sunt enim multi qui omnino Graecas non ament litteras, plures qui philosophiam; reliqui[2] etiam si haec non improbant,[3] tamen earum rerum disputationem principibus civitatis non ita decoram putant.[4] Ego autem cum Graecas litteras M. Catonem in senectute didicisse acceperim, P. autem Africani historiae loquantur in legatione illa nobili quam ante censuram obiit Panaetium unum omnino comitem fuisse, nec litterarum Graecarum nec philosophiae iam ullum auctorem
6 requiro. Restat ut iis respondeam qui sermonibus eius modi nolint personas tam graves inligari. Quasi vero clarorum virorum aut tacitos congressus esse oporteat aut ludicros sermones aut rerum conloquia leviorum! Etenim si quodam in libro vere est a nobis philosophia laudata, profecto eius tractatio optimo atque amplissimo quoque dignissima est, nec quid-

[1] audierat *Ernesti.* [2] reliqui qui *codd. multi.*
[3] *ed.*: improbent *codd.*
[4] putent *codd. fere omnes.*

[a] To the kings of Egypt and Asia in alliance with Rome, 144 B.C. Scipio Africanus Minor was censor 142 B.C.

[b] Cicero's *Hortensius.*

the chief among philosophers for intellect and learning, he kept him in his company both when quaestor and when a few years later he became general, and having the powerful memory that I have spoken of already he easily learnt from frequent repetition doctrines that he would have been quite capable of learning from a single hearing. Moreover, he took a marvellous delight in reading the books about which Antiochus used to discourse to him.

5 And I am sometimes afraid lest in regard to men of this character my desire to magnify their fame may actually diminish it. For there are many people who have no love for Greek literature at all, and more who have none for philosophy; while the residue even if they do not disapprove of these studies nevertheless think that the discussion of such topics is not specially becoming for great statesmen. But for my own part, as I have been told that Marcus Cato learnt Greek literature in his old age, while history states that Publius Africanus, on the famous embassy [a] on which he went before his censorship, had Panaetius as absolutely the sole member of his staff, I need not look any further for someone to support the claims either of Greek literature or of philosophy.

Combination of study and affairs in the best tradition of Roman life.

6 It remains for me to reply to the critics who are unwilling to have public characters of such dignity entangled in conversations of this nature. As if forsooth persons of distinction ought to hold their meetings in silence, or else engage in frivolous conversation or discussion on lighter topics! In fact, if there is truth in the praise of philosophy that occupies a certain volume [b] of mine, it is obvious that its pursuit is supremely worthy of all persons of the highest character and eminence, and the only precaution that

quam aliud videndum est nobis quos populus Romanus hoc in gradu conlocavit nisi ne quid privatis studiis de opera publica detrahamus. Quodsi cum fungi munere debebamus non modo operam nostram numquam a populari coetu removimus sed ne litteram quidem ullam fecimus nisi forensem, quis reprendet otium nostrum, qui in eo non modo nosmet ipsos hebescere et languere nolumus sed etiam ut plurimis prosimus enitimur? Gloriam vero non modo non minui sed etiam augeri arbitramur eorum quorum ad popularis inlustrisque laudes has etiam minus
7 notas minusque pervolgatas adiungimus. Sunt etiam qui negent in iis qui in nostris libris disputent fuisse earum rerum de quibus disputatur scientiam: qui mihi videntur non solum vivis sed etiam mortuis invidere.

III. Restat unum genus reprehensorum quibus Academiae ratio non probatur. Quod gravius ferremus si quisquam ullam disciplinam philosophiae probaret praeter eam quam ipse sequeretur. Nos autem quoniam contra omnes dicere quae[1] videntur solemus, non possumus quin alii a nobis dissentiant recusare: quamquam nostra quidem causa facilis est, qui verum invenire sine ulla contentione volumus idque summa cura studioque conquirimus. Etsi enim omnis cognitio multis est obstructa difficultatibus, eaque est et in ipsis rebus obscuritas et in iudiciis nostris infirmitas

[1] dicere quae *Reid*: qui dicere quae *codd.*, qui scire sibi *Cant.*

---

[a] *i.e.*, the *dramatis personae* of the dialogues that follow.
[b] *Cf.* 'preach Christ of contention,' *Philippians* i. 16, and *Hebrews* i. 3, *Thessalonians* ii. 2.

need be observed by us whom the Roman nation has placed in this rank is to prevent our private studies from encroaching at all upon our public interest. But if at the time when we had official duties to perform we not only never removed our interest from the national assembly but never even put pen to paper save on matters of public business, who will criticize our leisure, if therein we not only are reluctant to allow ourselves to grow dull and slack but also strive to be of service to the greatest number of men? At the same time in our judgement we are not merely not diminishing but actually increasing the fame of those persons [a] to whose public and distinguished glories we also append these less known
7 and less well advertised claims to distinction. There are also people who declare that the personages who debate in our books did not really possess a knowledge of the subjects debated; but these critics to my eye appear to be jealous of the dead as well as of the living.

III. There remains one class of adverse critics who do not approve the Academic system of philosophy. This would trouble us more if anybody approved any set of doctrines except the one of which he himself was a follower. But for our part, since it is our habit to put forward our views in conflict with all schools, we cannot refuse to allow others to differ from us; although we at all events have an easy brief to argue, who desire to discover the truth without any contention,[b] and who pursue it with the fullest diligence and devotion. For even though many difficulties hinder every branch of knowledge, and both the subjects themselves and our faculties of judgement involve such a lack of certainty that the most

The Academic philosophy defended against dogmatism.

ut non sine causa antiquissimi et doctissimi invenire se posse quod cuperent diffisi sint, tamen nec illi defecerunt neque nos studium exquirendi defatigati relinquemus; neque nostrae disputationes quidquam aliud agunt nisi ut in utramque partem dicendo eliciant et tamquam exprimant aliquid quod aut
8 verum sit aut ad id quam proxime accedat. Nec inter nos et eos qui se scire arbitrantur quidquam interest nisi quod illi non dubitant quin ea vera sint quae defendunt, nos probabilia multa habemus, quae sequi facile, adfirmare vix possumus; hoc autem liberiores et solutiores sumus quod integra nobis est iudicandi potestas nec ut omnia quae praescripta a quibusdam et quasi imperata sint defendamus necessitate ulla cogimur. Nam ceteri primum ante tenentur adstricti quam quid esset optimum iudicare potuerunt, deinde infirmissimo tempore aetatis aut obsecuti amico cuipiam aut una alicuius quem primum audierunt oratione capti de rebus incognitis iudicant, et ad quamcumque sunt disciplinam quasi tempestate delati ad eam tamquam ad saxum adhaerescunt.
9 Nam quod dicunt omnino se credere ei quem iudicent fuisse sapientem, probarem si id ipsum rudes et indocti iudicare potuissent (statuere enim qui sit sapiens vel maxime videtur esse sapientis); sed, ut potuerint,[1] potuerunt omnibus rebus auditis, cognitis etiam re-

[1] potuerint *inseruit Lambinus.*

[a] *Exprimant*, a metaphor from sculpture; no doubt the word properly denoted the preliminary model in clay.

ancient and learned thinkers had good reason for distrusting their ability to discover what they desired, nevertheless they did not give up, nor yet will we abandon in exhaustion our zeal for research; and the sole object of our discussions is by arguing on both sides to draw out and give shape to[a] some result that may be either true or the nearest possible ap-
8 proximation to the truth. Nor is there any difference between ourselves and those who think that they have positive knowledge except that they have no doubt that their tenets are true, whereas we hold many doctrines as probable, which we can easily act upon but can scarcely advance as certain; yet we are more free and untrammelled in that we possess our power of judgement uncurtailed, and are bound by no compulsion to support all the dogmas laid down for us almost as edicts by certain masters. For all other people in the first place are held in close bondage placed upon them before they were able to judge what doctrine was the best, and secondly they form judgements about matters as to which they know nothing at the most incompetent period of life, either under the guidance of some friend or under the influence of a single harangue from the first lecturer that they attended, and cling as to a rock to whatever
9 theory they are carried to by stress of weather. For as to their assertion that the teacher whom they judge to have been a wise man commands their absolute trust, I would agree to this if to make that judgement could actually have lain within the power of unlearned novices (for to decide who is a wise man seems to be a task that specially requires a wise man to undertake it); but granting that it lay within their power, it was only possible for them after hear-

liquorum sententiis, iudicaverunt autem re semel audita atque[1] ad unius se auctoritatem contulerunt. Sed nescio quo modo plerique errare malunt eamque sententiam quam adamaverunt pugnacissime defendere quam sine pertinacia quid constantissime dicatur exquirere.

Quibus de rebus et alias saepe nobis multa quaesita et disputata sunt et quondam in Hortensii villa quae est ad Baulos, cum eo Catulus et Lucullus nosque ipsi postridie venissemus quam apud Catulum fuissemus. Quo quidem etiam maturius venimus quod erat constitutum, si ventus esset, Lucullo in Neapolitanum, mihi in Pompeianum navigare. Cum igitur pauca in xysto locuti essemus, tum eodem in spatio consedimus.

10 IV. Hic Catulus, "Etsi heri," inquit, "id quod quaerebatur paene explicatum est, ut tota fere quaestio tractata videatur, tamen exspecto ea quae te pollicitus es, Luculle, ab Antiocho audita dicturum." "Equidem," inquit Hortensius, "feci plus quam vellem, totam enim rem Lucullo integram servatam oportuit. Et tamen fortasse servata est; a me enim ea quae in promptu erant dicta sunt, a Lucullo autem reconditiora desidero." Tum ille, "Non sane," inquit, "Hortensi, conturbat me exspectatio tua, etsi nihil

[1] atque *inseruit Lambinus.*

[a] *i.e.*, the colonnade or *xystus* in which they had been strolling.

ing all the facts and ascertaining the views of all the other schools as well, whereas they gave their verdict after a single hearing of the case, and enrolled themselves under the authority of a single master. But somehow or other most men prefer to go wrong, and to defend tooth and nail the system for which they have come to feel an affection, rather than to lay aside obstinacy and seek for the doctrine that is most consistent.

Dramatis personae.

Beside many other occasions on which we have engaged in long investigations and discussions of these subjects, there was one at Hortensius's country-house at Bauli, Catulus, Lucullus and we ourselves having come there on the day after we had been at Catulus's. We had in fact arrived there rather early because Lucullus had the intention of sailing to his place at Naples and I to mine at Pompei, if there was a wind. So after a little talk in the colonnade, we then sat down on a seat in the same walk.[a]

Lucullus, in defence of Antiochus, reports his polemic against Scepticism (§§ 10-62).

IV. Here Catulus said, "It is true that our inquiry of yesterday was almost fully cleared up, so that nearly the whole of the subject now appears to have been handled; but nevertheless I am waiting with interest for you, Lucullus, to fulfil your promise of telling us the doctrines that you heard from Antiochus." "For my part," said Hortensius, "I could wish that I had not gone so far, for the whole subject ought to have been reserved in its entirety for Lucullus. And yet perhaps it has been reserved, for it was the more obvious points that were expounded by me, whereas I look to Lucullus to give us the more abstruse doctrines." "Your expectancy, Hortensius," rejoined Lucullus, "does not, it is true, upset me, although there is nothing that so much

est iis qui placere volunt tam adversarium, sed quia non laboro quam valde ea quae dico probaturus sim, eo minus conturbor; dicam enim nec mea nec ea in quibus, si non fuerint, non vinci me malim quam vincere. Sed mehercule, ut quidem nunc se causa habet, etsi hesterno sermone labefactata est, mihi tamen videtur esse verissima. Agam igitur sicut Antiochus agebat (nota enim mihi res est, nam et vacuo animo illum audiebam et magno studio, eadem de re etiam saepius), ut etiam maiorem exspectationem mei faciam quam modo fecit Hortensius."

11 Cum ita esset exorsus, ad audiendum animos ereximus; at ille "Cum Alexandriae pro quaestore" inquit "essem, fuit Antiochus mecum, et erat iam antea Alexandriae familiaris Antiochi Heraclitus Tyrius, qui et Clitomachum multos annos et Philonem audierat, homo sane in ista philosophia, quae nunc prope dimissa revocatur, probatus et nobilis; cum quo Antiochum saepe disputantem audiebam, sed utrumque leniter. Et quidem isti libri duo Philonis, de quibus heri dictum a Catulo est, tum erant adlati Alexandriam tumque primum in Antiochi manus venerant: et homo natura lenissimus (nihil enim poterat fieri illo mitius) stomachari tamen coepit. Mirabar, nec enim umquam ante videram; at ille

---

[a] Lucullus was sent by Sulla to Alexandria, 87–86 B.C., to try to raise a fleet.

[b] *i.e.*, by Cicero.

handicaps people desirous of winning approval, but I am less upset because I do not mind how far I am successful in gaining assent for the views that I expound; for the doctrines that I am going to state are not my own, nor are they ones about which, if they are unsound, I should not wish rather to be refuted than to carry the day. But I protest that even though my case was shaken by yesterday's discussion, it nevertheless appears to me to be profoundly true—at least as it stands at present. I will therefore adopt what used to be the procedure of Antiochus (for I am familiar with the subject, since I used to hear him with undistracted attention and with great interest, even more than once on the same topic), so as to cause even more to be expected of me than
11 Hortensius did just now." On his beginning in this strain we aroused our attention to listen to him; whereupon he proceeded: "When I was deputy-quaestor at Alexandria,[a] Antiochus was in my company, and Antiochus's friend, the Tyrian Heraclitus, was at Alexandria already; he had been for many years a pupil of both Clitomachus and Philo, and was undoubtedly a person of standing and distinction in the school of philosophy in question, which after having been almost abandoned is now being revived[b]; I often used to hear Antiochus arguing with Heraclitus, both however in a gentle manner. And indeed those two volumes of Philo mentioned yesterday by Catulus had then reached Alexandria and had then for the first time come into Antiochus's hands; whereupon though by nature one of the gentlest of people (in fact nothing could have been kinder than he was) he nevertheless began to lose his temper. This surprised me, as I had never seen

Heracliti memoriam implorans quaerere ex eo viderenturne illa Philonis aut ea num vel e Philone vel ex ullo Academico audivisset aliquando. Negabat; Philonis tamen scriptum agnoscebat, nec id quidem dubitari poterat, nam aderant mei familiares, docti homines, P. et C. Selii et Tetrilius Rogus qui se illa audivisse Romae de Philone et ab eo ipso illos duos
12 libros dicerent descripsisse. Tum et illa dixit Antiochus quae heri Catulus commemoravit a patre suo dicta Philoni[1] et alia plura, nec se tenuit quin contra suum doctorem librum etiam ederet qui Sosus inscribitur. Tum igitur cum et Heraclitum studiose audirem contra Antiochum disserentem et item Antiochum contra Academicos, dedi Antiocho operam diligentius, ut causam ex eo totam cognoscerem. Itaque complures dies adhibito Heraclito doctisque compluribus et in iis Antiochi fratre Aristo et praeterea Aristone et Dione, quibus ille secundum fratrem plurimum tribuebat, multum temporis in ista una disputatione consumpsimus. Sed ea pars quae contra Philonem erat praetermittenda est, minus enim acer est adversarius is qui ista quae sunt heri defensa negat Academicos omnino dicere; etsi

[1] [Philoni] ? *Reid.*

---

[a] *i.e.*, the New Academy, as § 12 *fin.*

[b] These persons are otherwise unknown.

[c] *i.e.*, at the beginning of the lost Book I. of the first edition of *Academica*; in the second edition the topic was transferred to Cicero and occupied the lost Book II.

[d] Sosus, like Antiochus a native of Ascalon, seems to have gone over from the Academy to Stoicism.

[e] *i.e.*, when a copy is made, that is the name written on it.

[f] See i. 12 n.

[g] *i.e.*, by Catulus, in the lost Book I. of the first edition,

him do so before; but he kept appealing to Heraclitus's recollection and asking him whether he really thought that those doctrines were Philo's, or whether he had ever heard them either from Philo or from any member of the Academy.[a] Heraclitus always answered No; but still he recognized it as a work of Philo's, and indeed this could not be doubted, for my learned friends Publius and Gaius Selius and Tetrilius Rogus[b] were there to say that they had heard these doctrines from Philo at Rome and had copied down the two books in question from Philo's
12 own manuscript. Then Antiochus put forward the views that yesterday Catulus told us[c] had been put forward in regard to Philo by his father, and also a number of others, and did not restrain himself even from publishing a book against his own teacher,[d] the book to which is given[e] the title of *Sosus*. On this occasion therefore when I heard both Heraclitus earnestly arguing against Antiochus and also Antiochus against the Academics, I gave my attention more closely to Antiochus, in order to learn from him his whole case. Accordingly when we had for quite a number of days had Heraclitus with us and quite a number of other learned men, among them Antiochus's brother Aristus,[f] and also Aristo and Dio, to whom he used to assign the greatest authority next to his brother, we spent a great deal of time in this single discussion. But we must pass over the part of it that was directed against Philo, for he is a less keen opponent who declares that those doctrines maintained yesterday[g] are not the doctrines of the Academy at all; for though what he says is

which bore his name; the subject was given to Cicero in the lost Book II. of the second edition (see p. 406).

enim mentitur, tamen est adversarius lenior. Ad Arcesilan Carneademque veniamus."

13 V. Quae cum dixisset, sic rursus exorsus est: "Primum mihi videmini"—me autem [nomine][1] appellabat—" cum veteres physicos nominatis, facere idem quod seditiosi cives solent cum aliquos ex antiquis claros viros proferunt quos dicant fuisse populares ut eorum ipsi similes esse videantur. Repetunt enim a[2] P. Valerio qui exactis regibus primo anno consul fuit, commemorant reliquos qui leges populares de provocationibus tulerint cum consules essent; tum ad hos notiores, C. Flaminium qui legem agrariam aliquot annis ante secundum Punicum bellum tribunus plebis tulerit invito senatu et postea bis consul factus sit, L. Cassium, Q. Pompeium; illi quidem etiam P. Africanum referre in eundem numerum solent. Duos vero sapientissimos et clarissimos fratres P. Crassum et P. Scaevolam aiunt Ti. Graccho auctores legum fuisse, alterum quidem (ut videmus) palam, alterum (ut suspicantur) obscurius. Addunt etiam C. Marium, et de hoc quidem nihil mentiuntur. Horum nominibus tot virorum atque tantorum expositis eorum se

14 institutum sequi dicunt. Similiter vos, cum perturbare ut illi rem publicam sic vos philosophiam bene iam constitutam velitis, Empedoclen, Anaxagoran, Democritum, Parmeniden, Xenophanem, Platonem

[1] [nomine] *ed.*
[2] enim a *Reid*: iam *aut* iam a *codd.*

not true, he is a milder adversary. Let us come to Arcesilas and Carneades."

V. When he had said this he started again as follows: "In the first place I feel that you gentlemen"—it was to me that he was actually speaking,—"when you cite the names of the old natural philosophers, are doing just what citizens raising a sedition usually do, when they quote some famous personages of antiquity as having been of the people's party, so as to make themselves appear to resemble them. For they go back to Publius Valerius who was consul in the first year after the expulsion of the kings, and they quote all the other persons who when consuls carried popular legislation about processes of appeal; then they come to the better known cases of Gaius Flaminius, who when tribune of the plebs some years before the second Punic War carried an agrarian law against the will of the senate and afterwards twice became consul, and of Lucius Cassius and Quintus Pompeius; indeed these people have a way of including even Publius Africanus in the same list. But they say that the two very wise and distinguished brothers Publius Crassus and Publius Scaevola were supporters of the laws of Tiberius Gracchus, the former (as we read) openly, the latter (as they suspect) more covertly. They also add Gaius Marius, and about him at all events they say nothing that is untrue. After parading all this list of names of men of such distinction they declare that they themselves are following the principle set up by them. Similarly your school, whenever you want to upset an already well-established system of philosophy just as they did a political system, quote Empedocles, Anaxagoras, Democritus, Parmenides,

(1) The New Academy perverts history: the ancients were dogmatic,

509 B.C.

232 B.C.

133 B.C.

etiam et Socratem profertis. Sed neque Saturninus, ut nostrum inimicum potissimum nominem, simile quidquam habuit veterum illorum, nec Arcesilae calumnia conferenda est cum Democriti verecundia. Et tamen isti physici raro admodum, cum haerent aliquo loco, exclamant quasi mente incitati—Empedocles quidem ut interdum mihi furere videatur—abstrusa esse omnia, nihil nos sentire, nihil cernere, nihil omnino quale sit posse reperire ; maiorem autem partem mihi quidem omnes isti videntur nimis etiam quaedam adfirmare, plusque profiteri se scire quam sciant. Quodsi illi tum in novis rebus quasi modo nascentes haesitaverunt, nihilne tot saeculis, summis ingeniis, maximis studiis explicatum putamus ? nonne cum iam philosophorum disciplinae gravissimae constitissent, tum exortus est, ut in optima re publica Ti. Gracchus qui otium perturbaret, sic Arcesilas qui constitutam philosophiam everteret, et in eorum auctoritate delitesceret qui negavissent quidquam sciri aut percipi posse ? Quorum e numero tollendus est et Plato et Socrates—alter quia reliquit perfectissimam disciplinam, Peripateticos et Academicos, nominibus differentes, re congruentes, a quibus Stoici ipsi verbis magis quam sententiis dis-

[a] *i.e.*, to put Arcesilas in a list of philosophers that includes Democritus is like classing a modern demagogue with the democratic statesmen of history. Saturninus, the colleague of Marius, finally went beyond him, and was killed by the mob.

Xenophanes, and even Plato and Socrates. But neither had Saturninus—to cite in particular the name of the enemy of my family—any feature resembling those men of old, nor can the chicanery of Arcesilas be compared with the modesty of Democritus.[a] And nevertheless your natural philosophers do rather rarely, when brought to a standstill at some topic, cry out in an excited sort of manner—Empedocles indeed in a way that sometimes makes me think him raving—saying that all things are hidden and that we perceive nothing, discern nothing, are utterly unable to discover the real nature of anything; although for the most part all your school seem to me at all events to be only too confident in some of their assertions and to profess to know more
15 than they really do. But if those old thinkers found themselves floundering like babies just born in a new world, do we imagine that all these generations and these consummate intellects and elaborate investigations have not succeeded in making anything clearer? Is it not the case that, just as in the noblest of states Tiberius Gracchus arose to disturb the atmosphere of peace, so when the most authoritative schools of philosophy had now come to a standstill, then there arose Arcesilas to overthrow the established philosophy, and to lurk behind the authority of those whom he asserted to have denied the possibility of all knowledge and perception? From the list of these we must remove both Plato and Socrates—the former because he left behind him a most consummate system of thought, the Peripatetic School and the Academy, which have different names but agree in substance, and from which the Stoics themselves disagreed more in terms

senserunt; Socrates autem de se ipse detrahens in disputatione plus tribuebat iis quos volebat refellere; ita cum aliud diceret atque sentiret, libenter uti solitus est ea dissimulatione quam Graeci εἰρωνείαν vocant; quam ait etiam in Africano fuisse Fannius, idque propterea vitiosum in illo non putandum quod idem fuerit in Socrate.

16 VI. "Sed fuerint illa vetera,[1] si voltis, incognita: nihilne est igitur actum quod investigata sunt posteaquam Arcesilas, Zenoni (ut putatur) obtrectans nihil novi reperienti sed emendanti superiores immutatione verborum, dum huius definitiones labefactare volt conatus est clarissimis rebus tenebras obducere? Cuius primo non admodum probata ratio, quamquam floruit cum acumine ingenii tum admirabili quodam lepore dicendi, proxime a Lacyde solo retenta est, post autem confecta a Carneade, qui est quartus ab Arcesila, audivit enim Hegesinum qui Euandrum audierat Lacydi discipulum, cum Arcesilae Lacydes fuisset. Sed ipse Carneades diu tenuit, nam nonaginta vixit annos, et qui illum audierant admodum floruerunt, e quibus industriae plurimum in Clitomacho fuit (declarat multitudo librorum), ingenii non minus in Hagnone,[2] in Charmada eloquentiae,

[1] veteribus *Bentley*.

[2] in Hagnone *Christ*: in hac nonne (*et alia*) *codd.*: in Aeschine *Davies*.

[a] Little or nothing is known of this philosopher or of the others mentioned in this section.

than in opinions. As for Socrates, he used to depreciate himself in discussion and to assign greater weight to those whom he wished to refute; thus, as he said something other than what he thought, he was fond of regularly employing the practice of dissembling that the Greeks call *irony*, which Fannius says was also a feature of Africanus, and one not to be deemed a fault in him, for the reason that Socrates had the same habit.

6 VI. "But let us grant if you wish that those ancient doctrines represented no real knowledge; has nothing then been achieved by their having been under examination ever since the time when Arcesilas, criticizing Zeno (so it is supposed) as making no new discoveries but only correcting his predecessors by verbal alterations, in his desire to undermine Zeno's definitions attempted to cover with darkness matters that were exceedingly clear? His system was at first not very much accepted, although he was distinguished both by acuteness of intellect and by a certain admirable charm of style, and at the first stage it was preserved by Lacydes only, but afterwards it was completed by Carneades, who is the fourth in line from Arcesilas, having attended the courses of Hegesinus [a] who had attended Evander, the pupil of Lacydes as Lacydes had been the pupil of Arcesilas. But Carneades himself held the school for a long time, for he lived to be ninety, and those who had been his pupils were of considerable eminence, Clitomachus being the one among them most distinguished for industry (as is proved by the large number of his books), though there was an equal amount of talent in Hagnon, of eloquence in Charmades, and of charm in Melanthius

and philosophy has progressed.

in Melanthio Rhodio suavitatis. Bene autem nosse
17 Carneaden Stratoniceus Metrodorus putabatur. Iam
Clitomacho Philo vester operam multos annos dedit; Philone autem vivo patrocinium Academiae non defuit. Sed quod nos facere nunc ingredimur ut contra Academicos disseramus, id quidam e philosophis et ii quidem non mediocres faciundum omnino non putabant, nec vero esse ullam rationem disputare cum iis qui nihil probarent, Antipatrumque Stoicum qui multus in eo fuisset reprehendebant; nec definiri aiebant necesse esse quid esset cognitio aut perceptio aut (si verbum e verbo volumus) comprehensio, quam κατάληψιν illi vocant, eosque qui persuadere vellent esse aliquid quod comprehendi et percipi posset inscienter facere dicebant, propterea quod nihil esset clarius ἐναργείᾳ (ut Graeci, perspicuitatem aut evidentiam nos, si placet, nominemus, fabricemurque si opus erit verba, ne hic sibi "—me appellabat iocans—" hoc licere putet soli): sed tamen orationem nullam putabant inlustriorem ipsa evidentia reperiri posse, nec ea quae tam clara essent definienda censebant. Alii autem negabant se pro hac evidentia quidquam priores fuisse dicturos, sed ad ea quae contra dicerentur dici oportere putabant, ne qui fallerentur.
18 Plerique tamen et definitiones ipsarum etiam eviden-

[a] See i. 41 n.

[b] A general term denoting things that are self-evident and do not require proof, used as a technical term by Zeno to denote the characteristic of καταληπτικὴ φαντασία.

of Rhodes. But the Metrodorus who was a pupil of Stratonicus was believed to have been well acquainted
17 with Carneades. Again Philo of your school for many years gave his attention to Clitomachus; and while Philo lived the Academy did not lack advocacy. But the undertaking upon which we are now entering, the refutation of the Academics, was entirely ruled out by some of the philosophers, and those indeed men of no inconsiderable standing, and they held that there was really no sense in arguing with thinkers who sanctioned nothing as proved, and they criticized the Stoic Antipater for spending much time in this; and they also asserted that there was no need to define the essential nature of knowledge or perception or (if we wish to give a literal translation) 'mental grasp,' the Stoic term *catalēpsis*,[a] and maintained that those who tried to prove that there is something that can be grasped and perceived were acting unscientifically, because there was nothing clearer than *enargeia*[b] (as the Greeks call it: let us term it perspicuousness or evidentness, if you will, and let us manufacture terms if necessary, so as not to let our friend here "—this was a jocular shot at me —" think that he has a monopoly of this licence): well, they thought that no argument could be discovered that was clearer than evidentness itself, and they deemed that truths so manifest did not need defining. But others said that they would not have opened proceedings with any speech in defence of this evidentness, but held that the proper course was for argument to be directed to answering the case for the prosecution, so that they might not be some-
18 how taken in. Still a good many of them do not object to definitions even of evident things them-

Philo's attack on Zeno went too far.

tium rerum non improbant et rem idoneam de qua quaeratur et homines dignos quibuscum disseratur putant. Philo autem dum nova quaedam commovet quod ea sustinere vix poterat quae contra Academicorum pertinaciam dicebantur, et aperte mentitur, ut est reprehensus a patre Catulo, et, ut docuit Antiochus, in id ipsum se induit quod timebat. Cum enim ita negaret quidquam esse quod comprehendi posset (id enim volumus esse ἀκατάληπτον[1]), si illud esset, sicut Zeno definiret, tale visum (iam enim hoc pro φαντασίᾳ verbum satis hesterno sermone trivimus), visum igitur impressum effictumque ex eo unde esset quale esse non posset ex eo unde non esset (id nos a Zenone definitum rectissime dicimus, qui enim potest quidquam comprehendi ut plane confidas perceptum id cognitumque esse, quod est tale quale vel falsum esse possit?)—hoc cum infirmat tollitque Philo, iudicium tollit incogniti et cogniti; ex quo efficitur nihil posse comprehendi—ita imprudens eo quo minime volt revolvitur. Quare omnis oratio contra Academiam ita[2] suscipitur a nobis ut retineamus eam

[1] καταληπτόν *edd. nonnulli.*
[2] ita *inseruit ed.*

selves, and they think that any fact is a suitable matter for investigation and that human beings deserve to have their views discussed. But Philo, in raising certain revolutionary doctrines because he was scarcely able to withstand the usual arguments against the obstinacy of the Academics, manifestly propounds what is not true, as he was blamed for doing by the elder Catulus, and also, as Antiochus proved, himself slipped into the very position that he was afraid of. For when he thus maintained that there was nothing that could be grasped (that is the expression that we choose in rendering *acatalēpton* [a]), if that 'presentation' of which he spoke (for we have by this time sufficiently habituated ourselves by our yesterday's conversation to this rendering of *phantasia*) was, as Zeno defined it, a presentation impressed and moulded from the object from which it came in a form such as it could not have if it came from an object that was not the one that it actually did come from (we declare that this definition of Zeno's is absolutely correct, for how can anything be grasped in such a way as to make you absolutely confident that it has been perceived and known, if it has a form that could belong to it even if it were false?)—when Philo weakens and abolishes this, he abolishes the criterion between the unknowable and the knowable; which leads to the inference that nothing can be grasped—so incautiously does he come round to the position that he most wants to avoid. Therefore the whole defence of the case against the Academy is undertaken by us on the line of preserving the process of defini-

[a] To be accurately expressed, the sense requires the positive *catalēpton.*

definitionem quam Philo voluit evertere; quam nisi obtinemus, percipi nihil posse concedimus.

19 VII. "Ordiamur igitur a sensibus, quorum ita clara iudicia et certa sunt ut si optio naturae nostrae detur et ab ea deus aliqui requirat contentane sit suis integris incorruptisque sensibus an postulet melius aliquid, non videam quid quaerat amplius. Nec vero hoc loco exspectandum est dum de remo inflexo aut de collo columbae respondeam, non enim is sum qui quidquid videtur tale dicam esse quale videatur. Epicurus hoc viderit, et alia multa; meo autem iudicio ita est maxima in sensibus veritas, si et sani sunt ac valentes et omnia removentur quae obstant et impediunt. Itaque et lumen mutari saepe volumus et situs earum rerum quas intuemur et intervalla aut contrahimus aut diducimus multaque facimus usque eo dum aspectus ipse fidem faciat sui iudici. Quod idem fit in vocibus, in odore, in sapore, ut nemo sit nostrum qui in sensibus sui cuiusque

20 generis iudicium requirat acrius. Adhibita vero exercitatione et arte, ut oculi pictura teneantur, aures cantibus,[1] quis est quin cernat quanta vis sit in sensibus? Quam multa vident pictores in umbris et in eminentia quae nos non videmus! quam multa quae nos fugiunt in cantu exaudiunt in eo genere exercitati, qui primo inflatu tibicinis Antiopam esse

[1] ut . . . cantibus *secl. Davies.*

[a] *i.e.*, an oar half in the water, as seen from the boat; this case of refraction and the changing colours of a pigeon's neck were instances of apparent deception of the senses much used by the Sceptics; *cf.* § 79.

tion which Philo wished to overthrow; and unless we succeed in upholding it, we admit that nothing can be perceived.

(2) Scepticism leads to inaction and to ignorance; the senses give material for knowledge and science.

VII. "Let us begin therefore from the senses, whose verdicts are so clear and certain that if human nature were given the choice, and were interrogated by some god as to whether it was content with its own senses in a sound and undamaged state or demanded something better, I cannot see what more it could ask for. Nor indeed is it necessary to delay at this point while I answer about the case of the bent oar [a] or the pigeon's neck, for I am not one to assert that every object seen is really such as it appears to be. Let Epicurus see to that, and a number of other matters; but in my judgement the senses contain the highest truth, given that they are sound and healthy and also that all obstacles and hindrances are removed. That is why we often desire a change of the light and of the position of the objects that we are observing, and diminish or enlarge their distances from us, and take various measures, until mere looking makes us trust the judgement that it forms. The same is done in the case of sounds and smell and taste, so that among us there is nobody who desiderates keener powers of judgement in the senses, each in its class. But when we add practice and artistic training, to make our eyes sensitive to painting and our ears to music, who is there who can fail to remark the power that the senses possess? How many things painters see in shadows and in the foreground which we do not see! how many things in music that escape us are caught by the hearing of persons trained in that department of art, who when the flute-player blows his first note say 'That is

aiunt aut Andromacham, cum id nos ne suspicemur quidem! Nihil necesse est de gustatu et odoratu loqui, in quibus intellegentia, etsi vitiosa, est quaedam tamen. Quid de tactu, et eo quidem quem philosophi interiorem vocant, aut doloris aut voluptatis, in quo Cyrenaici solo putant veri esse iudicium quia sentiatur? Potestne igitur quisquam dicere inter eum qui doleat et inter eum qui in voluptate sit nihil interesse, aut ita qui sentiat non apertissime
21 insaniat? Atqui qualia sunt haec quae sensibus percipi dicimus, talia secuntur ea quae non sensibus ipsis percipi dicuntur sed quodam modo sensibus, ut haec: 'Illud est album, hoc dulce, canorum illud, hoc bene olens, hoc asperum.' Animo iam haec tenemus comprehensa, non sensibus. 'Ille' deinceps 'equus est, ille canis.' Cetera series deinde sequitur, maiora nectens, ut haec, quae quasi expletam rerum comprehensionem amplectuntur: 'Si homo est, animal est mortale, rationis particeps.' Quo e genere nobis notitiae rerum imprimuntur, sine quibus nec intellegi quidquam nec quaeri disputarive potest.
22 Quodsi essent falsae notitiae (ἐννοίας enim notitias appellare tu videbare)—si igitur essent hae falsae aut eius modi visis impressae qualia visa a falsis discerni

---

[a] Plays of Pacuvius and Ennius respectively.
[b] *i.e.*, in the dialogue of the day before, in the lost first edition of Book I.

Antiope' or '*Andromache*,'[a] when we have not even a suspicion of it! It is unnecessary to talk at all about the faculties of taste and smell, which possess a certain discernment, although it is of a defective sort. Why speak of touch, and indeed of the internal tactual sense, as the philosophers call it, perceptive of either pain or pleasure, the sole basis, as the Cyrenaics think, of our judgement of truth, caused by the mere process of sensation? Is it therefore possible for anybody to say that there is no difference between a person experiencing pain and a person experiencing pleasure, or would not the
21 holder of this opinion be a manifest lunatic? But then whatever character belongs to these objects which we say are perceived by the senses must belong to that following set of objects which are said to be perceived not by actual sensation but by a sort of sensation, as for example: 'Yonder thing is white, this thing is sweet, that one is melodious, this fragrant, this rough.' This class of percepts consists of comprehensions grasped by our mind, not by our senses. Then 'Yonder object is a horse, yonder a dog.' Next follows the rest of the series linking on a chain of larger percepts, for instance the following, which embrace as it were a fully completed grasp of the objects: 'If it is a human being, it is a rational mortal animal.' From this class of percept are imprinted upon us our notions of things, without which all understanding and all investigation and dis-
22 cussion are impossible. But if false notions existed (I understood you to employ[b] 'notions' to render *ennoiai*)—well, if there were these false notions or notions imprinted on the mind by appearances of a kind that could not be distinguished from false ones,

non possent, quo tandem iis modo uteremur? quo modo autem quid cuique rei consentaneum esset, quid repugnaret, videremus? Memoriae quidem certe, quae non modo philosophiam sed omnem vitae usum omnesque artes una maxime continet, nihil omnino loci relinquitur. Quae potest enim esse memoria falsorum? aut quid quisquam meminit quod non animo comprehendit et tenet? ars vero quae potest esse nisi quae non ex una aut duabus sed ex multis animi perceptionibus constat? Quam[1] si subtraxeris, qui distingues artificem ab inscio? non enim fortuito hunc artificem dicemus esse, illum negabimus, sed cum alterum percepta et comprehensa tenere videmus, alterum non item. Cumque artium aliud eius modi genus sit ut tantum modo animo rem cernat, aliud ut moliatur aliquid et faciat, quo modo aut geometres cernere ea potest quae aut nulla sunt aut internosci a falsis non possunt, aut is qui fidibus utitur explere numeros et conficere versus? quod idem in similibus quoque artibus continget quarum omne opus est in faciendo atque agendo, quid enim est quod arte effici possit, nisi is qui artem tractabit multa perceperit?

23 VIII. "Maxime vero virtutum cognitio confirmat percipi et comprehendi multa posse. In quibus solis inesse etiam scientiam dicimus (quam nos non comprehensionem modo rerum sed eam stabilem quoque et immutabilem esse censemus), itemque sapientiam,

[1] quas *Walker.*

---

[a] *Artifex* denotes the pursuer of an *ars*, an organized body of knowledge, a science, whether theoretical or applied in practice. It includes here the musician (also regarded as a poet), but the practice of music seems to be envisaged as

how pray could we act on them ? how moreover could we see what is consistent with any given fact and what inconsistent ? At all events no place at all is left for memory, the one principal foundation not only of philosophy but of all the conduct of life and all the sciences. For how can there possibly be a memory of what is false ? or what can anyone remember that he does not grasp and hold in his mind ? But what science can there be that is not made up of not one nor two but many mental percepts ? And if you take away science, how will you distinguish between the craftsman[a] and the ignoramus ? for we shall not pronounce one man to be a craftsman, and the other not, just casually, but when we see the one retain what he has perceived and grasped, and the other not. And as one class of sciences is of such a nature as only to envisage facts mentally, and another such as to do or to make something, how can the geometrician envisage things that are either non-existent or indistinguishable from fictitious things, or the player on the harp round off his rhythms and complete his verses ? and the same result will also occur in the other crafts of the same class which are solely exercised in making and doing, for what can be effected by a craft unless its intending practitioner has accumulated many percepts ?

True perception is indispensable for moral conduct and rational knowledge,

VIII. "The greatest proof however of our capacity to perceive and grasp many things is afforded by the study of Ethics. Our percepts alone we actually pronounce to form the basis of knowledge (which in our view is not only a grasp of facts but a grasp that is also permanent and unchangeable), and likewise

based on knowledge of its theory. At § 142 the craftsmen instanced are a painter and two sculptors.

artem vivendi, quae ipsa ex sese habeat constantiam. Ea autem constantia si nihil habeat percepti et cogniti, quaero unde nata sit aut quo modo. Quaero etiam, ille vir bonus qui statuit omnem cruciatum perferre, intolerabili dolore lacerari potius quam aut officium prodat aut fidem, cur has sibi tam graves leges imposuerit cum quam ob rem ita oporteret nihil haberet comprehensi, percepti, cogniti, constituti. Nullo igitur modo fieri potest ut quisquam tanti aestimet aequitatem et fidem ut eius conservandae causa nullum supplicium recuset, nisi iis rebus ad-
24 sensus sit quae falsae esse non possint. Ipsa vero sapientia si se ignorabit sapientia sit necne, quo modo primum obtinebit nomen sapientiae? deinde quo modo suscipere aliquam rem aut agere fidenter audebit cum certi nihil erit quod sequatur? cum vero dubitabit quid sit extremum et ultimum bonorum ignorans quo omnia referantur, qui poterit esse sapientia? Atque etiam illud perspicuum est, constitui necesse esse initium quod sapientia cum quid agere incipiat sequatur, idque initium esse naturae accommodatum. Nam aliter adpetitio (eam enim volumus esse ὁρμήν), qua ad agendum impellimur et id adpetimus quod est visum, moveri non potest;
25 illud autem quod movet prius oportet videri, eique credi, quod fieri non potest si id quod visum erit

of wisdom, the science of living, which is its own source of consistency. But if this consistency had nothing that it grasped and knew, whence, I ask, or how would it be engendered? consider also the ideal good man, who has resolved to endure all torments and to be mangled by intolerable pain rather than betray either his duty or his promise—why, I ask, has he saddled himself with such burdensome rules as this when he had no grasp or perception or knowledge or certainty of any fact that furnished a reason why it was his duty to do so? It is therefore absolutely impossible that anybody should set so high a value upon equity and good faith as to refuse no torture for the sake of preserving it, unless he has given his assent to things that cannot possibly be
24 false. As for wisdom herself, if she does not know whether she is wisdom or not, how in the first place will she make good her claim to the name of wisdom? next, how will she venture with confidence to plan or execute any undertaking when there will be nothing certain for her to act upon? indeed, when she will be hesitating in ignorance of what the final and ultimate good to which all things are to be referred really is, how can she possibly be wisdom? This other point moreover is manifest: there must be a first principle established for wisdom to follow when she embarks on any action, and this first principle must be consistent with nature; for otherwise appetition (our chosen equivalent for the term *hormē*), by which we are impelled to action and seek to get an object
25 presented to our vision, cannot be set in motion; but the thing that sets it in motion must first of all be seen, and must be believed in, which cannot take place if an object seen will be indistinguishable from

discerni non poterit a falso ; quo modo autem moveri animus ad adpetendum potest si id quod videtur non percipitur accommodatumne naturae sit an alienum ? Itemque si quid officii sui sit non occurrit animo, nihil umquam omnino aget, ad nullam rem umquam impelletur, numquam movebitur ; quodsi aliquid aliquando acturus est, necesse est id ei verum quod
26 occurrit videri. Quid quod, si ista vera sunt, ratio omnis tollitur quasi quaedam lux lumenque vitae ? tamenne in ista pravitate perstabitis ? Nam quaerendi initium ratio attulit, quae[1] perfecit virtutem cum esset ipsa ratio confirmata quaerendo ; quaestio autem est adpetitio cognitionis, quaestionisque finis inventio ; at nemo invenit falsa, nec ea quae incerta permanent inventa esse possunt, sed cum ea quae quasi involuta fuerunt aperta sunt, tum inventa dicuntur—sic et initium quaerendi et exitus percipiundi et comprendendi tenetur. Argumenti conclusio, quae est Graece ἀπόδειξις, ita definitur : 'ratio quae ex rebus perceptis ad id quod non percipiebatur adducit.'

27 IX. " Quodsi omnia visa eius modi essent qualia isti dicunt, ut ea vel falsa esse possent neque ea posset ulla notio discernere, quo modo quemquam aut conclusisse aliquid aut invenisse diceremus, aut quae esset conclusi argumenti fides ? Ipsa autem philosophia, quae rationibus progredi debet, quem

[1] quod (=quaerendum, quaestio) ? *ed.*

---

[a] Cicero seems to be translating some such phrase as φῶς καὶ φέγγος τοῦ βίου.

[b] The sense seems to require 'research which': for *virtus*, or its Stoic equivalent *sapientia*, as *ratio perfecta* cf. i. 20, ii. 30 *fin.*

[c] *Involuta aperire* is a translation of ἐκκαλύπτειν, denoting

a false one; but how can the mind be moved to appetition if it does not perceive whether the object seen is consistent with nature or foreign to it? And moreover if it has not struck the mind what its function is, it will never do anything at all, never be driven towards any object, never make a movement; whereas if it is at some time to do something, what strikes it must seem to it to be true. What about the total abolition of reason, 'life's dayspring and source of light,'[a] that must take place if your doctrines are true? will your school continue steadfast in such perversity all the same? For it is reason that initiated research, reason[b] which has perfected virtue, since reason herself is strengthened by pursuing research; but research is the appetition for knowledge, and the aim of research is discovery; yet nobody discovers what is false, and things that remain continually uncertain cannot be discovered: discovery means the 'opening up of things previously veiled'[c]—this is how the mind holds both the commencement of research and the final act of perceiving and grasping. Therefore this is the definition of logical proof, in Greek *apodeixis*: 'a process of reasoning that leads from things perceived to something not previously perceived.'

IX. "In fact if all sense-presentations were of such a kind as your school say they are, so that they could possibly be false without any mental process being able to distinguish them, how could we say that anybody had proved or discovered anything, or what trust could we put in logical proof? Philosophy herself must advance by argument—how will she find a

and for philosophy, which Carneades entirely undermined.

a process of argument; the conclusion is seen to be contained in the premisses.

habebit exitum? Sapientiae vero quid futurum est? quae neque de se ipsa dubitare debet neque de suis decretis quae philosophi vocant δόγματα, quorum nullum sine scelere prodi poterit; cum enim decretum proditur, lex veri rectique proditur, quo e vitio et amicitiarum proditiones et rerum publicarum nasci solent. Non potest igitur dubitari quin decretum nullum falsum possit esse sapientis, neque satis sit non esse falsum sed etiam stabile, fixum, ratum esse debeat, quod movere nulla ratio queat; talia autem neque esse neque videri possunt eorum ratione qui illa visa e quibus omnia decreta sunt nata negant
28 quicquam a falsis interesse. Ex hoc illud est natum quod postulabat Hortensius, ut id ipsum saltem perceptum a sapiente diceretis, nihil posse percipi. Sed Antipatro hoc idem postulanti, cum diceret ei qui adfirmaret nihil posse percipi unum tamen illud dicere percipi posse consentaneum esse, ut alia non possent, Carneades acutius resistebat; nam tantum abesse dicebat ut id consentaneum esset, ut maxime etiam repugnaret: qui enim negaret quicquam esse quod perciperetur, eum nihil excipere; ita necesse esse ne id ipsum quidem, quod exceptum non esset,
29 comprendi et percipi ullo modo posse. Antiochus ad istum locum pressius videbatur accedere: quoniam enim id haberent Academici decretum (sentitis enim iam hoc me δόγμα dicere), nihil posse percipi, non debere eos in suo decreto sicut in ceteris rebus

[a] ἀσφαλῆ καὶ ἀμετάπτωτον ὑπὸ λόγου Sextus, *A.M.* vii. 151.

way out? And what will happen to Wisdom? it is her duty not to doubt herself or her 'decisions,' which philosophers term *dogmata*, any of which it will be a crime to abandon; for the surrender of such a 'decision' is the betrayal of the moral law, and that sin is the common source of betrayals of friends and country. Therefore it cannot be doubted that no 'decision' of a wise man can be false, and that it is not sufficient for them not to be false but they must also be firmly settled and ratified, immovable by any argument[a]; but such a character cannot belong or seem to belong to them on the theory of those who maintain that the sense-presentations from which all decisions spring differ in no way from false presentations. From this sprang the demand put forward by Hortensius, that your school should say that the wise man has perceived at least the mere fact that nothing can be perceived. But when Antipater used to make the same demand, and to say that one who asserted that nothing could be perceived might yet consistently say that this single fact could be perceived, namely that nothing else could, Carneades with greater acumen used to oppose him; he used to declare that this was so far from being consistent that it was actually grossly inconsistent: for the man who said there was nothing that was perceived made no exception, and so not even the impossibility of perception could itself be grasped and perceived in any way, because it had not been excepted. Antiochus used to seem to come more closely to grips with this position; he argued that because the Academics held it as a 'decision' (for you realize by now that I use that term to translate *dogma*) that nothing could be perceived, they were bound not to

fluctuare, praesertim cum in eo summa consisteret, hanc enim esse regulam totius philosophiae, constitutionem veri falsi, cogniti incogniti; quam rationem quoniam susciperent, docereque vellent quae visa accipi oporteret, quae repudiari, certe hoc ipsum ex quo omne veri falsique iudicium esset percipere eos debuisse; etenim duo esse haec maxima in philosophia, iudicium veri et finem bonorum, nec sapientem posse esse qui aut cognoscendi esse initium ignoret aut extremum expetendi, ut aut unde proficiscatur aut quo perveniendum sit nesciat; haec autem habere dubia nec iis ita confidere ut moveri non possint[1] abhorrere a sapientia plurimum.[2] Hoc igitur modo potius erat ab his postulandum ut hoc unum saltem, percipi nihil posse, perceptum esse dicerent. Sed de inconstantia totius illorum sententiae, si ulla sententia cuiusquam esse potest nihil adprobantis, sit ut[3] opinor dictum satis.

30 X. "Sequitur disputatio copiosa illa quidem sed paulo abstrusior—habet enim aliquantum a physicis,—ut verear ne maiorem largiar ei qui contra dicturus est libertatem et licentiam, nam quid eum facturum putem de abditis rebus et obscuris qui lucem eripere conetur? Sed disputari poterat subtiliter quanto

[1] possit *? ed.*
[2] <quam> plurimum *? ed.*
[3] sit ut: est *Ernesti.*

[a] *i.e.*, in Antiochus's *Sosus*, see § 12. *Cf.* § 38.
[b] For this reproach against the Sceptics *cf.* §§ 38, 61, 109.
[c] *Cf.* i. 19.

waver in their own 'decision' as they did in everything else, particularly when it was the keystone of their system, for this was the measuring-rod that applied to the whole of philosophy, the test of truth and falsehood, of knowledge and ignorance; and that since they adopted this method, and desired to teach what sense-presentations ought to be accepted and what rejected, they unquestionably ought to have perceived this decision itself, the basis of every criterion of truth and falsehood; for (he said) the two greatest things in philosophy were the criterion of truth and the end of goods, and no man could be a sage who was ignorant of the existence of either a beginning of the process of knowledge or an end of appetition, and who consequently did not know from what he was starting or at what he ought to arrive; but to be in doubt as to these matters and not to feel immovably sure of them was to be very widely remote from wisdom. On these lines therefore they ought to have been required rather to say that this one thing at least was perceived—the impossibility of perceiving anything. But about the inconsistency of the whole of their theory, if anybody holding no positive view at all can be said to have any theory, enough, as I think, may have been said.

(3) The argument from psychology: knowledge, derived from sensation, is the basis of virtue.

X. "Next comes [a] a discussion which though very fully developed is a little more recondite, for it contains a certain amount of matter derived from natural philosophy; so that I am afraid that I may be bestowing greater liberty and even licence upon the speaker who is to oppose me, for what can I suppose that one who is endeavouring to rob us of light [b] will do about matters that are hidden in darkness? [c] Still, it would have been possible to discuss in minute detail

quasi artificio natura fabricata esset primum animal omne, deinde hominem maxime, quae vis esset in sensibus, quem ad modum primo visa nos pellerent, deinde adpetitio ab his pulsa sequeretur, tum[1] sensus ad res percipiendas intenderemus. Mens enim ipsa, quae sensuum fons est atque etiam ipsa[2] sensus est, naturalem vim habet quam intendit ad ea quibus movetur. Itaque alia visa sic arripit ut iis statim utatur, alia quasi recondit, e quibus memoria oritur, cetera autem similitudinibus construit, ex quibus efficiuntur notitiae rerum, quas Graeci tum ἐννοίας, tum προλήψεις vocant. Eo cum accessit ratio argumentique conclusio rerumque innumerabilium multitudo, tum et perceptio eorum omnium apparet et eadem ratio perfecta his gradibus ad sapientiam per-
31 venit. Ad rerum igitur scientiam vitaeque constantiam aptissima cum sit mens hominis, amplectitur maxime cognitionem et istam κατάληψιν, quam ut dixi verbum e verbo exprimentes comprensionem dicemus, cum ipsam per se amat (nihil enim est ei veritatis luce dulcius), tum etiam propter usum. Quocirca et sensibus utitur et artes efficit quasi sensus alteros et usque eo philosophiam ipsam corroborat ut virtutem efficiat, ex qua re una vita omnis apta sit.[3] Ergo ii qui negant quicquam posse comprendi

[1] tum *ed.*: tum ut *codd.*
[2] ipse *Ernesti.*
[3] est *Halm.*

[a] *Adpetitio* is Cicero's version of ὁρμή, see § 24 n.

the amount of craftsmanship that nature has employed in the construction first of every animal, then most of all in man,—the power possessed by the senses, the way in which we are first struck by the sense-presentations, next follows appetition[a] imparted by their impact, and then we direct the senses to perceive the objects. For the mind itself, which is the source of the sensations and even is itself sensation, has a natural force which it directs to the things by which it is moved. Accordingly some sense-presentations it seizes on so as to make use of them at once, others it as it were stores away, these being the source of memory, while all the rest it unites into systems by their mutual resemblances, and from these are formed the concepts of objects which the Greeks term sometimes *ennoiai* and sometimes *prolēpseis*. When thereto there has been added reason and logical proof and an innumerable multitude of facts, then comes the clear perception of all these things, and also this same reason having been by these stages made com-
1 plete finally attains to wisdom. Since therefore the mind of man is supremely well adapted for the knowledge of things and for consistency of life, it embraces information very readily, and your *catalēpsis*, which as I said we will express by a literal translation as 'grasp,' is loved by the mind both for itself (for nothing is dearer to the mind than the light of truth) and also for the sake of its utility. Hence the mind employs the senses, and also creates the sciences as a second set of senses, and strengthens the structure of philosophy itself to the point where it may produce virtue, the sole source of the ordering of the whole of life. Therefore those who assert that nothing can be grasped deprive us of these things that are the very

haec ipsa eripiunt vel instrumenta vel ornamenta vitae, vel potius etiam totam vitam evertunt funditus ipsumque animal orbant animo, ut difficile sit de temeritate eorum perinde ut causa postulat dicere.

32 "Nec vero satis constituere possum quod sit eorum consilium aut quid velint. Interdum enim cum adhibemus ad eos orationem eius modi, si ea quae disputentur vera sint, tum omnia fore incerta, respondent: 'Quid ergo istud ad nos? num nostra culpa est? naturam accusa, quae in profundo veritatem, ut ait Democritus, penitus abstruserit.' Alii autem elegantius, qui etiam queruntur quod eos insimulemus omnia incerta dicere, quantumque intersit inter incertum et id quod percipi non possit docere conantur eaque distinguere. Cum his igitur agamus qui haec distinguunt, illos qui omnia sic incerta dicunt ut stellarum numerus par an impar sit quasi desperatos aliquos relinquamus. Volunt enim (et hoc quidem vel maxime vos animadvertebam moveri) probabile aliquid esse et quasi veri simile, eaque se uti regula et in agenda vita et in quaerendo ac disserendo.

33 XI. "Quae ista regula est veri et falsi, si notionem veri et falsi, propterea quod ea non possunt internosci, nullam habemus? Nam si habemus, interesse oportet ut inter rectum et pravum sic inter verum et falsum: si nihil interest, nulla regula est, nec potest is cui est visio veri falsique communis ullum

---

[a] The favourite charge of the Sceptics against the dogmatic schools.

[b] *Cf.* i. 44 n.

[c] Doubtless a reference to the exposition of Catulus at the beginning of the lost Book I. of the first edition.

[d] *Quasi* marks *veri simile* as an explanation of *probabile* used to translate *πιθανόν*.

tools or equipment of life, or rather actually overthrow the whole of life from its foundations and deprive the animate creature itself of the mind that animates it, so that it is difficult to speak of their rashness [a] entirely as the case requires.

2 "Nor indeed can I fully decide what their plan is or what they mean. For sometimes when we address them in this sort of language, 'If your contentions are true, then everything will be uncertain,' they reply, 'Well, what has that to do with us? surely it is not our fault; blame nature for having hidden truth quite away, in an abyss, as Democritus says.' [b] But others make a more elaborate answer, and actually complain because we charge them with saying that everything is uncertain, and they try to explain the difference between what is uncertain and what cannot be grasped, and to distinguish between them. Let us therefore deal with those who make this distinction, and leave on one side as a hopeless sort of persons the others who say that all things are as uncertain as whether the number of the stars is odd or even. For they hold (and this in fact, I noticed,[c] excites your school extremely) that something is 'probable,' or as it were [d] resembling the truth, and that this provides them with a canon of judgement both in the conduct of life and in philosophical investigation and discussion.

A distinction without a difference.

3 XI. "What is this canon of truth and falsehood, if we have no notion of truth and falsehood, for the reason that they are indistinguishable? For if we have a notion of them, there must be a difference between true and false, just as there is between right and wrong; if there is none, there is no canon, and the man who has a presentation of the true and the

If the true is indistinguishable from the false, 'evidence' is destroyed.

habere iudicium aut ullam omnino veritatis notam. Nam cum dicunt hoc se unum tollere ut quicquam possit ita[1] videri ut non eodem modo falsum etiam possit[2] videri, cetera autem concedere, faciunt pueriliter. Quo enim omnia iudicantur sublato reliqua se negant tollere : ut si quis quem oculis privaverit, dicat ea quae cerni possent se ei non ademisse. Ut enim illa oculis modo agnoscuntur, sic reliqua visis, sed propria veri, non communi veri et falsi nota. Quam ob rem sive tu probabilem[3] visionem sive probabilem et quae non impediatur, ut Carneades volebat, sive aliud quid proferes quod sequare, ad visum
34 illud de quo agimus tibi erit revertendum. In eo autem, si[4] erit communitas cum falso, nullum erit iudicium, quia proprium[5] communi signo notari non potest ; sin autem commune nihil erit, habeo quod volo, id enim quaero quod ita mihi videatur verum ut non possit item falsum videri. Simili in errore versantur cum convicio veritatis coacti perspicua a perceptis volunt distinguere, et conantur ostendere esse

[1] ita <verum> *Baiter.*
[2] possit *Lambinus* : possit ita *codd.*
[3] *Faber* : improbabilem *codd.*
[4] si <ei> *? Reid.*
[5] proprium *Halm* : proprium in *codd.*

---

[a] κοινὴ φαντασία τοῦ τε ἀληθοῦς καὶ ψεύδους, Sextus.

[b] Perhaps we should emend 'any true thing,' *cf.* § 34. The clause refers to the possibility that an hallucination, a visual image not corresponding to a real object, may exactly resemble a visual image presented by a real object.

[c] φαντασία πιθανὴ καὶ ἀπερίσπαστος, a sensation which (1) at first sight, without further inquiry, seems true, and also (2) when examined in relation to all the other sensations

false that is common to both[a] cannot have any criterion or any mark of truth at all. For when they say that they only remove the possibility of anything[b] presenting an appearance of such a sort that a false thing could not present the same appearance, but that they allow everything else, they act childishly. Having abolished the means by which all things are judged, they say they do not abolish the remaining sources of knowledge; just as if anybody were to say that when he has deprived a man of his eyes he has not taken away from that man the possible objects of sight. For just as the objects of sight are recognized only by means of the eyes, so everything else is recognized by means of sense-presentations; but they are recognized by a mark that belongs specially to what is true, and is not common to the true and the false. Therefore if you bring forward 'probable presentation,' or 'probable and unhampered presentation,'[c] as Carneades held, or something else, as a guide for you to follow, you will have to come back to the sense-presentation that we
34 are dealing with. But if this has community with a false presentation, it will contain no standard of judgement, because a special property cannot be indicated by a common mark; while if on the contrary there is nothing in common between them, I have got what I want, for I am looking for a thing that may appear to me so true that it could not appear to me in the same way if it were false. They are involved in the same mistake when under stress of truth's upbraiding they desire to distinguish between things perceived and things perspicuous, and try to prove that there is such a thing as something perspicuous which although

received at the same time (which might turn one's attention away from it, περισπᾶν) is found to be consistent with them.

aliquid perspicui, verum illud quidem impressum in
animo atque mente, neque tamen id percipi atque
comprendi posse. Quo enim modo perspicue dixeris
album esse aliquid cum possit accidere ut id quod
nigrum sit album esse videatur, aut quo modo ista
aut perspicua dicemus aut impressa subtiliter cum
sit incertum vere inaniterne moveatur? Ita neque
color neque corpus nec veritas nec argumentum nec
35 sensus neque perspicuum ullum relinquitur. Ex hoc
illud iis usu venire solet ut quicquid dixerint a quibusdam interrogentur: 'Ergo istuc quidem percipis?'
Sed qui ita interrogant, ab iis irridentur; non enim
urguent ut coarguant neminem ulla de re posse contendere nec adseverare sine aliqua eius rei quam sibi
quisque placere dicit certa et propria nota. Quod
est igitur istuc vestrum probabile? Nam si quod
cuique occurrit et primo quasi aspectu probabile
36 videtur id confirmatur, quid eo levius? Sin ex cir-
cumspectione aliqua et accurata consideratione quod
visum sit id se dicent sequi, tamen exitum non habebunt, primum quia iis visis inter quae nihil interest
aequaliter omnibus abrogatur fides; deinde, cum
dicant posse accidere sapienti ut cum omnia fecerit
diligentissimeque circumspexerit exsistat aliquid
quod et veri simile videatur et absit longissime
a vero, ne si[1] magnam partem quidem, ut solent

[1] ne si *Mdv.*: si *codd.*

a true imprint on the mind and intellect is nevertheless incapable of being perceived and grasped. For how can you maintain that something is perspicuously white if it can possibly occur that a thing that is black may appear white, or how shall we pronounce the things in question either perspicuous or accurately imprinted if it is uncertain whether the mental experience is true or unfounded? In this way neither colour nor solidity nor truth nor argument nor sensation nor anything perspicuous is left. This is why it is their usual experience that, whatever they say, some people ask them 'Then anyway you do perceive that, do you?' But they laugh at those who put this question; for their effort is not aimed at proving that it cannot ever happen that a man may make a positive assertion about a thing without there being some definite and peculiar mark attached to the thing that he in particular professes to accept. What then is the probability that your school talk about? For if what a particular person happens to encounter, and almost at first glance thinks probable, is accepted as certain, what could be more frivolous than that? While if they assert that they follow a sense-presentation after some circumspection and careful consideration, nevertheless they will not find a way out, first because presentations that have no difference between them are all of them equally refused credence; secondly, when they say that it can happen to the wise man that after he has taken every precaution and explored the position most carefully something may yet arise that while appearing to resemble truth is really very far remote from truth, they will be unable to trust themselves, even if they advance at all events a large part of the way,

'Probability' is useless guess-work.

dicere, ad verum ipsum aut quam proxime accedant, confidere sibi poterunt. Ut enim confidant, notum iis esse debebit insigne veri, quo obscurato[1] et oppresso quod tandem verum sibi videbuntur attingere? Quid autem tam absurde dici potest quam cum ita loquuntur, 'Est hoc quidem illius rei signum aut argumentum, et ea re id sequor, sed fieri potest ut id quod significatur aut falsum sit aut nihil sit omnino'? Sed de perceptione hactenus; si quis enim ea quae dicta sunt labefactare volet, facile etiam absentibus nobis veritas se ipsa defendet.

37 XII. "His satis cognitis quae iam explicata sunt, nunc de adsensione atque adprobatione, quam Graeci συγκατάθεσιν vocant, pauca dicemus—non quo non latus locus sit, sed paulo ante iacta sunt fundamenta. Nam cum vim quae esset in sensibus explicabamus, simul illud aperiebatur, comprendi multa et percipi sensibus, quod fieri sine adsensione non potest. Deinde cum inter inanimum et animal hoc maxime intersit quod animal agit aliquid (nihil enim agens ne cogitari quidem potest quale sit), aut ei sensus adimendus est aut ea quae est in nostra potestate sita

38 reddenda adsensio. At vero animus quodam modo eripitur iis quos neque sentire neque adsentiri volunt; ut enim necesse est lancem in libra[2] ponderibus im-

[1] *Lambinus*: obscuro *codd.*
[2] libram *codd. nonnulli.*

[a] *i.e.*, different from what it seems.
[b] *i.e.*, the mental acceptance of a sensation as truly representing the object; *cf.* i. 40. [c] § 20.

as they are in the habit of saying, towards the actual truth, or indeed come as near to it as possible. For to enable them to trust their judgement, it will be necessary for the characteristic mark of truth to be known to them, and if this be obscured and suppressed, what truth pray will they suppose that they attain to? What language moreover could be more absurd than their formula, 'It is true that this is a token or a proof of yonder object, and therefore I follow it, but it is possible that the object that it indicates may be either false [a] or entirely non-existent'? But enough on the subject of perception; for if anybody desires to upset the doctrines stated, truth will easily conduct her own defence, even if we decline the brief.

37 XII. "Now that we are sufficiently acquainted with the matters already unfolded, let us say a few words on the subject of 'assent' [b] or approval (termed in Greek *syncatathesis*)—not that it is not a wide topic, but the foundations have been laid a little time back. For while we were explaining [c] the power residing in the senses, it was at the same time disclosed that many things are grasped and perceived by the senses, which cannot happen without the act of assent. Again, as the greatest difference between an inanimate and an animate object is that an animate object performs some action (for an entirely inactive animal is an utterly inconceivable thing), either it must be denied the possession of sensation or it must be assigned a faculty of assenting as a

(4) Certainty is needed for action: assent to phenomena underlies all rational conduct.

38 voluntary act. But on the other hand persons who refuse to exercise either sensation or assent are in a manner robbed of the mind itself; for as the scale of a balance must necessarily sink when weights are put in it, so the mind must necessarily yield to clear

positis deprimi, sic animum perspicuis cedere: nam quo modo non potest animal ullum non adpetere id quod accommodatum ad naturam adpareat (Graeci id οἰκεῖον appellant), sic non potest obiectam rem perspicuam non adprobare. Quamquam, si illa de quibus disputatum est vera sunt, nihil attinet de adsensione omnino loqui; qui enim quid percipit adsentitur statim. Sed haec etiam sequuntur, nec memoriam sine adsensione posse constare nec notitias rerum nec artes; idque quod maximum est, ut sit aliquid in nostra potestate, in eo qui rei nulli adsentietur non erit: ubi igitur virtus, si nihil situm est in ipsis
39 nobis? Maxime autem absurdum vitia in ipsorum esse potestate neque peccare quemquam nisi adsensione, hoc idem in virtute non esse, cuius omnis constantia et firmitas ex iis rebus constat quibus adsensa est et quas adprobavit. Omninoque ante videri aliquid quam agamus necesse est eique quod visum sit adsentiatur.[1] Quare qui aut visum aut adsensum tollit, is omnem actionem tollit e vita.

40 XIII. "Nunc ea videamus quae contra ab his disputari solent. Sed prius potestis totius eorum rationis quasi fundamenta cognoscere. Componunt igitur primum artem quandam de iis quae visa dicimus, eorumque et vim et genera definiunt, in his quale sit id quod percipi et comprendi possit, totidem verbis quot Stoici. Deinde illa exponunt duo quae

[1] adsentiamur *Davies*: adsentiri *Lambinus*.

[a] See § 30 n. [b] See i. 32 n.

[c] *Quasi* marks a tentative rendering of θεμέλιοι as does *quandam* just below one of τέχνη φαντασιῶν; and apparently also *quasi contineant* renders some other Greek technical term, perhaps συνέχειν; *cf.* §§ 20, 107.

[d] *Id . . . possit* = τὸ καταληπτόν.

presentations: since just as no animal can refrain from seeking to get a thing that is presented to its view as suited to its nature (the Greeks term it *oikeion*), so the mind cannot refrain from giving approval to a clear object when presented to it. Nevertheless, assuming the truth of the positions discussed, all talk whatever about assent is beside the mark; for he who perceives anything assents immediately. But there also follow [a] the points that without assent memory, and mental concepts of objects, and sciences, are impossible; and most important of all, granting that some freedom of the will exists, none will exist in one who assents to nothing; where then is virtue, if nothing rests with ourselves?

39 And what is most absurd is that men's vices should be in their own power and that nobody should sin except with assent, but that the same should not be true in the case of virtue, whose sole consistency and strength is constituted by the things to which it has given its assent and so to say approval.[b] And speaking generally, before we act it is essential for us to experience some presentation, and for our assent to be given to the presentation; therefore one who abolishes either presentation or assent abolishes all action out of life.

40 XIII. Now let us examine the arguments usually advanced by this school on the other side. But before that, this is an opportunity for you to learn the 'foundations'[c] of their whole system. Well, they begin by constructing a 'science of presentations' (as we render the term), and define their nature and classes, and in particular the nature of that which can be perceived and grasped,[d] at as great a length as do the Stoics. Then they set out the two propositions

(5) The New Academy's theory expounded: true sensations are indistinguishable from false ones, so perception cannot be trusted.

quasi contineant omnem hanc quaestionem: quae ita videantur ut etiam alia eodem modo videri possint nec in iis quicquam intersit, non posse eorum alia percipi, alia non percipi; nihil interesse autem, non modo si omni ex parte eiusdem modi sint, sed etiam si discerni non possint. Quibus positis unius argumenti conclusione tota ab iis causa comprenditur; composita autem ea conclusio sic est: 'Eorum quae videntur alia vera sunt, alia falsa; et quod falsum est id percipi non potest. Quod autem verum visum est id omne tale est ut eiusdem modi falsum etiam possit videri; et quae visa sunt[1] eius modi ut in iis nihil intersit, non potest[2] accidere ut eorum alia percipi possint, alia non possint. Nullum igitur est
41 visum quod percipi possit.' Quae autem sumunt ut concludant id quod volunt, ex his duo sibi putant concedi, neque enim quisquam repugnat: ea sunt haec, quae visa falsa sint, ea percipi non posse, et alterum, inter quae visa nihil intersit, ex iis non posse alia talia esse ut percipi possint, alia ut non possint. Reliqua vero multa et varia oratione defendunt, quae sunt item duo, unum, quae videantur, eorum alia vera esse, alia falsa, alterum, omne visum

[1] *edd.*: sint *codd.* [2] *edd.*: posse *codd.*

[a] Two objects entirely alike, A' and A'', present the same appearance a; but so also do two objects only superficially alike—though not really alike entirely, they are indistinguishable by the senses: X and Y both present the same appearance x. We may have the presentation x and think it comes from X when it really comes from Y, X not being there: in this case we do not *perceive* X. Therefore when we have the presentation x and think it comes from X and X *is* there, we cannot be said to *perceive* X. Therefore perception is impossible.

that 'hold together' the whole of this investigation, namely, (1) when certain objects present an appearance of such a kind that other objects also could present the same appearance without there being any difference between these presentations, it is impossible that the one set of objects should be capable of being perceived and the other set not capable; but (2), not only in a case in which they are alike in every particular is there no difference between them, but also in a case in which they cannot be distinguished apart. Having set out these propositions, they include the whole issue within a single syllogistic argument; this argument is constructed as follows: 'Some presentations are true, others false; and what is false cannot be perceived. But a true presentation is invariably of such a sort that a false presentation also could be of exactly the same sort; and among presentations of such a sort that there is no difference between them, it cannot occur that some are capable of being perceived and others are not. Therefore there is no presentation that is
41 capable of being perceived.'[a] Now of the propositions that they take as premisses from which to infer the desired conclusion, two they assume to be granted, and indeed nobody disputes them: these are, that false presentations cannot be perceived, and the second, that of presentations that have no difference between them it is impossible that some should be such as to be capable of being perceived and others such as to be incapable. But the remaining premisses they defend with a long and varied discourse, these also being two, one, that of the objects of presentations some are true, others false, and the other, that every presentation arising from a true object is

quod sit a vero tale esse quale etiam a falso possit
42 esse. Haec duo proposita non praetervolant, sed ita dilatant ut non mediocrem curam adhibeant et diligentiam; dividunt enim in partes, et eas quidem magnas, primum in sensus, deinde in ea quae ducuntur a sensibus et ab omni consuetudine, quam obscurari volunt, tum perveniunt ad eam partem ut ne ratione quidem et coniectura ulla res percipi possit. Haec autem universa concidunt etiam minutius; ut enim de sensibus hesterno sermone vidistis, item faciunt de reliquis, in singulisque rebus, quas in minima dispertiunt, volunt efficere iis omnibus quae visa sint veris adiuncta esse falsa quae a veris nihil differant; ea cum talia sint, non posse comprendi.

43 XIV. "Hanc ego subtilitatem philosophia quidem dignissimam iudico sed ab eorum causa qui ita disserunt remotissimam. Definitiones enim et partitiones, et horum luminibus utens oratio, tum similitudines dissimilitudinesque et earum tenuis et acuta distinctio fidentium est hominum illa vera et firma et certa esse quae tutentur, non eorum qui clament nihilo magis vera illa esse quam falsa. Quid enim agant si, cum aliquid definierint, roget eos quispiam num illa definitio possit in aliam rem transferri quamlubet? Si posse dixerint, quid dicere habeant cur illa vera definitio sit? si negaverint, fatendum sit, quoniam vel illa vera definitio transferri

[a] *Lumina*, a technical term of rhetoric, used to translate σχήματα.

of such a nature that it could also arise from a false object. These two propositions they do not skim over, but develop with a considerable application of care and industry; they divide them into sections, and those of wide extent: first, sensations; next, inferences from sensations and from general experience, which they deem to lack clarity; then they come to the section proving the impossibility of perceiving anything even by means of reasoning and inference. These general propositions they cut up into still smaller divisions, employing the same method with all the other topics as you saw in yesterday's discourse that they do with sensation, and aiming at proving in the case of each subject, minutely subdivided, that all true presentations are coupled with false ones in no way differing from the true, and that this being the nature of sense-presentations, to comprehend them is impossible.

(6) Preliminary criticism of the New Academy: it invalidates definition and reasoning.

XIV. "In my own judgement this minuteness although no doubt highly worthy of philosophy is at the same time absolutely remote from the position of the authors of this line of argument. For definitions and partitions, and language employing figures [a] of this class, as also comparisons and distinctions and their subtle and minute classification, are the weapons of persons who are confident that the doctrines they are defending are true and established and certain, not of those who loudly proclaim that they are no more true than false. For what would they do if, when they have defined something, somebody were to ask them whether that particular definition can be carried over to any other thing you like? If they say it can, what proof could they put forward that the definition is true? if they say it cannot, they would have to

non possit in falsum, quod ea definitione explicetur id percipi posse, quod minime illi volunt. Eadem
44 dici poterunt in omnibus partibus. Si enim dicent ea de quibus disserent se dilucide perspicere, nec ulla communione visorum impediri, comprendere ea se posse fatebuntur. Sin autem negabunt vera visa a falsis posse distingui, qui poterunt longius progredi? occurretur enim sicut occursum est; nam concludi argumentum non potest nisi iis quae ad concludendum sumpta erunt ita probatis ut falsa eiusdem modi nulla possint esse: ergo si rebus comprensis et perceptis nisa et progressa ratio hoc efficiet, nihil posse comprendi, quid potest reperiri quod ipsum sibi repugnet magis? Cumque ipsa natura accuratae orationis hoc profiteatur, se aliquid patefacturam quod non appareat et quo id facilius adsequatur adhibituram et sensus et ea quae perspicua sint, qualis est istorum oratio qui omnia non tam esse quam videri volunt? Maxime autem convincuntur cum haec duo pro congruentibus sumunt tam vehementer repugnantia, primum esse quaedam falsa visa, quod cum volunt declarant quaedam esse vera, deinde ibidem inter falsa visa et vera nihil interesse:

[a] *i.e.*, a thing misconceived (not 'an unreal thing').

[b] *Cf.* § 34 *init.*

admit that, since even this true definition cannot be applied to a false object,[a] the object explained by the definition can be perceived, and this they will not allow at any price. The same argument it will be possible to employ at every section of the discussion.

44 For if they say that they can see through the matters that they are discussing with complete clearness, and are not hampered by any overlapping [b] of presentations, they will confess that they can 'comprehend' them. But if they maintain that true presentations cannot be distinguished from false ones, how will they be able to advance any further? for they will be met as they were met before; since valid inference is not possible unless you accept the propositions taken as premisses as so fully proved that there cannot possibly be any false propositions that resemble them: therefore if a process of reasoning that has carried through its procedure on the basis of things grasped and perceived arrives at the conclusion that nothing can be grasped, what more self-destructive argument could be discovered? And when the very nature of accurate discourse professes the intention of revealing something that is not apparent, and of employing sensations and manifest presentations to facilitate the attainment of this result, what are we to make of the language of these thinkers who hold that everything does not so much exist as seem to exist? But they are most completely refuted when they assume as mutually consistent these two propositions that are so violently discrepant, first, that some presentations are false, a view that clearly implies that some are true, and then in the same breath that there is no difference between false presentations and true ones: but your first assump-

at primum sumpseras tamquam interesset—ita priori posterius, posteriori superius non iungitur.

45 "Sed progrediamur longius et ita agamus ut nihil nobis adsentati esse videamur; quaeque ab his dicuntur sic persequamur ut nihil in praeteritis relinquamus. Primum igitur perspicuitas illa quam diximus satis magnam habet vim ut ipsa per sese ea quae sint nobis ita ut sint indicet. Sed tamen ut maneamus in perspicuis firmius et constantius, maiore quadam opus est vel arte vel diligentia ne ab iis quae clara sint ipsa per sese quasi praestigiis quibusdam et captionibus depellamur. Nam qui voluit subvenire erroribus Epicurus[1] iis qui videntur conturbare veri cognitionem, dixitque sapientis esse opinionem a perspicuitate seiungere, nihil profecit, ipsius enim opinionis errorem nullo modo sustulit.

46 XV. "Quam ob rem cum duae causae perspicuis et evidentibus rebus adversentur, auxilia totidem sunt contra comparanda. Adversatur enim primum quod parum defigunt animos et intendunt in ea quae perspicua sunt ut quanta luce ea circumfusa sint possint agnoscere; alterum est quod fallacibus et captiosis interrogationibus circumscripti atque decepti quidam, cum eas dissolvere non possunt, desciscunt a veritate. Oportet igitur et ea quae pro perspicuitate responderi possunt in promptu habere,

[1] [Epicurus] *Baiter.*

[a] *Quasi quibusdam* mark *praestigiis* as a translation of *σοφίσματα*, paraphrased by *captionibus*.

tion implied that there is a difference—thus your major premiss and your minor are inconsistent with one another.

From sense-perception reason evolves knowledge.

"But let us advance further and proceed in such a manner as not to appear to have been unduly partial to our own views; and let us go through the doctrines of these thinkers so thoroughly as to leave nothing passed over. First then what we have termed 'perspicuity' has sufficient force of itself to §17. indicate to us things that are as they are. But nevertheless, so that we may abide by things that are perspicuous with more firmness and constancy, we require some further exercise of method or of attention to save ourselves from being dislodged by 'trickeries'[a] and captious arguments from positions that are clear in themselves. For Epicurus who desired to come to the relief of the errors that appear to upset our power of knowing the truth, and who said that the separation of opinion from perspicuous truth was the function of the wise man, carried matters no further, for he entirely failed to do away with the error connected with mere opinion.

(7) Logical fallacies of the New Academy: its *sōri'ae.*

XV. "Therefore inasmuch as things perspicuous and evident are encountered by two obstacles, it is necessary to array against them the same number of assistances. The first obstacle is that people do not fix and concentrate their minds on the perspicuous objects enough to be able to recognize in how much light they are enveloped; the second is that certain persons, being entrapped and taken in by fallacious and captious arguments, when they are unable to refute them abandon the truth. It is therefore necessary to have ready the counter-arguments, of which we have already spoken, that can be advanced in

de quibus iam diximus, et esse armatos ut occurrere possimus interrogationibus eorum captionesque dis-
47 cutere, quod deinceps facere constitui. Exponam igitur generatim argumenta eorum, quoniam ipsi etiam illi solent non confuse loqui. Primum conantur ostendere multa posse videri esse quae omnino nulla sint, cum animi inaniter moveantur eodem modo rebus iis quae nullae sint ut iis quae sint. Nam cum dicatis, inquiunt, visa quaedam mitti a deo, velut ea quae in somnis videantur quaeque oraculis, auspiciis, extis declarentur (haec enim aiunt probari Stoicis quos contra disputant), quaerunt quonam modo falsa visa quae sint ea deus efficere possit probabilia, quae autem plane proxime ad verum accedant efficere non possit, aut si ea quoque possit, cur illa non possit quae perdifficiliter,[1] internoscantur tamen, et si haec,
48 cur non inter quae nihil sit[2] omnino. Deinde cum mens moveatur ipsa per sese, ut et ea declarant quae cogitatione depingimus et ea quae vel dormientibus vel furiosis videntur non numquam, veri simile est sic etiam mentem moveri ut non modo non internoscat vera illa visa sint anne falsa sed ut in iis nihil intersit omnino: ut si qui tremerent et exalbescerent vel ipsi per se motu mentis aliquo vel obiecta terribili

[1] perdifficiliter <internoscantur> ? *Reid.*
[2] intersit *Muller.*

defence of perspicuity, and to be armed so that we may be able to meet their arguments and shatter their captions; and this I have decided on as my
47 next step. I will therefore set out their arguments in classified form, since even they themselves make a practice of orderly exposition. They first attempt to show the possibility that many things may appear to exist that are absolutely non-existent, since the mind is deceptively affected by non-existent objects in the same manner as it is affected by real ones. For, they say, when your school asserts that some presentations are sent by the deity—dreams for example, and the revelations furnished by oracles, auspices and sacrifices (for they assert that the Stoics against whom they are arguing accept these manifestations)—how possibly, they ask, can the deity have the power to render false presentations probable and not have the power to render probable those which approximate absolutely most closely to the truth? or else, if he is able to render these also probable, why cannot he render probable those which are distinguishable, although only with extreme difficulty, from false presentations? and if these, why not
48 those which do not differ from them at all? Then, since the mind is capable of entirely self-originated motion, as is manifest by our faculty of mental imagination and by the visions that sometimes appear to men either when asleep or mad, it is probable that the mind may also be set in motion in such a manner that not only it cannot distinguish whether the presentations in question are true or false but that there really is no difference at all between them: just as if people were to shiver and turn pale either of themselves as a result of some mental emotion or in consequence

re extrinsecus, nihil ut esset qui distingueretur tremor ille et pallor neque ut quicquam interesset inter intestinum et oblatum. Postremo si nulla visa sunt probabilia quae falsa sint, alia ratio est ; sin autem sunt, cur non etiam quae non facile internoscantur ? cur non ut plane nihil intersit ? praesertim cum ipsi dicatis sapientem in furore sustinere se ab omni adsensu quia nulla in visis distinctio appareat.

49 XVI. "Ad has omnes visiones inanes Antiochus quidem et permulta dicebat et erat de hac una re unius diei disputatio ; mihi autem non idem faciendum puto, sed ipsa capita dicenda. Et primum quidem hoc reprehendendum quod captiosissimo genere interrogationis utuntur, quod genus minime in philosophia probari solet, cum aliquid minutatim et gradatim additur aut demitur. Soritas hoc vocant, quia acervum efficiunt uno addito grano. Vitiosum sane et captiosum genus ! Sic enim adscenditis : 'Si tale visum obiectum est a deo dormienti ut probabile sit, cur non etiam ut valde veri simile ? cur deinde non ut difficiliter a vero internoscatur ? deinde ut ne internoscatur quidem ? postremo ut nihil inter hoc

[a] Apparently the technical term is jestingly used to describe the arguments just summarized.

[b] σωρειτὴς συλλογισμός, the conclusion of one syllogism forming the major premiss of the next. Each step may either add a small point, as in the example above, or subtract one, as in the practical illustration of the fallacy that gave it its name (*ratio ruentis acerui*, Horace) : from a heap of grain one grain at a time is taken away—at what point does it cease to be a heap ?

of encountering some terrifying external object, with nothing to distinguish between the two kinds of shivering and pallor, and without any difference between the internal state of feeling and the one that came from without. Lastly, if no false presentations at all are probable, it is another story; but if some are, why are not even those that are difficult to distinguish? why not those that are so much like true ones that there is absolutely no difference between them? especially as you yourselves say that the wise man when in a state of frenzy restrains himself from all assent because no distinction between presentations is visible to him.

These fallacies exposed: the differences between false and true sensations.

49 XVI. "In answer to all these 'unfounded sense-presentations'[a] Antiochus indeed used to advance a great many arguments, and also he used to devote one whole day's debate to this single topic; but I do not think that I had better do the same, but state merely the heads of the argument. And as a first point one must criticize them for employing an exceedingly captious kind of argument, of a sort that is usually by no means approved of in philosophy—the method of proceeding by minute steps of gradual addition or withdrawal. They call this class of arguments *sōritae*[b] because by adding a single grain at a time they make a heap. It is certainly an erroneous and captious kind of argument! for you go on mounting up in this way: 'If a presentation put by the deity before a man asleep is of such a character that it is probable, why not also of such a character that it is extremely like a true one? then, why not such that it can with difficulty be distinguished from a true one? then, that it cannot even be distinguished? finally, that there is no difference between the one and the other?'

et illud intersit ? ' Huc si perveneris me tibi primum
quidque concedente, meum vitium fuerit ; sin ipse
50 tua sponte processeris, tuum. Quis enim tibi dederit
aut omnia deum posse aut ita facturum esse si possit ?
quo modo autem sumis ut, si quid cui simile esse
possit, sequatur ut etiam difficiliter internosci possit ?
deinde, ut ne internosci quidem ? postremo, ut
eadem sint ? ut, si lupi canibus similes, eosdem dices
ad extremum. Et quidem honestis similia sunt
quaedam non honesta et bonis non bona et artificiosis
minime artificiosa ; quid dubitamus igitur adfirmare
nihil inter haec interesse ? Ne repugnantia quidem
videmus ? nihil est enim quod de suo genere in aliud
genus transferri possit. At si efficeretur ut inter visa
differentium generum nihil interesset, reperirentur
quae et in suo genere essent et in alieno ; quod fieri
51 qui potest ? Omnium deinde inanium visorum una
depulsio est, sive illa cogitatione informantur, quod
fieri solere concedimus, sive in quiete sive per vinum
sive per insaniam : nam ab omnibus eiusdem modi
visis perspicuitatem, quam mordicus tenere debemus,
abesse dicemus. Quis enim, cum sibi fingit aliquid
et cogitatione depingit, non simul ac se ipse commovit atque ad se revocavit sentit quid intersit inter

If you reach this conclusion owing to my yielding to
you each successive step, the fault will have been
mine; but if you get there of your own accord, it
50 will be yours. For who will have granted you either
that the deity is omnipotent, or that even if he can
do as described he will? and how do you make such
assumptions that, if it is possible for x to resemble
y, it will follow that only with difficulty can x and y
be known apart? and then, that they cannot even
be known apart? and finally, that they are identical?
for example, if wolves are like dogs, you will end by
saying that they are identical. And it is a fact that
some honourable things are like dishonourable ones
and some good things like not good ones and some
artistic things like inartistic ones; why do we hesitate therefore to aver that there is no difference
between these? Have we no eye even for incon-
gruities? for there is nothing that cannot be carried
over from its own class into another class. But if it
were proved that there is no difference between
presentations of different classes, we should find presentations that belonged both to their own class and
to one foreign to them; how can this possibly occur?
51 Consequently there is only one way of routing the
difficulty about unreal presentations, whether depicted by the imagination, which we admit frequently
to take place, or in slumber or under the influence of
wine or of insanity: we shall declare that all presentations of this nature are devoid of perspicuity,
to which we are bound to cling tooth and nail. For
who when feigning to himself an imaginary picture
of some object, the moment he bestirs himself and
recalls his self-consciousness does not at once perceive the difference between perspicuous presentations

perspicua et inania? Eadem ratio est somniorum. Num censes Ennium cum in hortis cum Servio Galba vicino suo ambulavisset dixisse: 'Visus sum mihi cum Galba ambulare'? At cum somniavit, ita narravit:

visus Homerus adesse poëta.

Idemque in Epicharmo:

Nam videbar somniare med ego esse mortuom.

Itaque simul ut experrecti sumus visa illa contemnimus neque ita habemus ut ea quae in foro gessimus.

52 XVII. "At enim dum videntur eadem est in somnis species eorumque[1] quae vigilantes videmus! Primum interest; sed id omittamus, illud enim dicimus, non eandem esse vim neque integritatem dormientium et vigilantium nec mente nec sensu. Ne vinulenti quidem quae faciunt eadem adprobatione faciunt qua sobrii: dubitant, haesitant, revocant se interdum, iisque quae videntur imbecillius adsentiuntur cumque edormiverunt illa visa quam levia fuerint intellegunt. Quod idem contingit insanis, ut et incipientes furere sentiant et dicant aliquid quod non sit id videri sibi, et cum relaxentur sentiant atque illa dicant Alcmaeonis:

[1] *Hermann*: eorum *codd.*

---

[a] The Italian Greek (239–169 B.C.) who initiated Latin poetry in Greek metres. He adapted Attic tragedies, *e.g.* *Alcmaeon*, quoted §§ 52, 89, and wrote Roman ones; but his greatest work was *Annales*, an epic of Roman history from which comes the part of a hexameter quoted. *Cf.* § 88.

[b] The chief Dorian comic poet, *c.* 540–450 B.C., lived at Hiero's court at Syracuse.

[c] The character in Ennius's tragedy: see § 51 n. and § 89.

and unreal ones? The same applies to dreams. Do you fancy that when Ennius [a] had been walking in his grounds with his neighbour Servius Galba he used to say, 'Methought I was walking with Galba'? But when he had a dream he told the story in this way:

> Methought the poet Homer stood beside me.

And the same in the case of Epicharmus [b]:

> For methought I had a dream that I myself was dead and gone.

And so as soon as we wake up we make light of that kind of visions, and do not deem them on a par with the actual experiences that we had in the forum.

52 XVII. "But you will say that at the time when we are experiencing them the visions we have in sleep have the same appearance as the visual presentations that we experience while awake! To begin with, there is a difference between them; but do not let us dwell on that, for our point is that when we are asleep we have not the same mental or sensory power and fulness of function as we have when awake. Even men acting under the influence of wine do not act with the same decision as they do when sober: they are doubtful and hesitating and sometimes pull themselves up, and they give a more feeble assent to their sense-presentations and, when they have slept it off, realize how unsubstantial those presentations were. The same happens to the insane: at the beginning of their attack they are conscious that they are mad, and say that something is appearing to them that is not real; and also when the attack is subsiding they are conscious of it, and say things like the words of Alcmaeon [c]:

Sed mihi ne utiquam cor consentit cum oculorum aspectu.

53 At enim ipse sapiens sustinet se in furore ne adprobet falsa pro veris. Et alias quidem saepe, si aut in sensibus ipsius[1] est aliqua forte gravitas aut tarditas, aut obscuriora sunt quae videntur, aut a perspiciendo temporis brevitate excluditur. Quamquam totum hoc, sapientem aliquando sustinere adsensionem, contra vos est; si enim inter visa nihil interesset, aut semper sustineret aut numquam. Sed ex hoc genere toto perspici potest levitas orationis eorum, qui omnia cupiunt confundere. Quaerimus gravitatis, constantiae, firmitatis, sapientiae iudicium, utimur exemplis somniantium, furiosorum, ebriosorum. Illud attendimus in hoc omni genere quam inconstanter loquamur? Non enim proferremus vino aut somno oppressos aut mente captos tam absurde ut tum diceremus interesse inter vigilantium visa et sobriorum et sanorum et eorum qui essent aliter ad-
54 fecti, tum nihil interesse. Ne hoc quidem cernunt, omnia se reddere incerta, quod nolunt (ea dico incerta quae ἄδηλα Graeci)? si enim res se ita habeant ut nihil intersit utrum ita cui videantur[2] ut insano an sano, cui possit exploratum esse de sua sanitate?

[1] ipsis ? *Reid.*

[2] *ed.*: videatur *codd.*

But my mind agrees in no way with the vision of my eyes.

But you will say that the wise man in an attack of madness restrains himself from accepting false presentations as true. So indeed he often does on other occasions, if his own senses happen to contain an element of heaviness or slowness, or if the presentations are rather obscure, or if he is debarred by lack of time from a close scrutiny. Although this admission, that the wise man sometimes withholds his assent, goes wholly against your school; for if presentations were indistinguishable, he would either withhold his assent always or never. But out of all this what is 'perspicuous' is the lack of substance in the case put by these thinkers, who aspire to introduce universal confusion. What we are looking for is a canon of judgement proper to dignity and consistency, to firmness and wisdom, what we find are instances taken from dreamers, lunatics and drunkards. Do we notice in all this department how inconsistent that talk is? If we did, we should not bring forward people who are tipsy or fast asleep or out of their minds in such a ridiculous fashion as at one moment to say that there is a difference between the presentations of the waking and sober and sane and of those in other conditions, and at another moment to say that there is no difference. Do they not even see that they make everything uncertain—a position which they repudiate (I use 'uncertain' to translate the Greek *adēla*)? for if objects are so constituted that it makes no difference whether they appear to anybody as they do to a madman or as they do to a sane person, who can be satisfied of his own sanity? to desire to produce this state of affairs is in

(8) Final criticisms of the New Academy.

quod velle efficere non mediocris insaniae est. Similitudines vero aut geminorum aut signorum anulis impressorum pueriliter consectantur. Quis enim nostrum similitudines negat esse, cum eae plurimis in rebus appareant? sed si satis est ad tollendam cognitionem similia esse multa multorum, cur eo non estis contenti, praesertim concedentibus nobis, et cur id potius contenditis quod rerum natura non patitur, ut non in[1] suo quidque genere sit tale quale est nec sit in duobus aut pluribus nulla re differens ulla communitas? Ut si[2] sint et ova ovorum et apes apium simillimae, quid pugnas igitur? Aut quid tibi vis in geminis? conceditur enim similes esse, quo contentus esse potueras; tu autem vis eosdem plane
55 esse, non similes, quod fieri nullo modo potest. Dein confugis ad physicos, eos qui maxime in Academia inridentur, a quibus ne tu quidem iam te abstinebis, et ais Democritum dicere innumerabiles esse mundos, et quidem sic quosdam inter sese non solum similes sed undique perfecte et absolute pares[3] ut inter eos nihil prorsus intersit [et eo[4] quidem innumerabiles],[5] itemque homines. Deinde postulas ut, si mundus ita sit par alteri mundo ut inter eos ne minimum quidem intersit, concedatur tibi ut in hoc quoque nostro mundo aliquid alicui sic sit par ut nihil differat, nihil

[1] non in *Halm*: non *codd.* [2] si *Müller*: sibi *codd.* [3] pares *Christ*: ita pares *codd.* [4] eos *edd.* [5] *secl. Halm.*

[a] *Ut non* depends on both *contenditis* and *non patitur* and introduces both *sit tale quale est* and *nec sit ulla communitas*. The assertion refuted by nature is that uniqueness and heterogeneity are not universal (*nulla re differens* renders ἀδιάφορος, and *communitas* ἐπιμιξία or ἀπαραλλαξία, 'undistinguishableness,' *cf.* § 34).

itself no inconsiderable mark of insanity. But the way in which they harp on cases of resemblance between twins or between the seals stamped by signet-rings is childish. For which of us denies that resemblances exist, since they are manifest in ever so many things? but if the fact that many things are like many other things is enough to do away with knowledge, why are you not content with that, especially as we admit it, and why do you prefer to urge a contention utterly excluded by the nature of things, denying that everything is what it is in a class of its own and that two or more objects never possess a common character differing in nothing at all[a]? For example, granting that eggs are extremely like eggs and bees like bees, why therefore do you do battle? Or what are you at in this matter of twins? for it is granted that two twins are alike, and that might have satisfied you; but you want them to be not alike but downright identical, which is absolutely impossible. Then you fly for refuge to the natural philosophers, the favourite butts of ridicule in the Academy, from whom even you can no longer keep your hands, and you declare that Democritus says that there are a countless number of worlds, and what is more that some of them to such an extent not merely resemble but completely and absolutely match each other in every detail that there is positively no difference between them, and that the same is true of human beings. Then you demand that if one world so completely matches another world that there is not even the smallest difference between them, it shall be granted to you that in this world of ours likewise some one thing so completely matches some other thing that there is no difference

The early physicists are out of date.

intersit; cur enim, inquies, cum ex illis individuis unde omnia Democritus gigni adfirmat, in reliquis mundis et in iis quidem innumerabilibus innumerabiles Q. Lutatii Catuli non modo possint esse sed etiam sint, in hoc tanto mundo Catulus alter non possit effici?

56 XVIII. "Primum quidem me ad Democritum vocas; cui non adsentior potiusque refello propter id quod dilucide docetur a politioribus physicis, singularum rerum singulas proprietates esse. Fac enim antiquos illos Servilios, qui gemini fuerunt, tam similes quam dicuntur: num censes etiam eosdem fuisse? Non cognoscebantur foris, at domi; non ab alienis, at a suis. An non videmus hoc usu venisse[1] ut, quos numquam putassemus a nobis internosci posse, eos consuetudine adhibita tam facile internosceremus uti ne minimum quidem similes esse

57 viderentur? Hic pugnes licet, non repugnabo; quin etiam concedam illum ipsum sapientem de quo omnis hic sermo est, cum ei res similes occurrant quas non habeat dinotatas, retenturum adsensum nec umquam ulli viso adsensurum nisi quod tale fuerit quale falsum esse non possit. Sed et ad ceteras res habet quandam artem qua vera a falsis possit distinguere, et ad similitudines istas usus adhibendus

[1] *Davies*: venire *codd.*

[a] The Stoics, *cf.* § 85.

or distinction between them; for what is the reason, you will say, why whereas in the rest of the worlds, countless numbers as they are, there not only can be but actually are a countless number of Quintus Lutatius Catuluses, arisen out of those atoms out of which Democritus declares that everything comes into existence, yet in this vast world another Catulus cannot possibly be produced?

Twins, and eggs, are really distinguishable.

XVIII. "In the first place indeed you summon me before Democritus; whose opinion I do not accept but rather reject, on the ground of the fact that is lucidly proved by more accomplished natural philosophers,[a] that particular objects possess particular properties. For suppose that the famous Servilius twins of old days did resemble each other as completely as they are said to have done: surely you do not think that they were actually identical? Out of doors they were not known apart, but at home they were; they were not by strangers, but they were by their own people. Do we not see that it has come about that persons whom we thought we should never be able to know apart we have come by the exercise of habit to know apart so easily that they did not appear to be even in the least degree alike? At this point although you may show fight I shall not fight back; indeed I will actually allow that the wise man himself who is the subject of all this discussion, when he encounters similar things that he has not got distinguished apart, will reserve his assent, and will never assent to any presentation unless it is of such a description as could not belong to a false presentation. But just as he has a definite technique applicable to all other objects to enable him to distinguish the true from the false, so to the resemblances you

est: ut mater geminos internoscit consuetudine oculorum, sic tu internosces si adsueveris. Videsne ut in proverbio sit ovorum inter se similitudo? tamen hoc accepimus, Deli fuisse complures salvis rebus illis qui gallinas alere permultas quaestus causa solerent; ii cum ovum inspexerant, quae id gallina
58 peperisset dicere solebant. Neque id est contra nos, nam nobis satis est ova illa non internoscere, nihil enim magis adsentiri par est hoc illud esse quasi[1] inter illa omnino nihil interesset; habeo enim regulam ut talia visa vera iudicem qualia falsa esse non possint; ab hac mihi non licet transversum, ut aiunt, digitum discedere, ne confundam omnia. Veri enim et falsi non modo cognitio sed etiam natura tolletur si nihil erit quod intersit, ut etiam illud absurdum sit quod interdum soletis dicere, cum visa in animos imprimantur, non vos id dicere, inter ipsas impressiones nihil interesse, sed inter species et quasdam formas eorum. Quasi vero non specie visa iudicentur, quae fidem nullam habebunt sublata veri et falsi nota!
59 Illud vero perabsurdum quod dicitis probabilia vos sequi si nulla re impediamini. Primum qui potestis non impediri cum a veris falsa non distent? deinde

[1] quasi *Madvig*: quam si *codd.*

[a] *Species* here combines the sense of 'appearances' with that of 'kinds' which it still bears in zoology; it translates εἴδη, and *quasdam* marks *formas* as an explanatory synonym.

adduce he has to apply practice : just as a mother knows her twins apart by having familiarized her eyes, so you will know them apart if you habituate yourself. Are you aware that the likeness of one egg to another is proverbial ? yet we have been told that at Delos at the time of its prosperity a number of people were in the habit of keeping large numbers of hens for trade purposes ; these poultry-keepers used to be able to tell which hen had laid an egg by merely looking at it. Nor does that go against us, for we are content not to be able to know those eggs apart, since to agree that this egg is the same as that egg, is nevertheless not the same thing as if there really *were* no distinction between them ; for I possess a standard enabling me to judge presentations to be true when they have a character of a sort that false ones could not have ; from that standard I may not diverge a finger's breadth, as the saying is, lest I should cause universal confusion. For not only the knowledge but even the nature of true and false will be done away with if there is no difference between them, so that even the remark that you have a way of occasionally making will be absurd—namely, that what you assert is not that when presentations are impressed on to the mind there is no difference between the imprints themselves, but that there is no difference between their 'species,' or so to say their class-forms.[a] As if forsooth presentations were not judged with reference to their class, and will have no reliability if the mark of truth and falsehood is abolished ! But the height of absurdity is your assertion that you follow probabilities if nothing hampers you. In the first place how can you be unhampered when there is no difference between true presenta-

The logical result of this theory is 'suspense of judgement.'

quod iudicium est veri cum sit commune falsi? Ex his illa necessario nata est ἐποχή, id est adsensionis retentio, in qua melius sibi constitit Arcesilas, si vera sunt quae de Carneade non nulli existimant. Si enim percipi nihil potest quod utrique visum est, tollendus adsensus est; quid enim est tam futtile quam quicquam adprobare non cognitum? Carneadem autem etiam heri audiebamus solitum esse eo[1] delabi interdum ut diceret opinaturum, id est peccaturum, esse sapientem. Mihi porro non tam certum est esse aliquid quod comprendi possit (de quo iam nimium etiam diu disputo) quam sapientem nihil opinari, id est numquam adsentiri rei vel falsae
60 vel incognitae. Restat illud quod dicunt veri inveniundi causa contra omnia dici oportere et pro omnibus. Volo igitur videre quid invenerint. 'Non solemus,' inquit, 'ostendere.' 'Quae sunt tandem ista mysteria, aut cur celatis quasi turpe aliquid sententiam vestram?' 'Ut qui audient,' inquit, 'ratione potius quam auctoritate ducantur.' Quid si utroque[2]? num peius est? Unum tamen illud non celant, nihil esse quod percipi possit. An in eo auctoritas nihil obest? Mihi quidem videtur vel plurimum; quis enim ista tam aperte perspicueque et perversa

[1] eo *inseruit Davies.*
[2] utrumque *codd. plurimi.*

[a] *i.e.*, a suspension of judgement.

tions and false? next, what criterion is there of a true presentation if one criterion belongs in common to a true one and a false? These considerations necessarily engendered the doctrine of *epochē*,[a] that is, 'a holding back of assent,' in which Arcesilas was more consistent, if the opinions that some people hold about Carneades are true. For if nothing that has presented itself to either of them can be perceived, assent must be withheld; for what is so futile as to approve anything that is not known? But we kept being told yesterday that Carneades was also in the habit of taking refuge in the assertion that the wise man will occasionally hold an opinion, that is, commit an error. For my part, moreover, certain as I am that something exists that can be grasped (the point I have been arguing even too long already), I am still more certain that the wise man never holds an opinion, that is, never assents to a thing that is
60 either false or unknown. There remains their statement that for the discovery of the truth it is necessary to argue against all things and for all things. Well then, I should like to see what they have discovered. 'Oh,' he says, 'it is not our practice to give an exposition.' 'What pray are these holy secrets of yours, or why does your school conceal its doctrine like something disgraceful?' 'In order,' says he, 'that our hearers may be guided by reason rather than by authority.' What about a combination of the two? is not that as good? All the same, there is one doctrine that they do not conceal—the impossibility of perceiving anything. Does authority offer no opposition at this point? To me at all events it seems to offer a very great deal; for who would have adopted doctrines so openly and manifestly

et falsa secutus esset, nisi tanta in Arcesila, multo etiam maior in Carneade et copia rerum et dicendi vis fuisset?

61 XIX. "Haec Antiochus fere et Alexandreae tum et multis annis post multo etiam adseverantius, in Syria cum esset mecum paulo ante quam est mortuus. Sed iam confirmata causa te hominem amicissimum" —me autem appellabat—" et aliquot annis minorem natu non dubitabo monere: Tune, cum tantis laudibus philosophiam extuleris Hortensiumque nostrum dissentientem commoveris, eam philosophiam sequere quae confundit vera cum falsis, spoliat nos iudicio, privat adprobatione, omnibus[1] orbat sensibus? Et Cimmeriis quidem, quibus aspectum solis sive deus aliquis sive natura ademerat sive eius loci quem incolebant situs, ignes tamen aderant, quorum illis uti lumine licebat; isti autem quos tu probas tantis offusis tenebris ne scintillam quidem ullam nobis ad dispiciendum reliquerunt; quos si sequamur, iis vinclis simus adstricti ut nos commovere nequeamus.

62 Sublata enim adsensione omnem et motum animorum et actionem rerum sustulerunt; quod non modo recte fieri sed omnino fieri non potest. Provide etiam ne uni tibi istam sententiam minime liceat defendere; an tu, cum res occultissimas aperueris in lucemque protuleris iuratusque dixeris ea te comperisse (quod

[1] omni *aut* omnino *edd.*

---

[a] The Catilinarian conspiracy, 63 B.C.

[b] Cicero used this expression in the senate, and it became a cant phrase with which he was often taunted.

[c] A likely emendation gives 'and it was known to me too.'

wrong-headed and false, unless Arcesilas had possessed so great a supply of facts and of eloquence, and Carneades an even much greater?

Common sense assumes the possibility of knowledge.

61 XIX. "These virtually were the teachings advanced by Antiochus in Alexandria at the time mentioned, and also even much more dogmatically many years afterwards when he was staying with me in Syria a little before his death. But now that my case is established, I will not hesitate to give some advice to you as a very dear friend"—he was addressing myself—"and a person some years my junior: Will you, who have lauded philosophy so highly, and have shaken our friend Hortensius in his disagreement with you, follow a system of philosophy that confounds the true with the false, robs us of judgement, despoils us of the power of approval, deprives us of all our senses? Even the people of Cimmeria, whom some god, or nature, or the geographical position of their abode, had deprived of the sight of the sun, nevertheless had fires, which they were able to employ for light; but the individuals whose authority you accept have so beclouded us with darkness that they have not left us a single spark of light to give us a glimpse of sight; and if we followed them, we should be fettered with chains that would prevent our being
62 able to move a step. For by doing away with assent they have done away with all movement of the mind and also all physical activity; which is not only a mistake but an absolute impossibility. Be careful too that you are not the one person for whom it is most illegitimate to uphold this theory of yours; what, when it was you who exposed and brought to light a deeply hidden plot[a] and said on oath that you 'knew about it'[b] (which I might have said too,

mihi quoque licebat[1] qui ex te illa cognoveram), negabis esse rem ullam quae cognosci comprendi percipi possit? Vide quaeso etiam atque etiam ne illarum quoque rerum pulcherrimarum a te ipso minuatur auctoritas." Quae cum dixisset ille, finem fecit.

63 Hortensius autem vehementer admirans, quod quidem perpetuo Lucullo loquente fecerat, ut etiam manus saepe tolleret (nec mirum, nam numquam arbitror contra Academiam dictum esse subtilius), me quoque iocansne an ita sentiens (non enim satis intellegebam) coepit hortari ut sententia desisterem. Tum mihi Catulus, "Si te," inquit, "Luculli oratio flexit, quae est habita memoriter accurate copiose, taceo, neque te quo minus si tibi ita videatur sententiam mutes deterrendum puto. Illud vero non censuerim ut eius auctoritate moveare, tantum enim te non modo monuit," inquit adridens, "ut caveres ne quis improbus tribunus plebis, quorum vides quanta copia semper futura sit, arriperet te et in contione quaereret qui tibi constares cum idem negares quicquam certi posse reperiri, idem te comperisse dixisses. Hoc quaeso cave ne te terreat; de causa autem ipsa malim quidem te ab hoc dissentire, sin cesseris non magnopere mirabor, memini enim Antiochum ipsum, cum annos multos alia sen-

[1] liquebat *Klotz.*

having learnt about it from you), will you assert that there is no fact whatever that can be learnt and comprehended and perceived? Pray take care again and again that you may not yourself cause the authority of that most glorious achievement also to be diminished." Having said this, he ended.

Hortensius however, indicating emphatic admiration, as he had in fact done all through Lucullus's discourse, frequently even raising his hands in wonder (and that was not surprising, for I do not think the case against the Academy had ever been argued with more minute precision), began to exhort me also, whether in jest or earnest (for I could not quite make out), to abandon my opinion. Thereupon Catulus said to me, "If Lucullus's speech has won you over—and its delivery showed memory, concentration and fluency—, I am silent, and I do not think you ought to be frightened away from changing your opinion if you think fit to do so. But I should not advise your letting his authority influence you; for he all but warned you just now," he said with a smile at me, "to be on your guard lest some wicked tribune of the people—and what a plentiful supply there will always be of them you are well aware—should arraign you, and cross-examine you in a public assembly as to your consistency in both denying the possibility of finding anything certain and asserting that you had discovered some certainty. Pray don't be alarmed by this; but as to the actual merits of the case, although I should it is true prefer you to disagree with him, if you give in I shall not be greatly surprised, for I remember that Antiochus himself in spite of having held other views for a number of

sisset, simul ac visum sit, sententia destitisse." Haec cum dixisset Catulus, me omnes intueri.

64 XX. Tum ego, non minus commotus quam soleo in causis maioribus, huius modi quandam orationem[1] sum exorsus. "Me, Catule, oratio Luculli de ipsa re ita movit ut docti hominis et copiosi et parati et nihil praetereuntis eorum quae pro illa causa dici possent, non tamen ut ei respondere posse diffiderem ; auctoritas autem tanta plane me movebat, nisi tu opposuisses non minorem tuam. Adgrediar igitur, si
65 pauca ante quasi de fama mea dixero. Ego enim si aut ostentatione aliqua adductus aut studio certandi ad hanc potissimum philosophiam me adplicavi, non modo stultitiam meam sed etiam mores et naturam condemnandam puto. Nam si in minimis rebus pertinacia reprehenditur, calumnia etiam coërcetur, ego de omni statu consilioque totius vitae aut certare cum aliis pugnaciter aut frustrari cum alios tum etiam me ipsum velim ? Itaque, nisi ineptum putarem in tali disputatione id facere quod cum de re publica disceptatur fieri interdum solet, iurarem per Iovem deosque penates me et ardere studio veri
66 reperiendi et ea sentire quae dicerem. Qui enim possum non cupere verum invenire, cum gaudeam si

[1] *Lambinus* : quadam oratione *codd.*

years abandoned his opinion as soon as he saw fit." After these words from Catulus, everybody looked towards me.

Cicero replies in defence of scepticism (§§ 64-end).

XX. Thereupon I, feeling quite as nervous as I usually do when I have a specially big case on, began what was almost a set speech on the following lines. "For my part, Catulus, Lucullus's speech on the actual merits of the issue has affected me as that of a scholarly, fluent and well-equipped person who passes by none of the arguments that can be advanced in support of the case put forward, though all the same not to the point of my distrusting my ability to answer him; yet his great authority was unquestionably working upon me, had you not set against it your authority which is no smaller. I will therefore set about it, after a few preliminary remarks on the subject of my own reputation, if I may use the term.

(1) Prefatory: his own desire for truth.

For if my own motive in choosing this particular school of philosophy for my adherence was some sort of ostentation or combativeness, I consider that not merely my folly but even my moral character deserves condemnation. For if in the most trifling matters we censure obstinacy and actually punish chicanery, am I likely to want either to join battle with others for the sake of fighting, or to deceive not only others but myself also, when the entire system and principle of the whole of life is the issue? Accordingly unless I thought it foolish in such a discussion to do what is customary occasionally in political controversy, I should swear by Jove and the gods of my household that I am fired with zeal for the discovery of the truth, and that I really hold the opinions that I am stating. For how can I fail to be eager for the discovery of truth, when I rejoice if I

simile veri quid invenerim? Sed, ut hoc pulcherrimum esse iudico, vera videre, sic pro veris probare falsa turpissimum est. Nec tamen ego is sum qui nihil umquam falsi adprobem, qui numquam adsentiar, qui nihil opiner, sed quaerimus de sapiente. Ego vero ipse et magnus quidem sum opinator (non enim sum sapiens) et meas cogitationes sic derigo, non ad illam parvulam Cynosuram qua

> fidunt duce nocturna Phoenices in alto,

ut ait Aratus, eoque derectius gubernant quod eam tenent quae

> cursu interiore brevi convertitur orbe,

sed Helicen et clarissimos Septemtriones, id est rationes has latiore[1] specie, non ad tenue elimatas. Eo fit ut errem et vager latius; sed non de me, ut dixi, sed de sapiente quaeritur. Visa enim ista cum acriter mentem sensumve pepulerunt accipio, iisque interdum etiam adsentior (nec percipio tamen, nihil enim arbitror posse percipi)—non sum sapiens, itaque visis cedo neque possum resistere; sapientis autem hanc censet Arcesilas vim esse maximam, Zenoni adsentiens, cavere ne capiatur, ne fallatur videre—nihil est enim ab ea cogitatione quam habemus de gravitate

[1] latiores ? *Reid.*

---

[a] The word *opinator* is coined to suit the pretended self-depreciation of the speaker.

[b] See *N.D.* ii. 104 n., 106: Cicero quotes his own translation.

have discovered something that resembles truth? But just as I deem it supremely honourable to hold true views, so it is supremely disgraceful to approve falsehoods as true. And nevertheless I myself am not the sort of person never to give approval to anything false, never give absolute assent, never hold an opinion; it is the wise man that we are investigating. For my own part however, although I am a great opinion-holder [a] (for I am not a wise man), at the same time the way in which I steer my thinking is not by that tiny star, the Cynosure, in which

> Phoenicians place their trust by night
> To guide them on the deep,

as Aratus [b] puts it, and steer the straighter because they keep to her who

> revolves upon
> An inner circle and an orbit brief,

but by Helicē and the resplendent Septentriones, that is, by these theories of wider aspect, not fined down and over-subtilized. The result is that I roam and wander more widely; but it is not I, as I said, but the wise man that is the subject of our inquiry. For when the presentations you talk of have struck my mind or my sense sharply I accept them, and sometimes I actually give assent to them (though nevertheless I do not perceive them, for I hold that nothing can be perceived)—I am not a wise man, and so I yield to presentations and cannot stand out against them; whereas the strongest point of the wise man, in the opinion of Arcesilas, agreeing with Zeno, lies in avoiding being taken in and in seeing that he is not deceived—for nothing is more removed from the conception that we have of

sapientis errore, levitate, temeritate diiunctius. Quid igitur loquar de firmitate sapientis? quem quidem nihil opinari tu quoque, Luculle, concedis. Quod quoniam a te probatur (ut praepostere tecum agam; mox referam me ad ordinem), haec primum
67 conclusio quam habeat vim considera: XXI. 'Si ulli rei sapiens adsentietur umquam, aliquando etiam opinabitur; numquam autem opinabitur; nulli igitur rei adsentietur.' Hanc conclusionem Arcesilas probabat, confirmabat enim et primum et secundum (Carneades non numquam secundum illud dabat, adsentiri aliquando: ita sequebatur etiam opinari, quod tu non vis, et recte, ut mihi videris). Sed illud primum, sapientem si adsensurus esset etiam opinaturum, falsum esse et Stoici dicunt et eorum adstipulator Antiochus; posse enim eum falsa a veris et quae non possint percipi ab iis quae possint distinguere.
68 Nobis autem primum, etiam si quid percipi possit, tamen ipsa consuetudo adsentiendi periculosa esse videtur et lubrica, quam ob rem, cum tam vitiosum esse constet adsentiri quicquam aut falsum aut incognitum, sustinenda est potius omnis adsensio, ne praecipitet si temere processerit; ita enim finitima sunt falsa veris eaque quae percipi non possunt eis quae possunt[1] (si modo ea sunt quaedam: iam enim videbimus) ut tam in praecipitem locum non debeat se sapiens committere. Sin autem omnino nihil esse quod percipi possit a me sumpsero et quod tu mihi

[1] eis quae possunt *inseruit Reid.*

the dignity of the wise man than error, frivolity or rashness. What then shall I say about the wise man's firmness? even you, Lucullus, allow that he never advances a mere opinion. And since you agree with this (to deal with you out of turn: I will soon return to a regular procedure), consider first
67 the validity of this syllogism: XXI. 'If the wise man ever assents to anything, he will sometimes also form an opinion; but he never will form an opinion; therefore he will not assent to anything.' This syllogism Arcesilas used to approve, for he used to accept both the major premiss and the minor (Carneades used sometimes to grant as minor premiss that the wise man sometimes assents, so that it followed that he also holds an opinion, which you will not allow, and rightly, as I think). But the major premiss, that if the wise man did assent he would also hold an opinion, both the Stoics and their supporter Antiochus declare to be false, arguing that the wise man is able to distinguish the false from the true and the
68 imperceptible from the perceptible. But in our view, in the first place, even if anything could be perceived, nevertheless the mere habit of assenting appears dangerous and slippery, and therefore since it is agreed that to give assent to anything that is either false or unknown is so serious a fault, preferably all assent is to be withheld, to avoid having a serious fall if one goes forward rashly; for things false lie so close to things true, and things that cannot be perceived to things that can (assuming there are such things, which we shall see soon), that it is the duty of the wise man not to trust himself to such a steep slope. But if on the contrary I assume on my own authority that there is nothing at all that can be

The danger of 'assent.'

das accepero, sapientem nihil opinari, effectum illud erit, sapientem adsensus omnes cohibiturum, ut videndum tibi sit idne malis an aliquid opinaturum esse sapientem. 'Neutrum,' inquies, 'illorum.' Nitamur igitur nihil posse percipi; etenim de eo omnis est controversia.

69 XXII. "Sed prius pauca cum Antiocho, qui haec ipsa quae a me defenduntur et didicit apud Philonem tam diu ut constaret diutius didicisse neminem, et scripsit de his rebus acutissime, et idem haec non acrius accusavit in senectute quam antea defensitaverat. Quamvis igitur fuerit acutus, ut fuit, tamen inconstantia levatur auctoritas. Quis enim iste dies inluxerit quaero qui illi ostenderit eam quam multos annos esse negitavisset veri et falsi notam. Excogitavit aliquid? Eadem dicit quae Stoici. Paenituit illa sensisse? Cur non se transtulit ad alios, et maxime ad Stoicos? eorum enim erat propria ista dissensio. Quid? eum Mnesarchi paenitebat? quid? Dardani? qui erant Athenis tum principes Stoicorum. Numquam a Philone discessit, nisi postea quam ipse
70 coepit qui se audirent habere. Unde autem subito vetus Academia revocata est? Nominis dignitatem

perceived, and accept your admission that the wise man forms no opinion, this will prove that the wise man will restrain all acts of assent, so that you will have to consider whether you prefer this view or the view that the wise man will hold some opinion. 'Neither of those views,' you will say. Let us therefore stress the point that nothing can be perceived, for it is on that that all the controversy turns.

69 XXII. "But first let us have a few words with Antiochus, who studied under Philo the very doctrines that I am championing for such a long time that it was agreed that nobody had studied them longer, and who also wrote upon these subjects with the greatest penetration, and who nevertheless in his old age denounced this system, not more keenly than he had previously been in the habit of defending it. Although therefore he may have been penetrating, as indeed he was, nevertheless lack of constancy does diminish the weight of authority. For I am curious to know the exact date of the day whose dawning light revealed to him that mark of truth and falsehood which he had for many years been in the habit of denying. Did he think out something original? His pronouncements are the same as those of the Stoics. Did he become dissatisfied with his former opinions? Why did he not transfer himself to another school, and most of all why not to the Stoics? for that disagreement with Philo was the special tenet of the Stoic school. What, was he dissatisfied with Mnesarchus? or with Dardanus? they were the leaders of the Stoics at Athens at the time. He never quitted Philo, except after he began to have an audience of

Argumentum ad hominem.

70 his own. But why this sudden revival of the Old Academy? It is thought that he wanted to retain

videtur, cum a re ipsa descisceret, retinere voluisse—quod erant qui illum gloriae causa facere dicerent, sperare etiam ut ii qui se sequerentur Antiochii vocarentur. Mihi autem magis videtur non potuisse sustinere concursum omnium philosophorum (etenim de ceteris sunt inter illos non nulla communia, haec Academicorum est una sententia quam reliquorum philosophorum nemo probet); itaque cessit, et, ut ii qui sub Novis solem non ferunt, item ille cum aestuaret veterum ut Maenianorum sic Academicorum
71 umbram secutus est. Quoque solebat uti argumento tum cum ei placebat nihil posse percipi, cum quaereret, Dionysius ille Heracleotes utrum comprehendisset certa illa nota qua adsentiri dicitis oportere—illudne quod multos annos tenuisset Zenonique magistro credidisset, honestum quod esset id bonum solum esse, an quod postea defensitavisset, honesti inane nomen esse, voluptatem esse summum bonum?—qui ex illius commutata sententia docere vellet nihil ita signari in animis nostris a vero posse quod non eodem modo posset a falso, is curavit quod argumentum ex Dionysio ipse sumpsisset ex eo ceteri sumerent. Sed cum hoc alio loco plura, nunc ad ea quae a te, Luculle, dicta sunt.

---

[a] *Novae Tabernae*, a row of silversmiths' and money-changers' booths skirting the Forum.

[b] Timber balconies added to shops round the Forum, to accommodate spectators at the games. Maenius was consul 338 B.C.

[c] Antiochus had refuted the doctrine that truth can be discerned because it commands the instinctive assent of the mind by pointing out that a prominent exponent of this doctrine had at different times assented to two contradictory opinions. Yet he himself later on underwent an equally violent change of opinion.

the dignity of the name in spite of abandoning the reality—for in fact some persons did aver that his motive was ostentation, and even that he hoped that his following would be styled the School of Antiochus. But I am more inclined to think that he was unable to withstand the united attack of all the philosophers (for although they have certain things in common on all other subjects, this is the one doctrine of the Academics that no one of the other schools approves); and accordingly he gave way, and, just like people who cannot bear the sun under the New Row,[a] took refuge from the heat in the shade of the Old Academy,
71 as they do in the shadow of the Balconies.[b] And as to the argument that he was in the habit of employing at the period when he held that nothing could be perceived, which consisted in asking which of his two doctrines had the famous Dionysius of Heraclea grasped by means of that unmistakable mark which according to your school ought to be the foundation of assent—the doctrine that he had held for many years and had accepted on the authority of his master Zeno, that only the morally honourable is good, or the doctrine that he had made a practice of defending afterwards, that morality is an empty name, and that the supreme good is pleasure?—in spite of Antiochus's attempt to prove from Dionysius's change of opinion that no impression can be printed on our minds by a true presentation of a character that cannot also be caused by a false one, he yet ensured that the argument which he himself had drawn from Dionysius should be drawn by everybody else from himself.[c] But with him I will deal more at length elsewhere; I turn now, Lucullus, to what was said by you.

72 XXIII. "Et primum quod initio dixisti videamus quale sit, similiter a nobis de antiquis philosophis commemorari atque seditiosi solerent claros viros sed tamen populares aliquos nominare. Illi cum res non[1] bonas tractent, similes bonorum videri volunt; nos autem ea dicimus nobis videri quae vosmet ipsi nobilissimis philosophis placuisse conceditis. Anaxagoras nivem nigram dixit esse: ferres me si ego idem dicerem? tu ne si dubitarem quidem. At quis est hic? num sophistes (sic enim appellabantur ii qui ostentationis aut quaestus causa philosophabantur)?
73 Maxima fuit et gravitatis et ingenii gloria. Quid loquar de Democrito? Quem cum eo conferre possumus non modo ingenii magnitudine sed etiam animi, qui ita sit ausus ordiri, 'Haec loquor de universis'? nihil excipit de quo non profiteatur, quid enim esse potest extra universa? Quis hunc philosophum non anteponit Cleanthi Chrysippo reliquis inferioris aetatis, qui mihi cum illo collati quintae classis videntur? Atque is non hoc dicit quod nos, qui veri esse aliquid non negamus, percipi posse negamus; ille verum plane negat esse; sensusque idem[2] non obscuros dicit sed tenebricosos—sic enim appellat

[1] non *inseruit Ascensius*.
[2] *Reid*: sensus quidem *codd.*

---

[a] § 13.

[b] Apparently he argued that black was the real colour of snow because snow is water and water of very great depth is very dark in colour.

[c] Sextus, *Adversus Mathematicos* vii. 265 Δημόκριτος ὁ τῇ Διὸς φωνῇ παρεικαζόμενος καὶ λέγων "τάδε περὶ τῶν ξυμπάντων."

[d] This proverbial expression, derived from the classification of the population ascribed to King Servius Tullius,

(2) Reply to Lucullus's first argument; all philosophers are really sceptical.

XXIII. "And first let us see what we are to make of your remark at the beginning,[a] that our way of recalling ancient philosophers was like the sedition-mongers' habit of putting forward the names of persons who are men of distinction but yet of popular leanings. Those people although they have unworthy designs in hand desire to appear like men of worth; and we in our turn declare that the views we hold are ones that you yourselves admit to have been approved by the noblest of philosophers. Anaxagoras said[b] that snow is black: would you endure me if I said the same? Not you, not even if I expressed myself as doubtful. But who is this Anaxagoras? surely not a sophist (for that is the name that used to be given to people who pursued philosophy for the sake of display or profit)? Why, he was a man of the highest renown for dignity and intellect. Why should I talk about Democritus? Whom can we compare for not only greatness of intellect but also greatness of soul, with one who dared to begin, 'These are my utterances about the universe'[c]?—he excepts nothing as not covered by his pronouncement, for what can be outside the universe? Who does not place this philosopher before Cleanthes or Chrysippus or the rest of the later period, who compared with him seem to me to belong to the fifth class[d]? And he does not mean what we mean, who do not deny that some truth exists but deny that it can be perceived; he flatly denies that truth exists at all; and at the same time says that the senses are (not dim but) 'full of darkness'[e]—for that is the term he uses

occurs here only. Horace, *Sat.* I. ii. 47, has 'in classe secunda' of 'second-class' merchandise.

[e] σκότιος.

eos. Is qui hunc maxime est admiratus, Chius Metrodorus, initio libri qui est de natura, 'Nego' inquit 'scire nos sciamusne aliquid an nihil sciamus, ne id ipsum quidem, nescire (aut scire), scire nos, nec
74 omnino sitne aliquid an nihil sit.' Furere tibi Empedocles videtur, at mihi dignissimum rebus iis de quibus loquitur sonum fundere; num ergo is excaecat nos aut orbat sensibus si parum magnam vim censet in iis esse ad ea quae sub eos subiecta sunt iudicanda? Parmenides, Xenophanes, minus bonis quamquam versibus sed tamen illi[1] versibus, increpant eorum adrogantiam quasi irati, qui cum sciri nihil possit audeant se scire dicere. Et ab eis aiebas removendum Socraten et Platonem. Cur? an de ullis certius possum dicere? vixisse cum iis equidem videor: ita multi sermones perscripti sunt e quibus dubitari non possit quin Socrati nihil sit visum sciri posse; excepit unum tantum, scire se nihil se scire, nihil amplius. Quid dicam de Platone? qui certe tam multis libris haec persecutus non esset nisi probavisset, ironiam enim alterius, perpetuam praesertim,
75 nulla fuit ratio persequi. XXIV. Videorne tibi non ut Saturninus nominare modo inlustres homines, sed etiam imitari numquam nisi clarum, nisi nobilem? Atqui habebam molestos vobis, sed minutos, Stil-

[1] illis *nonnulli codd.*

---

[a] See § 14. [b] *Ibid.*

for them. His greatest admirer, the Chian Metrodorus, at the beginning of his volume *On Nature* says: 'I deny that we know whether we know something or know nothing, and even that we know the mere fact that we do not know (or do know), or know at
74 all whether something exists or nothing exists.' You think that Empedocles raves,[a] but I think that he sends forth an utterance most suited to the dignity of the subject of which he is speaking; surely therefore he is not making us blind or depriving us of our senses if he holds the opinion that they do not possess sufficient force to enable them to judge the objects that are submitted to them? Parmenides and Xenophanes—in less good verse it is true but all the same it is verse—inveigh almost angrily against the arrogance of those who dare to say that they know, seeing that nothing can be known. Also you said[b] that Socrates and Plato must not be classed with them. Why? can I speak with more certain knowledge about any persons? I seem to have actually lived with them, so many dialogues have been put in writing which make it impossible to doubt that Socrates held that nothing can be known; he made only one exception, no more—he said that he did know that he knew nothing. Why should I speak about Plato? he certainly would not have set out these doctrines in so many volumes if he had not accepted them, for otherwise there was no sense in setting out the irony of the other master, especially
75 as it was unending. XXIV. Do you agree that I do not merely cite the names of persons of renown, as Saturninus did, but invariably take some famous and distinguished thinker as my model? Yet I had available philosophers who give trouble to your school,

ponem Diodorum Alexinum, quorum sunt contorta et aculeata quaedam sophismata (sic enim appellantur fallaces conclusiunculae); sed quid eos colligam cum habeam Chrysippum, qui fulcire putatur porticum Stoicorum? Quam multa ille contra sensus, quam multa contra omnia quae in consuetudine probantur! At dissolvit idem. Mihi quidem non videtur; sed dissolverit sane: certe tam multa non collegisset quae nos fallerent probabilitate magna nisi videret
76 iis resisti non facile posse. Quid Cyrenaici tibi[1] videntur, minime contempti philosophi? qui negant esse quicquam quod percipi possit extrinsecus: ea se sola percipere quae tactu intumo sentiant, ut dolorem, ut voluptatem, neque se quo quid colore aut quo sono sit scire sed tantum sentire adfici se quodam modo.

"Satis multa de auctoribus—quamquam ex me quaesieras nonne putarem post illos veteres tot saeculis inveniri verum potuisse tot ingeniis tantis[2] studiis quaerentibus. Quid inventum sit paulo post videro, te ipso quidem iudice. Arcesilan vero non obtrectandi causa cum Zenone pugnavisse, sed verum
77 invenire voluisse sic intellegitur. Nemo umquam superiorum non modo expresserat sed ne dixerat quidem

[1] tibi *inseruit Durand.* [2] tantis *? Reid*: tantisque *codd.*

---

[a] The Stoa Poikilē at Athens, the meeting-place of the school, which took its name from it.
[b] In § 16.

although they are petty in their method, Stilpo, Diodorus, Alexinus, the authors of certain tortuous and pungent *sophismata* (as the term is for little syllogistic traps); but why should I bring in them, when I have Chrysippus, supposed to be a buttress of the Stoics' Colonnade[a]? What a number of arguments he produced against the senses, and against everything that is approved in common experience! But he also refuted those arguments, you will say. For my own part I don't think that he did; but suppose he did refute them, yet undoubtedly he would not have collected so many arguments to take us in with their great probability if he had not been aware that
3 they could not easily be withstood. What do you think of the Cyrenaics, by no means despicable philosophers? they maintain that nothing external to themselves is perceptible, and that the only things that they do perceive are the sensations due to internal contact, for example pain and pleasure, and that they do not know that a thing has a particular colour or sound but only feel that they are themselves affected in a certain manner.

(3) Scepticism follows from the uncertainty of perception.

"Enough about authority—although you had put the question[b] to me whether I did not think that with so many able minds carrying on the search with such zealous energy, after so many ages since the old philosophers mentioned, the truth might possibly have been discovered. What actually has been discovered permit me to consider a little later, with you yourself indeed as umpire. But that Arcesilas did not do battle with Zeno merely for the sake of criticizing him, but really wished to discover the truth, is
7 gathered from what follows. That it is possible for a human being to hold no opinions, and not only

posse hominem nihil opinari, nec solum posse sed ita necesse esse sapienti; visa est Arcesilae cum vera sententia tum honesta et digna sapiente. Quaesivit de Zenone fortasse quid futurum esset si nec percipere quicquam posset sapiens nec opinari sapientis esset. Ille, credo, nihil opinaturum quoniam esset quod percipi posset. Quid ergo id esset? Visum, credo. Quale igitur visum? Tum illum ita definisse, ex eo quod esset, sicut esset, impressum et signatum et effictum. Post requisitum, etiamne si eiusdem modi esset visum verum quale vel falsum. Hic Zenonem vidisse acute nullum esse visum quod percipi posset, si id tale esset ab eo quod est ut eiusdem modi ab eo quod non est posset esse. Recte consensit Arcesilas ad definitionem additum, neque enim falsum percipi posse neque verum si esset tale quale vel falsum; incubuit autem in eas disputationes ut doceret nullum tale esse visum a vero ut non eiusdem modi etiam a
78 falso possit esse. Haec est una contentio quae adhuc permanserit. Nam illud, nulli rei adsensurum esse

that it is possible but that it is the duty of the wise man, had not only never been distinctly formulated but had never even been stated by any of his predecessors; but Arcesilas deemed this view both true and also honourable and worthy of a wise man. We may suppose him putting the question to Zeno, what would happen if the wise man was unable to perceive anything and if also it was the mark of the wise man not to form an opinion. Zeno no doubt replied that the wise man's reason for abstaining from forming an opinion would be that there was something that could be perceived. What then was this? asked Arcesilas. A presentation, was doubtless the answer. Then what sort of a presentation? Hereupon no doubt Zeno defined it as follows, a presentation impressed and sealed and moulded from a real object, in conformity with its reality. There followed the further question, did this hold good even if a true presentation was of exactly the same form as a false one? At this I imagine Zeno was sharp enough to see that if a presentation proceeding from a real thing was of such a nature that one proceeding from a non-existent thing could be of the same form, there was no presentation that could be perceived. Arcesilas agreed that this addition to the definition was correct, for it was impossible to perceive either a false presentation or a true one if a true one had such a character as even a false one might have; but he pressed the points at issue further in order to show that no presentation proceeding from a true object is such that a presentation proceeding from a false
78 one might not also be of the same form. This is the one argument that has held the field down to the present day. For the point that the wise man will

sapientem, nihil ad hanc controversiam pertinebat;
licebat enim nihil percipere et tamen opinari—quod
a Carneade dicitur probatum, equidem Clitomacho
plus quam Philoni aut Metrodoro credens hoc magis
ab eo disputatum quam probatum puto. Sed id omittamus. Illud certe opinatione et perceptione sublata
sequitur, omnium adsensionum retentio, ut, si osten-
dero nihil posse percipi, tu concedas numquam adsensurum esse.[1]
79 XXV. "Quid ergo est quod percipi possit, si ne
sensus quidem vera nuntiant? Quos tu, Luculle,
communi loco defendis; quod ne ita[2] facere posses,
idcirco heri non necessario loco contra sensus tam
multa dixeram. Tu autem te negas infracto remo
neque columbae collo commoveri. Primum cur?
nam et in remo sentio non esse id quod videatur, et
in columba pluris videri colores nec esse plus uno.
Deinde nihilne praeterea diximus? Maneant[3] illa
omnia, iacet[4] ista causa. Veraces suos esse sensus
dicit. Igitur semper auctorem habes, et eum qui
magno suo periculo causam agat! eo enim rem
demittit Epicurus, si unus sensus semel in vita men-
80 titus sit, nulli umquam esse credendum. Hoc est
verum esse, confidere suis testibus et in pravitate[5]
insistere! Itaque Timagoras Epicureus negat sibi umquam, cum oculum torsisset, duas ex lucerna flam-

[1] esse: sit necesse *? Reid.*
[2] ita *Müller*: id *codd.*
[3] manent *Reid.*
[4] iacet *Reid*: lacerat, iaceat *codd.*
[5] in pravitate *Reid*: inportata, inportane *codd.*

[a] §§ 19 ff. [b] See § 19.
[c] The third person, used of the person addressed, is rather contemptuous.

not assent to anything had no essential bearing on this dispute ; for he might perceive nothing and yet form an opinion—a view which is said to have been accepted by Carneades ; although for my own part, trusting Clitomachus more than Philo or Metrodorus, I believe that Carneades did not so much accept this view as advance it in argument. But let us drop that point. If the acts of opining and perceiving are abolished, it undoubtedly follows that all acts of assent must be withheld, so that if I succeed in proving that nothing can be perceived, you must admit that the wise man will never assent.

(4) Even the senses are uncertain:

9 XXV. "What is there then that can be perceived, if not even the senses report the truth ? You defend them, Lucullus, by a stock argument[a] ; but it was to prevent your being able to do it in that way that I had gone out of my way yesterday to say so much against the senses. Yet you assert[b] that the broken oar and the pigeon's neck don't upset you. In the first place why ? for in the instance of the oar I perceive that what is seen is not real, and in that of the pigeon that several colours are seen and really there are not more than one. In the next place, surely we said much beside that ! Suppose all our arguments stand, the case of you people collapses. His own senses, quoth he,[c] are truthful ! If so, you always have an authority, and one to risk his all in defence of the cause ! for Epicurus brings the issue to this point, that if one sense has told a lie once in a man's

Examples from the sense of sight:

0 life, no sense must ever be believed. This is true candour—to trust in one's own witnesses and persist in perversity ! Accordingly, Timagoras the Epicurean denies that he has ever really seen two little flames coming from the lamp when he has screwed up

mulas esse visas; opinionis enim esse mendacium, non oculorum. Quasi quaeratur quid sit, non quid videatur! Sit hic quidem maiorum similis; tu vero, qui visa sensibus alia vera dicas esse, alia falsa, qui ea distinguis? Et desine,[1] quaeso, communibus locis; domi nobis ista nascuntur! Si, inquis, deus te interroget sanis modo et integris sensibus num amplius quid desideres, quid respondeas? Utinam quidem roget! audiret[2] quam nobiscum male ageret! Ut enim vera videamus, quam longe videmus? Ego Catuli Cumanum ex hoc loco cerno et e regione[3] video, Pompeianum non cerno, neque quicquam interiectum est quod obstet, sed intendi acies longius non potest. O praeclarum prospectum! Puteolos videmus, at familiarem nostrum C. Avianium fortasse in porticu Neptuni ambulantem non vide-
81 mus; at ille nescio qui qui in scholis nominari solet mille et octingenta stadia quod abesset videbat: quaedam volucres longius. Responderem igitur audacter isti vestro deo me plane his oculis non esse contentum. Dicet me acrius videre quam illos pisces fortasse qui neque videntur a nobis et nunc quidem sub oculis sunt neque ipsi nos suspicere possunt; ergo ut illis aqua, sic nobis aër crassus offunditur.

[1] Sed desine *edd.* (Desine *vel* Desiste *Reid*).
[2] *Davies*: audires, audies *codd.*
[3] et e regione *Reid*: regionem *codd.*

[a] Presumably a public resort at Puteoli, the modern Pozzuoli.
[b] Pliny, *Nat. Hist.* vii. 85, repeats this astounding story on Cicero's authority, although he gives the distance as 135,000 paces; and he quotes from Varro that the telescopic person's name was Strabo, and that from Libybaeum in Sicily he saw the Punic fleet sail from Carthage.

an eye, since it is a lie of the opinion, not of the eyes. As though the question were what exists, not what seems to exist! However, Timagoras may be allowed to be true to his intellectual ancestry; but as for you, who say that some sense-presentations are true and some false, how do you distinguish them apart? And do pray desist from mere stock arguments: those are products we have a home supply of! If a god, you say, were to inquire of you whether, given healthy and sound senses, you want anything more, what would you reply? Indeed I wish he would make the inquiry! he would be told how badly he was dealing with us! For even granting that our sight is accurate, how wide is its range? I can make out Catulus's place at Cumae from where we are, and can see it straight in front of me, but I can't make out his villa at Pompei, although there is nothing in between to block the view, but my sight is not able to carry any further. O what a glorious view! We can see Puteoli, but we can't see our friend Gaius Avianius, who is very likely taking a
81 stroll in the Colonnade of Neptune[a]; whereas that somebody or other who is regularly quoted in lectures used to see an object two hundred and twenty-five miles off,[b] and certain birds can see further. Therefore I should boldly answer that deity of your friends that I am by no means satisfied with the eyes that I have got. He will say that my sight is keener than that of the fishes down there, very likely, which we cannot see though they are under our eyes at the very moment, and which also themselves cannot see us above them; it follows that we are shut in by an opaque envelope of air as they are by one of water.

At amplius non desideramus[1]! Quid? talpam num desiderare lumen putas? Neque tam quererer cum deo quod parum longe quam quod falsum viderem. Videsne navem illam? stare nobis videtur, at iis qui in navi sunt moveri haec villa. Quaere rationem cur ita videatur; quam ut maxime inveneris, quod haud scio an non possis, non tu verum te[2] testem habere, sed eum non sine causa falsum testimonium dicere
82 ostenderis. XXVI. Quid ego de nave? vidi enim a te remum contemni; maiora fortasse quaeris. Quid potest esse sole maius, quem mathematici amplius duodeviginti partibus confirmant maiorem esse quam terram? Quantulus nobis videtur! mihi quidem quasi pedalis. Epicurus autem posse putat etiam minorem esse eum quam videatur, sed non multo; ne maiorem quidem multo putat esse, vel tantum esse quantus videatur, ut oculi aut nihil mentiantur aut non multum. Ubi igitur illud est 'semel'? Sed ab hoc credulo, qui numquam sensus mentiri putat, discedamus, qui ne nunc quidem, cum ille sol, qui tanta incitatione fertur ut celeritas eius quanta sit ne cogitari quidem possit, tamen nobis
83 stare videatur. Sed ut minuam controversiam, videte quaeso quam in parvo lis sit. Quattuor sunt capita quae concludant nihil esse quod nosci percipi comprehendi possit, de quo haec tota quaestio est: e quibus primum est esse aliquod visum falsum,

[1] desiderant *Christ*. [2] te *inseruit Davies*.

[a] § 19.
[b] Latin arithmetic expressed the proportion of 19 to 1 by saying that '19 is greater than 1 by 18 parts.'
[c] See § 79 *fin*.

But, you say, we don't wish for more! What, do you think a mole doesn't wish for light? And I should not quarrel with the deity so much about the limited range of my sight as about its inaccuracy. Do you see yonder ship? To us she appears to be at anchor, whereas to those on board her this house appears in motion. Seek for a reason for this appearance, and however much you succeed in finding one—though I doubt if you can—you will not have made out that you have got a true witness but that your witness is
2 for reasons of his own giving false evidence. XXVI. Why do I talk about a ship? for I saw [a] that you think the illustration of the oar contemptible; perhaps you want bigger examples. What can be bigger than the sun, which the mathematicians declare to be nineteen times the size of the earth [b]? How tiny it looks to us! to me it seems about a foot in diameter. Epicurus on the other hand thinks that it may possibly be even smaller than it looks, though not much; he thinks that it is not much larger either, or else exactly the size that it appears to be, so that the eyes either do not lie at all or else not much. What becomes then of that 'once' [c] of which we spoke? But let us quit this gullible person, who thinks that the senses never lie,—not even now, when the sun up there, that is travelling with such rapidity that the magnitude of its velocity cannot even be conceived,
3 nevertheless appears to us to be standing still. But to narrow down the controversy, pray see how small a point it is on which the issue turns. There are four heads of argument intended to prove that there is nothing that can be known, perceived or comprehended, which is the subject of all this debate: the first of these arguments is that there is such a thing

secundum non posse id percipi, tertium inter quae visa nihil intersit fieri non posse ut eorum alia percipi possint, alia non possint, quartum nullum esse visum verum a sensu profectum cui non adpositum sit visum aliud quod ab eo nihil intersit quodque percipi non possit. Horum quattuor capitum secundum et tertium omnes concedunt; primum Epicurus non dat, vos quibuscum res est id quoque conceditis; omnis
84 pugna de quarto est. Qui igitur P. Servilium Geminum videbat, si Quintum se videre putabat, incidebat in eius modi visum quod percipi non posset, quia nulla nota verum distinguebatur a falso; qua distinctione sublata quam haberet in C. Cotta qui bis cum Gemino consul fuit agnoscendo eius modi notam quae falsa esse non posset? Negas tantam similitudinem in rerum natura esse. Pugnas omnino, sed cum adversario facili; ne sit sane: videri certe potest, fallet igitur sensum, et si una fefellerit similitudo, dubia omnia reddiderit; sublato enim iudicio illo quo oportet agnosci, etiamsi ipse erit quem videris qui tibi videbitur, tamen non ea nota iudicabis, qua dicis oportere, ut non possit esse
85 eiusdem modi falsa. Quando igitur potest tibi P.

---

[a] Identical pictures may be formed in the mind (1) truly, when one of the senses is affected by an external object, and (2) falsely, when we mistake one object for another, or when we merely imagine we see an object. In the latter case the mental picture is not 'perceived' in the technical sense here assumed. Therefore it is not 'perceived' in the former case either. [b] See § 56.

as a false presentation; the second, that a false presentation cannot be perceived; the third, that of presentations between which there is no difference it is impossible for some to be able to be perceived and others not; the fourth, that there is no true presentation originating from sensation with which there is not ranged another presentation that precisely corresponds to it and that cannot be perceived.[a] The second and third of these four arguments are admitted by everybody; the first is not granted by Epicurus, but you with whom we are dealing admit that one too; the entire battle is about the fourth. If therefore a person looking at Publius Servilius Geminus[b] used to think he saw Quintus, he was encountering a presentation of a sort that could not be perceived, because there was no mark to distinguish a true presentation from a false one; and if that mode of distinguishing were removed, what mark would he have, of such a sort that it could not be false, to help him to recognize Gaius Cotta, who was twice consul with Geminus? You say that so great a degree of resemblance does not exist in the world. You show fight, no doubt, but you have an easy-going opponent; let us grant by all means that it does not exist, but undoubtedly it can appear to exist, and therefore it will cheat the sense, and if a single case of resemblance has done that, it will have made everything doubtful; for when that proper canon of recognition has been removed, even if the man himself whom you see is the man he appears to you to be, nevertheless you will not make that judgement, as you say it ought to be made, by means of a mark of such a sort that a false likeness could not have the same character. Therefore seeing that it is possible for Publius

Indistinguishable resemblances.

Geminus Quintus videri, quid habes explorati cur non possit tibi Cotta videri qui non sit, quoniam aliquid videtur esse quod non est? Omnia dicis sui generis esse, nihil esse idem quod sit aliud. Stoicum est istuc quidem nec admodum credibile, nullum esse pilum omnibus rebus talem qualis sit pilus alius, nullum granum. Haec refelli possunt, sed pugnare nolo; ad id enim quod agitur nihil interest omnibusne partibus visa res nihil differat an internosci non possit etiamsi differat. Sed si hominum similitudo tanta esse non potest, ne signorum quidem? Dic mihi, Lysippus eodem aere, eadem temperatione, eodem caelo atque[1] ceteris omnibus centum Alexandros eiusdem modi facere non posset? qua igitur
86 notione discerneres? Quid si in eiusdem modi cera centum sigilla hoc anulo impressero, ecquae poterit in agnoscendo esse distinctio? an tibi erit quaerendus anularius aliqui, quoniam gallinarium invenisti Deliacum illum qui ova cognosceret? XXVII. Sed adhibes artem advocatam etiam sensibus. Pictor videt quae nos non videmus, et simul inflavit tibicen a perito carmen agnoscitur. Quid? hoc nonne videtur contra te valere, si sine magnis artificiis, ad quae pauci accedunt, nostri quidem generis admodum, nec videre nec audire possimus? Iam illa praeclara, quanto artificio esset sensus nostros

[1] atque *Reid*: aqua *codd.*

---

[a] See §§ 50, 54, 56.
[b] Lysippus had sole permission from Alexander to make statues of him; he made a great many.
[c] See § 57. [d] See § 20. [e] § 30.

Geminus Quintus to appear to you, what reason have you for being satisfied that a person who is not Cotta cannot appear to you to be Cotta, inasmuch as something that is not real appears to be real? You say that everything is in a class of its own,[a] and that nothing is the same as what some other thing is. That is, it is true, a Stoic argument, and it is not a very convincing one—that no hair or grain of sand is in all respects the same as another hair or grain. These assertions can be refuted, but I don't want to fight; for it makes no difference to the point at issue whether an object completely within sight does not differ at all from another or cannot be distinguished from it even if it does differ. But if so great a resemblance between human beings is impossible, is it also impossible between statues? Tell me, could not Lysippus,[b] by means of the same bronze, the same blend of metals, the same graver and all the other requisites, make a hundred Alexanders of the same shape? then by what mode of recognition would you tell them apart? Well, if I imprint a hundred seals with this ring on lumps of wax of the same sort, will there possibly be any mode of distinction to aid in recognizing them? Or will you have to seek out some jeweller, as you found that poultry-keeper [c] at Delos who recognized eggs? XXVII. But you call in the aid of art [d] to plead in defence even of the senses. A painter sees things that we do not, and a musical expert recognizes a tune as soon as a flute-player has blown a note. Well, does not this seem to tell against you, if without great artistic acquirements, to which few people, of our race indeed very few, attain, we are unable either to see or to hear? Again those were remarkable points [e] about the high artistic skill shown

mentemque et totam constructionem hominis fabri-
87 cata natura. Cur non extimescam opinandi temeritatem? Etiamne hoc adfirmare potes, Luculle, esse aliquam vim, cum prudentia et consilio scilicet, quae finxerit vel, ut tuo verbo utar, quae fabricata sit hominem? Qualis ista fabrica est? ubi adhibita? quando? cur? quo modo? Tractantur ista ingeniose, disputantur etiam eleganter; denique videantur sane, ne adfirmentur modo. Sed de physicis mox (et quidem ob eam causam ne tu, qui id me facturum paulo ante dixeris, videare mentitus); sed ut ad ea quae clariora sunt veniam, res iam universas profundam, de quibus volumina impleta sunt non a nostris solum sed etiam a Chrysippo; de quo queri solent Stoici, dum studiose omnia conquisierit contra sensus et perspicuitatem contraque omnem consuetudinem contraque rationem, ipsum sibi respondentem inferiorem fuisse, itaque ab eo armatum
88 esse Carneadem. Ea sunt eius modi quae a te diligentissime tractata sunt. Dormientium et vinulentorum et furiosorum visa imbecilliora esse dicebas quam vigilantium siccorum sanorum. Quo modo? Quia, cum experrectus esset Ennius, non diceret se vidisse Homerum sed visum esse, Alcmaeo autem

sed mihi ne utiquam cor consentit . . .

[a] See i. 29 n. [b] § 17. [c] § 55.
[d] §§ 47-53. [e] See § 51 n.

in Nature's fabrication of our senses and mind and the whole structure of a human being. Why should I not be extremely afraid of rashness in forming opinion? Can you even assert this, Lucullus, that there is some force, united I suppose with providence [a] and design, that has moulded or, to use your word,[b] fabricated a human being? What sort of workmanship is that? where was it applied? when? why? how? You handle these matters cleverly, and expound them in a style that is even elegant; well then, let us grant that they *appear*, only provided that they are not affirmed. But with the natural philosophers we will deal soon (and that with the object of saving you, who said just now [c] that I should go to them, from *appearing* to have told a falsehood); whereas, to come to matters less obscure, I will now pour forth the facts of the universe, about which volumes have been filled not only by our school but also by Chrysippus; of whom the Stoics are in the habit of complaining that, while he carefully sought out all the facts that told against the senses and their clarity and against the whole of common experience and against reason, when answering himself he got the worst of it, and thus it was he that furnished weapons to Carneades. My points are of the sort that have been handled very industriously by you.[d] Your assertion was that presentations seen by people asleep and tipsy and mad are feebler than those of persons awake and sober and sane. How? Because, you said, when Ennius [e] had woken up he did not say that he had seen Homer but that he had seemed to see him, while his Alcmaeon says

Hallucinations are real while they last.

> But my mind agrees in no wise . . .

Similia de vinulentis. Quasi quisquam neget et qui experrectus sit eum somniasse se[1] et cuius furor consederit putare non fuisse ea vera quae essent sibi visa in furore! Sed non id agitur; tum cum videbantur quo modo viderentur, id quaeritur. Nisi vero Ennium non putamus ita totum illud audivisse

o pietas animi . . .,

si modo id somniavit, ut si vigilans audiret; experrectus enim potuit illa visa putare, ut erant,[2] somnia, dormienti vero aeque ac vigilanti probabantur. Quid? Iliona somno illo

mater, te appello . . .

nonne ita credidit[3] filium locutum ut experrecta etiam crederet? Unde enim illa

age adsta, mane, audi; iteradum eadem ista mihi—?

num videtur minorem habere visis quam vigilantes fidem?

89 XXVIII. "Quid loquar de insanis? Qualis tandem fuit adfinis tuus, Catule, Tuditanus? quisquam sanissimus tam certa putat quae videt quam is putabat quae videbantur? Quid ille qui:

video, video te. vive, Ulixes, dum licet?

nonne etiam bis exclamavit se videre cum omnino

[1] somniasse se *Müller*: somnia reri *Reid*: somniare *codd.*
[2] erant *Mdv.*: erant et *codd.*
[3] *Halm*: credit *codd.*

---

[a] Presumably part of the dream about Homer, § 51 n.
[b] Quoted from the *Iliona* (see p. 662) of Pacuvius (see p. 393).
[c] Apparently this comes from an *Ajax Furens*, but no Latin tragedy on this subject is recorded.

There are similar passages about men tipsy. As if anybody would deny that a man that has woken up thinks that he has been dreaming, or that one whose madness has subsided thinks that the things that he saw during his madness were not true! But that is not the point at issue; what we are asking is what these things looked like at the time when they were seen. Unless indeed we think that, if Ennius merely dreamt that passage

> O piety of spirit . . .[a]

he did not hear the whole of it in the same way as if he had been listening to it when awake; for when he had woken up he was able to think those appearances dreams, as they were, but he accepted them as real while he was asleep just as much as he would have done if awake. Again, in that dream of Iliona,

> Mother, on thee I call . . .,[b]

did she not so firmly believe that her son had spoken, that she believed it even after waking up? For what is the cause of her saying

> Come, stand by me, stay and hear me; say those words to me again—?

does she seem to have less faith in her visual presentations than people have when they are awake?

89 XXVIII. "What shall I say about those who are out of their mind? What pray are we to think of your relative Tuditanus, Catulus? does anybody perfectly sane think that the objects that he sees are as real as Tuditanus thought that his visions were? What was the condition of the character who says

> I see, I see thee. Live, Ulysses, whilst thou mayest—?[c]

did he not actually shout out twice over that he saw,

non videret? Quid? apud Euripidem Hercules cum ut Eurysthei filios ita suos configebat sagittis, cum uxorem interemebat, cum conabatur etiam patrem, non perinde movebatur falsis ut veris moveretur? Quid? ipse Alcmaeo tuus, qui negat 'cor sibi cum oculis consentire,' nonne ibidem incitato furore

unde haec flamma oritur?

et illa deinceps

incedunt, incedunt,[1] adsunt, me expetunt.

Quid cum virginis fidem implorat—

fer mi auxilium, pestem abige a me, flammiferam hanc vim quae me excruciat!
caeruleo incinctae angui[2] incedunt, circumstant cum ardentibus taedis—?

num dubitas quin sibi haec videre videatur? Itemque cetera:

intendit crinitus Apollo
arcum auratum laeva[3] innixus,
Diana facem iacit a luna[3]—

90 qui magis haec crederet si essent quam credebat quia videbantur? apparebat[4] enim iam 'cor cum oculis consentire.' Omnia autem haec proferuntur ut illud efficiatur quo certius nihil potest esse, inter visa

[1] *sic edd.*: incede incede *codd.*
[2] angui *Columna*: igni *codd.*
[3] *sic anonymus apud Reid*: luna . . . laeva *codd.*
[4] *ed.*: apparet *codd.*

[a] See § 52.
[b] In bending a bow the left arm being more forward seems to do more work than the right.—The MS. text makes Apollo lean on the moon and Diana fling her torch from her left hand!

although he was not seeing at all? Or Hercules in Euripides, when he was transfixing his own sons with his arrows as if they were those of Eurystheus, when he was making away with his wife, when he was attempting to make away with his father too,—was he not being affected by things false in the same manner as if the things by which he was affected had been true? Again, Alcmaeon himself whom you quote,[a] who says that 'his mind agrees not with his eyes,'—does he not in the same passage spur on his frenzy and cry

> Whence does this flame arise?

and then the words

> They come, they come! Now, now they are upon me!
> 'Tis me they seek!

What when he appeals to the maiden's loyalty for aid—

> Help me, drive the venom off, the flaming violence that torments me!
> Girt with steely snake they come, they ring me round with burning torches?

surely you do not doubt that he seems to himself to see these things? And similarly the rest:

> Apollo of the flowing locks
> Against me bends his gilded bow
> With all the force of his left arm[b];
> Dian her torch flings from the moon—

0 how would he have believed these things more if they had really been true than he actually did believe them because they seemed to be? for as it was it seemed that 'mind with eyes agreeth.' But all these things are brought forward in order to prove what is the most certain fact possible, that in respect of

vera et falsa ad animi adsensum nihil interesse. Vos autem nihil agitis cum illa falsa vel furiosorum vel somniantium recordatione ipsorum refellitis; non enim id quaeritur, qualis recordatio fieri soleat eorum qui experrecti sint aut eorum qui furere destiterint, sed qualis visio fuerit aut furentium aut somniantium tum cum movebantur. Sed abeo a sensibus.

91 "Quid est quod ratione percipi possit? Dialecticam inventam esse dicitis veri et falsi quasi disceptatricem et iudicem. Cuius veri et falsi, et in qua re? In geometriane quid sit verum aut falsum dialecticus iudicabit an in litteris an in musicis? At ea non novit. In philosophia igitur? Sol quantus sit quid ad illum? quod sit summum bonum quid habet ut queat iudicare? Quid igitur iudicabit? quae coniunctio, quae diiunctio vera sit, quid ambigue dictum sit, quid sequatur quamque rem, quid repugnet? Si haec et horum similia iudicat, de se ipsa iudicat; plus autem pollicebatur, nam haec quidem iudicare ad ceteras res quae sunt in philosophia multae atque
92 magnae non est satis. Sed quoniam tantum in ea arte ponitis, videte ne contra vos tota nata sit, quae primo progressu festive tradit elementa loquendi et ambiguorum intellegentiam concludendique ratio-

---

[a] See §§ 26, 27.

[b] τῶν ἀληθῶν καὶ ψευδῶν λόγων διαγνωστική Sext. *P.H.* ii. 229.

[c] *i.e.*, dialectic, or rather λογική, which included both διαλεκτική, or logic in the modern sense, and ῥητορική, *elementa loquendi* below.

the mind's assent there is no difference between true presentations and false ones. But your school achieve nothing when you refute those false presentations by appealing to the recollection of madmen or dreamers; for the question is not what sort of recollection is usually experienced by those who have woken up or have ceased to be mad, but what was the nature of the visual perception of men mad or dreaming at the moment when their experience was taking place. But I am getting away from the senses.

"What is it that the reason is capable of perceiving? Your school says that dialectic was invented[a] to serve as a 'distinguisher'[b] or judge between truth and falsehood. What truth and falsehood, and on what subject? Will the dialectician judge what is true or false in geometry, or in literature, or in music? But those are not the subjects with which he is acquainted. In philosophy therefore? What has the question of the size of the sun to do with him? what means has he to enable him to judge what is the supreme good? What then will he judge? what form of hypothetical judgement or of inference from alternative hypotheses is valid, what proposition is ambiguous, what conclusion follows from any given premiss and what is inconsistent with it? If the reason judges these and similar matters, it judges about itself; but the promise that it held out went further, as to judge merely these matters is not enough for all the other numerous and important problems contained in philosophy. But since your school sets so much store by that science,[c] see that it is not essentially entirely against you, when at the first stage it gaily imparts the elements of discourse, the solution of ambiguous propositions and the theory of

(5) Dialectic does not give certainty.

The *sōrites* fallacy is irrefutable,

nem, tum paucis additis venit ad soritas, lubricum sane et periculosum locum, quod tu modo dicebas esse vitiosum interrogandi genus. XXIX. Quid ergo? istius vitii num nostra culpa est? Rerum natura nullam nobis dedit cognitionem finium ut ulla in re statuere possimus quatenus; nec hoc in acervo tritici solum unde nomen est, sed nulla omnino in re—minutatim interrogati, dives pauper, clarus obscurus sit, multa pauca, magna parva, longa brevia, lata angusta, quanto aut addito aut dempto
93 certum respondeamus non[1] habemus. At vitiosi sunt soritae. Frangite igitur eos, si potestis, ne molesti sint; erunt enim, nisi cavetis. 'Cautum est,' inquit; 'placet enim Chrysippo, cum gradatim interrogetur (verbi causa) tria pauca sint anne multa, aliquanto prius quam ad multa perveniat quiescere, id est quod ab iis dicitur ἡσυχάζειν.' 'Per me vel stertas licet,' inquit Carneades, 'non modo quiescas; sed quid proficit? sequitur enim qui te ex somno excitet et eodem modo interroget: "Quo in numero conticuisti, si ad eum numerum unum addidero, multane erunt?"—progrediere rursus quoad videbitur.' Quid plura? hoc enim fateris, neque ultimum te paucorum neque primum multorum respondere posse; cuius generis error ita manat ut non videam quo non possit accedere.
94 'Nihil me laedit,' inquit, 'ego enim ut agitator

[1] [non] *Halm.*

[a] See § 49. The argument is that the mere existence of the Sorites shows that there is no such thing as logical certainty or absolute knowledge.

the syllogism, but then by a process of small additions comes to the *sōrites*,[a] certainly a slippery and dangerous position, and a class of syllogism that you lately declared to be erroneous. XXIX. What then? is that an error for which we are to blame? No faculty of knowing absolute limits has been bestowed upon us by the nature of things to enable us to fix exactly how far to go in any matter; and this is so not only in the case of a heap of wheat from which the name is derived, but in no matter whatsoever—if we are asked by gradual stages, is such and such a person a rich man or a poor man, famous or undistinguished, are yonder objects many or few, great or small, long or short, broad or narrow, we do not know at what point in the addition or subtraction to give a definite
93 answer. But you say that the *sōrites* is erroneous. Smash the *sōrites* then, if you can, so that it may not get you into trouble, for it will if you don't take precautions. 'Precautions have been taken,' says he, 'for the policy of Chrysippus is, when questioned step by step whether (for example) 3 is few or many, a little before he gets to "many," to come to rest, or, as they term it, *hēsychazein*.' 'So far as I am concerned,' says Carneades, 'you may not only rest but even snore; but what's the good of that? for next comes somebody bent on rousing you from slumber and carrying on the cross-examination: "If I add 1 to the number at which you became silent, will that make many?"—you will go forward again as far as you think fit.' Why say more? for you admit my point, that you cannot specify in your answers either the place where 'a few' stops or that where 'many' begins; and this class of error spreads so widely that
94 I don't see where it may not get to. 'It doesn't

callidus prius quam ad finem veniam equos sustinebo, eoque magis si locus is quo ferentur equi praeceps erit: sic me,' inquit, 'ante sustineo, nec diutius captiose interroganti respondeo.' Si habes quod liqueat neque respondes, superbe; si non habes, ne tu quidem percipis. Si quia obscura, concedo, sed negas te usque ad obscura progredi. Inlustribus igitur rebus insistis. Si id tantum modo ut taceas, nihil adsequeris, quid enim ad illum qui te captare vult utrum tacentem inretiat te an loquentem? sin autem usque ad novem verbi gratia sine dubitatione respondes pauca esse, in decumo insistis, etiam a certis et inlustrioribus cohibes adsensum; hoc idem me in obscuris facere non sinis. Nihil igitur te contra soritas ars ista adiuvat quae nec augendi nec minuendi[1] quid aut primum sit aut postremum docet.

95 Quid quod eadem illa ars quasi Penelope telam retexens tollit ad extremum superiora? utrum ea vestra an nostra culpa est? Nempe fundamentum dialecticae est quidquid enuntietur (id autem appellant ἀξίωμα, quod est quasi effatum) aut verum esse aut falsum; quid igitur? haec vera an falsa sunt: 'Si te mentiri dicis idque verum dicis, mentiris[2]'? Haec scilicet inexplicabilia esse dicitis, quod est

[1] nec augentis nec minuentis *Halm.*

[2] mentiris *Klotz* (*cf.* § 96): mentiris verum dicis *codd.*: mentiris an verum dicis *Schutz.*

touch me at all,' says he, 'for like a clever charioteer, before I get to the end, I shall pull up my horses, and all the more so if the place they are coming to is precipitous: I pull up in time as he does,' says he, 'and when captious questions are put I don't reply any more.' If you have a solution of the problem and won't reply, that is an arrogant way of acting, but if you haven't, you too don't *perceive* the matter; if because of its obscurity, I give in, but you say that you don't go forward till you get to a point that is obscure. If so, you come to a stop at things that are clear. If you do so merely in order to be silent, you don't score anything, for what does it matter to the adversary who wants to trap you whether you are silent or speaking when he catches you in his net? but if on the contrary you keep on answering 'few' as far as 9, let us say, without hesitating, but stop at 10, you are withholding assent even from propositions that are certain, nay, clear as daylight; but you don't allow me to do exactly the same in the case of things that are obscure. Consequently that science of yours gives you no assistance against a *sōrites*, as it does not teach you either the first point or the last in the process of increasing or diminishing. What of the fact that this same science destroys at the end the steps that came before, like Penelope unweaving her web? is your school to blame for that or is ours? Clearly it is a fundamental principle of dialectic that every statement (termed by them *axiōma*, that is, a 'proposition') is either true or false; what then? is this a true proposition or a false one—'If you say that you are lying and say it truly, you lie'? Your school of course says that these problems are 'in-

and so also is *The Liar*.

odiosius quam illa quae nos non comprehensa et non percepta dicimus.

XXX. "Sed hoc omitto, illud quaero: si ista explicari non possunt nec eorum ullum iudicium invenitur ut respondere possitis verane an falsa sint, ubi est illa definitio, effatum esse id quod aut verum aut falsum sit? Rebus sumptis adiungam ex iis sequendas esse alias, alias improbandas,[1] quae sint in
96 genere contrario. Quo modo igitur hoc conclusum esse iudicas: 'Si dicis nunc lucere et verum dicis, lucet; dicis autem nunc lucere et verum dicis[2]; lucet igitur'? Probatis certe genus et rectissime conclusum dicitis, itaque in docendo eum primum concludendi modum traditis. Aut quidquid igitur eodem modo concluditur probabitis aut ars ista nulla est. Vide ergo hanc conclusionem probaturusne sis: 'Si dicis te mentiri verumque dicis, mentiris; dicis autem te mentiri verumque dicis; mentiris igitur'; qui potes hanc non probare cum probaveris eiusdem generis superiorem? Haec Chrysippea sunt, ne ab ipso quidem dissoluta. Quid enim faceret huic conclusioni: 'Si lucet, lucet; lucet autem; lucet igitur'? cederet scilicet, ipsa enim ratio conexi, cum concesseris superius, cogit inferius concedere. Quid ergo haec ab illa con-

[1] sequenda esse alia, alia improbanda *? ed.*
[2] lucet . . . dicis *inseruit Manutius.*

[a] ἄπορα.
[b] *alias, alias = effata alia, alia* (attracted to the gender of *rebus*).

soluble,'[a] which is more vexatious than the things termed by us 'not grasped' and 'not perceived.'

XXX. "But I drop this point and ask the following question: if the problems in question are insoluble and no criterion of them is forthcoming to enable you to answer whether they are true or false, what becomes of the definition of a 'proposition' as 'that which is either true or false'? Taking certain premisses I will draw the conclusion that, of two sets of propositions, to be classed as contradictory, one set is to be adopted and the other set to be rejected.[b]
96 What judgement do you pass on the procedure of the following syllogism—'If you say that it is light now and speak the truth, it is light; but you do say that it is light now and speak the truth; therefore it is light'? Your school undoubtedly approve this class of syllogism and say that it is completely valid, and accordingly it is the first mode of proof that you give in your lectures. Either therefore you will approve of every syllogism in the same mode, or that science of yours is no good. Consider therefore whether you will approve the following syllogism: 'If you say that you are lying and speak the truth, you are lying; but you do say that you are lying and speak the truth; therefore you are lying'; how can you not approve this syllogism when you approved the previous one of the same class? These fallacies are the inventions of Chrysippus, and even he himself could not solve them; for what could he make of this syllogism—'If it is light, it is light; but it is light; therefore it is light'? Of course he would agree; for the very nature of hypothetical inference compels you to grant the conclusion if you have granted the premiss. What then is the difference between this

clusione differt: 'Si mentiris, mentiris; mentiris autem; mentiris igitur'? Hoc negas te posse nec adprobare nec improbare; qui igitur magis illud? si ars, si ratio, si via, si vis denique conclusionis
97 valet, eadem est in utroque. Sed hoc extremum eorum est: postulant ut excipiantur haec inexplicabilia. Tribunum aliquem censeo videant: a me istam exceptionem numquam impetrabunt. Etenim cum ab Epicuro, qui totam dialecticam et contemnit et inridet, non impetrent ut verum esse concedat quod ita effabimur, 'Aut vivet cras Hermarchus aut non vivet,' cum dialectici sic statuant, omne quod ita disiunctum sit quasi 'aut etiam aut non' non modo verum esse sed etiam necessarium, vide quam sit cautus[1] is quem isti tardum[2] putant; 'Si enim,' inquit, 'alterutrum concessero necessarium esse, necesse erit cras Hermarchum aut vivere aut non vivere; nulla autem est in natura rerum talis necessitas.' Cum hoc igitur dialectici pugnent, id est Antiochus et Stoici; totam enim evertit dialecticam, nam si e contrariis disiunctio—contraria autem ea dico, cum alterum aiat, alterum neget—si talis disiunctio falsa potest esse, nulla vera est;
98 mecum vero quid habent litium, qui ipsorum disciplinam sequor? Cum aliquid huius modi inciderat, sic ludere Carneades solebat: 'Si recte conclusi,

[1] catus *Lambinus*: acutus *Reid.*
[2] bardum ? *Reid.*

[a] In civil suits the praetor did not try the facts but issued an instruction to an inferior court to cast the defendant *if* certain facts were proved, and sometimes also *unless* certain other facts were proved: the latter clause was an *exceptio.* If the praetor refused to grant an *exceptio*, the defendant might appeal to a tribune, who could procure the grant by

syllogism and the former one—'If you are lying, you are lying; but you are lying; therefore you are lying'? You say that you are unable either to agree to this or to disprove it; how then are you more able to deal with the other? if science, reason, method, in fact if the syllogistic proof is valid, it is the
7 same in either case. But the farthest length they go is to demand that these insoluble problems should be deemed an exception. My advice to them is to apply to some tribune[a]: they will never get that 'saving clause' from me. For as they will not get Epicurus, who despises and laughs at the whole of dialectic, to admit the validity of a proposition of the form 'Hermarchus will either be alive to-morrow or not alive,' whereas dialecticians lay it down that every disjunctive proposition of the form 'either *x* or not-*x*' is not only valid but even necessary, see how on his guard the man is whom your friends think slow; for 'If,' he says, 'I admit either of the two to be necessary, it will follow that Hermarchus must either be alive to-morrow or not alive; but as a matter of fact in the nature of things no such necessity exists.' Therefore let the dialecticians, that is, Antiochus and the Stoics, do battle with this philosopher, for he overthrows the whole of dialectic, if a disjunctive proposition consisting of two contrary statements—'contrary' meaning one of them affirmative, the other negative—if a disjunctive proposition of this sort can be false, none is true; but what quarrel have they with me, who am a disciple of their own school? When any situation of this nature occurred, Carneades used to play with the matter thus: 'If my conclusion is

threatening if it were not given to annul the whole of the praetor's instruction.

teneo[1]; sin vitiose, minam Diogenes mihi reddet' (ab eo enim Stoico dialecticam didicerat, haec autem merces erat dialecticorum). Sequor igitur eas vias quas didici ab Antiocho, nec reperio quo modo iudicem 'Si lucet, lucet' verum esse (ob eam causam quod ita didici, omne quod ipsum ex se conexum sit verum esse), non iudicem 'Si mentiris, mentiris' eodem modo esse conexum. Aut igitur et[2] hoc et illud aut nisi hoc ne illud quidem iudicabo.

XXXI. "Sed ut omnes istos aculeos et totum
tortuosum genus disputandi relinquamus ostendamus-
que qui simus, iam explicata tota Carneadis sententia
Antiochi ista conruent universa. Nec vero quicquam ita dicam ut quisquam id fingi suspicetur: a
Clitomacho sumam, qui usque ad senectutem cum
Carneade fuit, homo et acutus ut Poenus et valde
studiosus ac diligens. Et quattuor eius libri sunt de
sustinendis adsensionibus, haec autem quae iam
99 dicam sunt sumpta de primo. Duo placet esse
Carneadi genera visorum, in uno hanc divisionem,
alia visa esse quae percipi possint, alia quae percipi
non possint, in altero autem alia visa esse probabilia,
alia non probabilia; itaque quae contra sensus
contraque perspicuitatem dicantur ea pertinere ad
superiorem divisionem, contra posteriorem nihil dici

[1] ⟨te⟩ teneo *Davies*. [2] et *inseruit ed.*

[a] Say £4. The professor mentioned was a minor Stoic, a Babylonian; he went with Carneades to Rome on the famous embassy, § 137. [b] *Cf.* § 75.

[c] φαντασίαι καταληπτικαί and ἀκατάληπτοι, πιθαναί and ἀπίθανοι.

correct, I keep to it; if it is faulty, Diogenes will pay me back a mina[a]' (for Diogenes as a Stoic had taught him dialectic, and that was the fee of professors of that subject). I therefore am following the methods of procedure that I learnt from Antiochus, and I cannot make out how I am to form the judgement that the proposition 'If it is light, it is light' is a true one (because I was taught that every hypothetical inference is true), but not form the judgement that 'If you are lying, you are lying' is an inference on the same lines. Either therefore I shall make both the former judgement and the latter one, or, if not the former, not the latter either.

(6) The constructive side of Carneades: 'probable' sensation is enough to guide th wise man.

XXXI. "But to leave all those stinging repartees and the whole of the tortuous class of argument[b] and to display our real position, as soon as the whole system of Carneades has been unfolded the doctrines of your Antiochus will come to the ground in complete collapse. However, I will not assert anything in such a manner that anybody may suspect me of inventing; I shall take it from Clitomachus, who was a companion of Carneades quite until old age, a clever fellow as being a Carthaginian, and also extremely studious and industrious. There are four volumes of his that deal with the withholding of assent, but what I am now going to say has been taken from Volume One. Carneades holds that there are two classifications of presentations, which under one are divided into those that can be perceived and those that cannot, and under the other into those that are probable and those that are not probable[c]; and that accordingly those presentations that are styled by the Academy contrary to the senses and contrary to perspicuity belong to the former division, whereas the latter division

oportere; quare ita placere, tale visum nullum esse ut perceptio consequeretur, ut autem probatio, multa. Etenim contra naturam est[1] probabile nihil esse, et sequitur omnis vitae ea quam tu, Luculle, commemorabas eversio; itaque et sensibus probanda multa sunt, teneatur modo illud, non inesse in iis quicquam tale quale non etiam falsum nihil ab eo differens esse possit. Sic quidquid acciderit specie probabile, si nihil se offeret quod sit probabilitati illi contrarium, utetur eo sapiens, ac sic omnis ratio vitae gubernabitur. Etenim is quoque qui a vobis sapiens inducitur multa sequitur probabilia, non comprehensa neque percepta neque adsensa sed similia veri; quae nisi probet, omnis vita tollatur.

100 Quid enim? conscendens navem sapiens num comprehensum animo habet atque perceptum se ex sententia navigaturum? qui potest? Sed si iam ex hoc loco proficiscatur Puteolos stadia triginta probo navigio, bono gubernatore, hac tranquillitate, probabile ei[2] videatur se illuc venturum esse salvum. Huius modi igitur visis consilia capiet et agendi et non agendi, faciliorque erit ut albam esse nivem probet quam erat Anaxagoras (qui id non modo ita esse negabat sed sibi, quia sciret aquam nigram esse unde illa concreta[3] esset, albam ipsam esse ne videri

[1] est *Müller*: esset *codd.* [2] ei *inseruit Lambinus.* [3] *Man.*: congregata *codd.*

[a] §§ 31, 53, 58.

must not be impugned; and that consequently his view is that there is no presentation of such a sort as to result in perception, but many that result in a judgement of probability. For it is contrary to nature for nothing to be probable, and entails that entire subversion of life of which you, Lucullus, were speaking[a]; accordingly even many sense-percepts must be deemed probable, if only it be held in mind that no sense-presentation has such a character as a false presentation could not also have without differing from it at all. Thus the wise man will make use of whatever apparently probable presentation he encounters, if nothing presents itself that is contrary to that probability, and his whole plan of life will be charted out in this manner. In fact even the person whom your school brings on the stage as the wise man follows many things probable, that he has not grasped nor perceived nor assented to but that possess verisimilitude; and if he were not to approve them, all
00 life would be done away with. Another point: when a wise man is going on board a ship surely he has not got the knowledge already grasped in his mind and perceived that he will make the voyage as he intends? how can he have it? But if for instance he were setting out from here to Puteoli, a distance of four miles, with a reliable crew and a good helmsman and in the present calm weather, it would appear probable that he would get there safe. He will therefore be guided by presentations of this sort to adopt plans of action and of inaction, and will be readier at proving that snow is white than Anaxagoras was (who not only denied that this was so, but asserted that to him snow did not even appear white, because he knew that it was made of water solidified and that

101 quidem)[a]; et quaecumque res eum sic attinget ut sit visum illud probabile neque ulla re impeditum, movebitur. Non enim est e saxo sculptus aut e robore dolatus; habet corpus, habet animum, movetur mente, movetur sensibus, ut esse[1] ei vera multa videantur, neque tamen habere insignem illam et propriam percipiendi notam, eoque sapientem non adsentiri, quia possit eiusdem modi exsistere falsum aliquod cuius modi hoc verum. Neque nos contra sensus aliter dicimus ac Stoici, qui multa falsa esse dicunt longeque aliter se habere ac sensibus videantur.

XXXII. "Hoc autem si ita sit, ut unum modo sensibus falsum videatur, praesto est qui neget rem ullam percipi posse sensibus! Ita nobis tacentibus ex uno Epicuri capite, altero vestro perceptio et comprehensio tollitur. Quod est caput Epicuri? 'Si ullum sensus visum falsum est, nihil percipi potest.' Quod vestrum? 'Sunt falsa sensus visa.' Quid sequitur? Ut taceam, conclusio ipsa loquitur nihil posse percipi. 'Non concedo,' inquit, 'Epicuro.' Certa igitur cum illo, qui a te totus diversus est, noli mecum, qui hoc quidem certe, falsi esse aliquid in
102 sensibus, tibi adsentior. Quamquam nihil mihi tam mirum videtur quam ista dici, ab Antiocho quidem

[1] esse *inseruit ed.*

[a] *i.e.*, Lucullus, whom Cicero is addressing, *cf.* §§ 80, 94.

1 water was black); and whatever object comes in contact with him in such a way that the presentation is probable, and unhindered by anything, he will be set in motion. For he is not a statue carved out of stone or hewn out of timber; he has a body and a mind, a mobile intellect and mobile senses, so that many things seem to him to be true, although nevertheless they do not seem to him to possess that distinct and peculiar mark leading to perception, and hence the doctrine that the wise man does not assent, for the reason that it is possible for a false presentation to occur that has the same character as a given true one. Nor does our pronouncement against the senses differ from that of the Stoics, who say that many things are false and widely different from what they appear to the senses.

Certainty is not needed for conduct.

XXXII. "If however this be the case, let the senses receive but a single false presentation, and he [a] stands ready to deny that the senses can perceive anything! Thus a single first principle of Epicurus combined with another belonging to your school results in the abolition of perception and comprehension, without our uttering a word. What is the principle of Epicurus? 'If any sense-presentation is false, nothing can be perceived.' What is yours? 'There are false sense-presentations.' What follows? Without any word of mine, logical inference of itself declares that nothing can be perceived. 'I do not admit Epicurus's point,' says he. Well then, fight it out with Epicurus—he differs from you entirely; don't join issue with me, who at all events agree with you so far as to hold that there is an element
2 of falsehood in the senses. Although nothing seems to me so surprising as that those doctrines should be

maxime, cui erant ea quae paulo ante dixi notissima. Licet enim hoc quivis arbitratu suo reprehendat quod negemus rem ullam percipi posse, certe levior reprehensio est; quod tamen dicimus esse quaedam probabilia, non videtur hoc satis esse vobis. Ne sit; illa certe debemus effugere quae a te vel maxime agitata sunt: 'Nihil igitur cernis? nihil audis? nihil tibi est perspicuum?' Explicavi paulo ante Clitomacho auctore quo modo ista Carneades diceret; accipe quem ad modum eadem dicantur a Clitomacho in eo libro quem ad C. Lucilium scripsit poëtam, cum scripsisset iisdem de rebus ad L. Censorinum eum qui consul cum M'. Manilio fuit. Scripsit igitur his fere verbis—sunt enim mihi nota, propterea quod earum ipsarum rerum de quibus agimus prima institutio et quasi disciplina illo libro continetur—sed
103 scriptum est ita: Academicis placere esse rerum eius modi dissimilitudines ut aliae probabiles videantur, aliae contra; id autem non esse satis cur alia posse percipi dicas, alia non posse, propterea quod multa falsa probabilia sint, nihil autem falsi perceptum et cognitum possit esse. Itaque ait vehementer errare eos qui dicant ab Academia sensus eripi, a quibus numquam dictum sit aut colorem aut saporem aut sonum nullum esse, illud sit disputatum, non

---

[a] 149 B.C.
[b] *Quasi* marks *disciplina* as an explanation of *institutio* used to translate some Greek term, perhaps σύστημα.

asserted, especially indeed by Antiochus, who was perfectly well acquainted with the arguments that I stated a little before. For even though anybody at his own discretion may criticize our statement that nothing can be perceived, that is a less serious criticism; but it is our assertion that there are some things that are probable that seems to your school to be inadequate. It may be; anyhow it is certainly up to us to get round the difficulties that you raised with the greatest insistency: 'Do you then see nothing? do you hear nothing? is nothing clear to you?' I quoted from Clitomachus a little earlier an explanation of the way in which Carneades treated the difficulties you refer to; let me give you the way in which the same points are dealt with by Clitomachus in the volume that he wrote to the poet Gaius Lucilius, although he had written on the same subjects to the Lucius Censorinus who was Manius Manilius's colleague in the consulship.[a] He wrote then in almost these words—for I am familiar with them, because the primary 'system' or doctrine[b] which we are dealing with is contained in that book—
03 but it runs as follows: 'The Academic school holds that there are dissimilarities between things of such a nature that some of them seem probable and others the contrary; but this is not an adequate ground for saying that some things can be perceived and others cannot, because many false objects are probable but nothing false can be perceived and known.' And accordingly he asserts that those who say that the Academy robs us of our senses are violently mistaken, as that school never said that colour, taste or sound was non-existent, but their contention was that these presentations do not contain a mark of truth and

inesse in iis propriam quae nusquam alibi esset veri
104 et certi notam. Quae cum exposuisset, adiungit dupliciter dici adsensus sustinere sapientem, uno modo cum hoc intellegatur, omnino eum rei nulli adsentiri, altero cum se a respondendo ut aut adprobet quid[1] aut improbet sustineat, ut neque neget aliquid neque aiat; id cum ita sit, alterum placere, ut numquam adsentiatur, alterum tenere, ut sequens probabilitatem ubicumque haec aut occurrat aut deficiat aut 'etiam' aut 'non' respondere possit. Etenim cum[2] placeat eum qui de omnibus rebus contineat se ab adsentiendo moveri tamen et agere aliquid, relinqui eius modi visa quibus ad actionem excitemur, item ea quae interrogati in utramque partem respondere possimus, sequentes tantum modo quod ita visum sit, dum sine adsensu; neque tamen omnia eius modi visa adprobari,[3] sed ea quae nulla re impedirentur.

105 Haec si vobis non probamus, sint falsa sane, invidiosa certe non sunt, non enim lucem eripimus, sed ea quae vos percipi comprehendique, eadem nos, si modo probabilia sint, videri dicimus.

XXXIII. "Sic igitur inducto et constituto probabili, et eo quidem expedito, soluto, libero, nulla re implicato, vides profecto, Luculle, iacere iam illud

[1] ut quid aut adprobet? *Reid.*
[2] etenim cum *Reid*: nec ut *codd.*
[3] adprobavit *cod. unus.*

certainty peculiar to themselves and found nowhere
104 else. After setting out these points, he adds that the formula 'the wise man withholds assent' is used in two ways, one when the meaning is that he gives absolute assent to no presentation at all, the other when he restrains himself from replying so as to convey approval or disapproval of something, with the consequence that he neither makes a negation nor an affirmation; and that this being so, he holds the one plan in theory, so that he never assents, but the other in practice, so that he is guided by probability, and wherever this confronts him or is wanting he can answer 'yes' or 'no' accordingly. In fact as we hold that he who restrains himself from assent about all things nevertheless does move and does act, the view is that there remain presentations of a sort that arouse us to action, and also answers that we can give in the affirmative or the negative in reply to questions, merely following a corresponding presentation, provided that we answer without actual assent; but that nevertheless not all presentations of this character were actually approved, but those that nothing hindered.

105 If we do not win your approval for these doctrines, they may no doubt be false, but certainly they are not detestable. For we don't rob you of daylight, but, whereas you speak of things as being 'perceived' and 'grasped,' we describe the same things (provided they are probable) as 'appearing.'

(7) Reply to Lucullus's second and fourth arguments: probability is enough ground for action.

XXXIII. "Now therefore that we have thus brought in and established 'probability,' and a probability rid of difficulties, untrammelled, free, unentangled with anything, you doubtless see, Lucullus, that all your former advocacy of 'perspicuity' now

tuum perspicuitatis patrocinium. Iisdem enim hic sapiens de quo loquor oculis quibus iste vester caelum, terram, mare intuebitur, iisdem sensibus reliqua quae sub quemque sensum cadunt sentiet. Mare illud quod nunc favonio nascente purpureum videtur, idem huic nostro videbitur, nec tamen adsentietur, quia nobismet ipsis modo caeruleum videbatur, mane ravum,[1] quodque nunc qua a sole conlucet albescit et vibrat dissimileque est proximo et continenti, ut etiamsi possis rationem reddere cur id eveniat, tamen non possis id verum esse quod videbatur oculis de-
106 fendere. Unde memoria, si nihil percipimus? sic enim quaerebas. Quid? meminisse visa nisi comprensa non possumus? Quid? Polyaenus, qui magnus mathematicus fuisse dicitur, is posteaquam Epicuro adsentiens totam geometriam falsam esse credidit, num illa etiam quae sciebat oblitus est? Atqui falsum quod est id percipi non potest, ut vobismet ipsis placet; si igitur memoria perceptarum comprensarumque rerum est, omnia quae quisque meminit habet[2] comprensa atque percepta; falsi autem comprendi nihil potest, et omnia meminit Siron Epicuri dogmata; vera igitur illa sunt nunc omnia. Hoc per me licet; sed tibi aut concedendum est ita esse, quod minime vis, aut memoriam mihi remittas oportet et fateare[3] esse ei locum, etiamsi

[1] ravum videbitur *? ed.*
[2] habet *? Reid*: habet ea *codd.*
[3] *Davies*: facile *vel* facere *codd.*

[a] See § 22.

collapses. For this wise man of whom I am speaking will behold the sky and earth and sea with the same eyes as the wise man of your school, and will perceive with the same senses the rest of the objects that fall under each of them. Yonder sea that now with the west wind rising looks purple, will look the same to our wise man, though at the same time he will not 'assent' to the sensation, because even to ourselves it looked blue just now and tomorrow it will look grey, and because now where the sun lights it up it whitens and shimmers and is unlike the part immediately adjoining, so that even if you are able to explain why this occurs, you nevertheless cannot maintain that the appearance that was presented to your eyes was true! If we perceive nothing, what is the cause of memory?—that was a question you were asking.[a] What? are we unable to remember sense-presentations unless we have comprehended them? What? Polyaenus is said to have been a great mathematician: after he had accepted the view of Epicurus and come to believe that all geometry is false, surely he did not forget even the knowledge that he possessed? Yet what is false cannot be perceived, as you yourselves hold; if therefore the objects of memory are things perceived and comprehended, all the things a man remembers he holds grasped and perceived; but nothing false can be grasped, and Siro remembers all the doctrines of Epicurus; therefore in the present state of things those doctrines are all true. This may be so as far as I am concerned; but you are either bound to allow that it is so, which is the last thing you are willing to do, or you must grant me memory and admit that it has a place, even if grasp and

Certainty is not indispensable for memory nor for the arts.

107 comprehensio perceptioque nulla sit. Quid fiet artibus? Quibus? iisne quae ipsae fatentur coniectura se plus uti quam scientia, an iis quae tantum id quod videtur sequuntur nec habent istam artem vestram qua vera et falsa diiudicent?

"Sed illa sunt lumina duo quae maxime causam istam continent. Primum enim negatis fieri posse ut quisquam nulli rei adsentiatur, et id quidem perspicuum esse.[1] Cum Panaetius, princeps prope meo quidem iudicio Stoicorum, ea de re dubitare se dicat quam omnes praeter eum Stoici certissimam putant, vera esse haruspicum responsa,[2] auspicia, oracula, somnia, vaticinationes, seque ab adsensu sustineat, quod is potest facere etiam[3] de iis rebus quas illi a quibus ipse didicit certas habuerunt,[4] cur id sapiens de reliquis rebus facere non possit? An est aliquid quod positum vel improbare vel adprobare possit, dubitare non possit? an tu in soritis poteris hoc cum voles, ille in reliquis rebus non poterit eodem modo insistere, praesertim cum possit sine adsensione ipsam

108 veri similitudinem non impeditam sequi? Alterum est quod negatis actionem ullius rei posse in eo esse qui nullam rem adsensu suo comprobet; primum enim videri oportet, in quo est[5] etiam adsensus, dicunt enim Stoici sensus ipsos adsensus esse, quos quoniam adpetitio consequatur, actionem sequi, tolli

[1] et id quidem p. esse *Reid*: at . . . est *codd.*
[2] responsa *inseruit Ernesti*: omnia ? *Reid.*
[3] etiam ? *Reid*: ut *codd.*: vel *Goerens.*
[4] habuerunt *Kaiser*: erint *codd.*
[5] est *Reid*: sit *codd.*

[a] ἀνεμπόδιστος, *i.e.*, not inconsistent with some other apparent truth.

7 perception are non-existent. What will happen to the sciences? What sciences? the ones that themselves confess that they make more use of conjecture than knowledge, or those that are only guided by appearance, and are not possessed of that method belonging to your school to enable them to distinguish what is true from what is false?

Suspense of assent is possible,

"But the two outstanding things that hold your case together are the following. The first is your statement that it is impossible for anybody to assent to nothing, and that this at all events is 'perspicuous.' Seeing that Panaetius, who in my judgement at all events is almost the chief of the Stoics, says that he is in doubt as to the matter which all the Stoics beside him think most certain, the truth of the pronouncements of diviners, of auspices and oracles, of dreams and soothsaying, and that he restrains himself from assent, which he can do even about things that his own teachers held to be certain, why should not the wise man be able to do so about everything else? Is there any proposition that he can either reject or approve, but is not able to doubt? will you be able to do so with *sōrites* arguments when you wish, but he not be able to call a similar halt in everything else, especially as he is able to follow mere resemblance to truth when unhampered,[a] with-
08 out the act of assent? The second point is the assertion of your school that no action as regards anything is possible in the case of a man who gives the approval of his assent to nothing; for in the first place the thing must be seen, and that includes assent, for the Stoics say that the sensations are themselves acts of assent, and that it is because these are followed by an impulse of appetition that action

and compatible with action.

autem omnia si visa tollantur. XXXIV. Hac de re in utramque partem et dicta sunt et scripta multa, sed brevi res potest tota confici. Ego enim etsi maximam actionem puto repugnare visis, obsistere opinionibus, adsensus lubricos sustinere, credoque Clitomacho ita scribenti, Herculi quendam laborem exanclatum a Carneade, quod, ut feram et immanem beluam, sic ex animis nostris adsensionem, id est opinationem et temeritatem, extraxisset, tamen (ut ea pars defensionis relinquatur) quid impediet actionem eius qui probabilia sequitur nulla re impedi-
109 ente ? 'Hoc,' inquit, 'ipsum impediet, quod statuet ne id quidem quod probet posse percipi.' Iam istuc te quoque impediet in navigando, in conserendo, in uxore ducenda, in liberis procreandis, plurimisque in rebus in quibus nihil sequere praeter probabile.

"Et tamen illud usitatum et saepe repudiatum refers, non ut Antipater sed ut ais 'pressius'; nam Antipatrum reprehensum quod diceret consentaneum esse ei qui adfirmaret nihil posse comprehendi id ipsum saltem dicere posse comprendi. Quod ipsi Antiocho pingue videbatur et sibi ipsum contrarium; non enim potest convenienter dici nihil comprendi posse si quicquam comprendi posse dicatur. Illo modo potius putat urguendum fuisse Carneadem: cum sapientis nullum decretum esse posset nisi compren-

[a] *i.e.*, the activity of reason.

[b] § 29.

follows, whereas if sense-presentations are done away with, everything is done away with. XXXIV. On this matter a great deal has been said and written both for and against, but the whole subject can be dealt with briefly. For even although my own opinion is that the highest form of activity [a] wars against sense-presentations, withstands opinions, holds back acts of assent on their slippery slope, and although I agree with Clitomachus when he writes that Carneades really did accomplish an almost Herculean labour in ridding our minds of that fierce wild beast, the act of assent, that is of mere opinion and hasty thinking, nevertheless (to abandon that section of the defence) what will hamper the activity of the man that follows probabilities when nothing hampers? 'The very fact,' says he, 'that he will decide that not even what he approves can be perceived, will hamper him.' Well then, that same fact will hamper you also in going a voyage, in sowing a crop, in marrying a wife, in begetting a family, in ever so many things in which you will be following nothing but probability.

"And putting that aside, you repeat the old, familiar and oft-rejected argument, not in Antipater's manner, but as you say 'coming more to grips with it' [b]; for Antipater, you tell us, was censured for saying that it was consistent for one who asserted that nothing could be grasped to say that that assertion itself could be grasped. This seemed stupid and self-contradictory even to Antiochus; for it cannot consistently be said that nothing can be grasped if anything is said to be able to be grasped. The way in which Antiochus thinks Carneades should preferably have been attacked was this—to make him admit that, since the wise man can have no

sum perceptum cognitum, ut hoc ipsum decretum quidem,[1] decretum[2] sapientis esse nihil posse percipi, fateretur esse perceptum. Proinde quasi sapiens nullum aliud decretum habeat et sine decretis vitam
110 agere possit! Sed ut illa habet probabilia non percepta, sic hoc ipsum, nihil posse percipi; nam si in hoc haberet cognitionis notam, eadem uteretur in ceteris; quam quoniam non habet, utitur probabilibus. Itaque non metuit ne confundere omnia videatur et incerta reddere. Non enim, quem ad modum si quaesitum ex eo sit stellarum numerus par an impar sit, item si de officio multisque aliis de rebus in quibus versatus exercitatusque sit, nescire se dicat; in incertis enim nihil est probabile, in quibus autem est, in iis non deerit sapienti nec quid faciat nec
111 quid respondeat. Ne illam quidem praetermisisti, Luculle, reprehensionem Antiochi—nec mirum, in primis enim est nobilis—qua solebat dicere Antiochus Philonem maxime perturbatum: cum enim sumeretur unum, esse quaedam falsa visa, alterum, nihil ea differre a veris, non attendere superius illud ea re a se esse concessum quod videretur esse quaedam in visis differentia, eam tolli altero quo neget visa a

[1] quidem: quid, quod, qui *codd. nonnulli.*
[2] decretum *inseruit ed.*

[a] § 27. [b] § 44.

'decision'[a] that is not grasped and perceived and known, therefore this particular decision itself, that it is the decision of the wise man that nothing can be perceived, is perceived. Just as if the wise man held no other decision and could conduct his life without decisions! On the contrary, he holds this particular opinion, that nothing can be perceived, in just the same way as he holds the 'probable' but not 'perceived' views that have been mentioned; for if he had a mark of knowledge in this case, he would employ the same mark in all other cases, but since he has not got it, he employs probabilities. Thus he is not afraid lest he may appear to throw everything into confusion and make everything uncertain. For if a question be put to him about duty or about a number of other matters in which practice has made him an expert, he would not reply in the same way as he would if questioned as to whether the number of the stars is even or odd, and say that he did not know; for in things uncertain there is nothing probable, but in things where there is probability the wise man will not be at a loss either what to do or what to answer. Nor yet, Lucullus, did you pass over the criticism made by Antiochus[b]—and no wonder, as it is one of the most famous—which Antiochus used to say Philo had found most upsetting: it was that when the assumption was made, first, that there were some false presentations, and secondly, that they differed in no respect from true ones, Philo failed to notice that whereas he had admitted the former proposition on the strength of the apparent existence of a certain difference among presentations, this fact was refuted by the latter proposition, his denial that true presentations differ

Truth is imperceptible, but not non-existent.

falsis vera differre ; nihil tam repugnare. Id ita esset si nos verum omnino tolleremus ; non facimus, nam tam vera quam falsa cernimus. Sed probandi species est, percipiendi signum nullum habemus.

112 XXXV. "Ac mihi videor nimis etiam nunc agere ieiune. Cum sit enim campus in quo exsultare possit oratio, cur eam tantas in angustias et Stoicorum dumeta compellimus? Si enim mihi cum Peripatetico res esset, qui id percipi posse diceret 'quod impressum esset e vero,' neque adhiberet[1] illam magnam accessionem, 'quo modo imprimi non posset e falso,' cum simplici homine simpliciter agerem nec magno opere contenderem, atque etiam si, cum ego nihil dicerem posse comprendi, diceret ille sapientem interdum opinari, non repugnarem, praesertim ne Carneade quidem huic loco valde re-
113 pugnante: nunc quid facere possum? Quaero enim quid sit quod comprendi possit; respondet mihi non Aristoteles aut Theophrastus, ne Xenocrates quidem aut Polemo, sed qui minor est, 'tale verum quale falsum esse non possit.' Nihil eius modi invenio; itaque incognito nimirum adsentiar, id est opinabor. Hoc mihi et Peripatetici et vetus Academia concedit, vos negatis, Antiochus in primis, qui me valde movet, vel quod amavi hominem sicut

[1] *Reid*: aderere, adhaerere *etc. codd.*

[a] *Species* = φαντασία.

[b] *i.e.*, Antiochus.

from false ones; and that no procedure could be more inconsistent. This would hold good if we abolished truth altogether; but we do not, for we observe some things that are true just as we observe some that are false. But there is 'appearance'[a] as a basis of approval, whereas we have no mark as a basis of perception.

(8) The Dogmatists disagree among themselves.

XXXV. "And even now I feel that my procedure is too cramped. For when there is a wide field in which eloquence might expatiate, why do we drive it into such confined spaces and into the briary thickets of the Stoics? If I were dealing with a Peripatetic, who would say that we can perceive 'an impression formed from a true object,' without adding the important qualification 'in a manner in which it could not be formed from a false one,' I would meet his frankness with frankness and would not labour to join issue with him, and if, when I said that nothing can be grasped, he said that the wise man sometimes forms an opinion, I would even refrain from combating him, especially as even Carneades does not vehemently combat this position; but as it is what can I do? For I put the question what there is that can be grasped; I receive the answer, not from Aristotle or Theophrastus, not even from Xenocrates or Polemo, but from a smaller person,[b] 'A true presentation of such a sort that there cannot be a false one of the same sort.' I do not encounter any such presentation; and accordingly I shall no doubt assent to something not really known, that is, I shall hold an opinion. This both the Peripatetics and the Old Academy grant me, but your school denies it, and Antiochus does so first and foremost, who influences me strongly, either because I loved the man as he

ille me, vel quod ita iudico, politissimum et acutissimum omnium nostrae memoriae philosophorum. A quo primum quaero quo tandem modo sit eius Academiae cuius esse se profiteatur. Ut omittam alia, haec duo de quibus agitur quis umquam dixit aut veteris Academiae aut Peripateticorum, vel id solum percipi posse quod esset verum tale quale falsum esse non posset, vel sapientem nihil opinari? Certe nemo: horum neutrum ante Zenonem magno opere defensum est. Ego tamen utrumque verum puto, nec dico temporis causa sed ita plane probo.

114 XXXVI. "Illud ferre non possum: tu cum me incognito adsentiri vetes idque turpissimum esse dicas et plenissimum temeritatis, tantum tibi adroges ut exponas disciplinam sapientiae, naturam rerum omnium evolvas, mores fingas, fines bonorum malorumque constituas, officia discribas, quam vitam ingrediar definias, idemque etiam disputandi et intellegendi iudicium dicas te et artificium traditurum, perficies ut ego ista innumerabilia complectens nusquam labar, nihil opiner? Quae tandem ea est disciplina ad quam me deducas si ab hac abstraxeris? vereor ne subadroganter facias si dixeris tuam, atqui ita dicas necesse est. Neque vero tu solus sed ad suam
115 quisque rapiet. Age, restitero Peripateticis, qui sibi

did me, or because I judge him as the most polished and the most acute of all the philosophers of our time. The first question that I put to him is, how pray can he belong to that Academy to which he professes to belong? To omit other points, what member of the Old Academy or of the Peripatetic school ever made these two statements that we are dealing with—either that the only thing that can be perceived is a true presentation of such a sort that there could not be a false one of the same sort, or that a wise man never holds an opinion? No one, without a doubt; neither of these propositions was much upheld before Zeno. I nevertheless think both of them true, and I do not say so just to suit the occasion, but it is my deliberate judgement.

Antiochus is not irrefragable

XXXVI. "One thing I cannot put up with: when you forbid me to assent to something that I do not know and say that this is most disgraceful and reeks with rashness, but take so much upon yourself as to set out a system of philosophy, to unfold a complete natural science, to mould our ethics and establish a theory of the chief good and evil and map out our duties and prescribe the career that I am to embark upon, and also actually profess to be ready to impart a criterion and scientific system of dialectic and logic, will you secure that I on my side when embracing all your countless doctrines shall never make a slip, never hold a mere opinion? What system pray is there for you to convert me to if you can withdraw me from this one? I am afraid you may be doing rather a presumptuous thing if you say your own system, yet all the same you are bound to say so. Nor indeed will you be alone, but everybody will hurry me into his own system. Come, suppose I stand out against

cum oratoribus cognationem esse, qui claros viros a se instructos dicant rem publicam saepe rexisse, sustinuero Epicureos, tot meos familiares, tam bonos, tam inter se amantes viros: Diodoto quid faciam Stoico, quem a puero audivi, qui mecum vivit tot annos, qui habitat apud me, quem et admiror et diligo, qui ista Antiochi[1] contemnit? 'Nostra,' inquies, 'sola vera sunt.' Certe sola, si vera, plura enim vera discrepantia esse non possunt. Utrum igitur nos impudentes qui labi nolimus,[2] an illi adrogantes qui sibi persuaserint scire se solos omnia? 'Non me quidem,' inquit, 'sed sapientem dico scire.' Optime! nempe ista scire quae sunt in tua disciplina. Hoc primum quale est, a non sapiente explicari sapientiam? Sed discedamus a nobismet ipsis, de sapiente loquamur, de quo ut saepe iam dixi omnis haec quaestio est.

116 "In tres igitur partes et a plerisque et a vobismet ipsis distributa sapientia est. Primum ergo, si placet, quae de natura rerum sint quaesita videamus. At[3] illud ante: estne quisquam tanto inflatus errore ut sibi se illa scire persuaserit? Non quaero rationes eas quae ex coniectura pendent, quae disputationibus huc et illuc trahuntur, nullam adhibent persuadendi necessitatem; geometrae provideant, qui se pro-

[1] Antiochi *? Reid* (*cf.* 98): Antiochia *codd.*
[2] nolumus *codd. plerique.*
[3] at *Reid*: velut *codd.*

the Peripatetics, who say that they are akin to the orators and that famous men equipped with their teaching have often governed the state, and suppose I resist the Epicureans, that crowd of friends of my own, so worthy and so affectionate a set of men: what shall I do with Diodotus the Stoic, whose pupil I have been from a boy, who has been my associate for so many years, who lives in my house, whom I both admire and love, and who despises the doctrines of Antiochus that you are putting forward? 'Our doctrines,' you will say, 'are the only true ones.' If they are true, certainly they are the only true ones, for there cannot be several true systems disagreeing with one another. Then is it we that are shameless, who do not wish to make a slip, or they presumptuous, who have persuaded themselves that they alone know everything? 'I don't say that I myself know,' says he, 'but that the wise man knows.' Excellent! no doubt you mean 'knows the doctrines that are in your system.' To begin with, what are we to think of this—wisdom being unfolded by a man that is not wise? But let us leave ourselves and speak about the wise man, on whom all this inquiry turns, as I have often said already.

116 "Wisdom then is divided by your own school, as it is also by most philosophers, into three parts. First therefore, if you agree, let us see what investigations have been made about natural science. But one thing first: is there anybody so puffed up with error as to have persuaded himself that he knows this subject? I am not asking about the theories that depend upon conjecture, that are dragged to and fro in debate, employing no convincing cogency; let the geometricians see to that, whose claim is that

(8a) The Dogmatists disagreement as to Physics.

fitentur non persuadere sed cogere, et qui omnia vobis quae describunt probant. Non quaero ex his illa initia mathematicorum quibus non concessis digitum progredi non possunt, punctum esse quod magnitudinem nullam habeat, extremitatem et quasi libramentum in quo nulla omnino crassitudo sit, lineamentum sine ulla latitudine.[1] Haec cum vera esse concessero, si adigam ius iurandum sapientem, nec prius quam Archimedes eo inspectante rationes omnes descripserit eas quibus efficitur multis partibus solem maiorem esse quam terram, iuraturum putas? Si fecerit, solem ipsum quem deum censet esse con-
117 tempserit. Quodsi geometricis rationibus non est crediturus, quae vim adferunt in docendo, vos ipsi ut dicitis, ne ille longe aberit ut argumentis credat philosophorum; aut si est crediturus, quorum potissimum? omnia[2] enim physicorum licet explicare, sed longum est; quaero tamen quem sequatur. Finge aliquem nunc fieri sapientem, nondum esse; quam potissimum sententiam eliget et disciplinam? etsi quamcumque eliget, insipiens eliget; sed sit ingenio divino, quem unum e physicis potissimum probabit? nec plus uno poterit. Non persequor quaestiones infinitas; tantum de principiis rerum e quibus omnia

[1] latitudine *Reid*: latitudine carentem *codd.*
[2] somnia? *Reid.*

[a] *Libramentum*, 'evenness,' applied primarily to the scales of a balance; *quasi* marks it as here used to explain *extremitatem*, which is a translation of πέρας (*i.e.* πέρας σώματος, the boundary of a solid, viz. a surface, ἐπιφάνεια).

they do not persuade but convince, and who prove all their propositions by their diagrams to the satisfaction of your school. I am not asking these people about those first principles of mathematics which must be granted before they are able to advance an inch—that a point is a thing without magnitude, that a 'boundary' or surface[a] is a thing entirely devoid of thickness, a line a thing without any breadth. When I have admitted the correctness of these definitions, if I put the wise man on his oath, and not until Archimedes has first, with him looking on, drawn all the diagrams proving that the sun is many times as large as the earth, do you think that he will take the oath? If he does, he will have shown contempt for the sun itself which he deems is a
117 god. But if he is going to refuse credence to the methods of geometry, which in their teaching exercise a compelling force, as your school itself asserts, surely he for his part will be far from believing the proofs of the philosophers; or else, if he does believe them, which school's proofs will he choose? for one might set out all the systems of the natural philosophers, but it would be a long story: all the same, I want to know which philosopher he follows. Imagine that somebody is becoming a wise man now, but is not one yet; what doctrine or system will he select to adopt? although whichever one he does select, the selection will be made by a man not wise; but suppose he be an inspired genius, which single one among the natural philosophers will he choose to approve? more than one he will not be able to. I am not asking about problems of unlimited vagueness: let us merely consider what authority he will approve in respect of the elements

constant videamus quem probet, est enim inter magnos homines summa dissensio.

118 XXXVII. "Princeps Thales, unus e septem cui sex reliquos concessisse primas ferunt, ex aqua dixit constare omnia. At hoc Anaximandro populari et sodali suo non persuasit; is enim infinitatem naturae dixit esse e qua omnia gignerentur. Post eius auditor Anaximenes infinitum aëra, sed ea quae ex eo orerentur definita; gigni autem terram, aquam, ignem, tum ex his omnia. Anaxagoras materiam infinitam, sed ex ea particulas similes inter se, minutas; eas primum confusas, postea in ordinem adductas mente divina. Xenophanes, paulo etiam antiquior, unum esse omnia neque id esse mutabile, et id esse deum, neque natum umquam et sempiternum, conglobata figura; Parmenides ignem qui moveat terram quae ab eo formetur; Leucippus plenum et inane; Democritus huic in hoc similis, uberior in ceteris; Empedocles haec pervolgata et nota quattuor; Heraclitus ignem; Melissus hoc quod esset infinitum et immutabile et fuisse semper et fore. Plato ex materia in se omnia recipiente mundum factum esse censet a deo sempiternum. Pythagorei ex numeris et mathematicorum initiis proficisci volunt omnia. Ex his eliget vester sapiens unum aliquem, credo,

[a] *Omnia*=τὸ πᾶν. [b] See i. 28 note *d*.

of which the universe[a] consists, for it is a subject extremely debated among the great.

Examples of their disagreement.

XXXVII. "At the head of the list Thales, the one of the Seven to whom the remaining six are stated to have unanimously yielded the first place, said that all things are made of water. But in this he did not carry conviction with his fellow-citizen and associate Anaximander; Anaximander said that there exists an infinity of substance[b] from which the universe was engendered. Afterwards his pupil Anaximenes held that air is infinite, but the things that spring from it finite, and that earth, water and fire are engendered, and then the universe of things out of these. Anaxagoras held that matter is infinite, but that out of it have come minute particles entirely alike, which were at first in a state of medley but were afterwards reduced to order by a divine mind. Xenophanes at a somewhat earlier date said that the universe is one, and that this is unchanging, and is god, and that it never came into being but has existed for ever, of a spherical shape; Parmenides said that the primary element is fire, which imparts motion to the earth that receives from it its conformation; Leucippus's elements were solid matter and empty space; Democritus resembled him in this but was more expansive in the rest of his doctrines; Empedocles taught the four ordinary elements that we know; Heraclitus, fire; Melissus, that the present infinite and unchangeable universe has existed and will exist always. Plato holds the view that the world was made by god out of the all-containing substance, to last for ever. The Pythagoreans hold that the universe originates out of numbers and the first principles of the mathematicians. From these teachers your wise

quem sequatur: ceteri tot viri et tanti repudiati
119 ab eo condemnatique discedent. Quamcumque vero sententiam probaverit, eam sic animo comprensam habebit ut ea quae sensibus, nec magis adprobabit nunc lucere quam, quoniam Stoicus est, hunc mundum esse sapientem, habere mentem quae et se et ipsum fabricata sit et omnia moderetur moveat regat. Erit ei persuasum etiam solem lunam stellas omnes terram mare deos esse, quod quaedam animalis intellegentia per omnia ea permanet et transeat; fore tamen aliquando ut omnis hic mundus ardore deflagret. XXXVIII. Sint ista vera (vides enim iam me fateri aliquid esse veri), comprendi ea tamen et percipi nego. Cum enim tuus iste Stoicus sapiens syllabatim tibi ista dixerit, veniet flumen orationis aureum fundens Aristoteles qui illum desipere dicat; neque enim ortum esse umquam mundum quod nulla fuerit novo consilio inito tam praeclari operis inceptio, et ita esse eum undique aptum ut nulla vis tantos queat motus mutationemque moliri, nulla senectus diuturnitate temporum exsistere ut hic ornatus umquam dilapsus occidat. Tibi hoc repudiare, illud autem superius sicut caput et famam tuam defendere necesse erit, cum[1] mihi ne ut dubitem quidem re-
120 linquatur. Ut omittam levitatem temere adsentien-

[1] cum *inseruit Goerens.*

[a] *Quaedam* marks a translation of some phrase like Diog. vii. 147 θεὸν δὲ εἶναι ζῷον ἀθάνατον λογικόν.

[b] A rendering of the two meanings of κίνησις.

man will doubtless select some single master to follow,
while the numerous residue of men of such distinction
19 will depart rejected and condemned by him. But
whatever opinion he approves, he will hold it in as firm
a mental grasp as he holds the presentations that he
grasps by the senses, and he will not be more firmly
convinced that it is now daylight than he is convinced,
being a Stoic, that this world is wise and is possessed
of an intelligence that constructed both itself and
the world, and that controls, moves and rules the
universe. He will also be convinced that the sun and
moon and all the stars and the earth and sea are gods,
because a 'vital intelligence'[a] permeates and passes
through them all; but that nevertheless a time will
come when all this world will be burnt out with
heat. XXXVIII. Suppose these facts of yours are
true (for you see now that I do admit the existence
of some truth), nevertheless I deny that they are
'grasped' and perceived. For when your Stoic wise
man aforesaid has told you those facts one syllable
at a time, in will come Aristotle, pouring forth a
golden stream of eloquence, to declare that he is
doting, since the world never had a beginning, because there never can have been a commencement,
on new and original lines, of so glorious a structure,
and since it is so compactly framed on every side
that no force could bring about such mighty movements of mutation,[b] no old age arise from the long
lapse of years to cause this ordered cosmos ever to
perish in dissolution. For you it will be obligatory
to spurn this view, and to defend the former one as
you would your life and honour, while to me it is not
20 even left to doubt. Not to speak of the frivolity of
those who assent without consideration, how valuable

tium, quanti libertas ipsa aestimanda est non mihi necesse esse quod tibi est! Quaero[1] cur deus, omnia nostra causa cum faceret (sic enim vultis), tantam vim natricum viperarumque fecerit, cur mortifera tam multa ac[2] perniciosa terra marique disperserit. Negatis haec tam polite tamque subtiliter effici potuisse sine divina aliqua sollertia (cuius quidem vos maiestatem deducitis usque ad apium formicarumque perfectionem, ut etiam inter deos Myrmecides aliquis minutorum opusculorum fabricator fuisse videatur):
121 negas sine deo posse quicquam. Ecce tibi e transverso Lampsacenus Strato, qui det isti deo immunitatem magni quidem muneris (et[3] cum sacerdotes deorum vacationem habeant, quanto est aequius habere ipsos deos!); negat opera deorum se uti ad fabricandum mundum. Quaecumque sint, docet omnia effecta esse natura, nec ut ille qui ex[4] asperis et levibus et hamatis uncinatisque corporibus concreta haec esse dicat interiecto inani—somnia censet haec esse Democriti, non docentis sed optantis,—ipse autem singulas mundi partes persequens quidquid aut sit aut fiat naturalibus fieri aut factum esse docet ponderibus et motibus. Ne ille et deum opere magno liberat et me timore! quis enim potest, cum ex-

[1] quaero *inseruit Reid.*
[2] ac *inseruit Reid.*
[3] et *Goerens*: sed *codd.*
[4] ex *inseruit Reid.*

[a] A Greek artist famous for his microscopic works, doubtless chosen here because of his appropriate name (or nickname) 'Son of an Ant.'

is the mere freedom of my not being faced by the same obligation as you are! I ask for what reason did the deity, when making the universe for our sakes (for that is the view of your school), create so vast a supply of water-snakes and vipers, and why did he scatter so many death-bringing and destructive creatures over land and sea? Your school asserts that this highly finished and accurately constructed world of ours could not have been made without some skill of a divine nature (indeed it brings down that majestic deity to minutely fabricating the bees and the ants, so that we must even suppose that the list of gods included some Myrmecides,[a] an artist whose works were on a minutely small scale): you assert that nothing can be created without a god. Lo, here you have Strato of Lampsacus cutting in, bent on bestowing upon your deity exemption from exertion on any extensive scale (and seeing that the priests of the gods have holidays, how much fairer it is that the gods themselves should have them!); he declares that he does not make use of divine activity for constructing the world. His doctrine is that all existing things of whatever sort have been produced by natural causes, although he does not follow the master who says that this world of ours was welded out of rough and smooth, hook-shaped or crooked atoms interspersed with void—he judges these doctrines to be dreams on the part of Democritus, the talk of a visionary, not of a teacher,—but he himself, reviewing the various departments of the universe one by one, teaches that whatever either is or comes into being is or has been caused by natural forces of gravitation and motion. Assuredly he frees the deity from a great task, and also me from alarm! for who

istimet curari se a deo, non et dies et noctes divinum numen horrere et si quid adversi acciderit (quod cui non accidit ?) extimescere ne id iure evenerit ? Nec Stratoni tamen adsentior nec vero tibi ; modo hoc, modo illud probabilius videtur.

122 XXXIX. "Latent ista omnia, Luculle, crassis occultata et circumfusa tenebris, ut nulla acies humani ingenii tanta sit quae penetrare in caelum, terram intrare possit. Corpora nostra non novimus, qui sint situs partium, quam vim quaeque pars habeat ignoramus ; itaque medici ipsi, quorum intererat ea nosse, aperuerunt ut viderentur. nec eo tamen aiunt empirici notiora esse illa, quia possit fieri ut patefacta et detecta mutentur. Sed ecquid nos eodem modo rerum naturas persecare aperire dividere possumus, ut videamus terra penitusne defixa sit et quasi radicibus suis haereat an media

123 pendeat ? Habitari ait Xenophanes in luna, eamque esse terram multarum urbium et montium : portenta videntur, sed tamen nec ille qui dixit iurare possit ita se rem habere neque ego non ita. Vos etiam dicitis esse e regione nobis in contraria parte terrae qui adversis vestigiis stent contra nostra vestigia,

holding the view that a god pays heed to him can avoid shivering with dread of the divine power all day and all night long, and if any disaster happens to him (and to whom does it not?) being thoroughly frightened lest it be a judgement upon him? All the same I do not accept the view of Strato, nor yet yours either; at one moment one seems the more probable, and at another moment the other.

The heavenly bodies are outside our ken,

2 XXXIX. "All those things you talk about are hidden, Lucullus, closely concealed and enfolded in thick clouds of darkness, so that no human intellect has a sufficiently powerful sight to be able to penetrate the heaven and get inside the earth. We do not know our own bodies, we are ignorant of the positions of their parts and their several functions; and accordingly the doctors themselves, being concerned to know the structure of the body, have cut it open to bring its organs into view, yet nevertheless the empiric school assert that this has not increased our knowledge of them, because it is possibly the case that when exposed and uncovered they change their character. But is it at all within our power similarly to dissect and open up and separate the constituents of the universe, in order to see whether the earth is firmly fixed deep down and holds so to speak by its own roots, or hangs suspended at the
3 centre? Xenophanes says that the moon is inhabited, and is a land of many cities and mountains: these seem marvellous doctrines, but nevertheless I am no more able to swear that they do not agree with the facts than their author could swear that they do. Your school even says that there are people opposite to us on the contrary side of the earth, standing with the soles of their feet turned in the

quos antipodas vocatis: cur mihi magis suscensetis qui ista non aspernor quam eis qui cum audiunt desipere vos arbitrantur? Hicetas Syracosius, ut ait Theophrastus, caelum solem lunam stellas supera denique omnia stare censet neque praeter terram rem ullam in mundo moveri, quae cum circum axem se summa celeritate convertat et torqueat, eadem effici omnia quae si stante terra caelum moveretur; atque hoc etiam Platonem in Timaeo dicere quidam arbitrantur, sed paulo obscurius. Quid tu, Epicure? loquere, putas solem esse tantulum? ego ne bis[1] quidem tantum! Et vos ab illo inridemini et ipsi illum vicissim eluditis. Liber igitur a tali inrisione Socrates, liber Aristo Chius, qui nihil istorum sciri
124 putant[2] posse. Sed redeo ad animum et corpus. Satisne tandem ea nota sunt nobis, quae nervorum natura sit, quae venarum? tenemusne quid sit animus, ubi sit, denique sitne an, ut Dicaearcho visum est, ne sit quidem ullus? si est, trisne partes habeat, ut Platoni placuit, rationis irae cupiditatis, an simplex unusque sit? si simplex, utrum sit ignis an anima an sanguis an, ut Xenocrates, numerus[3] nullo corpore (quod intellegi quale sit vix potest)? et quidquid est, mortale sit an aeternum? nam

[1] *Reid*: ego ne vobis *codd.*: egone? ne bis *Lambinus.*
[2] *ed.* (*cf.* § 74): putat *codd.*
[3] numerus *Bentley*: mens *codd.*

---

[a] Plato, *Timaeus* 40 B.
[b] See § 82.
[c] See § 122, where however the mind is not introduced.
[d] *Republic*, *e.g.*, 439 D ff. τὸ λογιστικόν, τὸ θυμοειδές and τὸ ἐπιθυμητικόν.
[e] Some Stoics said fire, others warm breath (πνεῦμα ἔνθερμον).
[f] Empedocles.

opposite direction to ours, whom you call 'antipodes': why are you more irritated with me who do not scoff at these doctrines of yours than with those who when they hear them think you are out of your minds? The Syracusan Hicetas, as Theophrastus asserts, holds the view that the heaven, sun, moon, stars, and in short all of the things on high are stationary, and that nothing in the world is in motion except the earth, which by revolving and twisting round its axis with extreme velocity produces all the same results as would be produced if the earth were stationary and the heaven in motion; and this is also in some people's opinion the doctrine stated by Plato in *Timaeus*,[a] but a little more obscurely. What is your view, Epicurus? say, do you really think that the sun is as small as it appears? for my own part I don't think it is twice as big either![b] Your school are laughed at by Epicurus, and you yourselves also in your turn mock at him. Mockery of that sort therefore does not touch Socrates and does not touch Aristo of Chios, who think that none of the things that you treat of can be known. But I return to the mind and the body.[c] Pray are we sufficiently acquainted with the nature of the sinews and the veins? do we grasp what mind is, where it is, and in fine whether it exists, or, as Dicaearchus held, does not even exist at all? If it does, do we know if it has three parts, as Plato[d] held, reason, passion and appetite, or is a simple unity? if simple, whether it is fire or breath[e] or blood,[f] or, as Xenocrates said, an incorporeal numerical formula (a thing the very nature of which is almost unintelligible)? and whatever it is, whether it is mortal or everlasting? for many arguments are put forward

and so is the nature of the mind

utramque in partem multa dicuntur. Horum aliquid vestro sapienti certum videtur, nostro ne quid maxime quidem probabile sit occurrit, ita sunt in plerisque contrariarum rationum paria momenta.

125 XL. "Sin agis verecundius et me accusas non quod tuis rationibus non adsentiar sed quod nullis, vincam animum cuique adsentiar deligam—quem potissimum? quem? Democritum: semper enim, ut scitis, studiosus nobilitatis fui. Urgebor iam omnium vestrum convicio: 'Tune aut inane quicquam putes esse, cum ita completa et conferta sint omnia ut et quidquid[1] movebitur corporeum[2] cedat et qua quidque cesserit aliud ilico subsequatur? aut atomos ullas e quibus quidquid efficiatur illarum sit dissimillimum? aut sine aliqua mente rem ullam effici posse praeclaram? et cum in uno mundo ornatus hic tam sit mirabilis, innumerabilis supra infra, dextra sinistra, ante post, alios dissimiles, alios eiusdem modi mundos esse? et ut nos nunc simus ad Baulos Puteolosque videamus, sic innumerabiles paribus in locis esse eisdem nominibus honoribus rebus gestis ingeniis formis aetatibus, eisdem de rebus disputantes? et si nunc aut si etiam dormientes aliquid animo videre videamur, imagines extrinsecus in animos nostros per corpus inrumpere? Tu vero ista ne asciveris neve fueris commenticiis rebus

[1] quidquid *Reid*: quod *codd.*
[2] corporeum *Reid*: corporum *codd.*

[a] Implying that Democritus holds the high position in philosophy that noblemen hold in society.

on both sides. Some part of these matters seems to your wise man to be certain, but ours has not a notion even what part is most probable, to such an extent do most of these matters contain equal reasons for contrary theories.

25 XL. "If on the other hand you behave with greater modesty and charge me not with not agreeing with your arguments but with not agreeing with any, I will overcome my inclination, and will choose, in order to agree with him—whom for preference? whom? Democritus: for, as you know I have always been a devotee of rank[a]! Now I shall be assailed with upbraiding by all of you: 'Can you really suppose that any such thing as empty void exists, when the universe is so completely filled and packed that whenever a bodily object is set in motion it gives place and another object at once moves into the place that it has left? or that any atoms exist out of which are made things that are all entirely unlike them? or that anything splendid can be produced without the action of some mind? and that when one world contains the marvellously ordered beauty that we see, there exist above it and below, on the right and on the left, in front and behind, countless other worlds, some unlike it and others of the same sort? and that just as we are now at Bauli and have a view of Puteoli, so there are innumerable other groups of people with the same names and distinctions and records, minds, appearances and ages, discussing the same subjects in similar places? and that, if now or if even when asleep we seem to see something with the mind, it means that images are forcing a way through the body into our minds from outside? *You* must not accept such notions, or give your assent to mere

adsensus: nihil sentire est melius quam tam prava
126 sentire!' Non ergo id agitur ut aliquid adsensu meo comprobem, quod[1] tu vide ne impudenter etiam postules, non solum adroganter, praesertim cum ista tua mihi ne probabilia quidem videantur; nec enim divinationem quam probatis ullam esse arbitror, fatumque illud esse[2] quo omnia contineri dicitis contemno—ne exaedificatum quidem hunc mundum divino consilio existimo; atque haud scio an ita sit. XLI. Sed cur rapior in invidiam? licetne per vos nescire quod nescio? An Stoicis ipsis inter se disceptare, cum iis non[3] licebit? Zenoni et reliquis fere Stoicis aether videtur summus deus, mente praeditus qua omnia regantur, Cleanthes, qui quasi maiorum est gentium Stoicus, Zenonis auditor, solem dominari et rerum potiri putat; ita cogimur dissensione sapientium dominum nostrum ignorare, quippe qui nesciamus soli an aetheri serviamus. Solis autem magnitudinem—ipse enim hic radiatus me intueri videtur, admonens ut crebro faciam mentionem sui—vos ergo huius magnitudinem quasi decempeda permensi refertis, ego me quasi malis architectis mensurae vestrae nego credere: dubium est uter nostrum sit—leviter ut dicam—inverecundior[4]?
127 Nec tamen istas quaestiones physicorum exter-

[1] quod *Davies*: quae *codd.*
[2] esse *om. Christ.*
[3] non <nobis> *? Reid.*
[4] *Morgenstern*: verecundior *codd.*

fictions : it is better to have no opinions than to have such wrong ones!' Oh, then, the object is not to get me to give the approval of my assent to something —a demand which it is surely actually impudent and not merely arrogant for *you* to make, especially as these dogmas of yours don't seem to me even probable ; for I don't as a matter of fact think that there is any such thing as the divination which your school accepts, and I make light of the existence of that destiny which your school declares to be the bond that holds the universe together—I do not even deem that this world was built on a divine plan ; and yet it may be so. XLI. But why am I dragged into disfavour? may I have your leave not to know what I do not know? Are the Stoics to be allowed to dispute among themselves but nobody allowed to dispute with the Stoics? Zeno and almost all the other Stoics think the aether a supreme deity, endowed with a mind whereby the universe is ruled, Cleanthes, the Stoic of the older families as it were, who was a disciple of Zeno, holds that the sun is lord and master of the world ; thus the disagreement of the wise compels us to be ignorant of our own lord, inasmuch as we do not know whether we are the servants of the sun or of the aether. Then the size of the sun—for this radiant sun himself seems to be gazing at me, reminding me to keep mentioning him —your school then report his size as if you had measured it with a ten-foot rule, while I declare that I mistrust this measurement of yours as I distrust incompetent architects : then is it doubtful which of us is—to speak frivolously—the more modest? And all the same I do not think that these physical investigations of yours should be put out of bounds.

Yet the study of nature has moral value

minandas puto. Est enim animorum ingeniorumque naturale quoddam quasi pabulum consideratio contemplatioque naturae; erigimur, altiores fieri videmur, humana despicimus, cogitantesque supera atque caelestia haec nostra ut exigua et minima contemnimus. Indagatio ipsa rerum cum maximarum tum etiam occultissimarum habet oblectationem; si vero aliquid occurrit quod veri simile videatur,
128 humanissima completur animus voluptate. Quaeret igitur haec et vester sapiens et hic noster, sed vester ut adsentiatur credat adfirmet, noster ut vereatur temere opinari praeclareque agi secum putet si in eius modi rebus veri simile quod sit invenerit.

Veniamus nunc ad bonorum malorumque notionem: at[1] paulum ante dicendum est. Non mihi videntur considerare cum[2] ista valde adfirmant earum etiam rerum auctoritatem si quae inlustriores videantur amittere. Non enim magis adsentiuntur nec adprobant lucere nunc quam cum cornix cecinerit tum aliquid eam aut iubere aut vetare, nec magis adfirmabunt signum illud si erunt mensi sex pedum esse quam solem, quem metiri non possunt, plus quam duodeviginti partibus maiorem esse quam terram. Ex quo illa conclusio nascitur: si sol quantus sit percipi non potest, qui ceteras res eodem modo quo magnitu-

[1] at *Reid*: et *codd.*
[2] cum *Reid*: cum physici *codd.*

For the study and observation of nature affords a sort of natural pasturage for the spirit and intellect; we are uplifted, we seem to become more exalted, we look down on what is human, and while reflecting upon things above and in the heavens we despise this world of our own as small and even tiny. There is delight in the mere investigation of matters at once of supreme magnitude and also of extreme obscurity; while if a notion comes to us that appears to bear a likeness to the truth, the mind is filled with the most humanizing kind of pleasure. These researches therefore will be pursued both by your wise man and by this sage of ours, but by yours with the intention of assenting, believing and affirming, by ours with the resolve to be afraid of forming rash opinions and to deem that it goes well with him if in matters of this kind he has discovered that which bears a likeness to truth.

Even you admit that all sensations have equal validity.

Now let us come to the concept of good and evil: but a few words must be said first. When they assert those doctrines so positively they seem to me to forget that they also lose the guarantee for facts that appear to be more clear. For their assent to or acceptance of the fact that daylight is now shining is no more positive than their assent to the belief that when a crow croaks it is conveying some command or prohibition, and if they measure yonder statue, they will not affirm that it is six feet high with greater positiveness than they will affirm that the sun, which they cannot measure, is more than nineteen times as large as the earth. From this springs the following train of argument: if it cannot be perceived how large the sun is, he that accepts all other things in the same way as he accepts the sun

dinem solis adprobat, is eas res non percipit; magnitudo autem solis percipi non potest; qui igitur id adprobat quasi percipiat, nullam rem percipit. Responderint posse percipi quantus sol sit: non repugnabo dum modo eodem pacto cetera percipi comprehendique dicant; nec enim possunt dicere aliud alio magis minusve comprehendi, quoniam omnium rerum una est definitio comprehendendi.

129 XLII. "Sed quod coeperam: quid habemus in rebus bonis et malis explorati? Nempe fines constituendi sunt ad quos et bonorum et malorum summa referatur; qua de re est igitur inter summos viros maior dissensio? Omitto illa quae relicta iam videntur—ut Erillum, qui in cognitione et scientia summum bonum ponit; qui cum Zenonis auditor esset, vides quantum ab eo dissenserit et quam non multum a Platone. Megaricorum fuit nobilis disciplina, cuius, ut scriptum video, princeps Xenophanes quem modo nominavi; deinde eum secuti Parmenides et Zeno (itaque ab his Eleatici philosophi nominabantur), post Euclides, Socratis discipulus, Megareus (a quo idem illi Megarici dicti); qui id bonum solum esse dicebant quod esset unum et simile et idem semper. Hi quoque multa a Platone. A Menedemo autem, quod is Eretrius[1] fuit, Eretriaci appellati; quorum omne bonum in mente positum et mentis acie qua verum

[1] *Lambinus*: Eretrias, Eretria, ex Eretria *codd.*

[a] *i.e.*, *summum bonum et summum malum*, 'the supreme good and the supreme evil.' *Finis* has come to be almost a synonym for *summum*, 'highest in the scale,' losing the sense of 'object aimed at.'

does not perceive those things; but the size of the sun cannot be perceived; therefore he that accepts it as if he perceived it, perceives nothing. Suppose their answer is that it can be perceived how large the sun is: I will not combat this provided that they say that everything else can be perceived and grasped in the same manner; for in fact it is impossible for them to say that one thing is grasped more, or less, than another, since there is one definition of mental grasp in relation to all objects.

XLII. "But to resume: in the matter of good and evil what certain knowledge have we got? Clearly the task is to determine the Ends which are the standards of both the supreme good and the supreme evil[a]; if so, what question is the subject of greater disagreement among the leading thinkers? I leave out the systems that appear to be now abandoned—for example Erillus, who places the chief good in learning and in knowledge; although he was a pupil of Zeno, you see how much he disagreed with him and how little with Plato. A famous school was that of the Megarians, whose founder, as I see it recorded, was Xenophanes whom I mentioned just now; next he was followed by Parmenides and Zeno (and so the school of thought derived from them the name of Eleatic) and afterwards by Euclides, the pupil of Socrates, a Megarian (from whom the same school obtained the title of Megarian); their doctrine was that the sole good is that which is always one and alike and the same. These thinkers also took much from Plato. But from Menedemus, who was an Eretrian, they received the designation of the Eretrian school; they placed their good wholly in the mind and in keenness of mental vision whereby the

(8b) The Dogmatists' disagreement as to Ethics: examples.

cerneretur. Elii[1] similia sed opinor explicata uberius
130 et ornatius. Hos si contemnimus et iam abiectos putamus, illos certe minus despicere debemus: Aristonem, qui cum Zenonis fuisset auditor, re probavit ea quae ille verbis, nihil esse bonum nisi virtutem nec malum nisi quod virtuti esset contrarium; in mediis ea momenta quae Zeno voluit nulla esse censuit. Huic summum bonum est in his rebus neutram in partem moveri, quae ἀδιαφορία ab ipso dicitur; Pyrrho autem ea ne sentire quidem sapientem, quae ἀπάθεια nominatur. Has igitur tot sententias ut omittamus, haec nunc videamus quae diu multumque
131 defensa sunt. Alii voluptatem finem esse voluerunt; quorum princeps Aristippus qui Socratem audierat, unde Cyrenaici; post Epicurus, cuius est disciplina nunc notior nec tamen cum Cyrenaicis de ipsa voluptate consentiens. Voluptatem autem et honestatem finem esse Callipho censuit, vacare omni molestia Hieronymus, hoc idem cum honestate Diodorus, ambo hi Peripatetici; honeste autem vivere fruentem rebus iis quas primas homini natura conciliet et vetus Academia censuit, ut indicant scripta Polemonis quem Antiochus probat maxime, et Aristoteles eiusque amici huc proxime videntur

[1] Elii (*vel* Eliaci) *Reid*: ulli, illi *codd.*: Herilli *Mdv.*

[a] The term is more often applied as an adjective to the things themselves, ἀδιάφορα, 'indifferent.'

truth is discerned. The school of Elis taught a similar doctrine, but I believe they expounded it in
0 a more copious and ornate style. If we look down on these philosophers and think them out of date, we are undoubtedly bound to feel less contempt for the following: Aristo, who, having been a disciple of Zeno, proved in practice what his master established in theory, that nothing is good except virtue, and nothing evil unless it is contrary to virtue; those motives of action which Zeno held to exist in things intermediate he deemed to be non-existent. Aristo's chief good is in these things to be moved in neither direction—he himself calls it *adiaphoria* [a]; Pyrrho on the other hand held that the wise man does not even perceive these things with his senses—the name for this unconsciousness is *apatheia*. Leaving on one side therefore all these numerous opinions, let us now look at the following which have long been
1 strongly championed. Others have held that the end is pleasure; their founder was Aristippus, who had been a pupil of Socrates, and from whom they get the name of the Cyrenaic school; after him came Epicurus, whose doctrine is now more famous, although on the actual subject of pleasure it does not agree with the Cyrenaics. But Callipho defined the end as being pleasure and moral goodness, Hieronymus as freedom from all annoyance, Diodorus the same combined with moral goodness—both the two latter were Peripatetics; but the Old Academy defined the end as living the moral life while enjoying those primary things which nature recommends to man—this is proved by the writings of Polemo, who is very highly approved by Antiochus; and also Aristotle and his adherents seem to come very near

accedere. Introducebat etiam Carneades, non quo probaret sed ut opponeret Stoicis, summum bonum esse frui rebus iis quas primas natura conciliavisset. Honeste autem vivere, quod ducatur a conciliatione naturae, Zeno statuit finem esse bonorum, qui inventor et princeps Stoicorum fuit.

132 XLIII. "Iam illud perspicuum est, omnibus his finibus bonorum quos exposui malorum fines esse contrarios. Ad vos nunc refero quem sequar, modo ne quis illud tam ineruditum absurdumque respondeat, 'Quemlibet, modo aliquem': nihil potest dici inconsideratius. Cupio sequi Stoicos: licetne—omitto per Aristotelem, meo iudicio in philosophia prope singularem—per ipsum Antiochum? qui appellabatur Academicus, erat quidem,[1] si perpauca mutavisset, germanissimus Stoicus. Erit igitur res iam in discrimine, nam aut Stoicus constituatur[2] sapiens aut veteris Academiae. Utrumque non potest, est enim inter eos non de terminis sed de tota possessione contentio, nam omnis ratio vitae definitione summi boni continetur, de qua qui dissident de omni vitae ratione dissident. Non potest igitur uterque esse sapiens, quoniam tanto opere dissentiunt, sed alter. Si Polemoneus, peccat Stoicus rei falsae adsentiens—nam vos quidem[3] nihil esse dicitis a sapiente tam alienum; sin vera sunt Zenonis, eadem

[1] quidem: autem ? *ed.*
[2] constituetur *Lambinus.*
[3] nam vos quidem *Davies*: num quidem *codd.*: namque idem *Reid.*

to this position. Also Carneades used to put forward the view—not that he held it himself but in order to combat the Stoics with it—that the chief good was to enjoy those things that nature had recommended as primary. Zeno however, who was the originator and first head of the Stoics, set it up that the end of goods is the morally honourable life, and that this is derived from nature's recommendation.

Some Stoic doctrines are challenged by Antiochus,

XLIII. "There follows the obvious point that corresponding to all the ends of goods that I have set out there are opposite ends of evils. Whom I am to follow now I leave to you, only do not let anyone make that very uneducated and ridiculous answer 'Any body you like, only follow somebody'; no remark could be more ill-considered. I am eager to follow the Stoics: have I permission—I don't say from Aristotle, in my judgement almost the outstanding figure in philosophy, but from Antiochus himself? he was called an Academic, and was in fact, had he made very few modifications, a perfectly genuine Stoic. Well then, the matter will now come to an issue: we must settle on either the Stoic wise man or the wise man of the Old Academy. To take both is impossible, for the dispute between them is not about boundaries but about the whole ownership of the ground, since the entire scheme of life is bound up with the definition of the supreme good, and those who disagree about that disagree about the whole scheme of life. They cannot therefore each of them be the wise man, since they disagree so widely; it must be one or the other. If Polemo's is, the Stoic wise man sins in assenting to a falsehood —for you certainly say that nothing is so alien from the wise man; if on the other hand Zeno's

in veteres Academicos Peripateticosque dicenda. Hic igitur neutri adsentietur? Sin, inquam,[1] uter
133 est prudentior? Quid? cum ipse Antiochus dissentit quibusdam in rebus ab his quos amat Stoicis, nonne indicat non posse illa probanda esse sapienti? Placet Stoicis omnia peccata esse paria, at hoc Antiocho vehementissime displicet; liceat tandem mihi considerare utram sententiam sequar. 'Praecide,' inquit, 'statue aliquando quidlibet!' Quid quod quae dicuntur[2] et acuta mihi videntur in utramque partem et paria? nonne caveam ne scelus faciam? scelus enim dicebas esse, Luculle, dogma prodere; contineo igitur me ne incognito adsentiar—quod mihi
134 tecum est dogma commune. Ecce multo maior etiam dissensio: Zeno in una virtute positam beatam vitam putat; quid Antiochus? 'Etiam,' inquit, 'beatam sed non beatissimam.' Deus ille qui nihil censuit deesse virtuti, homuncio hic qui multa putat praeter virtutem homini partim cara[3] esse, partim etiam necessaria. Sed ille vereor ne virtuti plus tribuat quam natura patiatur, praesertim Theophrasto multa diserte copioseque contra[4] dicente. Et hic metuo ne vix sibi constet qui cum dicat esse quaedam et corporis et fortunae mala, tamen eum qui in his omnibus sit beatum fore censeat si sapiens sit. Distrahor—tum hoc mihi probabilius tum illud

[1] *Reid*: adsentiens si nunquam *codd.*
[2] quid quae dicuntur quid (*et alia*) *codd.*: *correxit Guiet.*
[3] cara *edd.*: clara *codd.*: praeclara *? Reid.*
[4] contra *inseruit Goerens.*

[a] *i.e.*, an opinion once decided, *decretum*, *cf.* § 27.

doctrine is true, the same verdict has to be passed against the Old Academics and the Peripatetics. Will Antiochus therefore agree with neither? or if
33 not, which of the two, say I, is the wiser? What then? when Antiochus himself disagrees in some things from these Stoic friends of his, does he not show that it is impossible for these views to be what the wise man must approve? The Stoics hold that all sins are equal, but with this Antiochus most violently disagrees; do please give me leave to deliberate which opinion to follow. 'Cut it short,' says he; 'do for once decide on something!' What of the fact that the arguments advanced seem to me both acute on either side and equally valid? am I not to be careful not to commit a crime? for you, Lucullus, said that it is a crime to abandon a dogma[a]; therefore I hold myself in so as not to assent to a thing unknown—that is a dogma that I share with you.
34 Look at an even much wider disagreement: Zeno thinks that the happy life is placed in virtue alone; what is the view of Antiochus? 'Yes,' says he, 'the happy life, but not the happiest.' Zeno was a god, he deemed that virtue lacks nothing: Antiochus is a puny mortal, he thinks that many things besides virtue are some of them dear to man and some even necessary. But I fear that Zeno assigns more to virtue than nature would allow, especially as Theophrastus says a great deal with eloquence and fullness on the opposite side. And as for Theophrastus, I am afraid it is hardly consistent of him both to say that certain evils of body and estate do exist, and yet to hold that a man for whom these are his entire environment will be happy if he is wise. I am dragged in different directions—now the latter view seems to

videtur. Et tamen, nisi alterutrum sit, virtutem iacere plane puto; verum in his discrepant.

135 XLIV. "Quid, illa in quibus consentiunt num pro veris probare possumus? Sapientis animum numquam nec cupiditate moveri nec laetitia ecferri? age, haec probabilia sane sint: num etiam illa, numquam timere, numquam dolere? Sapiensne non timeat ne patria deleatur? non doleat si deleta sit? Durum, sed Zenoni necessarium, cui praeter honestum nihil est in bonis; tibi vero, Antioche, minime, cui praeter honestatem multa bona, praeter turpitudinem multa mala videntur, quae et venientia metuat sapiens necesse est et venisse doleat. Sed quaero quando ista fuerint ab[1] Academia vetere decreta, ut animum sapientis commoveri et conturbari negarent. Mediocritates illi probabant, et in omni permotione naturalem volebant esse quendam modum. Legimus omnes Crantoris veteris Academici De Luctu; est enim non magnus verum aureolus et, ut Tuberoni Panaetius praecipit, ad verbum ediscendus libellus. Atque illi quidem etiam utiliter a natura dicebant permotiones istas animis nostris datas, metum cavendi causa, misericordiam aegritudinemque clementiae; ipsam iracundiam fortitudinis quasi cotem esse dicebant, recte secusne alias

[1] ab *ins* edd.

[a] *Cf.* § 27.

me the more probable, now the former. And yet I firmly believe that unless one or other is true, virtue is overthrown; but they are at variance on these points.

and even those that he accepts are paradoxical;

XLIV. "Again, those tenets on which they agree surely cannot be approved by us as true? The doctrine that the mind of the wise man is never moved by desire or elated by joy? well, granted that this may be probable, surely the following tenets are not so too, that he never feels fear and that he never feels pain? would the wise man feel no fear lest his country might be destroyed? no pain if it were? A hard doctrine, although unavoidable for Zeno, who includes nothing in the category of good save moral worth; but not at all unavoidable for you, Antiochus, who think many things good beside moral worth, and many bad beside baseness—things that the wise man is bound to fear when they are coming and to regret when they have come. But I want to know when the Old Academy adopted 'decisions'[a] of that sort, asserting that the mind of the wise man does not undergo emotion and perturbation. That school were upholders of the mean in things, and held that in all emotion there was a certain measure that was natural. We have all read the Old Academician Crantor's *On Grief*, for it is not a large but a golden little volume, and one to be thoroughly studied word by word, as Panaetius enjoins upon Tubero. And the Old Academy indeed used to say that the emotions in question were bestowed by nature upon our minds for actually useful purposes—fear for the sake of exercising caution, pity and sorrow for the sake of mercy; anger itself they used to say was a sort of whetstone of courage—whether this was right or not let us con-

136 viderimus. Atrocitas quidem ista tua quo modo in veterem Academiam inruperit nescio ; illa vero ferre non possum, non quo mihi displiceant (sunt enim Socratica pleraque mirabilia Stoicorum, quae παράδοξα nominantur), sed ubi Xenocrates, ubi Aristoteles ista tetigit (hos enim quasi eosdem esse vultis) ? illi umquam dicerent sapientes solos reges, solos divites, solos formosos, omnia quae ubique essent sapientis esse, neminem consulem praetorem imperatorem, nescio an ne quinquevirum quidem quemquam, nisi sapientem, postremo solum civem, solum liberum, insipientes omnes peregrinos, exsules, servos, furiosos ? denique scripta[1] Lycurgi, Solonis, duodecim tabulas nostras non esse leges ? ne urbes quidem aut
137 civitates nisi quae essent sapientium ? Haec tibi, Luculle, si es adsensus Antiocho familiari tuo, tam sunt defendenda quam moenia, mihi autem bono modo tantum quantum videbitur.

XLV. " Legi apud Clitomachum, cum Carneades et Stoicus Diogenes ad senatum in Capitolio starent, A. Albinum qui tum P. Scipione et M. Marcello consulibus praetor esset, eum qui cum avo tuo, Luculle, consul fuit, doctum sane hominem ut indicat ipsius historia scripta Graece, iocantem dixisse Carneadi : ' Ego tibi, Carneade, praetor esse non videor [quia sapiens

[1] praescripta ? *Reid.*

---

[a] This is done in the *Tusculan Disputations.*

[b] *i.e.*, allow you to advance them.

[c] With Critolaus they came on an embassy from Athens, 155 B.C.

[d] This interpolation spoils the joke, which turns on the Academician's doctrine of the uncertainty of all things.

sider on another occasion.[a] How indeed that ferocity of yours forced an entrance into the Old Academy I do not know; but I cannot approve [b] those doctrines, not because they seem unsatisfactory to me (for most of the 'surprising arguments,' the so-called *paradoxa* of the Stoics belong to Socrates), but where did Xenocrates hint at those views, or Aristotle (for you maintain that Xenocrates and Aristotle are almost identical)? could *they* ever say that wise men alone are kings, alone wealthy, alone handsome, that all the things anywhere existing belong to the wise man, that no one is consul or praetor or general, no one even a police-magistrate, except the wise man, and finally that he only is a citizen and a free man, and that all those not wise are foreigners and exiles and slaves and madmen? in fact that the rules given under the hand of Lycurgus and Solon, and our Twelve Tables, are not laws? that there are no cities even nor states save those that are the work of wise men? You, Lucullus, if you have accepted the views of your associate Antiochus, are bound to defend these doctrines as you would defend the walls of Rome, but I need only do so in moderation, just as much as I think fit.

while Carneades questions other Stoic doctrines.

XLV. "I have read in Clitomachus that when Carneades and the Stoic Diogenes [c] were on the Capitol attending on the senate, Aulus Albinus, who was praetor at the time, in the consulship of Publius Scipio and Marcus Marcellus,—he was a colleague of your grandfather, Lucullus, as consul, and his own history written in Greek shows him to have been a decidedly learned man,—said to Carneades in jest: 'In your view, Carneades, I am not a real praetor [because I am not a wise man [d]], nor is this a real

non sum][1] nec haec urbs nec in ea civitas.' Tum ille: 'Huic Stoico non videris.' Aristoteles aut Xenocrates, quos Antiochus sequi volebat, non dubitavisset quin et praetor ille esset et Roma urbs et eam civitas incoleret; sed ille noster est plane, ut supra
138 dixi, Stoicus, perpauca balbutiens. Vos autem mihi verenti ne labar ad opinationem et aliquid adsciscam et comprobem incognitum (quod minime vultis), quid consilii datis? Testatur saepe Chrysippus tres solas esse sententias quae defendi possint de finibus bonorum, circumcidit et amputat multitudinem—aut enim honestatem esse finem aut voluptatem aut utrumque; nam qui summum bonum dicant id esse si vacemus omni molestia, eos invidiosum nomen voluptatis fugere, sed in vicinitate versari, quod facere eos etiam qui illud idem cum honestate coniungerent, nec multo secus eos qui ad honestatem prima naturae commoda adiungerent; ita tris relinquit sententias quas putet probabiliter posse
139 defendi. Sit sane ita, quamquam a Polemonis et Peripateticorum et Antiochi finibus non facile divellor nec quicquam habeo adhuc probabilius—verum tamen video quam suaviter voluptas sensibus nostris blandiatur. Labor eo ut adsentiar Epicuro aut Aristippo: revocat virtus vel potius reprendit manu, pecudum illos motus esse dicit, hominem iungit deo.

[1] *Reid.*

city nor its corporation a real corporation.' 'In the view of our Stoic friend here you are not,' replied Carneades. Aristotle or Xenocrates, the masters of whom Antiochus made himself out to be a follower, would not have doubted either that Albinus was a praetor or Rome a city or its inhabitants a corporation; but our friend Carneades, as I said above, is a downright Stoic, though stammering on a very few points. As for yourselves however, seeing that I am afraid I may slip into forming opinions and adopt and approve something that I do not know (which you specially disapprove of), what advice do you give me? Chrysippus often solemnly avows that from among possible views as to the chief good there are only three that can be defended—a crowd of others he lops off and discards: for he holds that the end is either moral goodness, or pleasure, or a combination of the two; for those who say that the chief good consists in our being free from all trouble are trying (he says) to avoid the unpopular word 'pleasure,' but don't get very far away from it, and the same is also the case with those who combine freedom from trouble with moral goodness, nor is it very different with those who to moral goodness join the primary advantages of nature: thus he leaves three opinions that he thinks capable of a probable defence. Suppose it is so, although I find it hard to be parted from the Ends of Polemo and the Peripatetics and Antiochus, and hitherto have got nothing more probable—but nevertheless I see how sweetly pleasure flatters our senses. I am slipping into agreeing with Epicurus or else Aristippus: virtue calls me back, or rather plucks me back with her hand; she declares that those are the feelings of the beasts of the field, and

In fact the contest is between Pleasure and Virtue

Possum esse medius, ut, quoniam Aristippus quasi
animum nullum habeamus corpus solum tuetur, Zeno
quasi corporis simus expertes animum solum com-
plectitur, ut Calliphontem sequar, cuius quidem sententiam Carneades ita studiose defensitabat ut eam
probare etiam videretur (quamquam Clitomachus
adfirmabat numquam se intellegere potuisse quid
Carneadi probaretur); sed si istum finem velim
sequi, nonne ipsa veritas et gravis et recta ratio
mihi obversetur, 'Tune,[1] cum honestas in voluptate
contemnenda consistat, honestatem cum voluptate
140 tamquam hominem cum belua copulabis?' XLVI.
Unum igitur par quod depugnet relicum est, voluptas
cum honestate; de quo Chrysippo fuit quantum ego
sentio non magna contentio. Alteram si sequare,
multa ruunt et maxime communitas cum hominum
genere, caritas amicitia iustitia, reliquae virtutes,
quarum esse nulla potest nisi erit gratuita, nam quae
voluptate quasi mercede aliqua ad officium impellitur,
ea non est virtus sed fallax imitatio simulatioque
virtutis. Audi contra illos qui nomen honestatis a
se ne intellegi quidem dicant, nisi forte quod glo-
riosum sit in vulgus id honestum velimus dicere;
fontem omnium bonorum in corpore esse, hanc
normam, hanc regulam, hanc praescriptionem esse
naturae, a qua qui aberravisset, eum numquam quid
141 in vita sequeretur habiturum. Nihil igitur me putatis,[2] haec et alia innumerabilia cum audiam, moveri?
Tam moveor quam tu, Luculle, nec me minus homi-

[1] tune *Reid*: tum *codd.*
[2] putabis *Manutius*: putas *Goerens.*

she links the human being with god. A possible line is for me to be neutral, so that, as Aristippus looks only at the body, as if we had no mind, and Zeno takes into consideration only the mind, as if we were without a body, I should follow Calliphon, whose opinion indeed Carneades was constantly defending with so much zeal that he was thought actually to accept it (although Clitomachus used to declare that he had never been able to understand what Carneades did accept); but if I were willing to follow that End, would not truth herself and the weight of right reason meet me with the reply: 'What, when the essence of morality is to scorn pleasure, will you couple morality with pleasure, like a human being with a beast?'

140 XLVI. There remains therefore one match to be fought off—pleasure *versus* moral worth: and on this issue Chrysippus, as far as I for my part can perceive, had not much of a struggle. If one should follow the former, many things fall in ruin, and especially fellowship with mankind, affection, friendship, justice and the rest of the virtues, none of which can exist unless they are disinterested, for virtue driven to duty by pleasure as a sort of pay is not virtue at all but a deceptive sham and pretence of virtue. Hear on the opposite side those who say that they do not even understand what the word 'virtue' means, unless indeed we choose to give the name 'moral' to what looks well with the mob: that the source of all things good is in the body—this is nature's canon and rule and injunction, to stray away from which will result in a man's never having an object to follow in
141 life. Do you people therefore suppose that when I am listening to these and countless other things, I am quite unaffected? I am just as much affected as

nem quam te putaveris. Tantum interest quod tu cum es commotus adquiescis, adsentiris, adprobas, verum illud certum comprehensum perceptum ratum firmum fixum vis esse,[1] deque eo nulla ratione neque pelli neque moveri potes, ego nihil eius modi esse arbitror cui si adsensus sim non adsentiar saepe falso, quoniam vera a falsis nullo discrimine separantur, praesertim cum iudicia ista dialecticae nulla sint.

142 "Venio enim iam ad tertiam partem philosophiae. Aliud iudicium Protagorae est qui putet id cuique verum esse quod cuique videatur, aliud Cyrenaicorum qui praeter permotiones intimas nihil putant esse iudicii, aliud Epicuri qui omne iudicium in sensibus et in rerum notitiis et in voluptate constituit; Plato autem omne iudicium veritatis veritatemque ipsam abductam ab opinionibus et a sensibus cogitationis
143 ipsius et mentis esse voluit. Num quid horum probat noster Antiochus? Ille vero ne maiorum quidem suorum—ubi enim aut Xenocraten sequitur, cuius libri sunt de ratione loquendi multi et multum probati, aut ipsum Aristotelem, quo profecto nihil est acutius, nihil politius? A Chrysippo pedem nusquam. XLVII. Quid ergo Academici appellamur? an abutimur gloria nominis? Aut cur cogimur eos sequi qui inter se dissident? In hoc ipso quod

[1] vis esse *Reid*: fuisse vis *vel* fuisse *vel* vis *codd.*

[a] See i. 25 note.

you are, Lucullus, pray don't think that I am less a human being than yourself. The only difference is that whereas you, when you have been deeply affected, acquiesce, assent, approve, hold that the fact is certain, comprehended, perceived, ratified, firm, fixed, and are unable to be driven or moved away from it by any reason, I on the contrary am of the opinion that there is nothing of such a kind that if I assent to it I shall not often be assenting to a falsehood, since truths are not separated from falsehoods by any distinction, especially as those logical criteria of yours are non-existent.

(8c) The Dogmatists' disagreement on Logic.

"For I come now to the third part of philosophy. One view of the criterion is that of Protagoras, who holds that what seems true to each person is true for each person, another is that of the Cyrenaics, who hold that there is no criterion whatever except the inward emotions, another that of Epicurus, who places the standard of judgement entirely in the senses and in notions of objects and in pleasure; Plato however held that the entire criterion of truth and truth itself is detached from opinions and from the senses and belongs to the mere activity of thought and to the mind. Surely our friend Antiochus does not approve any doctrine of these teachers? On the contrary he does not even accept anything from his own ancestors —for where does he follow either Xenocrates, who has many volumes on logic[a] that are highly thought of, or Aristotle himself, who is assuredly unsurpassed for acumen and finish? He never diverges a foot's length from Chrysippus. XLVII. Why then are we called the Academics? is our use of that glorious title a mistake? Or why is the attempt made to force us to follow a set of thinkers who are divided among

in elementis dialectici docent, quo modo iudicare
oporteat verum falsumne sit si quid ita conexum est
ut hoc, 'si dies est, lucet,' quanta contentio est!
Aliter Diodoro, aliter Philoni, Chrysippo aliter placet.
Quid? cum Cleanthe doctore suo quam multis rebus
Chrysippus dissidet? quid? duo vel principes dialecticorum, Antipater et Archidemus, opiniosissimi
144 homines, nonne multis in rebus dissentiunt? Quid
me igitur, Luculle, in invidiam et tamquam in con-
tionem vocas, et quidem, ut seditiosi tribuni solent,
occludi tabernas iubes? quo enim spectat illud cum
artificia tolli quereris a nobis, nisi ut opifices con-
citentur? Qui si undique omnes convenerint, facile
contra vos incitabuntur! expromam primum illa
invidiosa, quod eos omnes qui in contione stabunt
exsules servos insanos esse dicatis; dein ad illa
veniam quae iam non ad multitudinem sed ad vosmet
ipsos qui adestis pertinent: negat enim vos Zeno,
negat Antiochus scire quicquam. 'Quo modo?'
inquies; 'nos enim defendimus etiam insipientem
145 multa comprendere.' At scire negatis quemquam
rem ullam nisi sapientem; et hoc quidem Zeno
gestu conficiebat: nam cum extensis digitis adversam
manum ostenderat, 'visum' inquiebat 'huius modi
est'; dein cum paulum digitos contraxerat, 'adsensus huius modi'; tum cum plane compresserat

[a] This word is coined by Cicero in jest. For *opinio* = δόξα or δόγμα *cf.* i. 39, 42.

themselves? Even on a matter that is among the very elements taught by the dialecticians, the proper mode of judging the truth or falsehood of a hypothetical judgement like 'if day has dawned, it is light,' what a dispute goes on! Diodorus holds one view, Philo another, Chrysippus another. Then, how many points of difference there are between Chrysippus and his teacher Cleanthes? Then, do not two of even the leading dialecticians, Antipater and Archidemus, the most obstinate dogmatists[a] of all mankind, disagree on many things? Why then, Lucullus, do you bring *me* into disfavour, and summon me before a public assembly, so to speak, and actually imitate seditious tribunes and order the shops to be shut? for what is the object of your complaint that we are abolishing the practical sciences, unless it aims at stirring up the craftsmen? But if they all come together from every quarter, it will be easy to stir them on to attack your side! I shall first expound the unpopular doctrine that all the persons then standing in the assembly are on your showing exiles, slaves and madmen; then I shall come to the point that concerns not the multitude but you yourselves now present: according to Zeno and according to Antiochus, you do not know anything! 'What do you mean by that?' you will say; 'for what we maintain is that even the unwise man can comprehend many things.' But you deny that anybody except the wise man *knows* anything; and this Zeno used to demonstrate by gesture: for he would display his hand in front of one with the fingers stretched out and say 'A visual appearance is like this'; next he closed his fingers a little and said, 'An act of assent is like this'; then he pressed his

Logic is certainly not necessary for the arts and crafts.

pugnumque fecerat, comprensionem illam esse dicebat (qua ex similitudine etiam nomen ei rei, quod ante non fuerat, κατάληψιν imposuit); cum autem laevam manum admoverat et illum pugnum arte vehementerque compresserat, scientiam talem esse dicebat, cuius compotem nisi sapientem esse neminem —sed qui sapiens sit aut fuerit ne ipsi quidem solent dicere. Ita tu nunc, Catule, lucere nescis, nec tu,
146 Hortensi, in tua villa nos esse! Num minus haec invidiose dicuntur? nec tamen nimis eleganter; illa subtilius. Sed quo modo tu, si comprehendi nihil posset, artificia concidere dicebas nec mihi dabas id quod probabile esset satis magnam vim habere ad artes, sic ego nunc tibi refero artem sine scientia esse non posse. An pateretur hoc Zeuxis aut Phidias aut Polyclitus, nihil se scire, cum in iis esset tanta sollertia? Quodsi eos docuisset aliquis quam vim habere diceretur scientia, desinerent irasci: ne nobis quidem suscenserent cum didicissent id tollere nos quod nusquam esset, quod autem satis esset ipsis relinquere. Quam rationem maiorum etiam comprobat diligentia, qui primum iurare 'ex sui animi sententia' quemque voluerunt, deinde ita teneri 'si sciens falleret' (quod inscientia multa versaretur in vita), tum qui testimonium diceret ut

[a] See § 22 note.

fingers closely together and made a fist, and said that that was comprehension (and from this illustration he gave to that process the actual name of *catalēpsis*, which it had not had before) ; but then he used to apply his left hand to his right fist and squeeze it tightly and forcibly, and then say that such was knowledge, which was within the power of nobody save the wise man—but who is a wise man or ever has been even they themselves do not usually say. On that showing you, Catulus, at the present moment, do not *know* that it is daytime, nor do you, Hortensius, *know* that we are at your country-house !
146 Surely these are not less unpopular arguments ? though they are not over-neatly put—the ones before were more clearly worked out. But just as you said [a] that if nothing can be comprehended, the practice of the arts and crafts collapses, and would not grant me that sufficient validity for this purpose is possessed by probability, so now I retort to you that art cannot exist without scientific knowledge. Would Zeuxis or Phidias or Polyclitus endure to admit that they knew nothing, when they possessed such great skill ? But if somebody explained to them what power is said to be possessed by knowledge, they would cease to be angry : indeed they would not feel a tinge of resentment even against us after it had been explained to them that we do away with a thing that nowhere exists but left to themselves what is sufficient for them. This theory is also supported by the precaution of our ancestors in requiring every juror to swear to give a verdict ' after the opinion of his own mind,' and afterwards to be held guilty of perjury ' if he gave a false verdict wittingly ' (because much that was unwitting occurred in life), and then

[a] 'arbitrari' se diceret etiam quod ipse vidisset, quaeque iurati iudices cognovissent ea non ut 'esse facta' sed ut 'videri' pronuntiarentur.

147 XLVIII. "Verum quoniam non solum nauta significat sed etiam Favonius ipse insusurrat navigandi nobis, Luculle, tempus esse, et quoniam satis multa dixi, est mihi perorandum. Posthac tamen cum haec quaeremus, potius de dissensionibus tantis summorum virorum disseramus, de obscuritate naturae deque errore tot philosophorum (qui de bonis contrariisque rebus tanto opere discrepant ut, cum plus uno verum esse non possit, iacere necesse sit tot tam nobiles disciplinas), quam de oculorum sensuumque reliquorum mendaciis et de sorite aut pseudomeno, quas plagas ipsi contra se Stoici texue-
148 runt." Tum Lucullus: "Non moleste," inquit, "fero nos haec contulisse; saepius enim congredientes nos, et maxume in Tusculanis nostris, si quae videbuntur requiremus." "Optume," inquam, "sed quid Catulus sentit? quid Hortensius?" Tum Catulus: "Egone?" inquit; "ad patris revolvor sententiam, quam quidem ille Carneadeam esse dicebat, ut percipi nihil putem posse, adsensurum autem non percepto, id est opinaturum, sapientem existumem, sed ita ut intellegat se opinari sciatque[1]

[1] sentiatque ? *Reid.*

---

[a] This foreshadows *De Finibus*, and possibly the preceding words also include *De Natura Deorum*, which was certainly written after the second edition of *Academica* was finished.

[b] See § 49 note. [c] See § 95.

enacted that a witness giving evidence should say that he ' thought ' even something that he had himself seen, and that the jury giving their verdict on oath should declare not that the facts which they had ascertained ' had occurred ' but that they ' appeared to have.'

147 XLVIII. " However, Lucullus, not only is our sailor signalling but even the west wind itself is whispering that it is time for us to be cruising, and also I have said enough ; so I ought to round off. On a later occasion however when we engage in these inquiries, let us by preference discuss the wide differences of opinion that exist among the men of greatest eminence, the obscurity of nature and the errors of all these philosophers (who disagree so violently about things good and their opposites [a] that, since there cannot be more than one truth, a large number of these famous systems must of necessity collapse), rather than the subject of the falsehoods told by our eyes and the rest of our senses, and the fallacies of ' the heap ' [b] and ' the liar ' [c]—traps Conclusi
148 that the Stoics have set to catch themselves." " I am not sorry," rejoined Lucullus, " that we have debated these subjects ; in fact we will meet more frequently, and particularly at our places at Tusculum, to investigate such questions as we think fit." " Excellent," said I, " but what is Catulus's view ? and Hortensius's ? " " My view ? " replied Catulus ; " I am coming round to the view of my father, which indeed he used to say was that of Carneades, and am beginning to think that nothing can be perceived, but to deem that the wise man will assent to something not perceived, that is, will hold an opinion, but with the qualification that he will understand that

nihil esse quod comprehendi et percipi possit; quare ἐποχήν illam omnium rerum comprobans[1] illi alteri sententiae, nihil esse quod percipi possit, vehementer adsentior." "Habeo," inquam, "sententiam tuam nec eam admodum aspernor; sed tibi quid tandem videtur, Hortensi?" Tum ille ridens: "Tollendum!" "Teneo te," inquam, "nam ista Academiae est propria sententia." Ita sermone confecto Catulus remansit, nos ad naviculas nostras descendimus.

[1] non probans *Mdv.*: improbans *Davies.*

---

[a] Possibly the Latin should be corrected to 'disagreeing.'

it is an opinion and will know that there is nothing that can be comprehended and perceived: and therefore although agreeing[a] with their rule of *epochē* as to everything,[b] I assent emphatically to that second view, that nothing exists that can be perceived." "I have your view," said I, "and I do not think it quite negligible; but pray, Hortensius, what do you think?" "Away with it!"[c] he replied with a laugh. "I take you," said I, "for that is the true Academic verdict." The conversation thus concluded, Catulus stayed behind, while we went down to our boats.

[b] *i.e.*, refusal to state any opinion, whether as certain or as probable: see § 104, and for the term, § 59.

[c] A *double entente*, (1) 'make a clean sweep' of assent, and (2) 'weigh anchor.'

INDEX TO ACADEMICA

(*Greek words in italics*)

acatalepton, ii. 18
Accius (see p. 388), i. 10
acervus, ii 147
active and passive, i. 24
adamare, fr. 4
adēla, ii 54
adiaphoria, ii. 130
Aelius Stilo (Roman knight and scholar), i. 8
aequor, fr. 3
Aeschines (pupil of Carneades), ii. 16
Aeschylus, i. 10
aestimatio, i. 36
Africanus, see Scipio
Agnon (*v.l.* Aeschines), ii. 16
agnosticism, i 45, ii. 14
Ajax Furens, ii. 89 n.
alabaster, fr. 11
Albinus, Postumius (praetor 155 B.C.), ii. 137
Alcmaeo (one of Seven against Thebes, slew his mother, haunted by Furies: title-part of play by Ennius), ii. 52, 88 f.
Alexander the Great, ii. 3, 85
Alexinus (Megarian philosopher), ii. 75
Amafinius (Roman Epicurean writer), i. 5
Anaxagoras (see p. 388), i. 40, ii. 72, 100, 118, 123
Anaximander (see p 388), ii. 118
Anaximenes (see p. 388), ii. 115
Andromacha (tragedy of Ennius), ii. 20
Antiochus (Academic, of Ascalon, d. 68 B.C.), i. 7, 16-24, 29, 31 f., 35; ii. 16 f., 20, 30, 37, 49, 123, 126, 131 ff.
Antiopa (tragedy of Pacuvius), ii. 20
Antipater (Stoic, of Tarsus), ii. 28, 109, 143
antipodes, ii. 123
Antiquities, Varro's, i. 8 f.
antistrophos, i 32
apatheia, ii. 130
Apollo, i. 16; ii. 89
Apology of Socrates, i. 16 n.
aporia, ii. 95
Arcesilas (see p. 389), i. 17, 35; ii. 7, 15 f., 21, 32
Archidemus (minor Stoic), ii 143
Archimedes (see p. 389), ii. 116
Aristippus (see p. 389), ii. 131, 139
Aristo (see p. 389), ii. 123
Aristo the Peripatetic (head of school *c* 225 B.C.), ii 12
Aristotle, i. 17-25, 29-34, 38; ii. 7, 16 f., 22, 47, 131
Aristus (of Ascalon, Academic, brother of Antiochus), i. 12; ii. 12
Asia (Roman province), ii. 1 ff.
assent, i. 45; ii. 37 ff., 67 f.
Athens, i. 12; ii. 69
atoms, i. 6, ii. 125
Atticus, i. 2, 14, 18, 37
axia, i. 36
axiōma, ii. 95

Bauli (between Misenum and Baiae in Campania), ii. 9, 125
Brutus (slayer of Caesar), i 12

Callipho (pupil of Epicurus), ii. 131, 139
captions, ii. 45 f.

INDEX TO ACADEMICA

Carneades (see p. 389), i. 45 f.; ii. 16, 28, 32, 40, 67, 78, 87, 112, 131, 137 f.
Cassius, L. (consul 125 B.C.), ii. 102
catalēpsis, *catalēpton*, i. 41; ii. 14, 145
Cato, Censorinus (consul 95 B.C.), ii. 5
Charmadas (Academic, pupil of Carneades), ii. 16
Chrysippus (see p. 390), ii. 73, 75, 93, 96, 138, 140, 143
Cimmerium, ii. 61
Cleanthes (see p. 390), i. 32; ii. 18, 126
Clitomachus (pupil of Carneades), ii. 16, 76, 97, 102, 108, 139
comprehension, i. 41 f.; ii. 16
concinnare, fr. 2
corpora=*atomoi*, ii. 121
corpuscula, i. 6
Crantor (Old Academy, *fl.* 300 B.C.), i. 35; ii. 135
Crassus, P. (consul 131 B.C.), ii. 13
Crates (Old Academy), i. 35
critērion, ii. 142
Cumae, i. 1; ii. 80
Cynosure (the Little Bear), ii. 66
Cyrenaics, ii. 20, 131, 142

Dardanus (minor Stoic), ii. 69
Delos (ravaged by army of Mithridates 80 B.C.), ii. 57, 86
Democritus (see p. 390), i. 6, 32, 44; ii. 14, 32, 55, 73, 118, 125
diadochos, i. 17
dialecticē, i. 30 n., 32; ii. 91
Diana, ii. 89
digladiari, fr. 12
Dio (Academic, of Alexandria), ii. 12
Diodorus (Megarian), ii. 75, 143
Diodorus (Syrian Peripatetic), ii. 131
Diodotus (see p. 390), ii. 115
Diogenes (of Babylon, see p. 390), ii. 98, 137
Dionysius (pupil of Zeno), ii. 71
dissection, ii. 122
dogmata, ii. 27, 29
dove's neck, i. 19; ii. 79

earth, motion of, ii. 123; divine, ii. 119

efficient causes, i. 6
eggs alike, ii. 54, 59, 86
eidē, ii. 58 n.
eirōneia, ii. 15, 74
ekkalyptein, ii. 26
Eleans, ii. 129
Empedocles (see p. 390), i. 44; ii. 14, 74, 124
enargeia, ii. 17
End, i. 22
Ennius (see p. 390), i. 10; ii. 20, 51 f., 88 f.
ennoiai, ii. 22, 30
Epicharmus, ii. 51
Epicurus, i. 5 f., 13, 27 f.; ii. 18, 79, 82, 89, 97, 120, 140, 142
epochē, ii. 59
Eretrians, ii. 129
Erillus (Stoic, pupil of Zeno), ii. 129
ethos, *ēthos*, i. 20
etymologia, i. 32
Euclides (founder of Megarian school), ii. 129
Euripides, i. 10; ii. 89
Eurystheus, ii. 89
Evander (Academic), ii. 16
exceptio, ii. 97
exponere, fr. 5
extremitas, ii. 116
exultare, fr. 13

Fannius, C. (consul 122 B.C.), ii. 16
fifth-class, ii. 73
Flaminius, C. (see p. 391), ii. 13
formae, ii. 58
Fortuna, i. 29

Galba, S. Sulpicius (praetor 187 B.C.), ii. 51
geometry, i. 6; ii. 23, 91, 116
Gracchus, Tiberius (tribune 133 B.C.), ii. 13

Hagnon (Academic, pupil of Carneades), ii. 16
hebes, fr. 6
Hegesinus (Academic), ii. 16
Helicē (the Great Bear), ii. 66
Heraclitus of Ephesus (see p. 391), ii. 118
Heraclitus Tyrius (associate of Antiochus), ii. 11 f.

INDEX TO ACADEMICA

Hercules, ii. 108
Hermarchus (see p. 391), ii. 97
hēsychazein, ii. 13
Hicetas (early Pythagorean), ii. 123
Hieronymus (Rhodian, Peripatetic), ii. 131
Homer, ii. 51, 88
hormē, ii. 24, 30 n.
Hortensius, Q. Hortalus (consul 69 B.C.), ii. 2, 9 f., 28, 148; (Cicero's dialogue), ii. 6 61
hy'ē, i. 24
Hyperides (Attic orator, middle 4th century B.C.), i. 10

idea, i. 30, 33
Iliona (daughter of Priam, wife of Thracian Polymnestor, who murdered Polydorus, her little brother entrusted to her maternal care), ii. 88
individua = *atomoi*, ii. 55
ingenerari, fr. 14
institutiam, i. 44
institutio, ii. 102
irony, ii. 15, 74

kalon, i. 23, 35
katalēpton, i. 41; ii. 17, 31
koinōnia anthrōpinē, i. 21

Lacydes (Academic), ii. 16
Latin, use of, i. 3 ff., 18
Leucippus (see p. 392), ii. 118
Liar, the, ii. 95, 147
Libo, L. Scribonius (consul 34 B.C., father-in-law of Pompey), i. 3
libramentum = *homalon* (see extremitas), ii. 116
light of reason, ii. 26
logikē, i. 30 n.
Lucullus (consul 74 B.C.), ii. 1 f., 11 etc.
Lyceum (gymnasium at Athens), i. 17
Lycurgus (Spartan law-giver), ii. 136
Lysippus (of Sicyon, sculptor *temp.* Alexander), ii. 85

Maeniana, ii. 70
Manilius (consul 149 B.C.), ii. 102
Marius (see p. 392), ii. 13
mathematics, ii. 82, 106, 116, 118
matter, i. 24, 27
Megarians, ii. 129
Melanthius (Academic, pupil of Carneades), ii. 16
Melissus (of Samos, Eleatic, pupil of Parmenides), ii. 118
memoria technica, ii. 2
Menedemus (founded Eretrian school, later 3rd century B.C.), i. 45
Menippus (Cynic philosopher and satirist of Gadara, middle 2nd century B.C.), i. 8
mentiens, ii. 95, 147
meros poleōs, i. 21
Metrodorus of Chios (see p. 393), ii. 73
Metrodorus of Stratonicea in Caria (pupil of Carneades), ii. 16, 78
Minervam, sus, i. 18
Mithridatic war, ii. 1, 3 (see n.)
Mnesarchus (Stoic), i. 46; ii. 69
mole, ii. 81
Monimus, i. 8
morbus = *pathos*, i. 38
Murena, C. Licinius (war in Pontus 83 B.C.), ii. 2
music, ii. 20, 22, 91
Myrmecides ('son of an ant,' miniature sculptor of Miletus or Athens), ii. 120

Naples, ii. 9
nature, Stoic standard of value, i. 36
necessity, ii. 29
Neptuni porticus, ii. 80
normae, fr. 8
Novae, ii. 70
numbers, Pythagorean, ii. 118

oikeion, ii. 38
oracles, ii. 47, 101

Pacuvius (see p. 393), i. 10; ii. 20, 88
painters, ii. 20, 80, 146
Panaetius (see p. 393), ii. 5, 107, 135
paradoxes, Stoic, ii. 132, 136, 144
Parmenides (see p. 393), i. 44; ii. 74, 118, 129
Penelope's web, ii. 95

INDEX TO ACADEMICA

peras, ii. 116 n.
Peripatetics, i. 6, 24; ii. 112, 131
perpendicula, fr. 8
perspicuousness, ii. 17, 105
phantasia, i. 40; ii. 18, 112
Philo of Larissa (see p. 394), i. 13; ii. 11, 17, 18, 32, 78
Philo of Megara (pupil of Diodorus), ii. 143
Phoenicians, ii. 66
phyta, i. 26 n.
Plato, i. 15 ff., 24, 29 ff., 38, 44; ii. 7, 17, 22, 118, 121, 124
point, definition of, ii. 116
poiotētes, i. 24 f.
Polemo (Academic), i. 17, 19, 37; ii. 16, 131, 132, 139
Polyaenus (friend of Epicurus), ii. 106
Pompei, ii. 80
Pompeianum, ii. 9, 80
Pompeius, Q. (consul 141 B.C.), ii. 13
Pontus (N.E. district of Asia Minor), ii. 2
porticus Neptuni, ii. 80; Stoicorum, ii. 75
Posidonius (see p. 394), ii. 82
preferred and rejected, i. 37
probability, fr. 19; ii. 32 f., 104 f.
prokopē, i. 20 n.
prolēpseis, ii. 30
pronoia, i. 29; ii. 87
Protagoras (see p. 394), ii. 142
providence, i. 29; ii. 87
purpurascere, fr. 7
Puteoli (Pozzuoli, Campanian seaport), ii. 80, 100, 125
Pyrrho (of Elis, Sceptic), ii. 130
Pythagoreans (see p. 394), ii. 118

quality, i. 24
quinta natura, i 39

Rabirius (Roman Epicurean writer), i. 5
refraction, fr. 3; ii. 19, 79, 82
Republic of Plato, ii. 124
research, ii. 26

Saturninus, L. Apuleius (tribune 103 and 100 B.C.), i. 14; ii. 7
Scaevola (consul 133 B.C.), ii. 13
Sceptics, i. 45; ii. 17, 28, 40, 43, 72, 76, 81, 104, 108, 110, 120, 125, 127
Scipio, P. Cornelius Aemilianus Africanus (consul 147 and 134 B.C.), ii. 5, 13, 15
Scipio, P. Cornelius Nasica (consul 155 B.C.), ii. 137
Scyllaeum bonum, ii. 139
Sellii, P. et S. (unknown), ii. 11
sēmeia, i. 32
Septentriones, ii. 66
Servilii (Publius, consul 252 and 248 B.C.), ii. 56, 84 f.
Servius Tullius, ii. 73 n.
Seven Wise Men, ii. 118
siccum, fr. 9
Siro (Epicurean, teacher of Virgil), ii. 106
Socrates, i. 15 ff., 21, 39, 44; ii. 14, 65, 74, 136, 145
Socratici, ii. 74
Solon, ii. 136
sophismata, ii. 45 n., 75
Sophists, ii. 72
Sophocles, i. 10
sōritēs, ii. 49, 92 ff., 107, 147
Sosus, ii. 12
species = *ideai*, i. 33; ii. 58, 112
Speusippus (see p. 395), i. 17, 34
Stars, ii. 32, 110, 119, 123
Stilbo (Στίλπων, Megarian philosopher, 3rd century B.C.), ii. 75
Strato (see p. 395), i. 34; ii. 121
Stratonicea. See Metrodorus
sun divine, ii. 116, 119, 126; size of, 82, 91, 118, 123, 126, 128; motion of, 82
sus Minervam, i. 18
syncatathesis, ii. 37
Syria, ii. 61
systēma, ii. 102

teleiōsis, i. 20
terminology, i. 5, 25
Tetrilius Rogus (unknown), ii. 11
Thales (of Miletus, earliest Greek philosopher, 636–546 B.C.), ii. 118
themelia, ii. 40 n.
Themistocles (Athenian statesman, b. 514 B.C., victor of Salamis), ii. 2
Theophanes (of Mitylene, counsellor and historian of Pompey), ii. 4
Theophrastus (see p. 395), i. 10, 33, 85; ii. 113, 123 134

INDEX TO ACADEMICA

Timaeus, ii. 123
Timagoras (unknown), ii. 80
Timon, i. 44 f.
tribunes, ii. 63, 97, 144
Tubero (consul 118 B.C.), ii. 135
Tuditanus (mentioned also Philippic III. 16 as insane), ii. 89
Tullia, i. 11 n.
Tusculan Disputations, ii. 135 n.
Tusculum (on Monte Albano, near Frascati, 10 m. S E. of Rome), ii. 148
Twelve Tables, ii. 136
twins, ii. 54

Ulysses (in Ajax Furens, author unknown), ii. 89
urinari, fr. 10

Varro, i. *passim*, fr. 22
vindicare, fr. 15
vipers, ii. 120

world-soul, i. 29; ii. 118 f., 126

Xenocrates (see p. 396), i. 17, 34, 39; ii. 113, 124, 136 f., 143
Xenophanes (see p. 396), ii. 74, 118, 123, 129

Zeno of Citium (see p. 396), i. 7, 18, 35, 42, 44; ii. 16, 66, 71, 76 f., 113, 126, 129 ff.
Zeno of Elia (see p. 396), ii. 129
Zeno of Sidon (Epicurean, contemporary of Cicero), i. 46
Zeuxis (Greek painter, late 5th cent. B.C.), ii. 146

Printed in Great Britain by R. & R. CLARK, LIMITED, *Edinburgh*

THE LOEB CLASSICAL LIBRARY

VOLUMES ALREADY PUBLISHED

LATIN AUTHORS

Ammianus Marcellinus. J. C. Rolfe. 3 Vols.
Apuleius : The Golden Ass (Metamorphoses). W. Adlington (1566). Revised by S. Gaselee.
St. Augustine : City of God. 7 Vols. Vol. I. G. E. McCracken. Vol. II. W. M. Green. Vol. IV. P. Levine. Vol. V. E. M. Sanford and W. M. Green. Vol. VI. W. C. Greene.
St. Augustine, Confessions of. W. Watts (1631). 2 Vols.
St. Augustine : Select Letters. J. H. Baxter.
Ausonius. H. G. Evelyn White. 2 Vols.
Bede. J. E. King. 2 Vols.
Boethius : Tracts and De Consolatione Philosophiae. Rev. H. F. Stewart and E. K. Rand.
Caesar : Alexandrian, African and Spanish Wars. A. G. Way.
Caesar : Civil Wars. A. G. Peskett.
Caesar : Gallic War. H. J. Edwards.
Cato and Varro : De Re Rustica. H. B. Ash and W. D. Hooper.
Catullus. F. W. Cornish ; Tibullus. J. B. Postgate ; and Pervigilium Veneris. J. W. Mackail.
Celsus : De Medicina. W. G. Spencer. 3 Vols.
Cicero : Brutus and Orator. G. L. Hendrickson and H. M. Hubbell.
Cicero : De Finibus. H. Rackham.
Cicero : De Inventione, etc. H. M. Hubbell.
Cicero : De Natura Deorum and Academica. H. Rackham.
Cicero : De Officiis. Walter Miller.
Cicero : De Oratore, etc. 2 Vols. Vol. I : De Oratore, Books I and II. E. W. Sutton and H. Rackham. Vol. II : De Oratore, Book III ; De Fato ; Paradoxa Stoicorum ; De Partitione Oratoria. H. Rackham.

THE LOEB CLASSICAL LIBRARY

Cicero: De Republica, De Legibus, Somnium Scipionis. Clinton W. Keyes.
Cicero: De Senectute, De Amicitia, De Divinatione. W. A. Falconer.
Cicero: In Catilinam, Pro Murena, Pro Sulla, Pro Flacco. Louis E. Lord.
Cicero: Letters to Atticus. E. O. Winstedt. 3 Vols.
Cicero: Letters to his Friends. W. Glynn Williams. 3 Vols.
Cicero: Philippics. W. C. A. Ker.
Cicero: Pro Archia, Post Reditum, De Domo, De Haruspicum Responsis, Pro Plancio. N. H. Watts.
Cicero: Pro Caecina, Pro Lege Manilia, Pro Cluentio, Pro Rabirio. H. Grose Hodge.
Cicero: Pro Caelio, De Provinciis Consularibus, Pro Balbo. R. Gardner.
Cicero: Pro Milone, In Pisonem, Pro Scauro, Pro Fonteio, Pro Rabirio Postumo, Pro Marcello, Pro Ligario, Pro Rege Deiotaro. N. H. Watts.
Cicero: Pro Quinctio, Pro Roscio Amerino, Pro Roscio Comoedo, Contra Rullum. J. H. Freese.
Cicero: Pro Sestio, In Vatinium. R. Gardner.
[Cicero]: Rhetorica ad Herennium. H. Caplan.
Cicero: Tusculan Disputations. J. E. King.
Cicero: Verrine Orations. L. H. G. Greenwood. 2 Vols.
Claudian. M. Platnauer. 2 Vols.
Columella: De Re Rustica, De Arboribus. H. B. Ash, E. S. Forster, E. Heffner. 3 Vols.
Curtius, Q.: History of Alexander. J. C. Rolfe. 2 Vols.
Florus. E. S. Forster; and Cornelius Nepos. J. C. Rolfe.
Frontinus: Stratagems and Aqueducts. C. E. Bennett and M. B. McElwain.
Fronto: Correspondence. C. R. Haines. 2 Vols.
Gellius. J. C. Rolfe. 3 Vols.
Horace: Odes and Epodes. C. E. Bennett.
Horace: Satires, Epistles, Ars Poetica. H. R. Fairclough.
Jerome: Select Letters. F. A. Wright.
Juvenal and Persius. G. G. Ramsay.
Livy. B. O. Foster, F. G. Moore, Evan T. Sage, A. C Schlesinger and R. M. Geer (General Index). 14 Vols.
Lucan. J. D. Duff.

LUCRETIUS. W. H. D. Rouse.
MARTIAL. W. C. A. Ker. 2 Vols.
MINOR LATIN POETS: from PUBLILIUS SYRUS to RUTILIUS NAMATIANUS, including GRATTIUS, CALPURNIUS SICULUS, NEMESIANUS, AVIANUS, with "Aetna," "Phoenix" and other poems. J. Wight Duff and Arnold M. Duff.
OVID: THE ART OF LOVE AND OTHER POEMS. J. H. Mozley.
OVID: FASTI. Sir James G. Frazer.
OVID: HEROIDES AND AMORES. Grant Showerman.
OVID: METAMORPHOSES. F. J. Miller. 2 Vols.
OVID: TRISTIA AND EX PONTO. A. L. Wheeler.
PETRONIUS. M. Heseltine; SENECA: APOCOLOCYNTOSIS. W. H. D. Rouse.
PHAEDRUS AND BABRIUS (Greek). B. E. Perry.
PLAUTUS. Paul Nixon. 5 Vols.
PLINY: LETTERS. Melmoth's translation revised by W. M. L. Hutchinson. 2 Vols.
PLINY: NATURAL HISTORY. 10 Vols. Vols. I-V and IX. H. Rackham. Vols. VI-VIII. W. H. S. Jones. Vol. X. D. E. Eichholz.
PROPERTIUS. H. E. Butler.
PRUDENTIUS. H. J. Thomson. 2 Vols.
QUINTILIAN. H. E. Butler. 4 Vols.
REMAINS OF OLD LATIN. E. H. Warmington. 4 Vols. Vol. I (Ennius and Caecilius). Vol. II (Livius, Naevius, Pacuvius, Accius). Vol. III (Lucilius, Laws of the XII Tables). Vol. IV (Archaic Inscriptions).
SALLUST. J. C. Rolfe.
SCRIPTORES HISTORIAE AUGUSTAE. D. Magie. 3 Vols.
SENECA: APOCOLOCYNTOSIS. *Cf.* PETRONIUS.
SENECA: EPISTULAE MORALES. R. M. Gummere. 3 Vols.
SENECA: MORAL ESSAYS. J. W. Basore. 3 Vols.
SENECA: TRAGEDIES. F. J. Miller. 2 Vols.
SIDONIUS: POEMS AND LETTERS. W. B. Anderson. 2 Vols.
SILIUS ITALICUS. J. D. Duff. 2 Vols.
STATIUS. J. H. Mozley. 2 Vols.
SUETONIUS. J. C. Rolfe. 2 Vols.
TACITUS: DIALOGUS. Sir Wm. Peterson; and AGRICOLA AND GERMANIA. Maurice Hutton.
TACITUS: HISTORIES AND ANNALS. C. H. Moore and J. Jackson. 4 Vols.
TERENCE. John Sargeaunt. 2 Vols.

TERTULLIAN: APOLOGIA AND DE SPECTACULIS. T. R. Glover; MINUCIUS FELIX. G. H. Rendall.
VALERIUS FLACCUS. J. H. Mozley.
VARRO: DE LINGUA LATINA. R. G. Kent. 2 Vols.
VELLEIUS PATERCULUS AND RES GESTAE DIVI AUGUSTI. F. W. Shipley.
VIRGIL. H. R. Fairclough. 2 Vols.
VITRUVIUS: DE ARCHITECTURA. F. Granger. 2 Vols.

GREEK AUTHORS

ACHILLES TATIUS. S. Gaselee.
AELIAN: ON THE NATURE OF ANIMALS. A. F. Scholfield. 3 Vols.
AENEAS TACTICUS, ASCLEPIODOTUS AND ONASANDER. The Illinois Greek Club.
AESCHINES. C. D. Adams.
AESCHYLUS. H. Weir Smyth. 2 Vols.
ALCIPHRON, AELIAN AND PHILOSTRATUS: LETTERS. A. R. Benner and F. H. Fobes.
APOLLODORUS. Sir James G. Frazer. 2 Vols.
APOLLONIUS RHODIUS. R. C. Seaton.
THE APOSTOLIC FATHERS. Kirsopp Lake. 2 Vols.
APPIAN'S ROMAN HISTORY. Horace White. 4 Vols.
ARATUS. *Cf.* CALLIMACHUS.
ARISTOPHANES. Benjamin Bickley Rogers. 3 Vols. Verse trans.
ARISTOTLE: ART OF RHETORIC. J. H. Freese.
ARISTOTLE: ATHENIAN CONSTITUTION, EUDEMIAN ETHICS, VIRTUES AND VICES. H. Rackham.
ARISTOTLE: THE CATEGORIES. ON INTERPRETATION. H. P. Cooke; PRIOR ANALYTICS. H. Tredennick.
ARISTOTLE: GENERATION OF ANIMALS. A. L. Peck.
ARISTOTLE: HISTORIA ANIMALIUM. A. L. Peck. 3 Vols. Vol. I.
ARISTOTLE: METAPHYSICS. H. Tredennick. 2 Vols.
ARISTOTLE: METEOROLOGICA. H. D. P. Lee.
ARISTOTLE: MINOR WORKS. W. S. Hett. "On Colours," "On Things Heard," "Physiognomics," "On Plants," "On Marvellous Things Heard," "Mechanical Problems," "On Indivisible Lines," "Situations and Names of Winds," "On Melissus, Xenophanes, and Gorgias."

Aristotle: Nicomachean Ethics. H. Rackham.
Aristotle: Oeconomica and Magna Moralia. G. C. Armstrong. (With Metaphysics, Vol. II.)
Aristotle: On the Heavens. W. K. C. Guthrie.
Aristotle: On the Soul, Parva Naturalia, On Breath. W. S. Hett.
Aristotle: Parts of Animals. A. L. Peck; Motion and Progression of Animals. E. S. Forster.
Aristotle: Physics. Rev. P. Wicksteed and F. M. Cornford. 2 Vols.
Aristotle: Poetics; Longinus on the Sublime. W. Hamilton Fyfe; Demetrius on Style. W. Rhys Roberts.
Aristotle: Politics. H. Rackham.
Aristotle: Posterior Analytics. H. Tredennick; Topics. E. S. Forster.
Aristotle: Problems. W. S. Hett. 2 Vols.
Aristotle: Rhetorica ad Alexandrum. H. Rackham. (With Problems, Vol. II.)
Aristotle: Sophistical Refutations. Coming-to-be and Passing-away. E. S. Forster; On the Cosmos. D. J. Furley.
Arrian: History of Alexander and Indica. Rev. E. Iliffe Robson. 2 Vols.
Athenaeus: Deipnosophistae. C. B. Gulick. 7 Vols.
Babrius and Phaedrus (Latin). B. E. Perry.
St. Basil: Letters. R. J. Deferrari. 4 Vols.
Callimachus: Fragments. C. A. Trypanis.
Callimachus: Hymns and Epigrams, and Lycophron. A. W. Mair; Aratus. G. R. Mair.
Clement of Alexandria. Rev. G. W. Butterworth.
Colluthus. *Cf.* Oppian.
Daphnis and Chloe. *Cf.* Longus.
Demosthenes I: Olynthiacs, Philippics and Minor Orations: I-XVII and XX. J. H. Vince.
Demosthenes II: De Corona and De Falsa Legatione. C. A. Vince and J. H. Vince.
Demosthenes III: Meidias, Androtion, Aristocrates, Timocrates, Aristogeiton. J. H. Vince.
Demosthenes IV-VI: Private Orations and In Neaeram. A. T. Murray.
Demosthenes VII: Funeral Speech, Erotic Essay, Exordia and Letters. N. W. and N. J. DeWitt.

THE LOEB CLASSICAL LIBRARY

Dio Cassius: Roman History. E. Cary. 9 Vols.

Dio Chrysostom. 5 Vols. Vols. I and II. J. W. Cohoon. Vol. III. J. W. Cohoon and H. Lamar Crosby. Vols. IV and V. H. Lamar Crosby.

Diodorus Siculus. 12 Vols. Vols. I-VI. C. H. Oldfather. Vol. VII. C. L. Sherman. Vol. VIII. C. B. Welles. Vols. IX and X. Russel M. Geer. Vol. XI. F. R. Walton.

Diogenes Laertius. R. D. Hicks. 2 Vols.

Dionysius of Halicarnassus: Roman Antiquities. Spelman's translation revised by E. Cary. 7 Vols.

Epictetus. W. A. Oldfather. 2 Vols.

Euripides. A. S. Way. 4 Vols. Verse trans.

Eusebius: Ecclesiastical History. Kirsopp Lake and J. E. L. Oulton. 2 Vols.

Galen: On the Natural Faculties. A. J. Brock.

The Greek Anthology. W R. Paton. 5 Vols.

The Greek Bucolic Poets (Theocritus, Bion, Moschus). J. M. Edmonds.

Greek Elegy and Iambus with the Anacreontea. J. M. Edmonds. 2 Vols.

Greek Mathematical Works. Ivor Thomas. 2 Vols.

Herodes. *Cf.* Theophrastus: Characters.

Herodotus. A. D. Godley. 4 Vols.

Hesiod and the Homeric Hymns. H. G. Evelyn White.

Hippocrates and the Fragments of Heracleitus. W. H. S. Jones and E. T. Withington. 4 Vols.

Homer: Iliad. A. T. Murray. 2 Vols.

Homer: Odyssey. A. T. Murray. 2 Vols.

Isaeus. E. S. Forster.

Isocrates. George Norlin and LaRue Van Hook. 3 Vols.

St. John Damascene: Barlaam and Ioasaph. Rev. G. R. Woodward and Harold Mattingly.

Josephus. 9 Vols. Vols. I-IV. H. St. J. Thackeray. Vol. V. H. St. J. Thackeray and Ralph Marcus. Vols. VI and VII. Ralph Marcus. Vol. VIII. Ralph Marcus and Allen Wikgren. Vol. IX. L. H. Feldman.

Julian. Wilmer Cave Wright. 3 Vols.

Longus: Daphnis and Chloe. Thornley's translation revised by J. M. Edmonds; and Parthenius. S. Gaselee.

Lucian. 8 Vols. Vols. I-V. A. M. Harmon. Vol. VI. K. Kilburn. Vol. VII. M. D. Macleod.

LYCOPHRON. *Cf.* CALLIMACHUS.
LYRA GRAECA. J. M. Edmonds. 3 Vols.
LYSIAS. W. R. M. Lamb.
MANETHO. W. G. Waddell; PTOLEMY: TETRABIBLOS. F. E. Robbins.
MARCUS AURELIUS. C. R. Haines.
MENANDER. F. G. Allinson.
MINOR ATTIC ORATORS. 2 Vols. K. J. Maidment and J. O. Burtt.
NONNOS: DIONYSIACA. W. H. D. Rouse. 3 Vols.
OPPIAN, COLLUTHUS, TRYPHIODORUS. A. W. Mair.
PAPYRI. NON-LITERARY SELECTIONS. A. S. Hunt and C. C. Edgar. 2 Vols. LITERARY SELECTIONS (Poetry). D. L. Page.
PARTHENIUS. *Cf.* LONGUS.
PAUSANIAS: DESCRIPTION OF GREECE. W. H. S. Jones. 5 Vols. and Companion Vol. arranged by R. E. Wycherley.
PHILO. 10 Vols. Vols. I-V. F. H. Colson and Rev. G. H. Whitaker. Vols. VI-X. F. H. Colson. General Index. Rev. J. W. Earp.
Two Supplementary Vols. Translation only from an Armenian Text. Ralph Marcus.
PHILOSTRATUS: THE LIFE OF APOLLONIUS OF TYANA. F. C. Conybeare. 2 Vols.
PHILOSTRATUS: IMAGINES; CALLISTRATUS: DESCRIPTIONS. A. Fairbanks.
PHILOSTRATUS AND EUNAPIUS: LIVES OF THE SOPHISTS. Wilmer Cave Wright.
PINDAR. Sir J. E. Sandys.
PLATO: CHARMIDES, ALCIBIADES, HIPPARCHUS, THE LOVERS, THEAGES, MINOS AND EPINOMIS. W. R. M. Lamb.
PLATO: CRATYLUS, PARMENIDES, GREATER HIPPIAS, LESSER HIPPIAS. H. N. Fowler.
PLATO: EUTHYPHRO, APOLOGY, CRITO, PHAEDO, PHAEDRUS. H. N. Fowler.
PLATO: LACHES, PROTAGORAS, MENO, EUTHYDEMUS. W. R. M. Lamb.
PLATO: LAWS. Rev. R. G. Bury. 2 Vols.
PLATO: LYSIS, SYMPOSIUM, GORGIAS. W. R. M. Lamb.
PLATO: REPUBLIC. Paul Shorey. 2 Vols.
PLATO: STATESMAN, PHILEBUS. H. N. Fowler; ION. W. R. M. Lamb.

THE LOEB CLASSICAL LIBRARY

PLATO: THEAETETUS AND SOPHIST. H. N. Fowler.
PLATO: TIMAEUS, CRITIAS, CLITOPHO, MENEXENUS, EPISTULAE. Rev. R. G. Bury.
PLOTINUS. A. H. Armstrong. 6 Vols. Vols. I-II
PLUTARCH: MORALIA. 15 Vols. Vols. I-V. F. C. Babbitt. Vol. VI. W. C. Helmbold. Vol. VII. P. H. De Lacy and B. Einarson. Vol. IX. E. L. Minar, Jr., F. H. Sandbach, W. C. Helmbold. Vol. X. H. N. Fowler. Vol. XI. L. Pearson, F. H. Sandbach. Vol. XII. H. Cherniss, W. C. Helmbold. Vol. XIV. P. H. De Lacy and B. Einarson.
PLUTARCH: THE PARALLEL LIVES. B. Perrin. 11 Vols.
POLYBIUS. W. R. Paton. 6 Vols.
PROCOPIUS: HISTORY OF THE WARS. H. B. Dewing. 7 Vols.
PTOLEMY: TETRABIBLOS. *Cf.* MANETHO.
QUINTUS SMYRNAEUS. A. S. Way. Verse trans.
SEXTUS EMPIRICUS. Rev. R. G. Bury. 4 Vols.
SOPHOCLES. F. Storr. 2 Vols. Verse trans.
STRABO: GEOGRAPHY. Horace L. Jones. 8 Vols.
THEOPHRASTUS: CHARACTERS. J. M. Edmonds; HERODES, etc. A. D. Knox.
THEOPHRASTUS: ENQUIRY INTO PLANTS. Sir Arthur Hort. 2 Vols.
THUCYDIDES. C. F. Smith. 4 Vols.
TRYPHIODORUS. *Cf.* OPPIAN.
XENOPHON: CYROPAEDIA. Walter Miller. 2 Vols.
XENOPHON: HELLENICA, ANABASIS, APOLOGY, AND SYMPOSIUM. C. L. Brownson and O. J. Todd. 3 Vols.
XENOPHON: MEMORABILIA AND OECONOMICUS. E. C. Marchant.
XENOPHON: SCRIPTA MINORA. E. C. Marchant.

DESCRIPTIVE PROSPECTUS ON APPLICATION

CAMBRIDGE, MASS. HARVARD UNIV. PRESS
LONDON WILLIAM HEINEMANN LTD

CPSIA information can be obtained
at www.ICGtesting.com
Printed in the USA
LVHW101759231021
701313LV00009B/217

9 781175 880628